THE CAMBRIDGE COMPANION TO

# THE AGE OF JUSTINIAN

This book introduces the Age of Justinian, which was both the last Roman century and the first flowering of Byzantine culture. Dominated by the policies and personality of emperor Justinian I (r. 527–565), this period of grand achievements and far-reaching failures witnessed the transformation of the Mediterranean world. In this volume, twenty specialists explore the most important aspects of the age, including warfare, urbanism, economy and the mechanics and theory of empire. They also discuss the impact of the great plague, the codification of Roman law, and the religious controversies of the day. Consideration is given to imperial relations with the papacy, northern barbarians, the Persians, and other eastern peoples, shedding new light on a dramatic and highly significant historical period.

Michael Maas is Professor of History and Director of the Program in Ancient Mediterranean Civilizations at Rice University.

The Cambridge Companion to

# THE AGE OF JUSTINIAN

*Edited by*

Michael Maas

*Rice University*

CAMBRIDGE UNIVERSITY PRESS
Cambridge, New York, Melbourne, Madrid, Cape Town, Singapore, São Paulo

Cambridge University Press
40 West 20th Street, New York, NY 10011-4211, USA

www.cambridge.org
Information on this title: www.cambridge.org/9780521817462



First published 2005

Printed in the United States of America

*A catalog record for this book is available from the British Library.*

*Library of Congress Cataloging in Publication Data*
The Cambridge companion to the Age of Justinian / edited by Michael Maas.
p. cm.
Includes bibliographical references and index.
ISBN 0-521-81746-3 (hardback) – ISBN 0-521-52071-1 (pbk.)
1. Byzantine Empire–History–Justinian I, 527–565. I. Maas, Michael, 1951–
DF572.C35 2004
949.5′013 – DC22 2004049266

ISBN-13 978-0-521-81746-2 hardback
ISBN-10 0-521-81746-3 hardback

ISBN-13 978-0-521-52071-3 paperback
ISBN-10 0-521-52071-1 paperback

*This book is dedicated with great respect and affection*
*to Peter Brown*
*on the occasion of his seventieth birthday.*

# Contents

## Part 2: Religion and Philosophy



## Part 3: Literature and the Arts



## Part 4: Peoples and Communities

# Illustrations and Maps

## Color Plates

*(Color plates appear between pages 266–267.)*



## Black and White Plates

*(Black and White plates appear between pages 426–427.)*

## Text Figures



## Maps

# Contributors

JOSEPH D. ALCHERMES is Associate Professor in the Department of Art History and Architectural Studies at Connecticut College.

LESLIE BRUBAKER is Reader in Byzantine Art History and Director of the Centre for Byzantine, Ottoman, and Modern Greek Studies at the University of Birmingham.

BRIAN CROKE is Executive Director of the Catholic Education Commission, Sydney.

FRED M. DONNER is Professor of Near Eastern History in the Department of Near Eastern Languages and Civilizations and the Oriental Institute of the University of Chicago.

PATRICK T. R. GRAY is Professor of Religious Studies in the School of Arts and Letters in the Atkinson Faculty of York University, Toronto.

GEOFFREY GREATREX is Associate Professor and Chair of the Department of Classics and Religious Studies at the University of Ottawa.

JOHN HALDON is Professor of Byzantine History in the Centre for Byzantine, Ottoman, and Modern Greek Studies and Head of the School of Historical Studies at the University of Birmingham.

KENNETH HOLUM is Professor of History at the University of Maryland.

PEREGRINE HORDEN is Reader in Medieval History, Royal Holloway, University of London.

CAROLINE HUMFRESS is Lecturer in Late Antique and Early Medieval History at Birkbeck College, London.

DEREK KRUEGER is Professor and Head of the Department of Religious Studies at the University of North Carolina at Greensboro.

NICHOLAS DE LANGE is Professor of Hebrew and Jewish Studies at the University of Cambridge.

A. D. LEE is Senior Lecturer in Classical Studies at the University of Nottingham.

MICHAEL MAAS is Professor of History at Rice University.

CHARLES PAZDERNIK is Assistant Professor of Classics at Grand Valley State University in Allendale, Michigan.

WALTER POHL is Director of the Institute of Medieval Research at the Austrian Academy of Sciences and teaches medieval history at the University of Vienna.

LUCAS VAN ROMPAY is Professor of Eastern Christianity in the Department of Religion at Duke University.

CLAIRE SOTINEL is *Maître de Conférences* in Roman History at the University of Bordeaux.

CLAUDIA RAPP is Associate Professor in the History Department at the University of California at Los Angeles.

CHRISTIAN WILDBERG is Professor of Classics at Princeton University.

# Abbreviations

| | |
|---|---|
| ACO | Acta conciliorum oecumenicorum |
| ANRW | Aufstieg und Niedergang der römischen Welt |
| AnTard | Antiquité Tardive |
| BMGS | Byzantine and Modern Greek Studies |
| BSOAS | Bulletin of the School of Oriental and African Studies |
| BZ | Byzantinische Zeitschrift |
| CAH13 | Cambridge Ancient History Vol XIII: The Late Empire, A.D. 337–425, ed. Averil Cameron and Peter Garnsey (Cambridge, 1998) |
| CAH14 | Cambridge Ancient History Vol XIV: Late Antiquity: Empire and Successors, A.D. 425–600, ed. Averil Cameron, Michael Whitby, and Bryan Ward-Perkins (Cambridge, 2000) |
| CCSG | Corpus christianorum, series graeca |
| CCSL | Corpus christianorum, series latina |
| CFHB | Corpus Fontium Historiae Byzantinae |
| ChHist | Church History |
| CollAvell | Collectio Avellana |
| CSCO | Corpus scriptorum christianorum orientalium |
| CSCO/Copt | Scriptores Coptici |
| CSCO/Syr | Scriptores Syri |
| CSEL | Corpus scriptorum ecclesiasticorum latinorum |
| DOP | Dumbarton Oaks Papers |
| EI(2) | Encyclopedia of Islam, new edition |
| EIr | Encyclopedia of Iran |
| FHG | Fragmenta Historicorum Graecorum |
| GOTR | Greek Orthodox Theological Review |
| IstMitt | Istanbuler Mitteilungen |

| | |
|---|---|
| JGR | Jus Graeco-romanum |
| JÖB | Jarhrbuch der Österreichischen Byzantinistik |
| JEChrSt | Journal of Early Christian Studies |
| JHS | Journal of Hellenic Studies |
| Jones, LRE | A.H.M. Jones, *The Later Roman Empire 284–602. A Social, Economic and Administrative Survey* (Oxford, 1964). |
| JRA | Journal of Roman Archeology |
| JRS | Journal of Roman Studies |
| MélRom | Mélanges d'archéologie et d'histoire, Ecole française de Rome |
| MGH AA | Monumenta Germaniae historica. Auctores antiquissimi |
| MittIÖG | *Mitteilungen des Instituts für Österreichische Geschictsforschung* |
| NPNF | *A Select Library of Nicene and post-Nicene Fathers* ed. P. Schaff and H. Wace (New York, 1887–1894; repr. Grand Rapids 1952–1956) |
| OCP | Orientalia christiana periodica |
| ODB | *Oxford Dictionary of Byzantium* |
| PG | Patrologiae cursus completus, series graeca |
| PL | Patrologiae cursus completus, series latina |
| PO | Patrologia orientalis |
| PLRE | Prosopography of the Later Roman Empire |
| RIDA | Revue internationale des droits de l'antiquité |
| SC | Sources Chrétiennes |
| Stein, Bas-Empire, 1&2 | Ernest Stein, *Histoire du Bas-Empire* I: *De l'état romain a l'état byzantin* (284–476) (edn. fr. J-R. Palanque, Paris-Bruges, 1959) II: De *la disparition de l'Empire d'Occident a la mort de Justinien* (476–565). (Paris, 1949); both repr. Amsterdam, 1968 |
| TM | Travaux et mémoires. Centre de recherche d'histoire et civilization de Byzance |

# Acknowledgments

It is a pleasure to thank friends and colleagues at several institutions who assisted in the preparation of this book. First of all, I wish to express my sincere gratitude to the A.G. Leventis Foundation, whose kind interest and generosity at the eleventh hour made the publication of this book possible. The School of Historical Studies, Institute for Advanced Study, Princeton, N.J., provided a most congenial atmosphere in which to plan the volume during the academic year 2000–2001. The American Philosophical Society also supported my research during that time. I warmly thank both institutions. Gale Stokes, when Dean of Humanities at Rice University, supplied funds for the color photographs. Catherine Howard, Kamila Bergen, and copy-editor Sage Rountree supplied invaluable assistance with the manuscript. Advice and aid came from Emily Albu, Joseph Alchermes, Morten Axboe, Susan Ashbrook Harvey, Matthias Henze, Carol Quillen, Julia Smith, Lisa Spiro, and as always, Paula Sanders. Beatrice Rehl at Cambridge University Press skilfully guided the entire project from its beginning; Kate Mertes expertly prepared the index; and Zachary Dorsey of TechBooks supervised the volume's production with exceptional efficiency. To all of them I am most grateful. Most of all I wish to thank the contributors to this volume for their patience and good humor.

# Select List of Ancient Sources

Agapetus. Sixth-century deacon, possibly of Hagia Sophia, whose *Mirror of Princes*, written between 527 and 548, advised Justinian on how to be a good ruler. Partial translation by Ernest Barker, *Social and Political Thought in Byzantium* (Oxford 1957), 54–63.

Agathias, c. 532–c. 580. A lawyer at Constantinople whose *Histories* continue Procopius's narratives: *Agathias, the Histories*, trans. J. D. Frendo (Berlin, 1975). In his *Kyklos*, or *Cycle*, he collected Greek epigrams, which are contained in the *Greek Anthology*, trans. W. R. Paton (Cambridge, Mass., 1916–1918).

Anonymous *Treaty on Strategy*. This discussion of defensive and offensive strategy was written by a professional soldier, probably in the sixth century. George T. Dennis, *Three Byzantine Military Treatises* (Washington, D.C., 1985).

Anonymous of Piacenza (see Piacenza Pilgrim).

Cassiodorus, c. 487–c. 580. Italian statesman and scholar. After his retirement from service under King Theoderic, he established a monastery at Vivarium in Calabria. His *Variae* or *Official Correspondence* collected edicts and letters he had written for Theoderic. *Variae*, trans. S. J. B. Barnish (1992) and *The Letters of Cassiodorus*, trans. Thomas Hodgkin (1886) contain selections. His *History of the Goths*, which no longer survives, was an important source for Jordanes. Charles C. Mierow, *The Gothic History of Jordanes* (1915).

Corippus, d. c. 567. This north African émigré to Constantinople wrote in Latin. His epic poem *Johannis* celebrated the victories of John Troglita over the Berbers in North Africa. *The Iohannis or de Bellis Libycis of Flavius Cresconius Corippus*, trans. George W. Shea (1998). His *Panegyric on Justin II*, which honors Justinian's successor, contains information about Justinian's death, Justin's succession, and political ideology. *Flavius*

*Cresconius Corippus, In Laudem Iustini Augusti minoris, libri IV*, trans. Averil. M. Cameron (1976).

Cosmas Indicopleustes (first half of the sixth century). An Alexandrian merchant who traveled on the Red Sea and possibly went to India, Cosmas wrote the *Christian Topography*, which describes his voyages and attempts to refute Ptolemaic and Aristotelian astronomy, believing that the world's shape imitates the tabernacle of Moses. *The Christian Topography of Cosmas*, trans. William McCrindle (London, 1897).

Cyril of Scythopolis, c. 525–c. 559. A Palestinian monk, whose *Lives of the Monks of Palestine* reveals much about ascetic practice in the desert monasteries of the sixth century. *Lives of the Monks of Palestine*, trans. R. M. Price and John Binns (Kalamazoo, Mich., 1991).

Evagrius Scholasticus, c. 536–after 594. A lawyer at Antioch, whose *Church History* covers the years 431–594, especially valuable for the post-Justinianic period. *Ecclesiastical History*, trans. Michael Whitby (2000).

John Malalas, c. 490–c. 575. An Antiochene bureaucrat who moved to Constantinople around 540 and wrote the *Chronicle*, or *Chronographia*, which tells the history of the world from the Creation to the death of Justinian. A valuable source for contemporary attitudes and beliefs. *John Malalas, The Chronicle*, translated by Elizabeth Jeffreys, Michael Jeffreys, Roger Scott, et al. (Melbourne, 1986).

John of Nikiu. A late-seventh-century Egyptian bishop who composed a chronicle in Greek (now lost), surviving only in Ethiopic, covering the period from Adam to the Arab conquest of Egypt. It is the only eyewitness account of the conquest. *The Chronicle of John, Bishop of Nikiou*, trans. R. H. Charles (London, 1916).

John Philoponos, c. 490–after 567 or 574. A Christian trained in Neoplatonic philosophy who taught at Alexandria, known especially for his criticism of Aristotle on many issues. *Philoponus: Against Aristotle on the Eternity of the World*, trans. Christian Wildberg (1987). Other works are also translated.

John the Lydian (John Lydus), 490–c. 565. A bureaucrat in the praetorian praefecture in Constantinople and an antiquarian scholar. He wrote three treatises that preserve much information from earlier sources while responding to contemporary controversies. *On Offices (De magistratibus)* is translated as *Ioannes Lydus On Powers or The Magistracies of the Roman State* by Anastasius C. Bandy (Philadelphia,

1983). *On Months* and *On Portents* have not yet been translated into English.

Junillus Africanus, d. c. 549. Chief legal officer at Constantinople after Tribonian's death, his *Handbook of the Basic Principles of Divine Law* presented a handbook of Christian exegesis for students. Translation by Michael Maas in *Exegesis and Empire in the Early Byzantine Mediterranean* (Tübingen, 2003).

Justinian, Roman emperor who reigned from 527–565. He was the author of many theological texts, some of which are translated by Kenneth P. Wesche, *On the Person of Christ* (Crestwood, N.Y., 1991). His *Corpus iuris civilis* (*Corpus of Civil Law*), which gathered prior Roman law and jurisprudence, consisted of the *Institutes, Code*, and *Digest*. He also published new laws called *Novellae* or *Novels*. P. Birks and G. MacLeod, trans., *Justinian's Institutes* (1987); J.A.C. Thomas, *The Institutes of Justinian* (1975); and Alan Watson, ed., *The Digest of Justinian* (1998). The *Novels* and the *Code* are translated (unreliably) by S. P. Scott in *The Civil Law* (Cincinnati, 1932).

Marcellinus Comes (Count Marcellinus). Sixth-century functionary at Justinian's court, he wrote a chronicle covering the eastern Mediterranean world during the years 379–534. As an eyewitness to events and a user of public documents, he is an important source for the reigns of Anastasius, Justin I, and Justinian. Brian Croke, *Chronicle of Marcellinus: Translation and Commentary* (Sydney, 1995).

Menander Protector. This late-sixth-century historian was a member of the palace guard under the emperor Maurice (r. 582–602). He composed a continuation of Agathias's *History* covering the period from 558–582. His work survives only as excerpts for a tenth-century Byzantine encyclopedia. R. C. Blockley, *The History of Menander the Guardsman* (Liverpool, 1985).

*Paschal Chronicle* (*Easter Chronicle*). The author of this early-seventh-century chronicle covering the Creation to 629 is unknown. It contains material on the Age of Justinian not found elsewhere. Michael Whitby and Mary Whitby, trans., *Chronicon Paschale 284–628 AD* (Liverpool, 1989).

Paul the Silentiary. A court official late in Justinian's reign, he composed a *Description of Saint Sophia* recited at the second dedication of the cathedral in 562. *Sancta Sophia*, trans. W. R. Lethaby and H. Swainson (London, 1894).

Peter the Patrician, c. 400–565. A lawyer and diplomat who served Justinian as master of offices for twenty-six years, he negotiated in Italy with the Goths and with Persian kings. Fragments of his writings survive. Some are translated into English by G. Greatrex and S. Lieu, *The Roman Eastern Frontier and the Persian Wars: Part II: 363–628 AD, Narrative Sourcebook* (London, 2002).

Photius, c. 810–c. 893. Patriarch of Constantinople, whose *Bibliotheca*, or *Library*, contains summaries and comments on hundreds of earlier Greek sources, many now lost. *Bibliothèque*, French trans. René Henry (1959–1977); *The Library of Photius*, trans. John N. Freese (1920) contains only the first 165 of Photius's summaries.

Piacenza Pilgrim. The account of this late-sixth-century traveler to the Holy Land contains much information about religious practice at holy sites, sacred geography, and architecture. John Wilkinson, *Jerusalem Pilgrims before the Crusades* (Warminster, Eng., 2002).

Procopius of Caesarea. The most important historian of Justinian's reign and an eyewitness to many events. His *Wars*, in eight books, deals with the Vandalic, Gothic, and Persian conflicts; *Buildings* celebrates Justinian's public works; and the *Secret History* or *Anecdota* is a vicious attack on the emperor, his court, and his policies. All Procopius's works are translated by H. B. Dewing and G. Downey (Cambridge, Mass., 1914–1940). *The Secret History*, trans., G. A. Williamson (London, 1966).

Pseudo-Joshua the Stylite. His chronicle, the earliest extant work of Syriac historiography, deals with Byzantine–Persian relations during the period 494–506. It describes the misfortunes of the city of Edessa in Syria. *The Chronicle of Pseudo-Joshua the Stylite*, trans. Frank R. Trombley and John W. Watt (Liverpool, 2000).

Romanos the Melode. Sixth-century deacon in Constantinople, whose hymns reflect contemporary piety and religious practice. Excellent translations of selected hymns: Ephrem Lash, trans. *St. Romanos the Melodist, Kontakia: On the Life of Christ* (1995) and R. J. Schork, *Sacred Song from the Byzantine Pulpit: Romanos the Melodist* (1995). His complete works are translated by Marjorie Carpenter, *Kontakia of Romanos, Byzantine Melodist*, 2 vols. (Columbia, Mo., 1970).

*Suda*. A lexicon written about 1000 that compiles much information about earlier historians and other writers. The *Suda* is now being translated online: www.stoa.org/sol.

Theophanes Confessor, c. 760–817. A historian whose *Chronographia* covers the years 285–813. *The Chronicle of Theophanes Confessor, in Byzantine and Near Eastern History, AD 284–813*, trans. Roger Scott and Cyril Mango (Oxford, 1997).

Theophylact Simocatta, early seventh century. The last historian writing in the classical tradition, he composed a narrative of the reign of emperor Maurice (582–602) as well as other works on natural history and theology. *The* History *of Theophylact Simocatta*, trans. Michael Whitby, and Mary Whitby (Oxford, 1986).

# Chronology

| | |
|---|---|
| c. 482 | Birth of Justinian |
| c. 495 | Justinian comes to Constantinople |
| 518 | Anastasius dies, Justin I becomes emperor |
| 521 | Consulship of Justinian |
| c. 525 | Marriage of Justinian and Theodora |
| 527 | Justinian becomes emperor |
| 528 | Law codification begins |
| 529 | First version of Justinian's *Code* appears; Academy in Athens closed; Samaritan revolt |
| 531 | Khusro I becomes Great King of Persia |
| 532 | Nika revolt; Eternal Peace with Persia signed |
| 533 | *Digest* published; Belisarius defeats Vandals |
| 534 | Belisarius celebrates triumph in Constantinople |
| 535 | Attack on Ostrogothic kingdom begins |
| 537 | Hagia Sophia dedicated in Constantinople |
| 540 | Khusro invades Syria and sacks Antioch |
| 542 | Plague epidemic begins; Jacob Baradaeus organizes anti-Chalcedonian church |
| 545 | Truce with Persia |
| 546 | Justinian issues edict condemning the Three Chapters |
| 548 | Death of Theodora |
| 550 | Attack on Visigothic Spain begins |
| 551 | Breach between Justinian and Pope Vigilius |
| 552 | Narses defeats Goths in Italy |
| 553 | Franks invade Italy; Fifth Ecumenical Council condemns Three Chapters |
| 554 | Italy pacified and reorganized through the "Pragmatic Sanction"; silkworm eggs smuggled into Roman empire |
| 558 | Dome of Hagia Sophia collapses; Avar envoys in Constantinople |

| | |
|---|---|
| 559 | Slavs and Kotrigur Huns attack Constantinople and are stopped by Belisarius |
| 562 | Fifty Years Peace (Eternal Peace) with Persia |
| 565 | Justinian endorses aphthartodocetism; Justinian dies, Nov. 14.; Justin II becomes emperor |
| 568 | Lombards invade Italy |
| c. 570 | Birth of Muhammad |
| 578 | Tiberius Constatine becomes emperor |
| 579 | Khusro I dies |
| 580s | Slav invasion of Greece |
| 582 | Maurice becomes emperor |
| 591 | Maurice restores Khusro II to Persian throne |
| 590 | Gregory the Great becomes pope |
| 602 | Phocas overthrows Maurice and becomes emperor |

# Maps

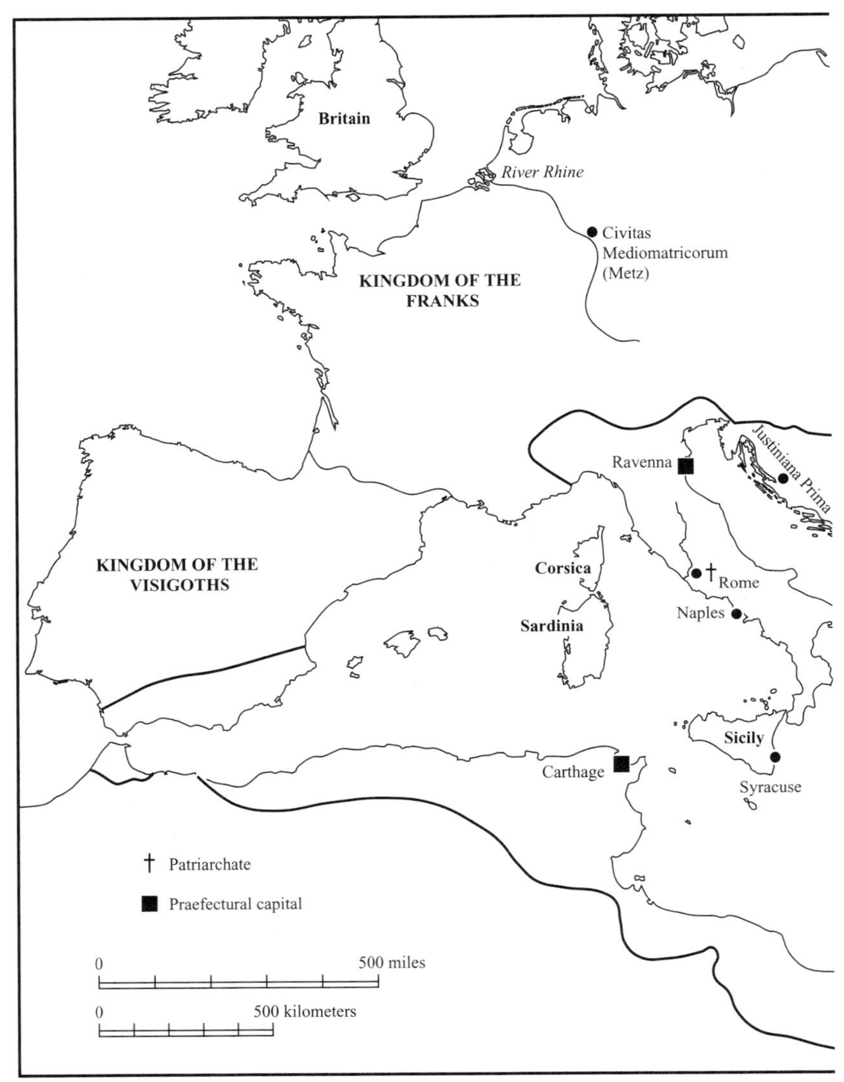


MAP 1. Justinian's empire in 565

N
River Danube
Cherson
Black Sea
Trebizond
ROMAN
EMPIRE
Constantinople
Nicaea
Ankyra
Thessaloniki
Caesarea
Sardis
Melitene
Aphrodisias
Edessa
Korykos
Athens
Ephesus
Antioch
Seleucia
River Euphrates
Emesa
Cyprus
Apamea
Epiphania
Crete
Damascus
Caesarea
Scythopolis
Jerusalem
Mediterranean Sea
Gerasa
Alexandria
Petra
River Nile

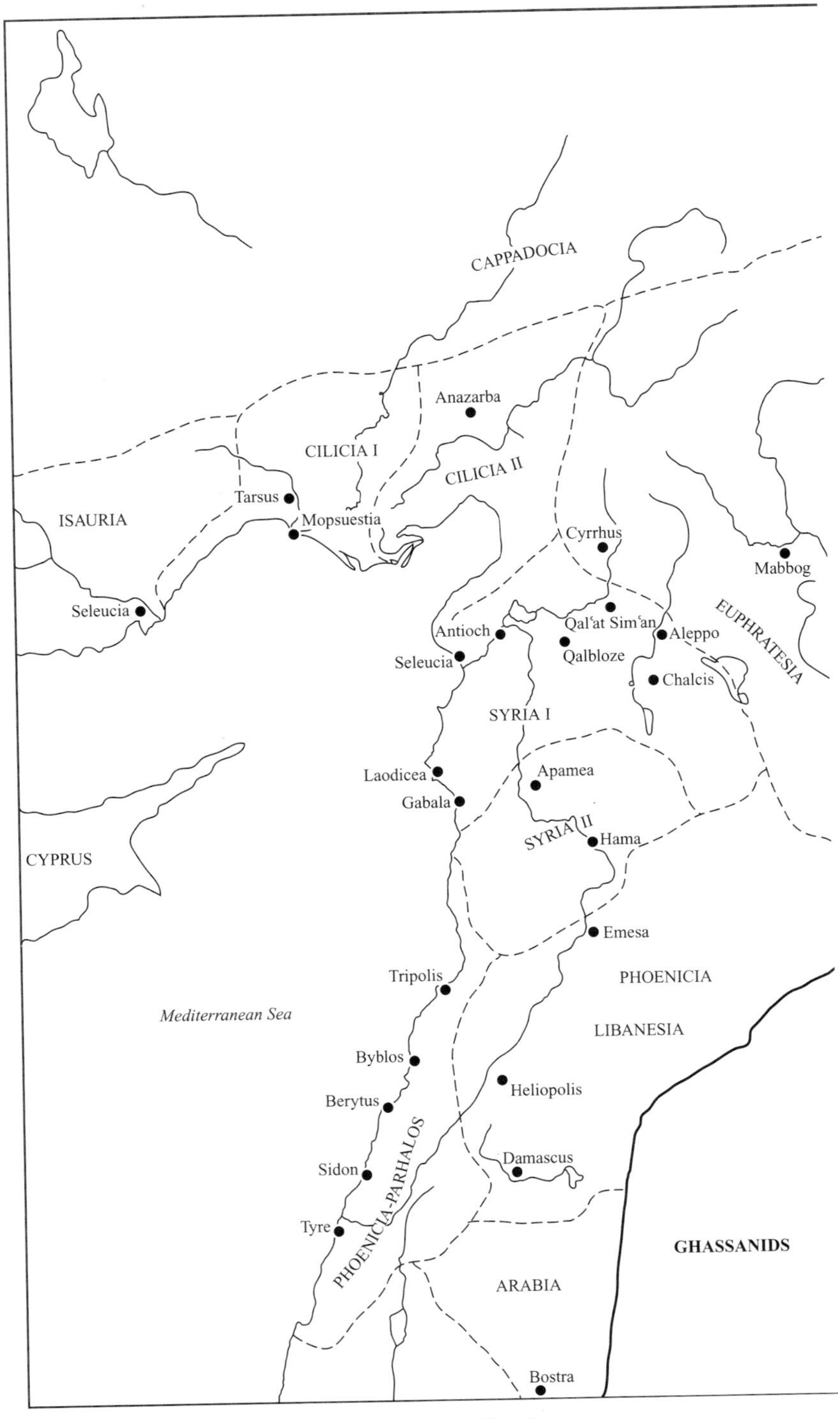


MAP 2. The eastern provinces of the Roman Empire

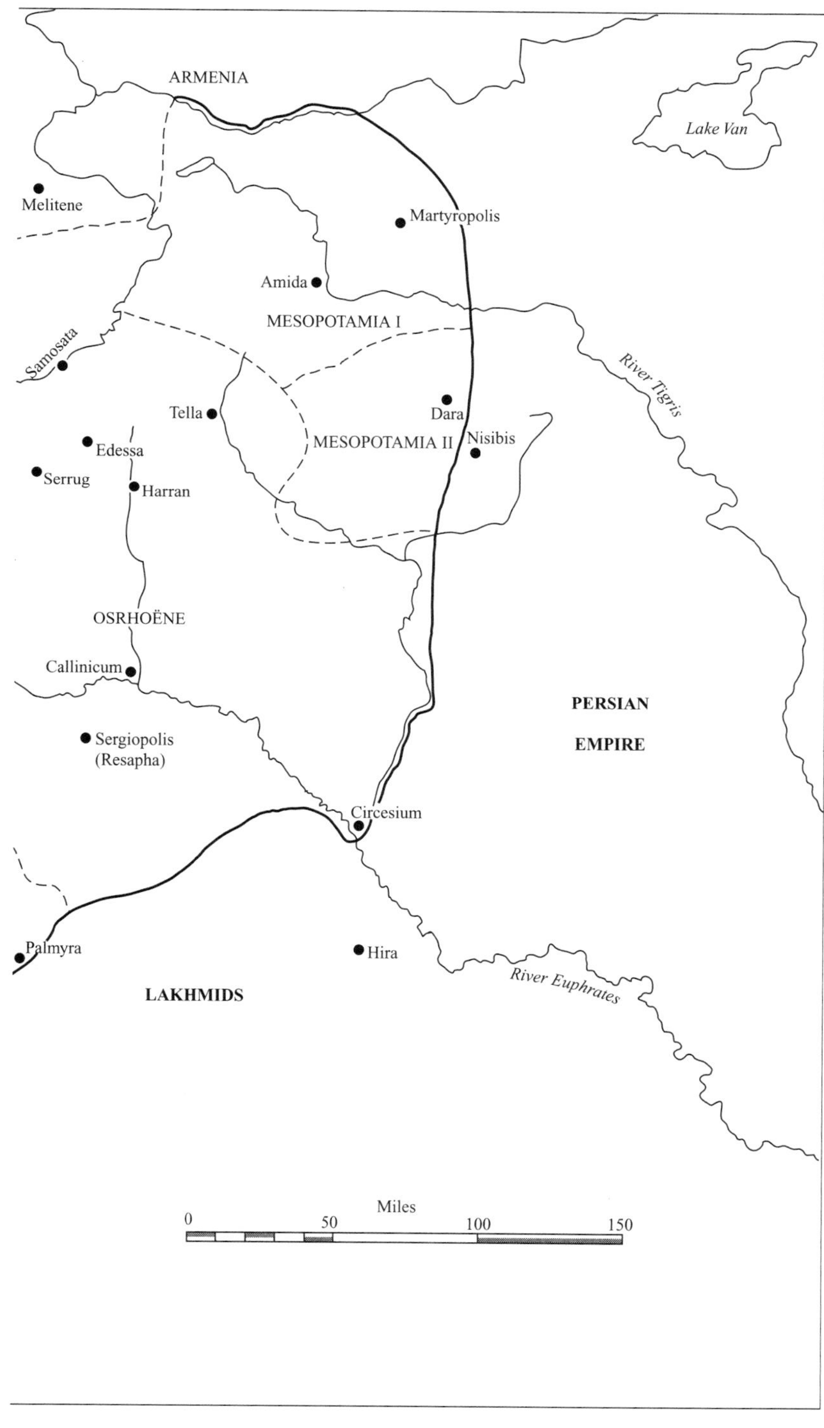
ARMENIA
Lake Van
Melitene
Martyropolis
Amida
MESOPOTAMIA I
Samosata
River Tigris
Tella
Dara
Nisibis
MESOPOTAMIA II
Edessa
Serrug
Harran
OSRHOËNE
Callinicum
PERSIAN
EMPIRE
Sergiopolis
(Resapha)
Circesium
Palmyra
Hira
River Euphrates
LAKHMIDS
Miles
0
50
100
150

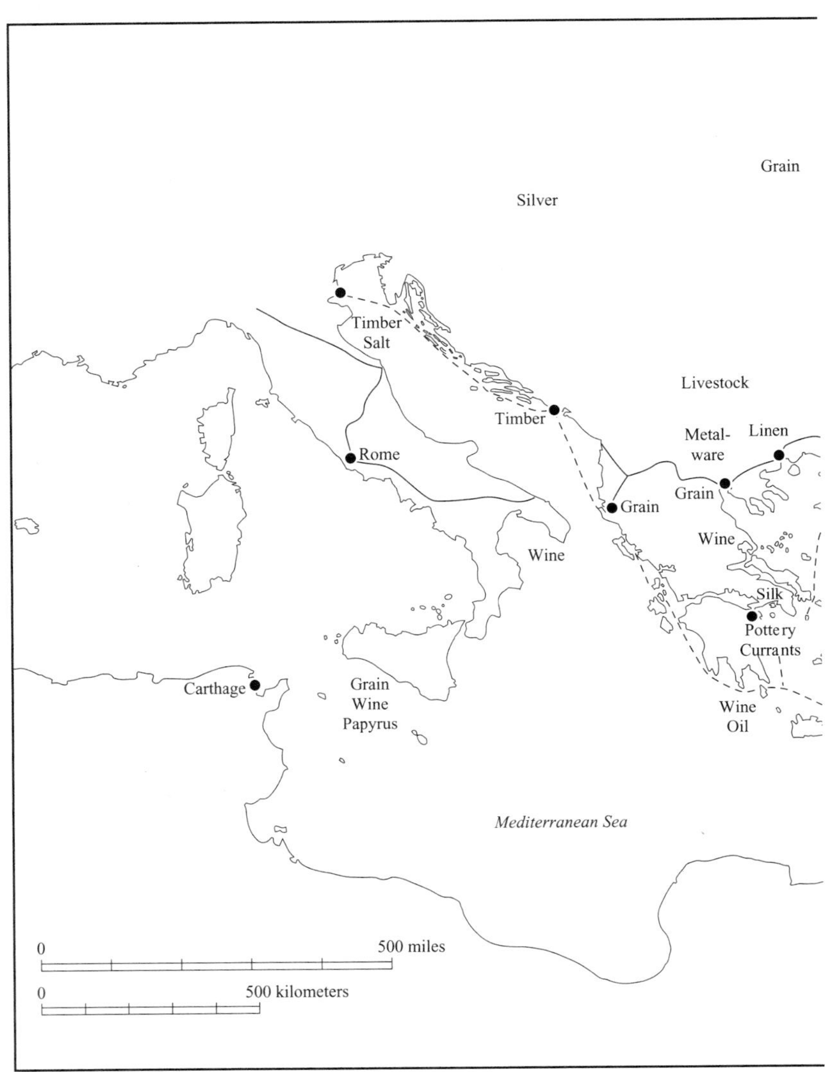


MAP 3. Resources, production, and trade in Justinian's empire

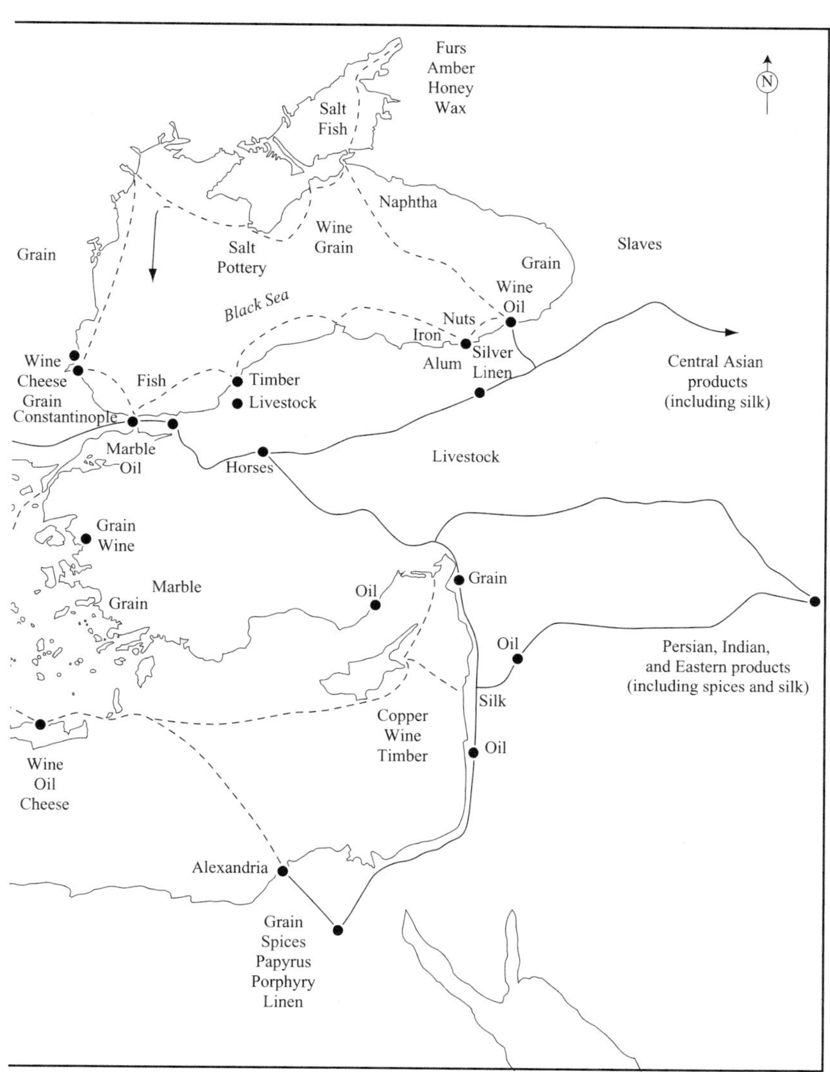

Furs
Amber
Honey
Wax
Salt
Fish
Naphtha
Wine
Grain
Salt
Pottery
Grain
Slaves
Grain
Wine
Oil
Black Sea
Nuts
Iron
Silver
Linen
Alum
Wine
Cheese
Grain
Fish
Timber
Livestock
Constantinople
Central Asian
products
(including silk)
Marble
Oil
Horses
Livestock
Grain
Wine
Marble
Grain
Oil
Grain
Oil
Persian, Indian,
and Eastern products
(including spices and silk)
Silk
Copper
Wine
Timber
Oil
Wine
Oil
Cheese
Alexandria
Grain
Spices
Papyrus
Porphyry
Linen
N

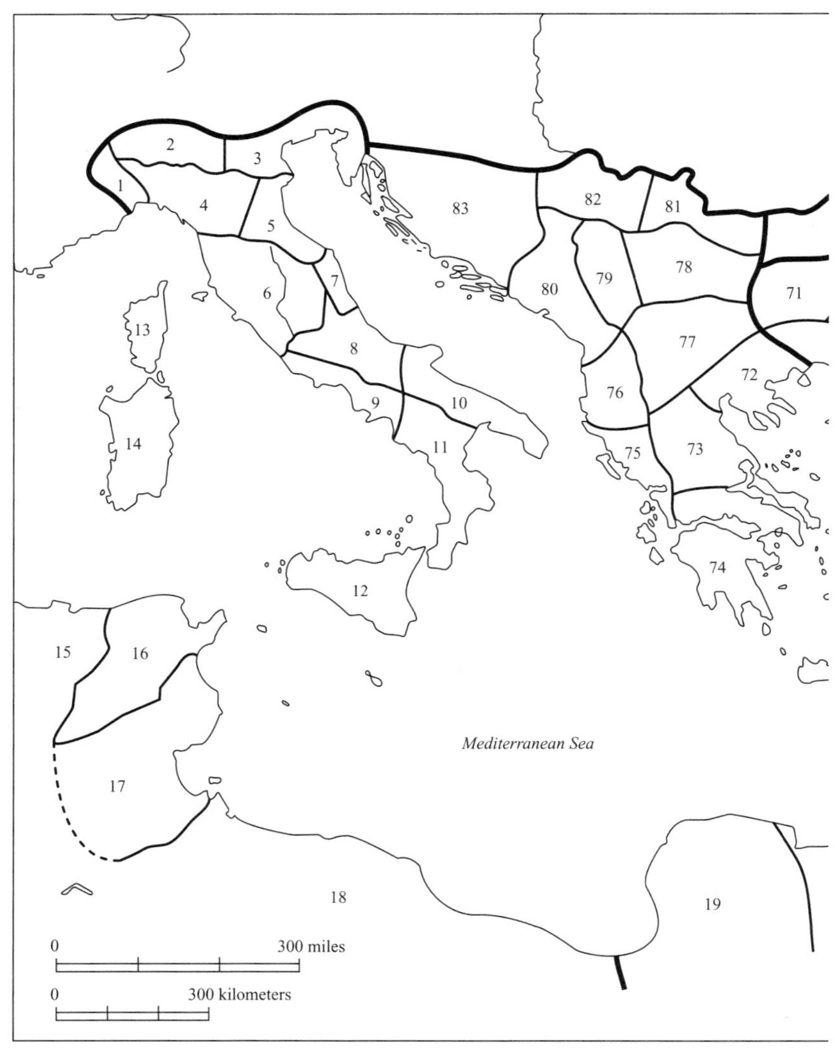


| | | |
|---|---|---|
| 1 Alpes Cottiae | 15 Numidia | 29 Palaestina II |
| 2 Aemilia | 16 Zeugitania | 30 Phoenice |
| 3 Venetia | 17 Byzacena | 31 Theodorias |
| 4 Liguria | 18 Tripolitania | 32 Cyprus (in *quaestura exercitus*) |
| 5 Flaminia | 19 Libya Pentapolis | 33 Phoenice Libanensis |
| 6 Tuscia et Umbria | 20 Libya Inferior | 34 Syria II |
| 7 Picenum | 21 Arcadia | 35 Syria I |
| 8 Samnium | 22 Thebais Inferior | 36 Euphratensis |
| 9 Campania | 23 Augustamnica II | 37 Osrhoene |
| 10 Apulia et Calabria | 24 Aegyptus I and II | 38 Mesopotamia |
| 11 Lucania et Bruttium | 25 Augustamnica I | 39 Armenia III |
| 12 Sicilia | 26 Palaestina III | 40 Armenia IV |
| 13 Corsica | 27 Palaestina I | 41 Armenia I |
| 14 Sardinia | 28 Arabia | 42 Armenia II |

MAP 4. Administrative organization of the empire

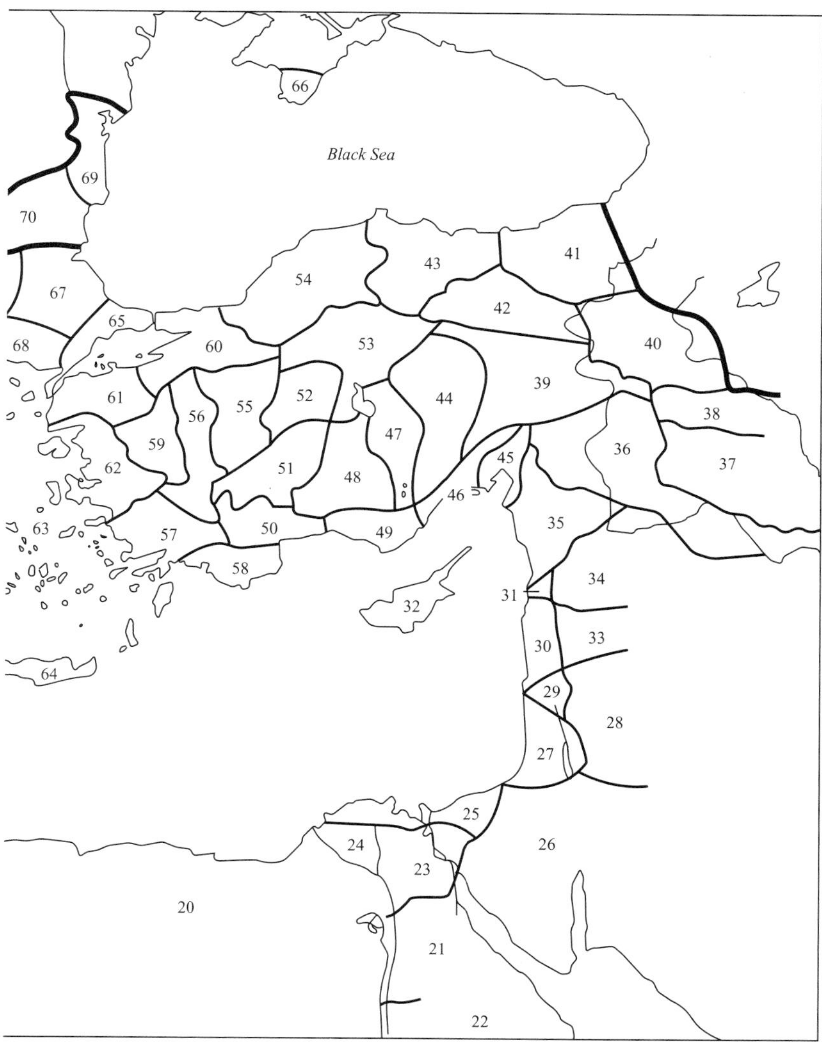


43 Helenoponus
44 Cappadocia I
45 Cilicia II
46 Cilicia I
47 Cappadocia II
48 Lycaonia
49 Isauria
50 Pamphylia
51 Pisidia
52 Galatia Salutaris
53 Galatia I
54 Paphlagonia
55 Phrygia Salutaris
56 Phrygia Pacatiana

57 Caria (in *quaestura exercitus*)
58 Lycia
59 Lydia
60 Bithynia
61 Hellespontus
62 Asia
63 Insulae (in *quaestura exercitus*)
64 Creta
65 Europa
66 Bosporus
67 Haemimontus
68 Rhodope
69 Sythia (in *quaestura exercitus*)
70 Mosia II (in *quaestura exercitus*)

71 Thracia
72 Macedonia I
73 Thessalia
74 Achaea
75 Epirus vetus
76 Epirus nova
77 Macedonia II
78 Dacia Mediterranea
79 Dardania
80 Praevalitana
81 Dacia ripensis
82 Moesis I
83 Dalmatia

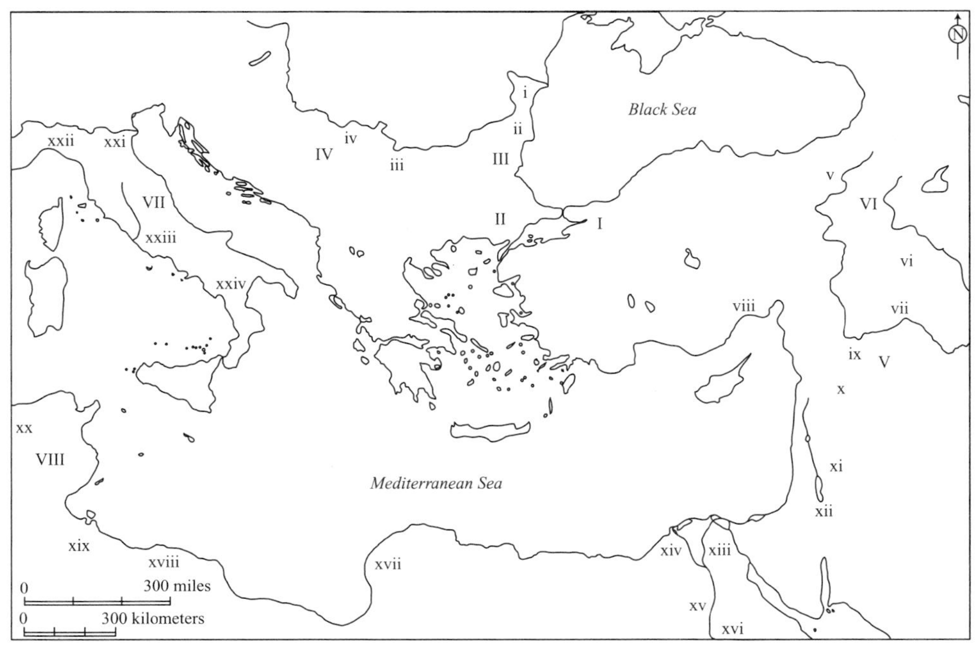


| | | | |
|---|---|---|---|
| I Magister militum praesentalis I | i Scythia | ix Syria | xvii Libya |
| II Magister militum praesentalis II | ii Moesia II | x Phoenice | xviii Tripolitania |
| III Magister militum per Thracias | iii Dacia | xi Arabia | xix Byzacena |
| IV Magister militum per Illyricum | iv Moesia I | xii Palaestina | xx Numidia |
| V Magister militum per Orientem | v Armenia | xiii Augustamnica | xxi Ravenna |
| VI Magister militum per Armeniam | vi Mesopotamia | xiv Aegyptus | xxii Liguria |
| VII Magister militum per Italiam (Exarchus Italiae) | vii Osrhoene | xv Arcadia | xxiii Roma |
| VIII Magister militum per Africam (Exarchus Africae) | viii Isauria | xvi Thebais | xxiv Neapolis |

MAP 5. Strategic arrangements in the mid–sixth century

# The Cambridge Companion to
# THE AGE OF JUSTINIAN

Part I

# STRUCTURES AND IDEOLOGIES OF EMPIRE

# 1: Roman Questions, Byzantine Answers

## Contours of the Age of Justinian

*Michael Maas*

Then appeared the emperor Justinian, entrusted by God with this commission, to watch over the whole Roman Empire and, so far as was possible, to remake it.

– Procopius of Caesarea, *Buildings* 2.6.6, trans. Dewing

## Introduction

The Age of Justinian stands at a historical milestone, marking a transition from antiquity to the Middle Ages in the Mediterranean world.[1] The period lasted for roughly a century, from the time that the young Justinian came down to Constantinople from his Balkan village around the year 500 to the regime of Phocas that began in 602, when the empire that Justinian had done so much to shape and that had been sustained with great effort by his successors plunged into a period of political instability. Throughout Justinian's era, recently called "the last of the Roman centuries,"[2] the monarchy begun by Augustus Caesar half a millennium earlier remained a going concern – even though it was now ruled from Constantinople, the "New Rome," even though most of its inhabitants spoke Greek rather than Latin, even though the old gods who had guided the empire to world rule were now pushed aside by the worshipers of Christ, and despite the uncomfortable fact that much of its territory in western Europe had been lost. Nevertheless, when the Age of Justinian came to a close on the eve of the Islamic conquests, the Roman Empire was still the strongest, best organized, and most resilient political community in Europe or the

Near East. It had a sound, even prosperous, economy, and its position in world affairs was relatively solid on all frontiers and commanding in some, so much so that recovery of lost territories again seemed a genuine possibility.[3] Yet somehow, during the century dominated by Justinian (he was sole ruler from 527 to 565, but influential from 518), the Roman Empire subtly changed internally: a new cultural entity that modern historians call Byzantium took shape.[4] Justinian's reign set the terms and, to some extent, the pace of this transformation. It was the chief catalyst in forging the Byzantine alloy, a world in which Christian, Roman, Greek, and many local elements fused to create a new medieval civilization within imperial borders. At the same time, in the lands surrounding the empire from Gaul to Arabia, other realms took distinctive medieval forms as well, influenced in part by Justinian's empire and the waves of change he helped set in motion (Maps 1 and 2).

While the Age of Justinian invites a before-and-after approach, and while scholars quite legitimately debate whether the period was "an end or beginning,"[5] it also requires investigation as a complex period in its own right. In the following chapters, we will find its distinctiveness in the ways Justinian responded to pressing problems inherited with the throne – problems framed by Roman traditions of world rule, theories of law and order, and experience of government. His answers to these Roman problems were generated by his own vision of a divinely supported autocracy. The emperor, of course, did not suspect that he was inaugurating medieval Byzantium. He meant only to distinguish his reign by overhauling an inherited Roman system of governance.[6] He believed that God had made him custodian of an empire that was very old but in disarray; already at the beginning of his reign men at court were positing that the Roman Empire in the west had ended in 476, when Romulus Augustulus, the last emperor in Italy, was deposed.[7] Justinian accordingly intended to restore Rome's venerable glory and give it additional luster as well, as a fully Christian state mirroring the splendors of heaven. These efforts to create a Roman realm unified by a single Christian faith under his authority touched the lives of millions of people, setting the course for imperial policies that long after his death continued to influence Europe and the Near East.

Justinian's record has fascinated historians since his own day, giving rise to a wealth of interpretations. Indeed, it is hard to be neutral about him. As an unscrupulous outsider and ideologue with visions of world domination, he has been compared to the Corsican Napoleon and the Georgian Stalin. His own mother was reputed to have said he was fathered by a devil.[8] In the Greek Orthodox Church, however, he is a saint. And his appeal lasts: a saturnine Justinian figures prominently in Prince Valiant comics in the Sunday papers.

The specific contours of the age that bears Justinian's name however, are not as well known as the man himself. Bracketed and overshadowed by the fall of the Roman Empire in western Europe in the fifth century and the rise of Islam in the seventh, the Age of Justinian in the sixth remains relatively unexplored by the reading public, though it has received much scholarly attention. Accordingly, the contributors to this volume have taken up a double challenge: to describe and evaluate the Age of Justinian as an epoch of far-reaching change and to address the particularity of the period in its own terms.

## Justinian and His Reign

The place to begin is with Justinian himself. The future emperor was born Petrus Sabbatius around 483 to a peasant family in the Latin-speaking Balkan village of Tauresium (modern Caričin Grad) in Thrace. We know nothing about his childhood, except that from an early age he benefited from the success of his uncle Justin, a stalwart soldier who had risen to command a palace regiment. The childless Justin brought Petrus Sabbatius to Constantinople, probably in his early teens, and formally adopted him. The intelligent boy received a good education, showing a special bent for theology but evidently not a strong interest in the non-Christian "classics" of Greek and Latin, which do not resound in his own later writings. He learned the politics of Constantinople, receiving commissions in elite palace guard units that did not require military campaigning. He had a talent for intrigue: when emperor Anastasius died in 518, Justinian worked behind the scenes to help ensure that his uncle Justin was chosen to be the new emperor. While we do not know the precise machinations that brought Justin to the throne, contemporaries believed that Justinian had a hand in them – and in the execution of several rivals immediately thereafter. By 519 he had the title of Count, followed by Master of Cavalry and Infantry at Court; his consulship came in 521, which he inaugurated with especially lavish celebrations; he gained the honorific status Patrician after 521 and Most Noble sometime before 527. At some point prior to April 527 Justinian married Theodora, once a prostitute and scandalous performer in the Hippodrome. Noted for her piety after the marriage, Theodora remained a close advisor to her husband until she died in 548.

On April 1, 527, his uncle made him co-emperor, and when Justin died four months later, Flavius Petrus Sabbatius Justinianus Augustus assumed the throne. In the fashion of conscientious Roman rulers before him, Justinian's initial impulse was to impose order on a realm that he believed to lack unity and firm direction. His tool would be Roman law legitimized by God. First the law must be put in order, however. At his command, a commission of lawyers produced a revised code of Roman law in 529, the *Codex Justinianus* (the *Code of Justinian*). Then they sifted some 2,000 works of previous Roman jurists to produce the *Digest* (or *Pandects*) in December 530. At the same time they produced a handbook for law students, called the *Institutes*, which also reformed legal studies throughout the empire. Though these projects were the product of a millennium of Roman law, in Justinian's sixth-century Christian hands, they bore the weight of new authority. Justinian insisted throughout all these legal works, whose rapid completion was interpreted as a sign of divine favor, that God had entrusted the government of the empire to him alone and that his laws should attempt to restore on earth the order that God had established in heaven.[9] On the heels of his legal reforms and in the same spirit, Justinian inaugurated a program of provincial reforms.[10]

In the short term these activities indicated the tone of Justinian's regime: self-righteously pious, overbearing, and bent on change. The long-term significance of this intimate association between imperial lawgiving and divine validation cannot be overstated for the development of Byzantine autocracy and later European ideas of kingship.

Justinian's need to meet his obligations to God by establishing order within the corpus of Roman law – as well as by establishing order throughout his realm through the agency of Roman law – is paralleled precisely in his approach to doctrinal diversity. From the beginning of his reign he attempted to eliminate heresy and establish one Christian doctrine throughout his domain, namely that formulation of belief established by the Council of Chalcedon in 451, as he interpreted it. He began protracted discussion with anti-Chalcedonians, including public debates with them in 532–533.[11] Chapters 9–11 explain the character of Christianity as it developed in the empire after Chalcedon and the consequences in the eastern and western Mediterranean of Justinian's attempts to establish unity. Here it is enough to say that the emperor's concern about maintaining order, a typically though not uniquely Roman preoccupation, found expression in efforts to establish uniformity of doctrine, a characteristically Byzantine solution that would become Justinian's new measure of imperial authority and social cohesion. This solution also required the suppression of polytheism, which was called a public crime.[12]

All was not law, religion, and reform, however. During the first five years of his reign, Justinian found himself embroiled in a war with Persia, ruled by the Sasanian dynasty and the traditional opponent of Rome in the east. Pursuing a military policy of "pragmatic engagement"[13] (characteristic of his approach to law and religion as well), Justinian extricated his armies from the war with Persia by 532. The emperor had little time to enjoy the peace, however. In mid-January 532 he almost lost his throne in an insurrection in Constantinople, the Nika revolt. Chanting "nika," which means "victory" in Greek, urban rioters demanded the removal of some high officials handpicked by the emperor. Aristocratic opponents, who had perhaps instigated the riots, attempted a coup. In the melee, fires destroyed the heart of the city and reached the palace. After painful deliberation, Justinian decided not to flee.[14] His generals Belisarius and Narses stopped the insurrection in its tracks by slaughtering thousands of the rioters in the Hippodrome. Justinian interpreted his survival as a sign of divine support. The intimate connection he envisaged between the imperial office and God would become a pillar supporting the Byzantine state.[15]

Buoyed by a reinforced sense of destiny, Justinian began ambitious projects of restoration. First came the construction of the enormous cathedral of Hagia Sophia (Holy Wisdom) near the palace in Constantinople.[16] Replacing an earlier church destroyed in the Nika revolt, Hagia Sophia embodied the spirit of Christian renovation that Justinian wished to be characteristic of his reign. The emperor also pursued an extensive building program throughout his realm, making his piety and solicitude for his subjects visible to all.

A second grand project, conquest of the Vandal kingdom based at Carthage, answered a pressing question: As Roman emperor, what should he do about the Roman provinces in the west lost for a century to heretical Germanic rulers?[17] Motivated as much by a desire to eliminate heresy as to regain Roman territories, Justinian launched an attack on the Arian Vandals in 533. His general Belisarius won an unexpectedly rapid victory with only 15,000 troops. Encouraged by this success, which was interpreted as a further sign of divine approval, in 535 Justinian attacked the Arian Ostrogoths who ruled Italy. Sicily fell easily, but it would take nearly twenty years of hard fighting before his armies defeated the Ostrogoths in 554.

If the 530s were a time of success and achievement for Justinian, the 540s witnessed only troubles. Hostilities with Persia resumed, causing a reallocation of military resources to the eastern front. Then in 542 a terrible outbreak of plague struck the empire, killing millions (Justinian himself nearly died) and substantially diminishing economic resources.[18] The next year, the so-called Three Chapters Controversy broke out as a result of the emperor's attempt to reconcile Chalcedonian and anti-Chalcedonian (Monophysite/Miaphysite) Christians in his eastern provinces while maintaining the support of the western clergy and the pope.[19] His efforts completely backfired. Not only did he fail to win doctrinal unity in the east, he alienated the western clergy through his efforts to interpret doctrine, something western clergymen felt was the prerogative of priests, not emperors.[20] Justinian's insistence on being a legitimate interpreter of sacred texts in the pursuit of doctrinal unity – as clear a statement of Byzantine kingship as one can imagine – resulted in a fissure between the Constantinopolitan church and the papacy that would last for generations.[21]

The last decades of Justinian's reign continued to be disappointing, as the hopes of the early years continued to sour. The war in Italy dragged on. In 548, Theodora, who had been such an astute counselor and aide, especially in negotiations with the eastern anti-Chalcedonians, died. The dome of Hagia Sophia cracked in 557 and partly collapsed the following year. In 559 Slav raiders accompanied by an army of Huns reached as far as the walls of Constantinople, forcing Justinian to call Belisarius out of retirement to organize the defense. Earthquakes struck the empire, civil disturbances rocked Constantinople, and ambitious men plotted against the aged emperor. Even the peace treaty concluded with Persia in 561–562 required heavy payments of gold from the Romans.

Justinian's tireless efforts for religious unity bore bittersweet fruit. Though bishops at the Fifth Ecumenical Council (the Second Council of Constantinople) finally anathematized the Three Chapters in 553, the rift with western clerics only deepened. His attempt to reach an understanding with the anti-Chalcedonians in the east failed as well, leading directly to the emergence of an independent anti-Chalcedonian clerical hierarchy.[22] Nevertheless, the bishops' acceptance of Justinian's claim to determine doctrine in 553 was an enactment of his view of imperial relations with the church – a Byzantine perspective put into action.[23] Yet even this development was imperiled in the last years of his life, when his bishops refused to accept aphthartodocetism, a heretical doctrine regarding the incorruptibility of Christ's body, which Justinian had espoused, claiming it to be compatible with Chalcedonian teachings.[24] The issue faded away when the emperor died on November 14, 565. Although ecstatic and hopeful early in his reign, the mood at Constantinople had changed by the end of Justinian's life to one of angry frustration. Justinian's funeral pall was embroidered with scenes of his military triumphs in the 530s that must have seemed a grim anachronism to the mourners who laid him to rest.[25]

## The Successors of Justinian

Justinian's successors, Justin II (556–578), Tiberius Constantine (578–582), and Maurice (582–602), maintained the general direction of Justinian's rule, though they adapted policy to circumstance.[26] During the watch of Justinian's immediate successor, his nephew Justin II, a war against Khusro II of Persia resulted in loss of Roman territory and its substantial revenues, the Lombards seized Italy, and Slavs and Avars gained a foothold in the Balkans. Under Tiberius Constantine, war with Persia continued, and in the west Tiberius attempted to recover Italian territory from the Lombards but failed. He created exarchs, new local administrators in Italy (in 584) and then in North Africa (in 591), who combined military and civilian responsibilities – a major administrative reform. The military situation worsened in the Balkans, where aggressive Avar forces probed the Roman defenses that were weakened by the withdrawal of troops for the Persian war. They captured the important city of Sirmium, and Slavic settlement continued. Domestically Tiberius tried to avoid involvement in the endemic religious disputes. He died in the late summer of 582 and was succeeded by his general Maurice, who had previously been the commanding general on the Persian front.

Because Tiberius had depleted the treasury, Maurice was forced to limit public expenditures and military pay, which earned him much disfavor. Like Tiberius, he attempted to maintain a tolerant posture in the continuing struggle between Chalcedonians and anti-Chalcedonians, without complete success, and he fell into serious quarrels with Pope Gregory. He was stymied in various attempts at reform.[27] Yet under his direction, war with Persia took such a positive turn that a new Persian monarch Khusro II, received Roman imperial support. He took command of Roman forces in the Balkans to confront the Avars and within a decade had reasserted Roman control there. In 602, he ordered his troops to winter in camps north of the Danube, a strategically sound decision, but his troops mutinied. Phocas, the soldier who led them, marched on Constantinople, killed Maurice, and claimed the throne, beginning a decade of misrule and political discontent that brought the Age of Justinian to an end.

## Contours of the Age

Having sketched in broad strokes the main events of the Age of Justinian, we turn now to examining its geopolitical, economic, religious, and intellectual contours.

### *The World around Justinian: Geopolitical Contours*

The geopolitical contours of the Age of Justinian were shaped by three forces. The most important was Persia, which expanded in the Near East and the Caucasus region at Rome's expense. The huge, multiethnic empire posed the greatest threat to Romans throughout the Age of Justinian, as warfare grew more frequent between the great powers.[28] Khusro I was Justinian's greatest adversary. His frequent invasions of Roman territory caused great damage to the rich cities of the region. The loss of revenues due to the continuing conflict and to Persian seizure of Roman property had a deleterious effect on the Roman economy, though it did not affect productivity. Only in the seventh century could either side envisage the complete overthrow of the other, a feat finally accomplished by the emperor Heraclius (r. 610–641) – just as Muslim armies were on the march.

The second force shaping the geopolitical contours of the age was the collapse of Roman authority in western Europe in the early fifth century, accompanied by the entry into the empire of diverse groups of fighting men and their dependents seeking new lands to settle.[29] These "barbarian invasions" resulted in the gradual loss of all Roman possessions west of the Balkans. Over several generations a number of aggressive new kingdoms slowly evolved on former Roman soil organized by different groups of settlers. By 527, when Justinian came to the throne, four major "successor" kingdoms exercized power in western continental Europe: the Ostrogoths in Italy, the Vandals in North Africa, the Visigoths in Spain, and the Franks, who held Gaul as well as lands beyond the Rhine River that Rome had never controlled. Their kings maintained a complex interrelationship with the vastly more numerous Roman populations whom they ruled with varying degrees of civility and with the Roman elites who collaborated in the new governments. The kings also maintained ties with the emperor in Constantinople, whose sovereignty in some formal but loose way they acknowledged. Because the new kings and the peoples they led were Arian Christians, while the Roman provinicials they ruled were Chalcedonians, two separate clergies and communities of faith existed side by side. In some cases, such as in Vandal Africa, there was occasional persecution of the Chalcedonian Romans. In society, politics, and religion, the new kingdoms experienced a complex internal evolution – an evolution influenced profoundly by Rome and eventually by Justinian and his policies.[30]

Justinian was eager to reassert Roman authority over these lost territories and to do away with the heretical Arian belief held by the new kings and their followers. Many discontented Romans who felt stranded in the new kingdoms emigrated to Constantinople and put additional pressure on Justinian to attack.[31] Justinian first set his sights on the Vandal kingdom based at Carthage. Belisarius won an easy victory there in 533, as noted above. Next came the war against Ostrogothic Italy, which began in 535 and lasted for twenty years because of the fierce resistance of the Ostrogoths and the indifference and occasional open resistance of the Italian population to Justinian's army of "liberation." During the long decades of the Italian war Justinian also struggled with a succession of popes over matters of doctrine and support of imperial policies, setting a pattern of relations between Constantinople and the western church for decades.[32] As the war in Italy was coming to a close, Justinian's forces managed to capture part of Spain's Mediterranean coast from the Visigothic king in 552.[33]

Justinian had no choice but to coexist with the Franks, who established a formidable new kingdom in the course of the fifth and sixth centuries in Gaul and in northern territories that had never been Roman. The kingdom of the Franks, based in the Loire-Rhine region under the Merovingian dynasty, became dominant from the Atlantic to the Elbe. The Merovingian king Clovis (r. 481–511) had adopted Catholicism, and so his Franks readily merged with the Gallo-Roman population, which gave the kingdom added strength. Though the Franks had a history of diplomatic relations with Constantinople, and though they were traditional enemies of the Ostrogoths, during Justinian's Italian war they were opportunistic, taking advantage of the moment against both Goths and Romans. Never as institutionally sophisticated as the Roman Empire, the Frankish realm nevertheless stood as the major power in western Europe throughout the Age of Justinian. The stability, civic organization, and even more the Catholicism (Chalcedonianism) of the Franks won high praise among some Romans in Constantinople.[34]

Justinian's death in 565 spared him open conflict with the Lombards, whose invasion of Italy in the late 560s was a direct consequence of his earlier machinations in Pannonia. They established a warlike kingdom in Italy that lasted until Charlemagne crushed it in 774. In addition to their rivalry with the Franks, the Lombards perpetually struggled with the Roman exarchs in Ravenna for control of Italy, and so they remained enmeshed with Constantinople throughout the reigns of Justinian's successors.

The third force shaping the geopolitical contours was the constant pressure inward toward the Mediterranean of different confederacies of peoples. To the north of the Danube loomed the Avars, steppe nomads driven westward from Central Asia by the Turks, who created a vast empire of subordinate peoples.[35] The Avars first appeared in the last years of Justinian's reign and immediately made an alliance with the emperor, who was pleased to have another pawn on his northern frontier. He paid them subsidies to stay at peace with Rome and to fight other northern enemies of Rome. The Avars soon became a terrible threat, however. Among the peoples in the Avar hegemony were Slavic groups. A mixture of many cultures and ethnic groups, Slav communities developed beyond Roman frontiers with no experience of Roman society and government. Bands of Slavs, sometimes in collaboration with Avars, began to cross into the Balkans in the last part of the sixth century, driving many Romans from their homes. By 600, emperor Maurice had cleared most of them from Roman territory, but after his death Avars and Slavs again gained control of most lands from Greece to the Danube, posing a constant threat to Constantinople and the empire.

In North Africa, tribesmen known collectively as Berbers pressed north against the settled farmlands of Roman North Africa.[36] These tribal groups for the most part did not speak Latin or Greek, though some were Christian and Romanized, forming enclaves of Romanized culture that lasted into the Islamic period.[37] The overthrow of the Vandal kingdom in 533 brought Roman troops into conflict with Berber tribes that were raiding freely toward the Mediterranean. Justinian's generals built a string of fortresses and won some important successes, but the Berbers remained a problem until the Muslim conquest of North Africa in the seventh century.

To the southeast of the Roman Empire on the northern fringes of Arabia, both Romans and Persians interacted with confederacies of Arabs, using them as pawns in their continuing conflicts. Though not a threat in the sixth century, after accepting Islam, these Arabs, in conjunction with armies from the Arabian peninsula, would utterly change the geopolitical contours of the Mediterranean world within a century of Justinian's death.[38]

This whirlwind tour of the neighbors of Justinian's empire shows vast territories developing new structures of power and identity while jousting with the Romans. Justinian's priorities had always lain on the Persian front, and by the end of the Age of Justinian there was an inevitable focus on the eastern Mediterranean. Islam's rise finished the story, and Byzantium became a regional power.

## *Economic Contours*

What were the consequences of these geopolitical developments on the economy of Justinian's age?[39] The evidence is patchy and much contested, but in a very general way, the Pirenne Thesis seems to hold true. This theory, developed by the Belgian medievalist Henri Pirenne in the years following World War I, discounted the role of Germanic invaders in breaking the economic unity of the Mediterranean and placed the onus instead on the Arab invasions of the seventh century.[40] If we add Persia to the equation, Pirenne's theory gains force.

In the fifth century the loss of the western provinces unquestionably injured the economic cohesiveness of the Mediterranean world. This does not mean that trade stopped, however, or that local economies collapsed altogether, but that a slow decline in economic activity was underway in the West.[41] One reason for the decline was the absence of the Roman administration that held together the empire's quilt of interlocking local and regional economies. This change reduced the scale of cities.[42] For example, grain from North Africa was no longer imported to the city of Rome after the establishment of the Vandal kingdom, which contributed to a reduction in the city's population. Low-value goods such as pottery as well as luxury items such as wine and textiles continued to be produced locally and shipped to distant markets,[43] but archaeologists have noted a general slowdown in exchange in the western Mediterranean's hinterlands during the Age of Justinian, due not to barbarian invasions but to various local factors. This led in turn to the further regionalization of the economy in the former western provinces.[44] As the economies of the different successor kingdoms went their separate ways, the foundation of the medieval economy in western Europe and North Africa slowly took shape.[45]

The economic situation differed in the eastern Mediterranean, where the Roman government still provided fiscal unity. Rigorous taxation continued to exploit local systems of production. The seizure of

Syrian wealth by Persians in the course of Justinian's century constituted a steady drain on resources, however, and the plague of the 540s further hurt the economy, though perhaps not as badly as has been thought.[46] The final loss of Syria and Egypt to the Arabs in the 630s and 640s created a debilitating crisis for the Byzantine state, causing a loss of revenues estimated at 75 percent.[47] We see then that the economic unity of the Roman Mediterranean dissolved unevenly: In the late sixth century, Gaza wine was still sent to Gaul, but in the late seventh century, Theodore of Tarsus, a Syrian cleric in Britain, had to explain what a melon was to his students.[48]

## *Religious Contours*

By the sixth century disputes over doctrine had become a familiar part of life in the Christian world, as large communities defined by faith and adherence to specific Christological positions emerged from the Near East to the Atlantic. These communities (which were not coterminous with kingdoms) took shape largely in response to the Council of Chalcedon, which in 451 had attempted to resolve the issue of the relation of the human and divine natures in Christ,[49] a matter that rested on interpretation of the Bible, first of all, in different languages, as well as a variety of other truth-bearing texts written by churchmen and church councils. There was frequently violent disagreement about the choice and interpretation of those texts and the proper method of explicating them. Arguments flared over the interpretive clout of various past authorities. What would be the relative authority of the pope, the church fathers, the church councils – and the emperor – in Justinian's new world order?[50]

The management of Christianity had been an imperial concern since Constantine's conversion to the faith in 312 for a very Roman reason: it was understood that the welfare of the empire depended on maintaining the good will of divinity. Naturally, Justinian jumped into the fray, and even before he took the throne he began to negotiate with the pope and other theologians and religious leaders on matters of doctrine and unity. As emperor he intended to establish uniform belief throughout the realm, thereby creating a unified empire pleasing to God. This involved mastering the complexities of Christological argument in Chalcedon's aftermath and then trying to establish himself in the hierarchy of legitimate textual interpreters. His tireless effort to resolve doctrinal disharmony failed spectacularly, but with significant consequences. As noted earlier, Justinian's autocratic posture poisoned the atmosphere in relations with Chalcedonians in the western Mediterranean.[51]

By attempting to intervene in doctrinal debate and to establish himself as a legitimate interpreter of sacred texts, Justinian set a Byzantine precedent. He went a long way to define a resilient Byzantine religious culture based on an interpretation of Chalcedon, rooted in Greek foundation texts and intimately linked to imperial authority. There was a downside, however. Despite his best efforts to broker a deal with eastern anti-Chalcedonian Christians, a fractious anti-Chalcedonian hierarchy soon established itself in Syriac-speaking lands as an independent religious presence. The anti-Chalcedonian communities continued to fragment during the reigns of Justinian's successors, making it impossible for Constantinople to reach any lasting accommodation with them.[52] The problem was made moot by the Islamic conquests in the seventh century, when these anti-Chalcedonian communities were taken from Constantinople's authority.

Allegiance to Chalcedonian doctrine was not limited to Romans or the inhabitants of lands once controlled by Rome. When Clovis, ruler of the Franks, converted to Catholicism (Chalcedonianism) in about 496, he found a way to challenge the authority of Visigothic enemies, who espoused Arian Christianity. Likewise in Spain, in 587, Reccared, the Visigothic king, converted to Catholicism, taking a step that would help create a more homogeneous medieval community.

Justinian also dealt with non-Christians: polytheists and Jews within the empire and polytheists beyond imperial borders. Let us look at each separately. Insistence upon uniform Christian belief entailed the suppression of the surviving polytheist worship, recently described as limited to "obdurate academics and illiterate peasants."[53] The first of these, whom we might call "intellectual pagans," have left no traces of cultic worship. They come to our notice only as a result of the emperor's charges against them. Though of course some people may have worshiped the old gods in secret, it is equally likely that their "paganism" lay in the realm of allegiance to intellectual traditions, especially philosophy, that could still be engaged independently of Christian interpretation.[54]

Large numbers of peasants from Spain to Syria continued to worship old gods. John of Ephesus converted thousands of nonbelievers to Christianity in Asia Minor and Syria in the 540s. The understanding of Christian beliefs cannot have been deep in such mass conversions. Clerics repeatedly had to admonish their flocks to abandon pagan habits.

By the end of the sixth century the term "pagan" had become a generalized insult hurled by bishops at one another.

Penalties were harsh. Christians caught sacrificing to the old gods were to be executed. Non-Christians were forbidden to hold public office, teach, or own property but were given a three-month grace period in which to convert and so keep their lands and jobs.[55]

Missionary activity had been essential to Christian practice since the time of Paul, but Justinian was the first emperor to make missions of conversion a matter of policy: in addition to John of Ephesus's activities, the emperor converted peoples in the Caucausus,[56] and further beyond imperial borders to Ethiopia,[57] and he (and his successors) made conversion an element in the diplomatic recognition of foreign kings from the northern steppe whenever possible.

For Jews, a minority in the empire, the Age of Justinian marked the beginning of a new phase in their history.[58] Though Justinian involved himself in the direction of the Jewish community in his realm (he encouraged Jews in Constantinople and perhaps the entire empire to use the Greek Septuagint), he did not actively persecute them. By the reign of Heraclius, however, forced conversions of Jews were an occasional feature of imperial policy. As a consequence of continued diminution of status in the empire and forced withdrawal from public life, Jewish communities turned inward, returning to Hebrew in liturgy, for example.[59]

What were the consequences of Justinian's religious policies? They produced a more unified Christian Roman society, resilient enough, as events of the subsequent decades demonstrated, to withstand attacks on many fronts, and eventually the onslaught of Islam.[60] In doing so, Justinian defined the empire as a community of orthodox faith and assumed control of its religious destiny.

Justinian's interventions in religious matters led to a further polarization of east and west, with the emergence of separate communities of faith throughout the Roman world, each based on its own language, sacred texts, Christological doctrine, and priestly hierarchies. These were the seeds of emerging medieval identities: Latin Christendom in western Europe (where Chalcedonian Christianity is referred to as Roman Catholicism); Greek Orthodox Byzantium; and the Syriac, Armenian, and Coptic realms.[61]

Finally, through his policies of conversion and missionary activity, as they were intertwined with diplomatic efforts, we see the first articulation of the medieval Byzantine Commonwealth, as Dimitri Obolensky termed it, in which Constantinople was the hub of a constellation of Christian ethnic communities beyond its borders.[62]

## *Intellectual Contours*

In terms of intellectual life, the Age of Justinian became a transitional phase between the classical past and the Byzantine future as non-Christian traditions of learning came under heated review. From this perspective, we see several interrelated developments that defined the intellectual contours of the age.

First, the Age of Justinian witnessed the intensification of Christianity in all aspects of intellectual life, often through the intervention of the emperor. Second, the system of education that had been characteristic of the Roman Empire for centuries broke down, a function of general changes in city life and imperial policy. Third, the period witnessed the gathering and codification of many sorts of knowledge for both utilitarian and preservative purposes. In the same way that the determination of basic texts was fundamental for religious exegesis, the assemblage of foundational texts for legal practice, grammar, philosophical inquiry, or the history of government institutions, stands out as a feature of the period. We will examine these briefly to see the Byzantine turn taken in each regard.

Intensification of Christian Influence Christian scholars had long debated the question "What has Athens to do with Jerusalem?" but during the sixth century tensions between Christian approaches and non-Christian traditions of knowledge became particularly acute, especially when refracted through the imperial lens. Justinian's effort to create a Roman society of uniform belief exacerbated the debate and served to break the links with the past. In suppressing polytheism and targeting the urban intelligentsia, he helped seal the fate of autonomous secular learning. He imposed the pejorative category of "pagan" on knowledge and activities that previously had been an unremarkable part of the cultural atmosphere of the empire. To put it broadly, at the beginning of the Age of Justinian, certain traditions of knowledge, especially in philosophy, art, and the writing of history, still existed independently of Christian appropriation. At the end of the sixth century, these autonomous cultural spheres had virtually disappeared, though not the material itself. Hereafter classical knowledge – law, philosophy, science – would be approached only from a Christian perspective. Such intellectual pluralism as made possible by these non-Christian perspectives would not be possible in another generation. Soon, much would be forgotten: by the eighth century, books would be a rarity and classical art viewed with suspicion and dread.[63]

The formal writing of history provides a good example of how choices were made about the proper relation of classical and Christian traditions of thought in the Age of Justinian. Historians who were Christian continued to write history in Greek in the classical tradition until the early seventh century, imitating the Attic style of the fifth-century BC historian Thucydides. This manner of writing history flourished at Constantinople, especially in the hands of Procopius and his continuators.[64] Procopius, the most Thucydidean, feigned ignorance of Christian beliefs and institutions although he was a Christian himself,[65] but nearly a century later Theophylact felt no need to employ such artifice and freely incorporated Christian material and explanations into his classicizing narrative.[66] He was the last to attempt traditional, classicizing historiography in this era.

As classical forms of historical narration fell by the wayside, Christian world chronicles took their place. They interpreted history within a Christian framework, starting at creation, covering biblical events and Christ's crucifixion, and then continuing to the present.[67] By the sixth century these chronicles provided an explanation of human history for all Christians, breaking with the classical, Greco-Roman past while connecting with the biblical past instead.[68] The chronicles written by the Antiochene lawyer John Malalas and by Count Marcellinus, an official at Justinian's court, are far more representative of widely held beliefs in the sixth century than the classicizing history of Procopius.[69] The concerns addressed in these chronicles reflect contemporaneous changes in popular piety.[70]

GATHERING AND CODIFYING KNOWLEDGE A growing sense of disconnection with the knowledge from and about the non-Christian past made the Age of Justinian a time of notable reorganization and codification of knowledge. For example, John the Lydian (John Lydus), a bureaucrat in the office of the praetorian prefect under Justinian, grew distressed because he saw imperial policies attacking men of high culture, the schools that nourished them, and the ties to the intellectual heritage of antiquity that shaped their understanding of the social universe. He compiled three antiquarian works to counter the ravages of time. These treatises, *On the Months, On Portents*, and *On Offices*, preserved data from a host of ancient authors yet responded to contemporary issues. *On Offices*, while presenting antiquarian data about the praetorian prefecture, considered the emperor as both the rehabilitator of the past and its destroyer. Other writers also produced collections: Hesychius wrote a biographical dictionary of pagan scholars; Stephanus compiled a huge geographical lexicon that was soon abridged and dedicated to Justinian. Peter the Patrician, a distinguished statesman in Justinian's service, wrote a history of the Bureau of the Master of Offices;[71] Priscian, a professor of grammar at Constantinople, wrote numerous works, including eighteen volumes on Latin grammar that drew liberally from a wide selection of classical Latin texts. Dedicated to the consul Julian, this massive work was the product of a patronage network in the imperial capital that linked literature to aristocratic munificence.[72] Priscian's massive work was soon condensed to create a book for use in schools,[73] as were other treatises. *A Handbook of the Basic Principles of Divine Law* was composed by Junillus, Justinian's chief legal officer in the 540s, to serve as a primer for students of biblical exegesis.

An emphasis on legal codification and condensation marked the age. Germanic kings produced law codes, as did the Persian monarch Khusro II Parviz (r. 591–628) in his *Book of a Thousand Decisions*, discussed in Chapter 20. Rabbis produced the Babylonian Talmud at about the same time, as we will see in Chapter 16. The most influential of all compilations of antique data, however, was Justinian's massive *Corpus of Civil Law*. It also was the source of a handbook, the *Institutes*, for students. At the emperor's instruction, furthermore, lawyers condensed and translated the Latin legal material into Greek in the late 530s.

Collections of knowledge with an educational goal in mind were not limited to Constantinople. We find individuals undertaking such encyclopedic tasks across the Mediterranean basin, wherever traces of Roman culture existed. In Italy under Ostrogothic rule, Boethius (c. 480–524) began an enormous project that addressed all knowledge systematically.[74] His contemporary, the Italian aristocrat Cassiodorus (c. 490–c. 582), who also served the Ostrogothic king, retired to his monastery at Vivarium, where he began a systematic gathering and reproduction of learning in an attempt to preserve classical learning and train scribes.[75] His *Institutions* discussed sacred and profane literature and offered appropriate bibliography. Perhaps more significantly, in the monastery his monks gathered classical texts, emphasizing practical studies such as agriculture, medicine, and natural history, in an attempt to preserve this material for later generations.[76] Around 529

Benedict founded the monastery of Monte Cassino in Italy. His *Rule* provided time for the monks to read every day, thereby leaving the door open for the copying of books in future generations. Farther still from Constantinople, Isidore of Seville in Spain (c. 570–636) composed many literary, historical, and encyclopedic works. The *Twenty Books of Etymologies or Origins* attempts to preserve an enormous amount of knowledge about law, medicine, and languages, as well as the standard Roman curriculum (the trivium and quadrivium), that might otherwise be lost.[77] Monasteries, the new homes of learning and copying manuscripts in the West, replaced urban centers of education and so altered the patterns of the flow of knowledge in the Mediterranean world. An inward turn to monastic life meant that the knowledge of antiquity acquired an existence apart from the political reverberations of Justinian's policies.

A new kind of Christian book developed in the Age of Justinian, the catena, that brought together the ecclesiastical need for authoritative text to use in doctrinal debate and the widespread tendency to summarize and codify. These works, first attributed to Procopius of Gaza (c. 460–530) created knowledge by proxy. They set out commentaries on biblical books that linked the interpretations of several previous clerics, often quoting them verbatim.[78] These chains of authoritative texts, which eventually came to substitute for reading the original works themselves, played an important role in late-sixth- and seventh-century doctrinal debates.[79]

Education The system of education in the Roman Empire changed significantly during the Age of Justinian, as the secular literary superstructure disintegrated due to imperial policy and, more indirectly, to the transformation of traditional city life.[80] The Roman educational system, which existed before the advent of Christianity, represented a view of culture and community that by the time of Justinian was not fully in keeping with Christian belief. How Justinian and his circle, who were both Christian and Roman, dealt with the differences speaks for the emergence of a Byzantine world in which secular education passed into Christian hands. During Justinian's reign imperial Christianity took a highly political stance toward classical learning. At the same time that Justinian's propaganda emphasized continuity with the Roman past, various parts of that legacy, particularly science and philosophy, were suspected of being pagan. There were purges of intellectuals, accusations against public officials, and book burnings. Traces survive of a debate among Christians at court about the nature of education. Advocates of a fully Christian curriculum, such as Justinian's legal minister Junillus, were on one side, while others, like the historian Procopius, who preferred traditional training in rhetoric, grammar, and classical literature, were on the other. Justinian took the middle road. While he reduced the financial support for teachers of traditional schools in some areas and insisted that all teaching be done by Chalcedonian Christians, he nevertheless subsidized teachers of grammar, rhetoric, medicine, and law in Italy when he reestablished Roman rule there in 554, "so that young men trained in liberal arts might continue to prosper in my empire."[81] In this way he would maintain an orthodox Christian hand on education and so keep God's favor. He did not take the step of creating fully Christian schools, such as that of Nisibis in Syria, known to Junillus and presumably others at court. Through this neglect, and through change to a more fully Christian perspective among the urban elite who in previous generations paid for traditional schooling, classical education slowly evaporated. By the seventh century the Psalter had become the primer for education, and training in law and medicine was limited to a very few. Across the Mediterranean monks took up the burden of education as much as they were able.

## THE IMPERIAL EPICENTER: CONSTANTINOPLE AND THE EMPEROR

At the focal point of the geopolitical, economic, religious, and intellectual shifts sketched here, there were two intertwined and unifying elements: the city of Constantinople itself and the emperor who dominated its life. Together they shaped the Byzantine character of the empire.[82]

In the sixth century, Constantinople fulfilled its potential as a Christian capital. It was seen as the juncture of human and divine affairs, where God's will was enacted by his political agent on earth, the emperor. Ritualized celebrations – of imperial arrival and departure, of addressing the public in the Hippodrome, of convening the Senate – enacted this imperial function, linking it to the Roman past and binding it to a Christian present. In the same urban context Christian liturgical patterns took shape, giving the city a spiritual geography manifest in churches, processions, and holy events. The emperor with the clergy thus played a crucial role in shaping Constantinople's religious and civic character. The Christian emperor dominated the city, the city embodied the empire, and the empire mirrored the kingdom of heaven.

In its guise as the hub of imperial administration, Constantinople became the focus of a different sort of attention: it was the goal for members of the provincial elite who in earlier generations may have sought honors in their own cities. Now the imperial bureaucracy offered an increasingly desirable opportunity for honor and preferment. Such service required closer links to the capital, so the city's claim to the attention of its elites increased. In addition to being the seat of government, in Justinian's determined hands Constantinople became a place where correct belief was established and, perhaps more important, where policies for its enforcement could be put in motion. Of course orthodox belief was a requirement for holding public office.

Though Justinian was a native Latin speaker and his legal codification was necessarily accomplished in that language, Greek served as the language of rule, worship, and everyday life. Latin and its handmaiden bilingualism faded away in the course of the century. Justinian and all his successors would issue their laws in Greek. Byzantium would be a Greek cultural realm.

The emperor pulled all these strands together, making himself the focus of his subjects' religious and political loyalties while at the same time determining the terms in which those loyalties could be expressed, a process that would continue into the next centuries.[83] Enacting a Christian vision of Roman imperial autocracy, Romans would serve him as he served God. During his reign the habit of calling Romans "subjects" rather than "citizens" intensified. The Roman community was changing from one defined primarily by law to a community defined first of all by faith.[84] Justinian spelled out a clear position for himself as well: his claim to be the motive force in scriptual interpretation and making of orthodoxy is mirrored precisely in his approach to Roman law. He claimed his authority to legislate came directly from God, making him both the embodiment of law and its sole interpreter for Romans.

To please God, Justinian embarked on an ambitious program of imperial restoration in many spheres. From the palace he maintained the age-old Roman vision of Mediterranean hegemony, sending his armies to reclaim Roman territory, drafting his orders to rebuild the fortresses and churches of his empire, and receiving embassies from the corners of the globe who had come to seek recognition, to threaten, or to sue for peace. But now in Justinian's view of Roman imperial action everything was refracted through a Christian lens. As an emperor who viewed himself as a restorer of Roman authority, Justinian became a radical facilitator of social change as he strove to create a fully Christian realm. His posture as restorer made him a bringer of civilization, a traditional service of Roman emperors. To Justinian and his successors, however, civilization now meant Christian life. The image of Justinian in San Vitale in Ravenna exemplifies this posture. In this mosaic, with Abraham, Melchisidek, and Christ as witnesses, Justinian claims a role for himself and his empire in the drama of Christian redemption. In this church Rome has become Byzantium.[85]

Many of the changes mentioned here found much fuller expression in the seventh century. As the chapters ahead will show, however, Byzantine chords were already sounding in the Age of Justinian.

## Notes

1 There are many excellent studies of Justinian and his age. For scholarly overviews, see the relevant chapters in *CAH* 14, *Late Antiquity: Empire and Successors, A.D. 425–600*, ed. Averil Cameron, Bryan Ward-Perkins, and Michael Whitby (Cambridge, 2000); John Moorhead, *Justinian* (London, 1994); and J. A. S. Evans, *The Age of Justinian: The Circumstances of Imperial Power* (London, 1996). Older but still reliable sources include Robert Browning, *Justinian and Theodora* (London, 1987); and John W. Barker, *Justinian and the Later Roman Empire* (Madison, Wis., 1966). John B. Bury, *History of the Later Roman Empire from the Death of Theodosius I to the Death of Justinian*, vol. 2, 1923 rep. 1958 is a masterful synthesis staying close to the ancient sources; Ernest Stein, *Histoire du Bas-Empire*, vol. 2 (Paris, 1949/Amsterdam, 1968) remains essential reading. Edward Gibbon's *Decline and Fall of the Roman Empire*, chaps. 40–44, never disappoints. Two recent monographs in German offer comprehensive overviews with bibliography: Mischa Meier, *Das andere Zeitalter Justinians* (Göttingen, 2003), emphasizing response to crisis and disaster, and Otto Mazal, *Justinian I. und seine Zeit. Geschichte und Kultur des Byzantinischen Reiches im 6. Jahrhundert* (Vienna, 2001), emphasizing art and culture.

2 Chris Wickham, "Overview: Production, Distribution, and Demand," in *The Sixth Century: Production, Distribution, and Demand*, ed. Richard Hodges and William Bowden (Leiden, 1998), 279.

3 See Peregrine Horden, "Mediterranean Plague in the Age of Justinian," Chap. 6 herein; see also the valuable discussions of Mark Whittow, *The Making of Byzantium, 600–1025* (Berkeley, Calif., 1996), 38–68; and Michael Whitby, "The Successors of Justinian," *CAH* 14.86–111. They challenge older interpretations of an empire fatally weakened by the plague and in a state of economic and social decline.

4 The inhabitants of the Roman Empire in the east continued to call themselves Romans (*Rhomaioi*) for another millennium, until Constantinople fell to the Turks in 1453. On periodization, see Averil Cameron, "The 'Long' Late Antiquity," in *Classics in Progress: Essays on Ancient Greece and Rome*, ed. T. P. Wiseman (Oxford, 2002), 165–191; *CAH* 14, "Conclusion," 972–981; and Vladimír Vavrínek, "The Eastern Roman Empire or Early Byzantium? A Society in Transition," in *From Late Antiquity to Early Byzantium*, ed. Vladimir Vavrínek (Prague, 1985), 9–20; on the seventh century, see John F. Haldon, *Byzantium in the Seventh Century: The*

*Transformation of a Culture* (Cambridge, 1990); and Averil Cameron, "Byzantium and the Past in the Seventh Century: The Search for Redefinition," in *The Seventh Century: Change and Continuity*, ed. Jacques Fontaine and J. N. Hilgarth (London, 1992), 250–276.

5 Pauline Allen and Elizabeth Jeffreys, eds., *The Sixth Century: End or Beginning?* (Brisbane, 1996).

6 Mischa Meier, *Das andere Zeitalter Justinians. Kontingenzerfahrung und Kontingenzbewältigung im 6. Jahrhundert n. Chr.* (Göttingen, 2003), plays in his title with Berthold Rubin's *Das Zeitalter Justinians*, vol. 1 (Berlin, 1960), vol. 2, ed. Carmelo Capizzi (Berlin, 1995); see Tony Honoré, *Tribonian* (London, 1978).

7 Brian Croke, *Count Marcellinus and His Chronicle* (Oxford, 2001), 195.

8 On Napoleon, see Peter Brown, *The Rise of Western Christendom: Triumph and Diversity, A.D. 200–1000* (Oxford, 1996), 122; on Stalin, see Tony Honoré, *Tribonian*, 28–30; on the devil, see Procopius, *Secret History*, 12.18–19.

9 See Caroline Humfress, "Law and Legal Practice in the Age of Justinian," Chap. 7 herein, and Charles Pazdernik, "Justinianic Ideology and the Power of the Past," Chap. 8 herein, for discussion and bibliography; see also Michael Maas, "Roman History and Christian Ideology in Justinianic Reform Legislation," *DOP* 40 (1986): 17–31.

10 See Maas, "Roman History and Christian Ideology," 17–18.

11 In this volume we will use the term "anti-Chalcedonian" to refer to those Christians who did not accept the decisions of the Council of Chalcedon, instead of the term "Monophysites," a seventh-century coinage that is generally used in scholarship today despite its original negative connotations. See Chap. 10 herein, Lucas Van Rompay, "Society and Community in the Christian East."

12 *CJ* 1.11.10; "From Justinian on, all pagans were condemned to civil death"; see Pierre Chuvin, *A Chronicle of the Last Pagans*, trans. B. A. Archer (Cambridge, Mass., 1990), 134; and see Chap. 13 herein, Christian Wildberg, "Philosophy in the Age of Justinian."

13 See Chap. 19 herein, Geoffrey Greatrex, "Byzantium and the East in the Sixth Century."

14 See Chap. 17 herein, Leslie Brubaker, "The Age of Justinian: Gender and Society," for discussion of Theodora's influence in this decision; on the Nika revolt, see Chap. 2 herein, John Haldon, "Economy and Administration: How Did the Empire Work?"; and see Averil Cameron, "Justin I and Justinian," in *CAH* 14.71–72.

15 See Gilbert Dagron, *Emperor and Priest: The Imperial Office in Byzantium*, trans. Jean Birrell (Cambridge, 2003), for a recent overview of later periods.

16 See Chap. 14 herein, Joseph D. Alchermes, "Art and Architecture in the Age of Justinian."

17 See Chap. 18 herein, Walter Pohl, "Justinian and the Barbarian Kingdoms."

18 See Horden, Chap. 6 herein, on the plague, and Haldon, Chap. 2, on the economy.

19 "The Three Chapters" refers to writings of fifth-century theologians Theodore of Mopsuestia, Theodoret of Cyrrhus, and Ibas of Edessa, which Justinian condemned as inconsistent with the Council of Chalcedon, even though the council itself had cleared them of wrong belief. See Chap. 11 herein, Claire Sotinel, "Emperors and Popes in the Sixth Century: The Western View."

20 For recent discussion and bibliography, see Michael Maas, *Exegesis and Empire in the Early Mediterranean: Junillus Africanus and the Instituta Regularia Divinae Legis, with a Contribution by Edward G. Mathews, Jr.* (Tübingen, 2003), 47–64.

21 See Sotinel, Chap. 11 herein.

22 See Chap. 9 herein, Patrick T. R. Gray, "The Legacy of Chalcedon: Christological Problems and Their Significance"; Maas, *Exegesis and Empire*, 42–71; and Pauline Allen, "The Definition and Enforcement of Orthodoxy," *CAH* 14.811–834.

23 Maas, *Exegesis and Empire*, 53.

24 Alois Grillmeier and Theresia Heinthaler, *Christ in the Christian Tradition*, trans. John Cawle and Pauline Allen. vol. 2.2. *Constantinople in the Sixth Century*. (Leiden, 1995), 467–47.

25 Corippus, *In Praise of Justin* (*In Laudem Iustini*), 1.276–290, and 3.1–27. See Cameron, "Justin I and Justinian," *CAH* 14.85, n. 134.

26 Michael Whitby, "The Successors of Justinian," *CAH* 14.86–111.

27 Whitby, "The Successors of Justinian," 102.

28 See Greatrex, Chap. 19 herein.

29 See Pohl, Chap. 18 herein.

30 Pohl, Chap. 18 herein.

31 See Croke, *Count Marcellinus and His Chronicle*, 78–101, on émigrés to Constatinople.

32 See Sotinel, Chap. 11 herein.

33 Gisela Ripoll Lopez, "On the Supposed Frontier between the *Regnum Visigothorum* and Byzantine Hispania," in *The Transformation of Frontiers from Late Antiquity to the Carolingians*, ed. Walter Pohl, Ian Wood, and Helmut Reimitz (Leiden, 2001), 95–115.

34 Agathias, *Histories*, 1.2, and see discussion in Pohl, Chap. 18 herein; Michael Maas, "'Delivered from Their Ancient Customs': Christianity and the Question of Cultural Change in Early Byzantine Ethnography," in *Conversion in Late Antiquity and the Middle Ages: Seeing and Believing*, ed. Kenneth Mills and Anthony Grafton (Rochester, N.Y., 2003), 172–174.

35 In Chap. 19 herein, Greatrex discusses the farther horizons of Justinian's world.

36 The name "Berbers", which comes from the Latin *barbari* or barbarians, was applied in the early years of the Muslim conquest in the seventh century.

37 C. R. Whitaker, "Berber," in *Late Antiquity: A Guide to the Postclassical World*, ed. Glen Bowersock, Peter Brown, and Oleg Grabar (Cambridge, Mass, 1999).

38 See Chap. 20 herein, Fred Donner, "The Background to Islam."

39 For further discussion, see Haldon, Chap. 2 herein and A. D. Lee, Chap. 5, "The Empire at War." I thank Michael Decker for discussing this material with me.

40 Pirenne began to develop his thesis in two essays: "Mahomet et Charlemagne," *La Revue Belge de Philologie et d'Histoire*, I (1922), 77–86, and "Un contraste économique: Mérovingiens et Carolingiens," *La Revue Belge de Philologie et d'Histoire*, II (1923), 223–35. His *Medieval Cities* (Princeton, 1925), and *Economic and Social History of Medieval Europe* (New York, 1937) expanded his discussion. *Mohammed and Charlemagne* (New York, 1939, French edition 1937) is the final statement of his ideas. See the essays in Hodges and Bowden, *The Sixth Century*; Michael McCormick, *Origins of the European Economy* (Cambridge, 2001), 1–6; John Moorhead, *The Roman Empire Divided, 400–700* (London, 2001), 248–270;

Bryan Ward-Perkins, "Specialized Production and Exchange," in *CAH* 14.346–391.

41 Chris Wickham, "Overview: Production, Distribution, and Demand," in Hodges and Bowden, *The Sixth Century*, 289, notes that the causes of the cumulative economic decline of the sixth century were primarily "endogenous not exogenous."

42 See Chap. 4 herein, Kenneth G. Holum, "The Classical City in the Sixth Century: Survival and Transformation."

43 Ward-Perkins, "Specialized Production and Exchange," 346–391.

44 Wickham, "Overview," 287.

45 Wickham, "Overview," 288; see also Richard Hodges, "Henri Pirenne and the Question of Demand in the Sixth Century," 3–14, and Paolo Delogu, "Reading Pirenne Again," 15–40, both in Hodges and Bowden, *The Sixth Century*.

46 See Horden, Chap. 6 herein.

47 See Michael Hendy, *Studies in the Byzantine Monetary Economy, c. 400–1450* (Cambridge, 1986), 620; Wickham, "Overview," 291.

48 On Theodore of Tarsus, see Michael Lapidge, "The Career of Archbishop Theodore," in *Archbishop Theodore: Commemorative Studies on His Life and Influence*, ed. M. Lapidge (Cambridge, 1995), 70.

49 Gray explains the nuances of the Chalcedonian and post-Chalcedonian positions in Chap. 9 herein.

50 Maas, *Exegesis and Empire*, 42–64.

51 See Sotinel, Chap. 11 herein.

52 Allen, "The Definition and Enforcement of Orthodoxy," 828–834.

53 Cyril Mango, "New Religion, Old Culture," in *The Illustrated History of Byzantium*, ed. C. Mango (Oxford, 2002), 111.

54 See Chap. 13 herein, Christian Wildberg, "Philosophy in the Age of Justinian."

55 Michael Maas, *John Lydus and the Roman Past: Antiquarianism and Politics in the Age of Justinian* (London, 1992), 69–82.

56 Michael Maas, "'Delivered from Their Ancient Customs,'" 160–169.

57 See Chap. 20 herein, Fred Donner, "The Background to Islam."

58 See Chap. 16 herein, Nicholas de Lange, "Jews in the Age of Justinian."

59 J. A. S. Evans, *The Age of Justinian: The Circumstances of Imperial Power* (London, 1996), 240–247; de Lange, "Jews in the Age of Justinian," Chap. 16 herein.

60 Averil Cameron, "Images of Authority: Elites and Icons in Late Sixth-Century Byzantium," in *Byzantium and the Classical Tradition*, ed. Margaret Mullett and Roger Scott (Birmingham, 1981), 205–234.

61 Similarly, Judaism turned from Greek to Hebrew in worship and the authority of the rabbis grew, while at the end of our period the community of Islam arose, founded on sacred text revealed in Arabic.

62 Dimitri Obolensky, *The Byzantine Commonwealth: Eastern Europe, 500–1453* (London, 1971); Garth Fowden, *Empire to Commonwealth: Consequences of Monotheism in Late Antiquity* (Princeton, N.J., 1993).

63 See Averil Cameron and Judith Herrin, eds., *Constantinople in the Early Eighth Century: The Parastaseis Syntomoi Chronikai* (Leiden, 1984), 1–53.

64 Michael Whitby, "Greek Historical Writing after Procopius: Variety and Vitality," in *The Byzantine and Early Islamic Near East: I. Problems in the Literary Source Material*, ed. Averil Cameron and Lawrence Conrad (Princeton, N.J., 1992), 25–80, provides a thorough overview.

65 Averil Cameron, *Procopius and the Sixth Century* (Berkeley, Calif., 1985), and Michael Whitby, "Greek Historical Writing after Procopius," 25–80.

66 Whitby, "Greek Historical Writing after Procopius," 51–52.

67 *Chronicon Paschale, 284–628 A.D.*, trans. Michael and Mary Whitby (Liverpool, 1989), ix; for the chronicle tradition, see Brian Croke and Roger Scott, "Byzantine Chronicle Writing," in *Studies in John Malalas*, ed. Elizabeth Jeffreys with Brian Croke and Roger Scott (Sydney, 1990), 25–54, and Croke, *Count Marcellinus and His Chronicle*, 145–169 and 257–265.

68 In the seventh century Islam would also break with its polytheist past and establish links with the biblical past.

69 Croke, *Count Marcellinus and His Chronicle*; Roger Scott, "Writing the Reign of Justinian: Malalas versus Theophanes," in Allen and Jeffreys, *The Sixth Century* (Brisbane, 1996), 20–34.

70 See Chap. 12 herein, Derek Krueger, "Christian Piety and Practice in the Sixth Century."

71 On these authors, see Maas, *John Lydus*, 55.

72 See Chap. 15 herein, Claudia Rapp, "Literary Culture under Justinian."

73 PLRE 2, Priscianus 2, 905; Barry Baldwin and Alice Mary Talbot, "Priscian," ODB, 1720; Albrecht Dihle, *Greek and Latin Literature of the Roman Empire from Augustus to Justinian*, trans. Manfred Malzahn (London, 1994), 443.

74 See Gian Biagio Conte, *Latin Literature: A History*, trans. Joseph B. Solodow, revised by Don Fowler and Glenn W. Most (Baltimore, 1987), 715–716.

75 See Maas, *Exegesis and Empire*, 33, for references and discussion.

76 For an overview, see Leighton D. Reynolds and Nigel G. Wilson, *Scribes and Scholars: A Guide to the Transmission of Greek and Latin Literature* (Oxford, 1968), 71–72.

77 Conte, *Latin Literature*, 721.

78 Reynolds and Wilson, *Scribes and Scholars*, 45.

79 Averil Cameron, "Byzantium and the Past in the Seventh Century: The Search for Redefinition," in *The Seventh Century: Change and Continuity*, ed. Jacques Fontaine and J. N. Hilgarth (London, 1992) 254.

80 Robert Browning, "Education in the Roman Empire," *CAH* 14.855–883.

81 Justinian, *Pragmatic Sanction* (*Constitutio Pragmatica*), appendix, 7.22 (Kroll 802).

82 See Chap. 3 herein, Brian Croke, "Justinian's Constantinople"; and Michael McCormick, "Emperor and Court," in *CAH* 14.135–163.

83 Cameron, "Images of Authority," 232.

84 See Pazdernik, Chap. 8 herein.

85 Maas, *John Lydus*, 16.

# 2: Economy and Administration

## How Did the Empire Work?

*John F. Haldon*

In the course of Justinian's reign, the apparatus of government dealt with continuing changes in social and economic relationships throughout the empire, altered relations between the imperial court and the church, and a series of reconquests of former imperial territory that were remarkably successful but expensive in manpower and cash. In this context of rapid change at home and abroad, flaws in the machinery of government came to the fore and must have been very clear to those who gave thought to the issue. In the early years of his reign, Justinian addressed problems in the administration of justice, finance, and the armies with a series of major administrative reforms intended to strengthen imperial power over the bureaucracy and the social elite. The institutional stasis that afflicted this bureaucracy, however, nullified all but the most persistent efforts at reform.[1] This chapter investigates the economic and administrative structures of Justinian's empire to see how they worked and how they changed under his influence.

## Economic Resources and Infrastructure

The sophisticated bureaucracy and administrative machinery that enabled the Roman state to function and to defend itself was not a monolith, but rather a constantly evolving set of institutional relationships and established social and economic structures. These changed in response to economic fluctuations and government demands as well as to tensions within late Roman society. This meant in practice that the government at Constantinople had to take account of several different levels of change: in the assessment, collection, and distribution of resources in kind, in manpower, and in cash; in the ambitions, vested interests, and economic situation of provincial and Constantinopolitan elites; in the demands for maintenance and recruitment of soldiers; and in the need to maintain a balance between the interests of those who managed the state's many different functions in the provinces and the capital and of the producing population. The government at Constantinople also had to deal with the damaged economies of certain exposed or border regions – sometimes quite extensive, as in the Balkans, sometimes quite small, as in certain regions along the eastern frontier. Accurately calculating the state's requirements in taxation was an especially difficult challenge, and in fact one rarely achieved – hence the vast range of supplementary taxes and impositions in kind and labour or services.

The extent to which these issues encroached upon the awareness of those in power varied with the times, of course. But it is clear that unlike his uncle and predecessor Justin I, Justinian was genuinely interested in the minutiae of government in the provinces, of the attitude of the provincials to the judicial system, of the problem posed by venal and corrupt fiscal administrators and provincial governors and their staffs, and of the way in which the Roman Empire should perceive itself and was to be perceived by outsiders. Given the nature of the changes that affected the late Roman world, the question we need to ask is whether or not Justinian's reforms had any chance of success in the long term, and what their short term results were. For as we shall see, their long-term results were, in fact, rather limited, constrained both by circumstances as well as by the way in which they were directed and the issues at which they were addressed.

The world of resources and producers, towns, cities, and villages, linked by a sophisticated and partly state-supervised road network, represents the physical backdrop to late Roman society, culture, and politics. This context limited the political programmes of different emperors and determined the ability of the late Roman government to respond to its enemies, deal with its neighbours, organise its administration, and recruit, move, and support its armies. It would be wrong to suggest that this physical context was the only factor: cultural constraints, traditional ways of doing things, and ideas about what could and could not be done all contributed. But it would be equally misguided to ignore the fundamental role of this physical environment in that history. Indeed, any attempt to understand the principles underlying Roman administration must begin with these features, for they directly affected how the government functioned.[2]

The late Roman world was dominated by three land masses (Asia Minor or Anatolia, very roughly modern Turkey; the Levant or Middle Eastern regions down to and including Egypt; and the Balkans), and by the Mediterranean and the Black seas, which united these to one another and to the outlying zones of Italy and the north African coastal provinces with their hinterlands. The climate of these very different regions determined the patterns of agricultural and pastoral exploitation. Asia Minor can be divided into three zones: central plateau, coastal plains, and the mountain ranges that separate them. The plateau is typified by extremes of hot and cold temperatures in summer and winter, in contrast to the milder and friendlier Mediterranean climate of the coastal regions, with the result that the density of agricultural activity and of population is generally very much higher in the latter than the former, where, with some exceptions in sheltered river valleys, a pastoral economy based on sheep, cattle, and horses predominates. The Balkans are in many ways more rugged and fragmented than Asia Minor, but if we include the broad Thracian plain, the plain of Thessaly and the fertile south Danubian plains, they are also productive and potentially quite rich. In contrast, the fertile Nile valley and the agricultural lands of Palestine and western Syria are much wealthier, while the long coastal plains of Tunisia produced both olives and cereals. Indeed, Rome imported most of the grain to support its population from Africa, just as Constantinople was heavily dependent upon Egypt to meet its needs. These were satisfied by state contracts with shippers organised in their own guild, who carried the requisite supplies and worked for the government at fixed tariffs and under government supervision in return for specific fiscal and legal privileges (in particular, exemptions from certain compulsory fiscal burdens).

The economic lifeblood of the Roman Empire was agrarian production. From the mountain valleys of the central Balkans to the fertile floodplain of the Nile, and from the coastal plains and hill country of southern Italy to the broad plains of northern Syria, agriculture was the mainstay of life, the essential foundation for the existence of towns and cities, and the basis for the state's taxation. Commerce and industry were, in places, essential elements of local, especially urban, economy; yet overall they played but a minor role in the economic life of the people of the Roman world. At any given time of the empire's existence, therefore, the great majority of its population was engaged in agricultural and pastoral production.[3]

Bread was the basic food of all the populations of the Mediterranean and Near or Middle Eastern zones, and cereals were therefore the dominant crop grown by the majority of rural producers. Egypt, with the Nile Valley's rich alluvial soils, produced by far the greatest quantity per head of the producing population, but the plains of northern Syria, the coastal regions of Asia Minor, Thrace, and Thessaly, and the north African provinces also produced substantial quantities of cereals, and North Africa provided the oil and grain for Rome. As well as wheat, a substantial element in the grain production of the empire was barley, with smaller amounts of millet, regarded generally as inappropriate for human consumption. Probably from the fourth century hard wheats – with a greater proportion of protein per volume – were gradually replacing the soft wheats that had hitherto dominated Mediterranean cereal agriculture, with important consequences for both diet and cereal production in the centuries to follow. Where the climate allowed – predominantly along the coastal plains of the Aegean and Mediterranean and in some sheltered inland districts – fruit, vines, and olives were also cultivated, sometimes extensively and, in the case of olives and vines, sometimes as cash crops to meet the demand from urban markets both near and far. Vegetables, pulses, and root crops were also cultivated throughout the region, usually on the basis of household garden plots rather than extensively, so that villages and towns were for the most part supplied with all the essentials of life – food, drink, clothing, the materials for housing and the livestock for transport – from their immediate hinterlands (Map 3).

But self-sufficiency was never absolute: villages were also part of a wider world of exchange consisting of several communities within a particular region, from which the inhabitants of one community could obtain goods and services they did not produce themselves, and through which – perhaps through holding an annual fair to celebrate a particular holy day – they might also attract trade and commerce from much farther afield. Only the largest cities, mostly those with access to ports and the sea, had the resources to import goods from further away than their own locality on a regular basis, and these were mostly luxuries. Rome and Constantinople imported bulk goods, chiefly grain and oil, on a large scale, but they were notable exceptions, with unusually large urban populations and substantial governmental and ecclesiastical bureaucracies. Such dependence on distant centres of production was possible only because it was paid for by the imperial government. Inland towns were generally entirely dependent on what was produced locally (although the wealthy might import luxuries and other commodities), and this varied strongly by season and region.[4]

Sowing, harvesting, and pattern of seasonal activities depended on location. For those regions dominated by a Mediterranean climate vegetables were harvested in June, cereals in July, after which the land was normally opened to livestock for pasturage and manuring. Ploughing and tilling generally took place in October and November, and planting followed immediately in order to take advantage of the winter rains and the seasonal humidity of the soil. But the cycle might be different in more arid regions: in Syria harvesting also took place in November, with ploughing and planting in July and August, for example. In those areas in which agricultural activity was supported by systems of irrigation, as in the Nile valley, or drier regions with very low annual rainfall, the pattern was different again. Returns on planting similarly varied: the highest average returns in fertile regions appear to have been of the order of 7:1 or 8:1, with variations in either direction. Lower returns in drier or less well-watered districts have been calculated at 5:1 but might be considerably lower. All these figures varied slightly across each district and according to the type of crop and seasonal climatic fluctuations. Livestock – sheep, goats, cattle, horses, and pigs – was a feature of most rural communities, but certain areas concentrated in stock raising more than in other spheres of production. The raising of mules and horses was essential for the state, both for the public postal and transport system as well as for the army. Substantial stud farms were maintained in parts of Asia Minor (Phrygia, Lydia, and Cappadocia), but are also known from North Africa, Italy, and Syria. The Anatolian plateau was dominated by stock farming, often on large ranchlike estates, and while agriculture played an essential role in the maintenance of the population, the richest landlords of the region seem generally to have based their wealth on this type of production. But stock farming played an important role throughout the East Roman world, and sheep and goats, along with pigs, formed an important element in the productive capacity of many rural communities, sharing with cereal production the attentions of the peasant farmer. Livestock was the source of many essential items: not just meat, skins, or milk, but also felt, glues, and horn, as well as bone and gut for both decorative and practical purposes.[5]

Raw materials such as wood, stone, and ores in particular were usually derived from more restricted contexts. The woodlands of the Mediterranean and the Black sea coasts produced timber for shipbuilding, and there is evidence that the government developed an organised policy for the exploitation of woodlands. Stone for building could be quarried throughout the empire, where the materials were available and appropriate, but certain types of stone, marble in particular, were quarried by specialists from particular sites. The much-sought-after high-quality marble of Prokonnesos, for example, was shipped all over the Mediterranean. Stonemasons similarly were in high demand and itinerant specialist groups are known to have been hired for particular building projects in Syria in the fifth and sixth centuries.[6]

Of the ores mined or collected in the Roman world, iron was probably the most important, needed for weapons and tools. Centres of iron mining included northeastern Anatolia and the central southern Black Sea coastal regions, and central Syria, although ores were also mined in the Taurus mountains and the south Balkans. Tin, generally alloyed with copper to make bronze or with zinc to make brass, was mined in the Taurus, but was also imported to the eastern Mediterranean from the southwestern parts of Britain; bronze was commonly used for low-value coins as well as for a huge range of household utensils, tools, and ornamental objects. The sources of copper remain uncertain, but the Caucasus and southern Pontic regions, north Syria, and the central Balkans and Spain seem to have supplied some of the empire's needs up to the sixth century.

Crucial to the empire's economy was gold obtained from the Caucasus, from Armenia, and to a lesser extent from the Balkans, although the location of Roman and Byzantine gold workings remains largely unclear. Silver was extracted in the Taurus, central Pontic Alps, and Armenia, as well as in the central Balkans. The state tried hard to control the import and export of gold and silver (their export was strictly prohibited) but with limited success. Control over stocks of precious metals was achieved partly through recycling, although this could not ensure a constant supply.[7]

One of the major features of the Roman world was the existence of a network of major arterial roads suitable for the rapid movement of men and materials from the inner provinces to the frontiers, and connecting these provinces to one another and to major political centres. But while this system of roads contributed crucially to the efficiency of the Roman army, it also made possible nonmilitary communications and the movement of goods, people, news, and ideas. During the later Roman period, however, and particularly from the later fourth and fifth centuries, the regular maintenance of roads, which was a state burden upon towns and their territories and which was administered and regulated at the local level, appears to have suffered a serious decline. In part, this reflected different priorities in the allocation and consumption of resources by those who governed urban centres. It may also reflect a decline in the necessary engineering skills in the empire, and especially in the army. One result of such changes, and the difficulties they brought for wheeled transport, was an increasing reliance upon beasts of burden for the movement of goods and people. The late Roman government laid down strict regulations on the size, loads, and use of different types of wheeled vehicle employed by the public transport system, which was divided into two branches, the slow post (oxcarts and similar heavy vehicles) and the fast post (faster moving pack animals, light carts, and horses or ponies). Roads varied in quality according to their function and the type of traffic for which they had originally been built: tracks or paths, paved and unpaved roads, roads that were suitable for wagons or wheeled vehicles, and roads that were not all receive mention in the sources. Roads that possessed some strategic value were generally better maintained, and throughout Justinian's reign and probably well into those of his successors this network was kept up fairly effectively.

Transport by water was immeasurably cheaper than by land, at least over medium and longer distances, and was generally also much faster. Long-distance movement of bulk goods such as grain was generally prohibitively expensive – the cost of feeding draught oxen, maintaining drovers and carters, paying local tolls, combined with the extremely slow rate of movement of oxcarts, multiplied the value of the goods being transported beyond the price of anyone who would otherwise have bought them. This does not mean that the bulk transport of goods over long distances did not take place, and there are examples of regular exports of goods from inland regions to areas very distant. But for the most part it was the state (to supply the armies), with some activity funded by wealthy private individuals, that was engaged in this. In contrast, the cost effectiveness of shipping, by which large quantities of goods could be carried in a single vessel managed by a small number of men, gave coastal settlements a huge advantage in terms of access to the wider world.[8]

## THE ECONOMY IN ACTION

Justinian's empire was a multiethnic, multilinguistic mélange of cultures, united chiefly through the fiscal administrative apparatus of the government. Roman law and Roman governance, at least at provincial level, served to reinforce the notion of a single state with a single ruler, the emperor. The issue and universal use of a coinage that bore the emperor's portrait bust and other symbols, along with an inscription invoking the emperor's right to rule, underlined and strengthened this political unity;[9] and already during Justinian's reign the Greek language and the church served as foci of a common cultural identity among the elites of the empire and as a reminder of the unity of the eastern Roman world. The existence of an empirewide system of taxation, alongside the imperial bureaucracy and the armies that it supported, made the word "empire" a political and financial reality.

The economy of the empire was more than just the activities of the state or its financial and administrative institutions, of course, or of the territories within imperial political control. Long-distance trade in the period up to the later sixth and early seventh century displayed particular patterns that reflected the prosperity of the regions where certain goods were produced.[10] Thus oil and grain were exported, along with the pottery in which they were transported, from North Africa throughout the Mediterranean world. Oil and wine similarly travelled from the Syrian coast to the western Aegean and south Balkan coastlands, whence they were reexported inland or further west to Italy and southern Gaul. The distribution of ceramic types can tell us a great deal about these movements, since many imports were carried in pottery containers (amphorae) of one sort or another, often very large, used for transporting and storing wine and oil as well as grains. They were transported chiefly by sea, often accompanied by other ceramic products, including fine tablewares, which were exported alongside the bulk goods. Finds of such pottery, in conjunction with knowledge of their centres of production, offer a fairly detailed picture of such trade. Some of these goods, indeed, travelled even further afield. In the later sixth century ships were still sailing from Egypt into the Atlantic and around to southwest England, trading corn for tin. This Mediterranean trade did not reflect private, market-led demand alone: it appears that much of the commerce in fine wares, for example, travelled in the ships of the great grain convoys from North Africa to Italy and from Egypt to Constantinople, the captains of the ships being permitted to carry a certain quantity of goods on their own account for private sale in return for a percentage of the price obtained.[11]

A marked difference existed between those centres of population and production with access to the sea and the inland towns and villages. The economy of the late Roman world was intensely local and regionalised, and this was reflected also in the attitudes and outlook of most of the population. Yet this means neither that the Roman world was poor in resources (although some regions were certainly poorer than others), nor that interregional commerce did not flourish. But the expense of transport, especially by land, meant that patterns of settlement and the demographic structure of the empire conformed to the limits of the resources locally available. And here, it was chiefly the major urban centres that were involved. The evidence of pottery, as already noted, is crucial in helping us understand patterns of production, exchange, and consumption in the late Roman world. Indicative of the strongly market-oriented nature of estate and smallholder production in North Africa, for example, is the fact that until the late fifth and early sixth century imports from this region were strongly represented throughout the eastern Mediterranean and Aegean regions. Commerce and exchange seem in no way to have been hindered by the political boundaries of the time. There then took place a reduction in regional north African ceramic production, a reduction in the variety and sometimes the quality of forms and types, especially of amphorae, and a corresponding increase of eastern exports to the West. The incidence of African imports to the eastern Mediterranean, for example, as reflected in both fine wares and in amphorae, declines sharply from about 480–490 on, recovering only partly after Justinian's destruction of the Vandal kingdom in the 530s and its partial incorporation into an eastern Mediterranean–centred network of exchange.[12] The incidence of Phocaean slip-coated wares, produced in the Aegean region and connected with the development of Constantinople as an imperial centre during the fourth century, increases in proportion as that of African wares decreases; while over the same period the importance of imported fine wares from the Middle East, especially Syria and Cilicia, also increases.[13] Aegean coarse wares – transport vessels such as amphorae, and cooking vessels, in particular – begin to compete with the western imports during the sixth century and finally to dominate from the decades around 600.[14]

The pattern of ceramic distribution thus reflects a variety of factors, including highly localised economic subsystems. Amphorae from both Palestine and north Syria are found in quantity in the Peloponnese and in Constantinople from the middle of the sixth century, for example, complemented by amphorae from western Asia Minor, presumably representing imports of olive oil and wine. From the late sixth and early seventh century there occurred a greater localisation of fine-ware production.[15] The economic implications of these patterns is that several overlapping networks of ceramic production and exchange complemented one another, and these were accompanied by similarly overlapping exchange patterns for the products that accompanied or were transported in these containers.

The ceramic record reflects two facets of economic activity: on the one hand, the movements of the state-controlled grain convoys and the "piggyback" commerce that accompanied and exploited the opportunities it offered; and on the other the networks of private enterprise and commerce reflecting the operations of large estate-based cultivation – especially in North Africa – as well as of smaller-scale cash-crop operations. But beneath this lay the vast substratum of simple peasant subsistence activities – subsistence, that is, that produced enough for the government to take in taxation as well as for landlords, whether individual private persons or corporate landlords such as the state and the church, to extract in rent. In addition, there were in several respects two economies in the Roman world. On the one hand, there was the economy of the state and government, representing a fairly straightforward relationship between producers, taxation, and the redistribution of the resources thus extracted to the army, court, government, and civil administration. The coinage issued by the government through its mints facilitated the smooth operation of this system. On the other hand, there was the economy of ordinary society, a vast web of intersecting pools of activity and resources tying town to countryside and vice versa, pools of activity that sucked in the state's coinage and circulated it around entirely different patterns of transaction and exchange from those of the state's fiscal system. Both were interrelated, yet both were in several respects autonomous, operating on different principles and responding to substantial shifts in context and circumstance in very different ways.[16]

When we put all this information together, the picture that emerges of late Roman commerce and trade is of an immensely complex pattern of intersecting local, regional and supraregional pools or networks of exchange, focused around the shores and major ports of the Mediterranean, the Adriatic, and the Aegean seas. Disruption of one area would thus affect comparable exchange zones in terms of reduction of supply or market demand, with all the consequences for local production, employment, and income this entailed. On the other hand, since these networks operated at different levels, and while they were fragile in certain respects, there was some flexibility, so that the dramatic shrinkage of one area of activity did not necessarily bring with it similar consequences throughout the whole system – the results of the Vandal occupation of North Africa in the first half of the fifth century, for example, were a series of relatively minor adjustments to markets and sources of supply, although with no doubt more or less drastic effects on particular communities or even households. Similar changes in local conditions, the background to which remains unclear, occurred in the later fifth and mid–sixth century in the eastern Aegean and in Palestine, but with only relatively modest consequences for neighbouring exchange zones – although the archaeological evidence is still relatively unexplored. But while such short-term shifts may have a direct impact on individuals and on the government at Constantinople (which would be especially concerned, for example, with the provisions in cereals and oil for the capital and other major cities), it is very doubtful whether the longer-term shifts would have been noticed, although the effects of major epidemics were certainly both noticed and described. Insofar as the regime at Constantinople was aware of economic issues (limited largely to the role of the imperial coinage at different levels of state and local demand), government policy can only have been reactive in this respect, if the symptoms of particular problems could even have been recognised. The accounts in Procopius and John the Lydian of the effects – however exaggerated – of the curtailment or cessation of the public post in certain areas of Asia Minor under Justinian would suggest as much.

## Society

Late Roman society was neither rigidly hierarchical nor inflexible. It was possible to move from relatively humble status to a position of considerable wealth and power, particularly through service in the army or another state service. Such opportunities were by definition very limited, however, so that the vast majority of the population undoubtedly remained in the social group into which they were born. As we have already seen, most people in the Roman world lived and worked in the country, as agricultural workers, or perhaps as rural artisans or skilled workers in specialist trades such as pottery production or smithing. The largest single group – although internally very varied by region and local tradition – was peasant tenant farmers, classified as *coloni adscripticii* or *coloni liberi*, the former tied tenants listed alongside their holdings in the tax register, the latter entered under their own names and paying their taxes directly rather than through their landlord, like the *adscripticii*. In other respects they differed little in legal and social status, being described in some texts as "slaves of the land," and tied to their holdings, from which they could be released only under certain conditions (although, by the same token, their tenancies were also protected insofar as landlords could not eject them – at least in theory). But they were technically all free persons and could take out leases on land in their own right, so that the dividing line between the two classes of *coloni* and other types of peasant leaseholder is often very difficult to draw. There was also a smaller group of free peasant landowners, often of the same economic and social condition as the *coloni*, again varying in density and frequency across the different regions of the empire according to the development of local traditions of landholding and landownership.[17]

Most land in the empire was held by a much smaller number of people and institutions – the church and the state represented the two largest corporate landlords – with members of the senatorial establishment making up the majority of individual landowners. But there was a great deal of variation within this group: in the provinces the leading private landowners, those with extensive properties and those more modestly endowed, the members of the provincial town councils, and representatives of the local provincial governor and the leading clergy in each city and territory, together constituted the local "establishment." The social elite also included all those who held a senatorial title, but this was a very wide range of people of vastly different social and economic situation, including the major landowners of the Roman world, at least as far as they held the senatorial rank or grade of *clarissimus*, the lowest of three classes of senator. Those holding state positions, active posts, may have held one of the higher grades. The middling and lesser landowners, the majority of members of the curial class, were not senators, but nevertheless shared the same cultural values as the elite.[18]

After numerous vicissitudes during the later third and fourth centuries, the senatorial order expanded rapidly during the fifth century, with the consequence that the status of the highest grade, the *illustres*, was enhanced at the expense of the lower, the *spectabiles* and *clarissimi*. *Clarissimi*, particularly those of curial status, were obliged to live in their own province; while under Marcian (r. 450–457), all such members were excused from involvement in the Constantinopolitan games and public festivals for which senators were officially financially responsible (and which only the wealthiest could, in any case, afford). By Justinian's reign, the senate at Constantinople – the actual senatorial assembly – consisted of men of *illustris* rank only.

Several changes seem to have followed the so-called Nika revolt in 532, in which Constantinopolitan senators appear to have been heavily involved. It is important to appreciate the nature of these changes, for they reflected a deliberate attempt by Justinian to exert a greater degree of authority over the leading elements in society. He carefully redefined the role and establishment of the senate, for example: senators henceforth played an active part in legal appeals to the imperial court, sitting together with the *consistorium* (a smaller group of the leading state officials and effectively the imperial cabinet),[19] and according to whether they held an office or not. While sons of senators inherited the grade of *clarissimus* only, the emperor could be petitioned for one of the higher grades. The grade of *spectabilis* lost in status and was associated mainly with lower administrative and military positions; those of *illustris* rank filled the active senate at Constantinople and dominated the middling and higher administrative and military positions. In the later 530s a new distinction appears within this grade, between ordinary *illustres*, and men of *magnificus* and then *gloriosus* rank (the latter soon appearing also as *gloriossisimus*). Justinian also rewarded some individuals who had held provincial offices, as well as *curiales*, with the title of *illustris*, thus further contributing to its loss of status and value. The net result was to emphasise the senate's dependency upon the imperial court and to strengthen the emperor's position in relation to the leading senators, even if this did not materially affect the ways in which senators could wield influence in the provinces through the ownership of land and tenure of office.[20]

Many senators also held emphyteutic leases of imperial estates, which were for the most part effective in perpetuity and operated on the principle that the property was leased in return for a usually fairly modest percentage on the produce from the land, or positions as *curatores* of imperial estates, which they could then exploit to their own advantage. Legislation of the sixth century from Justinian and his immediate successors shows that members of the provincial senatorial elite in particular were recognised by the government as major offenders in this respect, more especially in connection with the administration of imperial estates, which was regulated through the fiscal department of the *res privata* in its various subdepartments and the *domus divinae*, imperial estates (see below). These "divine houses" were managed through a number of regional subdepartments throughout the empire: in southern Thrace, Egypt, Syria, Phoenice, Mesopotamia, Asia Minor (especially Cappadocia), Greece, North Africa, Italy, and Dalmatia.[21] The *curatores* who ran them were the highest-ranking officials on the imperial domains, entirely separate from the civil and fiscal administrative unit or units across which they lay, and exercised also the equivalent judicial authority. They were thus persons of great power and members of the highest grade of the senate. Their management of these estates was notoriously exploitative – many peasant freeholders voluntarily sold out to the imperial estate nearest them in order to enjoy the favourable tax status they possessed.[22] Middling officials below the *curatores* likewise took advantage of their position and authority and like the *curatores* even maintained private estate militias, as did many wealthier private landlords.[23] In some cases the interests of the *domus divinae* seem to have succumbed almost entirely to the land- and revenue-grabbing activities of local provincial magnates. This is made apparent in a *novel* of Justinian issued in 536 concerning the proconsul of Cappadocia and the affairs of that diocese, according to which the imperial estates had been fragmented and fallen into private hands.[24] While the levels of exploitation and corruption varied enormously across the empire, it is quite clear that the wealthiest elements of the state administration and senatorial establishment benefited from the established arrangements, and it was largely these issues that Justinian's reforms were designed to address.

## Government

To a large extent civil government was the same as fiscal administration. The exception was the office and responsibilities of the immensely powerful *magister officiorum*, or master of offices. First attested in 320, the master of offices was a permanent member of the *consistorium* and was in effect the head of the empire's central administration.[25] He directed most palatine bureaus (apart from the fiscal departments) and took charge of the day-to-day functioning of the palace. In addition, he had authority over the imperial guard regiments (*scholae palatinae*), was responsible for the emperor's safety, and controlled the *agentes in rebus*. He could draw senior officers from this body of officials, who served as imperial agents seconded to a wide range of duties across the empire. They kept a close watch on provincial officials, maintained the public post, and served as special deputies to implement particular government policies. They were also imperial spies (Fig. 1).[26]

The *magister officiorum*'s great influence was reinforced by the fact that he was also in charge of the government corps of interpreters, which during the later fifth and sixth centuries played a significant role in diplomacy. In Justinian's reign, the best example is the *magister officiorum* Peter the Patrician.[27] The *magister officiorum*'s duties also included some economic activities. From the 390s the supervision of the imperial armaments factories was transferred from the praetorian prefects to his authority, and he was responsible for the billeting and provisioning of troops, with the assistance of local officials. His legal authority was also broad – in 443 he was awarded judicial authority over the soldiers of the *limitanei*, units based along and behind the frontiers;[28] in

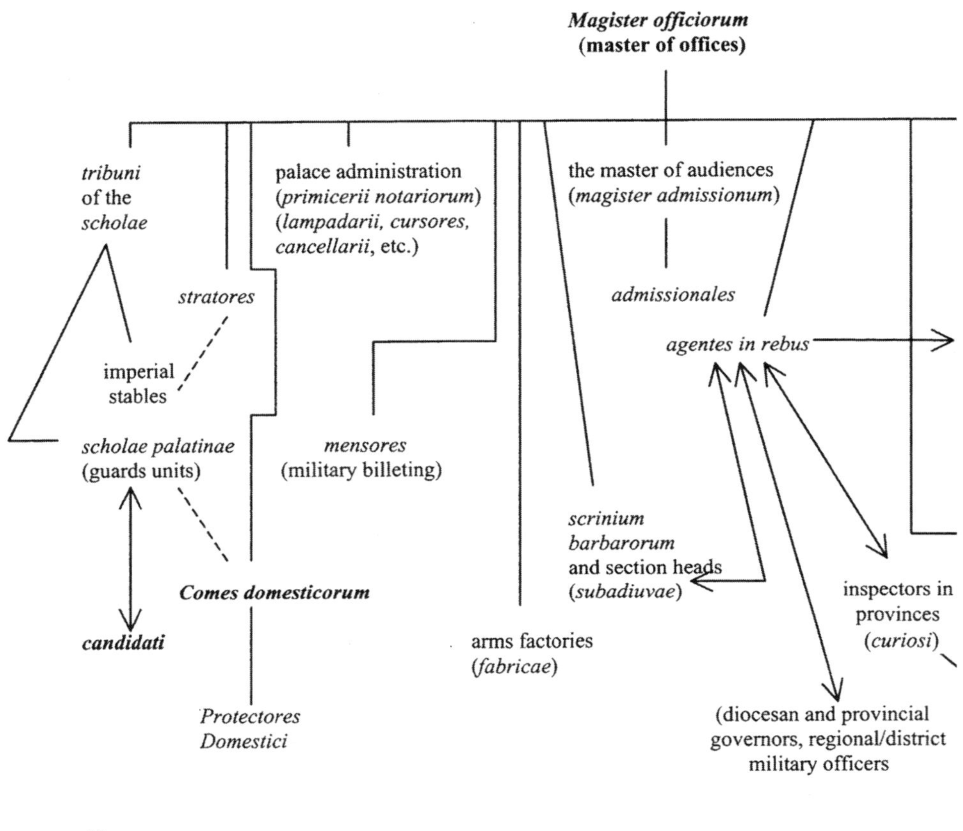


FIGURE 1. Structural chart I: The imperial and civil fiscal administration, c. 560.

529 Justinian made the *magister*, together with the *quaestor sacri palatii* at Constantinople, the senior appeal judge for military courts.[29] Although he was of equal status and rank to the praetorian prefects, his authority nevertheless meant that he could keep an eye on the fiscal bureaux of the palace as well.

The main function of the constantly evolving administration had come to be the assessment, collection, and redistribution of fiscal resources, in whatever form, towards the maintenance of the state. Justice

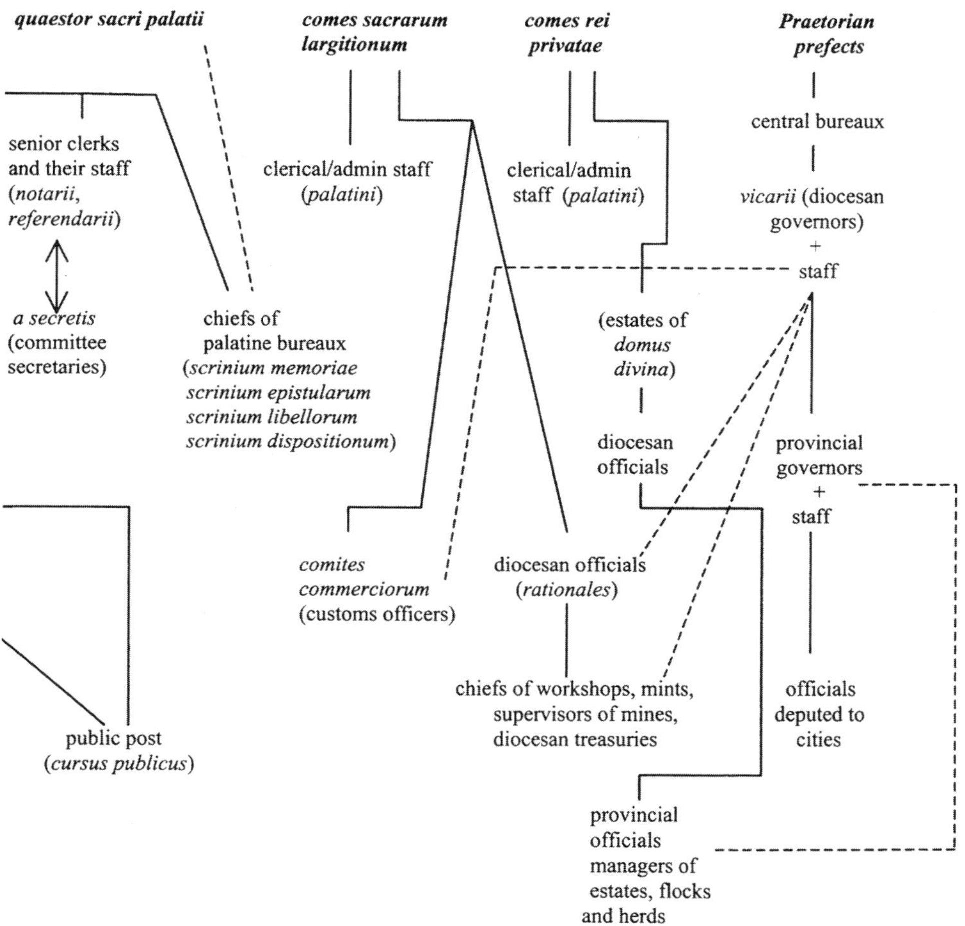


FIGURE 1. (*Cont.*)

was associated with the different levels of government: at the lowest local level, the city, progressing upwards through provincial, diocesan, and prefectural courts – so that the judicial hierarchy paralleled the fiscal administration. The amount of tax required by the government varied year by year according to the international political situation and according to internal requirements. By the sixth century, revenue extraction and assessment were organised through three separate departments, the praetorian prefectures, the "sacred largesses" (*sacrae largitiones*) and the "private fisc" (*res privata*). The most important was the praetorian prefecture, which calculated, collected, and redistributed the land-tax assessment. Each prefecture comprised a specific territory, although they were reorganised and redistributed on several occasions. At the beginning of the sixth century there were two prefectures in the eastern empire: Oriens (stretching from Moesia and Thrace in the Balkans around to upper Libya in Africa), and Illyricum. The other prefectures, namely Italy, Africa, and the Gauls, including Britain, had been lost – or had ceased to exist – during the fifth century.[30]

Each prefecture was subdivided into dioceses (the Roman form of the Greek word *dioikesis*, or "directorate"), under a deputy, *vicarius*, of the praetorian prefect. Each diocese was divided into provinces under provincial governors. The lowest unit of administration was then the city, *civitas* or *polis*, each with its district, *territorium*, upon which the assessment and collection of taxes ultimately devolved.

The structure of both prefectures followed the same pattern except that the prefecture of the east – *Oriens* – with its headquarters at Constantinople, was more complex, and its prefect certainly more powerful, than the others. Each diocese was supervised through a specific department (*scrinium*) at Constantinople. There were departments for Constantinople, for arms production, for the purchase of the grain dole for Constantinople, and for the military rations. There was also a praefectural *arca* or treasury that administered the main income from the assessment of land and produce. Department heads had staffs responsible for the accounts of their particular province. These departments could send out inspectors and other officials to supervise provincial and diocesan fiscal affairs, and they also despatched officials to collect arrears of tax.

Taxes were raised in a variety of forms, but the most important regular tax was the land tax. This could be raised in money, although much of it was actually raised in kind – grains and other foodstuffs – and deposited in a vast network of state warehouses, where it could be drawn on by both soldiers and civil administrators, who received a large portion of their salaries in the form of rations. As the financial situation of the government improved during the fourth and fifth centuries, so these rations came increasingly to be commuted again for cash, providing the producers were able to obtain it – but the government always kept available the option of raising revenues in kind, especially when military requirements demanded it. The prefectures, through their diocesan and more particularly their provincial levels of administration, were also responsible for the maintenance of the public post, the state weapons and arms factories, and provincial public works. The latter – maintenance of roads, bridges, granaries, the provision of crafts and skills for particular tasks – were provided through special levies or impositions upon the population, or specific groups within the population, depending on the task.[31]

The other finance departments, the sacred largesses (*sacrae largitiones*) and the private fisc (*res privata*), had more limited functions. The *largitiones* were responsible for bullion from mines and the mines themselves, minting coin, state-run clothing workshops, and the issue of military donatives – regular and irregular gifts of coin to the troops for particular occasions such as an imperial birthday. Its income was drawn from a few surviving taxes in gold and silver, import duties, donations from municipalities and the senate at imperial accessions, as well as the fees for commutation of military recruits and horses. Its most important asset was probably the mints, which produced coin at Constantinople, Thessaloniki, Carthage, and Ravenna (both bronze and gold coin), and at Nicomedia, Cyzicus, Alexandria, and Antioch (bronze coinage).[32] By the sixth century there had developed some ten *scrinia* or sections within the *largitiones* at Constantinople (dealing with revenues, accounts, donatives, mints, bullion and copper, diocesan reserves, clerical records, the imperial wardrobe, and palace silversmiths); there were in addition local branches in each diocese, with representatives in the cities and provinces to administer the revenues drawn from civic lands (which the *largitiones* administered after the middle of the fifth century) and from other income, such as the cash for the commutation of miltary service or the provision of horses for the army.[33]

The private fisc (*res privata*), under its count (*comes*), was essentially responsible for the income derived as rents from imperial lands. It was as complex as that of the *comes sacrarum largitionum*, with different sections responsible for its various tasks, and administered very substantial domains on behalf of the emperor. During the sixth century its responsibilities were divided between the income destined for state purposes and that employed to maintain the imperial household, and a new department, the *patrimonium*, was established under Anastasius. Indeed, as a result of the needs of the palace establishment, the *praepositus sacri cubiculi*, director of the sacred bedchamber, who was in charge of the imperial household, had been given authority over the imperial estates in Cappadocia by the end of the fourth century.[34] During Justinian's reign this separation of authority was further developed as the different aspects of government and imperial household administration

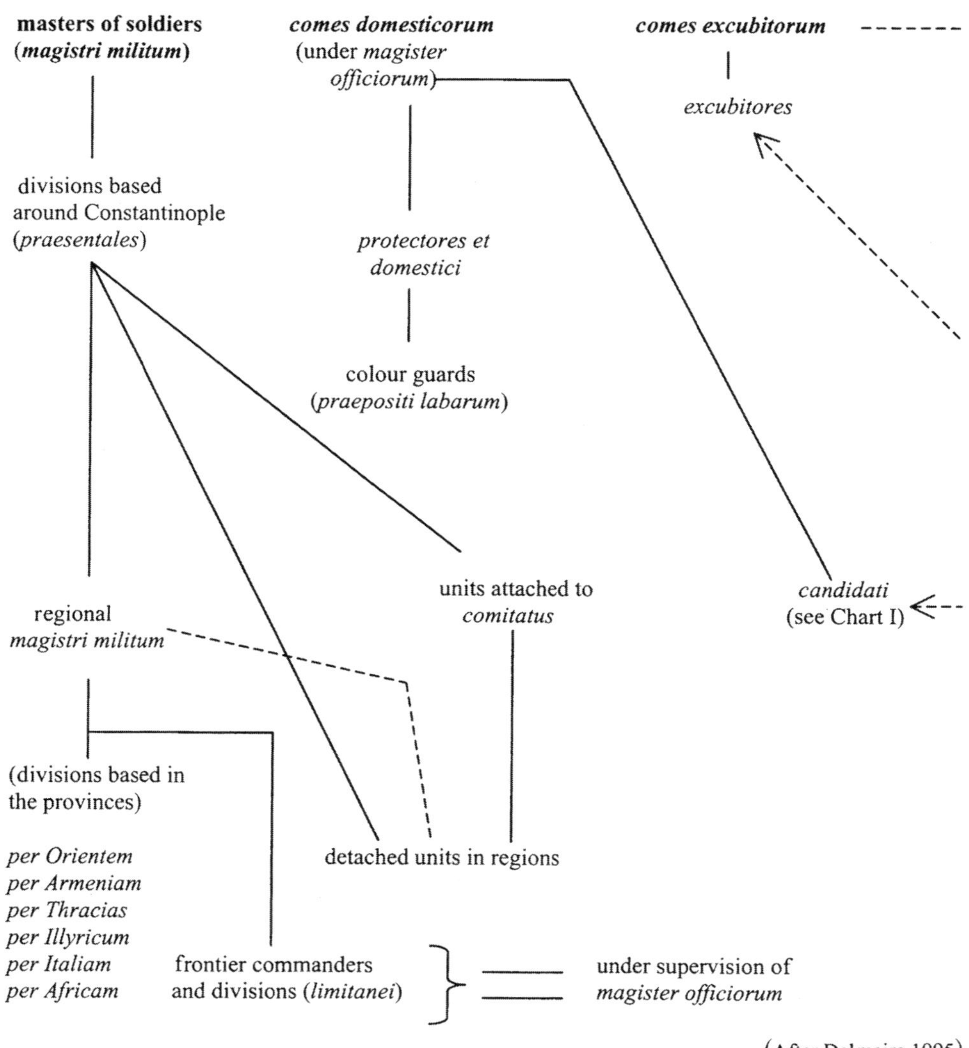


FIGURE 2. Structural chart II: The imperial military and palatine administration, c. 560.

required their own dedicated sources of income, as we shall see below[35] (see Fig. 2).

A fundamental principle of late Roman taxation was to ensure the extraction of the maximum level of revenue without damaging the social

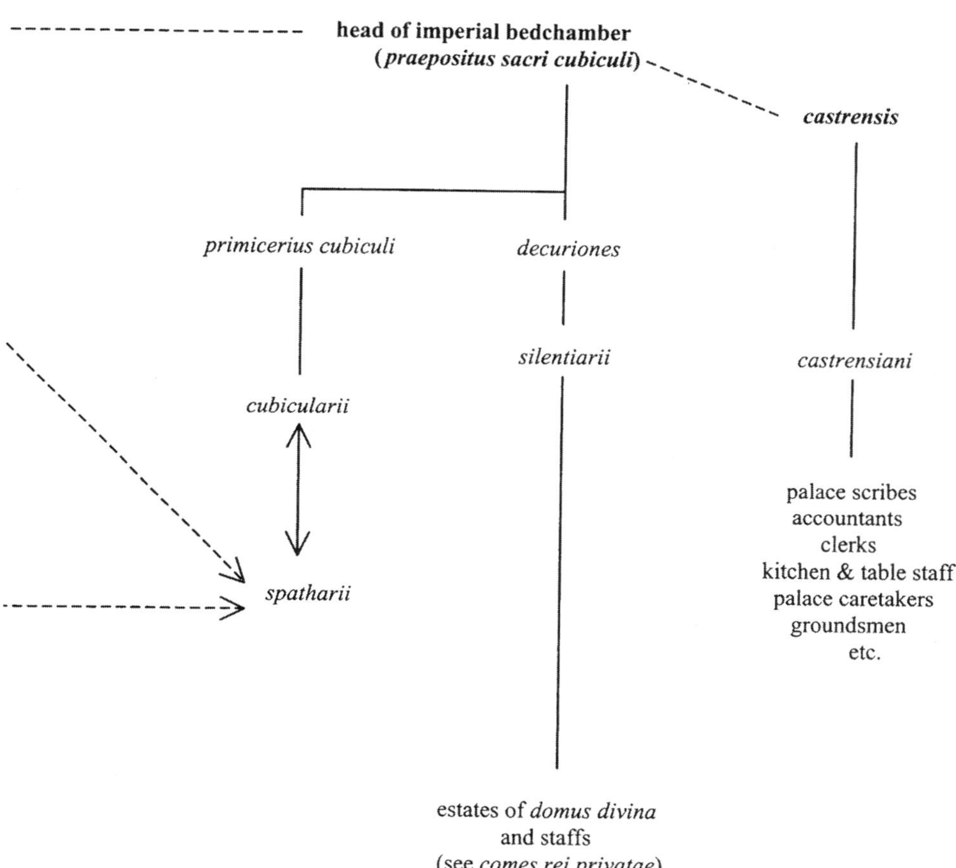


FIGURE 2. (*Cont.*)

basis of rural production. It is difficult to say with certainty, however, that imperial legislation that had the effect of protecting peasant producers was always intended to achieve this result. Tax was assessed according to a formula tying land – determined by area, quality, and type of crop – to labour power, a formula referred to as the *capitatio-iugatio* system.

Land that was not farmed or used for pasture was not taxed directly, but revenues could still be extracted by taxing neighbouring landlords. The tax burden was reassessed at intervals, originally in cycles of five, then of fifteen years, although in practice it took place far more irregularly. Price inflation and depreciation of the coinage meant that the system was always precarious, and the government evolved in consequence a series of alternative strategies for collecting and redistributing resources, most obviously in the military rations, through which food, livestock, manufactured goods, and produce of other sorts could be issued directly to those who required them.

The regular taxation of land was supplemented by a wide range of extraordinary taxes and corvées, including obligations to provide hospitality for soldiers and officials, maintain roads, bridges, fortifications, and to provide such requirements as charcoal or wood. In addition, the way stations and hostels of the public post were maintained through impositions on particular groups or individuals, who were then in theory exempted from a range of other fiscal dues, including military service.[36]

## Justinian, *Renovatio*, and the Imperial Administration

This machinery of state sounds both all-encompassing and efficient, and indeed, in relative terms, it was remarkably effective in supporting the state and its army. But in its day-to-day operations it was subject to a great number of faults and problems. The most obvious of these were geography and distance. In this premodern world, communications were often slow, distance from the capital made central supervision patchy, and uniform political authority and civil security were frequently difficult to maintain. This ramshackle administrative apparatus bred inefficiency and corruption that weakened the entire imperial system. Unscrupulous fiscal officials exploited the unprotected taxpayers. Military officials and soldiers exploited their power for their own benefit, while influential, wealthy men avoided their civic obligations in local and central government. The ordinary population had few sources of assistance apart from their own courts, themselves run in most cases by the very officials against whose interests most complaints might be made. This was by no means lost on the court or those officials and members of society – the clergy in particular – who wished for a more equitable system, and numerous imperial rescripts and novels illustrate this fact.

But, as noted in the introductory comments, the structure and institutional conservatism of the main organs of imperial administration rendered many – but by no means all – reforms ineffective. Justinian displayed a keen interest in both the practical efficiency of his administration and in its implications for his subjects. The changes that he introduced reflected not only his own interests. At least as importantly, perhaps more so, they reflect the views of his most senior and influential senior officials, such as John the Cappadocian. Such initiatives, introduced for the most part during the first fifteen years of his reign, were encouraged not only by a serious engagement with questions of the efficiency of administrative practice, but also by an ideologically motivated concern on Justinian's part to make manifest his role as the God-appointed emperor whose divinely guided hand would steer the ship of state to a secure future by reestablishing its former greatness.[37]

The reforms can be divided roughly into two basic types. The first, which followed military conquests, demanded the establishment of imperial administration to impose imperial authority, Roman law, and imperial taxation. The second type of reform consisted of ad hoc and short-term responses to specific problems in the empire, including imperial action directed at venality and corruption, the slowness of the judicial system, and the inefficiencies or unfairness of the fiscal apparatus.[38]

Of the first type, the establishment of a praetorian prefecture for the recovered territories of Italy in 537, and for Africa in 534, illustrates this facet of the expanding imperial power most clearly.[39] These prefectures were part of Justinian's strategy of reconquest. The structures that were put in place reflect existing administrative and military organisation and practice. The second type illustrates the emperor's personal engagement with the day-to-day affairs of the empire, covering major issues of law and the operation of the courts, finance and taxation, military organisation, and civil administration, as well as minor but still important matters of precedence, privilege, and corruption. The great majority of the major changes were introduced under the prefecture of John the Cappadocian, and while it is clear that he, rather than the emperor, must receive the credit for devising the reforms and implementing them, this does not mean that Justinian was not himself keenly interested in the issues involved (Map 2).

The reforms were unpopular because they challenged corruption and malfeasance among the Constantinopolitan and provincial governing establishment. The reforms prohibited the sale of provincial governorships and bolstered the authority of the "defenders of the city" (*defensores civitatis*) in consideration of the municipal perspective. The aim was to put an end to the corruption and exploitation by government officials in the provinces, and in order to achieve this a single text of instructions was devised for provincial governors.[40] Provincial organisation was also affected, a response to specific regional and local conditions, including brigandage, the need better to coordinate civil and military affairs in frontier regions or to prevent the military bullying the civil authority. Perhaps most significantly for longer-term developments, several diocesan vicariates were abolished. This seems to have been a reflection of both the increasing importance of the prefecture as the major fiscal administrative department (at the expense of the *sacrae largitiones*, which operated at diocesan and municipal levels only) and thus the simplification of the three-level administrative infrastructure of the empire to a two-level system: prefecture and province. These changes affected a substantial part of the eastern prefecture – the dioceses of Pontica, Asiana, and Oriens, which included Egypt – and involved both the amalgamation of some provinces into larger units, the combination of civil and military authority in the hands of several of the governors involved, and in the case of Cappadocia the creation of a new post, the proconsul, who held the position of both governor and count of the royal house (*comes domorum*), in charge of the imperial estates in the region (Map 4).[41]

Two major changes to the empire's military organisation involved the creation of a unified command of the Long Walls, now placed under the praetor of Thrace (in 535), and the post of quaestor of the army (*quaestor exercitus*) in 536. This brought together the Danubian provinces of Moesia II and Scythia with the Aegean islands and parts of western Asia Minor to better provide for the garrisons and field units operating on the frontier, which had suffered for over a century from raiding and the presence of imperial troops.[42] A number of other changes affected the security and day-to-day administration of Constantinople,[43] the movement of supplies and arms for the imperial armies,[44] the administration of the public post, and the operation of the judicial system. The latter issue was intimately bound up with the provincial administrative reforms – by appointing the new proconsuls and provincial governors at *spectabilis* rank and paying them properly (often consolidating the salaries of two former positions into one), Justinian and his advisers intended to limit the constant flow of appeals to the prefect's court at Constantinople and to establish a much more effective provincial judiciary (Map 5).

Justinian and John the Cappadocian have received much criticism for their handling of the public post. According to Procopius and John the Lydian, it was radically curtailed throughout the eastern prefecture, restricted to the imperial military routes from the capital to the eastern frontier.[45] To what extent this is accurate cannot be known, but we do know a reduction in the scope and expense of the public post did take place, with effects on local economy, or at least on the economics of exchange.[46] Yet it should be remembered that Justinian was not the first to introduce economies of scale in the public post – some adjustments and reductions in the scope of the service had already been introduced under Leo in the 460s or 470s.[47]

All these activities with respect to administration and military organisation are only one part of a whole, of course. Justinian's interest in religious affairs and dogma, the politics of his own imperial position, his building activity, his codification of the law, his enormous output of new constitutions and imperial rescripts, all testify to his vision of the paramount position of the God-protected Roman Empire in the world of men, and of his own position as supreme, God-appointed ruling authority in that empire. In this respect, the administrative changes introduced in his reign aimed not just at realising this vision in general terms, but also in exercising his duties as a just and fair ruler who cared for his subjects through the exercise of imperial benelovence (*philanthropia*) applied in practical terms to the way his government functioned.

The administrative problems his reforms attempted to address could not be resolved by this rather piecemeal tinkering with the system. Within a few years of the removal from power of John the Cappadocian in 541, several of the changes were abolished with harmful results. For example, the reduction in status or abolition of several diocesan *vicarii* in favour of governors of *spectabilis* rank in Pontica, Asiana, and Oriens meant that bandits and brigands could simply move across the borders to avoid pursuit. This was addressed either by the appointment of special officers with powers of pursuit over several provinces or by the restoration of the power of the *vicarii* (as in Pontica in 542). In the case of Thrace and the Long Walls, the *vicarius* of Thrace was revived to administer the civil business of the region, where the recently established praetor appears to have been less successful.[48] Yet the emperor continued to show a real concern for both government efficiency and the welfare of his subjects, in particular issuing laws on fiscal matters and justice, so that it is not possible to argue that the earlier series of reforms was the work of John the Cappadocian alone.

Justinian was also concerned with how provincial governors intervened in the governance of the towns in their districts. One of the most vexed questions of this period of late Roman social and economic history is that of the evolution of towns and cities, and in particular of their ruling elites who supplied the town councillors (*curiales*). To what extent were cities "in decline," and what do we mean by this phrase? Archaeological investigation, as well as a reexamination of the written sources for the problem, has shown that no simple answer is possible, even if general tendencies can be sketched out. For although cities lost much of their fiscal independence as administrators from the provincial governors came to play an increasingly interventionist supervisory role for fiscal reasons during the fifth and sixth centuries,[49] many cities remained relatively wealthy. Drawing from their possession of considerable lands cultivated by tenants within the city's territory, urban elites invested considerable sums in church building, as well as in some secular public works. While there were substantial changes in the physical appearance of many towns and in the use of public and private space in urban contexts, and while these reflect also a major shift in the patterns of investment of local elites, this does not mean that there also took place any substantial reduction in economic or exchange activity in those cities that retained their local role. There were, however, strong regional variations, reflecting local conditions: cities in the central and northern Balkans had already undergone very substantial changes in structure by the later fifth century, as new types of settlement emerged in response to changed economic and political circumstances and as older centres of population had to change. Cities in Asia Minor experienced such shifts only in the early seventh century and later.[50] Yet behind these transformations lay other, systemic shifts in relationships stimulated by, but also promoting longer-term social and cultural trends: the role and economic situation of the *curiales*, for example; increasing polarisation between the wealthy state elite and the less wealthy provincials; the Christianisation of urban centres; changes in the relationship between Constantinople and the provinces; and many other factors.[51]

In fact, both literary sources and the archaeological evidence from the south Balkans and Asia Minor suggest that urban centres continued to fulfil their role as local foci of exchange and small-scale commodity production as well as for the social activity of the landowners and the wealthy of their districts, at least until the 620s in most cases, later in others. There may thus have been as much wealth circulating in urban environments as before, but the difference was that the city as a municipality had limited access to it.[52] The church played a fundamental role in all this, as a receiver, administrator, and investor of social wealth in all forms – art, architecture, land and rents, livestock, and precious metals. There was little a government could do to affect these long-term trends; but for reasons of fiscal justice and because cities as such played such a significant role in Roman tradition and perceptions, Justinian intervened to prevent provincial governors appointing their own representatives over cities.[53]

In reviewing Justinian's reforms and interventions in the administration of the empire, therefore, it is possible to see his programme as dictated largely by his own ideological priorities, but with a strongly pragmatic and, to a certain extent, philanthropic element. The tensions between the welfare of his subjects, the efficient running of the state's fiscal and judicial machinery, and the vested interests of the metropolitan and regional social elites of the empire determined the effectiveness of his measures. Given the possibilities of seeing beyond immediate cultural and managerial horizons, his achievements should not be underestimated. But his reforms in provincial fiscal administration tended to strengthen rather than challenge existing trends, for example, in the relationship between the prefecture and the department of the *largitiones*: as the diocesan level of prefectural administration played a decreasing role in fiscal and judicial matters, so the *largitiones* became less important as an independent fiscal department and may even have ceased to operate as such by the end of Justinian's reign. The result was its absorption during the seventh century into one of the increasingly independent fiscal subdepartments of the prefecture.[54]

Similar observations might be made about the administration of the affairs of the cities. While ostensibly protecting towns and their autonomy, increased central supervision indirectly contributed to a decrease in municipal independence, reinforced in turn by the fact that the church, through its bishops, played an increasingly important role in city affairs, recognised and sanctioned by the government at Constantinople. The desire of key members of local elites to become members of the imperial establishment, at however great a distance (through titles and positions in the ramified palatine hierarchy), further contributed to the erosion of municipal financial independence.

In the longer term, it seems clear that Justinian's actions addressed only the symptoms of a much deeper set of problems. These included changing social relationships within the establishment, a strained tax base, a strategically overstretched army, and a fluctuating economic climate linked to demographic decline (to say nothing of the effects of the pestilence that struck the empire in the 540s). These problems developed in a context of changing international political-military relationships that would shortly transform the world in which the Roman state had to survive and the structures through which it could do so. It is also apparent that the nature of the reforms and other initiatives Justinian introduced across his reign, their short- or medium-term effect, and their implementation all likewise reflected the fundamental fact that the imperial government also depended heavily on the talents, willpower, political savvy and character of individuals such as the emperor and his top officials – men such as John the Cappadocian or Peter the Patrician. As with any autocratic system of rule, therefore, the effectiveness of late Roman government and administration was heavily inflected by this structural weakness.

The cost of Justinian's expansionist endeavours was considerable. Italy itself was devastated, its rural and urban economies shattered; the army was neither adequately supplied nor its ranks filled. State revenues could not meet greater military needs. The enormous cost of warfare in ancient states is summed up strikingly by the anonymous compiler of a sixth-century treatise on strategy, who notes that the greater part of the state's income is expended each year on the army.[55] And within ten years of the final reconquest of Italy, the invasion of the Lombards (from 568) had destroyed what little peace the peninsula had enjoyed. Henceforth it became increasingly marginal to imperial interests – although its ideological significance remained considerable for years.

In addition to the exhaustion of resources resulting from these vast campaigns of reconquest and the constant drain of also fighting with the Sasanid Empire, various forms of bubonic plague were endemic from the 540s, taking a huge cost in lives and morale.[56] From the 570s, the infiltration of groups of Slav immigrants across the Danube and into the Balkans, penetrating even into the Peloponnese by the 590s, the constant wars with the Persians, and the wars with the Turkic Avars in the Balkans represented a massive expenditure in resources, cash, and manpower. During the reign of Justin II (565–578), the state's fiscal exactions became ever more burdensome, so that his successor, Tiberius II Constantine (578–582), had to remit all taxes for a year in order to give the peasant producers time to recover.[57] Under his successor, Maurice (582–602), the fiscal and military crisis finally came to a head in the form of an increasingly oppressive tax regime, rigorous persecution of ideologically hostile populations (the Miaphysites in Syria and Egypt), and, finally, a major mutiny of the Balkan armies and the emperor's own deposition and murder. While it would be incorrect to ascribe all of this to Justinian's expansionism or his other activities, there can be no doubt that the strategic overextension of the empire, combined with a declining population and the systemic fiscal problems faced by the government, played a leading role in propelling the empire into a very different world from that which the young Justinian inherited in 527.[58]

## Notes

1 Averil Cameron, *The Mediterranean World in Late Antiquity* (London, 1993), 81–103, summarizes some of these issues.

2 For physical geography, see Richard J. A. Talbert, *Barrington Atlas of the Greek and Roman World* (Princeton, N.J., 2000), which offers information on roads, communications, and land use; and for some general considerations, see P. Horden and N. Purcell, *The Corrupting Sea: A Study of Mediterranean History* (Oxford, 2000), 9–25, 175–230. Michael F. Hendy, *Studies in the Byzantine Monetary Economy, 300–1453* (Cambridge, 1985), begins with a detailed discussion of the physical geography, demography, and land use of the empire from the fourth century; see also M. Kaplan, *Les Hommes et la terre à Byzance du VIe au XIe siècles* (Paris, 1992), 5–24.

3 Jones, *LRE*, 464–465, gives some indications of the proportions involved.

4 Several works deal with the relationship between town and countryside, the structures of rural life, and how urban centres were supplied. See, for example, J. H. W. G. Liebeschuetz, *The Decline and Fall of the Roman City* (Oxford, 2001); Jean Durliat, *De la ville antique à la ville byzantine. Le problème des subsistances* (Rome, 1990); and the essays in Gian Pietro Brogiolo, N. Gauthier, and N. Christie, eds., *Towns and Their Territories between Late Antiquity and the Early Middle Ages* (Leiden, 2000). For good surveys with the older as well as the most recent literature, see *CAH* 13: *The Late Empire, A.D. 337–425*, ed. Averil Cameron and Peter Garnsey (Cambridge, 1998), especially chap. 10, by P. Garnsey and C. R. Whittaker, "Trade, Industry, and the Urban Economy," 312–337; and chap. 12, by Bryan Ward-Perkins, "The Cities," 371–410.

5 See Jones, *LRE*, 767–823, many of the conclusions of which have since been revised: see *CAH* 13, chap. 9, by C. R. Whittaker, "Rural Life in the Later Roman Empire," 277–311; *CAH* 14. *Late Antiquity: Empire and Successors, A.D. 425–600* (Cambridge, 2000), especially chap. 13, by B. Ward-Perkins, "Specialised Production and Exchange," 346–391. For patterns of agricultural production and the seasons, see Kaplan, *Les Hommes et la terre à Byzance*, 25–87; and for rural society in general, B. Ward-Perkins, "Land, Labour, and Settlement," *CAH* 14, chap. 12, 315–345.

6 See J.-P. Sodini, "Le Commerce des marbres à l'époque protobyzantine," in *Hommes et richesses dans l'empire byzantin*, vol. 1, *Ire–VIIe siècle* (Paris, 1989), 163–186; *CAH* 14, chap. 31, by M. Mundell Mango, "Building and Architecture," 918–971.

7 See Jones, *LRE*, 834–839; O. Davies, *Roman Mines in Europe* (Oxford, 1935); K. Greene, *The Archaeology of the Roman Economy* (Berkeley, Calif., 1986), 142–148; J. C. Edmondson, "Mining in the Later Roman Empire and Beyond," *JRS* 79 (1989): 84–102; and Michael McCormick, *Origins of the European Economy: Communications and Commerce, A.D. 300–900* (Cambridge, 2001), 42–53.

8 See Jones, *LRE*, 824–844; Hendy, *Studies in the Byzantine Monetary Economy*, 554–561, 602–608; *CAH* 14:371–373; McCormick, *Origins of the European Economy*, 64–114, and Horden and Purcell, *The Corrupting Sea*.

9 See the classic essay by Norman H. Baynes, "Eusebius and the Christian Empire," *AIPHOS* 2 (1934): 13–18 (reprinted in N. H. Baynes, *Byzantine Studies and Other Essays* [London, 1955], 168–172); modern treatment in *CAH* 14, chap. 6, by M. McCormick, "Emperor and Court," 135–163.

10 Overview in B. Ward-Perkins, "Specialised Production and Exchange," *CAH* 14, chap. 13, 369–381.

11 McCormick, *Origins of the European Economy*, 98ff.

12 See the survey articles of C. Panella, "Gli scambi nel Mediterraneo Occidentale dal IV al VII secolo dal punto di vista di alcune 'merci,'" *Hommes et richesses dans l'empire byzantin*, 1:129–141; C. Abadie-Reynal, "Céramique et commerce dans le bassin égéen du IVe au VIIe siècle," *Hommes et richesses dans l'empire byzantin*, 1:143–159.

13 See J. W. Hayes, "Pottery of the Sixth and Seventh Centuries," in *Acta XIII Congressus Internationalis Archaeologiae Christianae*, 3:542; J. W. Hayes, "Problèmes de la céramique des VIIe–IXe siècles à Salamine et à Chypre," in *Salamine de Chypre, histoire et archéologie: État des recherches*, Colloques internationaux du CNRS 578 (Paris, 1980), 375–387.

14 P. Reynolds, *Trade in the Western Mediterranean, A.D. 400–700: The Ceramic Evidence*, BAR Int. Series 604 (Oxford, 1995), 34–35 and 118–121; D. P. S. Peacock and D. F. Williams, *Amphorae and the Roman Economy* (London, 1986); Abadie-Reynal, "Céramique et commerce," 155–157; J. W. Hayes, *Late Roman Pottery* (London, 1972), 418; and J. W. Hayes, *Excavations at Saraçhane in Istanbul*, vol. 2, *The Pottery* (Princeton, N.J., 1992), 5–8.

15 Hayes, *Excavations at Saraçhane*, 12–34; J.-M. Spieser, "La céramique byzantine médiévale," in *Hommes et richesses dans l'empire byzantin*, vol. 2, *VIIIe–XVe siècle* (Paris, 1991), 249–260.

16 See overviews of the late Roman economy in *CAH* 14, chap. 13, "Specialised Production and Exchange," 346–391, and McCormick, *Origins of the European Economy*, 25–119. For the economy and the role of coinage, see Hendy, *Studies in the Byzantine Monetary Economy;* Greene, *The Archaeology of the Roman Economy*, 44–57, 61–63; and C. Morrisson and J.-P. Sodini, "The Sixth-Century Economy," in *The Economic History of Byzantium from the Seventh through the Fifteenth Century*, ed. A. Laiou et al. (Washington, D.C., 2002), 171–220.

17 John F. Haldon, *Byzantium in the Seventh Century: The Transformation of a Culture* (Cambridge, 1990; 2nd rev. ed., 1997), 125–128; Ward-Perkins, "Land, Labour, and Settlement," 315–345.

18 For senatorial land ownership and acquisition, see M. Kaplan, *Les Hommes et la terre à Byzance du VIe au XIe siècles* (Paris, 1992), 155ff., 169–183.

19 See Jones, *LRE*, 333ff.; Stein, *Bas-Empire*, 2:432; and *Nov.* 62.1 (a. 537).

20 Stein, *Bas-Empire*, 2:429–432; Jones, *LRE*, 529–535. For Justinian, see *Nov.* 62, 1ff. (a. 537), 70 (a. 538).

21 R. Delmaire, *Largesses sacrées et* res privata. L'aerarium *impérial et son administration du Ive au Vie siècle*, Collection de l'École française à Rome 121 (Rome, 1989); Delmaire, *Les Institutions du Bas-Empire romain de Constantin à Justinien*, vol. 1, *Les institutions civiles palatines* (Paris, 1995), 140ff.; M. Kaplan, "Quelques aspects des

'maisons divines' de Justin II à Héraclius," in *Mélanges N. Svoronos* (Paris, 1986), 70–96; Kaplan, *Les Hommes et la terre*, 137ff., 140–142, 151. For older literature and discussion of the sources, see Jones, *LRE*, 412–427; Stein, *Bas-Empire*, 2:423ff., 472ff., 748ff.

22 For analysis of the legislative texts and other sources, see Kaplan, "Quelques aspects des 'maisons divines.'"

23 For detailed studies, see Kaplan, "Quelques aspects des 'maisons divines'"; D. Feissel, "Magnus, Mégas, et les curateurs des 'maisons divines' de Justin II à Héraclius," *TM* 9 (1985): 465–476.

24 *Nov. Iust.* 30, Chap. 7.

25 First mention is *CTh.* xvi, 10.1. Still the best survey of late Roman administration in English is Jones, *LRE*. For a good summary of central administrative departments, see R. Delmaire, *Largesses sacrées et* res privata.

26 A. E. R. Boak, *The Master of Offices in the Later Roman and Byzantine Empire* (New York, 1919), in A. E. R. Boak and J. E. Dunlop, *Two Studies in Late Roman and Byzantine Administration* (New York, 1924); Jones, *LRE*, 368–369, 575–584; M. Clauss, *Der Magister Officiorum in der Spätantike* (Munich, 1980); A. D. Lee, *Information and Frontiers: Roman Foreign Relations in Late Antiquity* (Cambridge, 1993), 41–48; Delmaire, *Les Institutions*, 75–95.

27 On Peter, see Stein, *Bas-Empire*, 2:723–729; P. Antonopoulos, *Petros patrikios: Byzantine diplomat, official, and author*, Historical Monographs 7 (Athens, 1990; in Greek). For the role of the master of offices in the field of diplomacy, see Lee, *Information and Frontiers*, 41–48.

28 *Nov. Th.*, 24.

29 *CJ*, 7.72.38.

30 The best survey of fiscal administration still remains that of Jones, *LRE*, 412–458; and see Stein, *Bas-Empire*, 1:174, 341; 2:67, 423ff., 472ff., 748ff. See also Hendy, *Studies in the Byzantine Monetary Economy*, 371–409; and *CAH* 14:170–181, with most recent literature. See also Delmaire, *Largesses sacrées et* res privata.

31 Jones, *LRE*, 448–462; *CAH* 14:174–175.

32 Jones, *LRE*, 437ff.; Hendy, *Studies in the Byzantine Monetary Economy*, 378–409 with literature.

33 Stein, *Bas-Empire*, 2:426–428, 766–769; Jones, *LRE*, 427–434; Delmaire, *Largesses sacrées et* res privata; Delmaire, "Le déclin des largesses sacrées," in *Hommes et richesses* 1:265–278; a general account in Delmaire, *Les Institutions*, 119–140.

34 Stein, *Bas-Empire*, 2:67 (with n. 1), 472–473, 748–749; Jones, *LRE*, 412–417; D. Feissel, "Magnus, Mégas et les curateurs des 'maisons divines,'" 465–476; Kaplan, "Quelques aspects des 'maisons divines'"; Kaplan, *Les Hommes et la terre*, 137–142; 149–152.

35 See Delmaire, *Les Institutions*, 140–147.

36 Jones, *LRE*, 830–834.

37 There are many sketches of Justinian's character and personality: see Stein, *Bas-Empire*, 2:275–283; Browning, *Justinian and Theodora*; Barker, *Justinian*; Cameron, *Procopius*; Maas, *John Lydus*. Justinian's own statement of the imperial ideology is neatly summarised in the opening section of the *Digests*; see *Digest Const. Deo auctore*, 1.8.

38 See Stein, *Bas-Empire*, 2:433–449, 463–483, for Justinian's leading ministers, especially John the Cappadocian; and Jones, *LRE*, 279–283.

39 See *CJ*, i, 1.27, for example, for Africa; and Stein, *Bas-Empire*, 2:319–328.

40 *Nov.* 8 (a. 535).

41 *Nov.*, 8, 24, 25, 28, 29 (a. 535), 30, 31 (a. 536), *Edict.* 13 (probably a. 539). For a detailed discussion, see Stein, *Bas-Empire*, 2:470–480.

42 On the praetor of Thrace, see *Nov.*, 26 (a. 535); On *Quaestura exercitus*, *Nov.*, 41 (a. 536).

43 *Nov.* 80 (a. 539)

44 *Nov.* 130 (a. 545)

45 Procopius, *Secret History*, 30.1.11; John the Lydian, *On Offices*, 3.61.

46 For discussion, see Hendy, *Studies in the Byzantine Monetary Economy*, 294–296; Jones, *LRE*, 284; Stein, *Bas-Empire*, 2:439–440.

47 Stein, *Bas-Empire*, 1:355 and n. 29; Jones, *LRE*, 833; cf. *CJ* 12.1.22 (a. 465 or a. 473).

48 See *Nov.* 145 (a. 553: Asiana); *Edict.*, 8 (a. 548: Pontica); *Nov.* 157 (a. 542: Osrhoene and Mesopotamia); Stein, *Bas-Empire*, 747–748 (but note that the middle Byzantine "count of the walls" has nothing to do with the Long Walls: see J. F. Haldon, *Byzantine Praetorians: An Administrative, Institutional, and Social Survey of the Opsikion and Tagmata, c. 580–900*, Poikila Byzantina 3 (Bonn, 1984), 271–275.

49 On reasons for the cities' loss of property, see W. Brandes and J. F. Haldon, "Towns, Tax, and Transformation: States, Cities, and Their Hinterlands in the East Roman World, ca. 500–800," in *Towns and Their Hinterlands between Late Antiquity and the Early Middle Ages*, ed. N. Gauthier (Leiden, 2000), 141–172.

50 Archibald Dunn, "The Transformation from *Polis* to *Kastron* in the Balkans (III–VII cc.): General and Regional Perspectives," *BMGS* 18 (1994): 60–80.

51 *CAH* 14, chap. 21, 570–637 (a: "Asia Minor and Cyprus," by C. Roueché; b: "Syria, Palestine, and Mesopotamia," by H. Kennedy; and c: "Egypt," by J. Keenan); and chap. 23, 701–730, "The Balkans and Greece, 420–602," by M. Whitby.

52 For literature and discussion of this vast and growing subject, see K. Holum in this volume. For a survey taking developments through into the ninth century, see L. Brubaker and J. F. Haldon, *Byzantium in the Iconoclast Era (ca. 680–850): A History* (Cambridge, 2005), chap. 7.

53 *Nov.* 134 (a. 556). See also *Nov.* 24–26 (a. 535) and 128 (a. 545) for the role of *vindices* in fiscal supervision of cities. On the ideological importance of cities, see Spieser, "L'Évolution de la ville byzantine de l'epoque paleochretienne a l'iconoclasme," in *Hommes et richesses dans l'empire byzantin*, vol. 1, *IVe–VIIe siècle*, ed. Catherine Abadie-Reynal (Paris, 1989): 101–104.

54 See Just., *Edict.*, 13, 11.2–3; 20; and discussion with literature in Haldon, *Byzantium in the Seventh Century*, 186–189; and Roland Delmaire, "Le Déclin des largesses sacrées," in Abadie-Reynal, *Hommes et richesses* 1:265–278.

55 George T. Dennis, ed., *The Anonymous Byzantine Treatise on Strategy*, in *Three Byzantine Military Treatises* (Washington, D.C., 1985), 1–136, esp. 13: "The financial system was set up to take care of matters of public importance that arise on occasion, such as the building of ships and of walls. But it is principally concerned with paying the soldiers. Every year most of the public revenues are spent for this purpose."

56 Procopius, *Wars*, 2. 22–23. For discussion of the plague, see P. Horden, "Mediterranean Plague in the Age of Justinian," Chap. 6 in this volume.

57 See *JGR*, 1, Coll. 1, nov. 9: Imp. Tiberii, *Peri kouphismon demosion* (on relief from public taxes) (a. 575). Tiberius began his reign formally in 578, but because of Justin II's illness actually took over some time before this date.

58 See Haldon, *Byzantium in the Seventh Century*.

# 3: Justinian's Constantinople

*Brian Croke*

Constantinople, Monday, August 11, 559. An unusual event is unfolding in the coolness of the early morning.[1] Justinian and his vast entourage of officials, servants, packhorses, and carts are assembling outside the walls of the imperial capital, by the Gate of Charisius. They are returning from Selymbria (modern Silivri), about sixty-five kilometres to the west, along the coast by the Sea of Marmara. Justinian, now in his late seventies, has been emperor for over thirty years. In all that time he has hardly set foot outside Constantinople. For the past few months, however, the aged sovereign and his court have been residing at Selymbria for extraordinary and urgent reasons. They had been engaged in the restoration of the Thracian Long Wall, which ran for sixty kilometres across the full length of the peninsula and constituted the outer defences of the capital.[2] The wall had been seriously damaged in an earthquake in December 557 and later overrun by a menacing band of Cotrigur Huns. Justinian's veteran general Belisarius had been dispatched to repulse the Huns, and the ensuing peace facilitated the imperial expedition to Selymbria.[3] The emperor's return to Constantinople in August 559 was announced and orchestrated. This was the traditional rite of welcome to a Roman city, the *adventus*. On entering the city he was formally greeted by the city prefect and other dignitaries, then ritually acclaimed by the Blue and Green circus factions in their colorful billowing costumes.[4]

## Location and Layout

Inside the Gate of Charisius a sparkling panorama opened up before Justinian. It was virtually the same vista he had encountered when he first set foot inside the city some sixty years earlier. Across the undulating hills and valleys before him, the horizon was punctured by statues of previous emperors resting atop tall columns, along with the glittering domes of many churches, especially the emperor's own renowned constructions of St. Irene and Sts. Sergius and Bacchus in the far distance. The greatest of all, however, Hagia Sophia, was temporarily diminished. Its dome had collapsed in the same earthquake that had affected the Long Wall, and it would take several more years to reconstruct. The morning summer sun would have highlighted the city's watery surrounds on three sides, forming a "garland around the city":[5] the Sea of Marmara to the right, the Bosporus directly ahead, and the narrower stretch of the Golden Horn to the left. Perched on a peninsula at the extremity of Thrace, Constantinople was strategically positioned at the narrow crossing from Europe to Asia and watched over the profitable sea-lane between the Mediterranean and the Black Sea. The sea was visible from almost anywhere in the city. It was the highway that conducted food supplies, building materials and luxury goods to the capital. It also linked the city with suburbs on the other side of both the Bosporus and the Golden Horn. The praetorian prefect maintained a fleet of three fast boats for crossing the straits on imperial business,[6] while in 528 Justinian joined Sykai to Constantinople by a bridge across the Golden Horn.[7] Being surrounded by water also made the capital vulnerable, however, necessitating enveloping sea walls from the mid–fifth century.[8]

The formidable walls protecting Constantinople on its landward side were completed in 413 and consisted of three layers of defence: two lines of wall, a castellated inner wall with a smaller curtain wall, and a substantial moat. At intervals along the wall were towers and gates, patrolled by soldiers. Much of the wall system is still standing, and part of it has recently been the subject of a controversial restoration.[9] On the steep ground at the northern end of the wall, but just beyond it, there stood the palace complex of Blachernai. The nearby Church of the Virgin was the original construction in the area and was completed by the empress Pulcheria around the mid–fifth century. Subsequently, in the reign of Leo I (457–474), a new chapel was built to take solemn possession of the Virgin's robe, which became a powerful Byzantine talisman. Around the turn of the sixth century, a palace was added to enable the emperor to spend time there. Justinian had himself rebuilt the church during the reign of his uncle Justin in the 520s and was a frequent visitor to Blachernai.[10]

Normally, returning from Selymbria and points nearer the city the emperor would enter through the Golden Gate close by the sea (see Map 6).[11] On this occasion Justinian had his own reason to break

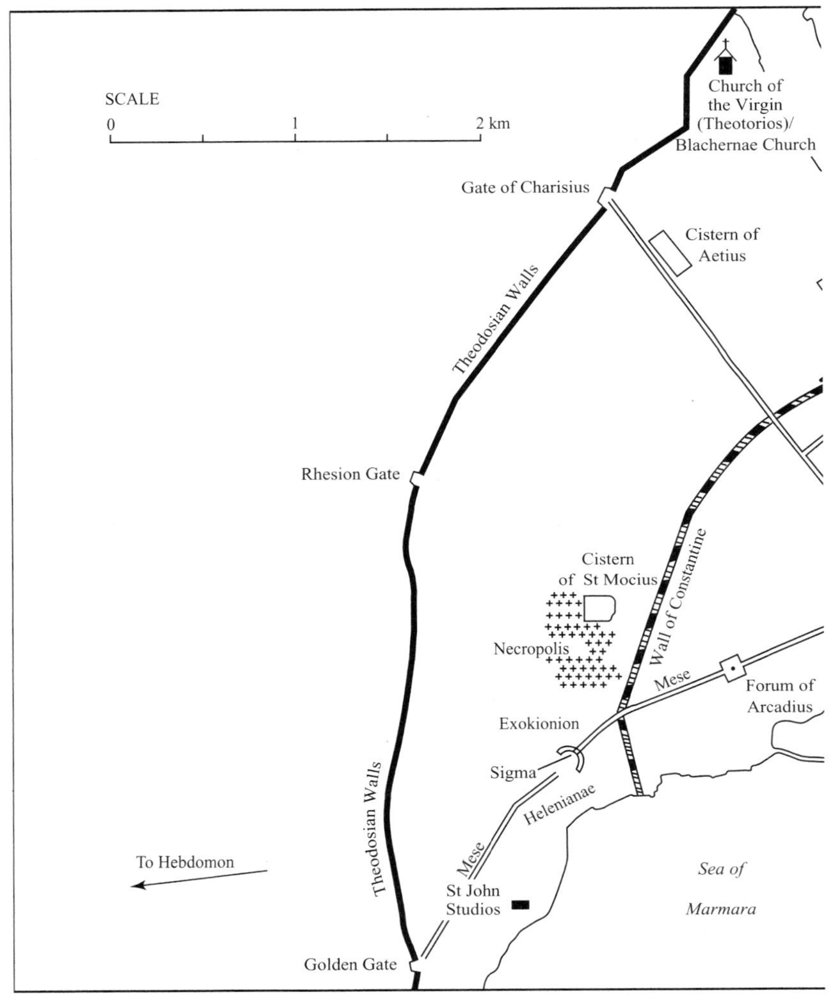


MAP 6. Justinian's Constantinople

with protocol and enter the city through the more northerly gate. A straight porticoed path lay ahead. As the procession advanced, the senators, soldiers, and Justinian on horseback passed on their left the large, open Cistern of Aetius, which was one of several such water storage facilities built on the city's high ground in the early 420s. Today it is a football field. Stretching across the landscape on both sides of the main thoroughfare were the city's extensive vegetable gardens. Soon the imperial party was passing through the Constantinian Wall, which marked the original perimeter of the city when it was first constructed in the

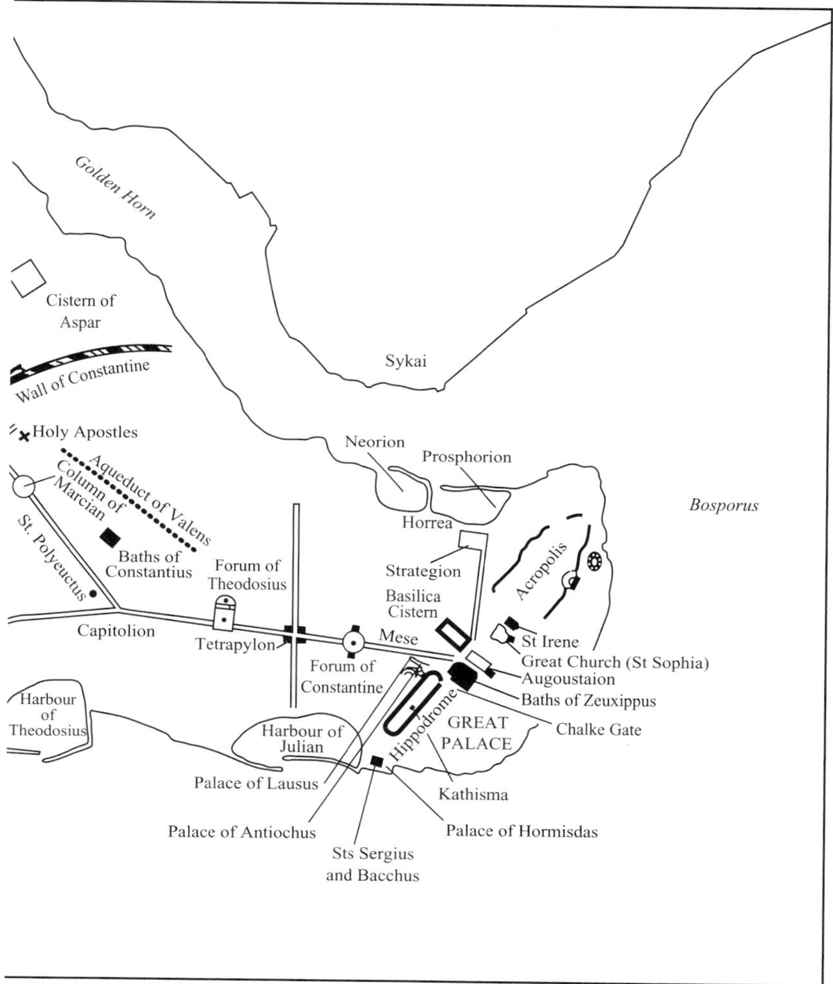


320s. The wall was now in a state of disrepair. From that point the city suddenly became more crowded, busy, and dense. Not far from the wall was the Church of the Holy Apostles, a grandiose cruciform edifice with multiple domes, completed by Justinian in 550 as a replacement for the original church built by Constantius II (337–361). Next to it was the mausoleum Constantine (305–337) built for himself, where most of Justinian's imperial predecessors now rested in marble sarcophagi. Justinian had built a new mausoleum nearby, and his wife Theodora, who died in 548, was its first occupant.[12] The emperor had taken this route through the city back to his palace precisely so that he could spend time at the tomb of Theodora and light candles to honor her memory.[13]

At the Church of the Holy Apostles the imperial party was swelled by the addition of another band of senators and officials, including the eunuchs of the imperial bedchamber. All of them would have been in the appropriate ceremonial dress, reflecting their carefully differentiated rank and status. They joined Justinian as he emerged from the Church of the Holy Apostles, where the imposing Aqueduct of Valens came into view. It had been conducting the city's water across a valley since its construction in the mid–fourth century. Nearby was the magnificent church of St. Polyeuktos, built in the early 520s by Justinian's rival, the imperial-blooded Anicia Juliana. When Justinian first arrived in Constantinople he will have passed the large basilica church of St. Polyeuktos built by the empress Eudocia. Her grandaughter Juliana had demolished the original church in the 520s and constructed what at the time was a building of unprecedented magnificence. The excavation of its remains last century has given some sense of its grandeur and opulence. As Justinian passed, he may well have recalled a personal encounter with Juliana when the magnificent building was just being finished.[14] As they advanced, just to the right, the imperial party could see the column of the emperor Marcian (451–457). Now they had virtually reached it, possibly at a small forum of Marcian.[15] Next en route was the key junction where the course Justinian had been following from the Gate of Charisius converged with the other route he might normally have been expected to follow, namely that through the Golden Gate. This route would have led him through the Forum of Arcadius with its historiated column and statue,[16] and the Forum Bovis,[17] then direct to the "Kapitolion" or Capitol.[18] Again, this was originally a Constantinian construction, modelled on the Capitol at Rome. Nearby stood many statues and the monument of "brotherly love" (Philadelphion), part of which survives in the embracing porphyry tetrarchs now in Venice.[19]

Justinian and his senatorial party then set off from the Capitol down the city's main artery, the so-called Middle Street (Mese), encountering along the way the serried ranks of the imperial officials itemised by Peter the Patrician: the emperor's personal staff (*protektores domestiki*), the full complement of over 5,000 guardsmen (*scholai*) in their dazzling white uniforms, the staff of the magister Peter (*magistrianoi*), and the prefects, including the prefect of the city who had previously welcomed him at the Gate of Charisius. Also present were the city's trade guilds: the skilled craftsmen responsible for the parade armour, the silversmiths and money lenders, and all the other merchants. It was a colourful and crammed procession, framed by the long porticos of the street.[20] Indeed, there was barely room for the emperor's horse to plod a path on a street designed to carry chariots in both directions. Above the packed crowd, visible to all, moved the emperor.[21] Justinian's ceremonial horseback entry to the imperial capital in 559 reflects his triumphal posture on the famous gold medallion in the Bibliothèque Nationale (Plates i & ii) and on the Barberini Ivory (Plate iii).

Moving along the double porticoed street, the emperor's party soon passed through the massive triumphal arch leading into the Forum of Theodosius (or Forum Tauri), built to commemorate the triumph of Theodosius I (379–395) over the Goths in the 380s. The arch supported statues of both Honorius, facing the west, and Arcadius, facing the east, and by Justinian's day the forum contained a large number of other statues. Deliberately imitating the Forum of Trajan at Rome, this forum's centrepiece was an imperial column with sculpted spiral reliefs depicting Theodosius's military triumphs.[22] Beneath this column foreign ambassadors were ceremonially welcomed to Constantinople, and it was here that the emperor was welcomed home whenever he returned from the west, as Justinian did on this occasion.

After being saluted, Justinian progressed further through the crowds until he reached the circular Forum of Constantine. By Justinian's day the Forum of Constantine was simply "the Forum," a central location for most imperial processions. Within this area with its massive gates at each end stood a tribunal to review troops, a senate house, and many statues, notably one of Apollo from Troy.[23] The central monument of the Forum was a porphyry column of the emperor, known in its present form as the Burnt Column. On top of it stood a statue of Constantine, later replaced by a cross.[24] Beneath it was buried the statue of Pallas, the city's traditional talisman.[25]

The double-storeyed porticoed Mese led out from the Forum of Constantine to the Augoustaion. Just before reaching the Augoustaion, Justinian passed by the main public entrance to the hippodrome, a large edifice pivotal to the life of the city. The hippodrome was the focus of regular programs of chariot racing and other entertainments "all of which," Agathias observed, "tend to have a profoundly disturbing effect on the minds of the young."[26] Much of the city's population could be accommodated in the hippodrome to cheer on their favourite charioteer as he circled the arena's axis, and to root for their preferred faction, predominantly Blue or Green. Justinian was the patron of the circus and sponsored the games.[27] He presided over the races from the imperial box (*kathisma*), which was also the place where he was presented to the city as the new emperor in April 527.[28] Very early in his reign (528), Justinian had remodelled the imperial box to make it more spacious and more conspicuous. At the same time he improved the view for the senatorial spectators.[29] The *kathisma* of the hippodrome was connected to the imperial palace through a spiral staircase.

As they reached the end of the Mese, Justinian's entourage skirted the Augoustaion square and approached the entrance to the imperial palace. The Augoustaion of 559 was considerably different from the original ceremonial space laid out by Constantine, and different again from the one modified in 459 by the addition of porticoes. It had been destroyed in 532 during the Nika riots and had been completely rebuilt by Justinian. It was now smaller than before and functioned more as a courtyard to the church of Hagia Sophia on its northeastern side. On the Augoustaion's other side stood the senate house, although by now senators mainly met with the emperor in the palace and the Baths of Zeuxippos, both of which had been rebuilt by Justinian after 532. The Augoustaion's main feature was a statue of Justinian on top of a high column erected in 543. The bronze statue was of the emperor on horseback holding an orb in his hand and facing east towards Persia (Plate iv). He was dressed in the martial uniform of Achilles, replete with ceremonial headdress.[30]

At last Justinian reaches the Chalke or "Brazen House," the grand entrance vestibule of the imperial palace, and his ceremonial return from Selymbria comes to an end. The accompanying senators and chamberlains have now dispersed; the emperor and his key staff are home. The triumphal return of Justinian to his palace sees him greeted by the *admissionalis*, the official who controlled entrance to the imperial presence, along with one of the *protectores* and the *triumphator*. The whole ceremonial was planned and supervised by the *magister officiorum*, Peter the Patrician, who tells us that he himself ordered the "triumphal salute" to be given at this point.[31] Had Justinian returned to the city through the Golden Gate, the ritual of triumph would have been performed there instead. The salute was accentuated and amplified by the emperor standing beneath the magnificent mosaics that covered the ceiling of the Chalke, representing his earlier triumphs over the Vandals and the Goths.[32] Along with two equestrian statues imported from Ephesus, they formed part of the lavish decoration of the Chalke, which had been completely rebuilt by Justinian after 532.[33]

Beyond the Chalke the imperial palace complex spread out across the terraced hillside and down to the water. Justinian's palace, which had evolved over the decades, was a sprawling collection of buildings and gardens connected by porticoed walkways. The palace's major spaces were the *consistorium* (a central room where the emperor sat in majesty to receive his visitors), the Tribunal of the Nineteen Couches or *Delphax* (an extensive terrace for special assemblies and investitures), the *Magnaura* (an audience hall) and the *Triklinos* (a large banquet room). The palace housed quite a horde, being home not only to the Emperor and his family but also to his senior officers and their families.[34] Justinian's main contribution was to rebuild and refurbish the Chalke and neighbouring structures.[35] Nothing much of the palace has been unearthed, except for some striking mosaics, but recent excavations have located some of its substructures and there are expectations of more to come.[36]

Justinian was now back in the imperial palace, where he spent most of his time with court officials as they dealt with a constant stream of appellants and special visitors, plus meetings with senior bureaucrats and generals. The systematic and notable centralization of power that characterised Justinian's reign created a busy life for the emperor.[37] In fact, Justinian was singled out by contemporaries for his diligence. The "sleepless emperor" could even be caricatured for spending long hours in the palace, day and night, on imperial business.[38] There were numerous documents for examination and briefing, new appointments, discussion and decision making, the reception of ambassadors, and imperial banquets. In between those obligations there was constant and extensive correspondence. Justinian had simply returned to the familiar hectic round of imperial business that had dominated his life for more than thirty years now and would continue to preoccupy him until his death in November 565.

## Governance and Sustenance

Inside the walls of Justinian's Constantinople lived around 500,000 people. As the imperial capital, the city was dominated by the needs and demands of the emperor, his court, and his palace. It was styled by Justinian in his laws as the "royal city," or "our fortunate city." Justinian, like his predecessors, took a close interest in Constantinople and occasionally made laws and other pronouncements designed to improve its financing and functioning. By Justinian's day the emperor never led his troops into battle but was still commander-in-chief of the army. His two senior generals attended the court at Constantinople, while most of the soldiers they commanded were stationed outside the city in nearby towns. So too, the majority of the emperor's palace guard (*scholae palatinae*), who lined the Mese to welcome him home in 559, was also stationed outside the city. The palace and the emperor himself were mainly protected by the *excubitores*, who could also be deployed outside the palace to provide an armed escort for those summoned to the imperial presence, to help restore order or prevent a serious civil disturbance from threatening the palace and the emperor. They were prominent, for example, during the Nika riots in January 532.[39]

Constantinople had its own civic administration, modelled on that of Rome. The city was originally divided into fourteen regions. Responsibility for local affairs in each region rested with a *curator* (or "regionarch") and five *vicomagistri*, who watched over the region at night and who reported to the city prefect. In general, the prefect was a senior member of the imperial court and had the authority to convene the senate. He had a large staff, a praetorium close to the palace, and his own carriage.[40] Prefectural responsibility extended to fire control, law and order, and civic amenities, including food and water.

Justinian's Constantinople was a city of consumers. Providing sufficient food and water for all the inhabitants of the enclosed capital was a permanent challenge. A disruption to routine could quickly bring disaster. The city's water supply originated over one hundred kilometres away in the mountains of Thrace and in streams closer in. The water was channelled through a long and complex system of aqueducts and tunnels all the way to Constantinople, where it was stored in large cisterns and distributed around the city's fountains and baths. Water was stored in the large open-air cisterns of Aetius (c. 420s), Aspar (c. 460), and Mocius (c. 500), which progressively supplied the growing city. They were complemented by numerous strategically located, covered cisterns.[41] Justinian's city prefect Longinus was responsible for the construction of the Basilica Cistern (Yerebatanserai), which still impresses visitors to Constantinople.[42] The city also boasted numerous private and public baths, including the Baths of Dagisthaeus completed by Justinian in 528,[43] as well as the largest and most elaborate of all – the Baths of Zeuxippos restored by Justinian after the Nika riots.[44]

The city's water supply was put under pressure every summer, sometimes seriously.[45] In November 562 a drought in the city's Thracian catchment was creating a water shortage, and thirsty people were fighting each other at the city's public fountains. By the following August (563) the prolonged drought had created an even more serious situation. Now the city's baths were closed and people were actually "murdered at the fountains," so desperate had some become.[46] The imperial court had avoided exposing itself to such pressure. One of the consquences of the chaos unleashed by the Nika riots in 532 was the difficulty of providing for those barricaded inside the palace complex. As a result Justinian ensured that in future the palace always had its own self-sufficient water supply from its own internal cistern.[47]

At the same time the emperor had a private granary and bakery built inside the palace, thereby reducing dependence on the city's grain supplies. All Constantinople's grain was imported, with most coming from Egypt's reliable annual yield. This supply line was also a long one, involving an annual armada of ships loaded with grain setting out for Constantinople and bringing assurance to the city by their safe arrival. A quick turnaround was required for the ships, always rushing to make two to three return trips per year.[48] Docking the grain ships required four to five kilometres of wharves across the harbours on both the Sea of Marmara and the Golden Horn.[49] No less enormous was the infrastructure required to unload, store, and transport the grain, then to bake the city's daily bread. The grain was unloaded quickly into nearby warehouses then distributed through a system of public and private bakeries throughout the city. In effect, Constantinople operated a duplex structure of food supply: one was a government-supplied daily ration to the city's inhabitants distributed at a designated point within each city region, the other was the private baking of bread for those not entitled to the government ration.[50]

Monitoring the levels of stored grain was crucial to the city's survival and civic stability. While this would have been done daily by the city prefect's staff, it was important for the emperor to demonstrate public assurance too. Each year, towards the end of summer, when supplies were dwindling, Justinian would set out on an elaborate expedition to inspect the granaries, accompanied by the city prefect, and then pronounce reassurance to the city.[51] There were times, however, when grain supply was seriously deficient. In May 555, for instance, a severe bread shortage lasted for three months until the first ships arrived from Alexandria. Justinian was at the hippodrome entertaining the Persian ambassador when chanting circus factions confronted the emperor in the imperial box with the hungry people's plight, whereupon he had the leaders of the Blue faction punished by the city prefect for their insolence.[52]

Besides grain, the imperial capital also had to import all its wine and oil. There were separate storehouses for these commodities, which arrived in large earthenware jars, and they formed part of the same distribution system, available as a periodic ration for those entitled or by private purchase.[53] Although not as serious as a deficiency of grain, shortages of wine and oil were also momentous events for the city's inhabitants. Justinian had to deal with a wine shortage in 546 and had experienced a scarcity of oil during the reign of his uncle Justin in 524.[54] Complementing the imported grain, wine, and oil were other foods supplied locally. There was an abundance of fish in the city's waterways.[55] Livestock, including cattle, were evidently traded in the open markets of the Forum Tauri and the Strategion, while a variety of meat was consistently available.[56] Both fish and meat were sold by butchers in the *macellum*, a walled area bordered by shops.[57] In February 545, resulting from a miscalculation in the date for the start of Lent, Justinian ordered that meat be sold for an extra week, but people were suspicious of the emperor's motives and boycotted the butchers. Some even tried to spoil the meat set out for sale by throwing dust and chalk over it.[58] Vegetables were plentiful year round, grown mainly in the gardens between the walls of Constantine and Theodosius, as well as beyond the walls.[59]

Justinian's Constantinople was highly combustible. Compact wooden structures, combined with permanent hearths for various essential purposes such as baking, smelting of metals, and glassblowing, made fire a perpetual risk and it could spread rapidly. Under the prefect's control were over five hundred *collegiati* or fire wardens, appointed by the various guilds. When fire broke out, the cry to summon them went up – "On the double, everyone."[60] Justinian decreed in 535 that the new praetor of the people should be assisted by thirty firefighters to help rescue property from the flames and would have authority to arrest anyone found looting a burning building.[61] There were major fires in April 550, December 560 (Harbour of Julian), October 561 (Caesarius quarter), and December 563 (destroying the hospital of Sampson, the atrium of Hagia Sophia, two monasteries near St. Irene and part of the church's narthex).[62] Sometimes fire resulted from rioting crowds, such as the most spectacular conflagration during the Nika riots in 532, when so much of the monumental centre of the city was burned down. One eyewitness looked back on a city "uninhabitable because of dust, smoke, and stench of materials being reduced to ashes, striking pathetic dread in those who beheld it."[63]

Even more destructive than these frequent blazes were the numerous earthquakes the city experienced during the reign of Justinian. Constantinople is part of an active seismic zone. Tremors in November 533 brought a large crowd into the Forum of Constantine where they prayed all night for the city to be spared. No one was hurt.[64] There were other minor earthquakes and tremors in 540–541, 545, 547, 551, 554, and 555,[65] but 557 was the year of seismic terror. A quake on Monday, April 16, frightened the city but caused no damage,[66] while another on Saturday, October 19, had the same effect.[67] Disaster finally struck, however, at midnight on December 14, when a very large earthquake rocked Constantinople and its environs, causing both the weakening of the dome of Hagia Sophia, which collapsed the following May, and the damage to the Long Wall that allowed the Cotrigur Huns to pass through early in 559. The city walls of Theodosius and Constantine were severely damaged, along with churches and other buildings. Many lives were lost. In sympathy Justinian went without his imperial crown for forty days.[68]

Every year thereafter the earthquake of 557 was commemorated at Constantinople with a liturgy of supplication.[69] In an undated law issued to the people of the city Justinian reminded them that loose public morals were the cause of God's anger manifest in any earthquake,[70] hence the need for propitiation. It was a message he reinforced in March 559 before setting out for Selymbria to deal with the consequences of divine wrath at the Long Wall.[71] Agathias, who lived through the 557 quake at Constantinople, observed that it had an immediate impact on people's behaviour. The rich gave to the poor, doubters turned to prayer, the vicious became suddenly virtuous – but soon they all lapsed back to their former ways.[72] The need for propitiation subsided until the next annual reminder. Besides earthquakes, an electrical storm in June 548 killed people in their sleep, and part of the column of Arcadius in his forum (Xerolophos) was shorn off.[73] There were violent winds, thunder, and lightning again on July 19, 555, which toppled the cross on the Rhesion gate (Yeni Mevlevihane Kapisi) of the land walls.[74] More lightning on July 13, 556, produced "many casualties."[75]

All these natural disasters ensured regular rebuilding and refurbishment in the city.[76] They also disrupted the regular routine of public life and created a demand for medical support and care. Justinian's Constantinople had the best possible physicians and some dedicated places for nursing the sick and injured. However, when the plague struck in 542, the city could barely cope with the horrendous loss of life and the pall of death that engulfed it. The plague returned in 558.[77] Funeral processions had to be abandoned, since there were so many corpses requiring rapid disposal. The city's dead were usually buried in cemeteries inside the Theodosian walls or in underground hypogaea.[78]

Another of the responsibilities of the city prefect was the maintenance of civic order and control of crime. A habitual challenge for the prefect was the rivalry maintained by the Blue and Green circus factions, together or separately, which regularly erupted into violence. The most famous occasion was the Nika riots in 532.[79] In 547, during the city's anniversary celebrations on May 11, the factions got out of control and the imperial guard was called in, resulting in heavy loss of life.[80] Much the same occurred in May 562.[81] Other factional riots broke out in October 562[82] and in 563.[83] There were yet other riots, including one over the debasement of coinage in 553, which forced Justinian to back down.[84]

Contemporaries were unnerved by the frequency and magnitude of such urban violence and looked for a decisive response from the emperor and the city prefect. In his firsthand account of the Nika riots, Marcellinus singles out the rioters as "criminal citizens" who may be contrasted to the "good citizens" who avoid throwing stones and who salute the public punishment of the perpetrators of violence. Procopius strongly criticised Justinian for letting the factions get out of hand.[85] John the Lydian explained the need for the emperor to take action against violence and looting in the city,[86] while John Malalas observed the general unpopularity of factional strife.[87] Still, clear action in response to these concerns was rare.[88] On his accession, Justinian issued a comprehensive decree outlawing violence.[89] In 535 he sought to curb civil unrest – arson, looting, and theft in particular – by upgrading the prefect of the night watch to the role of *praetor plebis*.[90] Evidently this law proved less than effective, so in 539 he decided to strike more directly at the root of the trouble by ruling that only officially registered arms manufacturers could make arms, and they could not sell them to any private person for any reason whatsoever.[91]

By the time of Justinian's rule, population density was aggravating civic tensions, potentially threatening security or self-sufficiency. Constantinople was firmly fixed in its physical limits. It could not afford to take on more inhabitants than it could support through its present mechanisms and resources, nor could it encroach on the open space required for cultivation. Still the city was like a magnet, constantly attracting supplicants and ambitious young men from everywhere. Each new generation of lawyers and soldiers set its sights on Constantinople. Many hoped and contrived to stay if they could. The city's delicate equilibrium of supply and demand for essential goods and services needed to be kept under strict observation. It is clear from the legislation of Justinian that the city and the emperor were constantly wrestling with a potential imbalance caused by crowds of complainants and refugees coming to Constantinople.[92] Some were even obtaining free rations illegally.[93] The number of farmers was a special concern. Yet the incursions of the Huns, Goths, and Bulgars in the Danubian and Balkan provinces inevitably propelled small farmers towards the capital in search of a different fortune.[94] Justinian issued many laws designed to address this concern and in 539 established a new position (*quaesitor*) with special responsibility for it. The *quaesitor* and his assistants would ascertain from all foreigners entering the city their identity, origin, and purpose in coming to Constantinople. Their motives were carefully scrutinised and, if litigious, then they must return home once their case was heard.[95] Justinian and Theodora built a hospice to shelter many of those visitors who satisfactorily completed their business and stayed until they had a place to lodge.[96] Justinian also tried to deal with those who claimed that they had been prevented from returning home by severe weather or illness.[97] Bishops were singled out for special treatment. They could no longer come to Constantinople without good reason and written explanation from their archbishop,[98] an instruction later reiterated and expanded by forcing a visiting bishop seeking an audience with the emperor to apply through the patriarch of Constantinople.[99]

Of particular concern during Justinian's reign was the large number of monks arriving in Constantinople fleeing persecution in the east, particularly after 536 when they were outlawed by imperial decree for dissenting from the orthodox Christology. Monks from Alexandria, headed by their bishop Theodosius, soon established monasteries and churches in the city.[100] Others arrived later from various parts, and in 539 Justinian charged the newly appointed *quaesitor* with examining the credentials of monks and nuns who had arrived in Constantinople.[101] Such scrutiny was then reinforced by another law forbidding the entry of any monk into the city without a letter of authorisation from his local patriarch.[102] In the decade or so between 536 and her death in 548, the empress Theodora had taken responsibility for giving succour at Constantinople to hundreds of Monophysite monks, whom she resettled in various underutilised mansions, including at the imperial palace of Hormisdas. Although her support for them was widely noted, it was always measured and it never contradicted Justinian. Following the initial influx in 537–538, the arrival of refugee monks at Constantinople was carefully monitored and regulated by Justinian.

## Society and Community

As a centre of power and influence, Justinian's Constantinople attracted people from a diversity of linguistic, cultural, and regional backgrounds.[103] The city streets resounded with a cacophany of Latin, Greek, and Syriac, Aramaic and Armenian, Coptic and Ethiopic, Gothic and Hunnic, Persian and Arabic. Justinian and his family were Latin-speaking Illyrians, while the diplomat Peter the Patrician was a Greek-speaking Illyrian, although he was born in Dara on the Persian frontier. Among the Africans were the rhetorician and grammarian Priscian, the poet Corippus, and the bishop Victor. There were famous Johns from Lydia and Cappadocia, as well as John Malalas from Antioch.[104] From Armenia came the generals Narses and Artabanes. The preeminent general Belisarius was a Latin speaker from the Balkans, but his secretary Procopius was a highly educated Greek speaker from Palestinian Caesarea. Procopius, Peter the Patrician, and many others – but probably not Justinian himself – were at home in both Greek and Latin. Increasingly, however, Greek was becoming the city's common language, so those who had mastered Latin, such as John the Lydian, could feel aggrieved that its use was declining even in the prefectural office.[105] In 535 Justinian decided that Greek should thereafter be the "language of state." It was the inevitable outcome of a long process.[106]

How this rich variety of individuals, families, and clans was spread throughout the city is difficult to determine. However, the *Notitia* of Constantinople – an official or quasi-official document from the reign of Theodosius II – provides a sound guide to the basic structure of the city and the spread of its population even in Justinian's day.[107] It enables us to conclude that the areas around the imperial palace (regions I and II) and in the western part of the city (regions X and XI) were relatively open and populated more by the city's aristocracy, while labourers, craftsmen, and unemployed people lived around the ports and fora and along the Mese. Regions IV to VIII comprised most of the areas of the craftsmen surrounding the porticoes of the Mese and the maritime districts, both around the harbour of Julian and along the Golden Horn. The *Notitia* also records how many freestanding houses or *domus* there were in each region, with the greatest number in region XI, an elegant area surrounding the church of the Holy Apostles.[108] The least populated was region V, which took in the Forum of Theodosius, the baths of Eudocia and Honorius, the cistern of Theodosius, the Troad, Valentinianic, and Constantinian granaries, as well as oil stores. This region also had the highest proportion of free bread outlets and the highest number of public bakeries.

Sixth-century Constantinople was a mélange of diverse communities, separated or bound by religion, language, and regional identity. The Chalkoprateia, for example, was a Jewish neighbourhood with its own synagogue,[109] and there were also definite communities of Goths who naturally tended to congregate together and probably had their own shops and churches. During Justinian's time the Alexandrians in the imperial capital, including the transplanted monks, had divided in response to the two current rivals for the patriarchal throne – Theodosius and Gainas. The Gaianitae and Theodosianitae built their own separate monasteries and churches in the city.[110] Then there were the Cappadocians, who, like the Isaurians of a previous generation, were always unpopular in Constantinople. A law of Justinian singled them out as being a nuisance,[111] and John the Lydian repeated some unkind anti-Cappadocian doggerel in common circulation.[112]

Latin was the language of a considerable proportion of the city's population. Yet there were several quite different Latin-speaking communities. First, there was the traditional senatorial aristocracy, with strong western connections. The Theodosian imperial dynasty, with branches in both east and west, survived at Constantinople in the family of Anicia Juliana, the daughter of the former western emperor Olybrius. She had long been resident there as patron of litterateurs and holy men, as well as being responsible for the construction of the grand church of St. Polyeuktos. She had also been involved in supporting papal embassies in Constantinople at the outset of Justin's reign. Latin studies flourished in her milieu.[113] Many other such families also lived on in Constantinople. Symmachus, consul in 485, had a mansion at Constantinople burnt out during the Nika riots.[114] There was certainly a steady flow of noble refugees from Italy during the war against the Goths in the 540s and 550s. Cassiodorus, Cethegus, and others were among them.

Another large group of Latin speakers in Constantinople was from Africa. Indeed, it was due to the pressure in Constantinople of African nobles, disenchanted or proscribed during the Vandal overlordship, that Justinian launched his expedition in 533.[115] The historian Procopius, the chronicler and courtier Marcellinus, as well as the exiled African bishop Victor of Tunnuna, all resident in Constantinople, refer to the presence in the city of many victims of Vandal persecution who had had their tongues cut out.[116] Like others, the Africans tended to live together and be buried together. For example, when Bishop Theodorus died in 565, he was buried alongside other victims of Huneric's persecution who had passed away in the city long ago.[117]

The third significant segment of Latin speakers were refugees and veterans from the Balkan provinces of Illyricum, where so many still had families and friends only a few days' travel away.[118] The family of

Justinian was numbered among them. Justin I, uncle of Justinian, left his hometown of Bederiana and came to Constantinople to find a worthwhile career in the army. He was followed later by his sister, Justinian's mother, and other family members later still.[119] Most of the known Illyrians at Constantinople were military men, but they were strongly engaged with theological and religious issues, especially in support of the orthodox Chalcedonian position and the authority of the bishop of Rome.[120]

The Constantinople of Justinian's time was crowded and boisterous, as it had long been and would remain. It was a city with buildings stacked so close together that there was very little room both inside and outside, while compact crowds of people and animals jostled each other.[121] An earthquake engendered panic because there was no nearby open space for people to congregate in safety.[122] Such density exacerbated social and communal friction arising from ethnic, sporting, and religious antagonisms and rivalries.[123] It also had an impact on sanitation, light, and neighbourly relations, as is evident from early laws regulating the distance between buildings.[124] A law of 538 refers to the proverbial "evil neighbour" who devises ways of getting around the prohibition on building closer than 100 feet from the sea in certain areas.[125] Building regulations, however, did little to contain the overcrowding problem.

## Ritual and Ceremonial

The pomp and majesty of the imperial court dominated Constantinople in the time of Justinian. The city functioned as the theatre for an elaborate and colourful ritual, with every movement of the imperial personage around the city carefully planned and stylised. The city had adapted progressively to this ceremonial role ever since emperors became permanently established there, from the time of Theodosius I (379–395) and Arcadius (392–408), when an emperor's main movements were wholly within the city itself. There now developed a new form of imperial self-representation focussed on the traditional virtues of the Roman imperial image. Moreover, during the fifth century Constantinople's imperial ritual became increasingly liturgified and sacralised.[126] Even the normal imperial movements in and around the city had become ritualised by elaborating the Roman *adventus* (arrival) and *profectio* (leaving). Justinian's return from Selymbria in 559 exemplifies the new convention, as does Theodora's *profectio* in August 528 to the hot springs at Pythia near Pylai (modern Yalova), where she was accompanied by an entourage of 4,000 including leading aristocrats and the officials of the imperial bedchamber.[127]

Since Constantinople was now the city where emperors were born, baptised, married, crowned, and were buried, each of these occasions gave rise to significant public ceremonial. Records survive of both Justinian's coronation and his funeral. Since he had already been crowned caesar (junior emperor) by his uncle in 525, the ceremony was much simpler when he became augustus on April 1, 527, with Theodora made augusta at the same time. It took place inside the palace, at the Tribunal of the Nineteen Couches, with the patriarch offering prayers and Justin crowning him as the assembled palace guards, court officials, and soldiers looked on.[128] By contrast, his funeral, in November 565, was a more public and more elaborate affair. Corippus describes the chanting, the music and incense, the dense crowds lining the Mese mourning as the bier of Justinian passed in solemn procession to his resting place beside his wife in the mausoleum at the Church of the Holy Apostles.[129] Theodora's funeral in June 548 would have involved a similar splendid procession.

The rhythm of the city's ceremonial was dictated by the rhythm of the annual calendar. In fact, the inhabitants of Justinian's Constantinople knew four different years simultaneously and marked the start of each of them with due ceremony and celebration: January 1 (consulship); April 1 (Justinian's regnal year); May 11 (birthday of the city); September 1 (tax year or indiction, liturgical year).[130] To minimise the confusion of overlapping years, Justinian decreed in 537 that the official method of reckoning and recording time on legal and other documents was to be the year of his reign.[131] Traditionally, the consulship had been a great Roman festival at which the new consuls for the year could demonstrate their generosity with lavish displays and handouts to the populace. Justinian's own consulships in 521 and 528 were said to be the most lavish ever,[132] although the diptych he issued in 521 was scarcely ornate.[133] In attempting to control the consulship more tightly, Justinian declared that he would be a perpetual consul, and he had the yearlong duties for others streamlined, compressing them into a single week.[134] By 542 the consulship had lapsed altogether.[135]

Throughout the liturgical year Constantinople witnessed regular public ceremonial and liturgy to mark feast days commemorating saints and martyrs, previous emperors, the opening of churches, earthquakes and other natural events, all of which engendered an official public proclamation, normally by the city prefect.[136] Many of these occasions involved religious processions.[137] Indeed, most of the liturgical processions recorded in later Byzantine calendars were already institutionalised in Constantinople by Justinian's day.[138] The common feature of all these processions and liturgical reenactments was the role of the imperial household and patriarch, integrated with the populace in a common cause of propitiation and celebration. The ritual and ceremonial of Justinian's Constantinople centered on the fora, which were settings for imperial events, with each new emperor seeking to eclipse his predecessors by giving his forum prominence on processional routes. This ritualised use of the city's main public spots played a major role in focussing the energies and interests of the people in the liturgical celebrations of the day.[139]

In the early years of Justinian's reign the most conspicuous ceremonial was devoted to the traditional celebration of triumph. Justinian could boast triumphs over the Persians and Bulgars in 530,[140] but most spectacular of all were the triumphs in 534 and 541, when the kings of the Vandals and Goths, along with their precious possessions, were paraded before the emperor and people of Constantinople.[141] These triumphs became the highlights of Justinian's reign. There are many other instances of the emperor celebrating at Constantinople news of an imperial victory, mainly local and short-term, such as receiving the keys of Verona and Brescia in 562.[142] Still, the emperor did not need to win military victories to be portrayed as victorious. He was ever-victorious, a triumphal ruler. It was simply part of the imperial ideology, so that when Justinian returned to the capital in 559 he entered and progressed triumphally through the city as if he had personally defeated the Cotrigur Huns and repulsed them by force of arms. He was even acclaimed as "victor." This was the first time a church had been included in the ritual of triumph.[143]

Considerable ceremonial and time was also taken up by Justinian receiving and entertaining foreign potentates. The Persian king never travelled to Constantinople, but most lesser rulers did. At the beginning of Justinian's reign in 527, Grepes, king of the Heruli, was honoured in the imperial capital and sponsored in baptism by the emperor.[144] A deputation "of the flower of the [Lazi] nation's nobility" was sent to Justinian and received the royal insignia from him.[145] The same pattern was followed in 528 by Grod, king of the Huns, then the Hun Askoum.[146] In 534 the Iberian king Zamanarzos, "accompanied by his wife and senators," came to the city. Justinian lavished him with gifts while Theodora "gratified his wife with jewellery of all kinds decorated with pearls."[147] The Persian king's ambassadors were always particularly honoured and entertained at Constantinople, as Yazdgushnasp (or Zich), and his family found in 547–548[148] and again in 555.[149] In 549 Justinian introduced the Ethiopian ambassador to the hippodrome crowd,[150] and at other times he received legations from the Heruli,[151] the Huns,[152] the Lombards,[153] and the Avars, whose appearance created quite a stir in the city.[154] Popes from "old Rome" were entertained by Justinian, too. Pope John came to Constantinople with great ceremony in 526 and celebrated Easter there; Pope Agapetus did likewise in 536 and Pope Vigilius in 547. None of them lived to see Rome again.

Justinian's singular contribution to Constantinople was the building of churches and monasteries. He built or rebuilt thirty-three of them. In the 520s, just before he came to the throne and just after, he built the churches of Sts. Peter and Paul and Sts. Sergius and Bacchus on his estate at the palace of Hormisdas, and he was responsible for the restoration of the church at Blachernai.[155] In the 530s there followed the replacement churches of Saint Irene and, most magnificent of all, Hagia Sophia, which was dedicated on December 27, 537, commencing with a procession from the church of Anastasia, in which Justinian advanced with the people on foot while the patriarch Menas was conveyed in the imperial carriage.[156] A similar procession took place on June 28, 550, for the dedication of the new Church of the Holy Apostles. Again Menas occupied the imperial carriage, balancing on his knees three caskets containing the relics of Andrew, Luke, and Timothy. Another empty imperial carriage preceded him.[157] Presumably Justinian was processing along the Mese on foot and would be conveyed back to the palace in the carriage. The process was repeated once more the following year, this time for the dedication of the church of St. Irene at Sykai, on the site now occupied by Arap Camii. The patriarch Menas began from Hagia Sophia, sitting in the imperial carriage with relics for the new church on his knee, with Justinian evidently using another carriage.[158] Then there was the dedication of the church of Theodora in August 562,[159] and a few months later, on December 24, was the grand occasion of the rededication of Hagia Sophia with its secure new dome.[160] This event gave rise to the celebrated encomium of Paul the Silentiary.[161]

Justinian's Constantinople was a vibrant and volatile city, noisy, smelly, and colourful. As the imperial capital, it provided the stage for his long and sedentary reign. The emperor possessed the city; he dominated it and secured it. During Justinian's reign the empire changed dramatically in political, economic, and social terms, but the emperor did not fundamentally change the life or organisation of Constantinople. When Justinian first entered the city, it was much the same size as he left it sixty to seventy years later. He had tried to ensure that the population was carefully monitored and its expansion strictly controlled. His particular contribution to the city itself was to enlarge its ritual and to integrate the growing number of churches into its ceremonial life, "a change which announces the Middle Ages," according to Cyril Mango.[162] The widespread destruction of the Nika riots in 532 provided an unforeseen opportunity to refurbish and reshape much of the ceremonial core of the city to this end. Most of what we know of Justinian's Constantinople comes from the contemporary literary records, including the first attempt to codify imperial ceremonial, such as the *adventus* of Justinian returning from Selymbria in August 559. In recent years there has been an effloresence of interest, new excavations, and much new research on Constantinople, including the sixth-century city. Justinian's Constantinople is slowly coming to life.

## Notes

1 The overseer of the occasion has left his description: Peter the Patrician, *On the Ceremonies*, in J. F. Haldon, *Constantine Porphyrogenitus: Three Treatises on Imperial Military Expeditions, CFHB, series vindobonensis* 28, (Vienna, 1990), 139.

2 J. Crow, "The Long Walls of Thrace," in *Constantinople and Its Hinterland*, ed. C. Mango and G. Dagron (London, 1995), 109–124; J. Crow and A. Ricci, "Investigating the Hinterland of Constantinople: Interim Report on the Anastasian Long Wall," *JRA* 10 (1997): 235–262.

3 Agathias, *Histories*, 5.14.6–20.8; Victor of Tunnuna, *Chronicle*, 162 (s.a. 560); John Malalas, *Chronicle*, 18.129; Theophanes, *Chronicle*, A.M. 6051.

4 Alan Cameron, *Circus Factions* (Oxford, 1976), 250–251.

5 Procopius, *Buildings*, 1.5.10.

6 John the Lydian, *On Offices*, 2.14.

7 *Chronicon Paschale*, 618.14–17 – this was probably the bridge of St. Callinicum at the head of the Golden Horn (R. Janin, *Constantinople byzantine* [Paris, 1964], 240–243).

8 On exposure to the sea, see P. Magdalino, "The Maritime Neighbourhoods of Constantinople: Commercial and Residential Functions, Sixth to Twelfth Centuries," *DOP* 54 (2000): 209–226. On sea walls, see C. Foss and D. Winfield, *Byzantine Fortifications* (Pretoria, 1986), 70–72.

9 Janin, *Constantinople*, 265–283; W. Müeller-Wiener, *Bildlexicon zur Topographie Istanbuls* (Tübingen, 1977), 286–307; Foss and Winfield, *Byzantine Fortifications*, 41–70.

10 Procopius, *Buildings*, 1.3.3; Müller-Wiener, *Bildlexicon*, 301–307.

11 J. Bardill, "The Golden Gate in Constantinople: A Triumphal Arch of Theodosius I," *AJA* 103 (1999): 671–696; C. Mango, "The Triumphal Way of Constantinople and the Golden Gate," *DOP* 54 (2000): 181–186.

12 Procopius, *Buildings*, 1.4.9–24.

13 Haldon, *Constantine Porphyrogenitus*, 139.

14 Described by Gregory of Tours, *On the Glory of the Martyrs*, 101.

15 Suggested by C. Mango, "The Development of Constantinople as an Urban Centre," in *The Seventeenth International Byzantine Congress: Main Papers* (New Rochelle, N.Y.), 117–136, reprinted in C. Mango, *Studies on Constantinople* (London, 1993), 46, but more or less retracted in "The Triumphal Way of Constantinople," 177.

16 Janin, *Constantinople*, 71–72; Müller-Wiener, *Bildlexicon*, 250–253; A. Berger, *Untersuchungen zu den Patria Konstantinopoleos* (Bonn, 1988), 356–357.

17 Janin, *Constantinople*, 69–71; Müller-Wiener, *Bildlexicon*, 253–254; Berger, *Untersuchungen*, 348–350.

18 Mango, "The Triumphal Way of Constantinople," 177.

19 Müller-Wiener, *Bildlexicon*, 266–267.

20 M. Mundell Mango, "The Porticoed Street at Constantinople," in *Byzantine Constantinople: Monuments, Topography, and Everyday Life*, ed. N. Necipoglu, vol. 33 of *The Medieval Mediterranean: Peoples, Economies, and Cultures, 400–1500* (Leiden, 2001), 44–45.

21 Haldon, *Constantine Porphyrogenitus*, 139, 141.

22 Janin, *Constantinople*, 64–68; Müller-Wiener, *Bildlexicon*, 258–265; Berger, *Untersuchungen*, 323–327. For relevant excavations, see R. Naumann, "Neue Beobachtungen am Theodosiosbogen und Forum Tauri in Istanbul," *IstMitt* 26 (1976): 117–141.

23 On the forum and its many statues, see Janin, *Constantinople*, 62–64; Müller-Wiener, *Bildlexicon*, 255–256; and Berger, *Untersuchungen*, 288–309.

24 Janin, *Constantinople*, 79; C. Mango, "Constantine's Column," in Mango, *Studies on Constantinople* (London, 1993), 1–6.

25 G. Dagron, *Naissance d'une capitale* (Paris, 1974), 39.

26 Agathias, *Histories*, 5.21.4.

27 Cameron, *Circus Factions*, 22, 217.

28 For the hippodrome: Dagron, *Naissance d'une capitale*, 320–347; R. Guilland, *Études de topographie de Constantinople byzantine* (Berlin, 1969), vol. 1, 369ff.; Müller-Wiener, *Bildlexicon*, 64–71; G. Dagron, *Constantinople Imaginaire* (Paris, 1984), 161–190; J. Herrin, "Byzance: Le palais et la ville," *Byzantion* 61 (1991): 214.

29 Marcellinus, *Chronicle*, *s.a.* 528, with B. Croke, *The Chronicle of Marcellinus* (Sydney, 1995), 124.

30 John Malalas, *Chronicle*, 18.94; Theophanes, *Chronicle*, A.M. 6036, with C. Mango, "The Columns of Justinian and His Successors," in Mango, *Studies on Constantinople* (London, 1993), 1–8.

31 Haldon, *Constantine Porphyrogenitus*, 139–141.

32 Procopius, *Buildings*, 1.10.15–18.

33 John Malalas, *Chronicle*, 18.85.

34 M. McCormick, "Emperor and Court," *CAH* 14:141.

35 For the palace: Janin, *Constantinople*, 106–121; Müller-Wiener, *Bildlexicon*, 229–230.

36 K. Dark and F. Ozgumus, "The Last Roman Imperial Palace? Rescue Archaeology in Istanbul," *Minerva* 12 (2001): 52–55, and, for a revaluation of previous excavations, J. Bardill, "The Great Palace of the Byzantine Emperors and the Walker Trust Excavations," *JRA* 12 (1999): 216–230.

37 M. Maas, *John Lydus and the Roman Past* (London, 1992), 14–15.

38 Procopius, *Wars*, 7.32.9; *Secret History*, 13.28–33; John the Lydian, *On Offices*, 2.15.

39 *Chronicon Paschale*, 626, and later riots in 547 (John Malalas, *Chronicle*, 18.99), 561 (John Malalas, *Chronicle*, 18.135), and 563 (John Malalas, *Chronicle*, 18.151).

40 Dagron, *Naissance d'une capitale*, 277–282; Theophanes, *Chronicle*, A.M. 6055 (prefect's carriage in 563).

41 C. Mango, "The Water Supply of Constantinople," in C. Mango and G. Dagron, *Constantinople and Its Hinterland* (London, 1995), 9–18; P. Bono, J. Crow, and R. Bayliss, "The Water Supply of Constantinople: Archaeology and Hydrogeology of an Early Medieval City," *Environmental Geology* 40 (2001): 1325–1333.

42 John Malalas, *Chronicle*, 18.17; *Chronicon Paschale*, 619, with Mango, "Water Supply," 11–12.

43 *Chronicon Paschale*, 618.

44 Procopius, *Buildings*, 1.10, with Janin, *Constantinople*, 222–224; Müller-Wiener, *Bildlexicon*, 51, and Berger, *Untersuchungen*, 378–379.

45 Procopius, *Buildings*, 1.11.10.

46 John Malalas, *Chronicle*, 18.139; Theophanes, *Chronicle*, A.M. 6055.

47 John Malalas, *Chronicle*, 18.71; *Chronicon Paschale*, 629.

48 Procopius, *Buildings*, 5.1.10.

49 C. Mango, *Le Développement urbain de Constantinople* (Paris, 1990), 120; Magdalino, "The Maritime Neighbourhoods of Constantinople," 211.

50 J. Durliat, "L'approvisionnement de Constantinople," in Mango and Dagron, *Constantinople and Its Hinterland*, 21–33. On *horrea:* M. Mundell Mango, "The Commercial Map of Constantinople," *DOP* 54 (2000): 192–193.

51 Constantine Porphyrogenitus, *On the Ceremonies*, 2.51.

52 John Malalas, *Chronicle*, 18.121; Theophanes, *Chronicle*, A.M. 6048.

53 C. Morrisson and J.-P. Sodini, "The Sixth-Century Economy," in *The Economic History of Byzantium: From the Seventh through the Fifteenth Century*, ed. A. Laiou (Washington, D.C., 2002), 206.

54 On wine, see John Malalas, *Chronicle*, 18.95; Theophanes, *Chronicle*, A.M. 6038; on oil, Marcellinus, *Chronicle*, s.a. 524.

55 John the Lydian, *On Offices*, 3.62.

56 Magdalino, "The Maritime Neighbourhoods of Constantinople," 214–215.

57 Mundell Mango, "Map," 193–194.

58 John Malalas, *Chronicle*, 18.96; Theophanes, *Chronicle*, A.M. 6038.

59 *Nov.*, 64 (538), with J. Koder, "Fresh Vegetables for the Capital," in Mango and Dagron, *Constantinople and Its Hinterland*, 49–56.

60 John the Lydian, *On Offices*, 1.50.

61 *Nov.*, 13.5 and 4(1).

62 On 550, see John Malalas, *Chronicle*, 18.108; on 560, Theophanes, *Chronicle*, A.M. 6053; on 561, Theophanes, *Chronicle*, A.M. 6054; on 563, Theophanes, *Chronicle*, A.M. 6056.

63 John the Lydian, *On Offices*, 3.70. Other fires resulting from riots occurred in 548 (John Malalas, *Chronicle*, 18.105) and 561 (John Malalas, *Chronicle*, 18.135).

64 John Malalas, *Chronicle*, 18.77, *Chronicon Paschale*, 629.10–20.

65 The episodes in 540–541 are preserved in Pseudo-Dionysius of Tel-Mahre, *Chronicle*, 82; 545 in Theophanes, *Chronicle*, A.M. 6038; 547 in John Malalas, *Chronicle*,

18.102; and Theophanes, *Chronicle*, A.M. 6040; 551 in Agathias, *Histories*, 2.15.1; 554 in John Malalas, *Chronicle*, 18.118; and Theophanes, *Chronicle*, A.M. 6034, 6046; 555 in Theophanes, *Chronicle*, A.M. 6047.

66 John Malalas, *Chronicle*, 18.123; Theophanes, *Chronicle*, A.M. 6049.

67 Theophanes, *Chronicle*, A.M. 6051.

68 John Malalas, *Chronicle*, 18.124; Theophanes, *Chronicle*, A.M. 6050; Agathias, *Histories*, 5.3.1–6.9.

69 Details in B. Croke, "Two Early Byzantine Earthquakes and Their Liturgical Commemoration," *Byzantion* 51 (1981): 124–125 (reprinted in *Christian Chronicles and Byzantine History* [London, 1992]).

70 *Nov.*, 77.

71 *Nov.*, 141.

72 Agathias, *Histories*, 5.5.4–5.

73 John Malalas, *Chronicle*, 18.103; Theophanes, *Chronicle*, A.M. 6041.

74 Theophanes, *Chronicle*, A.M. 6047.

75 Theophanes, *Chronicle*, A.M. 6048.

76 Mango, "The Development of Constantinople," 124–125.

77 John Malalas, *Chronicle*, 18.127; Theophanes, *Chronicle*, A.M. 6050; Agathias, *Histories*, 5.10.1–7.

78 G. Dagron, "'Ainsi rien n'échappera à la réglementation,' État, Église, corporations, confréries: À propos des inhumations à Constantinople (IVe–Xe siècles)," in *Hommes et richesses dans l'Empire byzantin*, ed. V. Kravari, J. Lefort, and C. Morrisson, vol. 2 (Paris, 1991), 157–161.

79 John Malalas, *Chronicle*, 18.71; G. Greatrex, "The Nika Riot: A Reassessment," *JHS* 117 (1997): 60–86; and J. B. Bury, "The Nika Riot," *JHS* 17 (1897): 92–119.

80 John Malalas, *Chronicle*, 18.99; Theophanes, *Chronicle*, A.M. 6039.

81 John Malalas, *Chronicle*, 18.135; Cameron, *Circus Factions*, 94.

82 John Malalas, *Chronicle*, 18.138; Theophanes, *Chronicle*, A.M. 6055.

83 Theophanes, *Chronicle*, A.M. 6055.

84 John Malalas, *Chronicle*, 18.117.

85 Procopius, *Secret History*, 7.

86 John the Lydian, *On Offices*, 2.30.5–6, cf. 1.50.9.

87 John Malalas, *Chronicle*, 18.151.

88 Cameron, *Circus Factions*, 272–273.

89 John Malalas, *Chronicle*, 17.18; *Chronicon Paschale*, 617.1–6.

90 *Nov.*, 13.

91 *Nov.*, 85.

92 *Nov.*, 8, pr. (535): "priests and town councillors, officials, landowners, farmers"; 102 (536); 69.1 (538); see Procopius, *Buildings*, 1.11.24–25.

93 *Nov.*, 88.2 (539).

94 Procopius, *Secret History*, 4.3.2, 6.1–3; *Wars*, 7.16.12–13, cf. H.-G. Beck, "Konstantinopel. Zur Sozialgeschichte einer frühmittelalterlichen Hauptstadt," *BZ* 58 (1965): 11–45 (reprinted in H.-G. Beck, *Ideen und Realitäten in Byzanz* [London, 1972]).

95 *Nov.*, 80. See further H.-G. Beck, "Grossstadt-Probleme: Konstantinopel vom 4–6 Jahrhundert," in H.-G. Beck, *Ideen und Realitäten in Byzanz* (London, 1972), 17–18.

96 Procopius, *Buildings*, 1.11.26–27.
97 *Nov.*, 49 pr. (537).
98 *Nov.*, 6.3 (535).
99 *Nov.*, 123.9 (544).
100 John of Ephesus, *Lives of the Eastern Saints* (PO 18.326–327); Ps.-Zachariah, *Ecclesiastical History*, 10.1; Victor of Tunnuna, *Chronicle*, 126 (s.a. 540).
101 *Nov.*, 80.
102 *Nov.*, 86.8.
103 C. Rapp, "A Medieval Cosmopolis: Constantinople and Its Foreign Inhabitants," in *Alexander's Revenge: Hellenistic Culture through the Centuries*, ed. J. Ma and N. Van Deusen (Reykjavik, 2002), 153–172.
104 B. Croke, "Malalas, the Man, and His Work," in *Studies in John Malalas*, ed. E. M. Jeffreys with B. Croke and R. Scott (Sydney, 1990), 10.
105 John the Lydian, *On Offices*, 3.42, 68.
106 G. Dagron, "Aux origines de la civilisation byzantine: Langue de culture et langue d'état," *Revue historique* 489 (1969): 29–76.
107 Details in A. Berger, "Regionen und Straßen im frühen Konstantinopel," *IstMitt* 47 (1997): 349–414.
108 P. Magdalino, "Aristocratic Oikoi in the Tenth and Eleventh Districts of Constantinople," in *Byzantine Constantinople: Monuments, Topography, and Everyday Life*, ed. N. Necipoglu (Leiden, 2000), 53–69.
109 Janin, *Constantinople*, 44.
110 Victor of Tunnuna, *Chronicle*, 126 (s.a. 540).
111 *Nov.*, 30.5.1 (535).
112 John the Lydian, *On Offices*, 3.57.2.
113 A. Momigliano, "Gli Anicii e la storiografia latina del VI secolo d.C.," *Entretiens Fondation Hardt* (Geneva, 1956), 249–290.
114 *Chronicon Paschale*, 623.7.
115 Ps.-Zachariah of Mytilene, *Historia Ecclesiastica*, 9.17.
116 Marcellinus, *Chronicle*, s.a. 484.2; Procopius, *Wars*, 2.8.4; Victor of Tunnuna, *Chronicle*, 51 (s.a. 479), also *Codex Justinianus*, 1.27.1, 4 (April 534), noted by the lawyer Evagrius (*Historia Ecclesiastica*, 4.14).
117 Victor of Tunnuna, *Chronicle*, 173 (s.a. 566–567).
118 *Buildings*, 4.4.2.
119 Procopius, *Wars*, 4.16.12–13.
120 B. Croke, *Count Marcellinus and His Chronicle* (Oxford, 2001), 88–101.
121 Zosimus, *New History*, 2.35.
122 Agathias, *Histories*, 5.3.6.
123 In Beck, "Grossstadt-Probleme," 17, and "Konstantinopel," 25–26.
124 Dagron, *Naissance d'une capitale*, 529–530 (including references).
125 *Nov.*, 63 cf. 165 (n.d.).
126 Dagron, *Naissance d'une capitale*, 91–92, 405–409, 454–458, 495; E. Patlagean, *Pauvreté économique et pauvreté sociale à Byzance, 4e–7e siècles* (Paris, 1977), 215; S. MacCormack, *Art and Ceremony in Late Antiquity* (Berkeley, Calif., 1981), 62ff.; S. Diefenbach, "Zwischen Liturgie und *civilitas*. Konstantinopel im 5. Jahrhundert und die Etablierung eines städtischen Kaisertums," in *Bildlichkeit und Bildorte von Liturgie. Schauplätze in Spätantike, Byzanz und Mittelalter*, ed. R. Warland (Wiesbaden, 2002), 21–47.

127 John Malalas, *Chronicle*, 18.25; Theophanes, *Chronicle*, A.M. 6025.
128 Peter the Patrician, in Constantine Porphyrogenitus, *On the Ceremonies*, 1.95.
129 Corippus, *Panegyric on Justin*, 3.1–61.
130 Janin, "Les Processions religieuses à Byzance," *Revue des études byzantines* 24 (1966): 73.
131 Justinian *Nov.*, 47 (537).
132 On 521, see Marcellinus, *Chronicle*, s.a. 521; On 528, *Chronicon Paschale*, 627.
133 A. Cutler, "The Making of the Justinian Diptychs," *Byzantion* 54 (1984): 75–115.
134 *Nov.*, 105.
135 R. S. Bagnall, Alan Cameron, S. R. Schwartz, and K. A. Worp, *Consuls of the Later Roman Empire* (Atlanta, 1987), 7–12.
136 M. McCormick, *Eternal Victory* (Cambridge, 1986), 190–195.
137 See Janin, "Processions," 69–68, for the processions, and Averil Cameron, "The Construction of Court Ritual: The Byzantine *Book of Ceremonies*," in *Rituals of Royalty: Power and Ceremonial in Traditional Societies*, ed. D. Cannadine and S. Price (Cambridge, 1987), 106–136, for the context of the *Book of Ceremonies*.
138 Croke, *Count Marcellinus and His Chronicle*, 122–124.
139 G. Dagron, "Le Christianisme dans la ville byzantine," *DOP* 31 (1977): 1–25; J. Baldovin, *The Urban Character of Christian Worship* (Rome, 1987), 182ff., 211–214; Croke, *Count Marcellinus and His Chronicle*, 116–124; A. Berger, "Imperial and Ecclesiastical Processions in Constantinople," *Byzantine Constantinople* (2001): 73–87; F. A. Bauer, "Urban Space and Ritual: Constantinople in Late Antiquity," *Acta ad Archaeologiam et Artium Historiam Pertinentia* 15 (2001): 27–61.
140 B. Croke, "Justinian's Bulgar Victory Celebration," *Byzantinoslavica* 41 (1980): 188–195 (reprinted in B. Croke, *Christian Chronicles and Byzantine History, Fifth–Sixth Centuries* [London, 1992]).
141 McCormick, "Victory," 65–67, 124–129.
142 John Malalas, *Chronicle*, 18.140; Theophanes, *Chronicle*, A.M. 6055.
143 McCormick, "Victory," 67.
144 John Malalas, *Chronicle*, 18.6.
145 Procopius, *Wars*, 3.13.1–3, 15.2.
146 John Malalas, *Chronicle*, 18.14, 18.21.
147 Theophanes, *Chronicle*, A.M. 6027.
148 Procopius, *Wars*, 2.28.39–41.
149 Agathias, *Histories*, 4.30.8.
150 John Malalas, *Chronicle*, 18.106; Theophanes, *Chronicle*, A.M. 6042.
151 Procopius, *Wars*, 6.15.30–33.
152 Procopius, *Wars*, 8.4.12–13.
153 Procopius, *Wars*, 8.27.2–4.
154 John Malalas, *Chronicle*, 18.125; Theophanes, *Chronicle*, A.M. 6050.
155 Procopius, *Buildings*, 1.3.3–5.
156 John Malalas, *Chronicle*, 18.86; Theophanes, *Chronicle*, A.M. 6030.
157 John Malalas, *Chronicle*, 18.109: 484.17–2; Theophanes, *Chronicle*, A.M. 6042; Procopius, *Buildings*, 1.4.17ff.
158 John Malalas, *Chronicle*, 18.113; Procopius, *Buildings*, 1.7; Theophanes, *Chronicle*, A.M. 6044.
159 John Malalas, *Chronicle*, 18.137.

160 John Malalas, *Chronicle*, 18.143; Theophanes, *Chronicle*, A.M. 6055.

161 R. Macrides and P. Magdalino, "The Architecture of Ekphrasis: Construction and Context of Paul the Silentiary's Poem on Hagia Sophia," *BMGS* 12 (1988): 47–82.

162 Mango, *Le Développement urbain de Constantinople*, 52, cf. P. Magdalino, "Medieval Constantinople: Built Environment and Urban Development," in *The Economic History of Byzantium: From the Seventh through the Fifteenth Century*, ed. A. Laiou (Washington, D.C., 2002), 530.

# 4: The Classical City in the Sixth Century

## Survival and Transformation

*Kenneth G. Holum*

In 533 Procopius of Caesarea, scouting for his general Belisarius, met a trader in Syracuse who was, by chance, both a "friend from childhood" and a "fellow-citizen" of Caesarea (*Wars*, 3.14). On two accounts, Procopius indicates, the man could be counted on for help with a dangerous mission, securing intelligence on the whereabouts of the enemy king and on Roman prospects for an invasion of Vandal Africa. The civic link between the two men, shared citizenship of Caesarea in Palestine, resembled the personal one, for both created claims of one person upon the other, and shared citizenship, like friendship, persisted despite long years abroad in trade or the imperial service. Further, in a hard spot it was apparently one's native city that counted, what Procopius elsewhere calls "my Caesarea" (*Secret History*, 11.25), not just being Roman, as both men obviously were, or belonging to the same ethnicity or to one religious persuasion or another. Describing this incident, Procopius suggests, quite by accident, that a robust personal identification with one's own native city, traditional in ancient Mediterranean culture, persisted in the reign of Justinian.

The incident invites broader investigation into the state of the Mediterranean cities in the sixth century. The agenda in this chapter is to discover whether cities like Caesarea still flourished, how faithful these cities remained to traditional urban forms, and, at least by implication, how firm a grip they still had on their inhabitants, especially on men like Procopius, members of the local elite of urban landowners. These questions are hotly debated nowadays, and clarity would be welcome on so central an issue.[1] The Mediterranean-style city (Greek *polis*,

Latin *municipium, civitas*) was the principal social organism, beyond the family and other kinship groups, with which not only Procopius but all ancient Mediterranean men and women identified and within which they elaborated their culture, so the demise of the cities, more than the "fall" of the empire itself, is as good a point as any to declare that the ancient Mediterranean world had run out of steam.

Taking the measure of sixth-century cities will require comparison not with modern cities but with the classical Mediterranean cities of the first and second centuries A.D., of the age of Augustus or of the Antonine emperors.[2] These cities were more densely settled than our own, made up of more or less continuously inhabited urban space, often constrained within fortification walls. With a few notable exceptions – Antioch, Alexandria, Rome itself, eventually Constantinople – they were smaller and more intimate than their modern counterparts, numbering only 10,000–50,000 persons inside the walls. Another peculiarity was the tight organic link between the built-up urban center, the polis itself, and the surrounding territory, with dependent villages, hamlets, and isolated farms doubling or tripling the overall population.[3] Within the fortifications, moreover, a proper city had certain typical furnishings. In the second century, the traveler Pausanias (10.4.1) denied the title "polis" to Panopieis in Phocis (central Greece), complaining that the place lacked municipal offices, a gymnasium and a theater, a marketplace, and water brought by aqueduct to a public fountain, all expected in an actual polis. Worse, its inhabitants lived in huts clinging to a mountain slope, not, as Pausanias would have liked, in contiguous houses along paved streets arranged on an orderly plan. Many cities had orthogonal grid plans, but even more characteristic were well-paved main streets flanked by colonnaded porticoes and punctuated by triumphal arches, public fountains (*nymphaea*), and plazas at the major intersections. Of course the typical polis differed from our own in more than buildings. Neither in the gymnasium or the public bath, where one exercised or bathed nude, nor in the theater or amphitheater, where the entire community witnessed the same combats of gladiators, beast fights, and other bloody and sensuous spectacles, were privacy or individuality held in high regard. Nothing typified the classical city more permanently than the predominance of a local elite of propertied families, the bouleutic or curial order (*bouleutai, decuriones, curiales*), so named because they sat together on the city council, *boule* or *curia*, to settle civic issues and to divide among themselves the administrative tasks required to run the city. These councilmen corresponded with no social group in a modern city. Lords of the most fertile land in a city's territory, together with the means of exploiting it – the rural estates, villages, and farmsteads of dependent farmers – they linked city and countryside in their own persons. Dwelling sometimes in the relative solitude of a rural villa, but more often in the teeming urban center, they upheld the city with their munificence as the proper setting for the display of wealth and influence. Hence cities were the artificial creations of the landed elite, or, as Peter Brown put it, "fragile excrescences in a spreading countryside."[4]

## THE SIXTH-CENTURY CITY: IMAGE AND REALITY

Literary texts about cities presume that cities of the ancient type still flourished, and indeed, they communicate a strong sense of continuity with earlier Mediterranean cities. In a Novel of 536 Justinian proclaimed the Caesarea of Procopius and his friend to be "ancient and renowned," a city founded long ago by a Greek hero named Straton, which Emperor Vespasian had then refounded after he defeated the Jews, and now was head of the province Palestine, a land replete with "noble cities" and "worthy and wise citizens" (*Novel* 103, *pr.*). The same idea of continuity characterizes the rhetorical instructions of Menander of Laodicea, written about 300 and still fashionable among rhetors two or three centuries later.[5] These instructions encouraged encomiums of a city's favorable setting within its subject territory, of its founding long ago by a god or hero (for which Justinian commended Caesarea), and especially of the beauty of a city's fortifications, baths, colonnades, groves, and temples, and the delights of its chariot races, theaters, and festivals (*Menander Rhetor*, pp. 349, 353, 383–384, 417, 431, 433). Contemplating departure from his native city, a speaker should anticipate intense longing for city and family, as in Homer's verse, "for there is nothing sweeter than one's parents and his native land" (433, cf. *Odyssey*, 9.34). Hence Menander assumes the intense identification with one's own city evident in Procopius and his friend. In his treatise praising Justinian's construction projects, *Buildings*, Procopius likewise highlighted the repertoire of buildings that made a city beautiful and comfortable – the porticoes, streets, and sewers, markets and theaters, aqueducts and baths – almost as if the author had in mind the rules of Menander, but by the sixth century churches and charitable institutions had replaced temples in the imagined city (*Buildings*, 2.10, 4.10.20–23, 5.2.3–5, 4.15–17, 6.4.1–5). Imperial palaces, too, are mentioned repeatedly, and the fortifications, more than a few centuries earlier, had become a defining feature. Hence when Justinian fitted out the town Vaga, in the province of Africa Proconsularis (Tunisia), with powerful defenses "he made it into a city and enabled the inhabitants to dwell in security" (6.5.13).

Helen Saradi has suggested that rhetorical literature exaggerated the physical attractions of cities in order to preserve, in the literary imagination, a resemblance of the antique city that was actually in full decline.[6] Hence it is worth comparing the literary sixth-century city with the corresponding archaeological remains. An instructive example, because it was a new foundation reflecting the builder's own conception, is Caričin Grad, which Justinian built in Dardania (Serbia) near the place of his birth as his name city, Justiniana Prima (see Fig. 5 in Chapter 14). Procopius styles this foundation "a most noble city," "large in size and well-populated," and praises "the magnitude of its colonnades, the beauty of its plazas," as well as its streets, magistrates' headquarters, shops, fountains, and baths, copiously supplied by an aqueduct, and numerous churches, including the archibishop's see, for Justinian designated the new city to be the metropolis of Illyricum (*Buildings*, 4.1.17–27, also Justinian, *Novel* 11). The panegyrist's words evoke a classical Mediterranean city of a distinct sixth-century style, yet on the ground Justiniana Prima occupies less than seven hectares, far smaller than any classical city, and could have accommodated at most a few hundred inhabitants. The main colonnaded streets intersected at a circular plaza only twenty-two meters in diameter. There appears to have been only one modest public bath, but seven basilical churches, as well as the archepiscopal cathedral with its baptistry and service buildings located on the site's fortified acropolis. Well-situated for security, the place also had a strong outer defensive wall with massive corner towers and monumental gates.[7] Clearly not a polis of the classical type, Justiniana Prima lacked the requisite scale and probably never accommodated the essential landed elite of the classical city in their urban mansions. Instead, it functioned, apparently, as a regional administrative and ecclesiastical center, and perhaps as a refuge (*Fliehburg*) for the neighboring agricultural population in times of invasion or other insecurity.

## The Prosperity of the Sixth-Century City

The example of Justiniana Prima shows that the ideological commitment to classical urbanism of the rhetorical sources needs testing against independent evidence, other literary sources, inscriptions, papyri, and

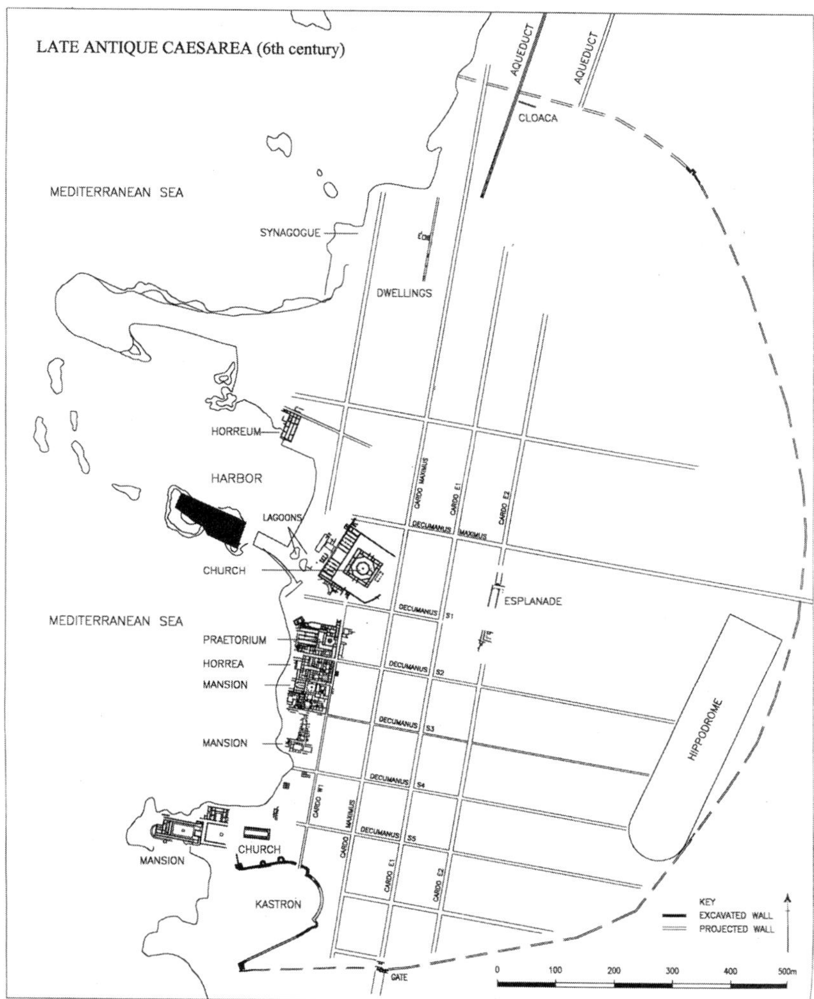


FIGURE 3. Caesarea Palaestinae in the sixth century. Drawing: Anna Iamim

especially archaeology. These show that some full-scale cities did indeed flourish in the Age of Justinian. Caesarea in Palestine, for example, the city of Procopius, appears to have reached a plateau of urban prosperity in the fifth century that persisted into the mid-sixth and beyond (Fig. 3).[8] A new fortification wall, built late in the fourth century or in the fifth, enclosed about ninety-five hectares, two or three times the space of its early Roman predecessor. Most of this urban space remains unexplored, and some of it may have been cultivated gardens, but so far every excavation within the perimeter has yielded evidence for sixth-century occupation, consisting generally of monumental public buildings, private houses, industrial installations, shops, and streets. Recent excavations have uncovered an entire seafront quarter of urban mansions, warehouses, and a governor's praetorium that were fully occupied and renewed through the sixth century and into the seventh. The sheer quantity of fifth- and sixth-century pottery is astounding, especially fragments of containers reflecting import of wine, oil, fish sauce, and other favorite commodities. Twin high-level aqueducts of the first and second centuries continued to flow in the sixth, and a ground-level aqueduct of the fourth century provided a copious flow for irrigation within the fortifications or the immediate suburbs, and perhaps also for industrial grain mills. In the sixth century street pavements were still being renewed, along with ceramic freshwater pipes and storm drains or sewers beneath them. To judge from inhabited space and urban infrastructure, Caesarea still flourished in the classical manner during the reign of Justinian.

A survey of similar data from elsewhere in the empire may yield an index of urban prosperity in various regions.[9] Apparently, the total number of cities remained roughly the same, but some of them suffered severe population loss, a sharp decline in the urban economy, and shrinkage of the inhabited core. In fact, many forfeited their character as ancient cities to become just the seats of bishops, garrison towns, or refuges (*Fliehburgen*) for the rural population. Justiniana Prima is a prime example. Where decline did set in, there was a correlation with the German conquests and settlements in the west, of Franks in Gaul, Visigoths in Spain, Vandals in Africa, and the Ostrogoths in Italy, and much later with the Arab conquest of the Levant. These conquests gradually brought new elites onto the scene who did not share the old commitment to Classical urbanism. As Ammianus Marcellinus acknowledged in the fourth century, when Germans seized Roman cities they elected to settle in the countryside, loathing the cities themselves "as if they were tombs surrounded by nets" (*Res gestae*, 16.2.12).

At the opposite extreme from Caesarea, the Roman cities of Britain, lacking defenses against marauding Irish, Picts, and Saxons, succumbed already during the fifth century. A dozen or so excavated sites have revealed only traces of subsequent occupation. Writing about 540, the British author Gildas lamented that "not even the cities of our land are occupied as they once were, but they lie empty, destroyed, and in ruins" (*The Ruin of Britain*, 26.2). Unlike Procopius, his near contemporary, Gildas identified himself with no city, and indeed he hardly mentions even one of the old cities in his account of the conquests.

On the continent, meanwhile, the situation remained less bleak, despite the German conquests. In the Iberian provinces, and in Gaul, Italy, and Africa, new fortification circuits enclosed less urban space, and street colonnades, forums, basilicas, public baths, amphitheaters, and hippodromes tended to fall into ruin. Yet many cities survived. Christian bishops resided universally in the old cities, and barbarian kings tended to base their administration on them. Hence the lawbook that the Visigothic king Alaric II issued in 509 requires a royal count (*comes civitatis*) in each Iberian city and expects the councilmen of each city to collect taxes. After virtual abandonment, Civitas Mediomatricorum (Metz) in northeastern Gaul became a residence of the Merovingian kings in the mid-sixth century and regained its lost urban character, but in a different urban style consisting of houses clustering about churches. After the reconquest of Africa in 533, Justinian financed an ambitious program of urban restoration there, especially refortification of the cities, but the urban space enclosed was much smaller than ever before. In the entire West, indeed, it was the cities of Ostrogothic Italy that most successfully preserved their ancient character in the Age of Justinian, but they suffered devastation from siege and countersiege in the long war of reconquest (536–554). In Italy another factor is visible that operated everywhere. Since about 300 the patronage of the urban elite that had financed urban construction in the Roman city's heyday had declined to almost nothing, while provincial governors, emperors, and Ostrogothic kings generally built in fewer places (e.g., cities of royal residence) and limited their activities to fortifications, palaces, baths, and above all churches. The new enthusiasm for dedicating churches diverted most of the available resources away from the traditional forms of monumental architecture.[10]

The Roman cities of the Danube, from Raetia in the west to Scythia on the Black Sea, had suffered heavily from Gothic and other Germanic invasions in the fourth and fifth centuries, from the Hun domination in the fifth, and later, toward the east, from the incursions of Avars, Slavs, and Bulgars. Refortification in the tetrarchic period (the early fourth century) had already reduced the defended urban space to a fraction of its earlier extent. In the sixth century Justiniana Prima, as administrative center and *Fliehburg*, suited the region admirably.

In the southern Balkans, however, in Asia Minor, the Levant, and Egypt, all Greek-speaking parts of the Roman Empire, cities still prospered in the Age of Justinian at a far higher level than in the Latin west. In Asia Minor,[11] Ephesus, most extensively excavated, received new fortification walls enclosing only one-third of the previous space, probably not until the early seventh century. At Sardis the so-called Byzantine shops, built about 400, flourished throughout the sixth century, and their inhabitants still supplied the city with pigments and dyes, jewelry, locks, glass vessels, and window panes, typical commercial activity in a prospering market center. At Aphrodisias a Christian church replaced the Temple of Aphrodite in about 500 in the city center, and in the ensuing century a minor boom appears to have taken place in both secular and religious building, to judge from the unusually rich collection of Greek inscriptions that has survived.[12] The builders included members of the local elite, who thus displayed their munificence in the traditional manner.

Ephesus, Sardis, and Aphrodisias were provincial capitals (*metropoleis*) in the Age of Justinian and thus profited from the economic activity of resident imperial personnel. A smaller city that lacked this advantage was Korykos in Cilicia (southern Turkey), a coastal site that has yielded a fascinating collection of Greek inscriptions from the fifth and sixth centuries. These reveal a small polis of the normal type with an aristocracy of notables, now called "landlords" (*ktetores*) and "town-dwellers" (*oiketores*), along with the usual magistrates and minor officials. Most of the texts are epitaphs on modest tombs, and a remarkable 456 of the total 589 give the tomb inhabitant's occupation. Some of the population in these epitaphs (8.2 percent) were in the government in one capacity or another, as local officials of the provincial governor, customs officers, or councilmen (*bouleutai*), while others (7 percent) worked in seafaring in this coastal city, for example, as fishermen or sailmakers. Yet as a group the Korykos epitaphs, like the contemporary shops at Sardis, reflect the supply and service sector of a representative *polis* economy that evidently still flourished in the Age of Justinian. Nearly 39 percent of the epitaphs commemorated tradesmen, merchants, or professionals, such as boot makers, potters, butchers, greengrocers, tavern keepers, stone masons, carpenters, and doctors.[13] A number of the epitaphs proclaim the tomb inhabitants' identity as *Korykaioi*, citizens of Korykos. Conspicuously missing from the epitaphs are the notables themselves, many of them town dwellers who apparently favored more elegant cemeteries adjacent to their country properties, as well as the far more numerous rural population of peasants and herdsmen whose labor delivered the agricultural products, rents, and taxes that formed the actual basis of the local economy.

Further to the east, beyond the Euphrates, ancient cities of the classical Mediterranean type lay exposed in the Age of Justinian to sieges and plundering expeditions of the Sassanian Persian king and his Lakhmid Arab allies. Edessa, however, the metropolis of Osrhoene, escaped destruction in the Persian wars of both 502–506 and 540–544 and appears to have prospered right through the Arab conquest of the seventh century. In the Syriac *Chronicle* of Pseudo-Joshua the Stylite, Edessa is a city of the traditional type, with a fortification wall and monumental gates, porticoed streets, a marketplace, a theater, public baths, subject villages in the surrounding territory, a local landowning elite, and churches in place of temples – all now ruled, it appears, mainly by the provincial governor and the local bishop (cc. 27–32, 36–46). Indeed, Edessa seems of special concern to the unknown author, who likely hailed originally from Edessa and thus identified with it, for he calls it "our city" and its ailing bishop "our bishop Mar Peter" (c. 95).

The cities of Syria likewise displayed social and economic vitality in the sixth century.[14] Best known from excavation is Apamea, the metropolis of Syria II, upstream from Antioch on the Orontes River. Severe earthquakes caused major damage there, as at Antioch, in 526 and 528, but the Persian king Khusro mostly spared Apamea in 540 after destroying much of Antioch. A generation later, in 573, the Persians thoroughly sacked and burned Apamea, and, according to contemporary sources, carried off with them to Persia no fewer than 292,000 chained male and female captives. The blow must indeed have been staggering, yet the figure seems inflated, because the Persians could not have managed or fed so many prisoners, and despite the demographic disaster Apamea did survive as a smaller city. In any case, until 573 money was available for large-scale urban renewal. After the earthquakes the authorities reconstituted the porticoes and repaved at least five hundred meters of Apamea's great north-south street, originally 22.8 meters wide but now reduced by sidewalks. Further, the emperor and the local bishop renewed and expanded the so-called Atrium Church as well as the city's cathedral, and the immensely wealthy elite continued to upgrade their urban mansions, adopting the fashionable floor pavements and wall revetments in multicolored marble (*opus sectile*) and elegant dining rooms equipped with the stone sigma tables and semicircular dining couches. After 573 such work continued, but with much smaller resources. In Apamea's territory, meanwhile, the emperor joined the church and private donors in organizing and financing construction of stone forts, defensive towers, and fortified churches in which rustics and villagers could find shelter from periodic plundering raids – a sure sign of concern that the rural population should remain in place and continue to pay rents and taxes.[15]

Further south, beyond the reach of Persian attacks, prosperity continued unabated. At the smaller city Epiphania (Hama), further up the Orontes, the city's cathedral, dedicated to the Virgin, was rebuilt in 595, and on the acropolis the elite occupied their luxurious mansions into the seventh century. At Gerasa in Arabia, nine of thirteen churches dated by inscriptions were built between 526 and 611, and two undated ones probably belong to the same period.[16]

Palestine reached its economic and demographic zenith during the fourth, fifth, and sixth centuries, because as the Christian Holy Land and goal of Christian pilgrimage it received lavish imperial and private investment in church building and charitable institutions.[17] Palestine's cities, Caesarea among them, definitely reflected this prosperity. Jerusalem itself received new fortifications in the fourth or fifth century that incorporated 120 hectares, making it the second-largest urban space in the country. The Madaba mosaic map (Plate 1) represents sixth-century Jerusalem, labeled the Holy City, as a contemporary might have imagined any prosperous sixth-century polis.[18] The image shows how the sixth-century city integrated religious architecture, now Christian churches, into the traditional urban framework. As before, fortification walls and gates constrain densely packed city buildings. Porticoed streets and plazas on the ancient plan accommodate the shops of craftsmen and traders, as at Sardis, and, during periodic Christian festivals, processions of Christian clergy and populace followed the streets to the principal churches, especially to the Holy Sepulcher at the city's center. Archaeological evidence corresponds admirably with the visual image. Excavations have revealed sixth-century occupation across the intramural space, as the Madaba map indicates. In the 1970s Nachman Avigad discovered a major episode of new construction that the map also depicts – extension of Jerusalem's porticoed main north-south street southward from the Holy Sepulcher to the Nea Church of the Virgin Mary *Theotokos*, a magnificent triple-apsed basilica 116 meters long. Procopius (*Buildings*, 5.6) credited Justinian himself with building the church, and an inscription found in the ruins confirms his account.[19]

Elsewhere in the region, the famous Nabataean city Petra, once thought destroyed in an earthquake of 551, proves to have been a flourishing city in the later sixth century. Newly discovered documentary papyri dating from 537 to 593 concern the estates of wealthy families who dwelled in Petra but owned agricultural estates in the surrounding villages and wadis cultivated by dependent renters. The local elite's identification with their venerable polis resounds among these documents in Petra's imposing titles: "Imperial Colony Antoniana, Distinguished, Holy, Mother of the Colonies, Hadriana, Petra, Metropolis of Third Palestina Salutaris."[20] Easily the most illuminating site in Palestine, however, is Scythopolis–Beth Shean, metropolis of Palaestina II, the object of large-scale excavations during the 1990s.[21] The city had expanded between the second century and the sixth, so a new fortification wall was thought necessary that enclosed about 134 hectares, on which inscriptions attest work early in the sixth century. This expansion enclosed previously unoccupied space next to the Roman hippodrome, which the urban builders reached by extending one of the main streets (Silvanus Street) southward in a project dated about 515. The new street and an eastward extension built in 522 were carefully paved with hard basalt blocks, and ceramic pipes beneath the pavements connected to the city water supply. According to the excavators, this period, around 450–540, was the city's prime. New construction in the city center included Silvanus Street itself with a large basilical hall on its west, the spacious Western Bath, a semicircular market building called the Sigma, all surrounding a newly-built late antique agora. Clearly ancient Scythopolis still flourished in the Age of Justinian, yet the excavators also discerned stagnation after midcentury that they associated in part with outbreaks of bubonic plague that began in 542.

## The Greater Cities

In the west Rome, Carthage, and Ravenna, and in the east Constantinople, Alexandria, and Antioch, deserve special attention, either because of their sheer size of population and economic heft, or because rulers exploited them exceptionally to organize imperial, royal, and episcopal power. Constantinople, the New Rome, receives detailed treatment in Chapter 3. For Procopius, it was the old Rome that remained "the grandest and most noteworthy of all cities under the sun," (*Wars*, 7.22.9), but in fact the city he visited early in the Gothic War suffered grievously from siege and countersiege in the hostilities of 536–554. Within the third-century fortifications, enclosing the huge expanse of 2,500 hectares, the population had already shrunk from around 800,000 in Constantine's time to perhaps 80,000 under the Ostrogoths early in the sixth century, most of them concentrated in the west of the city near the bend of the Tiber, from the foot of the Palatine and the Capitoline hills down to the river and on the right bank in Trastevere. Many of the old senatorial families had already died out, or their children had retreated into the religious life, abandoning their urban mansions on the hills to the east or in the circumferential greenbelt inside the walls. The war then finally ruined the aristocracy, for many of the families that survived abandoned their estates and took refuge in the East.[22] Around its dwindling population, meanwhile, the physical city decayed. The ancient city prefect (*praefectus urbi*) still held office under the Ostrogothic kings and after the Gothic war, and under him were officials in charge of building maintenance and restoration as well as dedicated funds for purchasing the necessary bricks and lime for mortar. Present during the first Gothic siege of 537–538, Procopius found the Romans to be "lovers of their city" (*philopolides*) beyond all others and observed that during the previous Ostrogothic regime "they had mostly preserved the city's buildings and their adornments even though under barbarian rule" (4.22.5–6). Yet new construction must already have despoiled the ancient monuments of the ancient center of their marble and other costly stones.[23]

This new construction was mostly churches. From their episcopal see at St. John's Lateran, Constantine's great basilica on the southern fringe, the Roman popes had presided over a construction program between 360 and 450 that left most of Rome's fourteen regions (except IV and VIII, nearest the ancient center) with spacious new basilicas. The pope himself bore the cost, along with the emperors and sometimes government officials or private donors. The popes, of course, had the means. As the senatorial aristocracy and the emperors abandoned Rome and central Italy, they bequeathed their estates to the see of Rome, which became the greatest landowner in the peninsula and in Sicily as well. New building continued later in the century with San Stefano Rotondo, completed in 483, a vast circular edifice in region II that accommodated 3,500 worshipers, and on a smaller scale under the Ostrogoths and throughout the sixth century, even during the long Gothic war. With these buildings the pope impressed his stamp on Rome, as its secular as well as its spiritual ruler. By the time of Gregory the Great (590–604), stability and a level of prosperity had returned, and Rome had taken on its medieval dress.[24]

In the third century, Carthage, a major seaport, exporter of grain and olive oil from a fertile hinterland, metropolis of Africa Proconsularis, had ranked as second city of the West, with perhaps as many as 300,000 inhabitants. The population had presumably decreased, but excavations in the 1970s and 1980s did reveal sixth-century occupation over much of the intramural space as well as villa development in nearby suburbs. When Belisarius had retaken the city in 536, Procopius asserts, Justinian began a building campaign that included restoring the existing fortifications, surrounding the Maritime Forum with porticoes, and constructing a public bath named for his consort Theodora, as well as several churches (*Buildings*, 6.5.8–11). Indeed, the Vandal kings who ruled in Carthage from 429 to 536 had consistently identified with and promoted the traditional city, the *Felix Karthago* of a royal coin legend, by maintaining the baths, celebrating chariot races in the circus, even supporting Latin poets like Florentinus who extolled King Thrasamund and Carthage itself early in the sixth century in a traditional *laudatio*.[25] By promoting the city Vandal kings conciliated less their own people than the old Roman elite, bearing in mind that taxes from their estates now accrued to the royal treasury. In Italy, under the Ostrogothic king Theoderic (493–526) and his successors, the same factor benefitted Ravenna. The kings restored the aqueducts, celebrated royal consulates with opulent shows, and engaged enthusiastically in the competitive church building that characterized Ravenna in the fifth and sixth centuries. The mosaics of San Apollinare Nuovo, San Apollinare in Classe, San Vitale, and the rest indicate a high level of material prosperity.[26]

Of the great eastern cities, Alexandria apparently flourished without major interruption through the sixth century. Extending over about 1,000 hectares within its ancient walls, it contained a relatively stable population of about 200,000.[27] Antioch in Syria I, of roughly the same scale as Alexandria, is similarly overbuilt today and mostly unavailable for excavation.[28] Procopius declares that a violent earthquake in 526, the same one that also devastated nearby Apamea, flattened major public buildings in Antioch and killed 300,000 of the population (*Wars*, 2.14.6). After the second quake in 528 the Antiochenes renamed their city Theopolis, City of God, but their hope of thus mollifying the deity proved vain. In his 540 invasion the Sassanian Khusro pillaged and burned the entire city, took its inhabitants captive, and resettled those who survived in his own country (2.8–10, 14.1–4). Nevertheless old Antioch soldiered on. Procopius claims that Justinian rebuilt Antioch literally from the ground up, ordering that the heaped ruins of the former city be carted away, that the streets and porticoes be laid out anew, along with new baths, a new theater, and the other paraphernalia of urbanism (*Buildings*, 2.10). Some of this is rhetorical exaggeration, but excavations in the 1930s did confirm pervasive devastation and reconstruction. Justinian's builders had rebuilt the city's main north-south street above its predecessor, but only twenty-six meters wide, ten meters narrower than before, still well paved with basalt blocks and lined by walks beneath the porticoes. Apparently Justinian's rebuilt city wall did shorten the original fortification perimeter in places, as Procopius asserts, but it nevertheless incorporated major segments of the old walls and gates.

## City and Countryside

If these cities, small or large, were of traditional Mediterranean type, then their prosperity in the Age of Justinian came ultimately not from trade or manufacture but from the soil of their own hinterlands. City and countryside constituted a continuum, as Peregrine Horden and Nicholas Purcell explain, with the city forming the mountain peak in the terrain of settlement, while the villages were the hills, and the fertile farmland was the valley.[29] Furthermore, the continuum between city and countryside was indeed partly economic, administrative, and ecclesiastical, but it remained nevertheless in essence a personal continuity between the urban landlords, the old *decuriones* or *bouleutai*, and their estates with the tenant farmers (*coloni, georgoi*) who tilled them. The landlords still put the rents they extracted from their tenants to work enhancing the city and their own lives within it. Again, Procopius shows this for Caesarea. The Samaritans of Palestine, he relates, rebelled in 529–530, and the emperor's soldiers crushed them mercilessly, slaughtering as many as 100,000, but in the slanted view of Procopius it was the Christian landlords of Caesarea, not the Samaritans, who suffered most (*Secret History*, 11.24–30). The Samaritans had cultivated the landlords' fields, and their destruction left Caesarea's farmland, "the finest in the world," devoid of cultivators, yet the emperor still demanded of the landlords the full amount of the taxes owed. Procopius exaggerates, as so often, for rhetorical purposes, but there was no reason for him to distort the prevailing continuity between the urban elite and Caesarea's countryside. The continuity existed likewise in the person named Evangelus, also mentioned by Procopius, one of Caesarea's advocates and hence a thoroughly urban person. This man had grown wealthy from his legal practice, owned vast rural estates, and had even purchased the entire village of Porphyreon, on the seacoast to the north of Caesarea, for the startling sum of 300 pounds of gold (30.18–20).

In Caesarea's case excavation of an urban quarter in the 1990s put the personal link between city and countryside on display. On a ridge paralleling the sea, exposed to cooling onshore breezes, the elite of Caesarea, presumably some of the Christian landlords that Procopius mentions, dwelled in elegant urban mansions in the fifth and sixth centuries (Fig. 3). These were palatial residences decorated with multicolored marbles, equipped with internal peristyles, formal reception and dining rooms, private baths, and in one case a sunken garden and loggia above the beach. Positioned along the same ridge as the mansions, in the intervals between them, were corridor or courtyard warehouses with grain bins and vaulted halls suited for storing wine and oil in jars or other products. From the spatial arrangement, it is reasonable to deduce that the same rich men owned both warehouses and mansions, that they numbered among the Christian landlords that Procopius mentions, and that Evangelus too may well have lived in such style. Warehouses in the city enabled landlords to store up the products from their estates for sale when supplies were low and the prices high. At Caesarea the proximity of the sea made such warehouses especially profitable, because somewhere within reach of Caesarea's ships a famine was bound to occur, and with it a sharp rise in prices.

The same personal continuity between city and countyside is evident everywhere in the East during the sixth century. In the new Petra papyri the deacon Theodoros and his relatives were the same type of landlords. When the anonymous Piacenza Pilgrim visited Apamea about 570, he reported that the "entire nobility" of the province resided there, presumably also city-dwelling landlords (Anonymous of Piacenza 46),[30] while the "city dwellers" and "landlords" at Korykos likewise represented continuity between Korykos and its farmland.

There were also, however, impersonal economic continuities between city and countryside that are evident in the archaeology of the Near Eastern village. The village, or *kome*, was a place like Porphyreon near Caesarea, or like Panopieis in Phocis, despised by Pausanias. Not cities themselves, lacking the requisite population, defensive walls, and organized urban plans, villages nevertheless were city-friendly. Villages characterized the countryside everywhere in the eastern Mediterranean, but most striking are several hundred villages in the limestone massif of northern Syria, north of Apamea and 40 kilometers east of Antioch.[31] These were small settlements of two-story houses, each accommodating one or several families, of narrow lanes rather than streets, a few communal baths, and on the periphery small churches with elegant stonework as well as numerous olive presses. Some villagers, perhaps, were tenants of large estate owners from Antioch, but most seem to have been independent smallholders. They raised animals, kept in the lower story of the houses, as well as wheat, lentils, vegetables, fruit trees, and especially the olive, and obviously they prospered mainly by shipping the oil and other products to the big neighboring cities, Apamea and

Antioch. Significantly, these villages reached the height of their prosperity around 450–550 but appear thereafter to have stagnated, just at the time when the Persian sack of Antioch in 540, as well as plague and earthquakes in the same period, struck a heavy blow to the regional economy. The shared pattern of prosperity confirms the economic link between city and countryside, likewise evident further south, in well-preserved villages of southern Syria, Arabia, and Palestine.[32]

The west of the Roman Empire, meanwhile, much of it dominated by Germanic kings, underwent what scholars sometimes call "ruralization," a process that was definitely not city-friendly. Through their bailiffs, the bishops administered ecclesiastical properties from what survived of the cities, but this was not the traditional personal link. Monasteries, likewise great landowners, were purely rural. Villages had never characterized Italy, Gaul, the Iberian Peninsula, and Britain, where the usual instrument of agricultural exploitation had been the rural villa, and villas had been rare in the East, except in the immediate environs of cities (like Daphne near Antioch). Traditionally, these villas in the West had consisted of both the *pars rustica* with barns, quarters for the estate personnel, and equipment like oil and wine presses, and the *pars urbana*, the luxurious stone-built habitation of the estate owner. Torre de Palma in eastern Portugal is a prime example.[33] The Gallic aristocrats Ausonius of Bordeaux in the fourth century and in the fifth Sidonius Apollinaris, bishop of Clermont, had divided time between cities and cherished estates in the countryside, but by the sixth century descendants of the Roman elite, and their German counterparts, dwelled more or less permanently on their rural estates, commonly in much reduced circumstances. The gradual decay of these villas under Germanic rule – the abandonment of the baths, postholes sunk through mosaics, installation of hearths in dining rooms and reception halls, subdivision into humble dwellings, eventual devolution into rustic villages – inevitably reflects likewise the decline of the Roman elite that promoted the city.

## Urban Buildings and Their Inhabitants

Public buildings in ancient cities, whether streets and plazas, public baths, or theaters, amphitheaters, and hippodromes, all created performance space[34] in which citizen behavior, whether ritualized in processions on Jerusalem's porticoed streets or during less scripted social interaction in the bath or amphitheater, communicated urban values and a sense of civic solidarity. Hence the rhetorical images of cities in Menander and Procopius, concentrating on buildings rather than persons, nonetheless raise a key issue, and estimating the state of cities in the Age of Justinian requires a look at their physical fabric. The evidence suggests the survival of major building types well into the sixth century, but it also points to significant transformations.

The infrastructure of fortification walls and streets remained a priority, especially in the East. Military threats made the fifth and sixth centuries an age of innovation in urban defensive architecture. As Procopius writes in the *Buildings*, Justinian lavished imperial resources on city fortifications. The refortification efforts of Ostrogothic kings in the towns of Italy, and of Justinian and his successors in the former Vandal kingdom, are well documented.[35] As for streets, urban authorities in the East, but less in the West, were still repairing the old pavements, water pipelines, and drains and putting down new streets of carefully fitted stone slabs, as at Caesarea and Scythopolis. The old porticoed thoroughfares, among the magnificent monuments of the ancient cities, were restored or constructed anew throughout the sixth century, including at Jerusalem, Antioch, and Apamea. These streets functioned equally as the setting of urban ritual and as linear markets, as in the case of the Byzantine shops at Sardis. In the meantime, the old agoras, *fora*, and palaestras, long since fallen into disuse, were reoccupied frequently as industrial quarters or neighborhoods of modest housing. In such quarters the space was not rigidly organized, and likewise waning in the Age of Justinian was the ancient distinction between public and private urban space. In the East temporary booths or shops in the porticoes were rebuilt in stone and then invaded the streets themselves, beginning the process that would transform the linear markets of the ancient city into the crowded and narrow suqs of the medieval Islamic towns.[36]

The "congenial pleasures of the bath," long an expected amenity, continued unabated in the sixth century, as did the association with both comeliness (*charis*) and good health (*hygieia*).[37] Christian admonitions about public display of the body perhaps encouraged the construction of smaller, more intimate facilities in which the plunge baths accommodated a single person instead of many, but the cause may have been partly a decline in public financing. Small baths indeed were sometimes *privata*, built by entrepreneurs to be run as a business. Two sixth-century examples have come to light at Caesarea, one linked to a church, the other perhaps servicing an adjacent suburban villa. Yet the older large public baths continued to function and new ones were built, generally lacking only the traditional palaestra and sometimes the large *frigidarium* (cold pool). In Italy public baths remained the most frequent beneficiaries of public and private patronage through the Ostrogothic period. The large western bath at Scythopolis in Palaestina II, constructed around 400, underwent continuous rebuilding and expansion through the first half of the sixth century. The spacious hot and warm rooms (*caldaria, tepidaria*) and the cold pools imply public nudity (not necessarily segregated by sex), nor does the adjacent public *latrina*, with narrow spaces for six simultaneous users, indicate much official regard for privacy. Yet to judge from the smaller, more intimate *privata*, the trend was toward greater modesty than in the old Roman cities.[38]

Every proper Roman city had at least one theater, while provincial capitals boasted amphitheaters also and perhaps a stadium, circus, or hippodrome. The spectacles remained popular in the sixth century, comprising chariot racing and beast hunts but also mimes, clowns, jugglers, tableaux, dancers, and musicians in various mixtures, always in a competitive setting. Theodora herself began as an actress who traveled to various cities (Procopius, *Secret History*, 9.28). She belonged to the Blue faction, which her consort Justinian later patronized (29.30). The factions of Blues and Greens, associations of professional performers, had branches in all the major cities in the sixth century, as well as fan clubs of young claqueurs occupying assigned sections in the theater or hippodrome who initiated rhythmical chants of partisans for one competitor or the other, at the same time glorifying a local benefactor or fair-minded governor, vilifying a heretical bishop, and always acclaiming the reigning emperor.[39] This highly ritualized behavior created a visible and vociferous community of spectators and prompted them to form and express a coherent political will, and it therefore tended to reinforce both civic identity and identification with a broader provincial and imperial society.[40] In the sixth century, though, the spectacles declined in frequency because bishops and other Christian moralists objected, and funding tended to dry up. Faction activity and performances continued in Italy under the Ostrogoths, and in 549 Totila celebrated what were apparently the last circus games in Rome.[41] Chariot racing seems to have collapsed about this time at Caesarea, where by mid-century stone robbing and building of modest structures had set in at the hippodrome site. No later than 600, Caesarea's deserted theater had been dismantled and its facade incorporated into the *kastron*, a spacious and heavily defended intramural fortress (see Fig. 3).

Four centuries earlier, cities had met the usual expenses of building and maintaining the urban infrastructure, baths, public spectacles, and

FIGURE 4. Caesarea Palaestinae, the Byzantine Esplanade, looking north. On the left is a reused marble statue of an unknown god, on the right a porphyry statue of Emperor Hadrian. Drawing: Anna Iamim

other services from rental of city-owned land or other properties and the munificence (*philotimia*) of wealthy councilmen. In the fourth century, however, the emperors, hard-pressed for cash, had confiscated city properties, only to return later one-third of the revenues to meet the cities' needs, always subject to the provincial governor's approval. A few private benefactors of the old type remained, as at Aphrodisias. Nevertheless, the financial means of most cities declined sharply, and money had to be scraped together from whatever sources.[42] In this climate only the emperor, working through the provincial governor, had the resources for major projects like city walls and aqueducts, and the city authorities typically received the governor's approval not for new construction but for repairs and bringing unfinished buildings to completion. At Caesarea, for example, an inscription from the later sixth century records that the governor Flavius Entolius permitted Flavius Strategius, "father of the city," to construct an arch, a wall, and a staircase "from city funds."[43] Excavations in the 1950s discovered the inscription and confirmed the modest scale of the Strategius project (Fig. 4). Included in the new work, flanking the arch and the stairs, were seated colossal statues of an unknown god and of the emperor Hadrian, both lacking their heads and extremities, the Hadrian statue seated on a stone throne that it did not fit. In characteristic fashion, Strategius thus incorporated ornaments of ancient Caesarea into the fabric of the sixth-century city, both saving money and confirming in stone the identification of his contemporaries with the city's illustrious past.[44]

Regression in urban building does not prove general impoverishment, because at the same time construction of religious buildings had soared. Leah Di Segni's recent count of dated inscriptions from Arabia and Palestine between 320 and 790 totaled 83 recording patronage of civil buildings and 153 of religious buildings, mostly churches, the latter reflecting both private and public patronage and bunched in the reign of Justinian. Italy and the West were similar.[45] Hence in church construction private benefactors of ancient type definitely remained in play, though building became an act of Christian penitence or a prayer for salvation of oneself and one's household as much as an expression of old-style conspicuous urban patronage.

By the Age of Justinian the Mediterranean cities had generally completed the process of "Christianizing." The pagan gods everywhere had yielded to Christian martyrs as the city's divine protectors, and a city's calendar of pagan religious festivals and processions had been reorganized around the memorials of the saints. This meant that temples and their precincts universally gave way to churches, but the process of "refiguring sacred space" differed remarkably from place to place.[46] In Jerusalem Constantine had created a general paradigm for the East by ordering the city's main temple to the Capitoline gods dismantled and the Church of the Holy Sepulcher built on the same site. This was in the city center, adjacent to the forum directly accessible from the porticoed north-south street (Plate I). Hence the sacred center would function as in pagan times in relation to the forum and the city's streets. Elsewhere, as at Aphrodisias, the old temples were themselves rebuilt as churches. In the West, however, the general pattern was different. When Constantine founded the great basilicas of Rome, he had avoided the monumental center, replete with pagan temples dear to the still-pagan aristocracy, and had positioned St. John's Lateran on the southern periphery located on imperial property. Similarly, in the cities of Gaul and Spain the bishops placed churches either outside city walls or away from the monumental centers. This had far-reaching implications, for new churches brought with them monasteries, hostels for strangers, the poor, and the sick, sometimes a bishop's palace, all in an underdeveloped urban quarter that now attracted settlement and commercial activity. Hence in the West, but not in the East, the positioning of churches dislocated the urban topography and hastened the decay of the old urban centers.[47]

## Ruling the Sixth-Century City

In a metropolis like Caesarea the provincial governor was the big man in the Age of Justinian, presiding over a staff of 100–300 clerks and other officials, commanding a force of soldiers or police to enforce order, and occupying an official palace or *praetorium* that was normally one of the most imposing edifices in the city.[48] In the East, and in restored Italy and Africa, there were more provinces than ever, so the powerful governor (*consularis, proconsul*) was a common urban phenomenon. They also approved all public construction projects, and as judges of first instance, as adminstrators and enforcers of taxation, their presence attracted numerous provincials to the metropolis and contributed to its prosperity.

The bishops were also big men.[49] Like the pope, they too had acquired rural estates and other income-producing properties for their sees by gift and bequest. This wealth, and the management of continuing private and imperial donations, made bishops the major urban builders, so they had the power to reshape the urban terrain by the insertion of churches. They also frequently managed secular urban construction, since they had both the expertise and men in the building trades among their clienteles. Hence in the Pseudo-Joshua *Chronicle* (c. 87) the emperor gives the bishop twenty pounds of gold in 504–505 to rebuild the city wall of Edessa. The bishop's reach had long since extended also to rural evangelizing and construction of village churches, so his undertakings helped maintain the ancient links between city and countryside. The bishops were definitely city-friendly. Since Constantine, moreover, the bishop's court, *episcopalis audientia*, had offered efficient, no-fault arbitration of property disputes and destructive altercations between powerful families. Above all, since the fourth and fifth centuries bishops had put forward a new concept of the Christian community, which on a local, practical level was coterminous with the city. To it the bishop regulated admission through baptism, and by excommunication he could exclude and marginalize the recalcitrant. Now for the first time, as Peter Brown has shown, the Christian community also encompassed the poor, always present but newly become visible.[50] In the Christian urban community, marshaling imperial and private wealth for the naked and hungry, for widows and orphans, as well as for the numerous lesser clergy and monks, invested the bishops with the highest moral authority.

In the emerging Frankish kingdom of sixth-century Gaul, a bishop like Severus of Arles or Gregory of Tours contested power in the city even with the royal count (*comes civitatis*),[51] but in the East the bishops general limited themselves to a more pastoral mode. There, and in the West too, what prevailed in the sixth century, to adopt the phase of A. H. M. Jones and J. H. W. G. Liebeschuetz, was the "regime of the notables," which around 500 replaced the old regime of the councilmen, the *curiales* or *bouleutai*. What actually happened is reasonably clear.[52] By the fourth century the councilmen, along with the old *duumviri* and other city magistrates, had passed their heyday. Enrolled in an official register, the *curiales* and *bouleutai* were still obliged in rotation to take on local administrative duties, above all collecting taxes for the imperial government, at the risk, if they could not deliver the full amount, of their own estates. Some failed and disappeared from the register and the local elite, while others sought from the emperor letters of office that made them *honorati* immune from local obligations. Though leakage thus occurred both down and up, councilmen, now called *politeuomenoi* in Greek, appear nevertheless in literary texts, inscriptions, and papyri in the sixth and seventh centuries, still collecting taxes and performing other civic duties, as in the Visigothic kingdom and at Petra. By the sixth century, as apparently at Korykos, many belonged in effect to a defined caste of relatively modest persons, whose tomb monuments resembled those of potters and greengrocers. Yet other councilmen had exploited their duties in tax collection, local construction, and food supply to amass even more wealth, often on the fringe of the law. Thus inside the old elite an inner circle of "first men" had risen, *principales* or *proteuontes*, still enrolled in the official register and under onerous obligations but nevertheless still powerful in the city.

Hence by 500 or so the emperors began to recognize a new urban regime. It combined the *honorati* resident in a city, identified typically as landlords, *ktetores*, or city dwellers, *oiketores*, with the bishop, himself often a scion of the local elite, and the "first men." In 545 Justinian issued an edict ordering that in all the cities the bishop should join with the first men and landlords to nominate the *pater tes poleos*, city father, the *sitones*, head of the grain supply, and similar administrators, and that each year the bishop and five "first men" should audit their accounts (*Novel*, 128.16). This was the regime of the notables. The city father typically handled secular construction projects. Prominent among other administrators was the *defensor*, in Greek *ekdikos*, responsible for low-level jurisdiction, arbitration of disputes, and generally for maintaining civil order.

So much is reasonably clear, but the meaning remains in dispute. Liebeschuetz interprets the new regime as "the end of civic politics," indeed as "the end of the ancient tradition of constitutional politics going back to Solon of Athens," while for Mark Whittow it was no more than an "institutional rearrangement."[53] It is true that the notables removed city politics from the council house, as Liebeschuetz asserts, and lodged it in the elegant reception halls and dining rooms of elite private mansions. Everywhere, as at Apamea and Caesarea, the mansions of the notables indeed "swallowed up" the public buildings, as Brown observed, and became the glory of the cities.[54] Yet with Whittow one wonders what had changed. Three centuries earlier Roman elites had also maintained their private mansions in town, and the *curiales* and *bouleutai* had always operated less through horizontal relationships of open debate and collective decision making and more through vertical ties of dependency, of estate ownership and patronage of persons and social institutions.

## Survival and Transformation

Hence sixth-century Mediterranean cities remained engrossing social organisms with which Procopius and others readily identified. Processes were working that would transform these cities beyond recognition, or even cause their extinction, among them depopulation, degradation of city centers, impoverishment of secular patronage, extraordinary demands upon city finances, regimentation of councilmen, and ruralization. Christianizing the cities and the ascendancy of bishops, on the other hand, strengthened the traditional community and helped sustain links between city and countryside, so some sixth-century trends were actually city-friendly. The results were as varied as the hundreds of cities themselves. Some cities still prospered, although plague, earthquake, and the plundering expeditions of Persians and Lakhmid Arabs devastated the East with monotonous regularity, as Germanic invasions had earlier in the West. What proved fatal in the West, however, was the decline of the old-style urban elite and arrival on the scene of new Germanic elites less attached to the traditional Mediterranean city. In the East the ancient traditions more often survived. In particular, it was not the "regime of the notables" that ended the cities, for the notables, too, were city-based and hence city-friendly. Instead, it was the Persian and Muslim conquests of the seventh century that would bring a decisive turn, for the Muslims would introduce not just a new religion but also new patterns of settlement and new forms of city. These, however, were still remote eventualities in the Age of Justinian.[55]

## Notes

1 See esp. A. H. M. Jones, *The Later Roman Empire, 284–602* (Oxford, 1964), 2:712–766; J. H. W. G. Liebeschuetz, *The Decline and Fall of the Roman City* (Oxford, 2001); and, for the variety of opinions, Luke Lavan, "The Late-Antique City: A Bibliographic Essay," in *Recent Research in Late-Antique Urbanism*, ed. Lavan (Portsmouth, R.I., 2001), 9–26.

2 E. J. Owens, *The City in the Greek and Roman World* (New York, 1991).

3 J. Rich and A. Wallace-Hadrill, eds., *City and Country in the Ancient World* (London, 1991).

4 Peter Brown, *The Making of Late Antiquity* (Cambridge, Mass., 1978), 3.

5 *Menander Rhetor*, ed. and trans. D. A. Russell and N. G. Wilson (Oxford, 1981), xi, xxiv–xxv.

6 Helen Saradi, "The *Kallos* of the Byzantine City: The Development of a Rhetorical *Topos* and Historical Reality," *Gesta* 34 (1995): 37–56.

7 Liebeschuetz, *The Decline and Fall of the Roman City*, 81, fig. 1.

8 See the papers and references in A. Raban and K. G. Holum, eds., *Caesarea Maritima: A Retrospective after Two Millenia* (Leiden, 1996), and K. G. Holum, A. Raban, and J. Patrich, eds., *Caesarea Papers 2* (Portsmouth, R.I., 1999).

9 See Liebeschuetz, *The Decline and Fall of the Roman City*, 29–103, with full bibliography.

10 B. Ward-Perkins, *From Classical Antiquity to the Middle Ages: Urban Public Building in Northern and Central Italy, AD 300–850* (Oxford, 1984).

11 See M. Whittow, "Recent Research on the Late-Antique City in Asia Minor: The Second Half of the Sixth C. Revisited," in Lavan, *Recent Research*, 137–153.

12 C. Roueché, *Aphrodisias in Late Antiquity* (London, 1989), 86–87.

13 F. R. Trombley, "Korykos in Cilicia Trachis: The Economy of a Small Coastal City in Late Antiquity (*Saec.* V–VI) – A Précis," *Ancient History Bulletin* 1 (1987): 16–23.

14 C. Foss, "Syria in Transition, A.D. 550–750: An Archaeological Approach," *DOP* 51 (1997): 189–269.

15 Foss, "Syria in Transition," 205–230; J. C. Balty, "Apamée au VIe siècle: Témoinages archéologiques de la richesse d'une ville," in *Hommes et richesses dans l'Empire byzantine*, ed. C. Morrison and J. Lefort (Paris, 1989), 1:79–92.

16 Foss, "Syria in Transition," 230–237; A. Walmsley, "Byzantine Palestine and Arabia: Urban Prosperity in Late Antiquity," in *Towns in Transition*, ed. N. Christie and S. T. Loseby (Aldershot, 1996), 126–158, esp. 139.

17 M. Avi-Yonah, "The Economics of Byzantine Palestine," *Israel Exploration Journal* 8 (1958): 39–51; cf. generally A. K. Walmsley, "Byzantine Palestine and Arabia: Urban Prosperity in Late Antiquity," in Christie and Loseby, *Towns in Transition*, 126–158.

18 H. Donner, *The Mosaic Map of Madaba* (Kampen, 1992).

19 N. Avigad, *Discovering Jerusalem* (Nashville, Tenn., 1980), 208–246.

20 L. Koenen, "The Carbonized Archive from Petra," *JRA* 9 (1996): 177–188; J. Frösén, A. Arjava, and M. Lehtinen, eds., *The Petra Papyri* (Amman, 2002), esp. 1, ll. 4–5.

21 Y. Tsafrir and G. Foerster, "Urbanism at Scythopolis–Bet Shean in the Fourth to Seventh Centuries," *DOP* 51 (1997): 85–146.

22 T. S. Brown, *Gentlemen and Officers: Imperial Administration and Aristocratic Power in Byzantine Italy, A.D. 554–800* (London, 1984), 21–37.

23 Ward-Perkins, *From Classical Antiquity to the Middle Ages*, esp. 38–48.

24 R. Krautheimer, *Three Christian Capitals: Topography and Politics* (Berkeley, Calif., 1983), 6–40, 93–121.

25 F. M. Clover, "*Felix Karthago*," in *Tradition and Innovation in Late Antiquity*, ed. F. M. Clover and R. S. Humphreys (Madison, Wis., 1989), 129–169.

26 Ward-Perkins, *From Classical Antiquity to the Middle Ages*, 72, 105–106, 128–129, 241–244; A. J. Wharton, *Refiguring the Post Classical City: Dura Europos, Jerash, Jerusalem, and Ravenna* (Cambridge, 1995), 105–147.

27 C. Haas, *Alexandria in Late Antiquity: Topography and Social Conflict* (Baltimore, 1997); also J. McKenzie, "Glimpsing Alexandria from Archaeological Evidence," *Journal of Roman Archaeology* 16 (2003): 35–63, esp. 58–61, with fig. 17.

28 Foss, "Syria in Transition," 190–197.

29 P. Horden and N. Purcell, *The Corrupting Sea: A Study of Mediterranean History* (Oxford, 2000), 100–101; cf. G. P. Brogiolo, N. Gauthier, and N. Christie, eds., *Towns and Their Territories between Late Antiquity and the Early Middle Ages* (Leiden, 2000).

30 For a translation of the Anonymous of Piacenza see John Wilkinson, trans., *Jerusalem Pilgrims before the Crusades* (Warminster, 2002), 129–51, c. 46 on p. 150.

31 G. Tate, *Les campagnes de la Syrie du nord*, vol. 1 (Paris, 1992), reviewed and summarized in C. Foss, "The Near Eastern Countryside in Late Antiquity," in *The Roman and Byzantine Near East*, ed. J. H. Humphrey (Ann Arbor, Mich., 1995), 218–223.

32 Y. Hirschfeld, "Some Aspects of the Late-Antique Village of Shivta," *JRA* 16 (2003): 395–408; more generally, see J. Shereshevski, *Byzantine Urban Settlements in the Negev Desert* (Beer-Sheva, 1991), with the cautionary comments of Foss, "Near Eastern Countryside," 223–231.

33 S. Mahony and J. Hall, "The Villa of Torre de Palma (Alto Alentejo)," *Journal of Roman Archaeology* 9 (1996): 275–294.

34 Paul Zanker, *Pompeii: Public and Private Life*, trans. D. L. Schneider (Cambridge, 1998), 3.

35 D. Pringle, *The Defence of Byzantine Africa from Justinian to the Arab Conquest* (Oxford, 1981); Ward-Perkins, *From Classical Antiquity to the Middle Ages*, 191–199.

36 H. Kennedy, "From Polis to Madina: Urban Change in Late Antique and Early Islamic Syria," *Past and Present* 106 (1985): 12–13.

37 K. M. D. Dunbabin, "*Baiarum Grata Voluptas*: Pleasures and Dangers of the Baths," *Proceedings of the British School at Rome* 57 (1989): 6–46; F. Yegül, *Baths and Bathing in Classical Antiquity* (Cambridge, 1992), 314–349.

38 For late-antique attitudes to public nudity, see Peter Brown, *The Body in Society: Men, Women, and Sexual Renunciation in Early Christianity* (New York, 1988), 315–317, 320, 437–438.

39 Alan Cameron, *Circus Factions: Blues and Greens at Rome and Byzantium* (Oxford, 1976), esp. 314–317; C. Roueché, *Performers and Partisans at Aphrodisias in the Roman and Late Roman Periods* (London, 1993).

40 Roueché, *Performers and Partisans*, 175–176, suggests on the contrary that the factions weakened local identity.

41 Ward-Perkins, *From Classical Antiquity to the Middle Ages*, 92–118.

42 Jones, *LRE*, 2:732–34, 737, 759; Ward-Perkins, *From Classical Antiquity to the Middle Ages*, esp. 1–48.

43 C. M. Lehmann and K. G. Holum, *The Greek and Latin Inscriptions of Caesarea Maritima* (Boston, 2000), no. 59.

44 J. D. Alchermes, "*Spolia* in Roman Cities of the Late Empire: Legislative Rationales and Architectural Reuse," *DOP* 48 (1994): 167–178; cf. Ward-Perkins, *From Classical Antiquity to the Middle Ages*, 203–229.

45 L. Di Segni, "Epigraphic Evidence for Building in *Palaestina* and *Arabia* (Fourth–Seventh C.)," in *The Roman and Byzantine Near East*, vol. 2, ed. J. H. Humphrey (Portsmouth, R.I., 1999), 149–178; Ward-Perkins, *From Classical Antiquity to the Middle Ages*, 51–84.

46 K. G. Holum, "The Christianizing of Caesarea Maritima," in *Die spätantike Stadt und ihre Christianisierung*, ed. G. Brands and H.-G. Severin (Wiesbaden, 2003), 151–164; Wharton, *Refiguring*.

47 In general, see Wharton, *Refiguring*, and the essays in Brands and Severin, *Christianisierung*; esp. B. Ward-Perkins, "Reconfiguring Sacred Space from Pagan Shrines to Christian Churches," 285–290.

48 Jones, *LRE*, 373–374, 434, 450–451, 565, 593–596, esp. 757–759, on governors in provincial capitals; Luke Lavan, "The *Praetoria* of Civil Governors in Late Antiquity," in *Recent Research*, 39–56.

49 Peter Brown, *Power and Persuasion in Late Antiquity: Towards a Christian Empire* (Madison, Wis., 1992), 118–158.

50 Peter Brown, *Poverty and Leadership in the Later Roman Empire* (Hanover, N.H., 2002).

51 W. Klingshirn, *Caesarius of Arles: The Making of a Christian Community in Late Antique Gaul* (Cambridge, 1994).

52 Jones, *LRE*, 2:724–763; K. G. Holum, "The Survival of the Bouleutic Class," in *Caesarea Retrospective*, ed. Raban and Holum, 615–627; Liebeschuetz, *The Decline and Fall of the Roman City*, 104–136; A. Laniado, *Recherches sur les notables municipaux dans l'Empire protobyzantin* (Paris, 2002).

53 Liebeschuetz, *The Decline and Fall of the Roman City*, 107, 117, 121; M. Whittow, "Ruling the Late Roman and Early Byzantine City: A Continuous History," *Past and Present* 129 (1990): 3–29.

54 Brown, *The Making of Late Antiquity*, 49.

55 Foss, "Syria in Transition"; Martin O. H. Carver, "Transitions to Islam: Urban Rôles in the East and South Mediterranean, Fifth to Tenth Centuries AD," in Christie and Loseby, *Towns in Transition*, 184–212.

# 5: The Empire at War

*A. D. Lee*

> Imperial majesty should not only be graced with arms but also armed with laws, so that good government may prevail in time of war and peace alike. The head of the Roman state can then stand victorious not only over enemies in war but also over trouble-makers, driving out their wickedness through the paths of the law, and can triumph as much by his devotion to the law as for his conquests in battle. Long hours of work and careful planning have, with God's help, given us success in both these fields. Barbarian nations brought beneath our yoke know the scale of our exertions in war. Africa and countless other provinces, restored to Roman jurisdiction and brought back within our empire after so long an interval, bear witness to the victories granted to us by the will of heaven. However, it is by the laws that we have already managed to enact and collect that all our peoples are ruled.
>
> – Justinian, *Institutes*, pr., *Nov.* 21, 533, trans. P. Birks and G. McLeod

War was undoubtedly an important feature of the Age of Justinian, most famously in the campaigns of reconquest that recovered North Africa from the Vandals and Italy from the Goths, but also in relations with Persia to the east, and with various tribal peoples along the lower Danube. As this extract from the preface to Justinian's handbook for law students makes clear, Justinian took an elevated view of the waging of war, presenting it, alongside law making, as one of his central, God-given duties. It is somewhat surprising, therefore, to discover that Justinian himself never led any of his campaigns in person, never even visited any of the theatres of war or the territory regained in the west; instead, he spent most of his reign ensconced in the imperial palace in Constantinople, rarely leaving the confines of the capital. This lack of direct involvement on his part in military affairs is explicable partly in terms of Justinian's own lack of military experience – despite holding the post of general for a number of years prior to his accession, this seems to have been a titular position, with no evidence of his actually engaging in military action of any sort[1] – and partly in terms of established tradition. Since the death of Theodosius I in 395 it had become extremely rare for emperors in Constantinople to campaign in person. This did not, however, prevent emperors from continuing to claim the credit for military successes – indeed, it became even more important that they do so, as Justinian appreciated. He was not slow to advertise military successes achieved under his aegis through such media as the equestrian statue in front of the Hagia Sophia, which presented Justinian as victor over the Persians, and the mosaic adorning the ceiling of the Chalke Gate of the palace, which depicted Justinian receiving the submission of the Vandals and the Goths.[2]

How were these successes achieved, and how typical were they? This chapter aims, among other things, to answer these questions, not by providing a narrative of the wars of Justinian's reign (which can be found in the existing literature),[3] but, first, by investigating the infrastructure of war making – the organisation, recruitment, and maintenance of the army – and, second, by assessing the effectiveness of the Roman army in the sixth century. The chapter will also examine war in this period from the rather different perspective of the communities that fighting directly affected.

The degree to which these questions can be answered satisfactorily is of course governed in large part by the amount and character of the evidence surviving from the sixth century. Archaeological and documentary materials (inscriptions and papyri) have some contribution to make, as do legal texts, but the literary sources necessarily take priority. Of these, the writings of the historian Procopius are of preeminent importance, above all the *Wars*, with their detailed account of campaigning during the first twenty-five years of Justinian's reign.[4] But caution must also be exercised, for the two fundamental features of the *Wars* that make them potentially so useful to the historian of military affairs are double-edged. The first feature, their very focus on warfare, derives from their genre as classicising history, but Procopius's aspiration to emulate the great models of classical historiography, particularly Herodotus and Thucydides, also means that his descriptions of battles and sieges can sometimes owe more to centuries-old generic stereotypes than to sixth-century realities.[5] The second feature, their claim to derive substantially from personal autopsy, derives from Procopius's privileged vantage point as secretary to Justinian's leading general, Belisarius, but his very proximity to Belisarius sometimes made it difficult for him to maintain a distinterested perspective on events.[6] "Sometimes" is the critical word here, for it is apparent that the *Wars* do also contain invaluable information on the character of warfare that has not obviously been constricted by generic straitjackets or tainted by personal bias.[7]

Procopius's *Wars* ended with the decisive defeat of the Goths in Italy in 552. Procopius's work evidently received a favourable reception, judging by the fact that a Constantinopolitan lawyer, Agathias, thought it worth continuing the story, describing mopping-up operations in Italy and ongoing conflict with Persian forces in the Caucasus. His account was in turn continued by Menander Protector from 557–558 to Justinian's death (565) and beyond (to 582), providing quite a detailed narrative framework of war making throughout Justinian's reign (although Menander's history is preserved only in the form of excerpts, albeit often substantial ones).[8] Mention ought also to be made of a narrative history of a rather different kind, the Syriac *Chronicle* attributed to Joshua the Stylite. Although its focus on the war between the empire and Persia during the reign of the emperor Anastasius (502–505) means that it predates Justinian's reign, this eyewitness account of early sixth-century warfare nevertheless provides an invaluable supplement to the classicising histories of Procopius and his continuators.[9]

A different genre of source material, military treatises, also warrants brief comment at the outset. As always, such works present the difficulty of discerning to what extent they are descriptive and to what extent prescriptive, although this issue becomes less problematic when they can be used in tandem with narrative histories such as those of Procopius and his continuators. An anonymous work, *On Strategy*, usually dated to Justinian's reign, contains material of relevance, interestingly set within a broader framework of political theory, while the *Strategikon* attributed to the emperor Maurice (582–602), although postdating Justinian's reign, has the potential to shed light on the Roman army of the sixth century from perspectives different from those provided by the narrative histories.[10]

## The Infrastructure of War Making

When the emperor Justinian considered the situation was as favourable as possible, both domestically and in his relations with

> Persia, he turned his attention to affairs in North Africa. But when he revealed to his officials that he was assembling an army against the Vandals and Gelimer, most of them were unhappy about it and regarded it as a mistake, recalling the expedition of the emperor Leo and the disaster of Basiliscus [in 468] and remembering how many troops had perished and how much money the state had lost. The men who were the most worried and had the most misgivings were the praetorian prefect . . . and the administrator of the treasury and those responsible for the collection of taxes, for they reckoned that they would have to produce large sums of money for the needs of the war, but would receive no leniency in the event of failure or extension of time in which to raise the sums. . . . But the only person who dared to say anything to the emperor with a view to preventing the expedition was John the Cappadocian, the praetorian prefect, a man of the greatest boldness and the cleverest man of his day.
>
> – Procopius, *Wars*, 3.10, trans. H. B. Dewing, with revisions

Procopius's account of the preliminaries to the Vandal expedition provides a valuable entrée into some of the issues connected with the infrastructure of war making. The opening sentence of the excerpt above, with its allusion to the recently concluded Endless Peace with Persia (532), implies that the empire's resources were not capable of sustaining major military commitments on more than one front simultaneously, at least for any significant length of time, while John the Cappadocian's intervention in the debate, and his reservations about the wisdom of the enterprise, reflects the central role of the praetorian prefect in the financing of war in this period, a natural corollary of that official's responsibility for the collection and distribution of imperial revenues.[11] Financial prudence was overruled by the demands of religious ideology – specifically, Justinian's concern to free the inhabitants of North Africa from the rule of the heterodox Arian Vandals – and John's concerns proved to be unfounded, at least in the short term. Against expectations, the Vandal regime was overthrown with relative ease by an army of 15,000 men, whose modest size was perhaps a concession to John's concerns. Despite this rapid success, it is clear that mounting a major campaign had potentially serious ramifications for the empire's resources and was not to be undertaken lightly. Moreover, such ramifications were additional to the continuous costs entailed by maintenance of a standing army, which placed a heavy burden on the empire even when it was not at war. What military infrastructure, then, did Justinian inherit, how did he adapt it over the course of his reign, and how was that infrastructure sustained in peace and in war?

Many of the salient organisational features of the army during the Age of Justinian reflect continuities from the military arrangements established by the emperor Constantine in the early fourth century.[12] The fundamental distinction between mobile field armies and more sedentary troops posted in frontier provinces remained in force, even if the terminology of *comitatenses* and *limitanei* is, necessarily, not employed by Procopius and others writing in Greek. At Justinian's accession in 527, the five regional field armies that had existed in the eastern half of the empire since the late fourth century were still in place, each under the command of a *magister militum* (two based near Constantinople, and one each in Illyricum, Thrace, and the East). Within a year, Justinian increased their number to six through the division of this last one into two (one for Armenia and the other for the eastern regions to the south), a move that perhaps reflected the growing importance of the Caucasus region in imperial thinking vis-à-vis Persia. In due course, similar commands were created for North Africa and Italy following their reconquest.[13] Procopius's claim in the *Secret History* that Justinian sought to wind down the *limitanei* does not tally with other evidence to the contrary and may reflect localised problems with pay in Procopius's native Palestine.[14]

Against this background of fundamental continuities, some changes are evident. Cavalry units were playing an increasingly important role in combat relative to infantry,[15] while two types of troop are more prominent in the sixth century – federates and *bucellarii*. The former had originally designated allied foreigners assisting Roman forces, but by Justinian's day the term had come to refer to valued cavalry units in the regular army, predominantly drawn from foreign peoples but including individuals from within the empire.[16] *Bucellarii* seem to have originated as the personal guards attached to commanders which, by the sixth century, could sometimes constitute substantial units in their own right.[17]

How large were the military forces at Justinian's disposal? The only specific statement in a sixth-century source is that of the historian Agathias, who gives a figure of 150,000.[18] There is, however, broad agreement that this figure errs on the low side, both because it occurs in a polemical context where it suits Agathias to portray Justinian as neglecting the army in his final years and because it does not tally with other, more circumstantial evidence.[19] One tenative suggestion for the actual number is something in the vicinity of 300,000 to 350,000.[20] It is highly unlikely to have exceeded this order of magnitude, in light of the figures contemporary sources give for the size of individual armies on campaign: the army of 52,000 the emperor Anastasius deployed in 503 is described by Procopius as the largest force assembled against the Persians before or since,[21] while armies during Justinian's reign are typically 15,000 to 30,000 men,[22] and the *Strategikon* considered a force of 15,000 to 20,000 large.[23] More generally, it is clear that major military commitments on two fronts – as in 540 when Justinian had to cope with the ongoing campaign against the Goths in Italy while also dealing with a Persian invasion of Syria – severely stretched available troops.

The prevailing view has been that, unlike its fourth-century counterpart, the Roman army of the sixth century relied on volunteers rather than conscription,[24] although evidence has been highlighted recently that is consistent with some degree of conscription, alongside continued use of hereditary obligation in the families of soldiers.[25] Continuing a centuries-old tradition, manpower from within the empire was supplemented by recruits from peoples beyond the empire's frontiers or recently settled within imperial territory – hence the presence of Heruls, Huns, and Lombards, among others, in Roman armies of the period.[26] An important issue for military manpower during Justinian's reign is the impact of the plague in the early 540s. There is little doubt that the plague caused major short-term dislocation in a wide variety of areas, including recruiting, but the question of its longer-term impact remains problematic. The claim that the demographic impact of the plague within the empire necessitated a major shift in recruitment patterns towards greater reliance on sources from outside the empire has proved difficult to sustain,[27] but the critical issue is the plague's effects on the rural population of the empire, from which military manpower was overwhelmingly drawn. Some evidence suggests significant agrarian depopulation in the aftermath of the plague,[28] yet it remains difficult to believe that the plague could have had as devastating an effect on the more dispersed population of the countryside as it clearly did on the major urban centres of the empire, while circumstantial evidence from at least some parts of the empire implies a robust rural population in the second half of the sixth century. "At least in the rural and upland areas most relevant to military recruitment the overall effect of the Plague may have been to terminate a period of population prosperity, but without necessarily immediately introducing a dearth of manpower; the resultant less buoyant level of population would obviously have been more vulnerable to future serious shocks."[29]

The army was the largest consumer not only of the empire's human resources, but also of imperial revenues, as a contemporary source acknowledged: "The financial system was set up to take care of matters of public importance that arise on occasion. . . . But it is principally concerned with paying the soldiers. Each year most of the public revenues are spent for this purpose."[30] This blunt and sobering assessment of the economic ramifications of the sixth-century army has been accepted as broadly accurate by scholars who have investigated the surviving data for the imperial budget, with quantitative estimates suggesting that the army accounted for between one-half and three-quarters of imperial expenditure.[31]

This broad-brush, macroeconomic overview can be fleshed out through investigation of the specific areas of expenditure required on behalf of the individual soldier. During the mid-third century, inflation had eroded the value of the cash payments (the *stipendium*) that in earlier centuries had been soldiers' primary recompense to such a degree that an alternative system of paying the troops in kind (the *annona*, comprising bread, meat, wine, and oil) had to be developed (in turn requiring the levying of taxes in kind); the *stipendium* lingered on in vestigial form through the fourth century, but by the sixth century had ceased to exist. The system based on the *annona*, however, also underwent modification with the passage of time: the levying of taxes in kind and their transport to where troops were stationed created major administrative headaches for the praetorian prefect and his officials, with corresponding pressure to allow the commutation of taxes in kind into money taxes. The result was that by the sixth century some units still received their income primarily in the form of foodstuffs, while others received theirs in cash. In general, the former arrangement applied particularly to units of *comitatenses*, the latter to the *limitanei*, but it is also apparent that there was some degree of regional variation. Soldiers also received cash donatives or bonuses upon the accession of a new emperor and at the five yearly anniversaries thereafter (an important way of reinforcing their sense of loyalty to the emperor); since the accession donative was roughly equivalent to the commuted value of two year's *annona*, and the quinquennial donatives to one year's *annona*, these bonuses represent significant supplements to soldiers' income. Finally, they were given cash allowances for the purchase of military clothing, armour, and weapons, the latter produced by imperial arms factories (*fabricae*).[32]

Of course, in addition to consuming human and material resources, running an institution the size of the army also required copious quantities of paperwork, some reflection of which is preserved in the sources. When the general Germanus arrived in Carthage in 536, his first recorded action was to inspect the army records listing the names of all the troops deployed in North Africa, while Egyptian papyri preserve valuable documentation pertaining to the sixth-century army, including instructions regarding recruitment (with a reference to unit registers) and data concerning the levying of the *annona*.[33]

This infrastructure possessed flexibility and scope for adaptation according to circumstances specific to different parts of the empire, as demonstrated by Justinian's establishment of the *quaestura exercitus* (quaestorship of the army) in 536, whereby the provinces of Moesia and Scythia on the lower Danube and the Asian provinces of Caria, Cyprus, and the Islands were detached from the praetorian prefecture of the east and placed under the authority of a new official, the quaestor of the army. The Danubian provinces, strategically critical but economically poor, had long struggled to support the troops stationed in them, a problem Justinian sought to solve by linking them in this way with the wealthier and more secure Asian provinces that could transport supplies via the Black Sea to the lower Danube. Although evidence about the subsequent history of this arrangement is limited, the post of quaestor was still in existence in the mid 570s, suggesting that it achieved some success.[34]

As John the Cappadocian appreciated, however, the real test of the infrastructure came when the empire was faced with having to mount a specific campaign. The largest expeditionary force known from the sixth century was that assembled by the emperor Anastasius in 503 to meet the Persian invasion of Mesopotamia, with the *Chronicle* attributed to Joshua the Stylite providing invaluable insight into the logistical challenges entailed by maintaining a force of 52,000 men in the field. The *Chronicle* records the appointment of a deputy praetorian prefect, Apion, based in Edessa, with specific responsibility for overseeing the production of sufficient bread for the Roman forces. Subsequently succeeded by Calliopius, Apion was then sent to Egypt to organise the baking and transport of bread to supplement that being produced in the theatre of war.[35] Another individual whose role may have been similar is referred to in the context of the campaign against another Persian invasion in 531, while the Vandal expedition in 533 included a "prefect," Archelaus, responsible for provisioning the army.[36] At 15,000 men, the force despatched in 533 was significantly smaller than that deployed in 503, yet even so it has been estimated that an army of this size would have needed, on a daily basis, something of the order of 30 tons of grain, 13 tons of fodder, and 30,000 gallons of water.[37] These were serious enough demands for armies operating out of fixed bases, as was the case in Mesopotamia in 503, but in the case of forces required to be more mobile, a substantial supply train comprising wagons and mules would have been necessary, in turn compromising the army's speed and flexibility.[38] The circumstances of the Gothic war, however, helped to reduce these problems: the substantial coastline of the Italian peninsula and the proximity of many urban centres to it, in combination with the naval superiority imperial forces enjoyed for much of the war, eased logistical support of Roman troops significantly.[39]

## The Effectiveness of the Army

> The Goths were quite unwilling to go out against them through fear of the forces of the Roman people which were not far away, thinking, of course, that they were soldiers and were remaining quiet because they had in mind some sort of ambush. . . . In the middle of the day, this Roman army suddenly made a rush against the enemy, and against expectation the Goths were routed . . . and climbed into the hills nearby. . . . But these Romans, though numerous, were not all soldiers, but were for the most part a mob of men without armour. For since the general was elsewhere, many sailors and servants in the Roman camp, eager to be involved in the war, mingled with that part of the army. And although by their mere numbers they did fill the barbarians with consternation and, as has been said, turn them to flight, yet because of their lack of order (*akosmia*), they lost the day for the Romans. For the intermixture of the aforementioned men caused the soldiers to be thrown into great disorder (*ataxia*).
>
> – Procopius, *Wars*, 5.29.23–28, trans. H. B. Dewing, with revisions

The question of military effectiveness can be approached from a variety of angles. If one starts with the obvious criterion of performance in battle, Justinian's armies emerge with considerable credit. On the eastern front, Belisarius defeated a substantially larger Persian army at Dara in 530,[40] as did Sittas and Dorotheus at Satala in the same year,[41] while Roman forces overcame Persian forces at the river Hippis in Lazica in 549.[42] The outcome of the Vandal campaign was rapidly settled in the space of three months towards the end of 533 as a result of Belisarius's victories at Ad Decimum and Tricamarum,[43] while North

African Berber tribesmen were defeated by Solomon at Mammes and Bourgaon in 535 and by John Troglita in Byzacena in 546–547 and on the "Plains of Cato" in 548.[44] Narses effectively brought the Gothic war in Italy to an end with victories over the Goths at Taginae (Busta Gallorum) and Mons Lactarius in 552 and over the Franks at Casilinus in 554.[45] On the lower Danube, Germanus inflicted a major defeat on the Slavic Antae in the years immediately prior to Justinian's accession, while Mundus defeated the Hunnic Bulgars in battle in 530.[46] All this implies troops and generalship of good quality, even after one adds into the equation the defeats suffered against the Persians at Callinicum in 531, against the Berbers at Cillium in 544 and at Marta in 547, and against the Goths at Faventia and Mugello in 542,[47] particularly since qualifying considerations can be suggested in relation to at least some of these defeats (the apparent extent of Persian losses at Callinicum implies theirs was a Pyrrhic victory, while poor coordination between commanders contributed to the debacle at Faventia).

Of course, performance in pitched battles is only one measure of military effectiveness, but it is an important one that deserves further consideration. One point that emerges from the detailed accounts that exist for many of the victories is the continuing centrality of infantry to success in pitched battles.[48] By the sixth century, cavalry had undoubtedly become an increasingly important element in the Roman army, and the advantages enjoyed by mounted Roman archers over spear-carrying Gothic cavalry seem to have been an important factor in the reconquest of Gothic Italy.[49] Nevertheless, the balance had not yet tipped decisively in favour of cavalry. To be sure, Dara, Ad Decimum, and Tricamarum were cavalry victories, but in the latter two cases only because forward cavalry units unexpectedly engaged and overcame the enemy before the Roman infantry had time to reach the battlefield. A striking feature of the combat in a number of other battles, however, is the way in which cavalry dismounted and fought on foot alongside infantry, as happened at Taginae and Mons Lactarius in Italy, Mammes in North Africa, and the river Hippis in Lazica.[50] Moreover, the fact that military handbooks of the period devote substantial attention to the training and manoeuvring of infantry corroborates the evidence of individual engagements.[51]

A second, related point is the way in which the discipline of Roman forces emerges as a decisive factor in many of the battle descriptions.[52] Although there is a temptation to dismiss this as nothing more than a reflection of traditional stereotypes, according to which non-Roman forces correspondingly lack discipline in battle, the sheer detail and variety of surviving battle descriptions from this period provide reassurance on this point, as does the passage at the head of this section, describing an episode from the first siege of Rome in 537–538, when the unplanned presence of a substantial number of nonprofessional combatants in an army resulted in disaster.[53] Moreover, the sources provide occasional clues as to the range of strategies by which discipline and morale were maintained, whether it be training exercises, stiff penalties for ill-disciplined behaviour, the promise of rewards for bravery and the prospect of booty, commanders using the language of comradeship to maintain a rapport with their men, or care for the wounded and proper burial of those killed in battle.[54] At the same time, it has to be recognised that failure on the part of the central government to ensure adequate payment of troops, as happened at some points during the Gothic war in particular, could have a fatal impact on morale and contribute to setbacks.[55]

As already intimated, however, performance in battle cannot be used as the sole criterion for gauging military effectiveness. First, the significance of individual battles needs to be assessed within a wider context, while, second, pitched battles were by no means the only form of warfare in this period. One example of the first point is provided by the Vandal expedition. The battles of Ad Decimum and Tricamarum were important in deciding the outcome of the expedition, but it must be acknowledged that Belisarius's success, achieved with a comparatively small force of 15,000 men, also owed much to the fact that, at the time of the invasion, the Vandal king Gelimer was distracted by revolts in Tripolitania and Sardinia.[56] Consider also the Gothic war in Italy, where weak and divided Gothic leadership contributed to Belisarius's rapid success in the early years of the war, while the emergence of an energetic and able leader in Totila and bickering amongst Roman generals played major parts in the military balance swinging back in favour of the Goths during the 540s. The impact of such contingent circumstances needs to be taken into account as part of any overall assessment.

As for other forms of fighting, siege warfare was another important dimension of military action during Justinian's reign, particularly in the Gothic war and in conflict with Persia. One would have expected to find imperial forces enjoying a significant advantage over the Goths in this sphere, where a long tradition of Roman technological expertise had the potential to make a major difference. That this tradition continued to be valued in the sixth century is evident from military treatises,[57] but its continued practice is, somewhat surprisingly, rather less evident in

Procopius's narrative of the Gothic war. Belisarius did deploy a range of different types of siege artillery in his defence of Rome in 537, to good effect,[58] but there is little if any mention of such devices in the numerous other sieges of the war. As for capturing cities, the use by imperial troops of simple and obvious aids such as ladders is occasionally mentioned,[59] but otherwise it was the Goths who tried, on one occasion, to use more ambitious assault equipment, in the form of towers and battering rams, albeit unsuccessfully.[60] For the most part, Belisarius and other imperial generals seem to have relied primarily on blockades to capture cities in the Italian peninsula, cutting off supplies of food and water and then waiting for hunger and dehydration to take effect, although this did not make for a speedy resolution. Imperial success in capturing cities was sometimes also aided by the non-Gothic Italian inhabitants' deciding that their interests were better served by abandoning the Gothic for the imperial cause, though this was by no means as widespread a trend as has sometimes been thought.[61]

Sieges were also an important feature of conflict with Persia during Justinian's reign, especially in the Caucasus, though here Roman success was hampered by the fact that, unlike the Goths, the Persians had significant capability and experience in siege warfare, whether in defence or attack (as demonstrated in the war of 502–505), while the loyalties of the Caucasian peoples were divided and even more prone to sudden changes than those of the inhabitants of Italy.[62]

In addition to siege warfare, mention should also be made of what is perhaps best described as irregular warfare – that is, some enemies' use of ambush and hit-and-run tactics designed to offset Roman advantages in more conventional modes of warfare and to wear down the Roman will to fight. This was an approach particularly suited to certain terrains, such as the desert regions of North Africa and Syria, where camels gave Berber and Arab tribesmen important advantages in terms of mobility across hostile environments.[63] It was a style of warfare also suited to the mountainous regions of the Caucasus and to parts of the lower Danube basin, where Slavic raiders tended to operate in small groups in heavily wooded country.[64] The Romans tried to counter such tactics by enlisting the help of allies able to operate effectively in such conditions and by trying to manoeuvre such enemies into situations where they had to give battle, but it remains the case that this was an area of warfare where Roman effectiveness was significantly reduced.

Justinian's armies, then, generally remained effective fighting forces in conventional forms of warfare and demonstrated some adaptability to changing circumstances so far as the use of cavalry and the bow was concerned. When they struggled in conventional campaigns, notably the Gothic war, the reasons can usually be traced to factors extraneous to the inherent fighting quality of the troops, notably problems with payment of soldiers and bickering amongst commanders. The greater challenges posed by enemies who avoided pitched battles and were better adapted to hostile terrains reveals the limitations of Roman flexibility in the military sphere, although diplomacy was often able to offset those limitations to varying degrees through the creation of judicious alliances – a reminder that warfare cannot be divorced from its political context.

## The Impact of War

> Because of this situation the inhabitants of Emilia left their homes and went to Picenum, thinking that, since that region was adjacent to the sea, it could not be suffering from a complete lack of food supplies. The inhabitants of Tuscany, no less than the others, were attacked by famine for the same reason, and the many who were living in the mountains ate loaves made from the acorns off oak trees, which they ground up just like grain. As was to be expected, many of these people fell victim to all manner of diseases, and there were only a few who threw them off and recovered. Indeed it is said that among the Roman farmers in Picenum no fewer than fifty thousand perished from starvation, and a great many more north of the Adriatic Sea.
>
> – Procopius, *Wars*, 6.20.18–22, trans. H. B. Dewing, with revisions

In focusing on the infrastructure of waging war and the effectiveness of the army, it is easy to lose sight of the impact of war on noncombatants, but it is an important ingredient in trying to gain a balanced understanding of warfare during Justinian's reign. An obvious starting point is that of the immediate short-term effects of war on civilians. While acknowledging the existence of considerable regional variation, a useful way of structuring such a survey is to consider urban communities first, before turning to the countryside.[65]

Warfare impinged most forcefully on urban communities in the context of sieges, as experienced by many Italian cities during the Gothic war and by those on the empire's eastern frontier with Persia. The heavy reliance on the strategy of blockade noted previously meant that some sieges were protracted – the city of Rome, for example, twice underwent lengthy investments of a year's duration in the space of a decade (537–538, 545–546) – with predictable consequences for food supply. Procopius's accounts of various sieges in Italy refer to communities brought to the point of consuming nettles, dogs, and mice, and even, in one instance, excrement; whether reports of cannibalism during the siege of Amida in 504–505 should be taken literally is another matter, though they surely reflect the understandable sense of utter desperation experienced by those trapped in such circumstances.[66] Perhaps also partly fuelled by the frustrations the length of some sieges generated in the attackers, the fall of some cities was accompanied by the massacre of inhabitants – most notoriously following the Gothic capture of Milan (538) and Tibur (545), but also by the Persians at Antioch (540) and by imperial troops at Naples (536), at least until they were restrained by Belisarius.[67] Those not killed were typically enslaved, which, in the case of those captured by the Persians, usually meant deportation to Iran – again, Antioch (540) was the most famous case, with Khusro apparently settling the prisoners in a specially built city, modelled on Antioch, near the Persian capital Ctesiphon.[68] In an analogous manner, the Romans sometimes removed captured enemy males from one theatre of war and redeployed them as troops in another distant theatre, as happened to Vandals posted to the eastern frontier, and Persians to Italy.[69]

Similar themes emerge from a consideration of the impact of warfare on rural inhabitants. With regard to sustenance, armies on campaign relied heavily on helping themselves to crops in the localities through which they passed. So, from the early stages of Belisarius's invasion of Italy, a report has survived to the effect that "a large [Gothic] army has arrived, known to be assigned to the defence of the state, and is reported to have ravaged the fields of Lucania and Bruttium, and to have lessened the wealth of those regions by enthusiastic robbery,"[70] while in the years immediately after the conclusion of the main conflict Pope Pelagius I is found writing to contacts in Gaul and North Africa requesting financial and material aid because of the devastation experienced by church estates in Italy as a result of the war.[71] As reported by Procopius in the passage at the head of this section, there was widespread famine across the countryside in Emilia, Tuscany and Picenum in the late 530s, with people resorting to living on acorns and grass and tens of thousands dying of starvation.[72] The reason for the shortage of food in this latter case appears to have been lack of manpower to plant and harvest crops, due partly to Gothic farmers serving in their army, partly to the flight of rural inhabitants from war-affected areas – perhaps into fortified urban settlements, perhaps further afield to regions less directly affected by conflict.[73] The demography of these parts may also have been affected by imperial forces enslaving Gothic inhabitants.[74] Archaeological evidence for the destruction and abandonment of villas in central and southern Italy in the 540s has been linked to the impact of the Gothic war,[75] while there is a reference in a legal document of the period from Ravenna to slaves "who have run away during these disturbed times,"[76] a phenomenon which must have been widespread.[77] At the same time, it is important to bear in mind that there will have been considerable regional variation in the impact of the war. "The total desolation of Italy in these years has certainly been exaggerated."[78]

Although there is much less in way of circumstantial evidence from North Africa on which to base conclusions, Procopius's assessment of the situation there following a decade or more of conflict with mutinous soldiers and with Berber tribesmen was pessimistic – "by reason of the previous wars and insurrections, the land remained for the most part destitute of human habitation."[79] While this is likely to contain a degree of overstatement, there is some corroboration in survey evidence that suggests "a decline in rural settlements in the sixth and seventh centuries."[80] There are repeated references to Slavic raiders carrying off provincials from the Balkans during the 540s and 550s,[81] while in the east, the complete absence of dated inscriptions between 540 and 550 from the otherwise abundant epigraphic record of the villages of the Syrian limestone massif has been interpreted as reflecting the deportation of significant numbers of rural inhabitants of the region by Persian forces in 540.[82] It is worth noting, however, that there are likely to have been some, admittedly limited, short-term benefits resulting from warfare, in the form of the programme of fortification construction initiated by Justinian in many parts of the empire, much of which is reflected in Procopius's panegyrical *Buildings*.[83] As the work on such structures was, by the sixth century, done by paid rather than forced labour,[84] it will have generated employment in localities, even if the financing did not always come from external sources.[85]

As one would have expected, then, demographic and economic dislocation emerge as the major ways in which warfare had immediate, short-term effects on communities in the main theatres of war during Justinian's reign. Of course, such dislocation can also have longer-term consequences, and indeed, as will have been apparent from some of the comments above, it is not always easy to maintain a clear distinction between short-term and longer-term effects. However, the circumstances of the sixth century particularly complicate any attempt to offer pronouncements about the more lasting effects of warfare. This is partly because of the need to take into account the impact of the plague in the 540s and its regular recurrence in subsequent decades, which also caused significant demographic and economic dislocation, and partly because in some regions, renewed warfare flared up soon after the end of Justinian's reign – notably in Italy, with the Lombard invasion of 568, in North Africa with the Berbers, and in the east, with Persia from 572 onwards.[86] In the specific case of Antioch, a succession of earthquakes in the 520s had already devastated the city before its sack by the Persians in 540.[87] Separating out the effects of these different events from those of war during Justinian's reign is obviously very difficult, especially with respect to archaeological evidence. In addition, there is the question of longer-term demographic and economic trends that can be traced back to the fifth century and which ultimately are likely to have exercised a more profound influence on sixth-century developments than did the wars of Justinian's reign.[88]

On the central issue of the fate of cities and towns, a vast modern literature leaves little doubt about the problems involved in determining the relative roles of a complex multiplicity of causes.[89] Consideration of two of the most important cities of the Italian peninsula illustrates the difficulties entailed in trying to generalise on this subject. On the one hand, Rome was clearly badly affected by the succession of lengthy sieges it underwent during the Gothic war, although at the same time it has been argued that the impact of warfare in the sixth century "only accelerated a process of deterioration that for centuries had worn down the city of Rome,"[90] while there is also some reason to doubt the more pessimistic demographic scenarios.[91] On the other hand, Naples appears to have been in a stronger economic position in the second half of the sixth century than it had been for some time, despite also undergoing a number of (admittedly shorter) sieges, though this may well have been a case of Naples benefiting at the expense of other, more severely affected communities in Campania.[92]

For the great majority of inhabitants of war zones during Justinian's reign, then, the direct impact of war is, unsurprisingly, likely to have been overwhelmingly negative. It is conceivable that those living in North Africa and Italy might have felt the hardships to be worthwhile if reincorporation into the empire had brought tangible benefits, but it is difficult to identify any of an enduring nature. They were once more subject to the demands of imperial tax collectors, who, by all accounts, seem to have been intent on making up for lost time.[93] Although the removal of Arian overlords ought to have been beneficial in the religious sphere, Justinian's policies in connection with the Three Chapters controversy served only to alienate religious sympathies in the West.[94] Against this background, a report that some inhabitants of Rome sent to Justinian's successor Justin II a petition critical of the new imperial governor of Italy acquires plausibility and provides a fitting epilogue to Justinian's grand schemes: "It would be better for the Romans to serve the Goths than the Greeks when the eunuch Narses is a ruler who subjects us to slavery and our most pious prince does not know it. Either deliver us from his hand, or we and the Roman citizens will serve the barbarians."[95]

## Notes

1 For references to the post, see *PLRE* 2, s.v. Iustinianus 7; the assumption of his lack of combat experience is, of course, an argument from silence, but if he had seen military action, one would have expected him or Procopius to have alluded to it, whether for good or ill.

2 On the equestrian statue, see Procopius, *Buildings*, 1.2.1–12; on the Chalke mosaic, Procopius, *Buildings*, 1.10.15–19. For further discussion of the issue of non-campaigning emperors in late antiquity, see A. D. Lee, "War and the State in Late Antiquity," in *The Cambridge History of Greek and Roman Warfare*, ed. H. van Wees, P. Sabin, and M. Whitby (forthcoming).

3 See, for example, J. B. Bury, *History of the Later Roman Empire from the Death of Theodosius to the Death of Justinian* (London, 1923), vol. 2, chaps. 16–19; E. Stein, *Histoire du Bas-Empire* (Paris, 1949), vol. 2, chaps. 6, 9–10; J. A. S. Evans, *The Age of Justinian* (London, 1996), 114–119, chap. 3. See also the chapters in this volume by W. Pohl "Justinian and the Barbanian Kingdoms" (Chap. 18) and G. Greatrex, "Byzantium and the East in the Sixth Century" (Chap. 19).

4 It is worth noting that while there are studies of Procopius's value as a source for aspects of the military history of the sixth century (e.g., A. Müller, "Das Heer Justinians (nach Procop und Agathias)," *Philologus* 71 [1912], 101–138), no overall detailed assessment of his value and limitations as a military historian exists, though G. Greatrex, *Rome and Persia at War, 502–532* (Leeds, 1998), makes a start with reference to the first book of the *Wars*, and E. A. Thompson, *Romans and Barbarians: The Decline of the Western Empire* (Madison, Wis., 1982), chap. 5, has some pertinent commentary on his account of the war in Italy.

5 See A. Cameron, *Procopius and the Sixth Century* (London, 1985), chap. 8; B. Shaw, "War and Violence," in *Late Antiquity: A Guide to the Postclassical World*, ed. G. Bowersock, P. Brown, and O. Grabar (Cambridge, Mass., 1999), at 132–133.

6 See, for example, his tendentious accounts of the battle of Callinicum (531) (for differing perspectives, see Cameron, *Procopius*, 158, and Greatrex, *Rome and Persia*, 194–195) and of the Persian campaign of 542 (M. Whitby, "Recruitment in Roman Armies from Justinian to Heraclius (ca. 565–615)," in *The Byzantine and Early Islamic Near East*, vol. 3, *States, Resources, and Armies*, ed. Averil Cameron [Princeton, N.J., 1995], at 74); on the Italian campaigns, see K. Hannestad, "Les Forces militaires

d'après la Guerre Gothique de Procope," *Classica et Mediaevalia* 21 (1960): 136–183. There is, of course, the further issue of his very negative portrayal of Belisarius in the opening chapters of the *Secret History*, though this relates to his personal life rather than his military competence.

7 See Shaw, "War and Violence," 132–133, citing Procopius's account of the siege of Rome in 538.

8 For discussion of Agathias and Menander, see M. Whitby, "Greek Historical Writing after Procopius: Variety and Vitality," in *The Byzantine and Early Islamic Near East*, vol. 1, *Problems in the Literary Source Material*, ed. Averil Cameron and L. I. Conrad (1992), 25–45.

9 For discussion, see F. R. Trombley and J. W. Watt, *The Chronicle of Pseudo-Joshua the Stylite* (2000), xi–li.

10 For discussion of the date and authorship of *On Strategy*, see G. T. Dennis, ed. and trans., *Three Byzantine Military Treatises* (Washington, D.C. 1985), 1–7; a case has been made attributing it to a certain Syrianus, author of another treatise, on naval matters (C. Zuckerman, "The Military Compendium of Syrianus Magister," *JÖB* 40 [1990]: 209–224), though for doubts about placing *On Strategy* in the sixth century, see A. D. Lee and J. Shepard, "A Double Life: Placing the *Peri presbeon*," *Byzantinoslavica* 52 (1991): 15–39. For discussion of the date and authorship of the *Strategikon*, see M. Whitby, *The Emperor Maurice and His Historian: Theophylact Simocatta on Persian and Balkan Warfare* (Oxford, 1988), 130–132.

11 For Procopius's presentation of this episode as a veiled critique of Justinianic policy, see R. Scott, "The Classical Tradition in Byzantine Historiography," in *Byzantium and the Classical Tradition*, ed. M. Mullett and R. Scott (Birmingham, 1981), 73–74.

12 For overviews of the army in the sixth century, see R. Grosse, *Römische Militärgeschichte von Gallienus bis zum Beginn der byzantinischen Themenverfassung* (Berlin, 1920), 272–320; Jones, *LRE*, 654–686; G. Ravegnani, *Soldati di Bisanzio in età Giustinianea* (Rome, 1988); M. Whitby, "The Army, c. 420–602" in *CAH* 14, ed. Averil Cameron, B. Ward-Perkins, and M. Whitby (2000), 288–314.

13 Jones, *LRE*, 655–656.

14 Jones, *LRE*, 661–662; P. J. Casey, "Justinian, the *Limitanei*, and Arab-Byzantine Relations in the Sixth Century," *Journal of Roman Archaeology* 9 (1996): 214–222.

15 See the section "Effectiveness" in this chapter.

16 Jones, *LRE*, 663–668.

17 Whitby, "Recruitment," 116–119.

18 Agathias, *Histories*, 5.13.7.

19 Jones, *LRE*, 684; Whitby, "Recruitment," 73–75; W. Treadgold, *Byzantium and Its Army, 284–1081* (1995), 59–64; Haldon, *War, State and Society in the Byzantine World* (*WSS*) (London, 1999), 99–100.

20 Haldon, *WSS*, 100–101.

21 Procopius, *Wars*, 1.8.4, Ps.-Joshua the Stylite, *Chronicle*, 54 (for the figure).

22 Jones, *LRE*, 684–685.

23 Maurice, *Strategikon*, 3.8, 10.

24 Jones, *LRE*, 668–670; J. Haldon, *Recruitment and Conscription in the Byzantine Army, c. 550–950* (Vienna, 1979), 20–40.

25 Whitby, "Recruitment," 79–83.

26 See Whitby, "Recruitment," 103–110, for references and discussion.

27 See J. L. Teall, "The Barbarians in Justinian's Armies," *Speculum* 40 (1965): 294–322, and the critique by Whitby, "Recruitment," 92–103.

28 P. Sarris, "The Justinianic Plague: Origins and Effects," *Continuity and Change* 17 (2002): 175–179.

29 Whitby, "Recruitment," 97. See further P. Horden, "Mediterranean Plague in the Age of Justinian," Chap. 6 in this volume.

30 Anonymous, *On Strategy*, 2.4 (trans. G. Dennis).

31 M. Hendy, *Studies in the Byzantine Monetary Economy, c. 300–1450* (1985): 157–159; M. Hendy, "Economy and State in Late Rome and Early Byzantium: An Introduction," in *The Economy, Fiscal Administration, and Coinage of Byzantium* (Northampton, 1989), study 1, 17; Treadgold, *Byzantium and Its Army*, 194–198.

32 Jones, *LRE*, 670–674.

33 Procopius, *Wars*, 4.16.3; *P. Rylands*, 609; *P. London*, 1663; *P. Cairo*, 67321.

34 Justinian, *Novel*, 41 (536); Justin II, *Novel*, 11 (575); Jones, *LRE*, 280.

35 Ps.-Joshua the Stylite, *Chronicle*, 54, 70, 77.

36 *PLRE* 2, s.v. Demosthenes 4, Archelaus 5; see also *PLRE* 3, s.v. Symmachus 2.

37 H. Elton, *Warfare in Roman Europe, AD 350–425* (Oxford, 1996), 237 (estimate for an army of 13,000 in the mid-fourth century).

38 Haldon, *WSS*, 289–291. Wagons receive occasional mention in Procopius's narrative: see *Wars*, 4.17.2, 6.5.2–3.

39 See, for example, Procopius, *Wars*, 5.8.6; 14.17. Totila did try to develop Gothic naval capacity during the 540s, which had at least some success in disrupting Roman maritime supply lines (Procopius, *Wars*, 7.13.5–7).

40 Procopius, *Wars*, 1.13–14, with discussion in Greatrex, *Rome and Persia*, 169–185, J. Haldon, *The Byzantine Wars* (Stroud, 2000), 28–35.

41 Procopius, *Wars*, 1.15.1–17, with discussion in Greatrex, *Rome and Persia*, 185–190.

42 Procopius, *Wars*, 8.8.

43 Procopius, *Wars*, 3.18–19 (Ad Decimum), 4.3 (Tricamarum).

44 Procopius, *Wars*, 4.11–12 (Solomon), Corippus, *Iohannis*, 5, 8.378–656 (John Troglita), with discussion in D. Pringle, *The Defence of Byzantine Africa from Justinian to the Arab Conquest* (Oxford, 1981), chap. 1.

45 Procopius, *Wars*, 8.29–32 (Taginae), 35 (Mons Lactarius), Agathias, *Histories*, 2.7–10 (Casilinus), with discussion in Haldon, *Byzantine Wars*, 37–44.

46 Procopius, *Wars*, 8.40.5–6 (Germanus); Marcellinus, *Chronicle*, s.a. 530 (Mundus).

47 Procopius, *Wars*, 1.18 (Callinicum, with discussion in Greatrex, *Rome and Persia*, 200–207), Procopius, *Wars*, 4.21 (Cillium), 4.28.47–48, Corippus, *Iohannis*, 6.497–773 (Marta), Procopius, *Wars*, 7.4–5 (Faventia, Mugello).

48 See Haldon, *WSS*, 193–197.

49 Procopius, *Wars*, 5.27.26–28; Thompson, *Romans and Barbarians*, 77–81, 86, 90–91.

50 Procopius, *Wars*, 8.31.5, 35.19; 4.11.50; 8.8.30–31.

51 Anonymous, *On Strategy*, 15–16, 18–25; Maurice, *Strategikon*, 12B.

52 See Haldon, *Byzantine Wars*, 40, 44. The problem posed by mutinous troops in North Africa in the late 530s was quite a different issue, a matter of political protest at lack of pay and other complaints and not one of discipline in the face of battle.

53 See also Procopius, *Wars*, 6.3.23–29.

54 On training, see Agathias, *Histories*, 2.1; on penalties, Procopius, *Wars*, 3.12.8–22, Agathias, *Histories*, 2.7; on rewards, Procopius, *Wars*, 7.1.8, 8.31.9, Theophylact

Simocatta, 2.6.10–11; on booty, Procopius, *Wars*, 4.21.24 (where Solomon's refusal implies the norm); on language of comradeship, Procopius, *Wars*, 3.12.20, 19.2; 4.15.16, 16.12; 5.28.6; 8.23.14; on the wounded and burial, Theophylact Simocatta, 2.6.12; Maurice, *Strategikon,* 12B.6. For increasing use of Christian symbols to motivate troops in the second half of the sixth century, see M. Whitby, "*Deus nobiscum*: Christianity, Warfare, and Morale in Late Antiquity," in *Modus Operandi: Essays in Honour of Geoffrey Rickman*, ed. M. Austin *et al.* (London, 1998), 195; note also Corippus, *Iohannis*, 8.318–369 (John Troglita sets up an altar in camp prior to battle).

55 For example, Procopius, *Wars*, 7.1.28–33; 11.13–16; see also 2.7.37.

56 Procopius, *Wars*, 3.10.22–34; 11.22–3; 14.9.

57 Anonymous, *On Strategy*, 9–13, Maurice, *Strategikon*, 10.1, 3.

58 Procopius, *Wars*, 5.21.14–22; 23.9–12; see also P. Southern and K. Dixon, *The Late Roman Army* (London, 1996), chap. 8.

59 For example, Procopius, *Wars*, 5.10.21–23.

60 Procopius, *Wars*, 5.21.3–12.

61 P. Amory, *People and Identity in Ostrogothic Italy, 489–554* (Cambridge, 1997), 165–194; in contrast with Thompson, *Romans and Barbarians*, 92–109, and J. Moorhead, "Italian Loyalties during Justinian's Gothic War," *Byzantion* 53 (1983), 575–596.

62 For specific instances of skill in sieges in the Caucasian theater, see Procopius, *Wars*, 8.11.27–38; 12.21–27. For convenient summaries of warfare in the Caucasus in this period, see D. Braund, *Georgia in Antiquity: A History of Colchis and Transcaucasian Iberia, 550 BC–AD 562* (Oxford, 1994), chap. 9, G. Greatrex and S. N. C. Lieu, *The Roman Eastern Frontier and the Persian Wars, Part II: AD 363–630* (London, 2002), chap. 8. See also Greatrex's section on Caucasus, in Chap. 19 in this volume, "Byzantium and the East in the Sixth Century."

63 On Berbers, see Averil Cameron, "Gelimer's Laughter: The Case of Byzantine Africa," in *Tradition and Innovation in Late Antiquity*, ed. F. M. Clover and R. S. Humphreys (Madison, Wis., 1989), 171–190, at 179; D. Mattingly and R. B. Hitchner, "Roman Africa: An Archaeological Review," *JRS* 85 (1995): 211 nn. 468–469 (further references); Arabs: B. Isaac, *The Limits of Empire: The Roman Army in the East* (Oxford, 1990), 235–249.

64 On the Caucasus, see n. 62; on the lower Danube, Whitby, *The Emperor Maurice*, 80–83.

65 In addition to the specific references here, helpful introductions to the experience of the relevant regions can be found in *CAH* 14, chaps. 19–20, 21b, 23.

66 Procopius, *Wars*, 6.21.26, 7.17.16–19; Ps.-Joshua the Stylite, *Chronicle*, 77.

67 Procopius, *Wars*, 6.21.39–42; 7.10.22; 2.8.34; 5.10.29.

68 Procopius, *Wars*, 2.9.14; 14.1–4; see also Ps.-Joshua the Stylite, *Chronicle*, 53 (Amida, 503).

69 Procopius, *Wars*, 4.14.17–18; 2.19.24–25; D. Hoffmann, "Der *numerus equitum Persoiustinianorum* auf einer Mosaikinschrift von Sant'Eufemia in Grado," *Aquileia Nostra* 32–33 (1961–1962): 81–98.

70 Cassiodorus, *Variae*, 12.5.3 (trans. S. Barnish). Compare Belisarius's need to remind his troops in Vandal North Africa to pay for supplies they obtained from locals (Procopius, *Wars*, 3.16.1–8), and the reputation of troops under his command in Italy for restraint in this respect (7.1.8–10), implying that such behaviour was unusual.

71 Pelagius I, *Letters*, 4, 9, 85.
72 Procopius, *Wars*, 6.20.15–21; there were also reports of cannibalism (6.20.27–31).
73 Procopius, *Wars*, 6.7.29; 17.1–2.
74 See Procopius, *Wars*, 6.7.25–34; 10.1.
75 A. Small and R. Buck, *The Excavations of San Giovanni di Ruoti*, vol. 1 (Toronto, 1994), 22, 28–29, 121; S. Barnish, "Pigs, Plebeians, and *Potentes:* Rome's economic hinterland, c. 350–600 AD," *Proceedings of the British School at Rome* 55 (1987): 182.
76 *P. Ital.*, 13. (*Die nichtliterarischen lateinischen Papyri Italiens aus der zeit 445–700.* Ed. J.O. Tjader. Lund, 1955).
77 See C. Wickham, *Early Medieval Italy* (London, 1981), 25.
78 Wickham, *Early Medieval Italy*, 26.
79 Procopius, *Wars*, 8.17.22 (trans. H. B. Dewing); see also 4.23.26–28; 28.52; and Cameron, "Gelimer's Laughter."
80 Mattingly and Hitchner, "Roman Africa," 189–196, 213 (quotation).
81 Procopius, *Wars*, 7.14.11; 13.24; 8.25.4.
82 F. Trombley, "War and Society in Rural Syria, c. 502–613 AD: Observations on the Epigraphy," *BMGS* 21 (1997): 176 n. 85. Note also the reports of Persian deportations of villagers in Armenia in 502 (Ps.-Joshua the Stylite, *Chronicle*, 48).
83 For a recent collection of important papers on the *Buildings*, see *AnTard* 8 (2000): 5–180.
84 Jones, *LRE*, vol. 1, 462.
85 Pringle, *Defence of Byzantine Africa*, 90–93; R. Coates-Stephens, "The Walls and Aqueducts of Rome in the Early Middle Ages, AD 500–1000," *JRS* 88 (1998): 167; Trombley, "War and Society in Rural Syria," 167–169.
86 Cf. T. S. Brown, *Gentlemen and Officers: Imperial Administration and Aristocratic Power in Byzantine Italy, AD 554–800* (London, 1984), chaps. 1–3; Pringle, *Defence of Byzantine Africa*, 39–43; Trombley, "War and Society in Rural Syria."
87 G. Downey, *A History of Antioch in Syria* (Princeton, N.J., 1961), chap. 18.
88 Cf. Barnish, "Pigs, Plebeians, and *Potentes*"; B. Ward-Perkins, "War, Disruption, and Economic Decline," *CAH* 14:383–386.
89 W. Liebeschuetz, *The Decline and Fall of the Roman City* (Oxford, 2001), offers one interpretation as well as a detailed guide to the literature. See also K. Holum, "The Classical City in the Age of Justinian: Survival and Transformation," Chap. 4 in this volume.
90 R. Krautheimer, *Rome: Profile of a City, 312–1308* (Princeton, N.J., 1980), 64.
91 R. Coates-Stephens, "Housing in Early Medieval Rome," *Proceedings of the British School at Rome* 64 (1996): 239–259.
92 P. Arthur, *Naples: From Roman Town to City-State* (London, 2002).
93 For example, Procopius, *Wars*, 7.1.32.
94 Cf. P. Gray, "The Legacy of Chalcedon: Christological Problems and Their Significance," Chap. 9 in this volume.
95 *Liber Pontificalis*, 63.3 (trans. R. Davis).

# 6: Mediterranean Plague in the Age of Justinian

*Peregrine Horden*

> During these times there was a pestilence, by which the whole human race came near to being annihilated.
>
> – Procopius, *Wars*, 2.22.1, trans. Dewing

Very occasionally the emperor Justinian deserves our sympathy. Epidemics are usually named after their victims: the biblical plague of the Philistines, for example, or the plague of Athens famously described by Thucydides. Yet the pandemic (worldwide epidemic) that struck the empire on an unprecedented scale during Justinian's reign, spreading to northern and western Europe, many parts of the Middle East, and possibly China, has always been treated differently. In the *Secret History* Procopius blamed the emperor's demonic machinations for all the natural disasters of his reign.[1] Even though Justinian himself contracted the disease and its ravages long outlasted him, historians of the sixth century, following Procopius's lead, have written of "the plague of Justinian."[2] This is unfair. In what follows attention will be confined for the most part to plague in sixth-century Byzantium. But the phenomenon is far larger, and to convey its "global" impact, extensive chronology, and questionable biological identity, I shall refer to it more neutrally as the early medieval pandemic (EMP).

## Itineraries

There had doubtless been localized epidemics aplenty in the later Roman and the early Byzantine empires. Yet, when the EMP arrived in 541, there had apparently not been a major one since the 520s. Looking back to approximately a century before his own time, the author of the *Paschal (Easter) Chronicle* recorded a Great Death under the year 529, which may well be a mistaken reference to the EMP.[3] Much later on, though more plausibly, the tenth-century universal chronicler Agapius of Hierapolis mentions a "terrible epidemic" that broke out in 525–526 and lasted for six years.[4] Even these epidemics apparently paled beside that of 541. In the first place it was probably a novel disease. Well before Justinian's time, there may, in the eastern Mediterranean, have been highly restricted outbreaks of a disease with similar symptoms.[5] But those symptoms had not been noticed since the first century AD. To its sixth-century victims this disease seemed wholly without parallel – and not only in symptoms, but in mortality and terrifying speed.

Before worrying further about diagnosis, let us look in more detail at the pandemic's initial phases to establish the geography and character of its movement.[6] (Map 7) The disease arrived on the Mediterranean scene at Pelusium (modern Tell el Farama), a small entrepôt at the extreme eastern edge of the Nile Delta, around the middle of July 541. It had perhaps been transmitted from central Africa via Zanzibar and the Christian Ethiopian kingdom of Axum. Once it had erupted in Pelusium it spread swiftly, presumably by boat, in two directions simultaneously, westward along the north African coast, eastward to coastal Palestine.

In the eastward direction, it has been plotted as first reaching Gaza, on the coast. It then turned inland as well as continuing along the Palestinian littoral, following shipping lanes and caravan routes. Constantinople remained untouched until March or April of 542. But once arrived, the plague raged in the capital until August. By the summer it had also reached Syria. Of major settlements, Antioch was struck first in the early summer of 542, followed by neighboring towns, and the small inland city of Zora in southern Syria. At about the same time, Myra on the Lycian coast and Sykeon in Galatia also succumbed. The disease was spreading rapidly across Asia Minor. By the autumn of 542 it had extended itself to Adarbigana (Media Atropatene) in modern Azerbaijan and reached the army of Persia, which had retreated there from its war with Byzantium.

In its western onslaught, the EMP crossed overland to devastate Alexandria in September 541. It may have been carried to Sicily in late 542. In early 543, it had probably reached Tunisia and was advancing across the Mediterranean reaches of Roman North Africa. It was present in Italy and Illyricum throughout 543, reaching Rome at the end of that year or very soon after. In 543 it is also attested in southern Gaul and

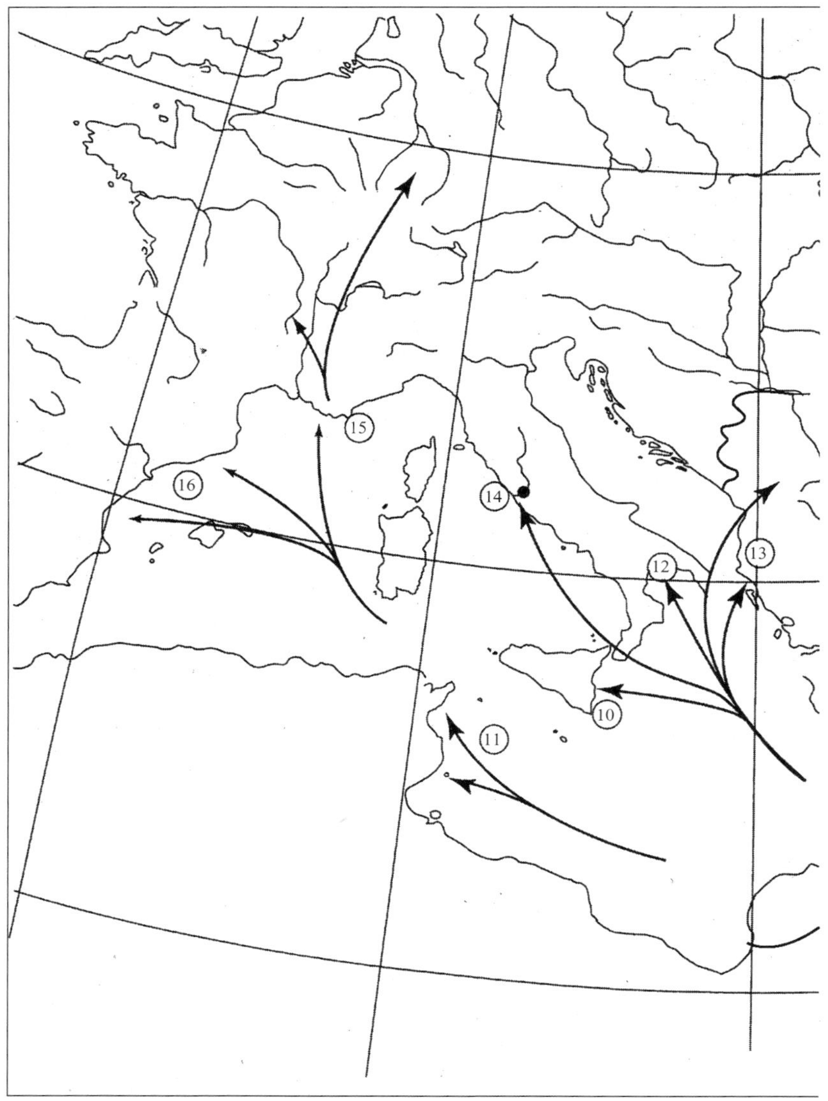


1. Pelusium, July 541
2. Gaza, Aug. 541
3. Jerusalem, 542
4. Antioch, summer 542
5. Myra, summer 542
6. Constantinople, Mar./Apr. 542
7. Sykeon, summer 542
8. Media Atropatene, fall 542

MAP 7. The first wave of the early medieval pandemic, (after Dionysios Stathakopoulos, *Famine and Pestilence in the Late Roman and Early Byzantine Empire: A Systematic Survey of Subsistence Crises and Epidemics* [Aldershot, 2004], chap. 6).

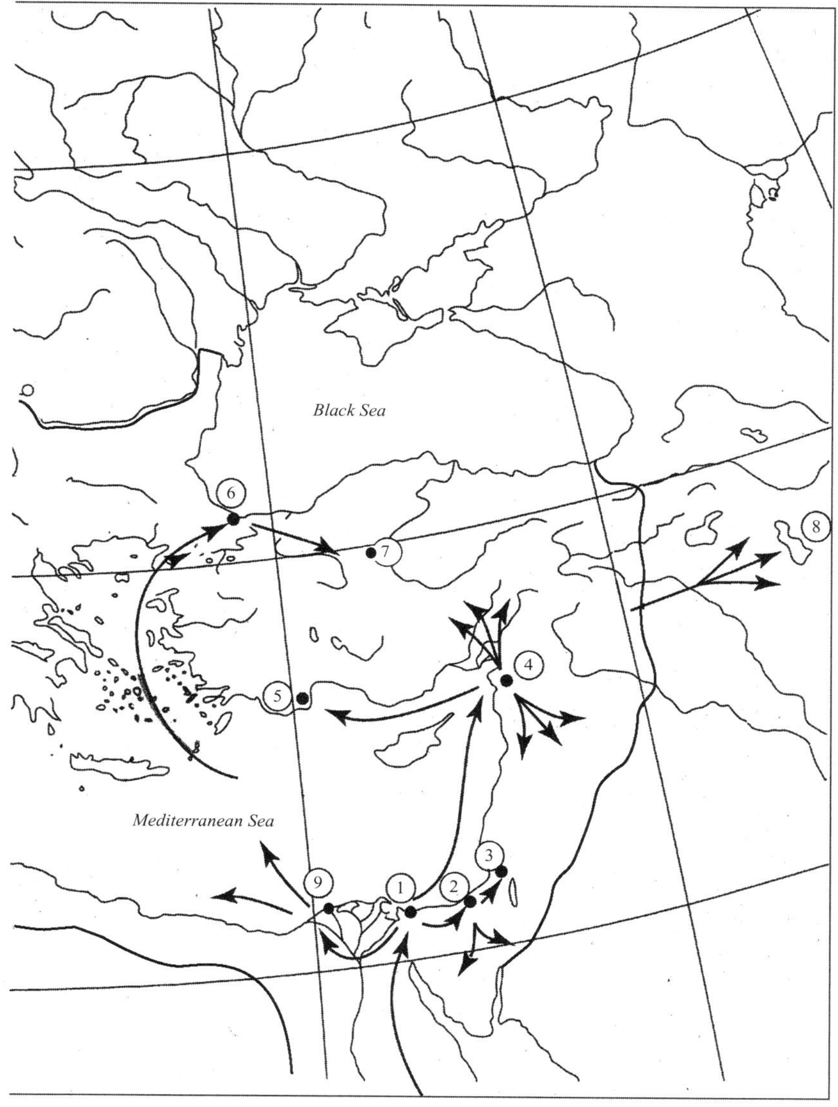


9. Alexandria, Sept. 541
10. Sicily, Dec. 542
11. Tunisia, Jan./Feb. 543
12. Italy, 543–544
13. Illyricum, 543
14. Rome, 543
15. Gaul, 543
16. Spain, 543

parts of Spain, although it seems to have subsided quite quickly in both areas.[7] On March 23, 543 Justinian issued a law in which he declared God's "education" (the epidemic) over; wages, which had soared, were to be restored to their preplague levels.[8] The plague had traversed the Mediterranean world and much of the Middle East in just under two years. It then mysteriously retreated, at least from Justinian's empire. But it may have reached Ireland in 544 or 545 and, just possibly, Wales in 547. There may also at this time have been "satellite" outbreaks as far apart as Finland and the Yemen.[9]

Doubtless the survivors of the 540s profoundly hoped that the pandemic really was over. In fact, so far as the Age of Justinian is concerned, this was only the first wave of many. Constantinople was struck again from February to July, 558, and Cilicia, Syria, and Mesopotamia in 560–561. A third wave reached Gaul in 571 and Constantinople in 573–574. A fourth wave broke in 590–591, with Rome and Antioch its leading casualties. A fifth wave was first evident in Thessaloniki in the summer of 597. It spread to Avar territory in 598, then moved to Constantinople, Asia Minor and Syria in 599, and North Africa in 599–600, finally attaining Ravenna and Verona in 600–601.

Thus battered, Justinian's century came to an end, but the pandemic did not. Eleven more visitations can be documented in the course of the seventh and early eighth centuries. They primarily affected the newly conquered "land of Islam," but there are some attested outbreaks in Byzantium and western Europe (including England in the 660s and perhaps Scandinavia), and others can be inferred because the pandemic had already shown itself to be no respecter of frontiers. The last epidemic in the Mediterranean was probably that which struck Naples in 747.[10] By 750 or quite soon after, the EMP had also disappeared from Islamic territories. It ceased almost as suddenly as it had begun.

I have surveyed the pandemic in these stark geographical and chronological terms first of all to give some idea of its scale. It affected all three continents of the then known world, although most of the Arabian peninsula, and perhaps the central Asian steppes, were free of it, their nomadic populations fortunately lacking the density necessary for its spread.[11]

Some of the geography and chronology given above is secure, based on reliable texts; other parts of it are more conjectural. The waves into which the chronology is divided are constructions of the most authoritative recent historians. They are a best attempt to make sense of the advance and retreat of the pandemic, its periodic disappearances – on average just over every eleven years[12] – until, for reasons that remain wholly obscure, it slipped quietly from the world stage. The combination of geography and chronology given above is also, crucially, based on the assumption that the pandemic, for all its interruptions, is a unitary phenomenon: that one disease is involved throughout, from Finland to the Yemen, Ireland to Iran.

What was that disease? The obvious historical question is still the most controversial. We have to take account of epidemiology – the overall pattern of the disease's behavior in the populations that it struck – as well as the symptoms described in our written evidence. Still, that written evidence is the indispensable starting point, and we need to "listen" to it. The student of the Age of Justinian is fortunate in that the best literary evocations of the EMP's impact fall within the sixth century.

## Descriptions

It is worth stressing first that the texts in question are not medical. Perhaps doctors wrote plague treatises in the sixth century as they would in the fourteenth; if so, nothing survives of them. The general medical texts of the period merely reproduce centuries-old material.[13] If we had only the medical "profession" to rely upon, we would not know of the pandemic's existence.

What we do have are vivid passages of historical writing. The most well known is that of Procopius in his narrative of the Persian Wars.[14] He had returned to Constantinople with Belisarius after the fall of Ravenna and was an eyewitness to the arrival of plague in the city. He describes its universality, which defied all rational explanation:

> It did not come in a part of the world nor upon certain men, nor did it confine itself to any season of the year, so that from such circumstances it might be possible to find subtle explanations of a cause, but it embraced the entire world, and blighted the lives of all men. . . . And it attacked some in the summer season, others in the winter, and still others at the other times of the year.

After mentioning its progress from coastland to interior, he sets out its "folk etiology," the way some people perceived its arrival.

> Apparitions of supernatural beings in human guise of every description were seen by many persons, and those who encountered them thought that they were struck by the man

> they had met in this or that part of the body, as it happened, and immediately upon seeing this apparition they were seized also by the disease.

Then he elaborates on the symptoms, which baffled even the greatest physicians:

> They had a sudden fever. . . . And the body shewed no change from its previous colour, nor was it hot as might be expected when attacked by a fever, nor indeed did any inflammation set in, but the fever was of such a languid sort from its commencement and up till evening that neither to the sick themselves nor to a physician who touched them would it afford any suspicion of danger. . . . But on the same day in some cases, in others on the following day, and in the rest not many days later, a bubonic swelling developed; and this took place not only in the particular part of the body which is called "boubon," that is, below the abdomen, but also inside the armpit, and in some cases also besides the ears, and at different points on the thighs.
>
> Up to this point, then, everything went in about the same way with all who had taken the disease. But from then on very marked differences developed. . . . For there ensued with some a deep coma, with others a violent delirium. . . . And in those cases where neither coma nor delirium came on, the bubonic swelling became mortified and the sufferer, no longer able to endure the pain, died. . . .
>
> Death came in some cases immediately, in others after many days; and with some the body broke out with black pustules about as large as a lentil and these did not survive even one day, but all succumbed immediately. With many also a vomiting of blood ensued without visible cause and straightaway brought death. . . .
>
> Now in those cases where the swelling rose to an unusual size and a discharge of pus had set in, it came about that they escaped from the disease and survived, for clearly the acute condition of carbuncle had found relief in this direction, and this proved to be in general an indication of returning health; but in cases where the swelling preserved its former appearance there ensued those troubles which I have just mentioned.

Then Procopius records the mortality – so great that the dead could not be buried in the customary fashion:

> Now the disease in Byzantium ran a course of four months, and its greatest virulence lasted about three. And at first the deaths were a little more than the normal, then the mortality rose still higher, and afterwards the tale of dead reached five thousand each day, and again it even came to ten thousand and still more than that. . . .
>
> At that time all the customary rites of burial were overlooked. For the dead were not carried out escorted by a procession in the customary manner, nor were the usual chants sung over them, but it was sufficient if one carried on his shoulders the body of one of the dead to the parts of the city which bordered on the sea and flung him down; and there the corpses would be thrown upon skiffs in a heap to be conveyed wherever it might chance.

To our second eyewitness. Traveling through regions recently devastated by the plague, John of Ephesus also includes the folk etiology of the plague's transmission from Egypt:[15]

> When this plague was passing from one land to another, many people saw shapes of bronze boats and figures sitting in them resembling people with their heads cut off. Holding staves, also of bronze, they moved along on the sea and could be seen going whithersoever they headed. These figures were seen everywhere in a frightening fashion, especially at night.

He is eloquent on the state of the countryside between Syria and Constantinople when the first "wave" was at its height:

> In these countries we saw desolate and groaning villages and corpses spread out on the earth, with no one to take up and bury them; other villages where some few people remained and went to and fro carrying and throwing the corpses like a man who rolls stones off his field, going off to cast it away and coming back to take another stone . . . [we saw] fields in all the countries through which we passed from Syria to Thrace, abundant in grain which was becoming white and stood erect, but there was none to reap or gather in.

Mortality in the capital exceeds even Procopius's estimates:

> Thus the people of Constantinople reached the point of disappearing, only few remaining, whereas of those only who had died on the streets – if anybody wants us to name their number, for in fact they were counted – over 300,000 were taken off the streets.

The symptoms are, however, reminiscent of Procopius's description:

> From now on the common people . . . could be seen to be smitten by a single great and harsh blow, and suddenly to fall, apart from a few. Not only those who died, but also those who escaped sudden death were struck with this plague of swellings in their groins, with this disease which they call *boubones*, and which in our Syriac language is translated as "tumours."

And not only people are afflicted:

> Also we saw that this great plague showed its effect on the animals as well, not only on the domesticated but also on the wild, and even on the reptiles of the earth. One could see cattle, dogs, and other animals, *even rats*, with swollen tumours, struck down and dying. (Emphasis added)

To these vivid evocations could be added the later testimony of the historian Evagrius, who saw plague not as divisible into waves but as lasting continuously from 542 until the time of his writing, the 590s.[16] For him too, the epidemic was universal, though utterly capricious in its geography and seasonality, sparing some cities but not others, seizing some quarters of cities but bypassing others, wiping out entire families while not touching any of those around them. Evagrius knew whereof he wrote. He contracted the disease as a schoolboy but survived; several members of his family and household perished, however. He describes symptoms different from those recorded by Procopius and John. In some, he writes, the plague was first evident in bloody and swollen eyes and moved down the body; others had severe diarrhea; others still buboes and fever. Some died suddenly after two or three days; others went mad. Some contracted the disease from the company of the sick; others who had lost members of their family tried to infect themselves and could not, as if the disease were thwarting them. Because Evagrius had firsthand experience of the pandemic, his account has sometimes been read rather straightforwardly; it is in fact a highly artful exploration of every conceivable contradiction in the disease's behavior.

## Diagnoses

For all students of the period, these texts and a few others like them are the materials for diagnosis. To the question of what the EMP was, three main answers have been given, one of them endemic (as it were) to historians of the sixth century, two others imported.

It is one of these imports that we might consider first. It provides in some ways the simplest response to any request for diagnosis. The plague was what its sufferers and observers said it was – no more, no less.[17] They – at least those who thought and wrote in Latin or Greek – characterized it as a *plaga* or *loimos* (or *thanatikon*).[18] They did not have a name for the disease (although writers in Arabic did, distinguishing this "plague" from other kinds of epidemic).[19] It was, simply, a great pestilence or mortality. But its particular etiology was conceived in culturally specific ways, such as headless supernatural seafarers, or an imbalance of humors caused by corrupt air, or divine chastisement. People experienced its symptoms as, variously, a severe fever, delirium, insomnia, acute pain in the *bubones*, and vomiting of blood.

And that is all there is to be said. Any given disease is at once a biological, a psychological, and a social phenomenon; and the biological must not be privileged in defining it. Today, diseases are isolated, named, and understood in the laboratory. Before the laboratory, however, different approaches prevailed: the diagnosis was more a judgment about the patient, and his or her environment, as a whole. The way the disease was conceptualized determined the way it was experienced, and that determined what it was. This approach to the problem of diagnosis is, in philosophical terms, a version of epistemological relativism. The nature of something is entirely relative to the way in which knowledge of it is acquired. Each age has its own culture and thus its own diseases. We cannot ask whether plague in the sixth century is the same as plague in the twenty-first – not because the answer is difficult, but because there are no criteria of sameness. There can therefore be no retrospective diagnosis, no imposition of our disease categories onto the very different ones of the past. Indeed, we might say that there are no *diseases*, there are only culturally specific *illnesses* – and our early medieval pandemic is one of them. Since the emperor contracted it and had his own experience of it, it really is, in that special sense, the plague of Justinian.

I have described this philosophically rigid approach in some detail because, though influential with respect to other periods, it has, so far, been alien to the historiography of the sixth century. When it arrives in late antique studies, it will encounter fierce resistance. Not surprisingly, historians of medicine and disease, reluctant to remain on the "surface" of the texts, and confident in the applicability to the remote past of the nosology of modern biomedicine, have long espoused retrospective diagnosis; and they have long known what the EMP really was. Theirs is the "endemic" approach to the question of diagnosis, to which we turn next before registering another import from outside the field.

The EMP was bubonic plague, *Yersinia pestis*, and its pulmonary and septicemic variants. It is a disease of rats (as John of Ephesus seemingly noted) and of their fleas, with human fleas and direct person-to-person transmission as occasional adjuncts. The details are familiar, are repeated in virtually any book with "plague" or "Black Death" in the title published before 2000, and need not be rehearsed at length here. I quote from the unexceptionable summary of a medically experienced historian:[20]

> Bubonic plague epidemics occurred as *Yersinia pestis*, a rodent disease that was communicated to humans through the bite of infected fleas. Humans have exceedingly poor immune defenses to this organism, and within 6 days of infection most victims develop a grossly swollen lymph node, a bubo, signifying the body's attempt to contain and arrest multiplication of *Y. pestis*. On the average, around 60 percent of those infected died within a week after the appearance of the bubo. . . .
>
> With the historically ironic exception of western Europe, *Y. pestis* today occurs naturally throughout the world among the wide variety of rodents and lagomorphs (i.e., rabbits and related species). . . . the "disease," then, is not always a disease, and it is ecologically very complex. Indeed, it is occasional ecological change or disturbance that brings

> susceptible rodents into contact with *Y. pestis*. Historically the most important of these rodents is considered to be *Rattus rattus*, the common, commensal black . . . house rat, that literally "shares man's table." When infected by *Y. pestis* these susceptible animals die quickly of an overwhelming infection, with blood levels of the microbe so high that their rat fleas imbibe large numbers of organisms. . . .
>
> Human plague usually arises after an epizootic plague has produced high mortality among susceptible rodents, when infected fleas, deprived of rodent hosts, begin to feed on humans. Although some historians speak of "endemic plague," no such phenomenon can exist. Humans do not normally carry the *Y. pestis* organism, and thus cannot infect fleas or otherwise pass the disease to new hosts. For human communities, plague is an acute infection ultimately derived from infected rodents. . . . Once a human is infected with *Y. pestis*, the organism rapidly replicates at the site of the flea bite. This area can subsequently become necrotic, where dead tissue blackens to produce a carbuncle or necrotic pustule often called "carbone" in many historical accounts. But in many cases the progress of infection is too rapid for this to happen. The lymphatic system attempts to drain the infection to the regional lymph node, where organisms and infected cells can be phagocytized (ingested by macrophages and white blood cells). That node becomes engorged with blood and cellular debris, creating the grossly swollen bubo. Because infected fleas usually bite an exposed area of the body, often a limb or the face, the location of the subsequent bubo is often visible. Frequent sites are the groin, the axilla, or the cervical lymph nodes. . . . the acute formation of a bubo, visible in 60 percent of bubonic plague victims, is pathognomonic of plague, meaning that no other disease commonly causes this reaction.

That seems to settle the matter. Those for whom retrospective diagnosis is philosophically permissible have mostly had no difficulty with the EMP. The telltale buboes are not only referred to in Byzantine histories such as those reviewed above; they appear in descriptions of plague sufferers that were written in Italy, Spain, Gaul, and Britain. To take only two further examples, for Gregory of Tours, writing in the 580s, this was *lues inguinaria*, "the groin plague"; for Paul the Deacon, recording around 790 an epidemic that struck northwest Italy in the sixth century, "there began to appear in the groins [*inguinibus*] of men . . . a swelling of the glands [*glandulae*], after the manner of a nut or date, presently followed by an unbearable fever."[21]

In such material there also seem to be represented the fever, delirium, diarrhea, and vomiting characteristic of modern cases of infection by *Yersinia pestis*; the black pustules that can form where the fleas bite; the rapid death that marks out the septicemic form of plague; the person-to-person transmission that is a sign of the pneumonic type (although the role of this in the EMP has been extensively and inconclusively debated);[22] and the patchy incidence combined with long-distance transmission (usually by shipborne infected rats or fleas) that has so often been a feature of later epidemics.

Ancient and modern pathology apparently match quite well. Moreover, discrepancies are easily explained by the nature of the ancient evidence. Some of the texts in question were written by eyewitnesses, but none of them can count as clinical descriptions. Complete accord with modern symptomatology would almost be suspicious. Even in modern times, not many people have wholly observed bubonic plague run its full course in a patient without either running away or intervening.

Today, then, virtually all students of the EMP reckon its diagnosis settled. The doubts come from outside, from those studying the Black Death of the fourteenth to seventeenth century. This is the last of the three possible approaches to diagnosis. The doubts will not easily be dispelled and those new to the plague of Justinian should be aware of them, even if ultimately they prefer one of the other two approaches just outlined: that of relativism (the disease was precisely what its sufferers said it was), or that of the conventional diagnosis (bubonic plague).

## Inferences

First, though, it needs to be shown why the Black Death may be relevant. The EMP is commonly held to be the earliest of three pandemics of plague that have so far affected the globe. The second was the Black Death, which struck Europe in the 1340s and continued to return in waves for almost twice as long as did the EMP, finally receding from western Europe only in the eighteenth century and maintaining its grip on the Ottoman Empire for a good deal longer. The third pandemic began more slowly in China in the second half of the nineteenth century, reaching Canton and Hong Kong in 1894, whence it spread around the world.[23]

Understanding of these pandemics is to some extent inferential and even based on circular reasoning. Since, on the conventional diagnosis, all three were pandemics of the same disease, the early authoritative accounts of the third pandemic not only include historical backgrounds but at times draw on the historical record of the second pandemic, the Black Death, to supplement the data available for the third.[24] These accounts are then treated by historians of the Black Death simply as scientific views of the third pandemic, independent of historical interpretation. So the history of the Black Death is to some extent explained using evidence of the modern pandemic that was originally based in part on narratives of the Black Death – circularity. The summary account of bubonic plague quoted above is an attempt by a historian with medical experience to generalize across the first two pandemics to make a biological history of the disease. While perfectly serviceable as a clinical description and epidemiology, it blends historical evidence and modern reports. I chose it precisely because it illustrates how such summaries can then become the starting point for further retrospective diagnosis, however explicit the author may be about the use made of history.

Since evidence for the first pandemic is so much sparser and more reticent than that for the Black Death, the latter is called upon to help interpret the former. In particular, estimates of the mortality caused by the EMP are inevitably colored by those for the Black Death. And in a less vicious circle than the one connecting the second and third pandemics, the plague of Justinian also becomes part of the historical background for the fourteenth-century plague, since few books on the Black Death fail to allow it a vignette in an early chapter.

The axiom that there have been three pandemics of the same disease also affects modern laboratory work. The pathogen is named *Yersinia pestis* after the man who first isolated the bacillus and after the "great pestilence" that was the Black Death in early modern England. The assumption that the second and third pandemics were biologically identical is thus built into its very name.[25] Three biovars (strains) of *Yersinia pestis* have been differentiated according to the degree to which they ferment glycerol, and their official names each correspond to one of the three presumed pandemics – *antiqua, mediaevalis*, orientalis.[26] Although there is certainly some historical evidence to support the attribution, nothing is settled, and the issue might have been less prejudiced by historically neutral terminology.

It is because of these multiple scholarly and scientific connections between pandemics that the scholarship of the plague of Justinian cannot be detached from recent work on the Black Death.

## Denials

The recent work can be summed up under the heading of "bubonic plague denial." The deniers have gathered momentum and garnered wide publicity in the years around the turn of the millennium. Yet aspects of their case have been aired for some time. In 1970, J. F. D. Shrewsbury argued on the basis of his (somewhat selective) "reading" of the third pandemic that the second one could not have killed one-half to one-third of Europe's population – as was, and is still, commonly thought – and that other diseases must have been involved.[27] He was taken to task for not giving sufficient "credit" to lethal pneumonic plague. His stance was not exactly one of denial, but it did bring to light some possible differences between second and third pandemics. In 1984, Graham Twigg published a book-length discussion of those differences and was either derided or ignored by medical historians. So powerful was their attachment to the bubonic paradigm that they felt no need even to engage with most of his arguments, let alone to refute them.[28] So, on the whole, and despite minor academic skirmishing, the matter rested for some time. Then, in the years around the turn of the millennium, two contradictory developments could be discerned.

On one hand, a few molecular biologists were able to extract DNA from the teeth of skeletons excavated from burial grounds very likely to contain plague victims of the later medieval and early modern periods. Comparison of the DNA with that of *Yersinia pestis* showed enough similarity for the biologists to proclaim (on the "one swallow *does* make a summer" principle) that the Black Death was an epidemic of bubonic plague and that all doubt about its identity had been removed.[29]

On the other hand, there was a return to, and amplified restatement of, Twigg's analysis of disquieting differences between the second and third pandemics – by two historical demographers, Susan Scott and Christopher J. Duncan, and by a historian of later medieval Europe, Samuel K. Cohn.[30] Both deny that *Yersinia pestis* could have been the primary agent of the Black Death and its subsequent waves. The symptoms and epidemiology were just too different.

There is space here neither to reflect adequately the detail of the deniers' hypotheses nor to convey the vigorous and knowledgeable counterattack that has been launched on behalf of the plague of Justinian by Robert Sallares.[31] It must suffice to report that, in effect, the jury is still out – and likely to remain so for some years, because the literature of plague in all its aspects and periods is now so large and variegated that almost any plausible position can find some empirical support, and because of continuing disagreements among biologists, epidemiologists, and historians alike about crucial data and their interpretation.

What the jury still has to deliberate on seems to me to be the following, mainly epidemiological, aspects of the modern pandemic. These aspects contrast it strongly with both of the first two pandemics and hence continue to unsettle the traditional diagnosis of the EMP as bubonic plague.[32]

First, despite its potentially global impact, the third pandemic inflicted nothing like the mortality now generally attributed to the EMP or the Black Death. We shall come back to the effects of the EMP below; but if, on a cautious estimate, the mortality of the first two pandemics was of the order of 20–30 percent, that of the early-twentieth-century pandemic, before vaccines were available, was of the order of 1 percent or less (as, e.g., in India, 1896–1917).

Second, both the earlier epidemics spread with astonishing rapidity compared to the plague's rate of advance in the later nineteenth and early twentieth centuries, even though it then had the advantage of diffusion by steamship or railway train. We saw the first waves of the EMP traversing the eastern Mediterranean in a matter of months. In South Africa in 1899, with steam trains to propel it, plague still moved inland at some 20 kilometers a year.

Third, the geography and seasonality of the modern pandemic are contrary to what historians expect. Bubonic plague is, first of all, a disease of rats and their fleas, and it cannot stray far from that zoological substructure. It should peak in spring or summer; yet, as we saw, Procopius states that the initial wave of the early medieval pandemic was felt throughout the year, and there are many other such anomalies in reports of both the first two pandemics. Following on from that, since the rat's flea, *Xenopsylla cheopis*, is the crucial vector in the transmission of bubonic plague from rodents to humankind, and since that flea requires a *sustained* summer temperature of 20–25°C to reproduce, the extension of plague pandemics to Scandinavia and Iceland, even to Britain, verges on the biologically impossible. Not just the occasional warm spell, but clusters of long, warm summers are required for the biology of fleas to accord with the chronology of recurrent epidemics.

Fourth, neither of the stopgaps proposed by defenders of bubonic plague to explain some of these anomalies really serves its purpose. The human flea is a very inefficient vector of plague and is now rarely espoused as a way of "detaching" the disease from its rodent base and explaining its rapid spread. The pneumonic form of plague, precisely because it is so lethal, will not sustain an epidemic beyond the geography of rats and their fleas. It burns itself out too quickly. In Manchuria in the early 1900s, living conditions among the migrant workers who became victims of pneumonic plague were so apt to produce an epidemic that an evil scientist might have designed them as a laboratory experiment.[33] Yet even in such ideal conditions (ideal for the bacillus, that is) the mortality was far lower than is postulated by historians of the first two pandemics.

Fifth, the DNA results referred to earlier are liable to the charges that they have, so far, proved unrepeatable, and that they may have arisen from contamination of the sample being analysed by DNA of *Yersinia pestis* already present in the laboratory. More importantly, these results, even if accepted, prove simply that bubonic plague was present at around the right time, not that it was the sole or even primary agent of the pandemic.[34]

That introduces a sixth point. Even the staunchest defenders of *Yersinia pestis* concede that diseases such as typhus could also have been involved in the first two pandemics. There is nothing biologically dubious about postulating mixed or overlapping epidemics of a number of different diseases. Perhaps bubonic plague was prevalent in the Mediterranean and other diseases predominated in the colder north, in epidemics whose chronological continuity with Mediterranean or Middle Eastern plagues was the result either of chance or of some interaction between the ecologies of plague and the other diseases that is currently obscure to us. Such a hypothesis of mixed or overlapping epidemics of course has obvious disadvantages. It invites the application of Ockham's razor in that it perhaps multiplies diseases beyond necessity. In this frustratingly difficult sphere of investigation, however, the conclusions that we adopt may have to be the least implausible, not the most convincing.

A final point under this heading of "denial": All the biological evidence suggests that plague evolved recently, perhaps as recently as 2,500 years ago, and has remained stable since.[35] The three biovars ("ancient," "medieval," and "oriental") are genetically very similar and seem to be equally infective and virulent. New strains have appeared through random mutation, some of them extremely recently. But the range of variation within which the bacillus has any chance of success is severely limited by the ecology of its hosts, the rat and the flea. Moreover, there is no evolutionary pressure for the bacillus to accommodate itself to humankind, because it is only relatively occasionally a disease of humanity. It has no "incentive" to become milder with each pandemic. That seems to rule out one possible explanation of why the first and second pandemics appear to have been vastly more serious than the third.

There are other questions that could be put to the first two pandemics – such as why hardly anyone in Europe, Byzantium, or Islam seems to have noticed the high and very visible mortality of rodents (and rodents only) that should have preceded an outbreak of plague, when the folk wisdom of the lands in which the modern pandemic originated is replete with warnings to evacuate the area of a rodent epizootic (animal epidemic).[36] (John of Ephesus, it will be recalled, referred to dead rats, but only in a lengthy catalog of smitten fauna.) But these are "softer" questions about cultural matters, almost impossible to answer with any confidence. The seven preceding questions are, however, matters of historical biology, epidemiology, and ecology on which progress ought to be possible. To these questions posed or implied by the deniers, upholders of the conventional diagnosis of the EMP must provide more substantial answers than they have so far managed.

As the debate continues, one other fundamental question deserves an airing: "So what?" That is, what turns on achieving the correct retrospective diagnosis of the EMP? The answer may be: "nothing." If correct, this is uncomfortable for both affirmers and deniers of *Yersinia pestis*. The reason nothing turns on the outcome of the debate is that both sides are trying to explain the evidence and the historical phenomena to which the evidence points. Neither side is trying to use its preferred diagnosis – bubonic or not-bubonic – as a way of either playing down the significance of the pandemic (as Shrewsbury did in his history of bubonic plague in Britain) or of showing that it has somehow been underestimated. Those who claim that the pandemic was not bubonic plague are simply trying, in the most economical way, to account for its speed of diffusion and the mortality it inflicted. They do not want to change our picture of the disease's impact. Those reaffirming the role of *Yersinia pestis* are claiming no more than that the traditional explanation is enough to account for its observable effects.

Arguments about diagnosis provide entertainment, and they are currently the focus of the most lively scholarship concerning any of the pandemics. That is why they have been conveyed here at length. But they do not necessarily advance historical understanding.

## Causes

If we cannot be certain of the EMP's biological identity, we are, a fortiori, unlikely to be able to give a causal explanation of its arrival. The first and most obvious subject against which to measure our scepticism is demography. In the eastern Roman Empire, it is now widely held, the two centuries preceding the pandemic of the 540s had been ones of economic expansion, a quickening of the monetary economy, and sustained demographic growth.[37] There were numerous periods of food stress and occasional famines – their frequency perhaps increasing in the 520s and 530s.[38] A new imperial elite acquired large estates and sucked a demographically expanding peasantry into its orbit. It was, perhaps, able to do this because, in many parts of the Byzantine world, the peasantry was too numerous to survive independently on ever smaller subdivisions of available land. Yet, despite the food shortages, there is no sign from the eastern Mediterranean of the sixth century, as there is from the Europe of the late thirteenth and early fourteenth century, that the population had generally grown substantially beyond its means. The EMP did not prick the Malthusian bubble in Byzantium. In general, explanations for its arrival of a demographic kind seem unpromising. At best they offer a context in which the disease could have spread rapidly and devastatingly. Something more obviously causal and more catastrophic is needed.

An earthquake is one type of candidate for that catastrophe. An earthquake preceded the outbreak of plague in India in 1993. Constantinople was shaken by earthquakes in 525, 533, 548, 554, 557, and 740. Only that of 557 is closely tied to the EMP, preceding a new wave of it by eight months.[39] But perhaps we should not expect the correlation to be too close. If rodents were involved in plague, then several years may have had to elapse between environmental disaster, changes in rat population, and epizootic. If the disease was not bubonic plague, then the biological or ecological preconditions of the EMP remain to be determined. And in any case, earthquakes are far from unusual in and around the Mediterranean. The German geographer Alfred Philippson wrote, for example, that no day passes without an earthquake somewhere in Greece.[40]

More promising than an earthquake as a cause of the EMP is climate. The climatological history of the sixth century is in its infancy, and from the scanty evidence so far available it would be rash to infer a general trend, for example toward greater precipitation, which might have encouraged a growth in rat population.[41] There were dry years in

530 (Constantinople) and 536 (Iran), but heavy snowfall in 540 (Syria). Yet what has quickened the pulse of scientists, historians, and even television audiences has been the "years without summer" or the "dust-veil event" of 536–537. The cause was low solar emissions or some dust-producing terrestrial disaster – perhaps the impact of an asteroid or comet, perhaps a major volcanic eruption (although none of these is so far clearly evidenced from the years in question).[42] The effect, widely noticed across the globe from Italy to China, and suitably registered in the very slow growth of tree rings, was twelve to eighteen months of faded sunlight, and a resulting period of poorer climate across the northern hemisphere.

Here, if anywhere, is a big ecological upset. In the eyes of believers, it heralded plague by causing a migration of plague-bearing rodents from their normal central African habitats.[43] More plausibly, though again only if *Yersinia pestis* was involved, the reduced temperatures of the 530s expanded the area within which plague survived enzootically among those African rodents. It pushed the perimeter of its reservoir almost to the coast opposite Zanzibar Island. Here, Byzantine Red Sea trade, especially an expanding trade in ivory, brought both seafarers and susceptible Mediterranean rats. On the return journey the rats took the disease north to Pelusium.[44] It may have been so, and it may have been that this "event" ushered in not only plague, but also the Avars, the weakening of the late Roman state, and the rise of Islam.[45] But the ecological connections between meteorology and history on this scale remain indistinct.

## Effects

What, then, was the impact of the early medieval pandemic on the Age of Justinian? To attempt even a partial answer to that question is virtually to rewrite the demographic, economic, social, cultural, and political history of the Mediterranean world in the later sixth and early seventh centuries. In that respect providing the answer falls to all contributors to this volume; it can hardly be restricted to a chapter on the pandemic itself. Perhaps significantly, only one other contribution (Chap. 2, by John Haldon) includes the EMP as an ingredient in major change.

There is no great surprise here. First of all, those who study the EMP directly tend to attribute a far greater effect to it than do those for whom it is, in disciplinary terms, peripheral. In recent decades only one influential plague denier has emerged among those who write on the pandemic: Jean Durliat.[46] He denies, not the diagnosis of bubonic plague, but the mortality and hence the wider effects. The descriptions of Procopius, John of Ephesus, Evagrius, and their kind may be rhetorical exaggerations, elite responses to localized panic. Beyond these few "supercharged" evocations, the written evidence worryingly fails us, either because it is imprecise about the nature of epidemics or because it does not mention the EMP where we should expect it. Without the major literary texts, Durliat asks in effect, what indices would we have of the plague's impact? There are no traces of it in the Egyptian papyri, and very few in the hagiography, our two most abundant documentary sources for "everyday life." The inscriptions of the period do not register it either. And there are, so far, no genuine plague pits known to archaeologists, no direct proof of the hastily improvised mass burials described by Procopius and widely known from the period of the Black Death.[47] Perhaps then the disease was confined to major cities and routes linking them. Even here, moreover, its impact remains uncertain because (as we see confirmed elsewhere in this volume) city life continued: "business as usual," in the words of another, similar, denier.[48]

Other scholars of plague are more or less united in rejecting this minimalist view. Although they must concede that the immediate impact of the EMP remains invisible in the urban archaeology and the field surveys of the sixth and earlier seventh centuries, Durliat's reassessment remains vulnerable on several counts. The record of inscriptions offers the clearest example. Improvised multiple burials would not have been recorded in inscriptions. And the majority of the dead would inevitably have been the poor, for whom epigraphic immortality was never in prospect. Again, if the epidemic was not a far more widespread and serious phenomenon than Durliat suggests, why did Justinian legislate at the end of the first wave to counteract major wage and price increases, and why was there famine in Constantinople one year later? *Contra* Durliat, mortality estimates similar to those given for the Black Death are widely and confidently repeated in the literature: figures ranging between 20 and 30 percent.[49] They are based not only on the texts quoted above but on the repeated impression of widespread panic, chaos, and disruption conveyed by a substantial corpus of written evidence, not only Latin and Greek but, still more, Syriac and Arabic.[50] Lawrence Conrad argues convincingly that, "as the witnesses responsible for these accounts spoke different languages (and often did not know others), represented different social, cultural, and religious viewpoints, and frequently lived at considerable chronological and geographical removes from one another, it is impossible to put these congruences down to the literary and emotional factors adduced by Durliat."[51]

There, however, clarity and consensus end – which may be one reason why the plague is mentioned, if at all, only in passing in many modern accounts of the period.[52] This, too, is unsurprising. A similar degree of ambivalence or caution prevails in the historiography of the Black Death. There was massive depopulation, not just from the initial pandemic but from recurrent waves of it – on average, one year in four between 1380 and 1480. The mechanisms of demographic recovery thus never had the chance to develop. This basic fact about prolonged demographic depression ought to color all socioeconomic interpretation of the later Middle Ages.[53] The problem for historians is that, in many cases, survivors of the pandemic prospered, in a land-rich, wage-inflationary environment. Demographic catastrophe was not, in the long term, matched by economic collapse. And if we cast the interpretative net more widely, there is no subject, from church sculpture to farming techniques, on which the Black Death can be said to have had a distinct and unequivocal impact: "Repeatedly we find that the Black Death was not an autonomous agent of change but worked in tandem with other processes."[54]

So it is with the early medieval pandemic: a major ingredient in the changes that we detect in the Age of Justinian and the seventh to eighth centuries, but only one such ingredient among several.[55] The EMP struck the Byzantine and Islamic Middle East less frequently than the Black Death did but was hardly a "light touch." Perhaps western Europe was more fortunate in the early Middle Ages; it is impossible to tell. In what follows, therefore, discussion is confined to the eastern Mediterranean, where the problems of interpretation seem slightly more tractable.

On one hand, the short-term impact (the "hammer-blow," as Peter Sarris puts it)[56] can, *pace* Durliat, be detected outside the usual literary evidence. Papyrology, for instance, records a quite rapid and marked improvement in the security of tenure enjoyed by Egyptian lessees of land from the mid-sixth century onward; presumably landlords suddenly found themselves in a buyers' market.[57] Nor is the history of coinage entirely unruffled by the EMP. The Byzantine state quickly responded to what must have been a drastic diminution of its tax revenues by reducing the size of its gold coinage, and perhaps also by tinkering with the weight of its copper issues.[58]

On the other hand, if we look to a broadly reliable index of manpower, recruitment to the army, it is far less clear that the state experienced insuperable difficulties.[59] In the later 540s and the 550s the armies of Byzantium fought successfully on three fronts: in Lazica, against the Moors in Africa, and, most decisively, in the Ostrogothic wars in Italy. Those who blame the pandemic for later defeats, inflicted first by the Persians, then by the armies of Islam, need to bear these successes of Justinian's reign in mind.

If there is so little certainty about the relations between the pandemic and such features of the political and military history of the period, still less can we pronounce on the role of plague in grander but vaguer phenomena like "the end of antiquity" or, à la Pirenne, the decline of the Mediterranean economy. A relatively sophisticated economy continued to function relatively unscathed well beyond the Age of Justinian in many parts of the empire – perhaps on much reduced populations, but not with that dramatic diminution of prosperity upon which several historians have insisted.[60] The "origins of the European economy," we are told by Michael McCormick, lie in the Carolingian world, not the tenth or eleventh century, where they had conventionally been placed.[61] That is, they lie in the period immediately following the EMP's recession from Europe. But there was too much else going on for the pandemic to be accorded a leading role in the economic *translatio imperii*.

## Uses

Michael McCormick treats plague as one way of tracking Mediterranean communications.[62] That prompts a final question: Is the EMP of any use? It was plainly not much use to its victims, other than in an eschatological sense; it was more obviously of use to those who survived into a world of greater economic opportunity. But has it anything to tell us today? If we could agree on a diagnosis, then we might enlarge our understanding of the ecology of the Age of Justinian. Until that unanimity is achieved, however, the way in which the disease spread by sea, by river, and from city to hinterland tells us, I submit, nothing that we did not already know. An unusual chronological cluster of inscriptions may, if interpreted as a sign of an epidemic, inform us that plague reached a locality where we had not previously suspected it. But this is progress at the microscopic level only. At the level of aerial photography, we use our already available evidence of Mediterranean communications and settlement to tell us about the likely behavior of the pandemic, not the other way around.

For all the immaculate scholarship that continues to be lavished upon it, the early medieval pandemic remains a black hole at the center of the Age of Justinian. It absorbs a great deal of our energy; it gives very little out.

## Notes

1 Procopius, *Secret History*, 18.36–44.

2 The pioneering work is Pauline Allen, "The 'Justinianic' Plague," *Byzantion* 49 (1979): 5–20. Dionysios Stathakopoulos, "The Justinianic Plague Revisited," *BMGS* 24 (2000): 256–276, surveys the literature.

3 Michael Whitby and Mary Whitby, ed. and trans., *Chronicon Paschale, 284–628 AD* (Liverpool, 1989), 111.

4 Alexander A. Vasiliev, ed., PO 8 (1912): 425. Here and throughout I am indebted to Dionysios Stathakopoulos for references and previews of works in press.

5 Robert Sallares, "Ecology, Evolution, and Epidemiology of Plague," in *The Justinianic Plague, 541–767 AD* (proceedings of conference held at the American Academy in Rome, December 2001), ed. Lester K. Little (Cambridge University Press, forthcoming), generously shown to me in typescript by its author, nn. 77, 212.

6 For full presentation of the evidence, see Dionysios Stathakopoulos, *Famine and Pestilence in the Late Roman and Early Byzantine Empire: A Systematic Survey of Subsistence Crises and Epidemics* (Aldershot, 2004), chap. 6, prefigured in Dionysios Stathakopoulos, "Crime and Punishment: The Plague in the Byzantine Empire, 541–749," in Little, *Justinianic Plague*. I cannot, however, always accept his speculative plotting of some of the disease's movements according to unusual chronological concentrations of funerary inscriptions.

7 See Alain Stoclet and Michael Kulikowski in Little, *Justinianic Plague*.

8 *Nov.*, 122.

9 J. R. Maddicott, "Plague in Seventh-Century England," *Past and Present* 156 (1997): 7–54; Stathakopoulos, *Famine and Pestilence*, 116.

10 Michael McCormick in Little, *Justinianic Plague*.

11 Lawrence I. Conrad, "Die Pest und ihr soziales Umfeld in Nahen Osten des früheren Mittelalters," *Der Islam* 73 (1996): 99–102; Peter Sarris, "The Justinianic Plague: Origins and Effects," *Continuity and Change* 17 (2002): 170 and n. 14.

12 Stathakopoulos, *Famine and Pestilence*, 123.

13 Marie-Hélène Congourdeau, "La Société byzantine face aux grandes pandémies," in *Maladie et Société à Byzance*, ed. Evelyne Patlagean (Spoleto, 1993), 25–26; Jean-Noël Biraben and Jacques Le Goff, "The Plague in the Early Middle Ages," in *Biology of Man in History: Selections from the "Annales: Économies, Sociétés, Civilisations"* ed. Robert Forster and Orest Ranum (Baltimore, 1975), 49 n. 3.

14 The following excerpts are from *Wars*, 2.22.1–10, trans. Dewing, 451–469.

15 The relevant (second) part of John's *Ecclesiastical History* survives in an eighth-century Syriac universal chronicle. Excerpts that follow are from Witold Witakowski, trans., *Pseudo-Dionysius of Tel-Mahre, Chronicle . . . Part III* (Liverpool, 1996), 77, 80–81, 86–87 (modified).

16 *The Ecclesiastical History of Evagrius*, 4.29, ed. J. Bidez and L. Parmentier (London, 1898), 177–179, trans. Michael Whitby, *The Ecclesiastical History of Evagrius Scholasticus* (Liverpool, 2000), 229–232.

17 Andrew Cunningham, "Transforming Plague: The Laboratory and the Identity of Infectious Disease," in *The Laboratory Revolution in Medicine*, ed. Andrew Cunningham and Penry Williams (Cambridge, 1992), 209–244; Cunningham, "Identifying Disease in the Past: Cutting the Gordian Knot," *Asclepio* 54 (2002): 13–34.

18 Dionysios Stathakopoulos, "Die Terminologie der Pest in Byzantinischen Quellen," *JÖB* 48 (1998): 1–7; Liliane Bodson, "Le Vocabulaire des maladies pestilentielles et épizootiques," in *Le Latin médical: la constitution d'un language scientifique,* ed. Guy Sabbah (Saint-Étienne, 1991), 215–241.

19 Lawrence I. Conrad, "*Ṭāʿūn* and *Wabā*': Conceptions of Plague and Pestilence in Early Islam," *Journal of the Economic and Social History of the Orient* 25 (1982): 268–307.

20 Ann G. Carmichael, "Bubonic Plague," in *The Cambridge World History of Human Disease*, ed. Kenneth F. Kiple (Cambridge, 1993), 628–630.

21 Gregory of Tours, *Libri Historiarum*, 10.1, trans. Lewis Thorpe, *Gregory of Tours, The History of the Franks* (Harmondsworth, 1974), 543; Paul the Deacon, *Historia Langobardorum*, 2.4, trans. W. D. Foulke, *History of the Langobards, by Paul the Deacon* (Philadelphia, 1907), 56.

22 The evidence is reviewed by Sallares, "Ecology," sec. 2.

23 Carol Benedict, *Bubonic Plague in Nineteenth-Century China* (Stanford, Calif., 1996).

24 Lien-Teh Wu, *Plague: A Manual for Medical and Public Health Workers* (Shanghai, 1936); L. Fabian Hirst, *The Conquest of Plague* (Oxford, 1953); R. Pollitzer, *Plague* (Geneva, 1954). See also Samuel K. Cohn, Jr., *The Black Death Transformed: Disease and Culture in Early Renaissance Europe* (London, 2002), 16.

25 For accounts of Yersin's achievement, see Cohn, *Black Death Transformed*, chaps. 1–2, and Cunningham, "Transforming Plague."

26 R. Devignat, "Variétés de l'espèce *Pasteurella pestis*: Nouvelle hypothèse," *Bulletin of the World Health Organisation* 4 (1951): 247–263, with Sallares, "Ecology," sec. 3.

27 J. F. D. Shrewsbury, *A History of Bubonic Plague in the British Isles* (Cambridge, 1970).

28 Graham Twigg, *The Black Death: A Biological Reappraisal* (London, 1984).

29 See, e.g., Didier Raoult et al., "Molecular Identification by 'Suicide PCR' of Yersinia Pestis as the Agent of Medieval Black Death," *Proceedings of the National Academy of Sciences of the U.S.A.* 97 (2000): 12880–12883. The literature is surveyed in Sallares, "Ecology," sec. 3.

30 Susan Scott and Christopher J. Duncan, *Biology of Plagues: Evidence from Historical Populations* (Cambridge, 2001); Cohn, *Black Death Transformed.*

31 Sallares, "Ecology."

32 I follow Graham Twigg, "Bubonic Plague: Doubts and Diagnoses," *Journal of Medical Microbiology* 42 (1995): 383–385.

33 Cohn, *Black Death*, 22–23.

34 James Wood and Sharon DeWitte-Aviña, "Was the Black Death Yersinial Plague?" *The Lancet, Infectious Diseases* 3 (2003): 327.

35 Sallares, "Ecology," fully reviews the genetic evidence. See also Scott and Duncan, *Biology of Plagues*, 63–65.

36 Cohn, *Black Death*, 17. Michael McCormick, "Rats, Communications, and Plague: Towards an Ecological History," *Journal of Interdisciplinary History* 34

(2003): 4, argues that early medieval texts do not distinguish rats from mice or other rodents. But that does not solve the problem: rodent mortality is very infrequently noticed in contemporary accounts of EMP.

37 Peter Sarris, "Rehabilitating the Great Estate: Aristocratic Property and Economic Growth in the Late Antique Eastern Empire," in *Recent Research on the Late Antique Countryside*, Late Antique Archaeology 2, ed. William Bowden, Luke Lavan, and Carlos Machado (Leiden, 2004), 55–71; Bryan Ward-Perkins, "Land, Labour, and Settlement," in *CAH* 14:319–321.

38 Stathakopoulos, *Famine and Pestilence*, 261–277.

39 McCormick, "Rats," 19; for wider context see *I terremoti prima del Mille in Italia e nell'area mediterranea*, ed. Emanuela Guidoboni (Bologna, 1989), 690ff.

40 *Das Mittelmeergebiet: Seine geographische und kulturelle Eigenart* (Leipzig, 1904), 28.

41 McCormick, "Rats," 20; Johannes Koder, "Climatic Change in the Fifth and Sixth Centuries?" in *The Sixth Century: End or Beginning?*, ed. Pauline Allen and Elizabeth Jeffreys (Brisbane, 1996), 270–285.

42 Joel D. Gunn, ed., *The Years without Summer: Tracing AD 536 and its Aftermath*, British Archaeological Reports Intermediate Series 872 (Oxford, 2000); David Keys, *Catastrophe: An Investigation into the Origins of the Modern World* (London, 1999), favors an eruption, perhaps of Krakatoa. M. G. L. Baillie prefers comets as his explanation for the EMP and much else; see his *Exodus to Arthur: Catastrophic Encounters with Comets*, 2nd ed. (London, 2000). Note also R. B. Stothers and M. R. Rampino, "Volcanic Eruptions in the Mediterranean before A.D. 630 from Written and Archaeological Sources," *Journal of Geophysical Research* 88 (1983): 6357–6371, a reference I owe to Morten Axboe.

43 Keys, *Catastrophe*, 18–19.

44 I follow unpublished work of Mark Horton of the University of Bristol, U.K.

45 As argued in Keys, *Catastrophe*.

46 Jean Durliat, "La Peste du VIe siècle: Pour un nouvel examen des sources byzantines," in *Hommes et richesses dans l'empire byzantin IVe–VIIe siècle* (Paris, 1989), 107–119, with the immediate response ("Rapport") by Jean-Noël Biraben, 121–125.

47 Michael McCormick's contribution to Little, *Justinianic Plague*, will contain a census of the archaeology of burials attributable to the EMP. For the meager trawl to date, see Stathakopoulos, *Famine and Pestilence*, 149–150.

48 Mark Whittow, *The Making of Orthodox Byzantium, 600–1025* (Houndmills, Eng., 1996), 66.

49 Stathakopoulos, *Famine and Pestilence*, 140; Allen, "The 'Justinianic' Plague," 11.

50 On social and religious responses to the EMP in Byzantium, see Stathakopoulos, *Famine and Pestilence*, 146–154.

51 Lawrence I. Conrad, "Epidemic Disease in Central Syria in the Late Sixth Century: Some New Insights from the Verse of Ḥassān ibn Thābit," *BMGS* 18 (1994): 56.

52 For a recent exception, in which plague, along with other environmental disasters of the 530s and 540s, becomes key to the whole subsequent, hyper-religious, tenor of Justinian's reign, see Mischa Meier, *Das andere Zeitalter Justinians* (Göttingen, 2003), esp. 340–341.

53 Colin Platt, *King Death: The Black Death and Its Aftermath in Late-Medieval England* (London, 1996), 177.

54 P. J. P. Goldberg, "Introduction," in *The Black Death in England*, ed. W. M. Ormrod and P. G. Lindley (Stamford, Eng., 1996), 13.

55 Conrad, "Die Pest und ihr soziales Umfeld," 102–112.

56 Sarris, "Justinianic Plague," 173.

57 Sarris, "Justinianic Plague," 178, cites Jairus Banaji, "Rural Communities in the Late Empire: Economic and Monetary Aspects" (PhD diss., University of Oxford, 1992), tab. 20.

58 Sarris, "Justinianic Plague," 175–177.

59 Michael Whitby, "Recruitment in Roman Armies from Justinian to Heraclius (*ca.* 565–615)," in *The Byzantine and Early Islamic Near East*, vol. 3, *States, Resources and Armies*, ed. Averil Cameron (Princeton, N.J., 1995), 61–124.

60 Ward-Perkins, "Land, Labour and Settlement," 327; Ward-Perkins, "Specialized Production and Exchange," in *CAH* 14:354, 388.

61 Michael McCormick, *Origins of the European Economy: Communications and Commerce, AD 300–900* (New York, 2001). For plague and economic change, see esp. 538–539. For plague and the overall "disease burden," 38–40.

62 McCormick, "Rats," esp. 25.

# 7: Law and Legal Practice in the Age of Justinian

*Caroline Humfress*

The vain titles of the victories of Justinian are crumbled into dust; but the name of the legislator is inscribed on a fair and everlasting monument. Under his reign, and by his care, the civil jurisprudence was digested in the immortal works of the Code, the Pandects [or Digest], and the Institutes: the public reason of the Romans has been silently or studiously transfused into the domestic institutions of Europe, and the laws of Justinian still command the respect or obedience of independent nations.

– Edward Gibbon, *The Decline and Fall of the Roman Empire*, Chap. 44

According to Edward Gibbon, writing in the late eighteenth century, the most important legacy of the Age of Justinian and indeed the most important legacy of the emperor himself lay in the field of law. Gibbon's assessment still rings true. Though the physical boundaries of medieval Europe were recast repeatedly on battlefields long after the Age of Justinian had ended, the law issued in his name still shapes legal culture today.

The "fair and everlasting monument" Justinian bequeathed to posterity is known today as the *Corpus iuris civilis*: three *codices* or books of law, promulgated between the years 529 and 534. The Justinianic *Codex*, the *Digest* (or *Pandects*), and the *Institutes* sought to harmonize 1,000 years of complex and checkered development in the citizen law of the Romans.[1] Justinian's new law books contained old wine in new skins; each book utilized and incorporated different types of legal source material from the Roman past, but each also reshaped that material, harmonizing disparate texts with each other, mapping the outline of a system of law in a single body (*corpus*) of interlocking texts. The resulting symphony (to use a sixth-century metaphor for what we today might term "codification") was then officially promulgated. Every text within the *Corpus*, no matter what its original source, now counted as binding imperial legislation issued jointly "in the name of our Lord Jesus Christ" and the sacred lord and emperor Justinian himself. Justinian thus legislated a single textual corpus of Roman law into existence within an explicitly Christian framework.

For the legal historian, the Age of Justinian is nothing short of pivotal. Medievalists and early modernists interested in the so-called reception of Roman law in later times and places must look back to Justinian and his law books, as classicists and historians interested in Roman republican or early imperial law must frequently look forward to them.[2] To borrow a metaphor from one preeminent scholar of the Roman law tradition, Justinian's *Corpus iuris civilis* is like a giant supermarket in which lawyers and historians alike shop for legal ideas and concepts.[3]

The enduring relevance of Justinian's law books presents a series of peculiar challenges to any historian interested in exploring law in the Age of Justinian itself. How should we place Justinian's law books within the legal culture of his time? All law was not Roman law in the Age of Justinian, yet there is an "almost irresistible temptation to judge all other laws in late antiquity by their relationship to Roman law."[4] Did law in the Age of Justinian really amount to what is contained within the pages of his *Corpus iuris civilis*? Was law, in practice, done by Justinian's books? In other words, we need to ask how exactly Justinian's legislative projects related to legal practice during his time.

## JUSTINIAN AND HIS LAW BOOKS

> We have by means of old laws not only brought matters into a better condition, but We also have promulgated new laws.
>
> – *CJ Const. Summa*, pr.

On February 13, 528, only six months after becoming sole emperor, Justinian announced to the senate of the city of Constantinople his intention of compiling a new book of Roman law. This imperial address had an important historical precedent: almost exactly a hundred years earlier, on March 26, 429, the emperor Theodosius II had announced his project of compiling an authoritative and comprehensive legal codex in the same senate house at Constantinople. Justinian, looking out from the seat of the New Rome, may also have had an eye on his Western contemporaries. Early sixth-century Burgundian and Visigothic kings had already ordered collections of existing Roman law to be made for them, seemingly for the benefit of their Roman subjects (and their own reputations). Justinian's legislation never refers to these codes, but the idea of "barbarian" kings promulgating Roman law must have cast a long shadow over his ambitions as emperor.

Justinian's 528 address to the Constantinopolitan senators began, "Those things which seem to many former Emperors to require correction, but which none of them ventured to carry into effect, We have decided to accomplish at the present time with the assistance of Almighty God."[5] With the Christian God's aid, Justinian's lawbook was to trump the imperial codes that had gone before it. Justinian was to succeed where (in his assessment) previous legislators had failed. Moreover, issued under the auspices of the eternal Godhead, Justinian's *Codex* was to be exclusively valid for all future times to come.[6]

The 528 project was entrusted to a specially appointed committee of ten, headed by the praetorian prefect John of Cappadocia. The commissioners' instructions were to collect together and revise a multitude of imperial constitutions from the emperor Hadrian (117–138 AD) up to Justinian himself. This legal source material was by no means uniform: it included (mostly pre-Constantinian) case-specific private rescripts, as well as imperial *epistulae* (letters) to individual officials and *edicta* (edicts) frequently directed at specific provinces (or the cities of Rome or Constantinople). Justinian's commissioners found the law in whatever imperial legislative texts they could, regardless of their original scope of application or circumstances of promulgation. So that no confusion might thereby arise, Justinian confirmed that every text included in his *Codex* would, by the very fact of its inclusion, "obtain the force of a general constitution."[7] Once the commissioners had selected their material, it then had to be grouped together according to subject matter, arranged in chronological order, and placed under appropriate titles or rubrics. A new single collection of clear, general, and certain legislation was thus envisaged. Its aim was to diminish the length and complexity of lawsuits and hence increase the public welfare. Accordingly, the commissioners were also instructed, when they deemed it necessary, to shorten, amalgamate, emend, simplify, and even reverse the meaning of the original imperial constitutions, thus rendering the past useful and applicable to the Age of Justinian.

The original imperial constitutions were to be harvested by the commissioners from law codes issued in the 290s under the reign of the emperor Diocletian (the *Codex Gregorianus* and *Codex Hermogenianus*), as well as Theodosius II's own *Codex Theodosianus* (finally validated for the Eastern empire on February 15, 438).[8] Justinian's legal commissioners were also instructed to excerpt "new" imperial constitutions (*Novellae* or *Novels*). For this new material the commissioners had to comb the collection of *Novellae* officially compiled by Theodosius II himself in the year 447, as a supplement to his 438 *Codex*. This collection of Theodosian *Novellae* had been originally presented as a gift from Theodosius in the Eastern half of the empire, to his coemperor Valentinian III in the West.[9] The *Codex Theodosianus* itself had already been "gifted" to the West so that its authority would extend empirewide. Valentinian III seemingly reciprocated these eastern gifts with a collection of his own new western laws.[10] Later fifth-century eastern and western emperors followed suit. After 476 and the deposition of the last western Roman emperor, these official collections of *Novellae* seem to have ceased and Justinian's legal commissioners had to raid the archives for individual constitutions issued by the eastern emperors Leo I (457–474), Zeno (474–491), Anastasius (491–518), and Justin I (518–527).

Nonetheless, the idea of collecting *Novellae* and "gifting" laws from East to West was not lost on Justinian and his bureaucrats. Exactly twenty years after the completion of the *Corpus iuris civilis*, Justinian announced a plan to collect together his own extensive *Novellae* – his legislation issued between 534 and 554 – and promulgate that collection for the new Western provinces (*Nov. App.* 7.11). This 554 collection never materialized.[11] Provisions had been made, however, after September 533, for the quick transmission of Justinian's lawbooks to the newly reconquered provinces of North Africa. In November 534, the completed set of *Codex, Digest*, and *Institutes* was also officially sent to Rome, before Belisarius's first military conquests in Italy. Justinian's legal reach – like his theological prowess – stretched out to Rome before his troops did.

The first edition of Justinian's *Codex* was promulgated in April 529, with the provision that it should take effect from the Christian festival of Easter that year, April 16. The city prefect at Constantinople was ordered to promulgate an edict announcing the existence of the new lawbook to all peoples, and to send out official copies of the book itself to each of the provinces.[12] This 529 *Codex*, however, was itself superseded in 534 by a second edition. It is this second edition, known technically as the *Codex repetitae praelectionis*, that survives today. Justinian was careful to spell out the fact that this second code superseded and replaced the first: from December 29, 534, the *Codex* of Justinian "should be copied in accordance with the second edition, as it was revised, and not in accordance with the first."[13] Why the need for a second authoritative edition?

During the compilation of the first code, Justinian and his commissioners had confronted head-on the complexity of Roman law and its historical sources. As much as Justinian might have wished otherwise, Roman law had not proceeded from the mouths of emperors alone. The written citizen law of the Romans had, in fact, long predated the first emperor. With the text of the Twelve Tables (450 BCE) as their common origin, praetors, legal experts or "jurists," and senators had all shared in assisting, supplementing, and amending the civil law, clarifying the legal conditions under which Romans had obligations, committed wrongs, or were subject to liabilities. Before the era of Justinian, praetors, senators, and legal experts each had (varying) claims to be in some sense developers, or at least creative interpreters, of the civil law. It had been explicitly provided for in 529 that Justinian's *Codex* of imperial legislation should be used alongside the texts of ancient Roman jurists, for the purposes of litigation: "The citation of the said constitutions of Our Code, with the opinions of the ancient interpreters of the law, will be sufficient for the disposal of all cases."[14] This attempt to run ancient jurisprudence alongside imperial legislation quickly revealed problems in guaranteeing the clarity and certainty of law. The "ancient interpreters of the law" by no means agreed with each other; neither did their reasoning necessarily agree with the imperial legislation in Justinian's *Codex*. On occasion, ancient juristic writings would turn up quotations from ancient imperial laws that Justinian's commission had already altered. Thus variant manuscript traditions of juristic writings and imperial laws continued to pose particular challenges to judges and litigants, despite Justinian's 529 *Codex*. This was no new uncertainty. The emperors Constantine, Valentinian III, and Theodosius II had each attempted to stabilize and fix the use of juristic literature in court disputes. True to form, Justinian was determined to outstrip his predecessors.

Almost immediately after promulgating the first *Codex* Justinian began to issue a series of "fifty decisions" (the *Quinquaginta decisiones*), legislative acts intended to resolve outstanding controversies in ancient juristic texts. These *Quinquaginta decisiones* are not extant and perhaps never were issued as a separate collected volume, although a number of them were incorporated into the *Codex* promulgated in 534. In the texts that survive, the opinions of the jurists are revised in the sense of being completed or "perfected" by Justinian's imperial laws: "Although

We are not ignorant of the opinion of Julius Paulus, and of certain other persons learned in the law, who have touched upon this question which we are at present discussing, they have not treated it in the most skilful manner. . . . We, however, decide in a more complete and general way."[15] Justinian's legislation constantly strove to correct "imperfections" and legal obscurities, whether they were found in ancient juristic texts, the laws of previous emperors, or, indeed, his own constitutions. Justinian even offered imperial perfectionism as a motive behind the compilation of the second edition in 534, the *Codex repetitae praelectionis*: "Nothing which has been begun by Us may be left imperfect."[16]

Justinian convened a second legal committee, headed by his imperial quaestor (a high-ranking palatine officer, responsible for the drafting and publication of imperial legislation), Tribonian, on December 15, 530. This committee was charged with preparing the *Codex repetitae praelectionis*. First, however, Tribonian was commissioned to preside over the compilation of the *Digest*. This second part of the *Corpus iuris civilis* was intended to reduce and harmonize nearly fourteen hundred years' worth of confused Roman jurisprudence into a single, concordant "most holy temple of justice."[17] Like the rubrics contained within the twelve books of Justinian's *Codex*, the order or structural architecture of the *Digest* was to imitate traditional classifications within the civil law as established by the *Edictum perpetuum* or *Perpetual edict* (a text compiled around 135 CE under the auspices of the emperor Hadrian, which codified all previous praetorian edicts). The titles and classificatory headings in the *Digest* were thus also intended to reference the rubrics already composed for Justinian's 529 *Codex*. The texts were intended to fit together, in both theory and practice.

The rationale behind the *Digest's* production was threefold. It was to be scholarly: a "boundless ocean of learning" was to be conserved, albeit in a much reduced form. It was to be academic: the text was targeted at the law schools and their system of education. And it was to be practical: law students were expected to display their knowledge of it in court.[18] The *Digest* would thus confront the problems associated with using ancient jurisprudence in concrete sixth-century legal contexts. Any juristic texts excluded from the *Digest*'s own fifty books could no longer be cited in court or relied upon in any legal transactions. Provisions were made for copies of the *Digest*, along with the 534 *Codex* and *Institutes*, to be produced cheaply (and in longhand) for the benefit of law students at Rome, Constantinople, and Beirut. The praetorian prefects of the East, Illyricum, and Libya were to be responsible for promulgating the new law books within their own jurisdictions.[19]

## Christianizing Roman Jurisprudence: Justinian's Digest and Institutes

The completion of the *Digest* project involved the collection, emendation, and reduction of over 1,500 separate books and more than 3 million lines of text written by classical Roman jurists stretching from the republic to the fourth century. As the work of Tony Honoré has established, the responsibility for excerpting, amending, and correctly ordering the juristic works was divided among the second law commission in a very precise fashion.[20] The commission's intensive program of work demanded legal expertise and a firm, controlling hand. Tribonian was undoubtedly the key figure, but Justinian's personal involvement cannot be doubted: "Our majesty too has at all times investigated and scrutinized what was being composed."[21]

The constitution *Deo auctore*, which ordered the composition of the *Digest* in 530, paints a highly rhetorical picture of an overwrought emperor imploring divine assistance for this seemingly impossible task:

> In our haste to extricate ourselves from minor and more trivial affairs and attain to a completely full revision of the law, and to collect and amend the whole set of Roman ordinances and present the diverse books of so many authors in a single volume (a thing which no one has dared to expect or to desire), the task appeared to us most difficult, indeed impossible. Nevertheless, with hands stretched up to heaven, and imploring eternal aid, we stored up this task too in our mind, relying upon God, who in the magnitude of his goodness is able to sanction and to consummate achievements that are utterly beyond hope. (Section 2)

In fact, according to the rhetoric of the constitution *Tanta*, the completion of the *Digest* in December 533 was nothing short of a providential act of divine generosity. Other such acts included the end of the Parthian wars, the extinction of the Vandal nation, and the reconquest of the whole of Libya for the Roman Empire.

We should take Justinian's rhetoric seriously. By ascribing the completion of this monumental volume to the "inspiration of heaven and the favor of the Supreme Trinity" (*Digest Const. Tanta* 1), and indeed by confirming the *Digest*'s authority in an imperial prologue issued "In the Name of Our Lord God Jesus Christ," Justinian effectively Christianized all the non-Christian classical juristic books contained within it. In other words, the Christian authority of the *Digest* was not achieved by a Christianization of the substantive principles of classical Roman law; Tribonian and his commissioners did not doctor their "pagan" juristic material in favor of more Christian precepts or rules. Nonetheless, the *Digest* was a Christian lawbook, inspired by God, aided by God, and promulgated in the name of Christ.

Through his official promulgation of the *Digest*, Justinian once again legislated a (Christian) textual monument into existence – in this case, transforming the opinions and writings of ancient jurists into his own. All the juristic texts within the *Digest* were given the force of imperial law: "So that all the most gifted authors whose work is contained in this book [i.e., the *Digest*] may have as much authority as if their studies were derived from imperial enactments and had been uttered from our own inspired mouth; for we ascribe everything to ourselves, since it is from us that all their authority is derived."[22] With his assertion that the authority of all the jurists was ultimately to be derived from the emperor, the drafter of this Justinianic text deliberately obscured a question that has vexed Roman legal scholars ever since. There is some historical evidence that the emperor Augustus may have granted a "right of response" (a *ius respondendi*) to certain top-class jurists. Whatever the historical reality of this Augustan grant, there is no legislative evidence that juristic authority per se depended on any act of imperial confirmation – before the Age of Justinian. After the promulgation of Justinian's *Digest*, no jurist was to be permitted to produce any independent juristic commentary. Indexes to the text were permitted "in such a way that no offense arises through interpretation."[23] Jurists were also allowed to translate Latin passages from the *Digest* into Greek, "in the same order and sequence as those in which the Roman words are written"[24] – an important reminder of the increasingly bilingual nature of Justinianic legal practice.

In a constitution issued in 529 and addressed to his praetorian prefect Demosthenes, who presided over one of the top-ranking legal courts in the empire, Justinian emphasizes the novelty concerning the relationship between the emperor and the law. Apparently his first legal commission had stumbled across a doubt in the ancient laws as to whether a judgment of the emperor should be considered a law. Justinian considered this "vain subtlety" to be contemptible and ordered its suppression.[25] Every interpretation of the laws by the emperor, whether in answer to petitions addressed to him, given in judgment, or "in any other way whatsoever," should be considered valid. Section 5 of the same law continues: "Therefore, these ridiculous doubts having been cast aside, the Emperor shall justly be regarded as the sole maker and interpreter of the laws; and this provision shall in no way prejudice the founders of ancient jurisprudence, because the Imperial Majesty conferred this privilege upon them." The story of Augustus and the *ius respondendi* thus provided a crucial historical context for Justinian's sixth-century claims to legal autocracy. Of course, late Roman emperors before Justinian had frequently adopted a rhetoric that placed all power within their hands. What was new with Justinian was his sustained attempt to make this rhetoric a reality, shoring up his position using arguments from the past.

We might well wonder whether Justinian does not protest too much. Alongside a certain insecurity over any lingering hints of independent juristic prestige, Justinian also seems to have been rather sensitive to any historical vestiges of independent praetorian legal authority. Shortly after issuing the second *Codex* in 534, Justinian and his praetorian prefect John of Cappadocia began a radical overhaul of provincial administration.[26] Justinian's *Novel* 24 (dated May 18, 535) was part of this overhaul. It orders the establishment of a praetor for the province of Pisidia, who was to have both military and civil jurisdiction "in imitation of former times." A brief account of the praetorian office under the republic and early empire then follows. During these times, the text states, the praetor was preeminent and superior to others in military affairs as well as in the execution of the laws, and in fact issued laws "with the force of statute" themselves (i.e., the Praetorian edicts; *Nov.* 24, pr.). The new 535 praetor of Pisidia, however, was to be firmly under the imperial thumb: taking the title of Justinianic praetor, he was to regulate his conduct by Justinian's instructions, render judgment in accordance with Justinian's laws, and, "above all things, keep the fear of God and of Us in mind, and never plan anything in contravention of Our precepts."

Justinian's attempt to tie the provinces to a strong imperial center is also evident from his *Novel* 47 (dated August 31, 537, and again addressed to John as praetorian prefect). This text ordered that all judicial and extrajudicial legal records must begin by acknowledging "God the creator" and then provide a record of their date. This date must be recorded first according to the relevant year of the rule of Justinian, "most sacred Augustus and emperor." Only after that should the date be entered in the customary fashion, according to either consular years or the year of the individual city. This reform in the standard dating practices was necessary "to the end that the government of the realm may be eternal and may outlast the laws and the celebrations that accompany them; so will the memory of our rule remain present for all occasions and times."[27] Every magistrate's act, every business transaction, court proceeding, or legal instrument would thus exist, like the texts of the *Corpus iuris civilis* itself, as a perpetual witness to Justinian's preeminent authority – an authority, moreover, that Justinian theorized was God-given. The first sentence of Justinian's *Novel* 72 (538) refers to "those who have received from God the power to make laws" and immediately adds "by which We mean the emperor."

Justinian and all magistrates with jurisdiction over criminal and civil cases had advisers. Every official court had assessors (legal experts) as well as legally trained advocates attached to its staff. According to Procopius, however, Justinian was apt to take his judicial advice from the wrong sources.[28] An extraordinary section of Justinian's *Novel* 8 corroborates Procopius, to a certain extent; it says that while Justinian was mulling over how best to stamp out corrupt provincial magistrates, he sought the advice of Theodora. The law that resulted (*Novel* 8 itself) was to be read out by bishops to their congregations on festival days: "In order that all persons may regard their magistrates as fathers, rather than as thieves and persons plotting to deprive them of their property."[29] The irony of this law, when seen in the context of Justinian and Theodora's own extensive confiscation of property for the imperial pocket, was not lost on their contemporaries.

In an attempt to ensure that his empire was supported by competent legal officials, Justinian ordered an overhaul of the legal educational system in 533. The *Digest*'s second preface, the *Constitutio Omnem*, was addressed from Justinian to eight professors at the law schools of Beirut and Constantinople; it details the new academic curriculum and flatters the scholarly labors of its addressees.[30] The key to the educational overhaul, however, was the promulgation of the Justinianic *Institutes* on November 21, 533. Tribonian and two professors from the schools of Beirut and Constantinople were employed to draft the text, which addressed itself to "young enthusiasts for law." Justinian christened these young enthusiasts, first-year law students, with the name "New Justinians."[31] Structured primarily around two texts written by the second-century law teacher Gaius, Justinian's *Institutes* were to provide students with: "An elementary framework, a cradle of the law, not based on obscure old stories but illuminated by the light of our imperial splendor . . . you have been found worthy of the great honor and good fortune of . . . following a course of legal education which from start to finish proceeds from the Emperor's lips."[32] The *Institutes*, which were promulgated in Latin, also specifically directed students' attention toward Justinian's most important legislative innovations to date: for example, on long-term possession (2.6, pr.); on making a will (2.10.10); and on statutory succession (3.2.3). This last example perfectly encapsulates the tension between old and new in Justinian's law: "Our pronouncement has completely redesigned the system and made it conform to the scheme of the Twelve Tables." Once again, innovation was framed as a return to the past.

Justinian's *Institutes* were also careful to point students toward the *Digest* and *Codex* for advice on tricky legal points.[33] Criminal law also had to be learned later. The "cradle of the law" thus looked forward to the time when first-year students would be capable of handling the grown-up material.

After five (long) years of studying Justinian's books of law, students were expected to become "leaders in advocacy, acolytes of justice, athletes and helmsmen of the courts."[34] The late-sixth-century historian Menander chose a different path:

> My Father Euphratas, who came from Byzantium, had no literary education. My brother Herodotus began to train towards a legal career but lost his enthusiasm for these studies. I myself thought that I ought not to abandon the law and should complete my studies, which I did to the best of my ability. But I did not take up the profession for which I was trained. For I had no desire to plead cases, or to haunt the Royal Stoa and impress the petitioners with my eloquence. I therefore neglected my career for the disgraceful life of an idle lay-about.[35]

Menander goes on to state that he took up writing history so that his life would not be completely futile. Not all law school graduates opted for careers in and around the Constantinopolitan courtrooms or the Palatine bureaucratic offices. As we shall see, there were other avenues for legal talent.

## Making Sense of the Emperors' Laws

> Our subjects are our constant care, whether they are alive or dead.
>
> – Nov. 43, pr.

The picture portrayed in Justinian's *Institutes* of law students at Beirut, Constantinople, and Rome constantly meditating upon imperial legislation can be borne out by legal writings outside the Justinianic corpus and contemporary literary accounts. Julian, a mid-sixth-century professor of law at Constantinople, thoughtfully provided his students with a short guide on how to look up different topics of law in the *Digest*, Justinianic *Codex*, and individual Justinianic *Novels*. This text is known today as the *Dictatum de Consiliariis* (*Instructions for Counsels*).[36] It gives an impression of Constantinopolitan legal practice as a highly professional and text-focused activity. Julian refers to the "grown-up" texts of Justinian's *Corpus*, together with the new laws (*Novellae*) that Justinian continued to issue. For example, Julian states:

> If you are looking for information about the production of witnesses, read *Code*, book 4, chap. 20, *Digest*, book 22 chap. 5, On Witnesses, and in the *Novels*, that same constitution, which is under the same heading, On Witnesses. But if a question is brought before you about heretical witnesses, then read the last constitution in *Code*, book 1 chap. 5. Read, too, however, the constitution in the *Novels* around 60, in which you will find that heretics of curial status can give testimony in every way.

Mastery of a single topic might require the perusal of many Justinianic texts. Julian considered book 9 of Justinian's *Codex* on criminal examinations to be especially important (or difficult): he states that it should be read every day. A meticulous reading of the constitutions on marriage in the *Novellae* is also advised – presumably because of the many legal innovations they contained, mostly in favor of women controlling either their children or their dowries. Julian also wrote summaries of 124 of Justinian's *Novellae* (known today as the *Epitome Juliani, Julian's Summaries*), for a course taught in Latin in the academic year 556–557. The following academic year, Julian was again teaching Justinian's new laws, this time in Greek.[37] The need for bilingual instruction came partly from the legislation itself: from 535 onward, laws addressed to officials within the eastern provinces were composed mostly in Greek, while laws directed to those in Illyria and Africa remained in Latin. Justinian's *Novellae* were a crucial part of legal practice, empirewide.

Further glimpses of legal practice can be gleaned from sixth-century literary accounts. Sometime in the early years of Justinian's reign, an individual named Zacharias Scholasticus (Zacharias the Advocate) wrote a hagiographical life story of Severus, Bishop of Antioch, covering the years between 512 and 518. Zacharias's *Life of*

*Severus* paints a vivid picture of life as a student at the famed law school of Beirut.[38] Zacharias relates how he and Severus devised a plan together to attend the classes of their professors regularly and to study the civil law diligently every day – taking Saturday afternoons off to read sacred scripture and the writings of the Church Fathers and attending church on Sunday. In a nice piece of legalese, Zacharias justifies having Sunday off from the civil law because "Sunday is the day that the same civil law orders should be consecrated to God." Zacharias also describes how Severus busied himself at Beirut studying the laws of emperors, "examining and going further into all the imperial edicts that comprised those of his time." Moreover, Severus, ever the overachiever: "wrote down comparisons of them [i.e., the imperial edicts] in the form of short commentaries, and he left notes and annotations for future generations, in the manner of notebooks, which were a useful means of eradicating errors in the records."[39] This comparative technique had long been essential to determining the practical application of imperial legislation. Justinian had attempted to dispense with one age-old problem in interpreting imperial laws by stating that all his legislation (unless it explicitly stated otherwise) had "general" empirewide application. Notwithstanding Justinian's assertions to the contrary, general imperial laws frequently conflicted with each other. A text of the third-century jurist Modestinus (included at *Digest* 1.4.4) stated that later laws repeal earlier laws to the extent that they are inconsistent with them. Justinian's *Codex* demanded the application of this same interpretative principle. Note, however, that neither Modestinus nor Justinian's commissioners intended later laws simply to repeal all earlier laws. Later laws repealed earlier laws only to the extent that they conflicted with them or added something to them. The techniques Severus had learned were essential to legal practitioners both before and after 534.

Despite Justinian's prohibition against any juristic commentaries on his *Codex*, *Digest*, or *Institutes*, the practice of Justinianic law still demanded the application of legal and rhetorical techniques of analysis on a case-by-case basis. Interpretative difficulties show up repeatedly in Justinian's early and late legislation alike. For example, a case that was judged on appeal in 535 gave the initiative to Justinian's *Novel* 2 (dated March 16). A woman, Gregoria, had petitioned the emperor regarding her lengthy and complex legal dispute with her daughter. Justinian accepted the woman's appeal and called them both to Constantinople. The daughter claimed the entire estate of her deceased father, relying on two former imperial constitutions to make her case. The judges at the first hearing must have been convinced, because the daughter had won her case. Before Justinian, however, the mother pleaded "that these constitutions were cruel, and unworthy of the clemency of our age. However, availing herself of the constitution promulgated by us, she alleged that this constitution could not be subordinated to the former ones."[40] The mother thus relied upon a more recent constitution promulgated by Justinian, which she interpreted as upholding her appeal. The daughter must have already argued that this new constitution did not in fact add anything new to the two former ones, despite her mother's interpretation. Justinian decided to enact another constitution, so that the difficult case could be finally decided in favor of the mother (who had perhaps swayed the emperor by her rhetorical appeal to the "clemency" of his age). This new law was to be observed in the case that had prompted it, as well as in all pending and future litigation. Its text was to be communicated to every city under Justinian's rule by Hermogenes, the master of the imperial offices, to whom it was addressed. Only two years later, however, Justinian issued yet another law on the same subject.

The prefaces to Justinian's *Novellae* frequently refer to the fact that new laws are necessary because concrete cases keep throwing up imperfections and complexities in the existing legislation. Prefaces were included as the first section of any imperial law at the time of its promulgation. They advertised general legislative policies and provided an imperial spin on any relevant current events. This information would be communicated empirewide when the laws were read out publicly, by imperial heralds, in the localities to which they were sent. The prefaces to Justinian's *Novellae* have perhaps been preserved only because Justinian never produced a collection of his new laws; if he had, they would have been cut as superfluous verbiage by the volume's compilers (as they had been in the 529 and 534 editions of the *Codex*). Justinian's *Novellae* thus offer a unique window through which to view the concrete circumstances that prompted most imperial legislation.

In the prefaces to Justinian's *Novellae* we are presented with a picture of Justinian constantly judging cases, hearing appeals, and being asked to decide complex points of law by imperial magistrates. The opening sentences of *Novel* 98 (issued December 16, 539) describe this constant activity using typical Justinianic legislative rhetoric:

> When things are always the same and just so, complicated laws are not required, since simplicity and integrity are maintained unmixed with all complexity, and use is made of laws that are eternal and divine and require no correction; in the

> whirlpool and turmoil that we now experience, however, our affairs need the governing wisdom that comes from laws. And so, since many lawsuits are passed on to us, who are hardly lazy about exercising judgment, we give our attention to each one; we take over all the inquiries considered doubtful by us and our judges, and, using the skill of the lawgiver, lay down what has to be done in each and every case.

Justinian's times are ever-changing; only laws fixed by God remain immutable, and a human legislator's task is incessant, dogged, and frequently keeps him awake at night. In the opening sentences of *Novel* 84 (539), the drafter of the text even apologizes for the many references to these motifs in the imperial laws.

Justinianic law making, then, by no means ended with his lawbooks. Any magistrate, lawyer, drafter of legal documents, or, indeed, any individual at all who wished to effect a transaction according to the law in force was expected to keep up with the legislative pace. The promulgation of new legislation was relentless, particularly for the years 535–542, but continuing right up to 565. Justinian, remember, never issued an official compilation of his *Novellae*, and this fact, coupled with the emperor's conviction that new legislation was constantly necessary, increased uncertainty later on in his reign concerning the law that was actually in effect, particularly in the two crucial fields of inheritance and ownership. This in turn increased the number of petitions and appeals addressed to the emperor and the courts at Constantinople. These appeals, of course, in their turn increased the number of new laws, as Justinian felt obliged to promulgate constitutions in response to problems thrown up by particular cases. His subjects complained. The preface to *Novel* 60 (537) adopts a defensive tone in response to this criticism: "For it is natural that some people will find fault with the mass of laws that are promulgated every day. Such people do not bear in mind that we are forced by pressing necessity to issue laws that are appropriate to the needs of government, since problems regularly arise unexpectedly which cannot be resolved by the existing body of laws." The later Byzantine emperor Leo, engaged in promulgating his Greek version of Justinian's *Corpus iuris civilis* (the *Basilica*) around 900 CE, saw Justinian as a failed and defective legislator – precisely because he did not know when to stop. In Leo's opinion, Justinian "ruined his first work [the *Corpus iuris civilis*] without knowing."[41]

Justinian's 528–534 project of codification had attempted to stabilize and fix the sources of law under the auspices of the immutable and eternal Christian God, but in practice Roman law – perhaps like the empire itself – proved an impossibly difficult terrain to control.

## Resolving Legal Disputes in the Age of Justinian

So far we have focused primarily upon the emperor and Constantinople as the center of legal practice, as Justinian himself did. He considered it unworthy of his reign that a law should be obeyed in one way at Constantinople and in another way in the provinces.[42] Likewise, all bureaucratic courts within the empire were expected to follow both the written and unwritten customs of the court of the praetorian prefect in the capital city. It would be a mistake, however, to assume that all dispute resolution took place according to this model. First, there was a complex system of different localized types of courts and legal jurisdictions empirewide. Second, there was the option of resolving private law disputes, as well as cases involving monks or clergy, before ecclesiastical authorities. Third, there were a number of extrajudicial options ranging from informal agreement to formal arbitration. We shall examine each in turn. Rather than seeing one as an alternative to the other, these three avenues were often used in practice as complementary and occasionally interlocking means of getting a case settled by law.

When a provincial inhabitant decided to pursue a case through the courts, his or her first recourse could be to the local town magistrate. The *defensor civitatis* (defender of the city) was another increasingly predominant option. Justinian's *Novel* 15 (535) spelled out the legal activities of these *defensores*; they were to register all wills, donations, and other such documents drafted within their locality, aid in tax collection, and supervise persons known for their bad behavior. They were also to have final judicial authority over cases involving fewer than three hundred *solidi* (pieces of gold). The final section of the text acknowledges that litigants (or their advocates) will try to get around the letter of this law by fraudulently estimating that the property under dispute was worth more than three hundred *solidi*, thereby enabling them to bring their action directly before the provincial governor. A further local option, specifically in rural areas, were *iudices pedanei* (itinerant judges). Justinian rationalized the structure of these traveling courts between 539 and 541.[43] He also acknowledged the challenges posed by low levels of literacy and shortages of skilled legal notaries, especially in the countryside.[44]

The next level of courts were those of the provincial governors – Justinian's judicial reforms granted all his new proconsuls and praetors the rank of *spectabiles*, and all magistrates of this rank were given the right of final judgment in cases involving fewer than five hundred *solidi*, a number quickly raised to 750. Some were also given appellate jurisdiction over a neighboring province.[45] Individuals petitioned provincial magistrates for the resolution of private law disputes, as well as cases involving criminal accusations. The magistrates were also responsible for maintaining public order and apparently relied upon a much-feared crew of informers to aid them in their task. Prosecuting a case through the various bureaucratic courts was invariably an expensive and lengthy process, despite Justinian's attempts to tackle both these areas. It was not unusual, if a case went to appeal, for the court costs to exceed the value of any disputed property.

There were also particular courts for special classes of people and special types of cases, as well as rules governing decisions over which court had jurisdiction in any given case.[46] In 535 and 539 Justinian established two new judges for Constantinople alone (the praetor of the plebs and the Constantinopolitan *quaesitor*); they were responsible for small claims, public order, and making sure that all those individuals whose cases ended up at Constantinople on appeal made it back home again.[47]

As well as creating new bureaucratic offices, the emperor could also delegate his authority to a named individual who would then act as judge for a particular case. Agathias's *Histories* purport to describe one such an event, a "show-piece" trial that took place according to Roman law and following customary Constantinopolitan procedure in the faraway land of the Colchi tribe. This trial is undoubtedly idealized in Agathias's narrative; he states that "... a court worthy of the traditions of Imperial Rome and Democratic Athens was set up at the foot of the Caucasus."[48] However, the historian intended his procedural details to ring true for his contemporary audience. Agathias states that the judge, sent specially from Constantinople by Justinian, donned the robes of the highest civil magistrates and took his seat on a raised tribunal. Trained shorthand writers were in attendance, as well as Constantinopolitan officials who were "especially well-versed in the niceties of legal procedure." Heralds were present, as were ushers with whips, as well as individuals specifically charged with the responsibility of administering torture (they carried iron collars and racks, as well as other instruments of torment). The accused took their positions to the left of the judge, the accusers to his right, and the trial commenced with the latter requesting a formal reading of the imperial mandate. Then came the accusers' speech. At this point, Agathias notes that the crowd of Colchians could not understand the accusers' terms or appreciate their rhetorical skill, but they "enthusiastically supported the efforts of the prosecution by echoing their intonation and imitating their gestures."[49] The ability of skilled pleaders to sway the mood of the crowd (and the judge) was a standard theme before and during Justinian's age. The defense then had its turn, delivering a speech composed of proofs, inferences, and deductions, three standard techniques in pleading a case at law taught at rhetorical schools. The magistrate listened to both sides before beginning his judicial inquisition.[50] After a written verdict had been given, the condemned men were paraded through the streets on mules. A herald then proclaimed "in a loud clear voice a general exhortation to respect the laws and refrain from committing murder."[51] The beheading of the defendants marked the end of the process. What stands out from Agathias's account, besides the details of how a sixth-century audience expected a criminal trial to proceed, is the reminder that legal trials could be public spectacles. Cases heard by legal officials, especially those of a high rank, could turn into theatrical occasions for performing the law.[52]

The Christian Church was rapidly developing its own claims to a distinct body of law, what we today might term "Canon law," during Justinian's reign. The emperor took on the role of executor for this ecclesiastical law: Justinian's *Novel* 131.1 (issued March 18, 545) confirmed the canons of the church as civil laws. Justinian even claimed to be the source of both secular and ecclesiastical jurisprudence in the preamble to his *Novel* 9 (April 14, 535, addressed to John, archbishop and patriarch of old Rome). Sentences of anathema and deposition issued by bishops in council were ratified by Justinian, just as if they had emanated from the *res publica* itself.[53] Indeed, placing texts of canon law side by side with texts of Roman law became an important and distinct aspect of legal practice in the later Byzantine Empire.[54]

The church was also consolidating its own bureaucratic structure, which included ecclesiastical courts, councils, and a system of judicial appeal for cases involving clergy or monks. Bishops had been permitted to hear cases relevant to Roman private law since the age of Constantine, and Justinian reinforced this practice at the same time as extending his control over it. Submitting a case for adjudication by a bishop undoubtedly held out the promise of a quicker and cheaper means of dispute resolution – although tips (*sportulae*) still had to be paid to the bishop's heralds, stenographers, and legal experts.

Justinian made use of Christian clerics in many different legal contexts. Bishops were expected to ensure that Christian slaves were released without price by Jewish, pagan, or heretical masters; they were ordered to hear (certain) cases where the provincial judge's neutrality or trustworthiness had been questioned. Likewise, they could sit in judgment over provincial judges themselves and report to the emperor where necessary; they were also expected to judge cases in cities or towns where there were no magistrates.[55] Monks were also utilized, in addition to their role as sacred invokers of God's divine beneficence over emperor and empire. In *Novel* 134.9 (issued May 556), Justinian ordered that women could not be held in prisons while they awaited judgment for criminal offenses; they had to be placed in convents or monasteries instead. The "reverend inmates" were to be the women's guards. Given this blurring of sacred and civil jurisdiction, it is little wonder that Justinian had to state explicitly that clergy and monks could not receive or collect taxes, nor could they act as agents for the transfer or alienation of public and private property or procurators in the conduct of civil litigation.[56]

The *defensores ecclesiae* (defenders of the church), on the other hand, had a specific imperial mandate to act in civil and criminal cases. The defenders' main purpose was to protect the individual legal interests of the particular church to which they were attached. Throughout Justinian's reign there is evidence for law school graduates opting for ecclesiastical careers. Zacharias Scholasticus names four of his contemporaries from the law school at Beirut (including Severus of Antioch) who swapped their togas for the monastic habit, their study of books of civil law for holy scripture.[57] However, converts from law to theology did not leave their legal training behind; they applied it in the service of monastic establishments and the church. The historian Evagrius Scholasticus studied law during Justinian's reign and later joined the office staff of Gregory, the patriarch of Antioch (570–592).[58]

The impossibility of splitting Justinian's empire into discrete units of church and state goes for legal texts as well as institutions and individuals. Bishops were expected to read imperial laws to their congregations, and in *Novel* 8, Justinian orders that his law is to be deposited in the Holy Church "as being itself dedicated to God, and written for the security of the men created by Him." Moreover, this text was to be engraved upon tablets of stone and placed at the portals of the Holy Church, so that everyone could have the opportunity of reading it. Imperial legislation was placed in Christian churches and Gospel texts were housed in Roman courtrooms. In 531 Justinian became the first emperor to require that before any kind of Roman civil or courtroom process could begin, all the participants – litigants and legal officials alike – had to swear an oath of Christian faith, while touching a copy of the Gospels.[59] Conveniently, Justinian had already ordered in 530 that the Gospels had to be placed in every Roman courtroom. The presence of the Gospels, stated Justinian, guaranteed the presence of God at every legal hearing.[60] This radical innovation is one of the most striking aspects of Justinianic courtroom practice.

Not all legal disputes, however, were pursued through the courts. Individuals could request that magistrates designate persons to decide controversies, or they could agree to such a person between themselves. The time-honored form of arbitration required that both parties swear mutual oaths before the case was begun, thereby agreeing to be bound by the result. A 529 constitution, included in Justinian's *Codex* at 2.55.4, advises that even when such arbitration was undertaken less formally, the parties' final agreement should be sworn on oath and then written down so that no one had any excuse for deceit later. The arbitrators did not necessarily have any legal knowledge. Justinian states that he is frequently harassed by persons who have selected arbiters absolutely ignorant of the law and with no experience of how to decide what is just. Having sworn an oath to abide by the decision, these persons subsequently decide that they got rough justice and appeal to have their cases heard a second time – thus committing calumny.[61] One way to bypass this problem, from the disputing parties' perspective, was to include elaborate clauses in the *dialyseis*, documents that recorded the arbitrated settlement of their dispute. A papyrus from the collection at Michigan, dated to around 527–538 and recording a *dialysis* from the Egyptian locale of Aphrodite, includes the following exhaustive clause:

> This general settlement has been concluded between [the parties to the dispute] for every removal and complete cutting out of the legal dispute concerning them and in accordance with this settlement the people of each party acknowledge to all others and each separately that they have no longer any claim against each other concerning whatsoever matter, small or big, written or unwritten, thought of or not thought of, remembered or not remembered, said or unsaid, judged or un-judged and that they for the future do not prosecute nor shall prosecute each other either in a law-court in the country nor in a law-court abroad or outside the law-courts, not they by themselves nor by a representative nor by a man

> of straw whosoever... because they have settled all points according to the aforesaid written decision and each party has in regard to all these points sworn.[62]

The purpose of this document was not only to record a settlement by arbitration, but also to stem every threat of a future lawsuit. Such clauses are also common in papyrological records of business transactions and contracts.

In a law issued in 531, Justinian forbade women to act as arbiters; they should safeguard their modesty and confine themselves to the roles that nature fitted them for.[63] It is clear from this text, however, that women *were* acting as arbiters and performing judicial duties. In fact, women frequently appear as vociferous legal participants in fifth- and sixth-century Egyptian papyri.[64]

Individuals could, of course, undertake to sort their disputes out between themselves. This kind of 'private' negotiation still needed to take account of the law in force. One example is provided by a papyrus in the Oxyrhynchus collection, dated March 17, 545.[65] It records a contract between two parties engaged in private negotiations over the ownership of a disputed property. A certain individual had mortgaged his estate to a monastery near Oxyrhynchus; but without the knowledge of the monastery, he had also previously mortgaged the same property to an important Oxyrhynchus landowner and Constantinopolitan senator. The double-crossing swindler died, and when the monks tried to claim his property they found they were disbarred. The monks were well aware of the law in force and thus acknowledged the senator's (prior) legal right to the estate in question. Nonetheless, representatives from the monastery traveled to Constantinople and begged that the senator and his heirs grant them the property, appealing to their piety (and promising to pray for their souls). The senator and his heirs agreed to compensate the monastery. As a parting shot, however, the senator's heirs required that the monastic representatives swear an oath promising not to pursue any element of this dispute through the courts at a future point in time. This oath was drafted by the same legal notary who seems to have been responsible for recording the settlement as a whole in 545. The monks swore that they would never attempt to oppose this agreement:

> in a local court or one beyond the frontier, nor out of court, not by petition directed to our victorious master [i.e., Justinian], that they will not make accusations among friends,

> not impugn the terms or part of [the agreement], either at law or in holy churches, nor say that they have suffered any fraud or neglect, because by confirmed reasoning and from accurate laws they have learned that they have no action or right of exaction lawfully.

Here we can see how individuals could negotiate disputes for themselves extrajudicially, acknowledging the imperial legislation in force and achieving a mutually agreeable resolution, even if that resolution was contrary to the strict letter of the law.

Any attempt to understand law in the Age of Justinian thus necessitates going beyond the pages of Justinian's *Codex*, *Digest*, and *Institutes*, piecing together imperial legislation and legal sources that survive outside that *corpus*, reading reports of judicial proceedings and legal transactions in sixth-century papyri, as well as evaluating literary accounts of legal activity recorded in different sixth-century texts. What emerges is a highly complex relationship between law on the one hand and society on the other – between the legislator in the imperial capital of Constantinople and a host of different legal practitioners, implementing, evading, and negotiating Justinian's texts of law in their own sixth-century settings.

## NOTES

My thanks to Professors Fergus Millar, Peter Garnsey, Charles Pazdernik, and Michael Maas for their generous and stimulating comments on earlier drafts of this essay.

1 The standard texts for the *Corpus iuris civilis* are *Justinian's Institutes*, trans. P. Birks and G. McLeod (London, 1987), using the edited text of P. Krueger; *Digest (Pandecta) of Justinian*, trans. A. Watson and others (Philadelphia, 1984), using the edited text of T. Mommsen and P. Krueger; and *Codex Justinianus*, ed. P. Krueger (Berlin, 1877). The only English translation of Justinian's *Codex*, by S. P. Scott in vol. 12 of his *The Civil Law* (Cincinnati, Ohio, 1932), is serviceable, if on occasion unreliable. All citations of the *Codex* in this essay follow Krueger's standard edition.

2 O. F. Robinson, *The Sources of Roman Law: Problems and Methods for Ancient Historians* (London, 1997), provides a useful overview. There is no standard account, in English, of law and legal practice in Justinian's age per se.

3 P. Stein, *Roman Law in European History* (New York, 1999), 2.

4 T. M. Charles-Edwards, "Law in the Western Kingdoms between the Fifth and the Seventh Century," *CAH* 14 260.

5 *CJ Const. Haec*, pr.

6 *CJ Const. Summa*, 2–3. Likewise *Digest Const. Tanta*, 12, refers to the Supreme Deity vouchsafing the "giving of the best laws, not merely for our own age but for all time, both present and future."

7 *CJ Const. Haec*, 2, repeated at *Const. Summa*, 3.

8 On the *Codex Theodosianus* and its forerunners, see J. F. Matthews, *Laying Down the Law: A Study of the Theodosian Code* (New Haven, Conn., 2000).

9 *Nov. Th.*, 2.2 (dated Oct. 1, 447).

10 On the reception of Theodosius's *Codex* in the West, see the *Gesta Senatus Urbis Romae* (printed as an introduction to the *Theodosian Code* in modern editions). For the transmission of Valentinian III's *Novellae* to the East, see *Nov. Th.*, 2.3.

11 Justinian's *Novellae* survived in various private collections; for a brief discussion of their complex transmission, see D. Liebs, "Roman Law," *CAH* 14:251–252. The standard edition of Justinian's *Novellae* (in parallel Greek and Latin text) is R. Schöll and W. Kroll (Berlin, 1895). An English translation exists in vols. 16 and 17 of S. P. Scott, *The Civil Law*, but is not reliable. For this reason all citations and translations of Justinian's *Novellae* in this essay are made from Schöll and Kroll.

12 *CJ Const. Summa*, 5.

13 *CJ Const. Cordi*, 4.

14 *CJ Const. Summa*, 3.

15 *CJ*, 2.55.5.3 to Julian praetorian prefect, 530.

16 *CJ Const. Cordi*, pr.

17 *Digest Const. Tanta*, 20.

18 *Digest Const. Omnem*, 5

19 See *Digest Const. Omnem*, 7, and *Digest Const. Tanta*, 12–13, 24.

20 Tony Honoré, *Tribonian* (London, 1978), 139–186. See also Honoré's article "Justinian's Codification: Some Reflections," *Bracton Law Journal* 25 (1993): 29–37.

21 *Digest Const Tanta*, pr.

22 *Digest Const. Deo auctore*, 6.

23 *Digest Const. Deo auctore*, 12.

24 *Digest Const. Tanta*, 21.

25 *CJ*, 1.14.12.2, 529.

26 Michael Maas, *John Lydus and the Roman Past: Antiquarianism and Politics in the Age of Justinian* (London, 1992), 27. For the 535–539 administrative reforms in general, see A. H. M. Jones, *LRE*, 279–282, and Michael Maas, "Roman History and Christian Ideology in Justinianic Reform Legislation," *DOP* 40 (1986): 17–31.

27 *Nov.*, 47.1.1.

28 Procopius, *Secret History*, 14.

29 *Nov.*, 8.1.

30 Liebs, "Roman Law," 253–258, provides a good overview.

31 *Digest Const. Omnem*, 2. The Roman law of the *Institutes* is explored in *A Companion to Justinian's Institutes*, ed. E. Metzger (Ithaca, N.Y., 1998).

32 *Inst. Const. Imp.*, 3.

33 See, for example, *Institutes*, 4.4.14.

34 *Digest Const. Omnem*, 6, translation by Honoré, *Tribonian*, 31. The historian Agathias, a law school graduate and practicing advocate at Constantinople, describes himself as being "kept at my desk in the *Basileios Stoa* from early morning until late evening busying myself with the incessant perusal of innumerable legal documents" (*Histories*, 3.1.4).

35 *Menander History*, frag. 1, 41.

36 The only modern edition of Julian's *Dictatum de Consiliariis* is in the volume *Iuliani Epitome Latina Novellarum Iustiniani*, ed. G. Hänel (Leipzig, 1873), 198–201. There is no English translation.

37 Liebs, "Roman Law," 252.

38 Zacharias Scholasticus, *Life of Severus*, ed. M. A. Kugener, PO 2 (Paris, 1907), 46–92. There is no English translation, but Kugener's edition provides a parallel Syriac-French text.

39 Zacharias Scholasticus, *Life of Severus*, 91; my thanks to Geoffrey Kahn for the translation of this passage from the Syriac.

40 *Nov.*, 2.1.

41 Emperor Leo, *Novel*, 1; passage trans. J. H. A. Lokin, "The *Novels* of Leo and Justinian," *Journal of Juristic Papyrology* 28 (1998): 138.

42 *CJ*, 8.10.13, 531. See also *Digest, Const. Deo auctore*, 10.

43 Maas, *John Lydus*, 34.

44 *Nov.*, 73.8–9, 538.

45 For further details of Justinian's complex judicial reforms and his modifications to rights of appeal, see Jones, *LRE*, 279–282.

46 See Liebs, "Roman Law," 240–241.

47 *Nov. Iust.*, 13 and 80.

48 Agathias, *Histories*, 4.1.2–11.3; quotation at 4.1.8.

49 Agathias, *Histories*, 4.7.1.

50 Agathias, *Histories*, 4.11.1.

51 Agathias, *Histories*, 4.11.3.

52 On this theme, see W. Davies, "Local Participation and Legal Ritual in Early Medieval Texts," in *The Moral World of the Law*, ed. P. Coss (Cambridge, 2000). The essay does not, however, discuss Justinian's age.

53 *Nov.*, 42, August 6, 536.

54 For mid- to late-sixth-century examples, see the introductory chapter to *Collectio Tripartita: Justinian on Religious and Ecclesiastical Affairs*, ed. N. van der Wal and B. H. Stolte (Groningen, 1994).

55 *CJ*, 1.3.54 (56).8, 533–534 and *Nov. Iust.*, 86.

56 *Nov.*, 123.6.

57 Zacharias Scholasticus, *Life of Severus*, 92. The phrases are Zacharias's own.

58 *Evag. Ecc. Hist*, xiv.

59 *CJ*, 2.58.2 pr.

60 *CJ*, 3.1.14.1–2.

61 *Nov.*, 82.11, 539.

62 *P. Mich.*, 8.659, ed. and trans. P. Sijpesteijn.

63 *CJ*, 2.55.6.

64 On the Egyptian papyri, with some discussion of the sixth century, see J. G. Keenan, "Egypt" in *CAH* 14:612–637. Also see T. Gagos and P. van Minnen, *Settling a Dispute: Towards a Legal Anthropology of Late Antique Egypt* (Ann Arbor, Mich., 1994).

65 *P. Oxy.*, 63.4397, ed. and trans. B. P. Grenfell.

# 8: Justinianic Ideology and the Power of the Past

*Charles Pazdernik*

> For [Justinian], being by nature an innovator and covetous of whatsoever does not belong to him, unable to abide by what is established, has longed to take over the entire earth, and has been striving to bring every kingdom into his power.
>
> – Procopius, *Wars*, 2.2.6

The words in the epigraph are the testimony of hostile witnesses, attributed by Procopius of Caesarea to envoys of the Ostrogothic king of Italy who have arrived at the court of Sasanid Persia in order to enlist support against Justinian's efforts to reconquer Italy.[1] Procopius himself qualifies these words in an aside: "[The Gothic envoys] were bringing as indictments against Justinian such things as would seemingly be encomiums for a worthy emperor, since he was striving to make his realm greater and much more splendid" (*Wars*, 2.2.14). While the historian discounts the motives of the speakers bringing the charges, his judgment as to the substance of the charges themselves is carefully nuanced. The very accomplishments that in the hands of Justinian's enemies supply material for invective, he states, might serve as the stuff of panegyric if viewed in a sympathetic light.

Justinian was a controversial and contradictory figure, whose policies and methods of self-presentation both attracted and repulsed contemporary observers. Two charges laid at Justinian's feet by the Gothic envoys are particularly relevant for the discussion that follows. The emperor is both an inveterate "innovator" and hostile to "what is established" – essentially two sides of the same coin.[2] Justinian's initiatives exposed tensions between the imperial office, which was capable of drawing upon deeply ingrained habits of loyalty and obedience from its subjects, and other sources of authority and legitimacy deeply embedded in the social fabric of late antiquity. Questions emerged with special urgency about what it meant to be a Roman, to govern (or to be governed) lawfully, and to perpetuate institutions and practices sanctioned by their antiquity. Much was at stake: to the extent that Justinian's rule could be characterized as neither "Roman" nor "lawful," to the extent that it demonstrated contempt for the legitimizing power of the past, the emperor jeopardized not merely his own position but also his vision of a society characterized by an unprecedented degree of order, unanimity, and concord – a vision he considered himself to have been uniquely and providentially appointed to realize.

As a devout Christian, Justinian professed a conception of human history that was providential and eschatological. Seeking to make the earthly monarchy over which he presided more nearly resemble the heavenly monarchy upon which he believed it to be patterned,[3] he was intolerant of pluralism and heterodoxy and prepared to use the resources of the state to regulate the lives and beliefs of his subjects. Until the Kingdom of God might be realized on earth, however, change was natural and inevitable, and needed to be managed by a strong hand and with unstinting effort. In his determination to translate principle into practice, to seize opportunities, and to articulate a vision of his role in the imperial office that elevated the pragmatic and opportunistic to the level of principle, Justinian emerges as a genuine ideologue and a radical, a ruler determined to remake the world in accordance with his ideals.

As a canny opportunist in a society suspicious of change, Justinian appreciated the instrumental value of portraying change as a development within, or a recovery of, traditional values. Accordingly, he presented himself as preserving the most ancient traditions of the office he held and of the Roman Empire he ruled. A case in point is the ceremony, held in the capital in 534, marking the destruction of the Vandal kingdom in North Africa the preceding year, which was intended to evoke the triumphal processions of Rome's imperial heyday.[4] Yet Justinian refused to be limited or constrained by tradition. Suitable precedents, when they mattered, might conveniently be discovered or drummed up by his clever and capable lieutenants;[5] tradition itself could be discredited for being obscure or self-contradictory. The emperor put himself forward as both a conservator and a reformer.

Alongside Justinian's appreciation of the power of the past must be placed his seemingly unshakable convictions about the indispensable nature of his own role in history and his ability to give effect to his will. Those convictions were severely tested throughout a long and eventful reign that witnessed, among other things, a bloody uprising against his throne, a quagmire in Italy and military disasters in the East, plague, and intractable resistance to his plans for achieving theological and ecclesiastical unity. Far from being chastened by such challenges, the emperor seized them as pretexts for exposing opponents, eliminating error, and consolidating control.

This chapter focuses principally upon the relationship between Justinianic ideology and the political legacy of Roman law. Justinian used legislation as both a medium to advertise his conception of the imperial office he inhabited and a means of exercising authority over the secular and the sacred, the public and the private. Yet Roman legal traditions and political discourse characteristically drew upon the priority and integrity of Roman law as a source of legitimacy distinguishable from, and potentially a counterweight to, encroaching imperial autocracy. Two figures, the late-fourth-century soldier and historian Ammianus Marcellinus and the sixth-century bureaucrat and antiquarian John the Lydian, testify to the relative standing of emperors and the law in their respective periods. John's writings respond to and problematize Justinian's efforts to circumscribe the polyvocal and autonomous qualities of Roman law and his decidedly mixed record of conserving the distinguishing features of the past.

Justinian's willingness to embrace change, to impress his personality upon his age and thus to affect decisively the course of history, and to do so across a broad range of human endeavor is remarkable in any historical period. Procopius, in the citations quoted here, subtly draws a parallel with the past that communicates a sense of both the promise of his age and its potential for disaster. The words he places in the mouths of the Gothic envoys are patterned upon accusations leveled against classical Athens – in an allusion that Procopius surely intended to be noticed and appreciated by his readers[6] – that are placed by Thucydides in the mouths of envoys from the rival city of Corinth during the diplomatic exchanges that preceded the outbreak of the Peloponnesian War. The Corinthians denounce the Athenians – another regime impatient with the status quo – as "innovators," a term, for readers of both Procopius and Thucydides, with connotations of revolution and social upheaval.[7]

## Roman Imperial Ideology and the Legacy of Roman Law

Ideology is an articulated and disseminated vision of "the way things ought to be" that may serve either to reinforce or to challenge the established order. The long process of conquest and acculturation that we call "Romanization" succeeded in predisposing the diverse peoples settled around the Mediterranean basin to believe that reciprocal ties of allegiance and responsibility existed between themselves and a figure in a distant capital who might be known indifferently to them as Caesar and recognized chiefly by means of images and slogans circulating on coins, statues and monuments in principal cities, and official portraits gracing the tribunals of local authorities.[8] Even after the collapse of central authority in the Latin West during the fourth and fifth centuries, the various successor kingdoms acknowledged a theoretical, if tenuous, deference to Constantinople.[9] The claims of the Roman emperors to universal jurisdiction, moreover, exercised a profound influence upon the development of European law and politics through the Middle Ages and beyond.[10]

Justinian was both the inheritor of this Roman imperial legacy and perhaps the single figure most responsible for establishing the form in which posterity would receive it. He distinguished himself from his predecessors and attributed a singular character to his achievements as emperor, not least in spearheading the creation of the *Corpus iuris civilis* and the elaboration of a remarkable program of legislative activism.[11] Justinian's use of legislation as a vehicle of self-promotion, together with his efforts to redefine the relationship between the imperial office and the body of Roman law, offers insight into the emperor's conception of his rule.[12] Because Caroline Humfress's contribution to this volume treats legal history, this chapter focuses on how legal sources, together with contemporary testimony, illuminate many larger social transformations, heralding a conception of government and imperial leadership that was perceptibly more absolute, more exclusively Christian and orthodox, and more dedicated to enforcing uniformity of thought and behavior than some observers thought to be achievable or desirable.

Historians of the Roman Empire customarily distinguish between a "principate" of roughly the first and second centuries of the common era and a "dominate" that emerges in the fourth, following a period of instability frequently designated the "third-century crisis." Fundamental to this distinction, which originates in late antiquity,[13] is the idea that whereas the emperors from Augustus (27 BCE–14 CE) to Marcus

Aurelius (161–180 CE) governed as *princeps*, a title with roots in the Roman Republic that indicated mere precedence within a body of fellow aristocrats (the position of being "first among equals"), emperors from the accession of Diocletian in 284 CE ruled as absolute monarchs claiming the title *dominus* (Greek *karios*, *despotes*) or "master," which appears on imperial coins from the fourth century onward.[14]

Emperors displayed their power in the fourth, fifth, and sixth centuries in a manner decidedly different from that of their predecessors, but it would be misleading to distinguish the emperors of the two periods by positing a fundamental difference in the nature of that power. Two of the most consequential checks upon the arbitrary exercise of power in the Roman Republic, the principle of collegiality, which insured that the acts of any magistrate could be annulled by the veto of a fellow magistrate of greater or equivalent authority, and the principle of limited tenure in office, were as extinct under the first of the emperors, Augustus, as they were under Justinian. The principal check upon the ability of any emperor to give effect to his will was the need to secure the compliance and cooperation of the greater number of his subjects. The most successful emperors found it expedient to be seen playing the role prescribed for them by public expectations and the traditions of their office – expectations and traditions that, as some of their subjects were aware, had changed over the course of time.

The intellectual, aristocratic, and professional elites who produced many of our sources were conscious of such changes and of the reality of the autocratic power vested in the imperial office; to mitigate the more unpredictable and threatening uses of that power, they maintained and manipulated an ideological investment in a vision of civil society founded upon the continuity and stability of the law (Latin *lex*, plural *leges*).[15] The resulting tension between the imperative of ruling a large and fractious empire effectively and decisively, on the one hand, while governing lawfully, on the other, was far-ranging in its consequences. Roman imperial ideology never repudiated the principle that a good emperor should not appear to be above the law and that he should do nothing contrary to the laws;[16] an emperor who failed to evince a correct understanding of his role within the state was susceptible of being branded a tyrant, an outcome that might not only authorize insurrection but also represent the settled judgment of history. Although the observance of such strictures was in large measure a matter of decorum and modes of imperial self-presentation, part of political theater rather than an insurmountable limitation on power,[17] emperors well understood the value of conserving respect for the law and the appearance of lawfulness as a critical underpinning of their authority. In seeking to preserve and to improve the law, Justinian for his part reaffirmed its centrality as a defining element of Roman civilization while also taking steps to identify it permanently with himself and to suppress its inherently polyvocal and disputatious nature.

As an extensively elaborated and systematic body of institutional knowledge, Roman law possessed attributes that help to explain why it retained its independent legitimizing force. The republican origin of the law had traditionally been closely associated with the expulsion of the Tarquins and with Romans' traditional hostility to monarchy. The history of the republic, and thus of *libertas* (liberty)[18] rested upon, as Livy put it, "the authority of laws superior to that of men."[19] By lending credence to that principle, Augustus succeeded in reconciling the rule of law with the reality of one-man rule. Having established his supremacy in a series of civil wars, Augustus distanced himself from extralegal expedients and refounded his rule on the basis of republican precedents.[20] As the pretense of popular participation in government was dispensed with, the notion took hold that the powers formerly held collectively by the Roman people had been duly delegated to the emperors, who exercised sovereignty on their behalf. This *lex regia*, as the *Corpus iuris civilis* calls it, established the emperor's legislative competence, which was expressed in the maxim "What the *princeps* (emperor) decides has the force of law."[21]

While an emperor's ability to make law was progressively acknowledged to be absolute,[22] a countervailing influence upon legislative initiative and interpretation in the area of private law continued to be exerted well into the sixth century by the writings produced during the classical period of Roman jurisprudence in the second and early third centuries. By giving expression to the conservative habits of mind characteristic of Roman legal reasoning, the classical jurists had ensured that legislative philosophy would always seek justification with reference to tradition and the sanction of the past.[23] Over time, juristic literature, which retained its private character despite the proximity of prominent jurists to imperial power,[24] itself acquired the sanction of the past. The Law of Citations of 426, which established a canon of juristic writings authorized for citation at legal proceedings and decided points of law (rather crudely, by the standards of earlier and later jurisprudence) on the basis of the majority of concurring opinions, evinced continuing respect for the pluralistic nature of juristic opinion and preserved it as a source of legal authority independent of the emperor.[25]

Justinian represented his own activities as a lawgiver as paradigmatic of his approach to the imperial office as a whole. A *constitutio* setting down standards for authenticating judicial documents declares, "The solicitude of Our Serenity is intent upon relieving the cares of our subjects, nor do we cease to investigate whether anything in our state is susceptible of correction."[26] Legislation provided an ideal medium through which to advertise Justinian's boundless energy, totalizing ambition, and accomplishments. The portrait of Justinian that emerges, then, is one of the emperor's own making. The legal history of the period therefore furnishes an approach to an examination of Justinian's "character," the stylized, self-serving portrait he constructed for himself in his legislation.

While this imperial portrait was presumably intended for consumption mainly by educated elites, the extent to which Justinian's lawmaking touched even the humblest social classes is illustrated by a *constitutio* of September 1, 537. The emperor complains that so many *adscripticii* (quasi-servile tenant farmers) have been challenging their status under a recently enacted law that the landowners have protested. Consequently a more restrictive restatement or clarification of the original policy is called for.[27] The fact that a significant number of humble persons attempted to assert what they believed to be their privileges under the original policy reminds us that law was not exclusively of interest to the privileged classes – even if, in this and other instances, the privileged managed to have the law "clarified" to their advantage.

The portrait that emerges is a complex and challenging one, not least because Justinian never aimed to conform to a static, idealized model of behavior based upon a canon of traditional imperial virtues. Consistent with his sense of election and mission was the conviction that his rule differed from that of his predecessors, whom he castigates on occasion for their laxness and complacency. Inseparable from his reforming zeal was his belief that he served a vengeful God who required propitiation. Imperial restoration through military and legal reform went hand in hand with campaigns of persecution and ecclesiastical controversy.[28] The boundless energy he was continually at pains to display, the relentless pursuit of perfection, the conviction that no project was too large or too small to engage his attention and furnish proofs of his determination – all of these qualities originate in his own imperial consistory, products of an unflagging determination to impress upon humanity a consciousness of the fact that they were living in the Age of Justinian.[29]

### "Laws, the Foundations of Liberty": Ammianus Marcellinus and John the Lydian on Emperors and the Law

The measures which had helped Diocletian to resolve the third-century crisis,[30] while emphasizing the emperor's distance from the rest of mankind, also defined every individual's position with respect to the all-important imperial center of power. Such patterns of allegiance powerfully reinforced the precarious unity of the state. The need for unity placed a strong premium upon cultural and political continuity for both emperors and subjects. But change had to be addressed as well. As the historiography of Ammianus Marcellinus illustrates, evolutionary narratives, incorporating biological metaphors of growth and decay, furnished one means of accounting for historical change while insisting upon the preservation of an unchanging, essential kernel of identity. Particularly for imperial bureaucrats like John the Lydian, who served on the staff of the praetorian prefect and whose *De magistratibus* (*On Offices*) tendentiously traces the origins of that office back to Romulus, the perpetuation of Roman institutions and customs preserved palpable links with the past demonstrating that their world retained its intrinsically and authentically Roman core.

A military officer and a native speaker of Greek, Ammianus retired to Rome and composed history in Latin, the surviving portions of which carry his narrative from the 350s down to 378 CE. His work acknowledges the reality of imperial autocracy while upholding the Roman ideal of government according to law. Roman history is encapsulated in three successive ages, constituting a single life-span. Three hundred years marked the period from Rome's birth to the end of childhood, during which the Romans fought merely local wars. Adulthood was accompanied by expansion beyond Italy and world conquest. Ammianus's own times witnessed the approach of Rome's old age: "And so the venerable city, having humbled the proud necks of fierce nations and rendered laws, the foundations and everlasting moorings of liberty, has like a thrifty parent, shrewd and wealthy, passed along to the Caesars, as if to her children, the management of her inheritance."[31] As a whole, Ammianus's portrait evokes a stately maturity and well-being, achieved through a universal order resting upon complete military, political, and social concord. Rome herself is an aged grande dame, doted upon by capable children and well-wishers. The establishment of *libertas* through law belongs, like other Roman achievements, to an earlier, more vigorous age. Yet law and the underpinning of civil society it supplies remain part of the inheritance entrusted to the emperors.

Ammianus pragmatically concedes that civil stability and security require the concentration of imperial authority and a corresponding diminution of freedom.[32] While acknowledging an emperor's right to defend his position (19.12.17), the historian knew that imperial self-interest could become an end in itself, and he looked to justice and the rule of law as the basis of imperial self-restraint. In his eyes, the neglect of the law, or the perpetuation of atrocities under the cover of law, was symptomatic of the absence of self-possession on an emperor's part, which in turn had a catastrophic impact on the rest of society. Just as good emperors protect the law, they deserve the protection of the law and the support of loyal subjects.

In contrast to Ammianus's measured assessment of Rome's continued vitality, and to the more precipitous sense of decline articulated by Zosimus early in the sixth century,[33] Justinian's presentation of his own regime, particularly from his accession in 527 until the capture of Ravenna in 540, radiated utter self-assurance: the drift of previous reigns, he asserted, had been decisively reversed, and the renewal and recovery (*renovatio*) of the Roman Empire was at hand.[34] Both John the Lydian and Procopius, his close contemporary, witnessed this "time of hope."[35] Like Ammianus, the two possessed a consciousness of the past and an intellectual and ideological investment in institutional and political continuity. Justinianic *renovatio* ideology was calculated to capture and mobilize the loyalties of such men. In discrediting his predecessors for squandering the Roman inheritance entrusted to their care, Justinian justified change as a return to an earlier, more felicitous period of imperial hegemony. Observers who interpreted this rhetoric as an investment in classical culture for its own sake, however, were bound to be disappointed.[36] While Justinian engaged and exploited antiquarian nostalgia, concrete initiatives the emperor pursued in the name of administrative efficiency, maximization of revenues, uniformity of religious belief, and regulation of public morals proved to be polarizing and alienating. John himself bitterly attributes economic devastation in his native province of Lydia to the emperor's rapacious fiscal officers and expresses with surprising candor his admiration for a prominent victim of Justinian's purges.[37]

Even so, John celebrated Justinian as the restorer of Roman greatness, as a patron of ancient culture, and as the defender of the traditions and prerogatives of the civil service as John had known them. Broad issues of cultural decline and rebirth were closely bound up with his investment in the prestige and institutional integrity of the prefecture itself. Consequently, one discovers in John a pervasive tension between the defining principles of Roman civilization as he understood them and Justinian's own much more equivocal ways of perpetuating them – a tension relating to both John's own bureaucratic preoccupations and his sense of the overarching direction being pursued by the state.[38]

Justinian's early victories over the Vandals in North Africa and the Ostrogoths in Italy as well as the success of his legal reform project offered hope that anything was indeed possible if only Justinian would set his mind to it.[39] Rhetoric and reality seemed to be tantalizingly aligned. John's work reproduces themes of imperial omnipresence and omnicompetence that originate, as we shall see, in the emperor's own propaganda: "And through [Justinian] the state is greater than it had been formerly because Libya has been restored to us . . . and because Rome itself, too, the mother of deeds, has been released by the sweat of the emperor from her bonds and from the power of the barbarians" (*On Offices*, 3.1).

This recollection of the triumph of Roman arms gives rise to a more ambitious statement: "All the distinctive features which once belonged to the state are being preserved with greater vigor."[40] Parallel to the recovery of Rome, the font and origin of Roman achievement, is the recovery of the law: "The laws, too, have been released from disorders and burdensome confusion, and justice is seen clearly, and the litigious regret their former vigilance over points of contention because thanks to the clarity of the laws no dispute is any longer left behind."

The emperor emerges victorious over both external and internal forces of disorder and oppression, releases from their bonds both the imperial city that inspires heroic action and the laws that define and govern civil life, and thereby demonstrates the indispensability and renewed vitality of the Roman imperial legacy and his own worthiness to serve as the guardian of that legacy.

In spite of these expressions of confidence, however, John's statements regarding the Roman constitution and the manner in which Justinian inhabited the imperial role intimate a deeper unease. In a sketch of Roman political history in *On Offices*, John seeks a reconciliation between the republican origins of Roman freedom and the consolidation of power under the emperors with reference to a concept of "lawful Roman emperorship," in which the will of the sovereign is firmly subordinated to the law. A series of contradictions in the regime's own self-presentation, however, points to a genuine dilemma regarding both the "lawful" and the "Roman" character of Justinian's rule.

At the beginning of *On Offices*, John distinguishes lawful rule from both tyranny, which had characterized early Roman government under kings before the establishment of the republic, and the imperium (Greek *autokratoria*) wielded by supreme military commanders, first by the consuls of the republic and later by the Caesars (1.3f.). Lawful emperorship is characterized by the elective character of the office, by an unstinting determination on the part of the emperor to disturb neither the laws nor the form of the state, and by an approach to government that involves the leading men of the state in the formulation of policy. Such an emperor shows himself to be both a father and a leader toward his subjects. The tyrant, in contrast, will behave rashly without regard either for the law or for the opinions of the aristocracy. "For, while the law is the wont of a king, a tyrant's wont *is* the law" (*On Offices*, 1.3).

These are commonplaces of sixth-century political discourse, with deep roots in Greco-Roman political speculation on the possibility of reconciling autocracy with the preservation of a civil order governed by the rule of law. The anonymous author of the sixth-century treatise *On Political Science* concentrates upon some notably Roman elements in his discussion of the "laws" of kingship, distinguishing between appointment by God and election by the people, insisting upon the legal inauguration of rule as essential to the auspiciousness of the reign, and underscoring the importance of collaboration with both the senate and the administration in the enforcement of the law.[41] This scrupulousness scarcely diminishes the king's ties to divinity: he governs the state in conformity with the Platonic Idea of the Good, participating in the divine likeness of the Almighty twice over, in respect of both his humanity and his kingship.[42] Such an emperor is a father to his people, governing in the first instance as an exemplar of virtue, a pedagogical tool for his subjects. Political will flows outward from him into the administration, setting in motion the machinery of civil life in which each citizen discharges his particular duties responsibly (5.9ff.). It is a bureaucrat's notion of the Christian *oikoumene* (inhabited world), conspicuously fitted out with citations from pagan political philosophy. The emperor heads a rigidly centralized and hierarchical civil order, initiating impulses that trickle down through society without directly intervening in the functioning of the apparatus.

Such restraint likewise seems to be at the heart of the *Ekthesis* of Agapetus, deacon of Hagia Sophia, who addressed this example of the "mirror of princes" genre to Justinian himself early in his reign. Kingly virtues include moderation and with it conscientious rule over the state (18, 68). The king should remain vigilant, like a helmsman (2), while remaining consistent and just: "Impose upon yourself the obligation of preserving the laws," Agapetus urges, "since no mortal can compel you" (27; see also 11, 13, 33–34). While conceding to the king an unlimited purview verging upon divinization, both the author of *On Political Science* and Agapetus insist upon self-control as the most exalted and, by implication, the most difficult application of kingly power. Kingship ought to be characterized not merely by distance from the rest of humanity, but by a restraint and moderation that cut to the heart of government.[43]

For his part, John states that the imperial office arose out of usurpation and that its power was mitigated as the result of Augustus's personal example and the preservation of continuities with the institutions of the republic.[44] The office of the Caesars, in assuming the imperium exercised by the consuls, did not avail itself of the emblems of tyrants but contented itself with the purple robe in performing public and military functions. John applauds such ceremonial self-restraint. However, a change occurred under Diocletian, "who, because he was the first to have placed on his head a jeweled diadem and adorned his dress and feet with gems, turned to the habits of royalty or, to speak the truth, of tyranny" (*On Offices*, 1.4).

Once the imperial office had adopted the trappings of absolutism, the nature of imperial power was reduced to a mirror of the emperor's temperament and capacity to live within the standards of lawful behavior. Romulus was a tyrant in view of his lawlessness and rashness, a fact John finds confirmed in the name *Quirinus* (a traditional name of Romulus): this John takes to be a title and glosses as *kurios*, master. "For," he continues, "tyrants like themselves to be called *kurios* and *despotes*, but not *basileus* [emperor]" (*On Offices*, 1.5). John recalls the distaste for the title *dominus* in the republic and early principate: such a title suited Marius and Sulla, but it was an affront to Augustus and Tiberius to suggest that they were lords over a nation of slaves.[45]

Of course, Justinian himself was addressed as *dominus* and *despotes* and was scarcely unique among Roman emperors in this respect.[46] John knows this but nonetheless claims that the practice is a mark of insolence introduced in earlier times as a misbegotten title of respect: Justinian, the most moderate of emperors, understanding the epithet to mean "good father," tolerated it so as not to discomfit those who supposed they were doing him honor.

John seems to conclude that Justinian rescues himself from the charge of tyranny, to which his participation in Diocletianic forms of imperial self-presentation would otherwise leave him exposed, on account of his correct understanding of what lawful Roman emperorship entails. Is Justinian therefore being urged to shun such practices and to adopt the more restrained habits of Augustus and Tiberius? In fact, the strategy John adopts in interpreting, in excusing, and perhaps in seeking to amend the objectionable conduct of emperors is as old as the Roman imperial office itself. Recent scholarship has demonstrated that such an invocation of the father-son relationship as an "ameliorative paradigm" for the emperor's relationship to his subjects, in opposition to the "invidious paradigm" of the master-slave relationship, was already a feature of elite discourse concerning the autocratic character of the emergent principate.[47]

While John is therefore participating in an old debate on the character of imperial authority, more recent developments had intensified that debate. John exposes deeper unease about the lawful character of Justinian's rule when he turns to a discussion of the Roman consulship. Though this had long been a purely ceremonial office, and had effectively ceased to exist in 541, some ten years before John wrote, he nonetheless hails the consulship as "the mother, as it were, of Roman liberty," established at the founding of the republic by Brutus, "the defender of freedom." "For it stands in opposition to tyranny, and, when it prevails, tyranny ceases to exist."[48] The demise of this magistracy, which is noted with bitter resentment by Procopius in the *Secret History*,[49] seems to imply, conversely, that tyranny has supplanted Roman liberty. It is characteristic of tyrants, as John observes in another context, to subvert ancient institutions.[50] However, echoing the language he used in discussing Justinian's understanding of the title *despotes*, John once again disposes of the specter of tyranny by appealing to the emperor's insight into the nature of his office: "Our father and most gentle emperor, by his reforms of affairs and bounties to his subjects, *is* a consul indefinitely, yet he becomes one formally[51] whenever he should wish to embellish his station, assuming the consular dignity as a more lofty rank than the imperial office" (*On Offices*, 2.8). Though the magistracy would henceforth be filled only exceptionally, and only by an emperor, John reassures himself that Justinian remains a consul in spirit.

John's trust in an emperor's capacity to use his power in the service of Roman liberty is tempered by his knowledge that no other check upon that power was readily to hand. In its essentials, his dilemma over the responsible use of imperial power is not all that different from the one that confronted elite observers of the evolving principate. What distinguishes John and the Age of Justinian, therefore, is not this abiding concern for the perpetuation of civil government in the face of absolutism, but rather John's alarm over the disappearance of the specifically "Roman" character of his civilization. Like Ammianus's image of Roman civilization as an inheritance handed along to successive generations, John imagines the praetorian prefecture itself as a family heirloom, a large silver bowl that, owing to the folly of succeeding generations, has been squandered.[52] Against the backdrop of such devastating cultural erosion, John is desperate to credit Justinian with whatever success he can muster in stemming the flow. In the absence of other possibilities, he has no alternative but to look upon the emperor as a redeemer.

John's ambivalence about Justinian is illustrated by his allusions to tyranny. Justinian allowed himself to be addressed as *despótēs*, which Augustus and Tiberius had refused to do; he had allowed the consulship to lapse, although the magistracy had preserved a living link with republican liberty. John can point only to Justinian's special insight into the nature of his role – his understanding that *despótēs* signifies "good father," and that his rule embodies the values represented by the consulship – in order to escape the implications of such contradictions. His explanations, though strained, are not necessarily insincere. The problem is that cultural collapse, from John's point of view, has created a vacuum that only the imperial office is available to fill. *Only* Justinian's enlightened approach to his office, John takes pains to point out, distinguishes his rule from tyranny. Other defining and legitimizing features of Roman civilization have withered away, leaving the figure of the emperor to assume their role. John's dilemma, finally, stems from his uncertainty whether Justinian's eagerness to occupy this vacated cultural territory heralds a genuine reawakening or signals merely an impulse toward self-aggrandizement and an ongoing monopolization of authority.

## "Our Own Inspired Mouth": Justinian and the Legacy of Roman Law

Well before he hoped to reconquer the West, Justinian aimed to make his mark upon the law.[53] The compilation of imperial *constitutiones*, initiated in 528,[54] was his first major enterprise. The preface to the *constitutio* that, some fifteen months later, authorized the first edition of the resulting *Codex* insisted upon the complementary functions of "arms and laws" in maintaining the integrity of the state and enabling the Romans to gain predominance over all other nations.[55] In following years, the emperor's ambitions encompassed the entire body of the law, the recovery of which he set on a par with the restoration of imperial authority over the West. The two objects constituted equal parts of a double legacy that Justinian became determined to rehabilitate. In the preface to the first of the "new" *constitutiones* promulgated after the completion of the *Corpus iuris civilis*, the emperor portrays himself turning his attention away from military triumphs abroad toward the project of achieving domestic concord in his legislative and judicial capacities.[56] This gesture unites Justinian's foreign and domestic policy, making arms and laws equivalent instruments of external and internal tranquility.

Publication of the *Codex* marked the first step in a process that did not simply preserve the law, but rather transformed it and reestablished it unambiguously as the product of Justinian's own legislative capacity. Henceforth the *novus codex Iustinianus* was to be the only valid source of citations of imperial *constitutiones*. The juristic writings, thus far untouched by Justinian's compilers, retained their authority, "insofar as citation of these *constitutiones* from our *Codex*, as supplemented by the works of the ancient jurists, will suffice for the resolution of every suit" (*Const. Summa*, 3). For the sake of practicality, however, the commission that produced the *Codex* had been expressly instructed to excise from the *constitutiones* included in the work any contradictions, excess verbiage, and obsolete rulings, restating the wording as necessary.[57] The resulting statute book did not so much repackage the law as reissue it, the interventions in the text having been validated by Justinian himself,[58] who thereby reauthorized the law and promulgated it "under the happy designation of our name."[59]

A second edition superseded the original *Codex* in 534.[60] The origins of this further revision, incorporating new enactments aimed in part at settling outstanding controversies,[61] lay in the emperor's decision to expand upon his achievement by turning to the juristic legal corpus. Under the direction of Tribonian, a second law commission collected, edited, and organized the writings of the jurists in fifty volumes, producing a reference library of the most authoritative citations on every aspect of jurisprudence.[62] The *Digest*, or *Pandects*, appeared in December 533 after three years of effort, three months after the initial Roman victory over the Vandals.[63] Following the completion of a new first-year law textbook, together with a wholly revised law syllabus, Justinian could truly boast that the whole body of the law had been reformed.[64]

In the *Digest* the radical implications of Justinian's legal program had their greatest impact. The compilation was an attempt to preserve a body of legal literature that had fallen out of circulation and was in danger of being lost.[65] It was not, however, a strictly historical enterprise. Only relevant and authoritative texts were to be included, once they had been altered, expanded, and rewritten to convey best the point being communicated.[66] No ambiguities, divergent opinions, or contradictions were to be introduced into the work, which was to be distinguished by total consistency and concord.[67] The variety of the opinions of the classical jurists was not to be preserved. To the contrary, this multiplicity of voices, we are led to believe, had plagued Roman jurisprudence from the very foundation of the city. The confusion and incomprehensibility of the laws throughout 1,400 years of Roman civilization is a recurring theme.[68] The *Digest*, in contrast, was intended to stand as "the temple of Roman justice," enclosing the body of the law, which was cleansed of its blemishes and rendered a self-sufficient whole.[69] Reference to the original texts in legal proceedings was forbidden,[70] nor were any commentaries on the *Digest* itself to be written, lest they lead to further confusion.[71]

Henceforth the authority of the citations preserved in the *Digest* would be attributable not to the jurists, but to the emperor. The compilation was to be regarded "as if uttered by our own inspired mouth."[72] Just as the legal capacity and power of the Roman people had been conferred upon the emperors by the *lex regia*, it was alleged, so too had the legal basis of the juristic writings originated in imperial authorization.[73] Once the private character of the juristic writings had been dispensed with, the emperor became the sole author of the law, its origin as well as its guarantor.

Justinian insisted, nevertheless, upon attributing the citations in the *Digest* to their original sources, substantiating his claim for the restoration of the ancient law and providing assurance of development within tradition rather than in spite of it.[74] Above all, the work was to be credited to God, under whose authority the emperor governed the empire, whose providence inspired the project and brought it to fruition.[75] The completion of the *Digest* testified to God's collaboration in the project and to the auspiciousness of the reign.[76] The emperor's authority, which was both Roman and Christian, delegated by the Roman people and by God,[77] assimilated to itself all other sources of legitimacy. In his totalizing ambition Justinian sought, moreover, to assert his supremacy over history, inasmuch as his attempts to discover historical precedents for his initiatives and to reconcile innovation with tradition constituted an authorized version of the past.[78]

Even as he celebrated his achievement in the *Digest*, however, the emperor stressed the inevitability of change:

> Now divine things are entirely perfect, but the character of human law is always to hasten onward, and there is nothing in it which can abide forever, since nature is eager to produce new forms. We therefore do not cease to expect that matters will henceforth arise that are not secured in legal bonds. Consequently, if any such case arises, let a remedy be sought from the emperor, since in truth God has set the imperial function over human affairs so that it should be able, whenever a new contingency arises, to correct and settle it and to subject it to suitable procedures and regulations.[79]

Change itself had to be conceptualized as a historical process, justifying and perpetuating a program of imperial activism. Justinian broke new ground in Roman legislative philosophy by pointing to nature as one source of unpredictable and disruptive change, giving rise to situations unforeseen in earlier legislation.[80] Government under such conditions is a process of continual maintenance and refurbishment; law, like medicine,[81] is an evolving body of precedent confirmed by practice. Holding it all together is the emperor, whom God has appointed to restore equilibrium through the law.

Consistent with his conception of his imperial role, Justinian portrayed himself as a paragon of activity. The *Novels* advertise his sleeplessness and burden of cares, his constant concern, and his foresight in providing for the needs of his subjects, improving their welfare, and enhancing the glory of the government.[82] The impression is of ceaseless, tireless, relentless scrutiny. The implied rebuke to Justinian's imperial predecessors for their insufficiencies is often made explicit.[83] The legal reform project had reinstated the already perishing and diminished respect accorded to legislation;[84] the conquests were recovering the ancient Roman birthright;[85] further reforms would more fully realize the benefits of good government.

Justinian's legal reforms attest to his conception of the universal competence and all-encompassing authority of the imperial office. To govern lawfully, the emperor first claimed the law as an extension of his own indubitable will. As we have seen, figures such as John the Lydian, for whom civil and administrative procedure was the focus of an ideological investment in cultural and political continuity, had to persuade themselves that Justinian's interventions in these areas betokened a return to old values. Justinian's own perspective was of course much larger. He viewed the law as the crystallization of his own unstinting efforts to preserve the state. The legitimizing power of tradition served as a means to that end.[86] The Roman constitution had been founded by God, as he saw it, and entrusted to the emperor for the care of all men.[87] The sole hope of survival depended upon divine favor.[88] His sense of election placed him at the center of an eschatological drama in which the fate of the world was his special responsibility. Consequently, no source of authority was reserved from his purview. Just as Justinian had assimilated the individual *loci* of Roman imperial and juristic law to himself, he declared that the canons of the four Christian ecumenical councils had the force of imperial *constitutiones* and subsequently observed, "If, for the welfare of our subjects, we have keenly enforced the civil laws, with whose execution God . . . has entrusted us, how much more keenly shall we look to the canons and divine laws established for the salvation of our souls?"[89] Though he was capable of describing himself as the most humble of God's servants,[90] he nonetheless called himself the father of his people and in that capacity presumed to associate himself with the Almighty directly.[91]

The extreme against which all of Justinian's claims to authority, secular and Christian, must be evaluated, finally, is his declaration of himself in a *constitutio* of December 537 as *nomos empsukhos*, the "incarnate law," to whom God has subjected the laws.[92] Such a claim, though latent in the direction to which imperial rule had run for centuries, had never been made by an emperor before, and Justinian did not repeat it.[93] It appears in a *Novel* setting out reforms in the consulship, the ultimate decline of which so disturbed John the Lydian.[94] Justinian sought to curb the enormous costs of the celebrations marking the consul's accession, which had caused candidates to shun the honor. Nonetheless, he exempted himself from his own sumptuary regulations, inasmuch as the emperor remained above the law. He thus reserved for the imperial office the right to assume the honor on a lavish scale, on the grounds that the consulship belongs to the emperor in perpetuity. John advanced this very claim as proof that the state preserved some vestige of Roman liberty under the rule of law. Could he have been unaware that Justinian's own words hinted at precisely the opposite conclusion?

# Epilogue

> In earlier times those who attended upon the emperor used to call him "emperor" (*basileus*) and his consort "empress" (*basilís*), and to address each of the other magistrates in accordance with his present rank; but if anyone upon venturing into dialogue with either [Justinian or Theodora] should mention the words *basileus* or *basilis* and fail to call them "master" (*despotes*) and "mistress" (*despoina*), or should attempt to refer to any of the magistrates as other than "slaves" (*douloi*), such a person would be considered empty-headed and too free of tongue, and as one who had erred most grievously and affronted those whom he certainly ought not to have affronted he would withdraw from the place.
>
> – Procopius, *Secret History*, 30.25–26

> In his left hand he holds a globe, by which the sculptor signifies that all the land and sea have been subjected to him, yet he has neither sword nor spear nor any other weapon, but a cross stands upon the globe which he carries, through which alone he has obtained his empire and victory in war.
>
> – Procopius, *Buildings*, 1.2.11

These passages, the first from Procopius's *Secret History*, the second from the *Buildings*, appraise the character of Justinian's tenure in the imperial office from dramatically opposed points of view. The former comments scathingly about court etiquette and relations between the imperial couple and their highest officials.[95] The latter respectfully contemplates the emperor as represented in a monumental equestrian statue in the heart of Constantinople.[96] In the former case Procopius affects to be an insider, one who knows well the dangers of an unbridled tongue; in the latter he speaks publicly as a grateful subject.[97]

The differing judgments Procopius presents in the two works are aptly illustrated by his comments on Justinian's handling of the law. The *Buildings*, like John the Lydian's *On Offices*, dutifully recapitulates the regime's own rationale for legal reform: "Finding the laws obscure because they had become more numerous than necessary, and in manifest confusion because they disagreed with each other, [Justinian] preserved them by cleansing them of the mass of their pedantry and controlling their discrepancies most rigorously" (*Buildings*, 1.1.10). The *Secret History*, in contrast, excoriates the emperor for the confusion his misrule has introduced into the law.[98]

The *Buildings* lauds the emperor's policy and discredits tradition, while the *Secret History* paints the emperor as the malign wrecker of established institutions. Panegyric and invective assess the same record of accomplishment from diametrically opposed points of view. What is clear in both cases is that a former dispensation has yielded to a new way of doing things, which was to be Justinian's way. The emperor's impatience with the old order shines through in either instance. In spite of the differing perspectives Procopius brings to the two works, together they evince a remarkable unanimity about the autocratic character of Justinian's rule.

The differences between the two works must therefore reflect the different ideological stances apparent in each. The *Secret History*'s "insider" voices prejudices and insecurities about Justinian that are also apparent in John the Lydian's *On Offices*, but whereas John's ostensible purpose is to insulate Justinian from charges of tyranny, Procopius dwells only upon the invidious connotations of the title *despotes* without seeking an ameliorating interpretation. The Justinian of the *Secret History*, whom Procopius compares to the paradigmatic bad emperor Domitian,[99] conforms to classic Greco-Roman depictions of the tyrant, the enemy of civil order and the rule of law. In the *Buildings*, the grateful subject gazing at the emperor's statue dwells only upon the providential nature of his election, his indispensable role as the agent of victory, and the extent to which his universal, benevolent, and paternalistic rule mirrors that of the Christian God in the heavens.

Just as Justinian's determination to make the law his own reveals his character and his conception of the imperial office, so too the concerns his subjects express about the standing of the law reflect their own priorities. The fact that Justinian embraced the law as a means to express his vision of himself and to offer a philosophy of legislative change attests to the continuing value of law as the underpinning of civil life and as a vehicle of political legitimization. By identifying himself so closely with the law, however, Justinian threatened to dispense with the Roman traditionalist's last consolation in the face of imperial despotism, that the laws were good even if their human executors were wicked. Whereas nominal subjection to the law denoted freedom and recalled some vestige of republican norms, the emperor's gestures toward making himself consubstantial with the law threatened to erode a living link to the past and to lay bare the autocratic reality of the imperial office.

Those who embraced Justinian's vision accepted not only the authority he wielded over them but also the unique nature of his election and their own direct relationship to him. Even for John the Lydian, the possibility that the emperor truly was motivated by paternal benevolence offered hope for a better future. At the same time, Justinian's determination to impose his vision not only upon the law but also upon the beliefs and actions of his subjects through the law was alienating even to persons whose investment in the Roman character of their civilization was tenuous, but who were nonetheless determined to live by their own lights. In spite of the artfulness with which Justinian engaged and exploited the values of his subjects, his attempt to forge a consensus about the nature and purposes of his rule and thus to unify his empire both geopolitically and ideologically was at best an imperfect success.

## Notes

I would like to acknowledge the comments and suggestions of Cyril Mango, John Matthews, and James Howard-Johnston; Peter Brown, Michael Maas, and Josh Ober; the members of the Legal History seminar, organized by Bill Nelson, at New York University School of Law (1997–1998); Miriam Aukerman; Caroline Humfress and Peter Garnsey; and Beatrice Rehl at Cambridge University Press.

1 Translations of Procopius are based on that of H. B. Dewing, with modifications.

2 Procopius makes substantially this same charge, in his own voice, in his *Anecdota* or *Secret History*, 6.21; see also 6.23–25; 7.1, 6–7, 31–32, 39–41. Comparable charges had been lodged against Constantine by the emperor Julian (Ammianus Marcellinus, *Res gestae*, 21.10.8).

3 The idea that an earthly monarchy ought to imitate a heavenly one is by no means exclusively, or originally, Christian. See D. M. Nicol, "Byzantine Political Thought," in J. H. Burns, ed., *The Cambridge History of Medieval Political Thought* (Cambridge, 1988), 51; on pre-Christian concepts of monarchy, E. R. Goodenough, "The Political Theory of Hellenistic Kingship," *Yale Classical Studies* 1 (1928): 55–102, remains fundamental.

4 *Wars*, 4.9. See, further, Michael McCormick, *Eternal Victory: Triumphal Rulership in Late Antiquity, Byzantium, and the Early Medieval West* (Cambridge, 1986), 124–129; and Sabine MacCormack, *Art and Ceremony in Late Antiquity* (Berkeley, Calif., 1981), 73–76.

5 See the examples documented in Michael Maas, "Roman History and Christian Ideology in Justinianic Reform Legislation," *DOP* 40 (1986): 17–31.

6 On other such allusions in Procopius, see Charles F. Pazdernik, "Procopius and Thucydides on the Labors of War: Belisarius and Brasidas in the Field," *TAPA* 130 (2000): 149–187; and now Anthony Kaldellis, *Procopius of Caesareta: Tyranny, History, and Philosophy at the end of Antiquity* (Philadelphia, 2004).

7 Thucydides, *History of the Peloponnesian War*, 1.70.2.

8 J. E. Lendon, *Empire of Honour: The Art of Government in the Roman World* (Oxford, 1997), 1–29, esp. 13ff.

9 See the essays in Walter Pohl, ed., *Kingdoms of the Empire: The Integration of Barbarians in Late Antiquity* (Leiden, 1997). For a summary of political and diplomatic history from 476–568, see Patrick Amory, *People and Identity in Ostrogothic Italy, 489–554* (Cambridge, 1997), 6–12, 43–59; and Tony Honoré, *Tribonian* (London, 1978), 18–19.

10 See Peter Stein, *Roman Law in European History* (Cambridge, 1999); Olivia F. Robinson, T. D. Fergus, and William M. Gordon, *European Legal History: Sources and Institutions*, 3rd ed. (London, 2000); Paul Vinogradoff, *Roman Law in Mediaeval Europe* (1909; reprint, Holmes Beach, Fla., 1994); and Franz Wieacker, *A History of Private Law in Europe*, trans. Tony Weir (Oxford, 1995).

11 I use the following conventions to refer to the *Corpus iuris civilis:* the *Codex Iustinianus* is referred to simply as the *Codex* (*CJ* in citations); the *Digesta* as the *Digest*; the *Institutiones* as the *Institutes* (*Inst.*); and the *Novellae* as the *Novels* (*Nov.*). In citations, "pr." designates the *principium*, or beginning, of each section or fragment of the material cited; similarly, "ep." denotes the *epilogus*. Where an individual imperial legislative enactment (*constitutio*, plural *constitutiones*) is referred to, the Latin term is used for the sake of clarity (*Const.* in references, together with the opening words of the document; e.g., *Const. Tanta*). Important pre-Justinianic legal sources include Gaius's *Institutes* (Gaius) and the *Codex Theodosianus* (*CTh*). Especially helpful on the conventions pertaining to Roman legal sources is A. Arthur Schiller, *Roman Law: Mechanisms of Development* (New York, 1978).

12 On political and military history, see J. B. Bury, *History of the Later Roman Empire from the Death of Theodosius I to the Death of Justinian*, vol. 2 (Oxford, 1923); Ernst Stein, *Histoire du Bas-Empire* (Paris, 1949); and J. A. S. Evans, *The Age of Justinian: The Circumstances of Imperial Power* (London, 1996). On administrative history, see A. H. M. Jones, *The Later Roman Empire, 284–602* (Oxford, 1964); on the legal history of the reign, see Honoré, *Tribonian* (London, 1978).

13 Sources such as John the Lydian impute to Diocletian the introduction of "Persian" court ceremonial (John Matthews, *The Roman Empire of Ammianus* [London, 1989], 231–252, esp. 244–249). The newness of these developments may have been overstated: see Andreas Alföldi, *Die monarchische Repräsentation im romischen Kaiserreiche* (Darmstadt, 1970).

14 See, further, D. Hagedorn and K. A. Worp, "Von ΚΥΡΙΟΣ zu ΔΕΣΠΟΤΗΣ: Eine Bemerkung zur Kaisertitulatur im 3./4. Jhdt.," *Zeitschrift für Papyrologie und Epigraphik* 39 (1980): 165–177; Gerhard Rösch, ΟΝΟΜΑ ΒΑΣΙΛΕΙΑΣ. *Studien zum offiziellen Gebrauch der Kaisertitel in spätantiker und frühbizantinischer Zeit* (Vienna, 1978).

15 The Latin word *ius* (plural *iures*) signifies various concepts covered by the word "law" in English; see Barry Nicholas, *An Introduction to Roman Law* (Oxford, 1962), 14ff.

16 P. A. Brunt, "Lex de imperio Vespasiani," *JRS* 67 (1977): 109.

17 Compare M. Morford, "How Tacitus Defined Liberty," *ANRW* II, 33.5 (1991): 3441: "There is an immense difference between the appearance of observing the laws . . . and the reality of autocratic behavior." See also Andrew Wallace-Hadrill, "Civilis Princeps: Between Citizen and King," *JRS* 72 (1982): 32–48, emphasizing imperial ritual as a serious means of articulating power.

18 *Libertas* in its political sense signifies primarily the absence of arbitrary or despotic uses of power as experienced by persons of free status; it also characterizes a civil order in which such persons are protected from such treatment. See P. A. Brunt, "*Libertas* in the Republic," in P. A. Brunt, *The Fall of the Roman Republic and Related Essays* (Oxford, 1988), 281–350; Jochen Bleicken, *Staatliche Ordnung und Freiheit in der römischen Republik* (Kallmünz, 1972); Chaim Wirszubski, *Libertas as a Political Idea at Rome during the Late Republic and Early Principate* (Cambridge, 1950); and

Matthew B. Roller, *Constructing Autocracy: Aristocrats and Emperors in Julio-Claudian Rome* (Princeton, N.J., 2001), 214–232.

19 Livy, *Ab urbe condita*, 2.1.1.

20 Augustus, *Res gestae*, 5ff.; see also Brunt, "Lex de imperio Vesp.," 114ff.; Ronald Syme, *The Roman Revolution* (Oxford, 1939).

21 "*Quod principi placuit legis habet vigorem*" (*Digest*, 1.4.1 pr. = *Inst.* 1.2.6), attributed to Ulpian. See also *Digest* 1.4.1.1; *Const. Deo auctore, 7* (= *CJ*, 1.17.1.7); and Gaius, *Institutiones*, 1.5. Brunt, "Lex de imperio Vespasiani," 110–113, examines the juristic background. See also W. W. Buckland, *A Text-Book of Roman Law from Augustus to Justinian*, 3rd ed., rev. Peter Stein (Cambridge, 1963), 6–20, esp. 15ff.; and Berthold Rubin, *Das Zeitalter Iustinians*, vol. 1 (Berlin, 1960), 125–127.

22 Brunt, "Lex de imperio Vespasiani," 108ff., suggests the emperor's total dispensation from the laws as early as Claudius and Nero; imperial *constitutiones* were acknowledged to be *leges* only later, although they had assumed such de facto authority in the second century (111ff.). See also Buckland, *Text-Book*, 3.

23 See Alan Watson, *The Spirit of Roman Law* (Athens, Ga., 1995), esp. 124ff., 146–157, which emphasizes that the Roman approach was atheoretical; the jurists were instead "very much tethered to the legal tradition that they themselves created" (126).

24 See Fergus Millar, *The Emperor in the Roman World* (Ithaca, N.Y., 1977), 94–97.

25 *CTh*, 1.4.3 (Nov. 7, 426), summarized in Buckland, *Text-Book*, 33ff. It had been incorporated in the first version of *CJ*; see the discussion in Honoré, *Tribonian*, 51ff., and more recently Jill Harries, *Law and Empire in Late Antiquity* (Cambridge, 1999), 33ff., and John Matthews, *Laying Down the Law: A Study of the Theodosian Code* (New Haven, Conn., 2000), 24–26. The compilers of the *Digest* were instructed to choose the more correct view without regard to the identity of the author (*Const. Deo auctore*, 5).

26 *Nov.*, 114 pr. (Nov. 1, 541).

27 *Nov.*, 54 pr. – 1; see also *CJ*, 11.48.24. See Jones, *LRE* vol. 2, 795–803, esp. 801ff. and n. 73. Further refinements to the policy were required in subsequent years.

28 On Justinian's purges, see (with caution) Pierre Chuvin, *A Chronicle of the Last Pagans*, trans. B. A. Archer (Cambridge, Mass., 1990); Polymnia Athanassiadi, "Persecution and Response in Late Paganism: The Evidence of Damascius," *JHS* 113 (1993): 1–29; Evans, *Circumstances*, 65–71; see also n. 37 below. On Justinian's religious policy, see Francis Dvornik, *Early Christian and Byzantine Political Philosophy* (Washington, D.C., 1966), 815–839; W. H. C. Frend, "Old and New Rome in the Age of Justinian," in *Relations between East and West in the Middle Ages*, ed. Derek Baker (Edinburgh, 1973), 11–28.

29 "It is important to appreciate that . . . Justinian is conscious of living in the age of Justinian" (Honoré, *Tribonian*, 16).

30 See n. 13.

31 Ammianus, *Res gestae*, 14.6.5. My translations of Ammianus are based upon that of J. C. Rolfe, with modifications. See Matthews, *Ammianus*, 250ff.; and John Matthews, "Ammianus and the Eternity of Rome," in *The Inheritance of Historiography, 350–900*, ed. Christopher Holdsworth and T. P. Wiseman (Exeter, 1986), 17–29. Honoré claims, on the basis of this passage (*Res gestae*, 14.6.5), that Ammianus was "the ancient historian who best understood the place of law in the Roman polity" (*Tribonian*, 33ff.).

32 Morford ("Tacitus," 3434ff.) attributes a compatible view to Tacitus in the principate. See also Wirszubski, *Libertas*, 163.

33 On Zosimus's view of Roman decline, see Walter A. Goffart, "Zosimus, the First Historian of Rome's Fall," *American Historical Review* 76 (1971): 412–441; Walter Emil Kaegi Jr., *Byzantium and the Decline of Rome* (Princeton, N.J., 1968), 114ff.; Michael Maas, *John Lydus and the Roman Past: Antiquarianism and Politics in the Age of Justinian* (New York, 1992), 48–52; also Brian Croke, "A.D. 476: The Manufacture of a Turning Point," *Chiron* 13 (1983): 81–119.

34 See Amory, *People and Identity*, 135–148; Averil Cameron, *The Mediterranean World in Late Antiquity, A.D. 395–600* (New York, 1993), 104–127; Honoré, *Tribonian*, 14–20; McCormick, *Victory*, 67ff.

35 The expression is Honoré's (*Tribonian*, 19).

36 The idea that Justinian sponsored a "classical revival" in literature and the arts has been largely discredited. See Averil Cameron, *Procopius and the Sixth Century* (London, 1985), 19–23.

37 See Maas, *John Lydus*, 18–23, 70–82. On Phocas (*PLRE* 2, s.v. Phocas 5), an admired patrician persecuted for paganism, see *On Offices*, 3.72ff.; *Wars*, 1.24.18; *Secret History*, 21.6.

38 See Maas, *John Lydus*, especially 83–96 on *On Offices*.

39 Compare *On Offices*, 2.5: the passage of time corrupts all things given to birth and decay, "but the emperor's excellence is such that whatever has perished in the past awaits regeneration through him." My translations are based, with modifications, upon that of Anastasius C. Bandy.

40 See also *On Offices*, 2.28: Justinian was eager to contribute to the common good and to "recall the entire dignity of the ancient form."

41 Anonymous, *Peri politikes epistemes* (*On Political Science*), 5.4. On its authorship, see Ernest Barker, *Social and Political Thought in Byzantium* (Oxford, 1957), 63–64; and C. M. Mazzucchi, ed., *Menae patricii cum Thoma referendario de scientia politica dialogus quae exstant in codice Vaticano palimpsesto* (Milan, 1982), xiii ff.

42 *Peri politikēs epistēmēs*, 5.7. Note also the Platonic color in Agapetus, *Ekthesis*, 3, 4.

43 See also Patrick Henry, "A Mirror for Justinian: The *Ekthesis* of Agapetus Diaconus," *Greek, Roman, and Byzantine Studies* 8 (1967): 281–308; Barker, *Social and Political Thought*, 63–68; Dvornik, *Early Christian and Byzantine Political Philosophy*, 706–711.

44 *On Offices*, 2.1ff. identifies both Marius and Sulla as tyrants; Pompey "emulated" Sulla (2.1), whereas Caesar "embraced the opposite faction and revered Marius and was captivated by his ways." The two men fought each other "as if they were heirs to the tyrants"; Caesar, victorious, declined the title of king (*basileús*, 2.2) and refused a crown. Instead he insisted upon holding a range of titles, symbolized by the triumphal garb he adopted, which John believes (mistakenly) to be the archetype of the vestments worn by Justinian to celebrate victory over the Vandals (*On Offices*, 2.2); see McCormick, *Victory*, 66. Octavian/Augustus did not at first make use of Caesar's regalia (*On Offices*, 2.3); following his defeat of Antony, however, he adopted all of Caesar's emblems. The implication that he thereby replicated Caesar's imperious demeanor as well as his prerogatives is alleviated by the remark that follows: "Nevertheless, he treated his subjects mildly."

45 For the references to Augustus (see also John the Lydian, *De mensibus* [*On the Months*], 4.112) and Tiberius, compare Suetonius, *Divus Augustus*, 53, *Tiberius*, 27.

46 See n. 14.

47 Roller, *Constructing Autocracy*, 213–288 (without reference to John the Lydian). Such discourse has "a long history in Greco-Roman political theory" (236, n. 39).

48 *On Offices*, 2.8; see also, 1.29–33.

49 *Secret History*, 26.12–15. The ordinary consulship had fallen vacant in the West after 534 and in the East in 536 and 537, upon which Justinian unsuccessfully attempted to reform it (*Nov.*, 105; see also n. 92). It was last held by a private individual in 541. See Jones, *LRE* vol. 1, 532ff.; Alan Cameron and Diane Schauer, "The Last Consul: Basilius and His Diptych," *JRS* 72 (1982): 126–145.

50 *On Offices*, 2.19, with reference to Domitian.

51 Literally, "he becomes one in vesture."

52 *On Offices*, 2.7. On this image, see Maas, *John Lydus*, 5–9.

53 Honoré suggests (*Tribonian*, 51) that the success of the legal program spurred the reconquest policy. After the Vandal defeat, the parallel between military and legislative success became explicit: *Const. Tanta/Dedoken*, pr., 23 (Dec. 16, 533).

54 *Const. Haec* (Feb. 13, 528) authorized a new collection of imperial *constitutiones* to supersede earlier compilations and incorporate all subsequent legislation. See Chap. 7 herein, Caroline Humfress, "Law and Legal Practice in the Age of Justinian."

55 *Const. Summa* (Apr. 7, 529), pr.: "The safety of the state proceeds out of two things, the force of arms and the observance of laws; for this reason, the fortunate race of the Romans, having established their own power, achieved precedence and control over all nations in former times, and will do so forever, if God is propitious." The notion is present in most of the prefaces of the *constitutiones* enacting the various elements of Justinian's program. Nor did it originate with him: Honoré collects earlier instances (*Tribonian*, 35, n. 373). Translations of these *constitutiones* and the *Digest* are based upon those by Alan Watson et al.

56 "Although we were formerly occupied with the concerns of the entire government, and could take thought of nothing of lesser importance, now [inasmuch as the external security of the state has been firmly restored] . . . private concerns addressed unceasingly by our subjects have also reached us, to each of which we shall give an appropriate form" (*Nov.*, 1, pr. [Jan. 1, 535]).

57 *Const. Haec*, 2; compare *Const. Summa*, 1. In contrast, the compilers of the Theodosian Code had included old rulings of historical and academic interest (*CTh*, 1.1.5 [Mar. 26, 429]). The second law commission of Theodosius II, which compiled the code, was nevertheless instructed (*CTh*, 1.1.6 [Dec. 20, 435]) to make alterations and emendations for clarity and brevity. See Matthews, *Laying Down the Law*, 55ff.

58 *Const. Cordi* (Nov. 16, 534), authorizing the second edition of the *Codex*, reports Justinian's instructions to the compilers, where there was any need of correction, "to act without hesitation, but confident, rather, in our authority" (3).

59 *Const. Haec*, pr. The idea is recapitulated in sec. 3; compare *Const. Summa*, 1.

60 *Const. Cordi*. This *constitutio* foresees (4) the necessity of further revisions to the *Codex*.

61 On the collection of *constitutiones* referred to as the Fifty Decisions (*Const. Cordi*, 1), see Humfress, Chap. 7 herein.

62 Authorized by *Const. Deo auctore* (Dec. 15, 530). On Tribonian's role see Honoré, *Tribonian*, 48–51, 139–141. A more ambitious compilation, combining juristic writings with the imperial codes, was contemplated by Theodosius II but not carried out: *CTh*, 1.1.5; compare 1.1.6.

63 *Const. Tanta/Dedoken* (Dec. 16, 533). On the desperate and miraculous character of the project, see *Const. Tanta/Dedoken*, pr., 12; *Const. Deo auctore*, 2; *Const. Imperatoriam*, 2.

64 Justinian's *Institutes* were promulgated in *Const. Imperatoriam* (Nov. 21, 533), the law syllabus in *Const. Omnem* (Dec. 16, 533): "That the whole body of law of our state has now been reformed and arranged . . . who knows this better than you do?" (*Const. Omnem*, pr., addressed to the members of the law commission).

65 Tribonian claims that most judges and lawyers, and even law professors, had so few reference materials at their disposal that the condensed but much larger selection of citations in the *Digest* actually seemed larger than the corpus from which they were excerpted: *Const. Tanta/Dedoken*, 17; compare *Const. Omnem*, 1.

66 *Const. Deo auctore*, 7ff.; *Const. Tanta/Dedoken*, 17.

67 *Const. Deo auctore*, 8. Following the completion of the *Digest*, Tribonian was prepared to concede some redundancy and omission (*Const. Tanta/Dedoken*, 13–16). He would not, however, brook the possibility of contradiction.

68 *Const. Deo auctore*, 1, 5; *Const. Imperatoriam*, 2; *Const. Tanta/Dedoken*, pr., where the image of "Roman jurisprudence . . . wavering this way and that in strife within itself" is especially vivid. John the Lydian recapitulates the idea (*On Offices*, 3.1). See the preceding section of this chapter.

69 *Hoc iustitiae Romanae templum* (*Const. Tanta*, 20). Integrity and sufficiency of the *Digest*: *Const. Deo auctore*, 2ff., esp. 5; *Const. Tanta/Dedoken*, pr.

70 *Const. Deo auctore*, 7; *Const. Tanta/Dedoken*, 19.

71 *Const. Deo auctore*, 12; *Const. Tanta/Dedoken*, 21. See Fritz Pringsheim, "Justinian's Prohibition of Commentaries to the *Digest*," *RIDA*, 2nd ser., 5 (1950): 383–415.

72 *Const. Deo auctore*, 6. The *Institutes* was also promulgated as an imperial *constitutio* and therefore had the force of law.

73 *Const. Deo auctore*, 7. Tribonian had also argued that the altered excerpts collected in the *Digest* ought rightly to be ascribed to the emperor, because "one who corrects something that is not done accurately deserves more praise than the original author" (6). See, further, Humfress, Chap. 7 herein. On the *lex regia*, see the second section of this chapter.

74 *Const. Tanta*, 10: "Now we had such great reverence for antiquity that by no means did we suffer these men to consign to oblivion the names of those learned in the law." Nevertheless, the *constitutio* continues, whatever is inappropriate in the citations has been emended.

75 *Const. Deo auctore*, pr.; *Const. Tanta/Dedoken*, pr. On the origins of Christian theories of empire, see Norman H. Baynes, "Eusebius and the Christian Empire," *Annuaire de l'Institut de Philologie et d'Histoire Orientale* 2 (1934): 13–18; reprinted in Norman H. Baynes, *Byzantine Studies and Other Essays* (London, 1960), 168–172; Wilhelm Ensslin, "Gottkaiser und Kaiser von Gottes Gnaden," *Sitzungsberichte der Bayerischen Akademie der Wissenshaften zu München, phil.-hist. Abt.* 6 (1943): 1–133; F. Edward Cranz, "Kingdom and Polity in Eusebius of Caesarea," *Harvard Theological Review* 45 (1952): 47–66; Dvornik, *Early Christian and Byzantine Political Philosophy*, 611–626.

76 *Const. Deo auctore*, 14: "in order that the complete work, divided into fifty books, may be offered to us in complete and eternal memory of the undertaking, and as a proof of the providence of Almighty God and for the glory of our rule and of your service."

77 Compare the address Justin I delivered upon his accession in July of 518: "'Having attained the throne by the will of Almighty God and by your unanimous choice, we call upon celestial providence.' All cried: 'Well-being to the world. As you have lived, so rule. Well-being to the state. Heavenly king (*basileús*), preserve the earthly one'" (*De ceremoniis*, 1.93, trans. A. A. Vasiliev, *Justin the First: An Introduction to the Epoch of Justinian the Great* [Cambridge, Mass., 1950], 68–82); on the attribution of this material to a contemporary sixth-century source, see J. B. Bury, "The Ceremonial Book of Constantine Porphyrogennetos," *English Historical Review* 22 (1907): 209–227.

78 Tribonian's historical interests are not reflected in other quaestors' legislation (Honoré, *Tribonian*, 223–242, 251–254; Tony Honoré, "Some Constitutions Composed by Justinian," *JRS* 65 [1975]: 107–123, esp. 123). See also Maas, "Reform Legislation," 27ff.

79 *Const. Tanta*, 18. Perhaps in anticipation of objections, the legislator hastens to add: "We are not the first to say this. It is of ancient descent" (*Const. Tanta*, 18). Appeal is made to precedents from the jurist Julian (compare *Digest*, 1.3.10–12) and the emperor Hadrian.

80 See Giuliana Lanata, *Legislazione e natura nelle novelle giustinianee* (Naples, 1984), esp. 165–187; also Maas, "Reform Legislation," 29–31; W. S. Thurman, "A Juridical and Theological Concept of Nature in the Sixth Century AD," *Byzantinoslavica* 32 (1971): 77–85; Honoré, *Tribonian*, 27 nn. 298–299; and Humfress in this volume.

81 For the comparison, see Honoré, *Tribonian*, 27ff., 254.

82 Honoré, *Tribonian*, 22.

83 *Nov.*, 30.11.2 (Mar. 18, 536): "We have good hope that God will grant us to rule over the rest of what, subject to the ancient Romans to the limits of both seas, they later lost by their easygoing ways." See also *Const. Tanta/Dedoken*, 19; *CJ*, 1.27.1.6 (534); *Nov.*, 8.11 (Apr. 15, 535); 28.4.2 (July 16, 535); 40 ep. (May 18, 536); 80.10 pr. (Mar. 10, 539).

84 *Nov.*, 17, introductory matter (Apr. 16, 535); compare 2 pr. (Mar. 16, 535).

85 *Nov.*, 30.11.2. (n. 83). Compare 1 pr.; 8.10.2 (Apr. 15, 535); 69.1 pr., ep. (June 1, 538, remarking on the extent of the restored empire).

86 See Maas, *John Lydus*, 38–48.

87 *Nov.*, 18 pr. (Mar. 1, 536); 133 pr. (Mar. 16, 539). Compare 77 pr. (uncertain); 59 pr. (Nov. 3, 537); 69 ep. (June 1, 538); 73 pr. 1 (June 4, 538); 81 pr. (Mar. 18, 539); 86 pr. (Apr. 17, 539).

88 *Nov.*, 109 pr. (May 7, 541). See also *Const. Deo auctore*, pr.; *Nov.*, 116 pr. (Apr. 9, 542); 135 pr. (uncertain); 141 pr. (Mar. 15, 559).

89 *Nov.*, 131.1 (Mar. 18, 545); 137 pr. (Mar. 26 565). Compare 6 pr. (Mar. 16, 535). See, further, Humfress, Chap. 7 herein.

90 For example, *CJ*, 1.27.1.5: "*per me, ultimum servum suum*" ("*through me, [God's] most humble servant*").

91 *Nov.*, 98.2.2 (Dec. 16, 539): "He who is, after God, the common father of all – for thus do we describe the holder of the imperial office – preserves this through the law."

92 *Nov.*, 105.2.4 (Dec. 28, 537): "But from everything which has been set down by us let the *tukhe* of the emperor be exempted, to which indeed God has subjected the laws, having bestowed it upon mankind as the incarnate law." Reference to the emperor's *tukhe* (*tyche*/"fortune") is perhaps intended to mitigate some of the

implications of the remark. On the history of this phrase, see Goodenough, "The Political Theory of Hellenistic Kingship"; Ensslin, "Gottkaiser und Kaiser von Gottes Gnaden," esp. 115ff; Artur Steinwenter, "Nomos Empsychos. Zur Geschichte einer politischen Theorie," *Anzeiger der Akademie der Wissenschaften, Wien, phil.-hist. Klasse* 83 (1946): 250–268; Herbert Hunger, "Kaiser Justinian I (527–565)," *Anzeiger der österreichischen Akademie der Wissenschaften, Wien, phil.-hist. Klasse* 102 (1965): 354ff.; G. J. D. Aalders, "ΝΟΜΟΣ ΕΜΨΥΧΟΣ," in *Politeia und Res Publica*, ed. Peter Steinmetz, Festschrift R. Starks (Wiesbaden, 1969), 315–329; Dvornik, *Early Christian and Byzantine Political Philosophy*, 716–722.

93 The phrase had been *applied to* an emperor before, by Themistius to Theodosius I (*Or.*, 19.228a4; see also 5.64b).

94 See the third section of this chapter and n. 49. Justinian may have been concerned about the opportunity the consulship offered for courting public favor. See Roger S. Bagnall, Alan Cameron, Seth R. Schwartz, and Klaas A. Worp, *Consuls of the Later Roman Empire* (Atlanta, Ga., 1987), 7–12.

95 On Theodora and the political role Procopius and other observers assign to her, see Charles F. Pazdernik, "'Our Most Pious Consort Given Us by God': Dissident Reactions to the Partnership of Justinian and Theodora, AD 525–48," *Classical Antiquity* 13 (1994): 256–281. I plan to examine Procopius's claim that imperial officials were obliged to identify themselves as *doûloi* more closely in a separate study.

96 *Buildings*, 1.2.1–12. See Glanville Downey, "Justinian as Achilles," *Transactions and Proceedings of the American Philological Association* 71 (1940): 68–78; Cyril Mango, *The Brazen House: A Study of the Vestibule of the Imperial Palace of Constantinople* (Copenhagen, 1959), 174ff.; Gervase Mathew, *Byzantine Aesthetics* (London, 1963), 81; MacCormack, *Art and Ceremony*, 77ff.; and McCormick, *Victory*, 68ff.

97 Compare especially *Secret History*, 1.1–3 with *Buildings*, 1.1.4ff.

98 *Secret History*, 7.31. Abuse of the law by the imperial couple and their ministers is a continuing refrain in the *Secret History;* see e.g. *Secret History* 7.7, 8.11, 11.1ff., 13.20–23, 14.8ff., 14.20, 16.22 (Theodora), 20.15ff. (on abuse of the quaestorship and the foibles of Tribonian; compare *Wars*, 1.24.16), and 21.16ff.

99 *Secret History*, 8.13ff.

# Part 2

# RELIGION AND PHILOSOPHY

# 9: The Legacy of Chalcedon

## Christological Problems and Their Significance

*Patrick T. R. Gray*

Perhaps the most astonishing failure of the Age of Justinian was the disintegration of the one Christian Church of the one Christian Empire into two distinct churches – what we now call Eastern Orthodoxy, on one hand, and the Oriental Orthodox (notably the Jacobite and the Coptic churches) on the other, a division only beginning to be healed in our own time. Remarkably, it seems that this division happened not, as a modern might think, because of nationalistic struggles against the empire, or any desire for autonomy by regional churches, but simply because church leaders, emperors, theologians, and monks, most of them devoted to the ideal of one church and one empire, were unable to resolve a longstanding theological dispute over how one was to understand and talk about Christ's divine-human reality, the debate over Christology. In the end, the dispute left behind it not only divided churches, a weakened empire, and a redefined role for the emperor, but also new ways of thinking and believing that mark the beginning of Byzantium proper and the end of late antiquity.

## The Background

### *Doctrinal Foundations and Founding Legends (100–400)*

The kind of Christianity that won the right to call itself the apostolic faith in the first two centuries CE established as authoritative the first three gospels and the teachings of Paul, all of which assumed the genuine humanity of Jesus.[1] That was to be a foundation of mainline

TABLE 9.1 *Time Line: Christological Controversies*

| | The Background |
|---|---|
| c. 180 | Condemnation of Jewish Christians as "Ebionites" |
| 268 | Trial of Paul of Samosata |
| 319 | Beginning of Arian Controversy |
| 325 | Council of Nicaea |
| 328–373 | Athanasius Bishop of Alexandria |
| 380s | Apollinarius fl. |
| 375–c. 390 | Diodore of Tarsus |
| 381 | First Council of Constantinople ends Arian Controversy and condemns Apollinarius |
| 392–428 | Theodore bishop of Mopsuestia |
| 412–444 | Cyril bishop of Alexandria |
| 423–c. 460 | Theodoret bishop of Cyrrhus |
| 428–431 | Nestorius bishop of Constantinople |
| 431 | Council of Ephesus |
| 433 | "Formula of Union" |
| 448 | Eutyches tried by synod in Constantinople presided over by Flavian |
| 449 | Leo of Rome sends his *Tome* to Flavian |
| | Dioscorus, patriarch of Alexandria, presides over council at Ephesus (the "Latrocinium") that condemns Flavian, exonerates Eutyches |
| 451 | Council of Chalcedon condemns both Nestorius and Eutyches, deposes Dioscorus. Reluctantly enunciates a statement of faith |
| | Immediate condemnations of Chalcedon as Nestorian by many in East, especially in Egypt, Syria, and Palestine |
| 478 | Marcianus and Martyrius in Palestine reach accord despite differing views on Chalcedon |
| 482 | *Henoticon* of Zeno enacted |
| 507–519 | First neo-Chalcedonians: Nephalius, John of Scythopolis, and John the Grammarian |
| | Severus argues against Neo-Chalcedonians |
| 512 | Severus becomes bishop of Antioch |
| | The Age of Justinian |
| 518–519 | Scythian monks' proposal |
| 525 | Justinian marries Theodora |
| c. 525 | John of Tella begins anti-Chalcedonian ordinations, a program met by repressive measures |
| 527 | Edict of Justin and Justinian vs. anti-Chalcedonians |

| | |
|---|---|
| 532 | Conversations held between Chalcedonians and anti-Chalcedonians in Constantinople |
| 532 or 533 | Leontius of Jerusalem writes work later known as *Against the Monophysites* |
| 533 | Edicts on Union by Hypostasis and "one of the Trinity suffered" |
| 538 | Death of Severus |
| 540s | Theodosius of Alexandria and Jacob Baradaeus in Syria ordain separate anti-Chalcedonian hierarchy |
| 544 | Decree against the Three Chapters |
| 547 | Pope Vigilius in Constantinople |
| 551 | Edict on the True Faith |
| 553 | Second Council of Constantinople |

Christology. It is significant, however, that heirs of the original Jewish Christians, who seem to have said that Jesus was *only* a human being, were by 180 being dismissed as heretics, and that in 268 Paul of Samosata was condemned as a heretic for, among other things, saying that Jesus was a man inspired in essentially the same way as a prophet was inspired. A second foundation of mainline Christology was emerging, the assertion that God was actually present and at work in Jesus in some way well beyond the divine inspiration or adoption any other human being might experience. John's gospel, with its language about the Word becoming flesh, was influential during the latter half of the second century in determining how the church would articulate this theme, especially as contemporary philosophy envisaged a mediating principle or "word" between the Absolute, or God, and the cosmos, a resonance already exploited by Justin Martyr around 150. The idea of the incarnation, the becoming flesh, of a second divine reality distinct from the Father (a reality known as the Son, Word, or Wisdom of God) became by the third century the dominant way of understanding what the church believed was involved.

The question about just how the divine Word was united with or incarnated in the human Jesus – in a strict sense *the* question of Christology – was put to one side in the Arian Controversy (319–381) that engulfed the church just as it was identifying itself with the empire of Constantine and his successors. The controversy concerned how the Word related to God the Father, with the ultimate victory going to the party (championed most eloquently by Athanasius, patriarch of Alexandria from 328 to 373), that argued, with the Council of Nicaea of 325, that the Word was absolutely and completely divine, "of one substance [consubstantial] with" God the Father. This conclusion was confirmed by the First Council of Constantinople in 381, and thereafter no one would be able to address Christology without taking as a given the Word's complete divinity. If anything, the outcome of the Arian Controversy strengthened the dominant Christology of the Word become flesh and identified it with the tradition and prestige of Alexandria.

The Arian Controversy also established the precedent of the church turning to the emperor to find and impose a resolution of its theological disputes, and of the emperor calling councils of bishops to enunciate the "faith of the church" he would then impose universally. It established, moreover, Nicaea's creed as the gold standard of orthodoxy, and Athanasius as the "star of orthodoxy" and, in his heroic resistance to heresy, the archetypal "martyr" for orthodoxy. The legend, too, of the rewinning for orthodoxy of a church hijacked by heretics was firmly planted in the church's imagination. All of these would inform and influence the sixth-century debate, but deepened by another legendary episode, this one involving a successor to Athanasius, Cyril of Alexandria.[2]

## *Cyril of Alexandria: Through Controversy to Peace (428–444)*

A companion and friend of Athanasius in the Arian Controversy, Apollinarius of Laodicea (c. 310–390), left a secret heritage that was to be decisive for the fifth century. He made a clever proposal to answer the christological question: the divine Word, he argued, took the place of a rational human soul in Christ, who was one nature, just as body and soul are one in an ordinary person. Though he was rapidly condemned (decisively by the First Council of Constantinople in 381) on the grounds that his solution compromised the full humanity of Jesus on which the salvation of his fellow humans depended, his followers succeeded in giving some of his writings a new life by ascribing them to heroes such as Athanasius. Through their pseudo-Athanasian texts, the fateful formula "one incarnate nature of God the Word" made its way to later Alexandrian theologians, to whom that formula seemed to follow John's gospel and Nicaea in asserting a single Word who really "became" flesh and was the one subject of all of Christ's actions, including being born. This meant that it came naturally to Alexandrians to call the Virgin Mary "the bearer of God" (*theotokos*). Also under the disguised influence of Apollinarius, they tended to think of the union of the divine and human in Christ on the analogy of the body-and-soul union in a human being.

Apollinarius and his Christology had been attacked by the founder of the quite different theological tradition of Antioch, Diodore of Tarsus, who emphasized the human Jesus revealed by the synoptic gospels. His pupil, Theodore of Mopsuestia, expressed the fundamental convictions of this tradition by saying that New Testament texts applicable to the human Christ should be distinguished from those applicable to the divine Word, and that, though Christ was certainly one person, there were two distinct natures in him, a divine and a human. A pupil of Theodore, Nestorius, who became patriarch of Constantinople (428–431), aroused the Alexandrians – whom he saw as crypto-Apollinarians – by supporting the view that the Virgin Mary was properly "bearer of Christ," not "bearer of God."

Cyril, patriarch of Alexandria (412–444), emerged as the champion of the rival majority Christological tradition as he defended the title *theotokos*. The Council of Ephesus (Ephesus I, 431) condemned Nestorius and his ideas, seeing itself as defending Nicaea, and Cyril was victorious. But his victory was flawed. Bishops from Antioch held a countercouncil and condemned him; Rome was on his side, but its own Western tradition was actually more like theirs, since it spoke of one person and two natures and distinguished the natures' operations.

A temporary resolution to this chaotic situation was made possible by Cyril, who in 433 sent John of Antioch a letter (often called the Formula of Union) in which he affirmed that, so long as the radical division of the one Christ associated with the name of Nestorius was rejected, Christ was "of two natures" and agreed it was acceptable to say specific biblical texts pertain to one or the other nature. Responding to claims that he had capitulated to the Antiochenes, Cyril began to use the pseudo-Athanasian formula "one incarnate nature of the Word of God" for the unity of Christ, and to affirm his duality by saying he was "out of two natures." Cyril's enormous prestige kept his more radical allies in check, and a kind of truce prevailed; after his death, however, the fact that he had changed his mind on the crucial point of two-natures language would cast a very long shadow indeed.

## *The Resumption of Hostilities (444–451)*

On Cyril's death the bishops of the Antiochene tradition could no longer suppress their jubilation at, as they saw it, having won the day; chief among them were Theodoret of Cyrrhus and Ibas of Edessa, names that were to haunt the sixth century. They boldly asserted their Christology, and Theodoret even refused to condemn Nestorius. In the sprawling and diverse patriarchate of Antioch, however, popular piety, often led by monks, tended to side with Cyril. Nothing could have been more calculated to alarm these simple souls than the seeming triumph of Nestorians. All the touchstones for orthodoxy – the one Christ, in whom the Word literally became flesh; Christ as one incarnate nature; the Virgin Mary as *theotokos* – seemed endangered. Nothing could have been more calculated, either, to undermine the moderates who agreed with the Cyril of 433 in accepting "two natures": they were immediately suspected of being in communion with open Nestorians. Nothing could have been better calculated, furthermore, to move the patriarchy of Alexandria and the formidable Dioscorus – Cyril's successor – to action. For him Alexandria's triumph at Ephesus I was the decisive thing, and taking Cyril's union of 433 as a serious acceptance of the orthodoxy of "two natures" rather than as a merely tactical move was a betrayal of all that Alexandria and the real Cyril stood for. Alarm bells rang all across the eastern part of the empire.

The lightning rod for events turned out to be Eutyches. He spoke out against talk of two natures and was condemned by a synod at Constantinople presided over by Flavian in 448. Whatever he actually thought, Eutyches's name is forever associated with the heresy of saying that the human and the divine were "mingled" in Christ. That was not what Eutyches was charged with, however. The actual charge (an astonishing one to make against a cyrillian conservative) was that he did not accept the authoritative teaching of Cyril. What he did not accept was the teaching of Cyril enunciated in the Formula of Union of 433. Eutyches' refusal to tolerate any acceptance of two-natures language as true to his cyrillian tradition and the insistence of Flavian and his synod to the contrary on the basis of the Formula of Union were the first shots in the battle that would consume the Age of Justinian, a battle fought out along the fault line between the Cyril of 431 and the Cyril of 433.

Dioscorus, with the support of Theodosius II (408–450), presided over another council at Ephesus in 449; it condemned Flavian and such "Nestorians" as Theodoret and Ibas. Saddled for history with Rome's dismissive caricature of it as the "Robber Synod" (*latrocinium*), this new council must have been seen by its members as vindicating the "real" Cyril and Ephesus, much as Constantinople in 381 had vindicated Athanasius and Nicaea, rewinning the church for orthodoxy.

Dioscorus's successors in the sixth century would never forget the stark reversal of that victory which was soon to follow, nor would they forget Dioscorus's humiliation.

## *The Council of Chalcedon: The Apple of Discord Is Thrown*

In 450, Theodosius fell off his horse and died.[3] His sister Pulcheria allied herself with Anatolius, the new patriarch of Constantinople, and Pope Leo I. She consolidated power by marrying Marcian, who succeeded Theodosius as emperor (450–457). They all sympathized with the deposed Flavian, and were outraged at Eutyches' "heresy" and Dioscorus's high-handedness. Leo was particularly offended because his careful setting out of the western Christology in his *Tome* – one person in Christ, but two natures, each having its own distinct operations – had not even been read in 449. Marcian decided to solve the impasse: he called the council that was to end all councils.

The council he called met at Chalcedon in 451. Destined to be the Fourth Ecumenical Council and the touchstone of Christological orthodoxy in the view of the West and Eastern Orthodoxy, it was also destined to be considered the great betrayal of Christological orthodoxy by much of the church in the East and the grounds for its separation from them. Chalcedon was thus a historic watershed.

Marcian sought a Christological statement from Chalcedon that would end all uncertainty and dispute, uniting the church and empire. The first instinct of the bishops, however, was to step back to the Union of 433. Accordingly, though Nestorius's and Eutyches' teaching was condemned, it was Dioscorus's conduct, not his teaching, that was condemned, leaving room for his possible reconciliation. Among the Antiochene bishops, Theodoret and Ibas were exonerated, but only after hard questioning and after they had clearly condemned Nestorius and his teaching. Leo's *Tome* was received with some enthusiasm. Pressed by the emperor to produce the desired definitive creed, the bishops' commission produced a statement (now lost) that evidently settled on a cyrillian sort of formula asserting that Christ was "out of two natures," leaving room for him to be "one incarnate nature" after the Incarnation.

The imperial commissioners would not hear of it. Dioscorus had accepted that very formula, they pointed out, and he had accepted Eutyches. Whether they were convinced of the necessity for clarity, or simply bowed to imperial direction and pressure – direction, it should be remembered, that the churches of the East accepted as the emperor's proper role – the bishops who remained took the fatal step of accepting a formula that said Christ was "recognized *in two natures*," balancing it with the assertion that he was also "in one person and hypostasis." They denied that this was a new creed, describing it simply as an "interpretation" of Nicaea.

Chalcedon's virtue was terminological clarity: it cut the Gordian knot by reserving the language of nature for describing the difference between the divine and human in Christ, unequivocally saying that he was "in two natures." It used the totally different terms "person" and "*hypostasis*" to assert the unity of Christ, adding also the adverbs "without division" and "without separation." At least terminologically, things were clearer. However, apart from the word "*hypostasis*," and the added adverbs, this language was exactly that used, in rather different ways, by the West and by Nestorius. If the majority of bishops at Chalcedon meant by this something more like what Cyril believed, they would have to explain how, and do so convincingly. The highly-charged atmosphere in the East did not bode well for them.

## *The Attempt to Impose Chalcedon: Marcian and Leo (451–474)*[4]

It is astonishing how many histories of doctrine used to conclude with Chalcedon, as if all Christological discussion and conflict were settled there. Nothing could be further from the truth. The West was happy enough, but then Chalcedon seemed to be enshrining what they traditionally believed. The Antiochene bishops could, if they put it artfully, claim that they were vindicated. For the rest in the East, three little words – "in two natures" – made Chalcedon a monumental disaster. Even before the council ended the dire news was announced: Chalcedon was a victory for Nestorianism! Chalcedon taught Nestorius' doctrine of two natures! The bishops who had subscribed to it were heretics! Yet the majority of those bishops had shown that they stood with Cyril, not with the Antiochene tradition, though in the end they had felt compelled to move away from Cyril's favored language to the language he had accepted in the Union of 433. What Chalcedon had done was to force on them a decision between the Cyril of 431 and the Cyril of 433. The faultline that had begun to appear with his change of mind in 433 became, as a result, a chasm. On each side of it, warring parties would marshal their forces and their arguments. On one side, from that moment on, stood Chalcedonians of several traditions, but the great majority moderate cyrillians; on the other side stood anti-Chalcedonians, all of them ardent cyrillians. [In modern times anti-Chalcedonians are usually called by the pejorative and anachronistic term "Monophysites," but the more neutrally descriptive term "anti-Chalcedonians" is used here.]

The limits of imperial power to impose a Chalcedonian solution were quickly reached: bishops could be deposed and replaced, but the people and monks were another question. Fervent resistance, supported from exile by deposed bishops, became a fact of life in the East. Fourth-century images of resistance were bound to be summoned up, and for a very long time the anti-Chalcedonians were going to understand their task as the re-winning of the Church and Empire for what they understood to be orthodoxy, on the model of the fourth-century re-winning by Athanasius and others of the Church and Empire for the Nicene faith. Only when that self-understanding faded late in Justinian's reign was all realistic hope of a unitive solution lost.

The majority of Chalcedonians in the East, though they stood with the Cyril of 433, were not in anything like as attractive a rhetorical position. Cast as heretics against, and betrayers of, what all agreed was a high point for orthodoxy (Ephesus), they had the unenviable task either of convincing the anti-Chalcedonians that they were not really heretics and traitors after all (while trying to dissociate themselves from the Nestorian taint of the two-natures language they used), or of suppressing anti-Chalcedonian resistance. The task was made all the more difficult by their communion with known Antiochenes like Theodoret and Ibas, whose opposition to Cyril, condemnation by Dioscorus and his council, and public celebration of their cause's triumph made their rehabilitation by Chalcedon unconvincing in the extreme.

While we know the outcome of the century-long controversy that was to follow, we need to remember that those who lived through it did not: to them, the possibility of a reconciliation was for a very long time quite real, and any other outcome was inconceivable. Tumultuous struggles ensued in the Eastern heartland of the Empire over subscription to Chalcedon, and the dogged anti-Chalcedonianism of Egypt and parts of Syria became a given. Yet there was universal resistance to the notion that the disagreement implied a real division between Churches. Emperors and Church-leaders alike continued to share an understanding of the one Empire united by the one Church, and were troubled by what was happening. Emperors were bound to attempt to exercise their authority and influence to achieve a resolution, and to seek widely for promising initiatives. Church-leaders on both sides were bound to address the rift too, and theologians would feel called upon to defend or explain positions.

Though Marcian's successor, Leo I (457–474), carried on the attempt to impose Chalcedonian conformity, we see also the beginnings of a quite different approach: in 458 he sent one of the anti-Chalcedonian patriarchs of Alexandria, as part of a negotiation, a collection of writings from the Church fathers (a florilegium) said to support "two natures." A first attempt was being made at arguing that, despite appearances, Chalcedon and the Chalcedonians were really orthodox, really in the tradition of the fathers. That initiative failed, but an important new option had opened up: reconcile the anti-Chalcedonians to Chalcedon. A much more extensive florilegium from Cyril would appear ca. 482, and be widely used by Chalcedonians to make their case. At the same time, however, anti-Chalcedonians were erecting new barriers: late in Leo's reign, they began to enshrine their Christology more explicitly in the worship of the Church by inserting into the hymn known as the *Trisagion* (*Thrice Holy*) an addition regarding the Son – "crucified for us" – that they believed no Chalcedonian could accept.

## *The Attempt to Move Back from Chalcedon: Zeno and Anastasius (474–517)*

After a short-lived usurpation that sided with the anti-Chalcedonians, the next emperor, Zeno (474–491), continued the policy of imposing Chalcedonian orthodoxy, and faced the inevitable resistance. In 482 he took a new tack in enacting the *Henoticon* (unitive statement) whereby each side was to draw back from insisting that the other side either accept or reject Chalcedon.[5] That is, there would be a withdrawal to a pre-Chalcedonian position based on common loyalty to Nicaea. In this, he seems to have adapted an approach recently tried with success in Palestine, where the patriarch Martyrius and the abbot Marcianus had reached a similar accord a few years earlier. The approach of the *Henoticon* would be maintained, in one form or another, right up until the Age of Justinian, a remarkable success story.

It could not be a success forever, though. Rome, though kept in the dark, had its informants in the form of the vigorously Chalcedonian "Sleepless Monks" of Constantinople, and eventually a major schism opened up between the churches of the East and Rome (known to history as the Acacian Schism, after Acacius, the patriarch of Constantinople who had written the *Henoticon*). In the East, some anti-Chalcedonians similarly decried anything short of complete condemnation of Chalcedon and Leo's *Tome*. Major rifts in the East were averted only by means of clever diplomacy.

When Anastasius I (491–518) became emperor by marrying Zeno's widow, the fragile peace achieved under the *Henoticon* was beginning to unravel over a hardening of positions. A brief opportunity, when a pro-*Henoticon* pope seemed to be in place in Rome, proved illusory, since Rome soon returned to intransigency. In the East, anti-Chalcedonians were undermining the intent of the *Henoticon* by arguing that it actually forbade adherence to Chalcedon. Anastasius seemed to shift in their direction when he supported the deposition of the Chalcedonian leadership in Antioch and in Constantinople. It was at this moment that the great anti-Chalcedonian theologian, Severus, ascended the throne of Antioch. At the end of his reign, however, Anastasius backed away from the anti-Chalcedonians, engaging in futile attempts to win Rome over and to restrain anti-Chalcedonians from outright and divisive domination of the churches in the East. He had been brought up short by the irreducible realities with which imperial policy had to deal: the refusal of Rome and some of its allies in the East to compromise Chalcedon, and the refusal of anti-Chalcedonians to accept it or its partisans.

As the tensions heated up again in the first decade of the sixth century, theological issues returned to the fore, and Anastasius's reign saw both sides produce genuine theologians who could engage the issues at a new level.

## *Engaging the Theological Issue: Neo-Chalcedonians and Anti-Chalcedonians (507–518)*

It was in Palestine that the most important option emerged, the articulation of Christology called by moderns "neo-Chalcedonianism." While Severus was still a monk there (in 507), he was challenged by another monk, Nephalius.[6] Nephalius was arguing something that had not been heard before: that Chalcedon had – unintentionally – given the wrong impression by using words "crudely" ("in two natures" is obviously intended) in its eagerness to exclude the error of Eutyches. Nephalius was thus recognizing the legitimacy of the concerns of the anti-Chalcedonians based on the appearance of Nestorianism in what Chalcedon said, while attempting to show them that there was no substance to those concerns. He proposed, as a legitimate way to say more clearly what Chalcedon really meant, expressions like "two united natures," suggesting that this was really just a different way of saying what the anti-Chalcedonians meant by "one incarnate nature." The thrust of Nephalius, as of neo-Chalcedonians after him, was to explain the intention of Chalcedon as expressing a pretty traditional Christology true to Cyril and the fathers, despite its use of formulae that appeared tainted by Nestorianism. Thus an entirely new, irenic approach to the divisive christological controversies entered the stage. It was the one approach that would come close – very close – to really restoring the peace of the church.

We know little about another of these Palestinian irenic theologians, John of Scythopolis, except that he used expressions such as "the Word suffered in the flesh" and "one of the Trinity who suffered," characteristically cyrillian ways of speaking of the unity of the Word become flesh, evidently arguing that a proper understanding of Chalcedon meant that one could use even such a formula (we remember that anti-Chalcedonians had recently been assuming that this was not possible for Chalcedonians.) He was dismissed by Severus. We know more about John the Grammarian, whom Severus attacked at length as a great danger. The "danger" lay precisely in the fact that John saw the Cyril of 433 as recognizing an underlying agreement between his tradition and the best of the Antiochene tradition. He was able to make a substantial case that (1) Cyril understood his own "one incarnate nature" as being exactly what Antiochenes meant when they spoke of "one person," and (2) Cyril realized the truth of speaking of "two natures," when "nature" was recognized as referring to the essence of things, since he and everyone had to admit that, while the incarnate Christ was of one essence ("consubstantial") with God, he was also of one essence with us. If John was correct, Chalcedon was true to Cyril and not at all Nestorian.

The response of Severus to these neo-Chalcedonian initiatives was definitive for what came later. In his *Philalethes* (*Friend of Truth*, by which he meant Cyril) he attacked a florilegium purporting to show Cyril as in favor of Chalcedon's position as a complete misrepresentation: the true Cyril believed rather that the Christ who could be conceived, but only in a purely theoretical way, as "out of two natures," needed to be thought of as actually and concretely one nature, just as body and soul can be conceived as being theoretically different natures out of which a person comes, but in actuality exist as only one nature. To achieve this "true" Cyril, however, Severus had to explain away the Cyril of 433 as using "crude language" that he did not really mean (much as Nephalius had argued, on the other side, that Chalcedon had used crude language.) In the name of his true, theologically purified Cyril, Severus rejected entirely the "Nestorian" distinction between divine and human operations enshrined at Chalcedon in Leo's *Tome* and in the statement of faith: all operations were simply those of the one incarnate Word. Severus's version of Cyril would guarantee the failure of any attempt to bridge the gap between Chalcedonians and anti-Chalcedonians.

## The Age of Justinian

### *Justin I (518–527): The Return to Imposing Chalcedon*

When Justin I (518–527) ascended the throne there was a return to the policy of imposing Chalcedon.[7] At his side was the powerful Vitalian, leader of a revolt against Anastasius in 514 based in his traditionally pro-Chalcedonian and pro-Western native province of Scythia. The symbol of anti-Chalcedonian ascendancy, Severus, was deposed and exiled to Egypt. Pope Hormisdas demanded the "correction," as he put it, of the erring churches of Syria and Egypt. It was a return to a policy that had been a conspicuous failure in the East under Marcian and Leo, and which could hardly be expected to succeed with anti-Chalcedonians who had had nearly seventy years to harden their vision of themselves as the embattled champions of orthodoxy, and who by now were inspired by their own "martyrs" for orthodoxy. The rest of Justin's reign shows him adjusting to those realities while attempting to retain the harmony with Rome and an officially Chalcedonian position. Justin's final policy may be summed up as making some accommodation to the fact of anti-Chalcedonian leadership in certain churches that could not easily be "corrected," while maintaining a position of official Chalcedonianism.[8]

### *Justinian Smells a Deal: The Scythian Monks' Proposal (518–519)*

Vitalian was not the only powerful influence in the court of Justin, and his death by assassination in 520 left his main rival, the emperor's nephew Justinian, in the position of influencing, and even directing, imperial policy on all matters religious. In any case, Justinian's accession to power (to be merely consolidated by his own elevation to the rank of Caesar in 527, and to the imperial throne itself a few months later) spells the beginning of the Age of Justinian for our purposes. It was to be an age marked not just by the personality and power of this extraordinary man and his equally extraordinary wife Theodora, but also by some of the most promising and ambitious new initiatives to reunite the church, both on the part of the court and on the part of church leaders.[9]

No issue is more contentious in understanding how the drama unfolded than the interpretation of Justinian's and Theodora's roles. Was he the demon-inspired enemy of the church? The architect of an intolerable "caesaropapism" that gave him illicit control of the church? A saint? A talented and learned theologian who imposed his own views on a pliant eastern church? An uxorious pawn in his wife's anti-Chalcedonian hands? The record supports none of these views, though all have been urged, but rather reveals an entirely pragmatic, vigorous, and clever practicioner of the emperor's traditional role, a man intent on one thing: brokering a deal.

Though Justinian first appears in the shadow of Vitalian and Justin, and though it is a truism that loyalty to Chalcedon was always and invariably a cornerstone of his policy as of theirs, our earliest glimpse of him addressing the christological controversies reveals a man not content to continue a policy that had been a conspicuous failure, the policy of suppressing one side or the other by force, but rather intent on finding a deal acceptable to both sides. Promising initiatives had begun to appear in Palestine, but Anastasius had not seen their potential. Not so Justinian. The first initiative Justinian himself came upon was one that he quickly siezed on and pursued. In 518 a group of Scythian monks were taking John of Scythopolis's approach – that "one of the Trinity was crucified" should be used to explain Chalcedon in a way that would correct the misunderstanding that Chalcedon was Nestorian. Their Chalcedon taught that the Word was the subject of all of the incarnate Christ's actions, so that the Son could properly be said to have been crucified. When they took their campaign to Rome, Justinian wrote to Pope Hormisdas opposing them, but days later changed his mind and vigorously urged the pope to accept their proposal positively for "the peace of the Church."

This about-face is extremely instructive: for one thing, it reveals that Justinian's fundamental agenda was – an emperor could have no other – to restore the peace of the church. It also reveals that Justinian was not concerned about the theological issues *per se*, since he seems to have been willing to move from one position to its opposite in mere days, and with no sign of a theological justification, simply because he suddenly realized the potential of the monks' initiative. The incident thus shows Justinian to be a pragmatic power broker looking for a deal that would do the job. It would be many years before he found what he was looking for, and by then it would be too late.

The fact that the very same Justinian and Justin, just before the latter's death in 527, promulgated an edict taking severe action against anti-Chalcedonians does not necessarily represent a reversal of policy. It was simply a fact that, if Justinian's succession to the imperial throne was to be secure, he required for a time the complete support of Rome and of the population of the city of Constantinople, which meant pleasing the pope and the Sleepless Monks with a show of Chalcedonian strictness. The pragmatic necessity of maintaining good relations with the West was all the more self-evident in the 530s, as wars to "restore" the West to the empire were launched. That the campaign by the anti-Chalcedonian bishop, John of Tella, to ordain a separate hierarchy of anti-Chalcedonians in Syria was met *pro tem* by strong repressive measures by no means implied a return to the old policy of repressing dissent. These measures were entirely and urgently pragmatic: if Justinian was to hold the empire together, the church could not be allowed to drift into deeper functional division before a deal could be found to end its internecine strife.

Finding that deal continued to be the most evident of all pragmatic necessities, and one Justinian never lost sight of. Given the failure that had met his predecessors' attempts to impose either the Chalcedonian or the anti-Chalcedonian position, and the demonstrated impossibility of drawing back from Chalcedon without alienating Rome and powerful forces in Constantinople, it was perhaps inevitable that Justinian would turn again and again to the one approach that might still be viable, the attempt to reconcile anti-Chalcedonians to Chalcedon. Justinian's marriage in around 525 to Theodora, born an anti-Chalcedonian, served that purpose admirably. Though Procopius's misogynistic *Secret History* is useless as an analysis of Justinian's and Theodora's motivations, he does make sense when he asserts that they made intentional use of their difference. It was double diplomacy: through Theodora, Justinian could recognize the reality of anti-Chalcedonians as part of his empire and negotiate with them; in his own capacity as a Chalcedonian, he could deal directly with Rome, Constantinople, and Chalcedonians in general.

## *The Conversations of 532*

Justinian's next known initiative came in 532, in the form of informal conversations he hosted between a few Syrian anti-Chalcedonian and some Chalcedonian bishops.[10] The meetings were set the task of finding ways of giving "satisfaction" to the anti-Chalcedonians on the objections they harbored. While the conversations, to the emperor's evident annoyance, were unsuccessful in finding a resolution, each side expressed some satisfaction, the Chalcedonians that they had made clear that Chalcedon was a useful advance in that it excluded Eutyches' ideas, the anti-Chalcedonians that they had cleared Dioscorus of the supposed charge of sharing Eutyches' ideas. It was a tiny step forward. The conversations much more readily identified the sticking-points: the issue of which Cyril – the one of 431, or the one of 433 – was authoritative; Chalcedon's "novelty" of saying "in two natures," rather than Cyril's "one incarnate nature"; the suspicion that Chalcedon and Leo's *Tome* were disguised Nestorianism; and the seeming confirmation of that suspicion by Chalcedon's exoneration of Theodoret and Ibas. When Justinian met with the anti-Chalcedonians after things had fallen apart, he sounded them out about a possible compromise deal: what if Chalcedon were construed simply as excluding Eutyches, if Theodoret and Ibas were condemned along with Theodore of Mopsuestia, and if both one- and two-natures formulae were accepted? He was politely but firmly told by the anti-Chalcedonians that it was not acceptable, no doubt because the two-natures formula remained part of it. Though that attempt failed, it seems to have triggered two separate initiatives, one coming from the church leadership, the other coming from the court. Drawn together with other initiatives by the guiding hand of an emperor ever more intent on finding the final deal that had evaded all of his predecessors, they would issue in the last and only integrated attempt at a solution, the Second Council of Constantinople of 553.

## *A Theologian's Initiative: Leontius of Jerusalem*

The first initiative out of the Conversations came from Palestine again, the matrix of previous irenic proposals. Leontius of Jerusalem may have been the "Leontius, representative of the monks of the holy city," who was among the Chalcedonian staff at the Conversations. What is certain is that his *Against the Monophysites* addresses most of the very issues on which the Conversations failed and attempts to take the ecumenical dialogue to a new level.[11] He openly invites his readers to part company with "a self-styled teacher of theirs, Severus," apparently convinced that there is no hope of reconciliation with him, but believing that others among the Syrians may be susceptible to his argument. He builds on Nephalius's approach. Against the charge Chalcedon introduced a novelty in the two-natures formula, he argues that both sides' formulae have their orthodox uses against heresy when they are properly understood, and that beneath the different ways of speaking lies substantive agreement on the faith both sides intend by their statements. That underlying common faith in the unity of Christ, he proposes, is best expressed as belief that Christ is in one hypostasis – thus taking up a neglected expression of Cyril and Chalcedon and developing it as a politically neutral vocabulary for voicing the common faith. (By "hypostasis" he means the concrete existing individual, in the way that water and a sponge come together in one entity, though the water and the sponge remain separate by nature; or in the way that fire and iron come together, though separate by nature again, in the one entity that is a red-hot ingot; or in the way that body and soul come together in one person – the metaphors are his.) Once that vocabulary for expressing Christ's unity is agreed upon, it becomes possible to speak of two natures (as meaning essences) in a perfectly orthodox way that does not compromise the concrete unity. Leontius likewise argues that when the fathers are read in terms of the underlying sense intended by their words, all of them agree that there is one hypostasis and two natures. On these bases, Leontius extends to the anti-Chalcedonians a remarkable and disarming invitation: "If you will confess along with us the tried and true doctrines, both speaking of one incarnate nature of the Word of God, and saying that there are two natures of Christ united in respect of His one hypostasis, while not disowning the Council and Leo and ourselves, we for our part anathematize even an angel from heaven, if he did not think and speak and write in this way, sooner than anathematizing you."

## *Putting Together a Comprehensive Approach (533–553)*

Justinian and his advisers must have seen the potential of Leontius's initiative, for in 533 Justinian published an edict proclaiming that "union by hypostasis" was part of the Chalcedonian faith. In the same year another edict said the same thing about the formula "one of the Trinity suffered" – Justinian had not forgotten the promise he had seen back in 519 in the Scythian monks' approach. It was not an approach that played any large part in Leontius's thinking, but that is just the point: Justinian was looking everywhere for a combination of approaches that would do the trick. He had failed with the combination he proposed at the end of the Conversations, but he had by no means given up. This time, the pope, John II, approved of the kind of formula Hormisdas had rejected and furthermore joined in condemning the Acoimetae for "Nestorianism." Some of the pieces were thus falling into place that promised to make the Chalcedonian position appear much more palatable, and much less tainted by Nestorianism, than had been possible before.

Ambitions in the West, where a Gothic invasion of Italy upset the whole agenda of reconquest, forced once again a temporary reorientation of imperial policy toward Rome in the mid-530s, and Pope Agapetus, taking refuge in Constantinople, made sure that a Chalcedonian was maintained as patriarch of Antioch against any possibility that Severus might return. A schism between two factions of the anti-Chalcedonians exiled in Egypt over minor points of doctrine, one that threatened to fracture the church even further, led Justinian to support the installation of the first Chalcedonian patriarch there in a long time.

The results were exactly the opposite of those intended: after Severus, who had never abandoned the dream of rewinning the Church of the Empire for anti-Chalcedonian "orthodoxy," died in 538, his exiled successor Theodosius began, as John of Tella had before him, to ordain a separate anti-Chalcedonian hierarchy. This task was carried on with great vigor by one of the bishops he consecrated, Jacob Baradaeus (after whom the Syrian anti-Chalcedonians are often called Jacobites.) The forces moving toward disintegration of the church were gaining ground on the forces attempting to reunite it.

By the mid-540s Justinian was able to return his attention to the second initiative coming out of the Conversations of 532, the possibility of clearing Chalcedonians of the taint of Nestorianism implied by Chalcedon's exoneration of Theodoret and Ibas. It was not enough, as Leontius had done, to say that a few closet Nestorians at Chalcedon did not spoil the whole council. The fact, too, that Theodore of Mopsuestia – the father of Nestorianism identified as such by Cyril – remained a "father of the church" among Antiochenes rankled with anti-Chalcedonians. Theodoret's widely circulated attacks on Cyril, and the tone of Ibas's *Letter to Maris the Persian* – the very letter Chalcedon consulted in exonerating him – roused deep suspicion. Memories going back to before 433 made these three names objects of hatred and derision. It did not help that, at the Conversations of 532, the Chalcedonians had tripped all over themselves on the Ibas question.

Whatever the neo-Chalcedonian theologians may have thought – we have no indication that any of them was eager to condemn the

Antiochenes – Justinian saw the chance of a breakthrough. He was encouraged most notably by his adviser, Theodore Askidas, a man implicated in the obscure but fiercely fought "Origenist" controversies (also over Christology, but of a particularly rarefied kind developed in the tradition of the third-century theologian Origen) of monastic factions in Palestine. In his most expansive understanding of his imperial role, Justinian marshaled his substantial resources to orchestrate for a less-than-eager Chalcedonian church the condemnation of the "Three Chapters": the person and work of Theodore of Mopsuestia, Theodoret's writings against Cyril, and Ibas's *Letter to Maris*. In the process an ecumenical council would be called, a pope would be humiliated and condemned, history would be rewritten, and the foundation would be laid for the modern West's detestation of Justinian and what it calls his caesaropapism.

Around 544 Justinian issued a decree condemning the Three Chapters. The central problem, of course, was Ibas, since Chalcedon itself exonerated him of Nestorianism on the basis of the very letter the anti-Chalcedonians despised. A novel solution rewriting history had been developed since the 532 debacle on this point, however: Ibas was indeed exonerated by Chalcedon, but only after he dramatically changed his mind – and the letter on the basis of which he was exonerated was not the *Letter to Maris*, which was certainly Nestorian, but some other letter! Though there was fierce resistance in the West, particularly in North Africa, where all of this was seen as a direct attack on Chalcedon, Justinian obtained a series of secret assurances from Pope Vigilius that he did condemn the Three Chapters and would work toward obtaining their condemnation in the West. With Vigilius safely within reach in Constantinople since 547, that project must have seemed eminently practicable to Justinian, especially as he had the means to assist the campaign with restored imperial power in the West. Meanwhile, the difficulty of Theodore of Mopsuestia's status as a father who had died in the faith of the church was undermined by an elaborately stage-managed inquiry that "discovered" that, on the contrary, Theodore had not been revered in his home city within living memory, and that his name on the diptychs had even been replaced – a nice touch! – by that of Cyril of Alexandria. A position was thus being prepared that would decisively detach the church from the Antiochene tradition for which Cyril, in 433, had recognized an orthodox understanding. Thereby it might appear acceptably orthodox to a faction that had never accepted the Cyril of 433.[12]

## *The Chalcedonians Agree: Constantinople II (553)*

Things moved swiftly forward. In 551 Justinian issued an edict, *On the True Faith*, which was to prove the charter document for Constantinople II. In it the various initiatives we have seen, at least those identified by the court as promising, were brought together: the Word as the subject of his own suffering "in the flesh"; the one Christ "composed" of two natures; difference in nature, but unity by hypostasis, or "hypostatic union"; "one incarnate nature of the Word of God" understood as meaning "one incarnate hypostasis or person," all supported by texts from Cyril and other fathers. The edict closed with thirteen anathemas, ten supporting this teaching and three, inevitably, condemning the Three Chapters. The deal Justinian and his advisers proposed for the Church was ready.

Things did not go as planned. Vigilius concluded that the West would see the condemnation of the Three Chapters as a betrayal of Chalcedon. The council met without him, and in the end condemned him. After lengthy comparison of the works of Theodore, and of the suspect work of Theodoret and Ibas, with those of recognizable champions of orthodoxy, it condemned the Three Chapters. In its anathemas, it enshrined the neo-Chalcedonian christological formulations. (In a separate session, it also condemned Origenism.)

How the council was received in the West is one of the more bizarre stories in this whole ill-fated affair. The first Latin acts of Constantinople II included the full story of Vigilius and his condemnation. Vigilius recanted completely by early in 554, and a new version of the Latin acts was prepared that entirely eliminated any mention of his resistance and condemnation, leaving the impression that he had entirely approved the council's decisions – yet another indication of Justinian's willingness to take whatever pragmatic steps were necessary to save the deal he had labored so hard to see put on the table. There was resistance to the council in the West for centuries (the Aquileian Schism), but eventually the revised acts prevailed as the official version in the West of what was understood to be an authoritative ecumenical council, with its neo-Chalcedonian Christology – the achievement in part of Gregory the Great! Paradoxically, and only by means of chicanery, success was thus eventually achieved in the West.[13]

It all came too late to bring the desired result in the East. Anti-Chalcedonians were beyond the point at which anything other than complete concentration on the one-nature formula could ever be widely accepted, and Constantinople II's failure to capitulate on that central point marked the moment at which the majority of anti-Chalcedonians realized fully that they had given up on their great dream of regaining the empire for orthodoxy as they understood it, and resigned themselves to going their own way as a church distinct from the official church of the empire. Justinian's successor, Justin II, after one further attempt, would abandon all hope of reconciliation in that direction and impose harsh measures.

## *A Changed World*

It is self-evident that the ecclesiastical and political geography was permanently altered by these developments.[14] Churches drifted apart, and provinces within which anti-Chalcedonian churches predominated would end up outside the empire. Justinian reshaped the imperial role in a much more proactive form by the vigor, even the desperation, with which he pursued the time-honored goal of keeping the church united by prodding, instructing, and bullying a church that showed little sign of being able to resolve its divisions.

A significant alteration in the intellectual world began, perhaps, with Cyril, when his ultimate appeal was not to scripture but to Athanasius's authority for the title *theotokos* for Mary. Certainly, when the great sixth-century controversy focused itself on rival claims to represent the authentic Cyril, the die was cast: theological argument was focused on arguments about what the "select fathers" of the first five centuries had said and meant. Sound theology became correct exegesis of the authoritative tradition of these fathers, no more, no less, a fact demonstrated when the Fifth Council determined the heterodoxy of Theodore of Mopsuestia solely on the basis of comparing his writings with the teachings of "the fathers."

Byzantine theology would never be the same. It would never again have the range of inquiry possible in a church that accepted both Antiochene and Alexandrian interpretations of scripture. The affair of the Three Chapters had effectively consolidated control of exegesis in the hands of the one person whose job it was to represent the mind of the church (and an exceedingly singleminded church it had become) – the emperor. The often fallible and brawling bishops of history became the sainted and infallible authorities for a monolithic, unchanging Christian tradition. Thinking that departed from them in the area of dogma, especially on the Trinity and on Christology, became impossible. The radical ideas of the theologian now known as Pseudo-Dionysius gained an audience in the Age of Justinian only by being passed off as dating from the apostolic age.

It should be noted, finally, that much of the transformation described here for theology finds parallels in other aspects of Justinian's reign. For instance, whereas the Theodosian Code preserved the twists, turns, and about-faces of legislation through the years, the Code of Justinian eliminated all of that in a monolithic harmony, much as the theological tradition was harmonized and, in the process, dehistoricized. Even the attempt to reconquer the Western Empire was an attempt to impose a monolithic idea at the expense of the historical reality of what the West had become. It was characteristic of the age, perhaps, to be haunted by a past it had, in large part, invented.

## Notes

1 Useful sources for primary material in translation include *The Seven Ecumenical Councils*, Nicene and Post-Nicene Fathers, ser. 2, vol. 14 (New York, 1900); Michael Maas, *Readings in Late Antiquity* (London, 2000); R. A. Norris, Jr., ed. and trans., *The Christological Controversy* (Philadelphia, 1980); W. H. C. Frend, *Creeds, Councils, and Controversies*, rev. ed., ed. J. Stevenson (London, 1989), and *A New Eusebius* (London, 1987); W. G. Rusch, ed. and trans., *The Trinitarian Controversy* (Philadelphia, 1980). Clear on doctrinal and church-historical issues are H. Chadwick, *The Church in Ancient Society: From Galilee to Gregory the Great*, Oxford History of the Christian Church (Oxford, 2001); J. N. D. Kelly, *Early Christian Doctrines* (San Francisco, 1978); and J. Quasten, *Patrology* (Westminster, 1983–1986).

2 Useful from this point on are W. H. C. Frend, *The Rise of the Monophysite Movement* (Cambridge, 1979); and J. Meyendorff, *Christ in Eastern Christian Thought* (Washington, D.C., 1969).

3 From this point on, see P. T. R. Gray, *The Defense of Chalcedon in the East (451–553)*. (Leiden, 1979).

4 On resistance to Chalcedon, see S. A. Harvey, *Asceticism and Society in Crisis* (Berkeley, Calif., 1990).

5 See the *Henoticon*, in Frend, *Rise*, 360–362, and Maas, *Readings*, 132ff. On the reign of Anastasius, see P. Charanis, *Church and State in the Later Roman Empire: The Religious Policy of Anastasius the First, 491–518* (Madison, Wis., 1939).

6 On the theologians, see R. C. Chesnut, *Three Monophysite Christologies* (Oxford, 1976); E. M. Ludwig, *Neo-Chalcedonism and the Council of 553* (Ph.D. diss., University of California at Berkeley, 1983); P. Rorem and J. C. Lamoureaux, *John of Scythopolis and the Dionysian Corpus* (Oxford, 1998), 23–36.

7 A. A. Vasiliev, *Justin the First* (Cambridge, Mass., 1950).

8 Some early historians of the period are Evagrius Scholasticus, *Ecclesiastical History*, ed. J. Bidez and L. Parmentier (London, 1898), trans. M. Whitby as *The Ecclesiastical History of Evagrius Scholasticus* (Liverpool, 2000); John of Ephesus, *Ecclesiastical History* II, partially preserved in *The Chronicle of Zuqnin, Parts III and IV*, trans. A.

Harrak (Toronto, 1999), 49–137; and Zacharias, *Ecclesiastical History*, CSCO 38 & 39, trans. F. J. Hamilton and E. W. Brooks as *The Syriac Chronicle Known as That of Zachariah of Mitylene* (London, 1899).

9 Primary sources are *CJ*, 1.5.12 (edict of 527); *Collectio avellana*, CSEL 35.2, 644ff., 648–649 (Justinian's letters to Hormisdas); Procopius, *Historia Arcana*, 11. A range of opinions on Justinian and Theodora appear in M. V. Anastos, "Justinian's Despotic Control over the Church as Illustrated by his Edicts on the Theopaschite Formula and his Letter to Pope John II in 553," *Mélanges G. Ostrogorsky* 2, 1–11, reprinted in Anastos, *Studies in Byzantine Intellectual History* (London, 1979), no. 4; R. Browning, *Justinian and Theodora* (London, 1971); A. Cameron, *Procopius and the Sixth Century* (London, 1985); J. A. S. Evans, *The Empress Theodora* (Austin, Tex., 2002), 67–104; L. Garland, *Byzantine Empresses* (London, 1999), 23–29; A. Gerostergios, *Justinian the Great, the Emperor and Saint* (Belmont, Mass., 1982); T. Honoré, *Tribonian* (Ithaca, N.Y., 1978), 5–30; and J. Moorhead, *Justinian* (London, 1994), 17ff., 38–40.

10 Surviving fragment of an anti-Chalcedonian account, evidently by John of Beit-Aphtona, and an ancient summary of the whole account, with translation: S. Brock, "The Conversations with the Syrian Orthodox under Justinian (532)," *OCP* 47 (1981): 92–117; statement of anti-Chalcedonians, in Frend, *Rise*, 362–366; Chalcedonian account (Lat.): Innocentius of Maronea, *Letter to Thomas, Priest of Thessalonica, about the Conversations with the Severians*, *ACO*, vol. 4, part 2, 169–184.

11 Leontius of Jerusalem, *Against the Monophysites*, PG, vol. 86, part 2, 1769A–1901A; forthcoming trans. by P. T. R. Gray, in Oxford Early Christian Texts. Studies include K. P. Wesche, *The Defense of Chalcedon in the Sixth Century* (Ph.D. diss., Fordham University, 1986); and K. P. Wesche, "Leontius of Jerusalem: Monophysite or Chalcedonian?" *St. Vladimir's Theological Quarterly* 31 (1987): 65–95.

12 On Justinian on Vigilius in acts of Constantinople II, see *ACO*, vol. 4, part 1, 11ff. For a report on the proceedings on Theodore of Mopsuestia, see *ACO*, vol. 4, part 1, 115–130. On edicts, see *CJ*, 1.1.6–8; on John II's acquiescence, *ACO*, vol. 4, part 2, 206–210; on Justinian's dogmatic writings, E. Schwartz, ed., *Drei dogmatische Schriften Justinians* (Munich, 1939; reprint, Milan, 1973.), trans. K. P. Wesche as *On the Person of Christ* (Crestwood, N.Y., 1991). Studies include J. L. Macdonald, *The Christological Works of Justinian* (Ph.D. diss., Catholic University of America, Washington, D.C., 1995).

13 On the acts of Constantinople II, see *ACO*, vol. 4, part 1, 3–231 and 248ff. See Justinian, *Edict on the True Faith*; and Schwartz, *Drei dogmatische Schriften*, 129–169, trans. K. P. Wesche, *On the Person of Christ*, 163–198. On reception in the West, see P. T. R. Gray and M. W. Herren, "Columbanus and the Three Chapters Controversy," *Journal of Theological Studies*, new ser., 45 (1994): 160–170.

14 Studies include P. Allen, "Neo-Chalcedonism and the Patriarchs of the Sixth Century," *Byzantion* 50 (1980): 5–17; A. Cameron, *Christianity and the Rhetoric of Empire* (Berkeley, Calif., 1991), 190–221; P. T. R. Gray, "Covering the Nakedness of Noah: Reconstruction and Denial in the Age of Justinian," in *Byzantinische Forschungen* 24 (1997): 193–206; Patrick T. R. Gray, "'The Select Fathers': Canonizing the Patristic Past," *Studio Patristica* 23 (1989): 21–36; Patrick T. R. Gray, "Through the Tunnel with Leontius of Jerusalem: The Sixth-Century Transformation of Theology," *The Sixth Century: End or Beginning?*, ed. P. Allen and E.

Jeffreys (Brisbane, 1996), 187–196; J. Herrin, *The Formation of Christendom* (Oxford, 1987), 121–127; M. Maas, *Exegesis and Empire in the Early Byzantine Mediterranean: Junillus Africanus and the Instituta regularia divinae legis* (Tübingen, 2003); and Maas, "Junillus Africanus' *Instituta Regularia Divinae Legis* in its Justinianic Context," in Allen and Jeffreys, *The Sixth Century*, 131–144.

# 10: Society and Community in the Christian East

*Lucas Van Rompay*

In the course of the sixth century the Christian world became irremediably divided over a dogmatic issue. The point of contention was whether one should speak of *two* natures in Jesus Christ, as it had been decided by the Council of Chalcedon (451), or of only *one* new nature, in which divinity and humanity were joined together.[1] This theological discussion strongly resonated in what we now call the Christian East – the eastern provinces of the Roman Empire and neighboring areas outside the empire, with their distinct linguistic and cultural characteristics.

Throughout his long reign, Justinian attempted to bridge the rift by winning the anti-Chalcedonians over to some sort of acceptance of the council, which since 518 had become the cornerstone of imperial religious policy. He failed, however, to achieve this goal. The opposition between the imperial church and the anti-Chalcedonians that existed at the beginning of Justinian's – indeed, from the beginning of Justin's – reign, was still there at his death. By that later date (565), not only had the opposition become much more articulate, the anti-Chalcedonians also had started building up their own ecclesiastical structure and had laid the foundations for the material and spiritual survival of their communities, which still exist today.

In fact, it is in Justinian's failed religious policy that we find the roots of a self-confident, powerful movement that was able to assert itself in spite of hardship and oppression. Although Justinian oppressed the anti-Chalcedonians and occasionally persecuted them, he also created the conditions that allowed them to exist, to shape their identity, and to negotiate their own domains of influence and power.

With regard to Justinian's failure to restore Christian unity, one may wonder whether by the sixth century the very idea of Christian unity had become a chimera. Throughout the fifth and sixth centuries, Christianity was expanding and various peoples within and outside the Roman Empire newly adopted Christianity. There was no question, therefore, of restoring Christian uniformity to its pre-Chalcedon situation – if such uniformity ever existed. It rather had to be imposed on an ever-growing diversity of nations and ethnicities. By definition, one might argue, doctrinal unity had become elusive, and the disagreement over Chalcedon was only one channel through which the inherent diversity of Christian belief and practice was being expressed.

The empire and the anti-Chalcedonian movement in the sixth century should, therefore, be envisioned not only in opposition, but also in interaction with each other. Throughout the sixth century, and in fact until the Arab invasions of Syria and Egypt, the Roman Empire and the anti-Chalcedonian movement lived together, most of the time accepting each other's existence and directing each other's course. They were uneasy partners in a Christian discourse that rejected diversity even while enacting it. It is only when we shift our focus from antagonism and opposition to coexistence and interaction that we are able to understand the sixth century as a period of intense creativity and productivity in literature, art, and spirituality for the anti-Chalcedonian communities, in spite of hardship and oppression.

The conflict over Chalcedon, with the division of eastern Christianity into Chalcedonian and anti-Chalcedonian communities, was by no means limited to the eastern provinces of the Roman Empire. The sixth century was an important period of Christian mission both inside and outside the empire, in large part because Justinian and the other emperors understood how to use Christian missionary activities in their foreign policy, protecting the borders of the empire and creating friendly neighbor states. The emperors did not always attempt to impose Chalcedonian beliefs on the missionaries and on the newly Christianized communities in Asia and Africa, but rather were willing, and occasionally forced, to accept anti-Chalcedonianism as the driving force behind the missions and the new Christian communities. Whether Chalcedonian or anti-Chalcedonian, the expansion of Christianity in Armenia, Georgia, Sasanian Persia, Arabia, Nubia, and Ethiopia served the interests of the Roman Empire and helped to create what has been called a "Byzantine commonwealth."[2]

Literature on Justinian and his religious policy is extensive,[3] but the other side of the conversation has received much less attention. The focus here will be on the formative history of the non-Chalcedonian communities, with much attention given to the texts and artifacts produced by these communities.

## The Accession of Justin and the Restoration of Chalcedon

On July 9, 518, Emperor Anastasius died at the age of eighty, without progeny. He was swiftly replaced by the sexagenarian Illyrian general Justin I.[4] Within a few weeks, steps were taken toward restoring Chalcedonian orthodoxy. Severus, patriarch of Antioch since 512, was summoned to the capital but chose to escape to Egypt, where he spent the rest of his life, until his death in 538. The centrality of Severus's name in the documents dealing with the changes in Constantinople in the summer of 518 shows that he was seen as the main representative of the anti-Chalcedonians, or at least of those anti-Chalcedonians who were seen as (potentially) troublesome in the eyes of the authorities.

In the capital, the new patriarch John II became the main proponent of the new policy. Communion with Rome, which had broken off in 484, was reestablished on Easter Sunday, 519. In Syria, in the course of the following months, bishops were urged to subscribe to an official document laying out the new policy or to give up their sees.[5] At that point, Severus already had left Antioch. Philoxenus – bishop of Mabbog and one of the most vociferous opponents of Chalcedon – was arrested. He was exiled to Philippoupolis, in Thracia (present-day Plovdiv in Bulgaria), where he was under the surveillance of the local Chalcedonian bishop, until he died in 524. Such treatment – house arrest in a remote location – was exceptional. Most bishops went into exile in Egypt, where they lived in relative freedom, while others gave up their sees and were allowed to stay in Syria.

In sharp contrast to the drastic purges in Syria and adjacent areas of Asia Minor (within the patriarchate of Constantinople), in Egypt anti-Chalcedonian bishops and their patriarch did not face any intervention. Patriarch Timothy IV of Alexandria (518–535) offered hospitality to his confrere Severus in the fall of 518. Other Syrian bishops also found a warm welcome in Egypt (Plate 2). They were received in cities and monasteries, from where some maintained contacts with their faithful in Syria through an exchange of letters or through messengers.

The difference in imperial policy applied in Syria and in Egypt is startling, and no satisfactory explanation for it has been offered so far.

One factor of significance must have been that whereas in Egypt there was overwhelming support for the anti-Chalcedonian cause, Syria was divided, with some areas profoundly attached to Chalcedon and others rejecting it. This division created instability, which at that point did not exist in Egypt. The emperor's master plan apparently aimed at providing a solution to the schism with Rome (which was an impediment to Byzantine policy in Italy) as well as to the instability in Syria. He may have intended to seriously weaken the anti-Chalcedonian movement by decapitating its hierarchy wherever there was unrest; its extinction at that point obviously was not one of his goals.

Less than two years after launching the first wave of oppression, the emperor moderated his approach in 520. He may have seen in the theopaschite formula (*Unus de Trinitate crucifixus*, "One of the Trinity was crucified"), popularized in Constantinople by the Scythian monks from 519 onward, a means to convince the anti-Chalcedonians on theological grounds and to lead them without coercion to a qualified acceptance of the council.[6] Moreover, in July 520, Vitalian, an influential proponent of the harsh policy, was assassinated. His disappearance left the emperor more freedom in his dealings with the anti-Chalcedonians. Another zealous Chalcedonian, Paul, who early in 519 had been elected patriarch of Antioch – to replace Severus – resigned in the spring of 521. In 520 or 521, both Severus and Philoxenus, in letters sent from their exile to their faithful in Syria, pleaded for a lenient attitude toward clergymen and laypeople who, after having fallen to the heretics (i.e., the Chalcedonians), repented and wished to come back to the orthodox faith.[7] This points to a relaxation of the oppression of the anti-Chalcedonians.

However, even before this relaxation, when the "cloud of persecution" was at its darkest, between 518 and 520, the same harshness was not found all over Syria. The events in Edessa, where resistance to the Council of Chalcedon was particularly strong, may serve to illustrate this.[8] When Bishop Paul was visited by the imperial inspectors in November 519, he refused to accept the council. This led to his deposition and arrest. However, he soon was released after a meeting with the patriarch, and he was able to resume his office, until he was again removed in 522 and exiled. The *Chronicle of Edessa*, a mid-sixth-century composition of Chalcedonian orientation, notes that the emperor himself ordered Paul's return to Edessa in 519, "in the hope that he would repent and accept the council."[9] Earlier in the same year, Paul had presided over the election of two anti-Chalcedonian bishops: Jacob, who until his death in November 521 served as bishop of Serug, and John, bishop of Tella, who was forced to resign in 521.

Vasiliev convincingly argued against the view, found in anti-Chalcedonian historiography, that the reign of Justin was one uninterrupted period of oppression and persecution. He drew attention to the evidence pointing not only to a moderation after the first two years, but also to the divergences existing within the imperial policy, which even in the first years of Justin's reign was "not absolutely ruthless" toward the anti-Chalcedonians, nor "stubbornly fanatical."[10]

Measuring the harshness of religious oppression and the ensuing hardship for the victims is, of course, a matter of subjective judgment. Even with its somewhat balanced approach, the imperial policy of these years prepared the ground for the creation of an ideology and a sense of identity that started disconnecting the anti-Chalcedonians – tentatively in the beginning and more radically a few decades later – from the all-encompassing authority of the emperor. It is important to note that the tribulations of expulsion, exile, vagrancy, and homelessness to which the opponents of imperial policy occasionally were condemned, or which they took upon themselves, perfectly matched the ascetic ideals and virtues of early Syrian Christianity. The oppression of anti-Chalcedonian laypeople, bishops, and monks and the expulsion of bishops from their sees and of monks from their monasteries provided the background against which historiographers and hagiographers portrayed models of excellent Christian behavior. John of Tella may serve as an example.[11] At Jacob of Serug's instigation, he was consecrated bishop of Tella against his will – so his biographer tells us – as he feared that his duties as bishop would distract him from his ascetic ideals. Only after his resignation as bishop, in 521, was he able to live up to the high standards of asceticism, wandering around, hiding himself and secretly ordaining priests. This holy man, the perfect example of the early Christian ascetic virtues, became one of the driving forces behind the movement of resistance. Oppression fostered the resilience of the victims and created new opportunities, ideologically and rhetorically. The anti-Chalcedonians were able to capitalize on this, not only because of their strength and resilience, but also because the oppression was never absolute and always left room for negotiation and for the anti-Chalcedonians' self-affirmation.

As a result of the Chalcedonian restoration within the empire, the opponents of the council were pushed back to the border areas and to the Christian communities outside the empire. Zealous preachers, such as Simeon of Bet Arsham, propagated the resistance against Nestorianism and Chalcedonianism in Persia, among East Syrians and Armenians.[12] The Arab *foederati* as well as the Christian communities of south Arabia and Ethiopia already had been exposed to anti-Chalcedonianism during the reign of Anastasius.[13] They were strengthened in their anti-Chalcedonian orientation during the reign of Justin I, when a powerful network was created, linking the council's opponents in Persia to those in south Arabia and in the Horn of Africa. In 520 or 521, Justin joined the Ethiopian *negus* in a military expedition against the allegedly Jewish king of the south Arabian Himyarites, who obstructed trade and harassed Christians. What must have been for Justin a pragmatic response to an unacceptable situation was perceived by the anti-Chalcedonians as a triumph of their form of Christianity. This south Arabian experience provided the anti-Chalcedonians with their first martyrs, men, women, and children allegedly massacred in the city of Najran by Jewish hands in defense of their orthodox (i.e., anti-Chalcedonian) faith. The rhetorical power of the ensuing literary creations was considerable.[14]

## Justinian: From the Edict on Heretics (527) to Direct Negotiations (532)

The opening sentences of the edict on heretics, issued jointly by the two *augusti* Justin and Justinian, in the summer of 527,[15] indicates the emperors' awareness that their policy of moderate oppression not only had failed to win back the anti-Chalcedonians to imperial orthodoxy but had actually strengthened the anti-Chalcedonian cause and transformed the scattered resistance into a coherent and well-organized network of dedicated people. As a corrective to the failed policy, a harsh approach was adopted once more.

As before, imperial strictures were not universally enforced. Egypt remained predominantly anti-Chalcedonian under patriarch Timothy IV and continued to serve as a safe haven for anti-Chalcedonians from Syria. In Antioch, however, the newly appointed patriarch, Ephrem of Amid (526–544), a former military commander, carried out the new policy with great determination.

As an immediate result of the new purge in the patriarchate of Antioch, the anti-Chalcedonians were entirely removed from power. All episcopal sees came into the hands of Chalcedonians, while many of the local priests eventually accepted Chalcedon or were replaced with Chalcedonians. With so many Syrian bishops already exiled and inactive in Egypt, this left a vacuum of anti-Chalcedonian leadership in Syria, which could easily have led to a complete takeover by the Chalcedonians. That this did not happen should be ascribed primarily to the fact that a number of monasteries in Syria remained fully committed to the anti-Chalcedonian cause and were able to secure popular support, not only in the countryside, but also in urban centers. Measures were taken to provide at least the lowest level of leadership.

First, the anti-Chalcedonian bishops in Egypt could provide some help. In several of his letters Severus described the churches of Syria and Egypt – the one existing in secret, while the other was enjoying freedom – as being in complete unity, constituting "one church which is compacted together in the orthodox faith, and confession and communion, and is most pure and free from association with the heretics."[16] Candidate priests and deacons, therefore, could be sent to Egyptian bishops for ordinations. This was not a full remedy to the existing need, either because of the long distance, or because the bishops in Egypt were reluctant to carry out the ordinations openly.[17] A more efficient solution, therefore, was worked out in the heartland of Syria. John of Tella, who had left his see in 521, moved from the monastery of Mar Zakkay, near Callinicum, to the countryside, where he started a new type of ministry as an itinerant bishop, secretly ordaining priests for the cities and villages, whereby "he liberated many from the communion of the heretics."[18] His biographer emphasizes that John had received "letters and permission from the Holy Patriarch Severus and from the metropolitan bishops who had fled to remote lands." The beginning of John's mission must be situated around the middle of the 520s.

John's activities did not remain unnoticed by the authorities and brought him to prominence within the anti-Chalcedonian movement. This must be the background against which, after a renewed mitigation in the imperial policy, he was included among the bishops who were invited to Constantinople for a theological discussion with Chalcedonians, probably in the spring of 532.

This is a most remarkable move on the part of Justinian, who now engaged in direct conversations with the Syrian anti-Chalcedonians. The three-day conference took place under Justinian's auspices, and on the third day the emperor himself made his appearance and took the lead in the discussion. Reports of the meeting are preserved, on the Chalcedonian side, in a Latin letter by Innocentius of Maroneia and, on the anti-Chalcedonian side, in one short, anonymous Syriac summary of the proceedings as well as in a more extensive, albeit incomplete, Syriac account.[19]

With this meeting the anti-Chalcedonians came closer to a formal recognition than they had ever been. For the first time the emperor and his entourage showed interest in and understanding of their viewpoint, which the emperor thought was not unorthodox.[20] Justinian went to great lengths in order to create room for the one-nature formula. But he requested that the anti-Chalcedonians rescind their condemnation of the council and the *Tome* of Leo, although they were expected to accept the council only as far as the expulsion of Eutyches was concerned, not its (dyophysite) definition of faith.[21] The anti-Chalcedonians rejected this pragmatic solution. Had they been frustrated by what they may have felt to be a political move void of genuine appreciation of their viewpoint? Were they perhaps reluctant to make such significant concessions in the absence of their leader Severus? Or had the ideological world of the anti-Chalcedonians in the eight decades following the council grown too far apart from mainstream Chalcedonianism?

Following this conference, Justinian did not give up his endeavors to reach if not a full agreement, then at least some kind of modus vivendi with the anti-Chalcedonians. Within a year after the conference he published a new "edict on faith" (533),[22] which avoided much of the disputed language and did not explicitly mention the Council of Chalcedon. In 535, Severus appeared in the capital at the emperor's invitation. His subsequent meetings with Anthimus, the new patriarch of Constantinople and participant in the conversations of 532, soon led to the latter's endorsement of the anti-Chalcedonian cause. Around the same time, in the middle of 535, Theodosius was elected patriarch of Alexandria, continuing the line of anti-Chalcedonian incumbents of that throne. Now, with anti-Chalcedonians on the sees of Constantinople and Alexandria and Severus well on his way to rehabilitation, it must have felt as if something of the climate prevailing in the later years of Anastasius had returned. However, just as in 518, a strong reaction – launched in the East by the Chalcedonian monks of Jerusalem and of Syria II (around the city of Apamea) – led to the reversal of the imperial policy in circumstances as dramatic as those of the year 518. The monks of Syria II were even better organized than they had been eighteen years earlier. The Monastery of St. Maron, possibly at the center of a federation of like-minded monasteries in the area, may have been instrumental in staging the resistance and in establishing contact with Pope Agapetus of Rome.[23] The pope appeared in Constantinople in 536. Anthimus resigned and was replaced with the Chalcedonian Menas. Anthimus was condemned, later in the same year, along with Severus, who was able to escape back to Egypt. Further measures for a purge of anti-Chalcedonians were taken. A three-year respite for the anti-Chalcedonians, which had begun in the spring of 532, thus came to an end.

## THE PIT OF THE ABYSS REOPENED (536–537)

In contrast with the situation of 518, this time Egypt was not spared imperial intervention. In 536 (or 537 – the sources are not unequivocal), Theodosius was forced to resign and was summoned to Constantinople, where he spent the rest of his life. His Chalcedonian successor was Paul of Tabennisi, who after two unsuccessful years resigned and was replaced with the Palestinian monk Zoilus. From the Egyptian perspective, it is with the deposition of Theodosius that the "very pit of the abyss was opened again in the days of the Emperor Justinian."[24] From now on, there would be two parallel hierarchies in Egypt as well as two patriarchs of Alexandria: a Chalcedonian one, installed by the emperor, and an anti-Chalcedonian one, living in exile or in one of the desert monasteries. The Chalcedonian patriarchs, in spite of the special powers with which they were invested,[25] had little popular support and were able only to create what has been called "a Byzantine enclave in the midst of a Coptic majority."[26]

Once Anthimus and Theodosius had been removed from power, the demise of the anti-Chalcedonian cause seemed to be complete. A bit more than a year later, Severus died in Egypt (on February 8, 538). Around the same time, John of Tella died in Antioch, at the age of fifty-five, humiliated and imprisoned by Ephrem of Antioch and his political allies. Things had never looked so bleak for the anti-Chalcedonians, both in Syria and in Egypt.

## TOWARD THE COUNCIL OF 553

Justinian, however, did not give up hopes to win the anti-Chalcedonians back to the imperial church. First, contacts with anti-Chalcedonian leaders continued. Somewhere between 537 and 548, the abbot of the important Pachomian monastery of Pbow, in upper Egypt, was summoned to Constantinople, where the emperor attempted to gain his support for the Chalcedonian cause. When the abbot failed to comply, he was deposed. He was able, however, to return to Egypt and to establish a new monastery at a short distance from his home monastery in Pbow, from which, apparently, anti-Chalcedonian monks had been expelled.[27]

Second, Justinian prepared another major strategic move. The neo-Chalcedonian theologians had come as close as possible to the anti-Chalcedonian Christology. Justinian's next step was aimed at clearing one further obstacle that prevented the anti-Chalcedonians from accepting the council. In his meeting with the Syrian bishops in 532, it had become clear once again that Chalcedonians and anti-Chalcedonians agreed on the condemnation of Diodore, Nestorius, and Eutyches, but in the view of the anti-Chalcedonians three names (often referred to as the "Three Chapters") needed to be added to that list: Theodore of Mopsuestia, Theodoret, and Ibas. These three names allegedly had found approval at the Council of Chalcedon, which therefore seemed to imply these theologians' orthodoxy. In Justinian's view, the three names could be removed from the council, and he was willing to subject them to a separate condemnation. This was pronounced first in imperial edicts of the 540s and subsequently by the Fifth Ecumenical Council (553). Though vindicating at the same time the Council of Chalcedon and (some of) the anti-Chalcedonian objections against it, the condemnation of the "Three Chapters" was hardly noticed by the anti-Chalcedonians and did nothing to bring them back to the imperial church.[28]

## New Anti-Chalcedonian Bishops Going East and South (ca. 542)

Much more consequential to the anti-Chalcedonian movement was a decision Justinian, or Theodora – it would be incorrect to separate them at this point or to see an opposition between them[29] – made in or around 542. At the request of the Arab Ghassanid phylarch Harith (Arethas), head of the *foederati* defending the eastern border of the empire, Theodora allowed Theodosius – the deposed patriarch of Alexandria who was living in the capital and after Severus's death acted as the head of the anti-Chalcedonians – to consecrate two bishops for the anti-Chalcedonians living under Ghassanid authority. The two men were Jacob Burdᶜânâ (or Burdᶜâyâ, Baradaeus in its Latin form), who would serve the northern border, and Theodore, who would be in charge of the southern parts. Both men were living in Constantinople. Theodore is often referred to as bishop of Bostra (present-day southern Syria). Jacob assumed the (possibly purely honorary) title of "metropolitan of Edessa."

There was no real need to ordain new bishops of anti-Chalcedonian sentiment, since a number were sitting idle in the capital. However, none of these retired bishops was sent to Harith. By starting with a new generation of bishops, who had not been involved in the

MAP 8. The spread of Miaphysitism in the Christian East.

power games of the previous years, the imperial couple may have intended to keep this resurgence of anti-Chalcedonian hierarchy, which apparently they could not deny to the Arab *foederati*, under strict control, severing it from its roots and quarantining it at the periphery of the empire. One would think, however, that they should have known better!

Jacob and Theodore embarked on their mission and started ordaining priests. Very little is known about Theodore,[30] while Jacob's role has received much more attention both in ancient sources and in modern scholarship.[31] Jacob worked as an itinerant bishop, much as John of Tella had done before him, visiting communities and monasteries and officiating at ordinations of priests. Ordinations had come to a virtual standstill due to the lack of anti-Chalcedonian bishops in Syria and Egypt. The demand for priests and the success of Jacob's mission indicate that the resistance to the Council of Chalcedon and to the imperial policy was still strong and could be rekindled whenever the means were available.

Was it perhaps due to the limited nature of his mission that Jacob never competed in authority with Theodosius of Alexandria, who, despite the restrictions imposed on him in Constantinople, acted as the uncontested leader of the anti-Chalcedonian movement? Ever since the days when Severus and many Syrian bishops found refuge in Egypt, there had been a remarkable unity between the anti-Chalcedonians in the two patriarchates in spite of the different cultural backgrounds, and no need was felt for a separate leader of the Syrian anti-Chalcedonians. Jacob, therefore, never was seen, nor saw himself, as a successor to Severus.

Before leaving the Constantinopolitan scene of the early 540s, it is worth pointing out that Theodore and Jacob were not the only anti-Chalcedonians to set off for mission work in remote lands. Around 542, two other companions of Theodosius, Julian and Longinus, were entrusted – by Theodora, so it seems – with a mission to the Nobades, the northernmost Nubian kingdom extending down the west bank of the Nile, between the First and the Third Cataracts. Just as in the case of Theodore and Jacob, there was a political dimension, for the conversion of the Nobades was intended to bring an end to the Nubian incursions into Roman Egypt. The bishop of the island of Philae, not far from Aswan, was closely involved in this mission, to which the destruction of the Isis temple at Philae on the orders of Justinian served as a prelude.[32]

The missions to the Ghassanids and to the Nubians, coordinated by Theodosius and his entourage, show that even when the situation of the anti-Chalcedonians within the empire was at its worst, they were able to expand their cause beyond the imperial borders. They did this not in an act of resistance against the empire, but ingeniously making their interest coincide with the emperor's broader concern for secure borders and reliable neighbors. In these border areas, Miaphysitism[33] became a key to imperial expansion! As a result of the Nubian mission in the mid-sixth century, Nubian Christianity became part of the anti-Chalcedonian fold, even though right from the beginning there was Chalcedonian competition – which, according to John of Ephesus, was supported by Justinian.[34]

Jacob Baradaeus was very cautious in the beginning. It took about ten years before he started consecrating bishops. A list preserved by John of Ephesus, covering the years 553 to 566, mentions twenty-seven bishops.[35] Twelve of them were consecrated at once in Constantinople (with a mandate given by Theodosius, John hastens to add) and sent to Egypt. The others were given dioceses in Syria and Asia Minor (including the Greek isles, where anti-Chalcedonians had settled). These bishops did not take residence in their dioceses, where their Chalcedonian counterparts would not have let them enter, but probably worked as itinerant bishops, based in nearby monasteries or even in Constantinople.

## The Beginnings of a New Church

With the consecration of this significant, albeit modest, number of bishops by Jacob, the foundation was laid for a new ecclesiastical structure. Still, in the mid-sixth century we are dealing not with the systematic construction of a new hierarchy, but only with an emergency measure, aimed at preventing the anti-Chalcedonian movement from dying out. With its headquarters in Constantinople and enjoying some sort of protection, if not of the emperor himself, then at least of the empress, this new organization did not place itself outside the Roman Empire. The anti-Chalcedonians still were very much part of the empire, in which they believed their orthodoxy one day would again prevail.

Jacob Baradaeus was instrumental in the creation of the new church structure both in Syria and in Egypt, but he never assumed a leadership role. When Theodosius was aging, Jacob took the initiative of consecrating a new patriarch of Antioch, around 558, twenty years after Severus's death. The candidate was Sergius, a Syrian priest who resided in Constantinople. Next to nothing is known about his activities as patriarch, which he probably carried out without leaving the capital, until his death in 560 or 561. Three years after Sergius's death, Theodosius proposed to Jacob Baradaeus to consecrate a new patriarch in the person of Paul, a native of Alexandria, who had lived for some time in Syria.[36] This Paul, in Syriac called *d-Bet Ukkâmê* and in Greek *Melanos* "the Black," had been Theodosius's assistant in Constantinople. His election and consecration, in 564, met with serious opposition among the clergy in Syria. Traveling back and forth between Alexandria, Constantinople, and Syria, he had a turbulent career as patriarch. He died in 578.

In 566, one year after Justinian, Theodosius died in Constantinople. No anti-Chalcedonian successor was elected as counterpart to the Chalcedonian patriarchs of Alexandria (Apollinarius, 551–570, and John, 570–580) for the next nine years. It was only in the middle of 575 that a certain Theodore, the Syrian abbot of a monastery in Egypt, was consecrated patriarch of Alexandria by three bishops, with the consent of Paul of Antioch. The Alexandrians, however, rejected him, and six weeks later another candidate, a certain Peter, was consecrated who, until his death in 578, served as patriarch. After his election, Peter declared Paul deposed and also attacked Jacob Baradaeus, who had consecrated Paul. When Jacob eventually accepted Paul's deposition and agreed to recognize Peter, a bitter struggle ensued in the course of which Paul's followers were called "Paulites," while Jacob's supporters started being called "Jacobites," a name that would stick forever with the Syrian anti-Chalcedonians. Relations between the two patriarchal sees became even more strained under Paul's and Peter's successors: Peter of Callinicum, patriarch of Antioch (581–591), and Damian, patriarch of Alexandria (578–606). The theological controversies between these two men led to mutual condemnations and to a schism between the two churches, healed only in 616.

## Divisions among the Anti-Chalcedonians: From Julianism to Tritheism and Beyond

We have been describing the steady growth of the anti-Chalcedonian, Miaphysite movement throughout the sixth century, carried on by a group of dedicated people who on the one hand were able to secure some sort of imperial approval and on the other hand did not lose touch with the common people in the monasteries, cities, and villages, both monks and laypeople. This picture needs some qualification.

Right from the early days of Severus's exile in Egypt, internal discussions and divisions plagued the anti-Chalcedonian community. Severus became involved in a devastating conflict with the exiled bishop Julian of Halicarnassus on the nature of Christ's human body. According to Severus, Christ's full participation in the human nature implied that his body, during his life on earth, was subject to corruption (*phthora*). Julian, on the contrary, argued that Christ's body transcended human corruptibility and was *aphthartos*, even though Christ of his free will – not out of necessity – submitted himself to corruption and suffering. This issue touched the heart of Miaphysite Christology.[37]

The Alexandrian patriarch Timothy IV (518–535) seems in his later years to have been inclined toward Julian's views,[38] and after Timothy's death the Julianist Gaianus was able to gain possession of the patriarchal throne. Three months later, however, he was deposed, at the emperor's instigation, and replaced with Theodosius. Theodosius was able to maintain his position only with the backing of the imperial army, while popular sentiment was in favor of Gaianus.[39] It is against this background that Justinian decided to remove Theodosius from power and to appoint a patriarch of his own choosing in the person of Paul of Tabennisi. As we have seen, in Constantinople Theodosius then became the leader of the (Severian) anti-Chalcedonians. For much of the remaining part of the sixth century, while Chalcedonians were sitting on the patriarchal throne in Alexandria, the Gaianites remained strong in Egypt and had their own hierarchy, at certain times including their own patriarch. It is only after the reign of Justinian that Severians or Theodosians regained power and were able to mark Coptic Orthodox tradition with their lasting imprint.

The aphthartodocetic controversy tore apart the monastic communities. In Syria, many monks sympathized with Julian's ideas, which seemed to echo some of the views expressed by Philoxenus of Mabbog, whose writings were copied and widely read in the sixth century.[40] The condemnation of the Julianists (called phantasiasts) by the abbot, priests, deacons, and brethren of an unnamed monastery in eastern Syria is recorded in a monumental Syriac inscription, probably of the sixth century.[41]

Material evidence of the split between Severian and Julianist monks may perhaps also be found in the Egyptian desert of Scetis (Wadi al-Natrun), where in the sixth century new residences were built at a short distance from existing monasteries. Basing himself on the Copto-Arabic *History of the Patriarchs of Alexandria* and related sources, Evelyn White argued that followers of Severus established these residences when the Julianists or Gaianites ousted them from their original monasteries.[42] Although no firm proof can be adduced, this theory linking the origin of the duplicate monasteries to the Gaianite schism has been generally accepted in recent literature.[43]

In Constantinople, Julian's ideas had a remarkable resurgence in the last writings of the emperor Justinian himself. His edict on the incorruptibility of Christ's body (564 or 565)[44] is difficult to understand. Even though the emperor's aphthartodocetic views most likely had a place within his Chalcedonian convictions,[45] they show once again how until his very last breath he attempted to describe the union of the natures in Christ in a language that would be acceptable to (a major segment of) the anti-Chalcedonians.

Meanwhile new discussions arose among the anti-Chalcedonians. They first had to do with the question whether the persons of the Trinity could be seen each as possessing his own individual substance (*ousia*) and nature (*physis*). Those who were willing to accept this idea were termed "tritheists" (believers in three Gods) by their opponents. Theodosius spoke out against this belief, but after his death the discussion was carried on. Adopted and further elaborated by the Alexandrian philosopher John Philoponus, the tritheist doctrine led to further divisions and constituted the background against which the conflict between Damian of Alexandria and Peter of Antioch originated, resulting in a schism between the two patriarchates. In spite of the vehemence with which the participants in these later theological discussions defended their position and reviled their opponents, the impact on popular belief seems to have been less strong and less enduring than in the case of the Julianist controversy. Tritheism and the discussions between Peter and Damian may have been felt as rather far removed from the core belief of Miaphysite Christianity.[46]

## ANTI-CHALCEDONIANISM AND THE FORMATION OF NEW IDENTITIES

The important question arises as to whether anti-Chalcedonian, Miaphysite Christianity, so firmly rooted in Egypt and Syria, also carried undertones of ethnic, cultural, and linguistic identity and even of political resistance.[47] If some of these elements were present, they seem to belong to the outcome of the process rather than to its beginnings. Theologically the anti-Chalcedonians had a strong case and could convincingly argue that their Christological interpretation was in agreement with the orthodox tradition of the imperial church, especially with the Alexandrian tradition that had triumphed at the Council of Ephesus. By officially distancing themselves from Eutychianism, they made it hard for their opponents to find fault with Miaphysite Christology. Powerful Chalcedonian refutations of Miaphysitism are lacking. In addition, the message of Miaphysitism was carried on by leaders and bishops who – in the tradition of Athanasius and Cyril – were able to rally the monks in support of what they saw as the orthodox faith. Monastic leaders joined with the bishops and several of them assumed episcopal authority themselves. The language of the resistance was Greek. There was very little regional or provincial about it.

Justin's return to the Chalcedonian interpretation of Christianity had its immediate effects on Syria and Asia Minor (whereas Egypt was spared), but anti-Chalcedonian sentiment by no means coincided with Syriac Christianity. Throughout the reigns of Justin and Justinian, the centers of the resistance were in Alexandria and Constantinople as much as, and even more than, they were in the Syrian countryside. The strong unity that was forged between the anti-Chalcedonian resistance in Syria and Egypt is a further indication of the transregional character of the movement. The ongoing contacts between the anti-Chalcedonian leaders and imperial circles in Constantinople again show that the anti-Chalcedonians up to the middle of the sixth century saw themselves as very much part of the empire. If there was antagonism, it was against the local Chalcedonian bishops or patriarchs, rather than to the empire as such. At the same time, there is reason to believe that within Justinian's vision of the empire there was room for some form of criticism of the Council of Chalcedon, not as an oddity of Syrian or Egyptian Christians, but as an authentic expression of orthodox belief.

It is in the interplay of these different factors, among which the imperial policy of alternately controlling, oppressing, and negotiating with anti-Chalcedonians – thereby reifying anti-Chalcedonian sentiment – was a very important one, that the anti-Chalcedonian movement gained full strength and gradually established itself as a structure of authority and power, ready to be transformed into a full-fledged church community once the Roman Empire had receded from the eastern lands after the rise of Islam.

The presence of the anti-Chalcedonians at the very center of the empire seems, therefore, to have been a decisive factor, granting the movement authority and legitimacy. On the other hand, however, one notices in the course of the sixth century deliberate attempts to implant anti-Chalcedonianism within Syriac and Egyptian tradition. Along with the first anti-Chalcedonian writings originally composed in Syriac by authors like Philoxenus of Mabbog (*fl.* ca. 480–524), a number of Greek anti-Chalcedonian writings began to be translated into Syriac, and to a lesser extent into Coptic. Some of these writings subsequently became classics in the literary tradition of the later Miaphysite churches.

The anti-Chalcedonian writings of Timothy, nicknamed Aelurus ("the cat"), patriarch of Alexandria between 457 and 477 (with interruptions), were translated into Syriac at an early date. Extracts from Timothy's writings fill the first half of ms. London, British Library, Add. 12,156, an impressive codex of anti-Chalcedonian testimonies in Syriac, written prior to the year 562.[48] Severus's writings, all originally composed in Greek, started being translated into Syriac during the author's lifetime. The homilies he pronounced as patriarch of Antioch, between 512 and 518, were collected, edited, and translated into Syriac in the next decades. Four incomplete manuscripts of the *Cathedral Homilies* from the sixth century are preserved, while portions exist of an early Coptic translation. Severus's writings against Julian are preserved in a Syriac translation which may go back to the year 528 and to the authorship of Paul of Callinicum. Along with the transmission of earlier Syriac compositions, notably of Ephrem the Syrian, and early sixth-century writings, such as the homilies of Jacob of Serug, the works of the Miaphysite leaders were incorporated into the literary tradition of the Syrian anti-Chalcedonians. There were theology, liturgy, biblical commentary, polemics, homilies, historiographical writings, and hagiography. These different genres all served as the literary expression of a communal identity. In spite of the increasing use of Syriac, the community in question was not primarily defined by linguistic boundaries, but rather by the orthodox Miaphysite faith.

In addition to the literary productivity, the sixth century also witnessed an outburst of Christian architecture in Syria. Several churches, mostly of the basilica type, either were built in the sixth century or underwent renovation and expansion in this period. In the hinterland of Antioch, between Antioch and Aleppo, and further south toward Apamea and Hama, dozens of churches can be found in what now is deserted land (Plate v).[49] Many of them are in ruins, with only their mosaics showing their original wealth,[50] while the architectural skeletons of others are almost intact, standing as silent witnesses to a period of intense religious and cultural life. Farther east, on the Euphrates River, German archaeologists recently excavated a monastery at Tall Biᶜa, near Raqqaᶜ, the ancient city of Callinicum (Fig. 6). The beautiful and well-preserved mosaics contain a few Greek inscriptions as well as two lengthy Syriac inscriptions, one dated to August 509 (mentioning bishop Paul of Callinicum, the later translator of Severus's works) and the other dated to April 595 (Plate vii). Since Callinicum was a center of the anti-Chalcedonians, we may be dealing with one of the important Miaphysite monasteries, perhaps with the monastery of Mar Zakkay (Zacchaeus), the monastery of John of Tella.[51]

To the cultural and artistic productivity of sixth-century Syria also belong a great number of Syriac manuscripts. Although we often cannot ascertain whether they originated in Chalcedonian or in non-Chalcedonian communities, a great number of sixth-century manuscripts were in Syrian Orthodox possession when they were transferred from Syria to the Syrian monastery in the Egyptian Wadi al-Natrun.[52] One sixth-century manuscript deserves to be singled out for its extraordinary illuminations: ms. Florence, Biblioteca Medicea Laurenziana, Plut. 1,56, known as the Rabbula Gospels,[53] dated to the year 586 (Plates viii and ix). It did not reach the West via Egypt but was transferred from the Syrian Orthodox monastery of Zagba, where it was produced (most likely near Apamea),[54] to Maronite monasteries in Lebanon, before being sent to Italy in the sixteenth century. The rich iconography and style of these illuminations seem to be a natural blend of late ancient Roman and Byzantine art on the one hand and local Syrian traditions on the other – a rare representative of what must have been a flourishing artistic tradition.

## Dyophysitism and Miaphysitism in Sasanian Persia

From the first decades following the Council of Chalcedon onward, opponents of the council spread their message beyond the borders of the Roman Empire. Philoxenus, one of the early Syrian spokesmen against the council, was of Persian origin. Although he operated within the Roman Empire, he maintained contacts with the Christians in Persia. In the same period, another Persian, Simeon of Bet Arsham, was active in the Sasanian Empire, preaching and writing in defense of the Miaphysite cause. In the writings of both men, the target of their polemics was first and foremost the dyophysite doctrine of the followers of Nestorius and Theodore of Mopsuestia, of which Chalcedonian dyophysitism – in their eyes – was a later offshoot.

In Justinian's day – one hundred years after Nestorius's condemnation at the Council of Ephesus – followers of Nestorius no longer constituted a threat within the Roman Empire. However, Nestorius still was very much alive in definitions of faith, as the heretic on whose condemnation there was virtual unanimity among Christians within the empire. Anti-Nestorian rhetoric (which in the sixth century included not only Nestorius himself, but also Diodore, Theodore, Ibas, and Theodoret), therefore, was frequently found among Chalcedonians. It allowed them not only to position themselves as clearly distinct from, and opposed to, Nestorianism, but also to give prominence to the common ground Chalcedonians and anti-Chalcedonians shared. It is this strategic use of Nestorianism that we find in several of Justinian's writings.

However, Nestorianism in the sixth century was more than a distant memory. At the end of the fifth century, Christians in the Sasanian Empire adopted a strict dyophysite Christology, which was largely defined as Nestorianism, even though it reflected Theodore of Mopsuestia's ideas rather than those of Nestorius.[55] The intellectual center of this nascent "Nestorian" church was the School of Nisibis, while the bishop of Seleucia-Ctesiphon (assuming the title of *catholicos*) was the head of the Christian community as it had been organized from the early fifth century. By adopting strictly dyophysite Christology, regarded as heretical in the imperial church, the Persian Christians placed themselves outside the ecclesiastical structures of the Roman Empire. They did not, however, sever their connections with Greek Christian tradition or with contemporary imperial Christianity. The sources of East Syriac Christian tradition are the writings of Greek Antiochene authors as well as a wide range of Greek patristic authors whose works continued to be translated and studied in the schools. Persian Christians also studied the Greek Aristotelian tradition and introduced Aristotle's works to the Sasanian (Zoroastrian) cultural elite – a prelude to the East Syrian Christians' role in the translation movement under the early Abbasids.

Several students of the School of Nisibis rose to important positions in the Persian Church. Mar Aba, who at a young age converted from Zoroastrianism, used his study period at Nisibis as a stepping-stone toward further explorations in the Greek Christian world. Between 525 and 533 he traveled extensively in the Roman Empire, to Edessa, Palestine, Egypt, Athens, and Constantinople. Called to the highest office of *catholicos*, which he held from 540 to 551, he worked on behalf of the Christian minority that was in the throes of division and instability. In a period of increased tension between the Sasanian and the Roman empires, he spent several years in exile and in prison.

Among Mar Aba's disciples, some made their name as teachers in Nisibis, interpreting and further developing the basic tenets of Antiochene theology. A preserved series of lectures delivered at the school in the mid-sixth century are attributed to Thomas and Cyrus, two men from Edessa.[56] Another disciple, Paul, from the region near the Persian Gulf, was consecrated, around 544, as bishop of the important city of Nisibis. In this capacity the Persian king sent him, shortly after 561, to Constantinople, where along with other East Syrian theologians he met with Justinian. A short extract of Paul's Syriac report of this meeting has been preserved.[57] One wonders whether in spite of Justinian's anti-Nestorian rhetoric Persian Christians still had a place in his view of the universal church.

There is another Paul, "the Persian," almost certainly to be distinguished from the bishop of Nisibis, who in 527 was in Constantinople and held a philosophical dispute with a Manichaean.[58] This Paul may perhaps be the "Paul, a Persian by name, who was educated at the Syrian School in the city of Nisibis" whom Junillus Africanus mentioned as his source of inspiration in the preface to his *Instituta regularia divinae legis*.[59]

The organization of the Persian church along with its distinct dyophysite theological orientation shaped the identity of Persian Christianity in the course of the fifth and sixth centuries, roughly contemporaneous to the creation of the non-Chalcedonian communal identity within the Roman Empire. One other element, which proved to be of decisive importance for the survival of the non-Chalcedonians within the Roman Empire, was less prominent in the early period in Persia. Asceticism may have been an important undercurrent in Persian Christianity, but its role in society seems to have been limited, perhaps due to the antiascetical attitude of Zoroastrian society. Around the middle of the sixth century, however, Abraham of Kashkar, a former student of the School of Nisibis, traveled to the desert of Scetis and to the Sinai, and upon his return introduced Egyptian monasticism on Mount Izla, north of Nisibis. The monastery founded by him became the center of a powerful monastic movement spreading all over Mesopotamia. "Just as in former days everyone who wanted to study and master pagan Greek philosophy would go to Athens, the famous city of the philosophers, (now) everyone desirous of being initiated into spiritual philosophy would go to the holy monastery of Mar Abraham and sign up for his sonship," according to one ninth-century author.[60] In the following decades the monastic movement gradually took over and incorporated the educational role of the schools.

Since the end of the fifth century Persian Christianity had been predominantly dyophysite, and the East Syrian Church enjoyed a special relationship with the Persian king. However, as briefly pointed out above, anti-Chalcedonians gradually established themselves in the country and started setting up their own communities, connected to the network of the anti-Chalcedonians within the Roman Empire. Around 530, John of Tella and Thomas of Dara were asked by "some believers" in Persia to send bishops who would be able "to fight valiantly for the orthodox faith which already had become extinct there due to the error of the miserable Nestorius, the worshipper of the man."[61] Around 540, there was a Miaphysite bishop in Persia, Ahudemmeh, whose consecration in some sources is attributed to the Armenian *catholicos* Christophorus (538 or 539–545), while other sources attribute his (second?) consecration as "metropolitan of the East" to Jacob Baradaeus (in 559).[62] However, it was only in the early seventh century, on the eve of the Muslim invasion, that a separate Miaphysite hierarchy started being built up in Persian territory. It had the city of Takrit as its center.

## Part of the Roman and Part of the Persian Empire: Armenian Christianity

Armenian Christianity, like Syrian Christianity, was divided between the Roman and the Persian empires. In the case of the Armenians, however, this did not lead to two doctrinally divergent communities, due perhaps to a strong sense of ethnic and cultural identity. After having been exposed to Antiochene dyophysite Christology in the first decades of the fifth century, the doctrinal orientation of the Armenian church shifted toward Constantinople in the years following the Council of Ephesus (431). Involved in their struggle for independence in 451, the Armenians were not present at the Council of Chalcedon. In later councils, they clearly and repeatedly rejected dyophysitism, associated with Nestorius as well as with the East Syrian church in Persia, situated at their southern borders. Official rejections of dyophysitism were on the agenda of the councils held at Dvin, in Persarmenia, in 505/06 and in 555. By the latter date, the Armenians were thoroughly familiar with the Miaphysite doctrine, which had spread in their country and was well received. However, a straightforward rejection of the Council of Chalcedon was not pronounced until the Council of 607. The various phases of the process leading to the creation of a decidedly Miaphysite

Armenian church remain enshrouded in darkness. According to some scholars, major anti-Chalcedonian writings, such as Timothy Aelurus's *Refutation of the Council of Chalcedon*, had been translated into Armenian in the late fifth century, thus setting the tone for an early rejection of the council.[63] The present-day consensus, however, seems to be that this work, a product of the so-called Hellenizing school of translation, appeared in Armenian only around the middle of the sixth century.[64]

Another difficult problem concerns the Julianist leanings of Armenian Christology, which have long been recognized by scholars. While Severus is occasionally condemned in sixth-century Armenian documents, the name of Julian, his opponent, is remarkably absent from contemporary texts, and nothing of his works is preserved in Armenian. This seems to indicate that the Armenian church did not officially endorse Julian's teachings. It has been suggested that the aphthartodocetic views of Armenian Christology did not stem from Julian but may have been shaped by the writings of Philoxenus of Mabbog, some of which were translated from Syriac into Armenian and circulated in Armenia around the middle of the sixth century.[65] It will be clear, therefore, that the Armenian Church, before joining the Miaphysite fold, had its own specific history, in which influences from various Christian communities in Syria as well as from Constantinople and the Greek world competed with each other. In this process, the Church of Georgia parted ways with the Armenian church, by formally adopting Chalcedonianism around 600.

## Anti-Chalcedonians and the Empire

Toward the end of the sixth century the anti-Chalcedonian movement had its centers of power within the empire in Constantinople, in the Syrian hinterland, and in the Egyptian monasteries. Equally important was the vitality of the communities outside the empire, which had developed and expanded throughout the sixth century, largely during the reign of Justinian. In the Persian Empire, Syrian and Armenian Miaphysites had been able gradually to strengthen their positions. Among the Arab *foederati*, the Ghassanid phylarchs on several occasions presented themselves as staunch protectors of the Miaphysite cause. Miaphysitism became the dominant confession among the Nubians, and Ethiopian Christianity assumed its Miaphysite identity. While Miaphysitism clearly became part of the national identity for those entities outside the empire (and still is today, in the case of Armenia and Ethiopia), there is little evidence that Miaphysites within the empire envisioned any sort of political or national separation.[66] The resistance to the Council of Chalcedon and the transformation of the purely theological issue into an anti-Chalcedonian worldview developed and reached full maturity within the empire, as expressed in the language of the empire. Even when using their distinct languages, the anti-Chalcedonian communities still were fully imbued with imperial concepts and ideologies. It would require different processes to produce, after Justinian, alienation and estrangement, and eventually a final separation, between the anti-Chalcedonian communities and the Roman Empire.

Up to the present day, Chalcedonianism and anti-Chalcedonian Miaphysitism exist alongside each other in the Christian communities of the Middle East. Miaphysitism is largely dominant among the Christians in Egypt, while the historical lands of Syria (including Syria, Lebanon, part of Turkey, and Israel/Palestine) are divided – just as they were in Justinian's day! – between Chalcedonians and anti-Chalcedonians. Both traditions foster the legacy of the Roman and early Byzantine world and both traditions have their own memories of the enigmatic imperial couple, Justinian and Theodora.[67]

## Notes

1 For the theological issues involved, see Patrick T. R. Gray, "The Legacy of Chalcedon: Christological Problems and Their Significance," in this volume. The technical terms defining the two positions are "Dyophysite" (two-nature) and "Miaphysite" (one-nature). Other names used for the anti-Chalcedonians include "Monophysite" and "Jacobite." These will be avoided in this essay, as the present-day non-Chalcedonian communities see them as inadequate descriptions of the traditions that they represent.

2 For this term, see Dimitri Obolensky, *The Byzantine Commonwealth: Eastern Europe, 500–1453* (New York, 1971), followed by Garth Fowden (who applied it to the sixth-century Middle East and North Africa), *Empire to Commonwealth: Consequences of Monotheism in Late Antiquity* (Princeton, N.J., 1993), esp. 100–137.

3 Most recently: Alois Grillmeier and Theresia Hainthaler, *Christ in Christian Tradition*, 2/2, *The Church of Constantinople in the Sixth Century*, trans. John Cawte and Pauline Allen (Louisville, Ky., 1995); 2/4, *The Church of Alexandria with Nubia and Ethiopia after 451*, trans. O. C. Dean Jr. (Louisville, Ky., 1996); Karl-Heinz Uthemann, "Kaiser Justinian als Kirchenpolitiker und Theologe," *Augustinianum* 39 (1999): 5–83; several articles in *Late Antiquity: Empire and Successors, A.D. 425–600*, ed. Averil Cameron, Bryan Ward-Perkins, and Michael Whitby, *CAH* 14 (Cambridge, 2000).

4 See A. A. Vasiliev, *Justin the First: An Introduction to the Epoch of Justinian the Great* (Cambridge, Mass., 1950).

5 See Ernest Honigmann, *Évêques et évêchés monophysites d'Asie antérieure au VIe siècle*, CSCO 127/Subs. 2 (Louvain, 1951); Albert Van Roey, "Les débuts de l'Église jacobite," in *Das Konzil von Chalkedon: Geschichte und Gegenwart* II, ed. A. Grillmeier and H. Bacht, 339–360 (Würzburg, 1953); T. Jansma, "Encore le Credo de Jacques de Saroug. Nouvelles recherches sur l'argument historique concernant son orthodoxie," *L'Orient Syrien* 10 (1965): 75–88, 193–236, 331–370, 475–510; W. H. C. Frend, *The Rise of the Monophysite Movement: Chapters in the History of the Church in the Fifth and Sixth Centuries* (Cambridge, 1972; reprinted with corrections, 1979). Two works by John of Ephesus, the *Lives of the Eastern Saints* and the *Ecclesiastical History*, are among our main sources for this period. It should be noted, however, that John wrote in the second half of the sixth century. Some of his views and interpretations may therefore have been retrojected to the earlier period. On John, see Susan Ashbrook Harvey, *Asceticism and Society in Crisis: John of Ephesus and the Lives of the Eastern Saints* (Berkeley, Calif., 1990).

6 André de Halleux, *Philoxène de Mabbog. Sa vie, ses écrits, sa théologie* (Louvain, 1963), 99; Patrick T. R. Gray, *The Defense of Chalcedon in the East (451–553)*, (Leiden, 1979), 48–50.

7 Severus, *Select Letters*, V,8, V,9, and V,12, ed. E. W. Brooks, *The Sixth Book of the Select Letters of Severus Patriarch of Antioch in the Syriac Version of Athanasius of Nisibis* 1:2 (Syriac text, London, 1904), 361–366 and 380–385; 2:2 (translation), 319–324 and 337–342; for Philoxenus, see De Halleux, *Philoxène*, 100 and 220–222.

8 See Jansma, "Encore le Credo," 193–236.

9 *Chronicle of Edessa*, ed. I. Guidi, *Chronica Minora* I. CSCO 1/Syr. 1 (1903; reprint, Louvain, 1955), 10, 14–15.

10 Vasiliev, *Justin the First*, 232 and 240; Gray, *The Defense*, 47–48.

11 Syriac text with Latin translation: E. W. Brooks, *Vitae virorum apud Monophysitas celeberrimorum*. CSCO 7–8/Syr. 7–8 (1907; reprint, Louvain, 1955), 29–95 (Syriac text) and 21–60 (translation).

12 Irfan Shahîd, *The Martyrs of Najrân: New Documents*, Subsidia Hagiographica 49 (Brussels, 1971), esp. 159–179; Nina Garsoïan, *L'Église arménienne et le grand schisme d'Orient*. CSCO 574/Subs. 100 (Louvain, 1999), 441–446.

13 Irfan Shahîd, *Byzantium and the Arabs in the Sixth Century*, vol. 2 (Washington, D.C., 1995), 693–715.

14 Shahîd, *The Martyrs of Najrân;* Grillmeier and Hainthaler, *Christ in Christian Tradition*, vol. 2/4, 305–323; Shahîd, *Byzantium and the Arabs in the Sixth Century* (Washington, D.C., 1995–2002), 2:29–733.

15 Vasiliev, *Justin the First*, 223, 225, and 241–250; Gray, *The Defense of Chalcedon*, 52–53.

16 Severus, *Select Letters*, 1:55, ed. Brooks, *The Sixth Book of the Select Letters of Severus*, 1:1 (Syriac text), 182–183; 2:1 (translation), 165.

17 See E. W. Brooks, ed., *John of Ephesus: Lives of the Eastern Saints*, vol. 2. PO 18. 4 (1924; reprint, Turnhout, 1974), 516–517 [314–315].

18 Elias, *Life of John of Tella*, in Brooks, *Vitae virorum*, 58–59 (Syriac text).

19 Sebastian Brock, "The Conversations with the Syrian Orthodox under Justinian (532)," *OCP* 47 (1981): 87–121 (with further references); Uthemann, "Kaiser Justinian," 27–34.

20 The Syriac account reports the following statement addressed by the emperor to the anti-Chalcedonian bishops: "I am not of the opinion, either, that you do

not think in an orthodox fashion, but you do not want to communicate out of excessive (scruples over) detail, and because of (certain) names which have been put on the diptychs." See Brock, "The Conversations," 108, par. 36.

21 Brock, "The Conversations," esp. 116–117.

22 Uthemann, "Kaiser Justinian," 34–37.

23 Harald Suermann, *Die Gründungsgeschichte der Maronitischen Kirche*, Orientalia Biblica et Christiana 10 (Wiesbaden, 1998), 101–113.

24 K. H. Kuhn, *A Panegyric on Apollo Archimandrite of the Monastery of Isaac by Stephen Bishop of Heracleopolis Magna*. CSCO 394–395/Copt. 39–40 (Louvain, 1978), 14 and 16–17 (Coptic text); 10–13 (translation). See Edward R. Hardy, "The Egyptian Policy of Justinian," *DOP* 22 (1968), 32–34; Leslie S. B. MacCoull, "'When Justinian Was Upsetting the World': A Note on Soldiers and Religious Coercion in Sixth-Century Egypt," in *Peace and War in Byzantium, Essays in Honor of George T. Dennis*, ed. Timothy S. Miller and John Nesbitt, 106–113 (Washington, D.C., 1995); David W. Johnson, "Anti-Chalcedonian Polemics in Coptic Texts, 451–641," in *The Roots of Egyptian Christianity*, ed. Birger A. Pearson and James E. Goehring (Philadelphia, 1986), 216–234.

25 See Anna Maria Demicheli, "La politica religiosa di Giustiniano in Egitto. Riflessi sulla chiesa egiziana della legislazione ecclesiastica giustinianea," *Aegyptus. Rivista italiana di egittologia e papirologia* 58 (1983): 236–238 and 247–257.

26 Demicheli, "La politica religiosa," 239; Grillmeier and Hainthaler, *Christ in Christian Tradition*, vol. 2/4, 60–65; Uwe Michael Lang, *John Philoponus and the Controversies over Chalcedon in the Sixth Century: A Study and Translation of the* Arbiter, Spicilegium Sacrum Lovaniense 47 (Louvain, 2001), 25.

27 See James E. Goehring, "Chalcedonian Power Politics and the Demise of Pachomian Monasticism," in Goehring, *Ascetics, Society, and the Desert: Studies in Egyptian Monasticism* (Harrisburg, Pa., 1999), 241–261.

28 For Philoponus's reaction to the council, see Lang, *John Philoponus*, 28–40.

29 See Hardy, "The Egyptian Policy of Justinian," 31–32; Gray, *The Defense*, 55–56.

30 See Shahîd, *Byzantium and the Arabs*, vol. 1, part 2, 850–860.

31 See Hendrik Gerrit Kleyn, *Jacobus Baradaeüs. De Stichter der Syrische Monophysietische Kerk* (Leiden, 1882); David D. Bundy, "Jacob Baradaeus. The state of research, a review of sources, and a new approach," *Le Muséon* 91 (1978): 45–86.

32 See Frend, *The Rise of the Monophysite Movement*, 297–301. On the Isis temple at Philae, see David Frankfurter, *Religion in Roman Egypt: Assimilation and Resistance* (Princeton, N.J., 1998), 105–106.

33 "Miaphysitism" is another term for anti-Chalcedonianism, indicating one nature of Christ but avoiding the negative connotations of Monophysitism. See note 1.

34 Grillmeier and Hainthaler, *Christ in Christian Tradition*, vol. 2/4, 263–276; Fowden, *Empire*, 116–119.

35 Honigmann, *Évêques et évêchés*, 172–173.

36 Ernest W. Brooks, "The Patriarch Paul of Antioch and the Alexandrine Schism of 575," *BZ* 30 (1929–1930): 468–476.

37 See Grillmeier and Hainthaler, *Christ in Christian Tradition*, vol. 2/2, 79–111.

38 Brock, "The Conversations," 90.

39 Hardy, "The Egyptian Policy of Justinian," 30; Demicheli, "La politica religiosa," 232–233; Grillmeier and Hainthaler, *Christ in Christian Tradition*, vol. 2/4, 46–47.

40 De Halleux, *Philoxène de Mabbog*, 459–460, with n. 2, and 503–505.

41 Sebastian P. Brock and David G. K. Taylor, *The Hidden Pearl: The Syrian Orthodox Church and Its Ancient Aramaic Heritage*, vol. 2 (Rome, 2001), 33 and 24 (photograph).

42 Hugh G. Evelyn White, *The Monasteries of the Wadi 'n Natrun*, vol. 2, *The History of the Monasteries of Nitria and Scetis* (New York, 1932), 232–235.

43 Aelred Cody, "Dayr al-Baramūs," *Coptic Encyclopedia* 3:789–791; Cody, "Dayr al-Suryān," *Coptic Encyclopedia*, 3:876–879; Otto F. A. Meinardus, *Two Thousand Years of Coptic Christianity* (Cairo, 1999), 166–167; Karel C. Innemée, "Deir al-Baramus: Excavations at the So-Called Site of Moses the Black, 1994–1999," *Bulletin de la Société d'archéologie copte* 39 (2000): 123–135.

44 Uthemann, "Kaiser Justinian," 79–83.

45 Michel van Esbroeck, "The Aphthartodocetic Edict of Justinian and Its Armenian Background," *Studia Patristica* 33 (1997): 578–585; Lang, *John Philoponus*, 26.

46 See Lang, *John Philoponus*, 11.

47 For some general observations, see Fergus Millar, "Ethnic Identity in the Roman Near East, 325–450: Language, Religion, and Culture," *Mediterranean Archaeology* 11 (1998): 159–176.

48 William Wright, *Catalogue of Syriac Manuscripts in the British Museum Acquired since the Year 1838 II* (London, 1871): 639–648.

49 See Georges Tchalenko, *Villages antiques de la Syrie du Nord. Le Massif du Bélus à l'époque romaine*, 3 vols. (Paris, 1953–1958).

50 See Pauline Donceel-Voûte, *Les pavements des églises byzantines de Syrie et du Liban. Décor, archéologie et liturgie*, vols. 1–2, Publications d'histoire de l'art et d'archéologie de l'Université catholique de Louvain 69 (Louvain-la-Neuve, 1988).

51 Manfred Krebernik, "Schriftfunde aus Tall Bi[c]a 1990, I. Funde aus dem byzantinischen Kloster," *Mitteilungen der Deutschen Orient-Gesellschaft zu Berlin* 123 (1991): 41–57; Gábor Kalla, "Christentum am oberen Euphrat. Das byzantinische Kloster von Tall Bi[c]a," *Antike Welt* 30 (1999): 131–142.

52 See Karel Innemée and Lucas Van Rompay, "La présence des Syriens dans le Wadi al-Natrun (Égypte). À propos des découvertes récentes de peintures et de textes muraux dans l'Église de la Vierge du Couvent des Syriens," *Parole de l'Orient* 23 (1998): 167–202. Around forty-two Syriac manuscripts (most of them coming from Egypt) are explicitly dated to the sixth century. See Brock and Taylor, *The Hidden Pearl*, 2:245. Many more are attributable to that period.

53 Carlo Ceccheli, Giuseppe Furlani, and Mario Salmi, *The Rabbula Gospels: Facsimile Edition of the Miniatures of the Syriac Manuscript Plut. I, 56 in the Medicaean-Laurentian Library* (Olten, 1959).

54 Marlia Mundell Mango, "Where Was Beth Zagba?" *Harvard Ukrainian Studies* 7 (1983): 405–430.

55 See Wilhelm Baum and Dietmar W. Winkler, *The Church of the East: A Concise History* (London, 2003), esp. 21–37.

56 William F. Macomber, *Six Explanations of the Liturgical Feasts by Cyrus of Edessa, an East Syrian Theologian of the Mid Sixth Century*, CSCO 355–356/Syr. 155–156 (Louvain, 1974).

57 Antoine Guillaumont, "Justinien et l'Église de Perse," *DOP* 23–24 (1969–1970): 39–66; Guillaumont, "Un colloque entre orthodoxes et théologiens nestoriens de Perse sous Justinien," *Académie des Inscriptions et Belles Lettres. Comptes rendus 1970* (Paris, 1970), 201–207.

58 Uthemann, "Kaiser Justinian," 25–27.

59 Michael Maas, *Exegesis and Empire in the Early Byzantine Mediterranean: Junillus Africanus and the* Instituta regularia divinae legis. Studien und Texte zu Antike und Christentum 17 (Tübingen, 2003), 17–18.

60 Thomas of Marga, *The Book of Governors: The Historia Monastica of Thomas Bishop of Marga, A.D. 840*, ed. E. A. Wallis Budge, vol. 1 (London, 1893; reprint, Piscataway, Md., 2003), 23.20–24.2.

61 Elias, *Life of John of Tella*, ed. Brooks, *Vitae virorum*, 60.22–61.2 (Syriac text).

62 Jean Maurice Fiey, *Jalons pour une histoire de l'Église en Iraq*, CSCO 310/Subs. 36 (Louvain, 1970), 128–131; Garsoïan, *L'Église arménienne*, 202 and 375.

63 Karekin Sarkissian, *The Council of Chalcedon and the Armenian Church* (London, 1965), 165–170.

64 Andrea B. Schmidt, "Die *Refutatio* des Timotheus Aelurus gegen das Konzil von Chalcedon. Ihre Bedeutung für die Bekenntnisentwicklung der armenischen Kirche Persiens im 6. Jh.," *Oriens Christianus* 73 (1989): 149–165; Garsoïan, *L'Église arménienne*, 238.

65 S. Peter Cowe, "Philoxenus of Mabbug and the Synod of Manazkert," *Aram* 5 (1993): 15–29.

66 Fowden, *Empire*, 133.

67 Susan A. Harvey, "Theodora the 'Believing Queen': A Study in Syriac Historiographical Tradition," *Hugoye: Journal of Syriac Studies* 4.2 (2001).

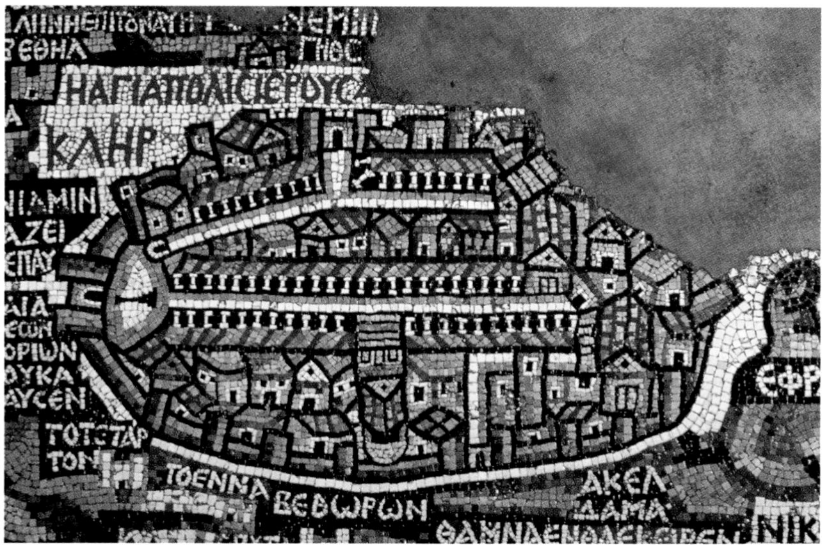


PLATE I. Jerusalem in the sixth century. Mosaic map from Madaba, Jordan, detail. Photo: Studium Biblicum Fransciscanum

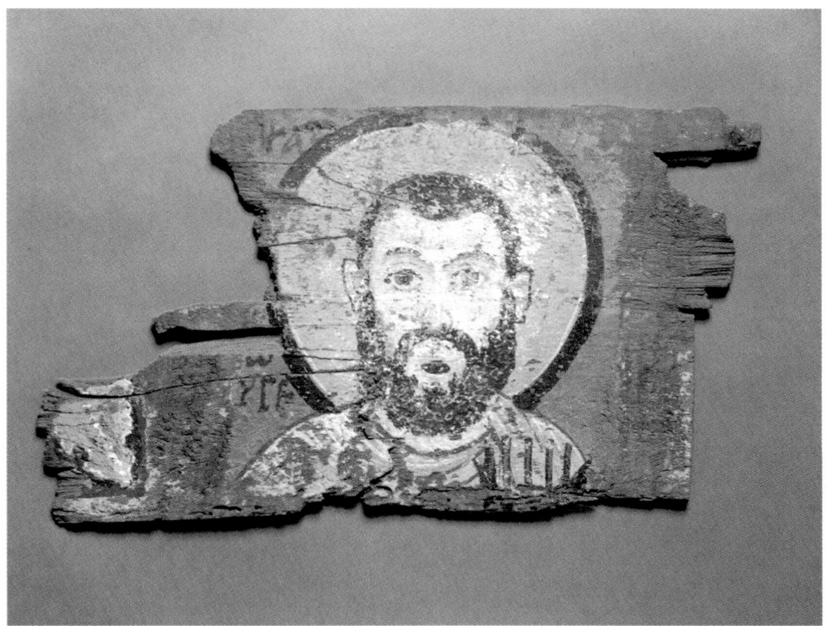

PLATE II. "Brother George the Scribe," monk's portrait and Coptic inscription on wood. From Bawit (sixth or early seventh century). Courtesy Newark Museum

PLATE III. Procession of Theodora and attendants, 547, mosaic panel, San Vitale, Ravenna. Photo: Scala/Art Resource, N.Y.

PLATE IV. Procession of Justinian, Archbishop Maximian, and attendants, 547, mosaic panel, San Vitale, Ravenna. Photo: Scala/Art Resource, N.Y.

PLATE V. Detail of reliquary box from the Holy Land now in the Vatican Museum, painted around 600 depicting five scenes from the life of Christ. From the lower left to the upper right: the Nativity, Baptism, and Crucifixion, the empty tomb, and the Ascension (see plate xiii). Palestine, c. 600. 23.7 × 18.0 cm. Photo: Museo Sacro, Vatican

PLATE VI. Blessing Christ, Monastery of St. Catherine, Mt. Sinai, sixth century. Photo: Studio Kontos/Photostock, Athens

PLATE VII. Transfiguration, Monastery of St. Catherine, Mt. Sinai, apse mosaic, c. 550
Photo: Studio Kontos/Photostock, Athens

PLATE VIII. Monastery of St. Catherine, Mt. Sinai, general view of monastery enclosure, c. 550. Photo: Joseph D. Alchermes

PLATE IX. Hagia Sophia, Istanbul, view looking east, 532–537. Photo: Werner Forman/Art Resource, N.Y.

PLATE X. Synagogue mosaic from Beth Alpha, Israel, showing the zodiac, with sun chariot in the center and the four seasons in the corners, c. 517–518. Photo: Collection N. de Lange

# 11: Emperors and Popes in the Sixth Century

## The Western View

*Claire Sotinel*

From a western Mediterranean point of view, the reign of Justinian may seem a brief parenthesis in the history of Europe, a failed attempt to resurrect an empire already dead. Justinian's reconquest of Italy was brought to nothing by the Lombard invasion of 568, and North Africa fell to Muslim armies within a century. From a Roman ecclesiastical perspective the balance sheet is even more negative. The sad story of the Three Chapters Controversy and the souring of relations between Constantinople and Rome contributed greatly to Justinian's reputation for divisive autocracy in ecclesiastical affairs.[1] This chapter does not seek either to defend the western attitude toward Justinian's religious politics or to clear his name. Instead it explores the "parting of the ways" between West and East signaled by these differing ecclesiastical perspectives.[2] In Justinian's day there was still no consensus about the emperor's place in Christian society, and the question of the relations between church authority and political power played a major role in the parting of East and West, especially in the West, where imperial power was weak. The eclipse of imperial authority in the West during the fifth century created new conditions for its churches and demanded new definitions of their relation to the emperor. Even in times of tension, Rome and Constantinople desired the unity of church and empire and the defense of Christianity, but the assumptions underlying these diverged significantly. The reunion of the western provinces with Constantinople during Justinian's reign highlighted and even reinforced these differences. Seeing the Age of Justinian as a major phase in this process of separation gives new insights on the Roman church and the complex history of its relations with Constantinople.

TABLE 11.1 *Sixth century popes*

| Name | Date of consecration | Date of burial |
|---|---|---|
| Symmachus | Nov. 22, 496 | July 19, 514 |
| (Lawrence 498–506) | | |
| Hormisdas | July 20, 514 | Aug. 6, 523 |
| John I | Aug. 13, 523 | May 18, 526 |
| Felix IV (III) | July 12, 526 | Sept. 530 |
| (Dioscorus Sept. 22, 530–Oct. 14, 530) | | |
| Boniface II | Sept. 22, 530 | Oct. 532 |
| John II | Jan. 2, 533 | May 8, 535 |
| Agapetus I | May 13, 535 | April 27, 536 |
| Silverius | June 536 | Dec. 2, 537 |
| Vigilius | Mar. 29, 537 | June 7, 555 |
| Pelagius I | April 16, 556 | Mar. 3/4, 561 |
| John III | July 17, 561 | July 13, 574 |
| Benedict I | June 2, 575 | July 30, 579 |
| Pelagius II | Nov. 26, 579 | Feb. 7, 590 |
| Gregory I | Sept. 3, 590 | Mar. 12, 606 |

## The Roman Church outside the Empire: Political Autonomy and Ecclesiastical Schism

From at least 476, when Odoacer seized the throne in Italy, the Italian churches stood beyond imperial control. Odoacer and his successor Theoderic the Ostrogoth officially ruled under the sovereignty of the emperor in Constantinople but in fact were the true political authorities with whom Italian Christian leaders had to deal.[3] The bishop of Rome essentially monopolized relations with Constantinople, but for everyday business, bishops had to deal with the local kings. The Italian bishops began to adopt a more active civic role. For the first time in their history some of them defended their cities during wars and negotiated with the king to obtain pardon for Romans who had fought on the wrong side. They went as ambassadors to redeem prisoners of war and discussed political matters with the emperor. Some bishops acted occasionally as agents of the king, controlling the distribution of money or food in times of crisis. For their part, until 526, Gothic kings seldom interfered in religious matters.[4] As a result, Italian bishops enjoyed more freedom and independence than they had since the conversion of Constantine.

Independence from Constantinople had two major consequences for the Roman church. First, a new balance of power developed between the clergy and the senatorial aristocracy, partly because of disagreements about how to deal with the emperor. New polarizations among the Roman elites, both clerical and lay, explain why papal elections were more fiercely disputed than ever.

The second consequence of having a distant emperor was that the Roman church assumed autonomy regarding doctrinal matters. The Acacian schism demonstrates this independent stance. The Roman church resented the publication of the *Henoticon* by Emperor Zeno (482) as an implicit condemnation of Chalcedon and of Pope Leo's *Tome*. In July 484, Pope Felix convoked an Italian council, which excommunicated Acacius, patriarch of Constantinople, in the name of the apostolic authority of Rome, a condemnation almost immediately reciprocated. The schism, which divided western and eastern churches until 518, caused a breakdown in papal relations with Constantinople. As there was no Roman *apocrisiarius* (permanent legate to the emperor) at the time, the main manifestation of failed communication between the Roman and Constantinopolitan churches is seen in the matter of the diptychs. These were lists of names of living and dead persons (patriarchs, bishops of provinces, presiding celebrants, emperors, and their families) who were to be proclaimed and commemorated by the deacon during the celebration of the mass.[5] In 484, Pope Felix struck the name of Acacius from the Roman diptychs and asked the Constantinopolitan church to do the same after Acacius's death (489). Though Acacius's successors proposed to make some concessions, Rome did not accept the *Henoticon*, nor did Constantinople remove Acacius's name from the diptychs.

The Acacian crisis marked a turning point in the relations between Rome and Constantinople because Pope Felix and his successors Gelasius, Symmachus, and Hormisdas had to find new ways to legitimate their disagreement with the religious policy of the East and to uphold the authority of the Roman see. They never discussed religious matters with the emperor, but they never broke communion, either.[6] More important, the popes defined their view of the relations between ecclesiastical and secular power. While Acacius justified his conciliatory attitude toward anti-Chalcedonian bishops[7] by the necessity of close cooperation with imperial policy, Gelasius contested this claim, asserting a prophetic model of ecclesiastical authority. What in the Middle Ages came to be known as the "theory of the two swords" was expressed by Pope Gelasius in a famous letter sent to Anastasius, probably written in 493, defining "the two principles which govern this world: the sacred authority of the bishops and the power of the kings."[8] Gelasius stressed the tensions between religious and secular orders, changing the emphasis of a tradition that had tended to stress harmony, or consensus, or sometimes confusion between them.[9] It may be that this attempt to define a hierarchy between the different kinds of power had been inspired by the necessity of adapting the model inherited from the Roman Empire to the new political order. On the whole, the ideas expressed by Gelasius were not new, not even specifically Christian, but his position was to become a guideline to most of his successors, not only in relation to a hostile emperor like Anastasius, but even to a benevolent one, like Justin or Justinian.[10]

In Italy, the question of the attitude toward the eastern churches was only one of the many issues that divided the elites. Most of the senators, together with part of the clergy, were in favor of a policy of union with the East, but eventually, the Gelasian attitude prevailed for the most part until the Three Chapters Controversy.

In Constantinople, the emperor Anastasius did not understand the Roman position. The failed attempts to settle the dispute in 515–517 only confirmed the depth of the disagreement. Attempts at reconciliation on both sides failed. The last letter addressed by Anastasius to Pope Hormisdas in 517 ended with the words, "We can tolerate being insulted and being made insignificant, but we cannot tolerate being ordered about."[11] This gives the measure of the crisis between Rome and Constantinople.

## *The Reconciliation between Rome and Constantinople: Toward a New Crisis?*

The situation changed dramatically when Justin became emperor in July 518 and adopted a conciliary attitude toward Rome. The very day of his proclamation, the names of Pope Leo and of bishops Euphemius and Macedonius, Chalcedonian patriarchs deposed by Anastasius, were restored to the diptychs. The first proposals of union made in the summer of 518 were no different from the policy followed by Anastasius, however, and the first letter sent by Justinian to "invite" the pope to Constantinople was written in polite but authoritarian style.[12] When Hormisdas answered, in January 519, without obeying the imperial summons and without yielding any point of the Roman demands, the emperor greeted the Roman legates led by the deacon Dioscorus with respect and put pressure on the patriarch of Constantinople, John, to make him accept a Roman document, usually called *libellus*, as a condition of reconciliation.[13] The union was made according to Rome's agenda: not only Acacius's name, but the names of all Constantinopolitan bishops after him, as well as the names of emperors Zeno and Anastasius, were to be erased from the diptychs. The emperor sent off letters to all the eastern churches inviting them to follow Constantinople.[14]

Whatever the reasons for such an about-face in imperial policy, the West celebrated the union of May 519 as the victory of Roman steadfastness as well as the triumph of Chalcedon. Indeed, for a moment at least, all the Roman requirements were met, and the *libellus* asserted that the apostolic see was the one "in which persists the total and true strength of the Christian religion."[15] Yet from the beginning, the union was celebrated in different ways in East and West. Both Rome and Constantinople desired the unity of the churches and the unity of the empire. But in the East, where the hope was for religious unity among all the churches, the union meant that the Roman church was reintegrated into the imperial system, in which the secular and the sacred spheres coincided. For the pope, however, the union meant that the new emperor fully accepted Roman authority in all ecclesiastical matters, disciplinary as well as doctrinal, and that religious matters were supposed to remain under ecclesiastical control. Thus the union of 518 was based on a misunderstanding that became very clear within a few years.

The influence of Rome on imperial religious policy regarding church discipline faded quickly. Although the Roman legates remained a few months in Constantinople, Justin ignored their suggestions.[16] In June 520, the Roman request to restore three eastern bishops who had been deposed in 512 for their Chalcedonian opinions was politely dismissed by the emperor.[17]

Nor did perfect harmony last concerning the unity of the church. The first flaws in the freshly restored union appeared in 520. In January, the emperor refused to send bishop Dorotheus of Thessalonica to Rome to be judged by the pope for refusing to sign the *libellus*. At the same time, Justin, together with Justinian and the patriarch John, raised the question of churches reluctant to remove from the diptychs the names of well-known Chalcedonian bishops who had died outside the communion of Rome. In July, the Roman legates left Constantinople, bearing letters from the new patriarch, Epiphanius, and from Justin and Justinian, congratulating the pope for the success of the legation but asking one more time for a less strict application of the *libellus*.

Justinian soon took control of religious policy, and relations with Rome became both closer and more fraught. He spoke with new authority in letters sent to Rome in September, asserting a theological opinion (about the theopaschite question, discussed in a later section). In addition, concerning the question of the *libellus*, he now urged Pope Hormisdas to "show that he deservedly had succeeded to the Apostle Peter." Then Justinian's tone hardened: "For after the topics about which you have received written information have been concluded, we shall not permit further controversy on religion to be agitated in our State nor is it fitting for your Sanctity to hear persons disputing about superfluous matters."[18] Hormisdas remained steadfast, but this had little effect on imperial policy: the names of Chalcedonian bishops who died outside the Roman communion remained in the diptychs of many eastern churches.

## *The Theopaschite Formula*

The so-called Theopaschite Formula further tested the new relations between Rome and Constantinople. For two years the emperor and pope discussed this formula promoted by a group of Chalcedonian monks (usually called Scythian monks)[19] that affirmed "One of the Trinity suffered in the Flesh."[20] Justinian initially opposed the Formula. When the Scythian monks traveled to Rome, they were looking for support against Justinian and the Roman legates in Constantinople, who had rejected the Formula in March 519. When they arrived in Rome, in the summer of 519, the pope as well as many members of the clergy and Senate welcomed them. Their Formula was discussed openly, while Justin and Justinian sent letters opposing them and asking the pope to expel them from Rome, in the interest of the peace of the church. During the summer, the positions changed. Pope Hormisdas rejected the Formula, whereas Justinian adopted it and tried to obtain both Hormisdas's support and the return of the monks to Constantinople.

How Justinian dealt with theology in the years before ascending the throne anticipates his later policies. He recognized the authority of the pope and asked him to give an authoritative opinion on the matter raised. He asked the pope to confirm his policies but not to act on them. Justinian had no need of Rome to know what was orthodox: for that, as he said in his letters to Rome, he had the tradition, the opinion of the fathers, including former popes, and the communion of the eastern bishops, primarily the bishop of Constantinople. When he had accepted the Roman position on Christological matters, he accepted it because he believed that the church of Rome had been orthodox since its foundation (therefore his insistence on the apostolicity of Rome). Yet Justinian thought the pope was tied by this orthodoxy just as much as any other Christian, lay or cleric. Justinian needed the authority of Rome to back his own religious policy but he did not allow Rome any autonomy in religious policy.

Pope Hormisdas took no account of Justinian's request and kept the debate on the Theopaschite Formula open. He refused to allow the monks to go back to Constantinople until he finally condemned the Theopaschite Formula as useless and dangerous, in March 521.[21] For the next five years, there was no correspondence between popes and emperors, and for fifteen years after that Justinian, although actively trying to reconcile Chalcedonian and non-Chalcedonian, did not consult Rome about religious matters. No pope felt the need for a permanent representative in Constantinople before 533. The union had been proclaimed and the names of Roman popes and eastern patriarchs entered on the diptychs, but this was all. The only way to avoid admitting the antagonism between Rome and Constantinople was by avoiding any actual dealings between them. This was possible only as long as Italy remained politically independent from the Empire.

## Impact of the Union between Rome and Constantinople on the Political Situation in Italy

The union between Rome and Constantinople was by no means a political action against Gothic rule in Italy.[22] The Italian population and clergy were divided on the issue of ties to Constantinople, among many other matters,[23] and their allegiance to the Gothic king varied as well. Some Italians fully cooperated with the Gothic king, others were more reserved, but none openly opposed his power. For those who favored union with Constantinople as well as for those who supported Gothic rule, there was only one res publica and one emperor. During his negotiations with the East, in 518–519, Hormisdas consulted Theoderic, and the Arian king was favorable to reconciliation among Catholics. True, the king's name does not appear in any of the many letters exchanged between Rome and Constantinople, but this does not indicate any hostility toward the Gothic king, or that Justin was already interested in changing the political setup in the West. If any such project was envisaged at this time by the emperor or by his nephew, we know nothing of it. Moreover, in the way he resisted imperial authority as soon as it diverged from his own agenda, Hormisdas showed no inclination to political rapprochement with the emperor. Yet the pope was far from being the only political actor in Italy, and the new condition of religious union actually changed the balance of power among the Roman aristocracy and clergy.

## *Religious Affairs and Italian Foreign Policy*

The Roman aristocracy played an important and complicated role in Italian ecclesiastical life, exercising some control over the church, participating in episcopal elections and in theological debate. There were many conflicts about the control of papal elections and about the use of ecclesiastical wealth.[24] Many Roman senators were involved in eastern policy and, like the clergy, the aristocracy was divided on the issue of what attitude to take toward Constantinople, but this had long been a private matter, a question of literary and theological preference.

In 523, it became a political question, when charges of treasonable communication with the imperial court were brought against the *patricius* Albinus.[25] Boethius, who was then master of offices, protested, insisting that if Albinus were guilty, so were he and the entire Senate. Boethius and his father-in-law Symmachus, who had tried to defend him, were imprisoned, tried, and condemned to death by the Ostrogothic king Theoderic. The details of this affair have been much discussed, but neither the actual reasons for the condemnations nor the chronology of the trial and execution are completely clear. Many scholars have linked the trial to religious questions, because Albinus and Boethius had been involved in discussions about the union with the East, and had been more open-minded about eastern theology than Hormisdas. According to these scholars, the new pope, John, was a close friend of Boethius,[26] and Theoderic resented his election as a change in Roman policy.[27]

It was in other ways a difficult time for the king. In 523, the political balance he had carefully built in the previous years came to an end in Burgundy and in Africa.[28] In 525 or 526, worried by news about Justin's policy toward the Arians in the East, Theoderic sent him an embassy to ask for a more lenient policy.[29]

## *Pope John in Constantinople and Aftermath*

Theoderic's embassy to Constantinople consisted of four senators and four Nicene bishops, including Pope John, the first Roman bishop to travel to Constantinople or even to leave Rome. The *Liber pontificalis* (*Book of the Pontiffs*, a collection of papal biographies) stresses that Theoderic compelled the pope to go to Constantinople, and that once there he was warmly received. The pope was asked to preside over the Easter celebration and to crown the emperor a second time. The successful embassy returned with rich gifts offered for the major Roman churches. However, when John arrived in Ravenna, he and his fellow legates were kept in custody by order of the king Theoderic, and John died a few days later, on May 18. John was immediately celebrated as a martyr, thus making Theoderic a persecutor.

We must stress that the story of Pope John, as we know it, is a western construction. Eastern sources are almost silent about his visit to Constantinople,[30] and no official document has survived. If theological issues were raised while the pope was in Constantinople, no trace of this survives, either. While there is no reason to doubt the historicity of John's voyage and death, or the discontent of the Gothic king, we must recall that history writing flourished in Rome during these years. The *Liber pontificalis* was elaborated in its present version in the first years of the sixth century. One of its goals was to create an ideal image of the papacy, including the relations between the Roman church and Constantinople. The story of the pope's embassy to Constantinople, his crowning of the emperor, and his martyrdom at the hands of a heretical barbarian king is heavily loaded with ideological content.

Despite the pontifical visit of 526, Constantinople and Rome went their separate ways until 533. The new pope Felix (526–530) had no dealings at all with the imperial court, a policy largely continued by his successor, Boniface (530–532).[31] In 532, however, Boniface asserted the rights of Rome over Illyricum, in answer to an appeal by the bishop of Larissa, who had been deposed by the patriarch of Constantinople, which worsened relations with the East. At his death, after a vacancy of two-and-a-half months, Mercurius was elected pope and took the name of John in January 533.

## *Justinian Takes the Throne*

Meanwhile, Justinian succeeded Justin as emperor in August 527. He actively repressed paganism and heresy and looked for a way to reconcile Chalcedonians and anti-Chalcedonians. The first fruit of his effort was the Theopaschite edict published in March 533, with a profession of faith stating that Jesus Christ "who was made man and was crucified is one of the consubstantial Trinity," but taking no account of Chalcedon.[32]

It was sent to Pope John II only three months later, after two of the Acoimetae monks,[33] who had been condemned in Constantinople for their opposition to this edict, had already submitted the case to the pope. Justinian asked John to give his agreement to his profession of faith and to condemn the monks as well as all those who rejected it. The emperor argued that this was the only way to increase the authority of the Roman see and to keep the unity of the church. The imperial letter respectfully called the pope "head of all the holy churches" but asked him to do no more than confirm what had already been decided and published in the East.[34] Once more, the Roman bishop acted as if he had been asked to be part of the decision: he consulted the African deacon and theologian Fulgentius of Ruspe and did not answer until March 534. This time he fully accepted Justinian's position, acknowledged the doctrinal decree, and condemned the monks as Nestorians.[35]

Justinian incorporated in the code of laws both his letter to John and the pope's answer. The pope's approval was of primary importance to him at this time. He had already embarked on the military conquest of the West. He had reconquered Africa from the Vandals in September 533, putting an end to more than a century of Arian domination. He was also negotiating with Theoderic's heirs to restore direct imperial authority over Italy. Legates sent to Pope John were instructed to discuss this matter with the regent Amalasuintha while they were in Italy. Seen from Rome, the situation was changing dramatically. In April 535, the murder of Amalasuintha launched the conquest of Italy. Restoration of direct imperial rule over Italy was imminent when John died in May 535.

## The Roman Church under Imperial Authority

The history of the relations between Rome and Constantinople from the beginning of Justinian's reconquest of Italy until the end of his reign is one of failed attempts to build a Christian empire that could reconcile imperial and papal definitions of authority in religious matters. Western and eastern opinion about this differed substantially by the end of the fifth century. As long as western and eastern objectives coincided, it was possible to mask these differences, as it had happened under the pontificate of Hormisdas and John II. Indeed, the pope and the emperor both desired the unity of the churches and the unity of the empire, as witnessed by the haste with which they celebrated any sign of union.

Success seemed near when Pope Agapetus visited Constantinople in 536, but the Three Chapters Controversy ruined the illusion forever.

## *The Apparent Victory of Pope Agapetus*

Agapetus was elected, apparently without any political intervention, in 535. Of aristocratic birth (still uncommon among popes at the time), he was supported by part of the Senate. At the same time he was on good terms with the Gothic king, as is proved by his friendship with Cassiodorus. He was the first pope to confront Justinian's new political order, and he was soon to assert his authority over western churches and his independence in relation to the emperor. After his swift recovery of Africa, Justinian had adopted an ambiguous attitude toward the Arians living there, probably aiming to reconcile the different religious communities. The Catholic clergy demurred. At the beginning of 535, a council of 220 bishops from the three African provinces appealed to the pope against the imperial policy that allowed Arian clerics converted to Catholicism to keep their rank in the clergy. At the same time, they addressed a petition to the emperor asking for a fuller restitution of properties confiscated by the Arians. The emperor satisfied the African demand without delay, by enacting the *Novella de Africana Ecclesia* (*Law Concerning the African Church*) on August 1, 535, ordering the immediate restitution of all ecclesiastical properties to the Catholic Church, and launching a systematic persecution against "Donatists, Jews, Pagans, Arians and other heretics."[36] At the same time (August 535), Agapetus answered the African request, taking advantage of this occasion to assert his authority in relation to the emperor. The pope accepted the hard line against Arians. He wrote to Justinian, explaining that he could not, "in accordance with his function," allow Arian clerics to keep their rank in the clergy.[37]

The same correspondence also raised the Illyrian question. A few months after *Novel* 11, which gave ecclesiastical autonomy to Justiniana Prima (Justinian's birthplace), the pope reasserted Roman authority over the whole Illyrian province and in October sent a legation of four Italian bishops and two Roman deacons to Constantinople to settle the case of the bishop of Larissa.[38] He intended to restore Roman influence over an area long contested by Rome and Constantinople. Agapetus's steadfastness, so highly praised in western sources, must not mislead us. His task was easy at a time when Justinian was looking for support in the West and when the Gothic king, Theodahad, was desperately trying to avoid war. More than ever, ecclesiastical and political matters were intertwined.

In May 535, the Senate and the king appealed to Justinian not to attack Italy. Cassiodorus wrote a letter on behalf of the Senate, which contained, in addition to other arguments, a plea by Rome herself: "My religion, which is your own, is known to be flourishing; why then do you try to do more for me? ... For, if Africa deserved to receive her freedom through you, it is cruel for me to lose a freedom which I have always possessed."[39] This plea did not prevent Justinian from attacking Sicily and Dalmatia in June 535. In this context of intense diplomatic activity, while he was dealing with the Byzantine legate Peter, King Theodahad sent Pope Agapetus to Constantinople to ask for a removal of imperial armies from Sicily, Dalmatia, and Italy, threatening to kill all the Roman senators if the emperor refused.[40] Pope Agapetus left Rome in the winter of 535–536, arriving in Constantinople in February or March. Once in the imperial capital, the pope concerned himself only with ecclesiastical matters and showed no intention of returning quickly to Rome.

In Constantinople, the legates Agapetus had sent in October informed him of the complex situation: the new patriarch of Constantinople, Anthimus, former bishop of Trebizond, who had been a Chalcedonian for a long time, was now a disciple of Severus of Antioch, whom the empress Theodora was protecting. Agapetus refused to communicate with him and asked to confront him in a public disputation, but Anthimus consented to resign the see of Constantinople. On March 13, 536, Agapetus could consecrate the new patriarch, Menas. Both he and the emperor signed a profession of faith written by western theologians, reasserting the faith of Hormisdas (as stated in the *libellus* of Hormisdas) and the *Tome* of Leo. The document included the Council of Constantinople in 381 among the four ecumenical councils and said nothing about the theopaschite formula.

For Rome, it was a major victory. It amounted to an admission by the emperor and by the patriarch of Constantinople that Rome had unique competence in defining orthodoxy. Once again, however, this victory was grounded on a misunderstanding. The emperor certainly acknowledged the importance of Rome as the first of all the ecclesiastical sees. He had said it many times before, and his insistence on obtaining the agreement of Rome was proof of his sincerity. But he did not give up his own search for a common theological ground between Chalcedonian and non-Chalcedonian theological positions. At the same time that he gave his assent to the "Roman" profession of faith, he was asking Agapetus to give his approval to the Theopaschite Formula and to the condemnation of the Acoimetae monks.

Agapetus was fully aware of the problem raised by Justinian's demand. He gave his agreement "not because we accept the authority of the teaching of a lay person, but because we confirm that the zeal of your faith is in conformity with the rules of our fathers."[41] Such an ambiguity was to remain the insecure basis of the relations between the Roman church and Constantinople.

Agapetus died suddenly on April 22. In Constantinople, his enemies called it a divine punishment. A synod was held in May and June 536, presided over by the patriarch Menas, with the participation of almost all the western clerics present in Constantinople. The council deposed Anthimus (this time from his see of Trebizond), condemned him as a heretic, and repeated the condemnation of Severus and his followers. After the council, the Italian legates left Constantinople to bury Agapetus in Rome. Only the Roman deacon Pelagius, who had been appointed *apocrisiarius* to the emperor by Agapetus, remained behind. Evidently Agapetus intended to keep close contact with Constantinople, contrary to what had happened after the 519 union.

### *Agapetus's Successor and War in Italy*

The news of Agapetus's death reached Rome in the spring. His successor, Silverius, was consecrated on June 8, under Gothic rule and without waiting for the return of the legation from Constantinople. He was Hormisdas's son and only a subdeacon at the time of his election. In the summer, the Byzantine army landed in Italy and successfully besieged Naples. The question of Roman (and clerical) loyalties was still open in Italy. The new king Vitigis, who had replaced Theodehad early in December, expected papal support.[42] But when the Byzantines arrived at the gates of the city, the Romans, and "more than any others, Silverius" decided that it was better to "receive the emperor's army."[43] On December 9, Belisarius peacefully entered Rome. After sixty years, Rome was back under direct imperial administration.

## JUSTINIAN AND ROME IN THE THREE CHAPTERS CONTROVERSY

With the pontificate of Silverius, we enter the troubled times of the Three Chapters Controversy. From this point on, our sources deserve special attention. They tell a story full of improbabilities and of contradictions, with many conflicts between the tendentious narratives and the few official surviving documents. Here we will not discuss the "fatal web of intrigues,"[44] but we will consider the sixth-century Roman version of the events to see how it contributed to a long-lasting western image of Byzantine imperial power.

## *Pope Vigilius*

While Justinian had chosen to back the Roman position on Severus and Anthimus, the empress Theodora was trying to undo Agapetus's work and to restore her Severan protégés. Both the emperor and his wife supported the deacon Vigilius, who had lived in Constantinople for many years and hoped to become pope. Vigilius hurried to Rome in the hope of being elected as successor to Agapetus, but he arrived too late. But during the siege of Rome, in March 537, Belisarius arrested Silverius for plotting with the Goths and exiled him. With Belisarius's support, Vigilius was elected pope the same day, and his election was not contested.

Rome remained under Gothic siege until spring 539, and Vigilius did not communicate with his *apocrisiarius* Pelagius or the emperor until 540. Only then did Justinian send a (lost) letter, to which Vigilius replied in September, giving a profession of faith and assuring the emperor that he was sincerely happy about the Byzantine military success. This letter shows Vigilius's sensitivity to the new problems raised by direct imperial control over Rome. He urged Justinian to do nothing new in matters of faith, or "against the see of the blessed Peter the apostle."[45] The emperor had much better relations with the *apocrisiarius* Pelagius, who was an influential actor on the religious scene in Constantinople.[46]

## *First Reactions to the Three Chapters Condemnation*

In 543 or 544, Justinian published the edict on the Three Chapters, so called because it involved the person of Theodore of Mopsuestia, some writings of Theodoret of Cyrrus, and a letter from Ibas of Edessa to a Persian bishop. The condemnation was the logical continuation of the search for unity with the moderate anti-Chalcedonians with whom Justinian had been engaged since he took the throne.[47]

The new Roman *apocrisiarius*, the deacon Stephen, warned the emperor and the patriarch Menas that Rome could on no account accept the condemnation of two bishops who had been cleared by the council of Chalcedon. Menas reluctantly consented to sign the edict, explaining that his agreement would not be definitive as long as the pope had not spoken. Stephen broke communion with him.[48] Meanwhile, in Rome, Vigilius made no official statement, nor did he break the relations with the East. In 545, when Justinian published *Novel* 131, setting up the new ecclesiastical organization of Illyricum, in which the bishop of Justiniana Prima "holds the place of the apostolic see of Rome," he could explain that this had been done "according to what has been settled by the very holy pope Vigilius."[49]

In November 545, events took a new turn. Byzantine soldiers abducted Vigilius while at mass and took him to Sicily, where he stayed for almost a year.[50] All the western sources say that Justinian wanted to exert pressure on Vigilius to obtain his agreement to the condemnation of the Three Chapters, but we must not underestimate the seriousness of the military situation. During the summer of 545, the Goths, led by king Totila, were marching against Rome. Vigilius left the city a few days before the Goths laid siege to it. It may have been for safety's sake, but western chroniclers claimed he could only have left Rome under political pressure, not of his own free will.

During the few months Vigilius spent in Sicily, a coherent western position developed. Pelagius, now back in Italy, had involved the African churches by seeking advice from the African deacon Ferrandus. This expert theologian had no doubt about the illegitimacy of any text that claimed to correct the decrees of Chalcedon – or to condemn the dead – and he contested Justinian's authority to deal with theological matters.[51] Bishop Datius of Milan pressed the pope to resist Justinian,[52] while the patriarch Zoïlos sent legates from Alexandria to present excuses for having signed the imperial edict. Vigilius approved the steadfastness of his *apocrisiarius* Stephen and the excommunication of Menas. When he left Sicily for Constantinople, he seemed like a new Agapetus – precisely as the African bishop Facundus of Hermiane, the most eminent opponent of the Three Chapters' condemnation in Constantinople,[53] described him.

For African or Roman experts, the Three Chapters Controversy had little to do with Christology. The issue was the status of the council and, more broadly, a need to clarify the respective roles of pope, council, and emperor in defining the true faith. They could differ to some extent on the competence of councils and popes, but in the tradition of Ambrose of Milan, Leo, Gelasius, Hormisdas, and Agapetus, they all agreed that no layman, not even an emperor, could interfere with defining the faith and interpreting scripture. For Justinian, on the other hand, the true faith had already been defined, and as a Christian emperor it was his duty to unite all the inhabitants of the empire under this faith. He was only clarifying some points that could mislead some believers, as he explained to the Illyrian bishops who protested against the condemnation of the Three Chapters. According to him, the pope was the leader of all other bishops, as long as he remained orthodox.

## *Vigilius in Constantinople*

When Vigilius arrived in Constantinople in late December 546, he was greeted with the same honors as his predecessors, but his sojourn in the imperial city was very different. The Roman clerics in Constantinople may have looked like a government in exile, with five of the seven deacons and the head of the pontifical chancery present with the pope. These men had no hope of returning to Rome in the near future, for Totila had taken the city after a long siege and threatened to destroy its walls and buildings. When he departed, he took all the senators with him and ordered the population to leave the city as well. According to contemporary historians, the city remained unoccupied for forty days. The pope was now entirely dependent on the emperor.

Vigilius did not surrender immediately to the imperial will, however. He excommunicated Menas in January 547 (and subsequently was excommunicated by him) and resumed communion with him only in June.[54] He then tried to find a middle way to reconcile Justinian's policy and western steadfastness by means of the publication, in 548, of the *Iudicatum*, a text condemning the Three Chapters explicitly without prejudice to Chalcedon.[55] This was seen as a betrayal by most of the West, including some of the pope's companions in Constantinople, whom he then excommunicated in 550.[56] Vigilius eventually came to an agreement with the emperor to keep silent about the Three Chapters as long as a general council had not settled the matter, and he withdrew his *Iudicatum*. But in July 551, Justinian submitted a new edict of condemnation to the pope, thus launching a new crisis. Vigilius left the palace and took refuge in a church dedicated to Saint Peter with a group of western clerics. There, he excommunicated all those who accepted Justinian's new edict. Thirteen western bishops signed the excommunication, which was not published at the time. Imperial soldiers attacked the group but could not pull them out of the church. After a while, and in exchange for imperial promises, Vigilius consented to return to his lodgings. The news aroused indignation among the Italian churches.[57] A few months later, in December 551, Vigilius fled again, this time to take refuge in the church of St. Euphemia in Chalcedon, from where he finally published the excommunications pronounced in the summer. This led to apparent success: the excommunicated eastern bishops signed a text requesting that the last imperial edict be withdrawn and condemning the violence against the pope. In June 552, Justinian had made his peace with Vigilius, who was back in Constantinople.[58]

This complex story is known mainly from western sources: Vigilius's own letters and encyclicals, treatises against the condemnation of the Three Chapters, and chronicles. The only eastern source for the period is the letter sent by the emperor to the Council of Constantinople, held in May–July 553,[59] in which Justinian revealed two accords concluded secretly with the pope. According to the emperor, as early as 547, Vigilius had written secret letters committing himself to condemning the Three Chapters, and in 551 (early summer), in exchange for the withdrawal of his *Iudicatum*, he had taken the most solemn oath to work for the condemnation. According to Justinian, all the papal policy in defense of the Three Chapters was grounded on perjury and should not be considered by the council. These conflicting accounts underline the depth of the misunderstanding between the pope and the emperor.

Between June 552 and January 553, the emperor and the pope decided to call a general council to settle the Three Chapters Controversy once and for all. Vigilius later asserted that he welcomed its convocation in January, but he was soon disappointed when Justinian refused to hold the council in Sicily, with equal representation of western and eastern bishops.[60] And so, when the council began on May 4, few western bishops attended.[61] Vigilius refused to take part in person, arguing that no pope had even been present in a general council. Instead, he wrote a new text, the *Constitutum*, which was presented to the emperor on May 25, after the council had already met six times and begun to deal with the Three Chapters.[62] Justinian refused even to read it and sent to the council a letter informing it that "the very religious pope of old Rome had made himself an alien to the catholic church by defending the impious chapters, and by putting himself out of the communion (of the fathers)." He added that the council had to keep "the union with the apostolic see" because "Vigilius's change of mind could not be allowed to ruin the unity of the churches."[63] The council then deposed the pope. During the last session, held a few days later, on June 2, the bishops published their decisions.

After the council, Justinian imprisoned or exiled the Roman and African clerics who persisted in opposing the condemnation. Six months later, Vigilius surrendered to the emperor. He sent a letter to patriarch Eutychius, asking to be restored to communion with him, which allowed them to celebrate Christmas mass together in Constantinople.

In February 554, Vigilius published a new *Iudicatum* condemning the Three Chapters in terms similar to those used by the council and condemning all their defenders, including his deacon Pelagius, who was still under arrest in a monastery.[64] Vigilius remained in Constantinople one more year,[65] and was finally allowed to leave Constantinople in spring 555. He died in Syracuse before the end of his journey.

Justinian probably knew that most Italian churches still opposed the condemnation of the Three Chapters, and he did not want to forfeit his victory. Therefore he needed the next pope to be reliable. He proposed the deacon Pelagius for the papacy, a choice not as surprising as it may seem. Although Pelagius had opposed Justinian's position, he had demonstrated his ability to deal with ecclesiastical matters when he was *apocrisiarius* and when he directed the administration of the Roman church (547–551). Even in his pamphlet defending the Three Chapters, he had attacked Vigilius's inconstancy much more than Justinian's policy.[66] Though we lack substantial evidence, we may suppose that Justinian and Pelagius came to some agreement. The Roman deacon resigned himself to condemning the Three Chapters and embarked for Italy. Despite a hostile reception in Rome, he was consecrated pope in April 556. Such a direct imperial intervention was unprecedented, but so was the situation in Rome: since 555, there had been no deacon left in the city to administer the church, and in 556 there were not enough bishops around Rome to consecrate Pelagius according to canon law.

## RECONSTRUCTING PAPAL AUTHORITY IN BYZANTINE ITALY

In 556, Justinian had at last gained full control of Italy. With the exception of some pockets of resistance in northern Italy, the war against the Ostrogoths was over; the Three Chapters had been condemned, and Justinian could rely on the bishops of Ravenna and Rome to enforce the decisions of the council. But the new pope had his own agenda. The conditions were far from those imagined by the Roman aristocracy in the early sixth century: the empire was restored, but Rome was no longer a center of power. The city itself had not recovered from its sack by Totila; most of the senators had been killed; many had left Rome for Constantinople, very few still lived in Italy, which was now a distant province of the Byzantine Empire. Together with the long war, plague and famine had laid waste the country. The failure of the papacy – as most western Catholics saw it – was one of the many signs of a bitter transformation of the world. How could Pelagius reassert papal authority in the face of western hostility to the condemnation of the Three Chapters? How could he resist an emperor on whom he so completely depended?

## *Regaining Roman Authority*

Pelagius's task was indeed difficult. As we have seen, news of the controversy in the West had been patchy and distorted. Many people believed that Vigilius had stood steady in the defense of the Three Chapters until his death; some even believed that Pelagius had killed him! With the exception of the bishop of Ravenna, there was almost complete unanimity against the condemnation. The controversy might be over in Constantinople, but it was only beginning in the West. African and Illyrian bishops had broken off communion with Rome, most Italian bishops refused communion with Pelagius on account of his betrayal of the Three Chapters, and Gallic clerics and laymen were worried that the new pope might be heretical.

Pelagius attempted to reconcile the apparently irreconcilable: accepting the decisions of the council of Constantinople, winning over the vast majority of western Christians, and restoring the credibility of his see. His policy rested on purely Roman and ecclesiastical grounds. He did not exploit imperial patronage. When he asserted his orthodoxy, which he had to do many times, he quoted the faith of his predecessors, the decisions of the four councils (but never those of Constantinople II), or communion with the eastern churches, never the emperor.[67] He never invoked the authority of the emperor or of the council, and in the Italian churches under his direct authority (in Italia Suburbicaria, south of the Po River) nor did he call on Byzantine authorities to restore unity. When he appealed to them after 559, it was on the pretext of disciplinary affairs, not reestablishing communion.[68] He met with success in these areas, but his efforts were thwarted in northern Italy.

## *Schism in Northern Italy*

In the provinces of Liguria, Venetia, and Histria, the metropolitan sees of Milan and Aquileia were not subject to the disciplinary authority of Rome. As followers of Datius of Milan, the churches were steadfast defenders of the Three Chapters, despite the Byzantine attempt, in 552–553, to control the election of a new bishop of Milan. After Vigilius's death, Milan and Aquileia had silently broken off communion with Rome, probably only by refusing to name Pelagius in the diptychs, but in early 559, a new Aquileian bishop, a monk named Paulus, was consecrated in Milan and publicly expressed his doubts about the orthodoxy of the Roman see.[69] Pelagius then asked the military authorities to arrest him, calling Paulus "execrated rather than consecrated",[70] but the Byzantine authorities paradoxically refused. The Byzantine officers in northern Italy needed the cooperation of the local bishops if they wanted to assert their authority in still restless areas. Agreement with local communities prevailed over communion with Rome.[71] The controversy had long-term consequences: schism in northern Italy persisted until 573 in the church of Milan, and until the beginning of the seventh century in the ecclesiastical province of Aquileia. Its history, soon to be complicated by the Lombard invasion of Italy in 568, need not be told here, but it is interesting to note that, in their conflict with papal authority, dissident bishops appealed to the emperor against Rome more often and more successfully than Rome appealed to Constantinople against schismatic churches.[72]

## *Rome and Constantinople in the Late Sixth Century*

This attempt to regain ecclesiastical authority independently from the emperor does not mean that Rome had recovered ecclesiastical autonomy or that communication with Constantinople had ceased. On the contrary, the rule was now for a newly elected pope to wait for imperial permission before being consecrated (John III in 561, Benedict I in 575, Gregory in 590). John III sent a profession of faith to Justinian in 562.[73] These popes did not challenge imperial authority, including imperial control of ecclesiastical elections. If Pope Pelagius II was consecrated without waiting for the imperial confirmation in 579, it was only because the Lombards were beseiging Rome. In 590, Gregory is said to have hoped that the emperor Maurice would refuse his election. There was a Roman *apocrisiarius* in Constantinople at least until 559, and from 579 onward the future pope Gregory served in that capacity.

The new pattern of relations between bishops and secular authorities that developed in Italy differed from that in the East. The contrast is striking. The Roman bishops did not discuss religious questions with the emperor in the forty years following Pelagius's consecration, or, if they did, no record survives of such discussions. There is no trace of any communication between Pelagius or his successor and Justinian during the last ten years of the emperor's reign. No letter sent to or received from the emperor has survived in Roman archives from 556 to 573, and the *Liber pontificalis* does not mention Justinian or his successors until the pontificate of Pelagius II. The last theological debates in Constantinople were not mentioned in the West, and Rome did not react in 565 to the deposition of the patriarch Eutychius, to whom Pelagius had sent Roman relics in 558–559.[74]

The lapse in communication was limited to religious matters only; the emperor was addressed in connection with pressing secular matters. For example, the Senate and the pope sent two delegations to Constantinople in 578 and 580 to ask for help against the Lombards.[75] A new balance between political loyalty and sacerdotal authority was taking shape that would find its completion in Gregory the Great's way of dealing with the emperor Maurice: Gregory accepted imperial rule, even when the emperor legislated on ecclesiastical matters, but he raised objections with great freedom when he thought a decision unfair.[76]

## Conclusion

The end of the Acacian schism and Justinian's active involvement in the West lets us assess the extent of the differences between West and East. By the end of the sixth century, the Roman bishops had accepted the institutional framework of the Christian Byzantine empire but not the model of a sacerdotal emperor. From the Three Chapters Controversy, western bishops had learned that direct contact with the emperor was better avoided.

Thanks to its prudent policy, Rome could regain authority over dissident or worried bishops (with the exception of the ecclesiastical province of Aquileia), thereby preserving a precious modicum of unity in a divided Europe. But the price was high: Rome turned away from the East as much as the East turned away from Rome. There was no schism, but the disagreement between eastern and western churches remained unresolved. Justinian's imperial model of the church did not find a place in the memory of the West, not even in Ravenna. On the contrary, men took pen in hand to compose histories and chronicles that defined and defended the Roman model of ecclesiastical authority. This is the explanation of the distorted account of events in the West often mentioned above. This historical writing did more than express the divisions between Rome and Constantinople. It helped deepen the divisions and establish the basis of future relations between East and West.

## Notes

1 Ernst Stein, *Histoire du Bas-Empire* (Paris, 1949) 2:279–283.
2 Philipp Rousseau, "Inheriting the Fifth Century: Who Bequeathed What?" in *The Sixth Century, End or Beginning?*, ed. Pauline Allen and Elizabeth Jeffreys (Brisbane, 1996), 1–19.
3 John Moorhead, *Theoderic in Italy* (Oxford, 1973); Patrick Amory, *People and Identity in Ostrogothic Italy, 489–554* (Cambridge, 1997).
4 Moorhead, *Theoderic in Italy*, 114–139; Thomas F. X. Noble, "Theoderic and the Papacy," in *Theoderico il grande e i Goti d'Italia: Atti del XIII Congresso internazionale di studi sull'Alto Medioevo. Milano 2–6 novembre 1992* (Spoleto, 1993), 395–423.
5 Robert F. Taft, *A History of the Liturgy of St. John Chrysostom*, vol. 4, *The Diptychs*, Orientalia Christiana Analecta 238 (Rome, 1991).
6 Felix, who had announced to Zeno the excommunication of Acacius, nevertheless sent a letter of congratulations to the new emperor Anastasius in April 491; his successors Gelasius, Anastasius, and Symmachus all sent letters to the emperor to announce their election.
7 Namely Acacius's reconciliation with Peter Mongus in Alexandria and the consecration of Peter the Fuller.
8 Gelasius to Anastasius, *Collectio Veronensis*, 8:20, in Thiel, ep. 12.
9 Jean Meyendorf, *Imperial Unity and Christian Divisions: The Church, 450–680 A.D.*, Church History 2 (Crestwood, N.Y., 1989), 207–210.
10 Walter Ullmann, *Gelasius I (492–496): Das Papsttum an der Wende der Spätantike zum Mittelalter* (Stuttgart, 1981).
11 Paul Robinson Coleman-Norton, *Roman State and Christian Church, a Collection of Legal Documents to A.D. 535* (London, 1966), no. 964.
12 Justinian to Hormisdas, *Coll. Avell.*, 44, CSEL, 35, 2:592–593, in Coleman-Norton, no. 549, 965.
13 Dioscorus to Hormidas, *Coll. Avell.*, 167, CSEL, 35, 2:618–621.
14 *Coll. Avell.*, 68–71, CSEL, 35, 2:614–616.
15 Exemplum libelli, *Coll. Avell.*, 116b, CSEL, 35, 2:521.
16 Election of the patriarch of Alexandria is in Hormisdas to Dioscorus = *Coll. Avell.* 105, CSEL, 35, 2:631; the patriarch of Antioch, Paul, seems to have been the Roman choice, but he had to be deposed in May 521: *Coll. Avell.*, 241–242, CSEL 35, 2:740–742.
17 *Coll. Avell.* 193, CSEL 35, 2:650–651, in Coleman-Norton, no. 557.
18 Justinian to Hormisdas, *Coll. Avell.*, 235, CSEL 35, 2:715–716, in Coleman-Norton, no. 988.
19 They are called this in some contemporary texts and were clearly of the same origin (Scythia Minor, modern Dobroudja) as Vitalian in Constantinople.
20 See Gray, Chap. 9 in this volume.
21 *Coll. Avell.*, 326, CSEL, 35, 2:716–22.
22 Charles Pietri, "Aristocratie et société cléricale dans l'Italie chrétienne aux temps d'Odoacre et de Théodoric," *MélRome* 93.1 (1981): 432–444; Noble, "Theoderic and the Papacy," n. 4.
23 See Amory, *People and Identity in Ostrogothic Italy*, 195–235.
24 Pietri, "Aristocratie et société cléricale dans l'Italie chrétienne," 417–467.
25 *PLRE* 2, Albinus 9:52.

26 *Prosopographie Chrétienne du Bas-Empire. Italie*, 2, Boethius, 314.

27 Meyendorf, *Imperial Unity and Christian Divisions*, n. 15, takes this hypothesis as granted. There is a more careful attitude in *Prosopographie Chrétienne du Bas-Empire. Italie*, 2, Iohannes, 28:1080.

28 The Franks invaded Burgundy after Sigismund's death, and the new Vandal King, Hilderic, imprisoned Amalafrida, Theoderic's sister and, according to Procopius, destroyed "all the Goths": Moorhead, *Theoderic in Italy*, 217.

29 Moorhead, *Theoderic in Italy*, 236–238; according to our Western sources, the embassy was sent to intercede for the return of Arian converts to their faith or of Arian churches to the Arian community.

30 See Theophanes, *Chronographia*, ed. Carl de Boor (Leipzig, 1883).

31 The ones who did not rally were reconciled by Agapetus in 535.

32 *Chronicon Paschale, 284–628 AD*, ed. Michael Whitby and Mary Whitby (Liverpool, 1989), 128–130.

33 See n. 12.

34 Justinian to John, in *Coll. Avell.*, 84, CSEL 35, 1:322–325.

35 John to Justinian, in *Coll. Avell.*, 84, CSEL 35, 1:320–328.

36 Yves Modéran, "Les Eglises et la reconquista byzantine: L'Afrique" in *Histoire du christianisme*, vol. 3, ed. Luce Pietri (Paris, 2000), 701–705.

37 *Coll. Avell.*, 88, CSEL, 35, 1:333–338.

38 Robert A. Markus, "Carthage – Prima Justiniana – Ravenna: Aspects of Justinian's *Kirchenpolitik*," *Byzantion* 49 (1979): 277–306; Charles Pietri, "La géographie de l'Illyricum ecclésiastique et ses relations avec l'Eglise de Rome (Ve–VIe siècles)," in *Villes et peuplement dans l'Illyricum protobyzantin*, Collection de l'École française de Rome 77 (Rome, 1984), 21–62.

39 Cassiodorus, *Variae*, 11. 13, ed. Sam J. B. Barnish (Liverpool, 1992), 153.

40 Liberatus, *Breuiarum*, 21; *Liber pontificalis*, ed. Louis Duchesne (Paris, 1886); *Vita Agapiti*, 287–288.

41 *Coll. Avell.*, 91, CSEL 35, 1:343.

42 Procopius, *Wars*, 5.9.26, ed. Henry Bronson Dewing, 115.

43 Procopius, *Wars*, 5.14. 4:143.

44 John N. D. Kelly, *The Oxford Dictionary of Popes* (Oxford, 1986), 59. Claire Sotinel, "Autorité pontificale et pouvoir impérial sous le règne de Justinien: Le pape Vigile," *Mélanges d'archéologie et d'histoire de l'École française de Rome* 104.1 (1992): 439–463; "Silverius," "Vigilius," "Pelagius I" in *Enciclopedia dei Papi* (Rome, 2000), 506–536.

45 *Coll. Avell.*, 92, CSEL, 35, 2:349–354.

46 *Prosopographie Chrétienne du Bas-Empire. Italie*, Pelagius 3.

47 See Gray, Chap. 9 in this volume.

48 Facundus Hermian, *Pro defensione Trium Capitulorum*, 4.4.3, *CCSL*, 90A: 123–124.

49 *Nov.* 131.3.

50 *Liber Pontificalis*, Vigilius; Victor Tunnunnensis, *Chronica ad a.* 542, *MGH AA* 11:201; *Epistula Clericorum Mediolanensium ad legatos Francorum, qui Constantinopolim proficiscebantur*, a cura di Ernst Schwartz, *Vigiliusbriefe* (Munich, 1940), 18–25.

51 Ferrandus, *Ep.*, 6, PL 67:921–928.

52 About Datius after he left Milan in 536, see *PLRE* 2 *Italie*, 532.

53 Facundus, *Pro defensione Trium Capitulorum*, *CCSL* 90A, 417–434.

54 Facundus, *Contra Mocianum*, 43–44, *CCSL* 90A, 410–411.

55 This lost document is quoted during the council of 553: *Concilium uniuersale constantinopolitanum sub Iustiniano habitum*, *ACO*, vol. 4, part 2 (Berlin, 1971), 11–12.

56 Vigilius Papa, *Epistula ad Rusticum et Sebastianum*, *ACO*, vol. 4, part 2, 188–194.

57 Vigilius, *Ep.* 1, 2, *Vigiliusbriefe*, 1–15; *Ep. clericorum Mediolanensiusm*, *ACO*, vol. 4, part 2, 22.

58 *Ep. clericorum Mediolanensiusm*, *ACO*, vol. 4, part 2, 22–25; Vigilius, *Constitutum de tribus capitulis, Coll. Avell.*, 83: 231–234.

59 *Vigilii iuramenti testificatio*, quoted by Justinian, *ACO*, vol. 4, part 1, 198–199.

60 Vigilius, *Constitutum de Tribus Capitulis, Coll. Avell.*, 83, CSEL 35: 232–234.

61 Evangelos Chrysos, *Die Bischofslisten des V. oekumenischen Konzils 553* (Bonn, 1966).

62 Vigilius, *Constitutum de Tribus Capitulis, Coll. Avell.*, 83.

63 Justinian, *ACO*, vol. 4, part 2, 8–14.

64 Vigilius, *Ep. Ex tribus capitulis*, *ACO*, vol. 4, part 2, 138–168.

65 *Nov.* 131.

66 Pelagius, *In defensione Trium Capitulorum*, ed. Robert Devreesse, Studi e testi 57 (Rome, 1957).

67 Pelagius, *Epistulae*, 3, 11, 19, ed. Pius M. Gassó and Columba M. Batlle, Scripta et documenta 8 (Montserrat, 1956), 6–10, 35–40, 55–61.

68 Pelagius, *Epistulae*, 61, 65, 69, 70 and 71:162, 171–173, 178–182.

69 *Prosopographie Chrétienne du Bas-Empire. Italie*, 2, Paulus 34:1680.

70 Pelagius, *Epistulae*, 24:73–78.

71 Pelagius, *Epistulae*, 75:189–190.

72 Robert A. Markus, *Gregory the Great and His World* (Cambridge, 1997): 125–142.

73 John of Malalas, *Chronographia* 18, *PG* 97:711a.

74 Pelagius, *Epistula*, 20:62–63.

75 Menander Protector, frags. 49 and 62, *Fragmenta Historicorum Graecorum* IV, ed. Charles Müller (Paris, 1928), 253, 263.

76 Markus, *Gregory the Great and His World*, 87–96.

# 12: Christian Piety and Practice in the Sixth Century

*Derek Krueger*

The sixth century represents a particularly dynamic period in the history of Christianity in the eastern Mediterranean, not merely for its articulation of ecclesiological divisions between those claiming adherence to the Council of Chalcedon and those rejecting it, but also for its impact on the development of Christian practices. A wide variety of written sources and material evidence – including histories, saints' lives, collections of miracle accounts, festal hymns, pilgrim's diaries and souvenirs, magical paraphernalia, images, and architecture – attests to significant changes in modes of piety, the ways Christians expressed and engaged in their religious life. The evidence presented here challenges models for understanding religion through neat distinctions between clergy and laity, between elite and popular pieties, and between religion and magic. Many innovations in liturgical practice disseminated by church leaders led to new modes of Christian self-conception for all participants. At the same time evolving forms of "popular" devotion such as pilgrimage and the seeking of miracles gained popularity with emperor and peasant alike. Although parallel developments occurred among non-Chalcedonian Christians, this essay emphasizes Constantinople and neo-Chalcedonian Christianity.

The fourth century had already seen the proliferation of new forms of Christian practice, including asceticism, pilgrimage, the veneration of saints, and the composition and dissemination of new liturgies. These practices continued during the Age of Justinian. But in contrast to the obvious novelty of the forms of fourth-century piety, the sixth century saw an elaboration and routinization of Christian practices as a feature of Byzantine culture. The synthesis of a truly imperial Christianity tied intimately to the biblical past was expressed grandly in architecture, art, and church plate. Certain trends emerge as particularly distinctive. The first was a movement toward higher levels of correspondence between pious practices and the events of the biblical narrative. Employing techniques of biblical typology, Christians sought the biblicization of many aspects of religious life. The second was the rise of an increasingly tactile and therapeutic piety focused on the ability of sacred places and material substances to contain and convey divine power. Together these developments reshaped Christian life in Byzantium.

## Liturgical Innovation

### *The Divine Liturgy*

Changes to the liturgy initiated by Chalcedonian patriarchs and disseminated throughout the Chalcedonian church demonstrate how new forms of Christian self-understanding could emerge from the top down. During the reign of Justin II (565–578), probably in either 565 or 577, Eutychius, the patriarch of Constantinople (552–565, 577–582), introduced a new *koinonikon*, or communion chant, for the celebration of the Divine Liturgy on Holy Thursday, the annual commemoration of Christ's Last Supper. Once the bread and wine had been consecrated and transformed by the Holy Spirit into the body and blood of Christ, the choir chanted, "At your mystical supper, Son of God, receive me today as a partaker, for I will not betray the sacrament to your enemies, nor give you a kiss like Judas, but like the thief I confess you: remember me, Lord, in your kingdom."[1]

According to the contemporary historian John of Ephesus, a non-Chalcedonian sharply critical of Eutychius, the innovation caused great controversy. John writes that Eutychius attempted to change the antiphon "which by ancient custom was in use in all the churches."[2] Moreover, the patriarch "wrote on tablets concerning Holy Thursday, and sent it to all the churches. And he ordered that the ancient one that was in use since the beginning be suppressed and that his own be used, threatening those who would dare to use still the old one and omit his own." According to John of Ephesus, "The clergy of all the churches, the convents and monasteries of men and women" were alarmed and troubled and the whole city was in revolt. When Justin II himself demanded to know why Eutychius had made his innovation, "changing the ancient customs," the patriarch responded, "Lord, what I composed is far more suitable than the old one." Although John of Ephesus depicts the emperor as prevailing against Eutychius, later evidence suggests otherwise. Liturgical historian Robert Taft believes that the troparion was promptly accepted into the liturgy in the years following Justin II's death in 578, and its place remained secure. Indeed, it remains an integral part of the Liturgy of St. John Chrysostom used regularly in Orthodox churches today.[3]

The objection which John of Ephesus describes presumably arose because the new hymn replaced a text that derived directly from the Bible, mostly likely an excerpt from Psalm 148. That standard and fixed Constantinopolitan communion hymn reads, "Praise the Lord from the heavens, praise him in the highest, Alleluia!"[4] Despite John's hostility to the new material, John reports (and here he is quite plausibly accurate) that Eutychius believed his substitution to be "far more suitable." Not only does this liturgical substitution reveal aspects of Eutychius's view of the liturgy, his innovation also reflects broader shifts in Christian self-understanding and liturgical formation in the sixth century, toward a greater emphasis on ritual performance as biblical reenactment.

The suitability of liturgical texts to their moment in the liturgical action had concerned Eutychius on at least one earlier occasion. A few years earlier, in a sermon titled "On Easter and the Holy Eucharist," Eutychius complained that the practice of chanting Psalm 24:7–10 during the Great Entrance seemed inappropriate. The text of the psalm reads: "Lift up your heads, O gates! and be lifted up, O ancient doors! that the King of Glory may come in." The Patriarch Eutychius regarded it as problematic to refer to the unconsecrated bread and wine carried during the procession to the altar as the King of Glory, since it had not been consecrated and had not yet become the body and blood of God. Eutychius had no objection to the psalm itself; in fact, the patriarch chanted these verses during the rededication of Hagia Sophia in 562, while entering the doors of the church. For Eutychius, the psalm was particularly apt here, while in the Great Entrance it was liturgically premature.[5]

In substituting the new hymn "At Your Mystical Supper" in place of a psalm text on Holy Thursday, Eutychius attempted to better integrate the words of prayer into the liturgical moment. Eutychius replaced a celebratory text emphasizing praise of the divine (a rather generic text appropriate at any time of year) with a text specifically invoking the dramatic action represented in the events of Holy Week. The new troparion called upon individual Christians not to be "like Judas," but rather to be "like the thief." The communicant calls on Christ to be accepted at the table as a repentant and redeemable sinner, not as Judas, whose kiss in the Garden of Gethsemane betrayed his Lord (Matthew 26:27), but rather as the thief crucified with Jesus at Golgotha (Luke 23:43), the one who asked Jesus to remember him, and to whom Jesus replied, "Truly I say to you, today you will be with me in Paradise."

The shift away from the biblical text of the psalm of praise to one that more fully embraces the biblical narrative inserts the members of the congregation into the liturgical drama at the appropriate point in the action. In regarding such a text as "far more suitable," Eutychius payed great attention to liturgy as performance. The new text provided an opportunity for communicants to enact their preference for one role in the biblical narrative over another. In distinguishing between Judas and the thief, the first associated with the Last Supper and the other with the Crucifixion, Eutychius's text encourages conformity with the identity of the thief, rather than the identity of Christ's betrayer. Despite its departure from a strictly biblical formula, the patriarch's new text attempted to shape the self-understanding of Christian communicants in greater conformity to the patterns of the liturgical calendar, tying the liturgical performance directly to the events being commemorated in the liturgy of Holy Thursday and about to be commemorated on Good Friday. Through the performance of the amended eucharistic rite, Eutychius's communicants approached the sacrament like characters in the biblical drama, reliving the life of Christ in the liturgy of the church. They aspired that when their lips touched the host, the body of Christ, it was not with the kiss of betrayal, but rather with devotion, feeding fully on their salvation. Eutychius demonstrates a particular interest in employing the liturgy in the formation of the Christian self, desiring to activate a specific Christian self-conception as redeemable sinner.

By articulating correspondence to the biblical past, emerging forms of piety shaped the experience of time and space, linking it to specific events both in the life of Christ and in the rest of the biblical narrative. The formation of Christian identity through typological correspondence with events in the biblical narrative had been a feature of Christian piety and practice since the earliest churches. Paul's congregations understood baptism as a dying and rising with Christ, and eucharist as a participation in the events of the night before Jesus died. And indeed, the second half of the fourth century saw not only the rapid increase in the number of Christian converts in the Roman Empire, but also a proliferation of the liturgical forms and catechetical instructions designed to situate Christian practice within the narrative of Christ's incarnation, life, crucifixion, death, resurrection, and ascension.[6] Not only did these events structure the Christian liturgical year from Christmas to Holy Week, Easter, and beyond, the liturgy served to construct a biblical reality, articulating and authenticating present Christian experience. Eutychius's adjustment to the liturgy fits this pattern and demonstrates sensitivity to the effectiveness of biblical typology in shaping Christian liturgical experience. As we shall see in a moment, the biblicization of Christian life can also be seen in the expansion of other forms of later sixth-century piety, especially in pilgrimage. In the eucharist itself, the effort to strengthen the connection between the liturgical performance and the biblical narrative to which it made persistent reference received visual expression in the Riha Paten. This silver repoussé plate with gilding and niello was crafted in Constantinople during the reign of Justin II for holding the eucharistic bread during the offering, consecration, and distribution (Plate x). The scene represented is the Communion of the Apostles. Here Jesus is depicted twice, distributing both the bread and the wine to his disciples at the Last Supper. Significantly, the Last Supper is depicted not merely as a historical event, but rather as a type for the ceremony in which the paten itself was to be employed. Jesus presides behind an altar table laid with a sumptuous cloth, a chalice, a paten, and other vessels necessary to the performance of the eucharistic rite. Like those hearing Eutychius's new chant, the Riha Paten called on the viewer to insert himself as a player in the biblical scene.

The trend toward increased reference to biblical history in the liturgy, which one scholar has called a "historicization," was not the only shift toward a richer configuration of liturgical experience.[7] The sixth century also saw a more mysticizing trend. The treatises *On the Ecclesiastical Hierarchy* and *On the Celestial Hierarchy* were most likely composed in the decade preceding 528, although they were attributed to Dionysius the Areopagite, a first-century student of Paul. The author emphasized that the eucharist both symbolized and effected the unity of divinity and humanity and conceived of the liturgy of the church as a participation in the eternal liturgy of heaven.[8] The connection to the angelic liturgy, already present in the New Testament book of Hebrews and famously articulated in the fourth century by John Chrysostom, found emphasis in the script for the Divine Liturgy in the years after the death of Justinian.[9]

The addition of the Cherubic Hymn, or *Cherubikon*, to the liturgy in 573–574 under the patriarch John III Scholasticus enhanced the impact of the eucharistic rite by pointing to heaven. An offertory hymn sung during the transfer of the bread and the wine to the altar, the

Cherubic Hymn invokes the eternal liturgy of the angels who encircle the throne of God: "We who mystically represent the Cherubim and sing the thrice-holy hymn to the life-giving Trinity, let us lay aside all worldly care to receive the King of All escorted unseen by the angelic corps. Alleluia."[10] The congregation's "mystical representation" of the angels moved beyond mere role playing to a true inhabiting of the scripted role. The Cherubic Hymn makes explicit reference to the biblical *Trisagion*, or Thrice Holy Prayer ("Holy, Holy, Holy Lord of Hosts, the whole earth is full of His glory"), which according to Isaiah 6:3 is sung by the angels circling the throne of God in heaven. The *Trisagion* had entered the liturgy, with some initial controversy, in the course of the fifth century. John Scholasticus's addition of the new Cherubic Hymn emphasized the point of singing the *Trisagion*. The *Cherubikon* made explicit what the performance of the angels' thrice-holy prayer left implicit, namely that those who sang the *Trisagion* joined themselves to the singing of the angels. By the logic of mystical representation, the Byzantine communicants participated in the heavenly liturgy, joining themselves not to the biblical past, but to the eternal present of God's divine choir.

The two hymns added in the fifteen years after the death of Justinian, "At Your Mystical Supper" and the *Cherubikon*, employ methods of figuration that correspond to long-established patterns of Christian scriptural interpretation. The first employs typology, connecting events to the biblical past, especially to the life of Christ; the second employs anagogy, a "drawing upward," referring ultimately to heavenly realities. It is worth emphasizing that neither of these techniques is literal: the eucharistic service is not literally taking place in the past, nor in the throne room of heaven. Rather the two hymns employ two different forms of allegory, invoking biblical and heavenly realities through performance. Eutychius's sensitivity to the liturgical season of Holy Week manifests his desire for a text more appropriate to the representation of the Last Supper.

Much recent scholarship in the study of religion has explored the category of performance to understand how religious practices produce, articulate and maintain norms for self-understanding and self-presentation within a given culture. In a manner analogous to theater, ritual activities involve the playing and ultimately the inhabiting of the mythic roles of sacred narrative.[11] Eutychius's hymn encourages a form of role playing in which participants figure themselves in attendance "at your mystical feast" hoping to be received "like" or "as if" they were the thief. The analogy here constructs identity with the past rather than emphasizing the difference between the present and the past. This typological self-positioning employs performance as a technology through which Christians might conform themselves to appropriate biblical models while rejecting others. Various other liturgical celebrations and lay practices introduced, interpreted, or expanded in the course of the sixth century employed this logic of performance in the formation of Christian self-understanding.

## *Romanos the Melodist and the Night Vigil*

Biblical narratives also provided inspiration for liturgical services outside the Divine Liturgy itself. Presentations of biblical models exhibited their formative power perhaps most eloquently in the hymns of Romanos the Melodist. Romanos arrived in Constantinople from Syria during the reign of Anastasius I (491–518). He served as cantor and composer at the Church of the Theotokos in the Kyrou district in the northwest of the capital through much of the reign of Justinian, dying sometime after 555. During his career, he provided the city with a wealth of liturgical hymns that imagined, enacted, and expanded scenes from biblical stories. Most of Romanos's sixty surviving hymns are lengthy chanted verse sermons keyed to specific days on the liturgical calendar, either to feasts in the cycle of the life of Christ or to the lectionary, the system assigning biblical readings to particular weeks of the year. Romanos's monumental achievement lay in his integration of liturgical performance and the liturgical calendar. In his hymns composed for the night vigils preceding the various Christological festivals, Romanos moved beyond inserting the Christian directly into the role of single characters. His poems combined typology with dialogue, allowing Romanos to dramatize the biblical narrative as an opportunity for theological reflection and for greater emotional involvement.

The context for his performances was the increasingly popular office of the night vigil, during which crowds of laypeople would join clergy at urban churches to anticipate the festivals of the Church.[12] In one hymn, Romanos describes the scene:

> The people, faithful in their love of Christ,
> have gathered to keep a night-long vigil with psalms and odes;
> unceasingly they sing hymns to God.
> So, now that [the Psalms of] David ha[ve] been sung
> and we rejoiced in the well-ordered reading of Scripture,

> Now let us raise a hymn to Christ and pillory the enemy [i.e., the Devil].
> For this is our lyre of understanding,
> and in this understanding Christ is our leader and teacher –
> he is the Master of All.[13]

Within the structure of the night vigil service, Romanos's hymns respond to a specific sequence of scriptural passages. The Gospel reading was the service's centerpiece, approached by the antiphonal chanting of psalms and the singing of familiar hymns. Then came Romanos's sung homily, during which a choir, or perhaps the entire assembly, would join in the refrain. The vigil likely continued with additional prayers and songs. In the passage quoted, Romanos explicitly likens his composition within the structure of the service to the psalmody that preceded the biblical lection. From the pulpit, the poet sings like David with the lyre, to search the deeper meaning of the biblical text.

In one of his most famous hymns, composed for the Christmas Eve vigil, Romanos heightens the drama through the use of the first person, temporal markers like "today," and verbs in the present tense.

> Today the Virgin gives birth to him who is above all being,
> and the earth offers a cave to him whom no one can approach.
> Angels with shepherds give glory,
> and magi journey with a star
> . . .
> (Prelude)
>
> Bethlehem has opened Eden, come, let us see;
> we have found delight in secret, come, let us receive. (1)

The events take place "today," in the liturgical present. In attendance at the nativity of Christ, Romanos invites the congregation to play witness to the action as if it were happening at this very moment.

Through dialogue especially, Romanos is able to render the biblical action in the here and now. The power of this technique for prompting and maintaining his audience's involvement in the tension of the biblical action proves most effective in Romanos's hymn "On Mary at the Cross," composed for the night vigil preceding Good Friday. Here the poet invents an extended conversation between Christ and his mother while the savior prepares to die on the cross. The poet invites his audience not only to observe Mary's anguish, but to share in it.[14]

Romanos also employs this anguish to articulate a theology of the crucifixion, as he uses the person of Mary to pose to Jesus himself the question, "Why did the savior have to die?" Romanos begins his prelude by emphasizing Mary's looking:

> Come, let us all praise him who was crucified for us,
> for Mary looked upon him on the Tree and said,
> "Though you endure the Cross, yet you are my Son and my
> God." (Prelude)

The last line, which serves as the refrain for all seventeen stanzas to follow, encapsulates the paradox of Mary's identity as the Theotokos, the one who gave birth to God. Romanos calls attention not only to Christ's suffering as the lamb of God, but to Mary's as well. And her confusion at her son's willingness to die shapes a theological probing of the crucifixion itself.

> As she saw her own lamb being dragged to slaughter,
> Mary, the ewe-lamb, worn out with grief, followed
> with the other women, crying out,
> "Where are you going, my child? For whose sake are you
> running this course so fast?" (1)

Through Mary's voice, the poet reminds the audience of Christ's innocence ("You are on your way, my child, to unjust slaughter") and his abandonment by his disciples, including Peter and Thomas. Through the course of the dialogue, Christ answers Mary and encourages her to put away her grief and focus on the triumph of his willing suffering.

> As Mary from her deep grief
> and great sorrow cried out thus and wept, he turned
> to her, he that had come from her, and cried,
> "Why are you weeping, Mother? Why are you carried away like
> the other women?
> Should I not suffer? Not die? How then shall I save Adam?" (4)

He explains to her the essential content of Good Friday, "In flesh I suffer, and in flesh I save" (6). Yet an intellectual apprehension of the crucifixion is not sufficient in itself, and the dialogue charts Mary's evolving emotional reconciliation to the death of her son. She tells him,

> "If I speak once more, do not become angry with me.
> I shall tell you what is on my mind, so that I may learn from you
> all that I wish.
> If you suffer, if you die, will you return to me?
> . . . . . . . . . . . . . . . . . . . . . . . . . . . . . . . . .
> "Shall I see you again?
> For this is what I fear." (11)

Jesus counsels her to have courage and patience while he accomplishes all the things that he must, fulfilling his Father's plan for the salvation of humanity: to die, to descend into Hell to conquer the Devil, and to rescue Adam and Eve by curing them of their mortality. The course of the dialogue charts Mary's transformation from lamenting mother to steadfast witness. As a beneficiary of the victory of divine love, Mary finally declares, "Let me come with you, for to see you heals me" (15). Using the persona of Mary, Romanos prepares his congregants to witness the events on the cross to be commemorated and performed in the Good Friday liturgy. Through dialectic, Romanos deepens both the theological and the emotional dimensions of the events.

Romanos's hymns do not merely rehash the biblical stories but rather plumb their dramatic depths for the characters involved. In their turn, the poems invite the listeners to enter into the story by identifying with Christ's interlocutors, with Peter, Thomas, the sinful woman, even with Judas.[15] By voicing the congregation's concerns through the mouths of these biblical players, Romanos allows for theological reflection and character development.[16] The festal hymns of Romanos the Melodist demonstrate how the emerging office of the night vigil provided opportunities for Christians to enter into the drama of the liturgical calendar. By amplifying and articulating the essential content of the festivals, Romanos added to the spectacle a dramatic and probing reencounter between the characters of the biblical narrative.

## *Processional Liturgies and the Urban Landscape*

Religious processions further enhanced the sanctification of time, and particularly of space. Liturgical parades had been a common feature of Christian practice in the city of Jerusalem already in the second half of the fourth century. Stational liturgies spread to Rome shortly thereafter as Christians marked that city as a Christian landscape.[17] By the sixth century such festive movement through the space of church buildings during the Divine Liturgy and marches from point to point within the city had become major aspects of Constantinopolitan worship as well. The sixth-century eucharistic service featured two processions. During the Liturgy of the Word (the first half of the Divine Liturgy, dedicated to the readings from scripture), deacons and priests processed with the Gospel book from the altar to the nave of the church, where the laity were gathered, then back into the sanctuary of the church, to the altar. This Little Entrance symbolized Christ's coming as the Word of God among the people in the incarnation. (The mosaics at San Vitale in Ravenna depict Justinian and Theodora participating in the Little Entrance [Plates III and IV]). The second procession, or Great Entrance, began the second half of the Divine Liturgy, the eucharistic service itself, with even greater pomp and ceremony. During this offertory, a deacon carried a paten with the eucharistic bread and a priest carried a chalice with the wine from the sacristy into the nave and then to the altar, symbolizing Christ's coming in the sacrament of his body and blood. These liturgical features influenced church architecture. Hagia Sophia in particular was designed to accommodate such elaborate liturgical processions better than the old basilica it replaced.[18]

Out of doors, Christians witnessed and participated in stational liturgies that processed from church to church through the various neighborhoods of the capital.[19] As the *Chronography* of Theophanes Confessor records, these processions were not limited to the festivals of the church; some arose in response to natural disasters. Constantinopolitans marched annually to commemorate an earthquake that had occurred in 554.[20] During a drought in August 562, the patriarch Eutychius led a procession out of the Church of St. Diomedes just beyond the Golden Gate, no doubt with prayers for rain.[21] Processions celebrated the dedications of churches. Constantinopolitans marched through the streets of the city for both the dedication and the rededication of Hagia Sophia. A procession carried relics formerly housed at Hagia Sophia to a new Church of Saint Irene across the Golden Horn.[22] Many processions involved both members of the clergy and members of the imperial family, indicating that the increase in ceremonial became an occasion for the display of both the emperor's piety and his political power. In one case the emperor and patriarch rode together in a chariot after an all-night vigil at the Church of St. Plato.[23] An emperor might even declare a procession after a military success: Emperor Maurice inaugurated an annual procession to the Church of the Virgin at Blachernae to mark the defeat of Khusro I in 588.[24] Such parades employed the entire urban landscape in the service of God.

## Lay Pieties and Practices

### *Pilgrims' Piety*

The second half of the sixth century witnessed an increased interest in pilgrimage to the Holy Land and to saints' shrines around the eastern Mediterranean basin as well as a shift in emphasis from a principally visual piety to one both visual and tactile. Christians had set forth on spiritually motivated journeys since Constantine the Great built major churches in Jerusalem and Bethlehem. Fourth-century travelers such as Egeria and Paula had desired principally to *see* the places where the events of the Old Testament and the life of Christ had taken place.[25] Pilgrims also traveled to see living holy men in action, living lives of remarkable asceticism. Laity and monastics alike toured the monasteries and hermitages of the Egyptian desert or journeyed to the hill in northwestern Syria, where, in the first half of the fifth century, Symeon the Stylite had stood atop a series of pillars. Such pilgrimages continued and were elaborated through the fifth century and into the sixth. By the reign of Justinian, religiously motivated travel to the Holy Land was common enough to become a literary trope in saints' lives. According to a biography composed shortly after his death in 564, Nicholas of Sion had made two pilgrimages to Jerusalem, "to adore the venerable wood of the Holy Cross and all the Holy Places."[26] Holy places, holy people, and the shrines associated with their tombs served as repositories of spiritual power which pilgrims could access through visitation, and increasingly through touch.

At play in the minds of these early Byzantine Christian travelers was the concept of the *eulogia*, whose primary sense of "blessing" or "benediction" came by extension to signify any conduit for transferring the divine or saintly power to others.[27] The *eulogia* became concrete in physical matter such as the bread of the eucharist, holy water or oil, and more mundane objects that a holy man had consecrated or blessed. The term also applied to the vessels, ampullae, and boxes in which such holy substances were stored or transported. More than souvenirs, these *eulogiai* were pieces of "portable sanctity,"[28] as effective as verbal blessing itself in transferring benefit to the faithful. That the term *eulogia* also referred to the consecrated host suggests that the therapeutic powers attached to the oil and earth collected by pilgrims applied also to the eucharist, itself a material substance able to convey health and salvation.

The greater emphasis on a tactile piety can be seen in the account composed by a pilgrim from the Italian town of Piacenza who traveled to the Holy Land around 570.[29] This pilgrim desired contact with the biblical narrative through materiality itself. Of his visit to Cana, "where the Lord attended a wedding" and changed water into wine, the Piacenza pilgrim reports that he reclined on the wedding couch and wrote the names of his parents on it. He filled one of the water pots, "which are still there," with wine and lifted it onto his shoulders. "I offered it at the altar, and we washed in the spring to gain a blessing" (4). He sat on the bench in Nazareth where the young Jesus sat (5). The goal extended beyond merely touching holy things to include obtaining bits of holy matter to take home. At the Lord's tomb, the scene of the resurrection, the Piacenza pilgrim reports, "Earth is brought to the tomb and put inside, and those who go in take some as a blessing" (18). Near Golgotha, he visited the basilica housing the Wood of the True Cross, upon which Christ had been crucified. Pilgrims knelt to kiss the wood and handled the placard that was nailed above Jesus' head reading "This is the King of the Jews." The faithful offered flasks filled with oil to receive the blessing of holiness through proximity to the cross, like an electric charge. "When the mouth of one of the little flasks touches the Wood of the Cross, the oil instantly bubbles over, and unless it is closed very quickly it all spills out" (20).

Material evidence corroborates this account of pilgrims' practices and offers further insight into the piety that sustained them. Around 600 a pilgrim visiting Jerusalem obtained a small lead flask or ampulla (4.6 cm) filled with oil that had come into contact with the wood of the cross. The object, now flattened and missing its neck, was cast with images on both sides signifying its contents (Plates xi and xii).[30] One side recalls the scene of the crucifixion at Golgotha as it might have appeared in the pilgrims' imagination or experience. The bust of Jesus hovers above an equal-armed cross. On the left and the right are the two thieves who were crucified with Jesus, grounding the scene in the historical past. But the scene also invokes the pilgrims' present. At the foot of the shaft supporting the cross, two figures venerate the True Cross, as pilgrims drawn to the life-giving spot. The inscription surrounding the image indicates the vessel's function and significance within the system of pilgrims' practices: "Oil of the Wood of Life of the Holy Places of Christ." The ampulla was manufactured to contain and transport oil collected at Golgotha, just as the Piacenza pilgrim describes. Pilgrims regarded this oil as a precious and life-giving substance; thus contained, the oil could be taken home and later used to assist in healing or to anoint the dead.

The ampulla's other side depicts another most important destination on the pilgrims' itinerary and its corresponding biblical referent. On Easter Sunday, the two Marys approach the tomb of Christ to anoint him properly. As they arrive, they are greeted by an angel of the Lord (on the left), who informs them that Christ has risen from the dead. The inscription above declares, "The Lord is risen." However, as Gary Vikan has noted, "the iconography is heavily weighted toward the contemporary Tomb relic at the expense of the Bible text."[31] The women carry not a spice jar, but rather a swinging censer, and the tomb itself is surmounted by a dome supported by columns. The scene depicts the architectural structure of the Anastasis (Resurrection) Rotunda as it had looked since the fourth century, and which the flask's owner would have seen when visiting the spot. The images thus connect the biblical past with the pilgrims' present. The women approaching the tomb function as stand-ins for the pilgrims themselves, as visitors to the tomb. As with the hymn "At Your Mystical Supper" and the vigil hymns of Romanos, pilgrimage invited participation in the biblical narrative through witnessing and reenactment. Jerusalem pilgrims inserted themselves into the biblical narrative by kneeling at the cross and approaching the tomb of the resurrection. Other pilgrims' *eulogiai* depicting the adoration of the magi suggest that pilgrims also understood themselves as latter-day wise men when they visited the spot where Jesus had been born to the Virgin Mary in Bethlehem.[32]

In addition to oil from the site of the True Cross, pilgrims collected water from the Jordan and dirt from the tomb of the resurrection. They placed these materials in containers, ampullae and boxes, in which they could transport them. The physical association of this spiritually charged matter with biblical sites conferred blessings upon those who possessed them or came into contact with them. The images and inscriptions on the containers explained and certified the sacred origin of the contents. Another pilgrim who also traveled around 600 brought back from Palestine a painted box with a sliding lid, now in the Museo Sacro of the Vatican (Plate xiii and Plate V).[33] Like the people witnessed by the Piacenza pilgrim, the owner of this box collected blessings in material form at many holy places while traveling. Inside the box are stones, dirt, wood, and cloth. The stones set into the interior's clay floor bear the inscriptions "From Bethlehem," "From Zion," "From the place of the Resurrection," and "From the Mount of Olives." These truly are bits of the Holy Land. The images painted in tempera and gold leaf on the lid attest to the origins of the contents in the Holy Land. Reading from lower left to upper right, they depict the nativity of Christ, his Baptism, his Crucifixion, the women arriving at his empty tomb to discover his resurrection, and his ascension into heaven on the Mount of Olives. The sequence not only refers to events from the life of Christ, but also alludes to the pilgrim's itinerary, during which he or she visited Bethlehem, the Jordan, Golgotha, the Church of the Anastasis (or Resurrection), and the Mount of Olives. As with the ampulla discussed above, the image of Christ's tomb depicts it not as it might have been in the first century, but rather how the dome over the tomb appeared at the time the pilgrim visited. The pilgrim's quest involved the procurement and transport of holy *stuff*. Moreover, the itinerary described the life of Christ not merely as preserved in the Gospels, but also as celebrated in the liturgical calendar of the church. The pilgrim's desire to visit these sites and expectations about what might be seen there had been formed and fed through years of participation in the annual cycle of Christological festivals: Christmas, Epiphany, Good Friday, Easter, and Ascension.

The proliferation of pilgrims' ampullae made of lead or clay surviving from the final decades of the sixth century and the early seventh demonstrate similar practices not only at Christological sites in the Holy Land, but also at shrines of a number of saints, including the shrine of Saint Menas across Lake Mareotis from Alexandria, a nearby shrine of Saint Thecla as well as her more traditional shrine at Seleucia in Isauria, and the shrine of Saint John the Evangelist at Ephesus, to name a few.[34] From these sites pilgrims collected holy water, oil, and in the case of Saint John, the dust from his tomb. Such substances might protect the traveler or cure the sick.

## *The Cult of the Saints: Shrines and Therapies*

Sixth-century Christians inhabited a world in which the miraculous was possible, and they employed many technologies for securing divine assistance. Like their pagan and Jewish precursors and contemporaries, sixth-century Christians continued to cast binding spells by inscribing curses on lead or papyrus to conjure the spirits who might help or harm them. They did so despite nominal condemnation from church and civil authorities and even persistent opposition from local holy men.[35] A great number of Christian "magical" texts survive on papyri from Egypt. These often invoke Christ and the angels and employ quotations from the Bible or the Christian liturgy, as well as Christian symbols such as the cross or the Chi-Rho. Amulets were intended to protect people or houses from evil spirits, while oracular texts sought to determine the future or the will of God.[36] Christians chanted spells – spells for healing, for protection from illness and evil, on their own behalf and for their children. They performed spells to assist in their erotic exploits, as well as curses to effect vengeance against their personal enemies. One sixth-century lead tablet from Dalmatia, designed to be worn as an amulet, begins with and ends with inscribed crosses. "In the name of the Lord, Jesus Christ," the curse denounces the "most foul spirit of Tartarus, whom the angel Gabriel bound with burning fetters." The text employs the River Jordan as a metaphor for the boundary between this world and hell and adjures the evil spirit to stay on the other side. The lead may have actually have been dipped in water from the Jordan obtained by a pilgrim.[37] Together with the church-sanctioned cults centered on relics and shrines and the wearing of amulets, the spells and their paraphernalia reinforce the view that many forms of Christian practice centered on seeking solutions to and therapies for everyday problems.

The therapeutic aspect of Christian practice was part of the cult of the saints. Saints' biographies recount healing and cures wrought by holy men both living and dead. These texts reinforced a worldview that both accounted for misfortune and prescribed technologies to avoid it. Such piety directed itself to the most practical of concerns: physical and mental illness, commerce and agriculture. The apparent efficacy of the cults of the saints, together with amulets, reliquaries, and magical texts, is well attested by their persistent employment. This aspect of early Byzantine religion was fundamentally therapeutic, directed toward remedies and solutions to basic human problems.

Among the thirty or so churches that Justinian commissioned for the city of Constantinople were a number dedicated to saints already popular in other parts of the empire.[38] Justinian and Theodora imported the cult of Saint Sergius from Resafa on the Syrian frontier to the imperial capital, building a remarkable octagonal church to him and his companion Bacchus near the imperial palace.[39] Justinian also erected churches to Saint Theodore, popular in Pontus, and another to Saint Thecla of Isauria.[40] Each of these foundations almost certainly involved the transfer of relics of the various saints to the capital city, transforming local or regional cults into imperial, and empirewide, phenomena.

Christians prayed and visited the shrines of saints in search of healing or protection. The emperor was no exception. One popular

Constantinopolitan healing shrine that came to prominence in the period was the Church of Cosmas and Damian, on a steep escarpment just above the Golden Horn (at modern Eyüp). A modest church had been erected on the spot in 439. The historian Procopius writes that "when the emperor himself once lay seriously ill, giving the appearance of being actually dead (in fact he had been given up by the physicians as being already numbered among the dead), these saints came to him here in a vision, and saved him unexpectedly and contrary to all human reason raised him up." Moreover, Justinian's cure was far from unique. Procopius continues by observing the general popularity of the shrine: "When any persons find themselves assailed by illnesses which are beyond the control of physicians, in despair of human assistance they take refuge in the one hope left to them, and getting on flat-boats they are carried up the bay to this very church." Justinian's miraculous cure occurred in a typical way, while the ailing suppliant slept at the shrine hoping for healing. This practice of incubation had its origins in ancient pagan cult and continued to be practiced into the fourth century at the shrine of Asclepius in Cilicia and at Epidaurus. By the fifth century, the practice had emerged in Christian form at the shrine of Saint Thecla at Seleucia.

According to Procopius, after his cure, Justinian "entirely changed and remodeled the earlier building" as a token of his gratitude.[41] With the infusion of imperial patronage, the shrine of Cosmas and Damian became a popular venue of last resort for the sick, the lame, and the possessed. According to legend, Cosmas and Damian had been doctors, and their work at the shrine emphasized how blurry the line might be between medicine and miracle. The sick would come to sleep in the shine's atrium and porticoes and pray during the day in the church itself. Attendants at the shrine collected wax and oil to prepare a salve called *kērōtē*, which they distributed to the suppliants during vigils on Saturday night. The ailing smeared the paste on their afflicted parts or ingested it. Many then waited to have the saints appear to them in a dream and heal them. At first, accounts of the miraculous cures worked at the shrine circulated orally: the healed returned to the shrine during its weekly vigils to testify to the shrine's efficacy, to glorify God, and to express their thanks to the saints through whom God worked their cure. The earliest written collections of miracles worked at the shrine were known to Sophronius, the patriarch of Jerusalem from 634–637, and thus were likely to have been composed before the end of the sixth century.[42]

Unlike the shrine of Saint Artemios, popular during the seventh century, which specialized nearly exclusively in male genital ailments, the Church of Cosmas and Damian engaged in general practice, treating a wide variety of conditions. According to the collections of miracle tales, the saintly pair cured people suffering from dropsy, demonic possession, paralysis, cancers, and abscessed bowels. They cured a deaf-mute and a man coughing up blood. In addition to Christians, they cured a Jew and a worshipper of Castor and Pollux, both of whom they converted. They healed across a wide range of social classes.

Cures were wrought in ways that seem peculiar to the modern reader, although they resemble the techniques of folk medicine. Nearly all involved the application or ingestion of some simple material substance available at the shrine. The *Miracles of Cosmas and Damian* itself displays a consciousness of how amusing some of the prescriptions might be. In one account, a gentleman associated with the imperial court suffered from a problem with urinary retention. The saints appeared to him in a dream and advised him to obtain some of Cosmas's pubic hair, burn it and mix it well with water, and drink it. Puzzled and greatly embarrassed, the courtier searched the church for such an odd bodily relic. Eventually he came across a shepherd who had brought to the shrine a lamb whom he had named for Saint Cosmas. Here was the solution! With a snip of the scissors at the right bit of the lamb's hairs, the man concocted and drank his medicine. Immediately and painlessly he released a huge amount of urine and was cured.

Devotees brought votives to shrines in thanksgiving for the receipt of miracles as well as other offerings. Saint Sabas was the founder of the monastic complex known as the Great Lavra (now Mar Saba monastery) in the Judean desert. In the years after his death in 532 many faithful visited his tomb, where Sabas's body was said to remain "sound and incorrupt."[43] Some brought votives to this and to nearby shines as a token in return for the saint's assistance. Cyril of Scythopolis, author of the *Life of Sabas* and a resident of the Great Lavra, tells of a circle of women who wove curtains for the nearby monasteries of Castellium and the Cave and presented them as offerings (80). A Saracen camel driver made yearly visits to the lavra to thank Sabas for keeping his camels safe on the treacherous path leading up from the Dead Sea to the monastery (82). Others made prayers to Sabas from afar to intercede with Christ on their behalf regarding their misfortunes. Two farmers became so ill at harvest time that they could not work. After they called on Sabas for intercession, the saint appeared to them in dream visions and brought news of their cures. On the anniversary of the receipt of their miracle, the beneficiaries would celebrate a public festival on their estate (79). Votives could take many forms; the edge of the Riha Paten bears an inscription indicating that it was donated to effect the repose of the souls of deceased members of a family and to insure the health and salvation of others: "For the peace of the soul of Sergia, [daughter] of John, and of Theodosius, and for the salvation of Megalos and Nonnous and their children" (Plate x).

The *Life of Nicholas of Sion* offers a sixth-century model of sanctity as well as rare glimpses into aspects of rural piety. Composed in the 560s, this biography of the abbot of the Monastery of Holy Sion in the hills above the Lycian port of Myra on the southwestern coast of Asia Minor reveals ongoing tensions with persisting pagan conceptions of the landscape. Pagan shrines and sacred trees and springs dedicated to the traditional spirits still filled Nicholas's world. The local population, only recently converted to Christianity, still regarded them as powerful. In the *Life*, Nicholas sets about ridding the landscape of these haunts for demons. Nicholas fells a sacred tree that the recently Christianized population has come to view as the source of many problems in the community and exorcizes unclean spirits from people, performing one of the standard functions of living local holy men (15–19, 26). And yet the Christianity that had come to this corner of Lycia continued to resemble the earlier rural paganism it replaced. Traditions of animal sacrifice endured, and Nicholas slaughters oxen at shrines in the surrounding villages to the Angel Gabriel, and to Saints George, Theodore, Michael, Apphianos, Demetrios, Irene, and Nicholas; Daniel the Prophet; and the Virgin. The focus of the cult had shifted, but many of the forms of pagan worship endured.

In many ways, Nicholas is a conventional saint: as in earlier saints' lives, the biographer represents the life of his hero through illustrating a great number of typological correspondences between the life of Nicholas and the life of Jesus. He calms a sea storm (30). His last words echo those of Christ on the Cross (78). Some of these Christological parallels demonstrate the hopes placed in the holy man under conditions of rural poverty and scarce food during times of famine. Like Jesus, Nicholas performs not one but two miraculous feedings. Once, he feeds an entourage of clerics by multiplying three loaves and three pints of wine, and later he blesses a single loaf of bread to feed a large team of craftsmen employed to build the shrine of Holy Sion (25, 45). The author presents Nicholas as an appropriate object of local veneration. A piety regarding holy men as living imitators of the incarnate Christ represented the potential for humans to live in conformity to the Gospel.

The Shrine of Holy Sion had been founded a generation earlier by a monk also named Nicholas as "a memorial and for the propitiation of his sins." By naming it for Zion itself, the founder attempted to bring the Holy Land closer to home, a local Zion. The connection is reinforced as the younger Nicholas himself goes on pilgrimage to Jerusalem. By the text's account, the church was "a glorious shrine," and Nicholas "loved this spot as greatly as if it were God's paradise. For there has appeared to him an angel of the Lord, saying: 'This spot is an antitype [or counterpart] of Holy Sion in Jerusalem'" (10). Even in remote regions of Justinian's empire, typology exerted the power to transform Christians' experience of their surroundings in terms of the biblical narrative. With the landscape's pagan impulses neutralized, albeit through a curious incorporation, the light of Holy Sion shined forth from Nicholas's shrine.

## *The Emergence of Icon Piety*

Long before iconoclasm, images played a significant role in Christian piety. Images of the saints appeared on pilgrims' ampullae. Art appeared on walls of churches in frescoes and mosaic, illustrating biblical scenes and depicting Christ and the saints. The sixth century also saw the spread of religious practices employing and often directed toward visual representations of holy men and women separate from their association with material substances. The apotropaic and therapeutic use of images, perhaps more than their use in worship, expanded greatly in the reign of Justinian and especially shortly thereafter, despite lacking a well-articulated theological rationale of the sort that would develop during and after the iconoclasm of the eighth and ninth centuries, when the veneration of icons became a firmly rooted practice distinctive of Byzantine Christianity. The cult of images that emerged in the sixth century bears striking relationship to the tactile piety already discussed, as the images of the saints were believed to render the saints present, and the material substances that bore their images were in turn believed to contain miraculous power.[44]

In a passage preserved in the *Greek Anthology*, the historian Agathias explains that an image of the archangel Michael in the Plate neighborhood of Constantinople encouraged contemplation and prayer.[45] But more evidence from this period points in the direction of less intellectual practices associated with icons. Images played a role in the cult of Symeon the Younger Stylite (521–592), who imitated the fifth-century Symeon the Elder by standing atop a pillar on the Wondrous Mountain, not far from the city of Antioch. According to the *Life of Symeon the Younger*, a woman childless after twenty years of marriage traveled from Rhosopolis in Cilicia to see the saint, who drove out a demon that had possessed her. When she returned home, the woman "set up an image of the saint in the inner part of her house." Subsequently the image itself began to perform miracles. Many locals came to see the image, believing that if only they could see Symeon's likeness, they would be healed.[46] An artisan from the city of Antioch whom the saint had exorcized set up an image of Symeon above the door of his workshop, adorned with lamps and a curtain.[47] In popular devotion to the saints, their images could stand in for the saints themselves, offering both healing and protection like *eulogiai* or amulets.

Nor was this piety limited to the cult of Symeon the Younger. According to the *Miracles of Cosmas and Damian*, a military officer from Constantinople carried an image of the two saints with him when he was stationed abroad, through which the saints were said to be present with their miracle-working power.[48] A woman who had been healed at the shrine itself proceeded to paint images of the saints "on all the walls of her house, being as she was insatiable in her desire of seeing them." Once suffering from a serious case of colic, she scraped some of the plaster from one of the images with her fingernails, put it in water and drank it. According to the text, "she was immediately cured of her pains by the visitation of the saints."[49] By the early seventh century, copies of the portrait of Saint Demetrius in his church in Thessalonica proliferated widely.[50]

The sixth century saw broad shifts in the practice of Christianity in Byzantium. While earlier forms of piety continued, patterns of Christian devotion in the reign of Justinian and, perhaps especially, in the subsequent decades transformed Christianity in the eastern Mediterranean from a late Roman enterprise to a more distinctively Byzantine one. Liturgical innovations and evolving modes of practice reveal the formation of a Chalcedonian Christian identity expressed through increased contact with the biblical narrative and with the maturing logic of a tactile and therapeutic piety. The adjustment of established practices and the introduction of new ones set about the formation of Byzantine orthodoxy, not merely a distinctive system of thought, but also a distinctive pattern of Christian practice. Through liturgical innovation, increased interest in pilgrimage and healing shrines, and the rise of icons, sixth-century Byzantine Christians remade the patterns of their piety and practice.

## Notes

1 Robert F. Taft, *The Precommunion Rites*, Orientalia Christiana Analecta 261 (Rome, 2000), 307–313; Taft, *The Great Entrance: A History of the Transfer of Gifts and Other Preanaphoral Rites of the Liturgy of St. John Chrysostom*, 2nd ed., Orientalia Christiana Analecta 200 (Rome, 1978), 54, 68–70, 487–488; and Thomas H. Schattauer, "The Koinonicon of the Byzantine Liturgy: An Historical Study," *OCP* 49 (1983): 109–110.

2 John of Ephesus, *Ecclesiastical History: Part 3*, ed. E. W. Brooks, CSCO 105–106: Scriptores Syri 54–55 (1935–1936; Louvain, 1952), 107–108; translation, 78; and see Taft, *Precommunion Rites*, 310; Writing in the twelfth century, George Cedrenus (*Historiarum Compendium*, PG 121:784) reported that Justin II introduced the troparion "At Your Mystical Supper" into the celebrations of Holy Thursday in 573–574, but there is no reason to prefer his account to that of John of Ephesus.

3 *Liturgies Eastern and Western*, ed. F. E. Brightman (Oxford, 1896; reprint, 1965), 1:394; and Taft, *Great Entrance*, 85–86, 98–112.

4 Schattauer, "Koinonicon," 101–103; Taft, *Precommunion Rites*, 305–306.

5 Taft, *Great Entrance*, 98–112.

6 See Jean Daniélou, *The Bible and the Liturgy* (1951; Notre Dame, Ind., 1956). Thomas Merton, "Time and the Liturgy," in *Seasons of Celebration* (New York, 1977), 45–61.

7 Paul Meyendorff, "Eastern Liturgical Theology," in *Christian Spirituality: Origins to the Twelfth Century*, ed. Bernard McGinn and John Meyendorff (New York, 1985), 350–363.

8 Text: Pseudo-Dionysius, *Corpus Dionysiacum*, ed. Beate Suchla et al., 2 vols. (Berlin, 1990–1991); translation: Pseudo-Dionysius, *The Complete Works*, trans. Colm Luibheid with forward and notes by Paul Rorem (New York, 1987). On the date, see Paul Rorem and John C. Lamoreaux, *John of Scythopolis and the Dionysian Corpus: Annotating the Areopagite* (Oxford, 1998), 9–11.

9 John Chrysostom, *On the Priesthood*, 3.4 (NPNF 1.9). Georgia Frank, "'Taste and See': The Eucharist and the Eyes of Faith in the Fourth Century," *Church History* 70 (2001): 619–643.

10 Taft, *Great Entrance*, 54–118.

11 On performance studies, see Catherine Bell, "Performance," in *Critical Terms for Religious Studies*, ed. Mark C. Taylor (Chicago, 1998), 205–224; Thomas F. Driver, *Liberating Rites: Understanding the Transformative Power of Ritual* (1990; Boulder, Colo., 1998); and Pierre Bourdieu, *The Logic of Practice*, trans. Richard Nice (Cambridge, 1990).

12 *Sancti Romani Melodi Cantica: Cantica Genuina*, ed. Paul Maas and C. A. Trypanis (Oxford, 1963) (hereafter, Romanos, *Hymns*). Translations of selected hymns are available in *St. Romanos the Melodist, Kontakia: On the Life of Christ*, trans. Ephrem Lash (San Francisco, 1995); and R. J. Schork, *Sacred Song from the Byzantine Pulpit: Romanos the Melodist* (Gainesville, Fla., 1995). Unless indicated, translations of Romanos are by Lash. Alexander Lingas, "The Liturgical Place of the Kontakion in Constantinople," in *Liturgy, Architecture, and Art in the Byzantine World: Papers of the XVIII International Byzantine Congress (Moscow, 8–15 August 1991) and Other Essays Dedicated to the Memory of Fr. John Meyendorff*, ed. Constantine C. Akentiev (St. Petersburg, 1995), 50–57 (with relevant additional bibliography); José Grosdidier

de Matons, "Liturgie et Hymnographie: Kontakion et Canon," *DOP* 34–35 (1980–1981): 31–43. On the cathedral vigil office, see also the excellent overview in Robert Taft, *The Liturgy of the Hours in East and West: The Origins of the Divine Office and Its Meaning for Today*, 2nd ed. (Collegeville, Minn., 1993), 165–190.

13 Romanos, "On the Man Possessed by Demons," *Hymns*, 11.1; my translation.

14 Gregory W. Dubrov, "A Dialogue with Death: Ritual Lament and the *Threnos Theotokou* of Romanos Melodos," *Greek, Roman, and Byzantine Studies* 35 (1994): 385–405.

15 Andrew Louth (in Lash, *Kontakia*, xvi) points to Romanos's "liturgical storytelling": "In each case, an event, as related in the Scriptures and celebrated in the Liturgy, is retold in such a way as to enable those who hear it to enter into it."

16 Herbert Hunger, "Romanos Melodos, Dichter, Prediger, Rhetor – und sein Publikum," *Jahrbuch für Österreichischen Byzantinistik* 34 (1984): 15–42; Susan Ashbrook Harvey, "Spoken Words, Voiced Silence: Biblical Women in Syriac Tradition," *Journal of Early Christian Studies* 9 (2001): 105–131; and Derek Krueger, "Writing and Redemption in the Hymns of Romanos the Melodist," *BMGS* 27 (2003): 2–44.

17 John F. Baldovin, *The Urban Character of Christian Worship: The Origins, Development, and Meaning of Stational Liturgy*, Orientalia Christiana Analecta 228 (Rome, 1987), 180.

18 See Thomas F. Mathews, *The Early Churches of Constantinople: Architecture and Liturgy* (University Park, Penn., 1971); and Baldovin, *Urban Character of Christian Worship*, 174–181.

19 Baldovin, *Urban Character of Christian Worship*, 187–189.

20 Theophanes the Confessor, *Chronographia*, 2 vols., ed. Carolus de Boor (Hildesheim, 1963); translated as *The Chronicle of Theophanes Confessor: Byzantine and Near Eastern History, A.D. 284–813* by Cyril Mango and Roger Scott, with the assistance of Geoffrey Greatrex (Oxford, 1997).

21 Theophanes, *Chron.*, 1:237.

22 Theophanes, *Chron.*, 1:228.

23 Theophanes, *Chron.*, 1:238.

24 Theophanes, *Chron.*, 1:265–266.

25 *Égérie, Journal de voyage*, ed. and trans. Pierre Maraval, SC 296 (Paris, 1982); English translation by John Wilkinson, *Egeria's Travels to the Holy Land*, 3rd ed. (Warminster, 1999); Jerome, *Ep.*, 108; and Georgia Frank, *The Memory of the Eyes: Pilgrims to Living Saints in Christian Late Antiquity* (Berkeley, Calif., 2000).

26 *The Life of Nicholas of Sion*, ed. and trans. Ihor Ševčenko and Nancy Patterson Ševčenko (Brookline, Mass., 1984), 13, 27.

27 On the development of the concept of *eulogia* in early Byzantine Christianity, see Gary Vikan, *Byzantine Pilgrimage Art* (Washington, 1982), 10–14; Derek Krueger, "Writing as Devotion: Hagiographical Composition and the Cult of the Saints in Theodoret of Cyrrhus and Cyril of Scythopolis," *Church History* 66 (1997): 709–713; and Cynthia Hahn, "Loca Sancta Souvenirs: Sealing the Pilgrim's Experience," in *The Blessings of Pilgrimage*, ed. Robert Ousterhout (Urbana, Ill., 1990), 85–96.

28 Vikan, *Byzantine Pilgrimage Art*, 13.

29 On the Piacenza Pilgrim: text: *Itineraria et Alia Geographica*, CCSL 175 (Turnhout, 1965), 127–153; English translation in John Wilkinson, *Jerusalem Pilgrims Before*

*the Crusades* (Warminster, England, 2002). See also Blake Leyerle, "Landscape as Cartography in Early Christian Pilgrimage Narratives," *Journal of the American Academy of Religion* 64 (1996): 119–143.

30 Vikan, *Byzantine Pilgrimage Art*, 20–24; M. C. Ross, *Catalogue of the Byzantine and Early Mediaeval Antiquities in the Dumbarton Oaks Collection, I: Metalwork, Ceramics, Glass, Glyptics, Painting*, (Washington, D.C., 1966–1999), n. 87.

31 Vikan, *Byzantine Pilgrimage Art*, 22; Gary Vikan, "Early Byzantine Pilgrimage *Devotionalia* as Evidence of the Appearance of Pilgrimage Shrines," in *Jahrbuch für Antike und Christentum Ergänzungsband* 20 (1995–1997): 1:337–388.

32 Gary Vikan, "Pilgrims in Magi's Clothing: The Impact of Mimesis on Early Byzantine Pilgrimage Art," in Ousterhout, *The Blessings of Pilgrimage*, 97–107.

33 Vikan, *Byzantine Pilgrimage Art*, 18–20; Robert P. Bergman, *Vatican Treasures: Early Christian, Renaissance, and Baroque Art from the Papal Collections* (Cleveland, Ohio, 1998), 30–33.

34 On such ampullae more generally, see Gary Vikan, *Byzantine Pilgrimage Art*; André Grabar, *Les ampoules de Terre Sainte (Monza, Bobbio)* (Paris, 1958); Stephen J. Davis, *The Cult of Saint Thecla: A Tradition of Women's Piety in Late Antiquity* (New York, 2001).

35 H. J. Magoulias, "The Lives of Byzantine Saints as Sources of Data for the History of Magic in the Sixth and Seventh Centuries A.D.: Sorcery, Relics, and Icons," *Byzantion* 37 (1967): 228–269.

36 *Ancient Christian Magic: Coptic Text of Ritual Power*, ed. Marvin Meyer et al. (San Francisco, 1994), 27–57.

37 John G. Gager, *Curse Tablets and Binding Spells from the Ancient World* (New York, 1992), 224.

38 Glanville Downey, "Justinian as a Builder," *Art Bulletin* 32 (1950): 262–266.

39 Procopius, *Buildings*, 1.4.1–9. Elizabeth Key Fowden, *The Barbarian Plain: Saint Sergius between Rome and Iran* (Berkeley, 1999), 130–133.

40 Procopius, *Buildings*, 1.2.28.

41 Procopius, *Buildings*, 1.6.5–8.

42 Ludwig Deubner, *Kosmas und Damian: Texte und Einleitung* (Leipzig, 1907); French translation: A.-J. Festugière, *Sainte Thècle, Saints Côme et Damien, Saints Cyr et Jean (Extraits), et Saint Georges [Miracles of Cosmas and Damian]* (Paris, 1971), 83–213.

43 Cyril of Scythopolis, *Life of Sabas:* text in *Kyrillos von Skythopolis*, ed. Eduard Schwartz, *Texte und Untersuchungen* 49.2 (1939): 85–200; translation: R. M. Price, *Cyril of Scythopolis: The Lives of the Monks of Palestine*, trans. R. M. Price and John Binns, Cistercian Studies 114 (Kalamazoo, Mich., 1991).

44 On the early stages of the Byzantine cult of icons, see Averil Cameron, "The Language of Images: The Rise of Icons and Christian Representation," in *The Church and the Arts*, ed. Diana Wood, Studies in Church History 25 (Oxford, 1992), 1–42; Leslie Brubaker, "Icons before Iconoclasm?" in *Morfologie sociali e culturali in Europa fra tarda antichità e alto Medioevo* (Spoleto, 1998), 2:1215–1254; and Hans Belting, *Likeness and Presence: A History of the Image before the Era of Art*, trans. Edmund Jephcott (Chicago, 1994), 78–114.

45 *Anthologia Graeca*, 1:34; text and translation: *The Greek Anthology*, 5 vols. (London: Heinemann, 1916–1918); trans. Cyril Mango, *The Art of the Byzantine Empire, 312–1453* (Toronto, 1986), 115.

46 *Life of Symeon the Younger*, 118; text: *La vie ancienne de S. Syméon Stylite le jeune (521–592)*, ed. Paul van den Ven, 2 vols. (Brussels, 1962–1970); trans. Mango, *Art of the Byzantine Empire*, 134.
47 *Life of Symeon the Younger*, 158; trans. Mango, *Art of the Byzantine Empire*, 134.
48 *Miracles of Cosmas and Damian*, 13; trans. Mango, *Art of the Byzantine Empire*, 138–139.
49 *Miracles of Cosmas and Damian*, 15; trans. Mango, *Art of the Byzantine Empire*, 139.
50 *Miracles of Saint Demetrius*, 82; text: *Le plus anciens recueils des Miracle de s. Démétrius*, ed. Paul Lemerle, 2 vols. (Paris, 1979–1981); trans. Mango, *Art of the Byzantine Empire*, 129–130.

# 13: Philosophy in the Age of Justinian

*Christian Wildberg*

No one reading the last chapters of Eduard Zeller's monumental *Philosophie der Griechen*, first published between 1844 and 1852, will fail to notice the barely veiled contempt that pervades his account of the final period of ancient Greek philosophy. Summarily treating the fifth and sixth centuries, he concludes that around this time Greek philosophy collapses not on account of external circumstances, but due to internal exhaustion. Zeller's almost wholesale condemnation of the period no longer stands, yet it would be foolish wholly to disagree with him. The sixth century *is* a period in which the philosophical glory that was Greece is wearing thin; philosophers, and especially pagan ones, are rare birds indeed, flocking together for shelter and survival in various parts of the empire. What they have to say *is*, in a sense, derivative and remains largely unintelligible today unless it is understood against the backdrop of the great philosophical past.

Judged from a different perspective, however, Zeller's view becomes problematic. One only has to take note of the sheer quantity of philosophical writing produced in this late period: it is staggering, and this is particularly true of the time of Justinian. To give but one example: of the roughly sixty different works printed in the Berlin edition of the Greek commentaries on Aristotle (*CAG*),[1] some twenty belong to the decades discussed in this volume. These also happen to be some of the most substantial and valuable works in the series, rivaling the great commentaries of a luminary such as Alexander of Aphrodisias of the second and third centuries CE. To this output we may add a considerable number of commentaries on Plato as well as other works of different genres, only some of which have survived. If nothing else, the several thousand pages of philosophical prose extant from this period bear witness to a robust intellectual life. One might be tempted, however, to make a familiar qualification that the vast majority of these texts are commentaries and hence do not constitute genuine philosophical achievements. But such complaints are largely out of place, especially since they presuppose and import a modern notion of what a commentary is. Today, we think of a commentary as a scholarly exercise that comprehensively informs the reader about the text commented on. In antiquity, however, philosophical commentaries were not in the first instance about *texts*, but about the *truth*, enshrined as it was thought to be in the transmitted text of, say, Plato or Aristotle. A philosopher was thus a commentator of a particular kind; we shall return to the particular hermeneutical problems and presumptions an approach such as this generated.

Zeller also failed to take into account that there must have been an audience for all this philosophical literature; part of this audience was, of course, made up of the students who flocked to places such as Alexandria, the most important remaining citadel of learning in Justinian's empire. The names of the philosophers of this period suggest a great deal of regional mobility, and the centers of learning attracted teachers and students from far and wide. In addition, intellectual exchanges over long distances seem to have presented few problems. When a young Christian grammarian in Alexandria, who was not even endowed with a chair in philosophy, set out to undermine the central pillars of Aristotle's natural philosophy, the Athenian Neoplatonists, by this time hiding in some remote spot and crippled by Justinian's anti-pagan persecutions, retaliated almost immediately with scathing invective. Wholly mistaken seems to be the view that the consumers of philosophical prose must have been predominantly die-hard pagans. Shortly before the time we are concerned with here, Christian rhetoricians like Aeneas of Gaza and Zacharias Scholasticus, who in his later life became bishop of Mytilene, wrote popular but nevertheless serious philosophical works in the genre and style of Socratic dialogues. Christians such as these not only studied Aristotle and Plato with care and intelligence, but also wrote for a broader audience of Christian elites. The evidence suggests that together with epigram, epic, and rhetoric, the genre of philosophy, too, was firmly embedded in the high culture that pervaded the late Roman Empire and transcended the ideological and religious boundaries that separated Christians and Hellenes. The last pagans clung to it as much as Christian intellectuals tried to appropriate it in all kinds of ways, not least in order to articulate the "orthodoxy" in an increasingly complex and ferocious debate about what precisely good Christians were supposed to believe. At the very least, then, if one is, like Zeller, wedded to the idea that the period we are dealing with is indeed a period of intellectual decline, the image should be one of a glowing sunset, rather than of the Argo collapsing under the weight of its own rot and decay.

## A Short Prosopography of Sixth-Century Philosophers

In order to bring some clarity to the sometimes confusing list of names of nowadays little-known philosophers active during the period in question, it is necessary to begin with a short prosopography. A history of philosophy in the Age of Justinian must include an account of two towering but very different figures, Damascius (c. 460–540) and Ammonius, (c. 440–517 or 526). The philosophical activities of both these men occur well before the accession of Justinian, but through their pupils they shaped the views and methods of their philosophical successors in the period that concerns us.

Ammonius was the son of Hermeias, a teacher of philosophy at Alexandria, who died when Ammonius was a child. As a young man, Ammonius received his education at Athens under Proclus (412–485), the head of the Platonic academy reconstituted by Plutarch of Athens at the beginning of the fifth century. After his training, Ammonius returned to Alexandria, where he managed to survive antipagan persecutions and riots that broke out in that city in the late eighties. Rumor had it that Ammonius had ingratiated himself with the local Christian authorities, possibly even, as Damascius insinuates, by conversion.[2] Zacharias, an early student of his, wrote a dialogue titled *On the Creation of the World, against the Philosophers*[3] in which Ammonius appears to be persuaded by his Christian interlocutor's reasoning that the universe cannot be co-eternal with its divine principle. Whatever the reliability of these reports about Ammonius's pro-Christian leanings, the fact is that he was an influential teacher of philosophy, styling himself as an expert on Aristotle, although he did not confine his teaching to him. We still possess four commentaries that bear his name (on Porphyry's *Introduction*, and on Aristotle's *Categories, On Interpretation*, and *Prior Analytics*), but only one of them seems to be by Ammonius's own hand, the commentary on the *On Interpretation*.

It appears that Ammonius preferred to have his lecture notes written up by his students, and several other extant Aristotelian commentaries derive in substance from his lectures. John Philoponus's commentaries on the *Prior Analytics*, the *Posterior Analytics*, the *On Generation and Corruption*, and the *On the Soul* all indicate in their titles that they were composed in association with Ammonius. In addition, Asclepius's *Metaphysics* commentary is in substance by Ammonius. By 517, when John Philoponus started to publish commentaries in his own name, Ammonius's influence seems to have waned. The end of Ammonius's tenure falls into a period when Justinian was just being groomed for the throne.

Damascius was born in Damascus, in the Roman province of Syria, not long after 460. In the late fifth century, he first became a professional rhetorician in Alexandria, where he attended courses taught by Ammonius Hermeiou. In the wake of Zeno's persecution of pagan intellectuals in 488–489, he fled the city with his mentor Isidore of Alexandria and eventually arrived at Athens. There he joined the circle of philosophers around Marinus, a pupil of Proclus and then head of the Neoplatonic school. Some twenty-five years later, around 515, Damascius himself assumed leadership of the school, but when Justinian persecuted the Athenian philosophers at the beginning of his reign, he and some or all of his associates fled again, this time to seek refuge in Persia.[4] The last we hear of him, apart from references to his work in the writings of his pupils, is an epitaph dedicated to one of his female slaves.[5]

Damascius worked predominantly on the exegesis of Plato. We possess almost complete commentaries on the *Parmenides*, the *Philebus*, and two commentaries on the *Phaedo*, based on lectures given on different occasions. His *Philosophical History*, better known as *The Life of Isidore*,[6] of which numerous fragments are extant in Photius's work (in the ninth century) and the Suda (in the tenth century), provides invaluable insight into the cultural history of philosophy in late antiquity and into the mobility of philosophers, their rivalries, and their personal idiosyncrasies. Damascius also taught on the *Timaeus*, the *Republic*, the *Phaedrus*, the *Sophist*, and the *Laws*, but none of these lectures survive.

Ammonius and Damascius had a brilliant pupil, Simplicius of Cilicia,[7] who, according to the historian Agathias, joined Damascius on his flight to Persia. Simplicius, a devout and outspoken pagan, studied as a young man under Ammonius in Alexandria, but then evidently thought the philosophical culture of Athens more in tune with his own sentiments. It is impossible to determine precisely the dates of his birth and death, but his great commentaries must have been written in the 530s and 540s. It is to Simplicius that we owe the most erudite commentaries on Aristotle produced in antiquity (on the *Categories*, *On the Heavens*, the *Physics*, and perhaps *On the Soul*; he also wrote a commentary on Epictetus's *Handbook*). One of the invaluable features of Simplicius's work is that it frequently summarizes and cites the opinions of earlier philosophers, including the pre-Socratics, and it is very often thanks to him that we possess so many and often quite substantial fragments of otherwise lost works.

A few other philosophers joined the philosophical exodus to the Persian court in 531 or 532. These were Priscian of Lydia, Eulamius of Phrygia, Hermes and Diogenes of Phoenicia and Isidore of Gaza.[8] Of these, only Priscian is more than a name.[9] If we suppose (although Agathias does not explicitly say so) that this group of philosophers all departed from Athens, the list is a striking testimony to the "international" character of philosophy at Athens and the regional mobility of intellectuals at the time. Also, we hear from later Byzantine sources of a number of women associated with the school, one Theodora (not the empress) and her younger sisters.[10] It is unclear from Simplicius's commentaries whether he had a circle of students. He certainly had readers, but by the middle of the century, we lose track of the Athenian school. The Neoplatonic school at Athens was private. The "Department of Philosophy" in the Egyptian capital was part of a public institution. Whereas the pagan philosophers of Athens were disposed of near the beginning of Justinian's reign, we possess ample evidence from Alexandria of lively philosophical activity, both pagan and Christian, right up to the end of the Justinianic era and beyond. After Ammonius, it may have been the case that the mathematician Eutocius of Ascalon assumed leadership of the school, presumably because Ammonius's most capable students near the end of his career were still quite young. A note in the *Prior Analytics* commentary of Elias, at any rate, refers to Eutocius's lectures on Porphyry's *Introduction*.[11]

One of Ammonius's pupils, Asclepius of Tralles, seems to have been mathematically inclined, and the commentary on Aristotle's *Metaphysics*, books 1–7, edited by him, does not have a good philosophical reputation. There can be no doubt that the real philosophical talent at the time was to be found in another figure who would acquire great historical importance and influence. This was the Christian John Philoponus, the "Lover-of-Work," also known as John the Grammarian, of Alexandria (c. 490–570). Philoponus was presumably Ammonius's star student and, self-appointed or not, editor of the great teacher's lecture notes. Steeped in the Aristotelian-Neoplatonic tradition, Philoponus developed into its most outspoken critic. He also had, although some have doubted this, an original mind, and part of his life's achievement, a millennium before Galileo, was to repudiate many a venerable doctrine of the Aristotelian tradition, and in a manner that demanded to be taken seriously by other philosophers. The onset of the so-called Dark Ages all but obliterated the culture that could have given his work the attention it deserved. For centuries, his reception in Byzantium and the West was minimal, but his work was widely read, translated, and studied in the Syriac and Arabic traditions. His influence in the Renaissance helped pave the way for the eventual demise of Aristotelianism in the natural sciences.

Philoponus's oeuvre comprises at least forty items on diverse subjects such as grammar, logic, mathematics, physics, psychology, cosmology, astronomy, theology, and church politics; even medical treatises have been attributed to him.[12] The most important philosophical works are his commentaries on Aristotle's *Categories, Physics*, and on parts of the *Meteorology*. It has already been noted that he edited, and perhaps doctored, Ammonius's lecture notes on the *Prior* and the *Posterior Analytics, Generation and Corruption*, and *On the Soul*. What is so remarkable about Philoponus is that he gradually transformed the usual format of explanatory commentary into open criticism of the presuppositions that underpinned the Aristotelian-Neoplatonic doctrine of the eternity of the world. Yet despite his considerable talent, Philoponus never turned philosophy into a career but devoted the second half of his life to theological commentary – and doctrinal controversy.

The title of *philosophos* passed to the pagan Olympiodorus of Alexandria (ca. 505–570), who as a young man must have heard Ammonius near the very end of his life. Olympiodorus, like his predecessors, taught Aristotle's treatises on logic and natural philosophy (his commentaries on the *Categories* and *Meteorology* still survive), but he also revived interest in teaching Plato. This may be surprising, because it is generally believed that Christians considered Plato's dialogues, and especially the Neoplatonic exegesis of them, much more controversial and explosive than Aristotle's sober ratiocinations. I am not sure that this is true. In any case, the surprise is mitigated by the fact that Olympiodorus, unlike his contemporary Simplicius, was not a pagan of the combative sort. Like most of the remaining cultivated pagans, he hoped for some form of peaceful cultural coexistence.[13] A look at his commentaries on the *Phaedo*, the *First Alcibiades*, and the *Gorgias*, all of which survive, reveals his toothless Platonism. One modern authority says about one such disappointing commentary, "it abounds in reminiscences and anecdotes about Ammonius, while the actual substance is of the poorest."[14]

Even after Olympiodorus, who taught until at least 565, we have evidence of a thriving philosophical tradition in Alexandria. We possess fascinating *Introductions to Philosophy* (lectures held for beginners), as well as commentaries on Porphyry's *Introduction* and Aristotle's *Categories*, but the manuscripts, which are clearly indebted to the works of Olympiodorus, are no longer clear about their own authors. We encounter good Christian names such as Elias and David, yet the texts do not betray any Christian commitment whatsoever.[15] If the names do refer to actual figures of the time, one could of course also reckon with the possibility that they were Jews or Samaritans. But prosopographical research does not yield anything concrete. Elias is an altogether mysterious figure; neither the Suda nor Photius nor anyone else in later Byzantium seems to know of any such philosopher. The same is true of David, except that his actual existence is well established by the Armenian philosophical tradition, which counts him as its towering founder, awarding him the magnificent epithet "The Invincible."[16] The texts attributed to David were evidently widely distributed and read, and an abbreviated and simplified version of his *Prolegomena to Philosophy* survives in Armenian (our earliest manuscripts date from the fourteenth century). The trouble is that the Armenian tradition also thinks of David the Invincible as a theologian of the fifth century, and it is impossible to believe that the Armenian theologian and the (Alexandrian) philosopher a century later were one and the same. Here, the cross-fertilization of intellectual traditions has given rise to a great deal of confusion. Quite possibly the texts now attributed to David first circulated as anonymous lecture notes and were only later attributed to an author with a Christian name for purposes of authentication. Much research remains to be done to clarify the extent and nature of philosophy at the end of the reign of Justinian and beyond.

In any case, the puzzling story of the Armenian "David the Invincible" should remind us that the time of Justinian was very much also a time in which Greek learning increasingly percolated into neighboring territories and cultures. Boethius, of course, comes to mind first, but only from a western perspective. Of prime importance for the Syrian philosophical tradition is Sergius of Ras Ayin,[17] who died in 536. He not only translated parts of Aristotle's logical works and certain treatises of Galen's as well as Porphyry's *Introduction* into Syriac but also composed logical and physical treatises in the spirit of Aristotle. We hear of Paul the Persian,[18] who was a Nestorian philosopher and theologian active at the Persian court of Khusro, and we have evidence of several philosophical works by him.[19] There must have been numerous figures of second rank, such as the Syrian Uranius, who was equally at home in Byzantium and Persia and whose pretentiousness and conceit so irritated Agathias.[20]

To be sure, other established centers of learning existed in the empire, notably Constantinople, Gaza, and Aphrodisias, but we are poorly informed about them for the time of Justinian. Agapius, a pupil of Proclus and teacher of John the Lydian, taught at Constantinople slightly before the time we are concerned with here. Voices of increasingly confident Christian intellectuals such as Aeneas of Gaza (c. 430–520) and Zacharias Scholasticus (c. 465 or 466–536), the later bishop of Mytilene, can be heard from Gaza in the late fifth century. Zacharias was more of a historian and rhetorician, not a full-blown philosopher, but he had studied under Ammonius Hermeiou in Alexandria. Both Aeneas and Zacharias had the opportunity to study not only Aristotelian logic and natural philosophy, but also the more advanced curriculum of Platonic dialogues such as *Phaedo* and *Timaeus*. Whereas Aeneas raises the topic of the nature of the soul, Zacharias discusses, in the form of Platonic dialogue, whether the world is co-eternal with the divine principle. His main interlocutor is a pupil of Ammonius; the Christian "Socrates" succeeds in converting him (not Ammonius, as is sometimes suggested) to Christianity, and the work ends with a triumphant enunciation of the Christian creed. In it, the work has embedded a subdialogue between Ammonius Hermeiou and an unnamed "Christianos," no doubt Zacharias himself, in which Ammonius appears to be at a loss how to defend the doctrine of the eternity of the world against the Christian's *elenchus*.

I emphasize this because John Philoponus, perhaps a generation younger than Zacharias, continues Zacharias's project of rebutting paganism on philosophical grounds. But instead of the "Socratic" dialogue, he chose the more established genre of the commentary. Moreover, by attacking Ammonius's great teacher Proclus and Aristotle himself, he surpasses Zacharias's work in scope and sophistication.

The works of Zacharias and John Philoponus are examples of the Christian appropriation of Neoplatonic philosophy for the purposes of giving Christian doctrine a foothold in reason. More remarkably still, in the Age of Justinian an entirely new phenomenon gained momentum, quite separate from the pursuits of the school philosophers and the contemporary theologians grappling with the question of the divine and human natures of Christ. This is the confluence of Christian mysticism and Neoplatonic metaphysics in the writings of Pseudo-Dionysius the Areopagite. This author's true identity is unknown. He claims to be a disciple of Paul, but theological speculations abound with Neoplatonism of the Proclean type. Ps.-Dionysius wrote his treatises (*The Ecclesiatical History, Mystical Theology, Divine Names*) around the turn of the century, and his reception begins to gain momentum with John of Scythopolis,[21] who wrote his annotations sometime between 537 and 543. He laid the foundation for Maximus the Confessor (of Chrysopolis, 580–662), the first great commentator on Ps.-Dionysius a century later.

This brief prosopography already gives an impression of the richness and diversity of philosophy at the time of Justinian. Although it seems true to say that the figure of the pagan sage became increasingly marginalized in the imperial society of the fifth and sixth centuries,[22] it is equally true to say that philosophical inquiry and debate, understood as a search for the truth, never ceased to be of central concern. There were enough scholars, both pagan and Christian, to keep philosophy alive, and we are now in a position to survey more specifically some of the major points of contention.

## Trends and Debates in Sixth-Century Philosophy

To illustrate the point that commentaries were not written to elucidate otherwise obscure texts but were the preferred genre of discourse to establish, negotiate, and criticize substantive philosophical claims, we now turn to some of the controversies that were discussed in a more or less open fashion. In an influential article, Karl Praechter once argued that one can distinguish clearly between different schools and directions within the broader Neoplatonic movement in late antiquity.[23] In particular, Praechter argued that the salient difference between the two major schools, the Athenian and the Alexandrian branch, lay in their different exegetical methods. Whereas the Athenian school (represented by Syrianus, Proclus, Damascius, and Simplicius) was heavily influenced, broadly speaking, by Iamblichus's tendency to bring out in any text, as far as possible, the understanding it offers of the intelligible world, the Alexandrian School (represented by Hierocles in the fifth century, and by Ammonius, Philoponus, Olympiodorus, Elias, and David in the sixth) tended toward a more sober and less metaphysical technique of interpretation. Praechter connected these observations with two sociocultural differences separating the schools: Alexandria had traditionally been a center of learning in the exact sciences (hence the preference for Aristotle) and possessed a large Christian intellectual community attending the Alexandrian philosophers' lectures and classes (which would temper the propagation of Platonism as an antigospel). Thus, as compared to the Athenians, the Alexandrian Neoplatonists were less of a sect (*hairesis*) and more of a collegium of higher education.

Praechter also suggested elsewhere that these hermeneutical and cultural differences, which put constraints on the way in which the philosophers in the two cities operated, eventually led to certain doctrinal differences.[24] In particular, Praechter thought that the Alexandrians embraced as the highest divine principle not the Neoplatonic One, but the Demiurge, in apparent harmonization with Christianity. This particular aspect of Praechter's construal of Alexandrian Neoplatonism has come under forceful attack by, among others, Ilsetraut Hadot, who has pleaded repeatedly for the doctrinal unity of the schools in question.[25] Koenraad Verrycken has done a great deal to clear up the doctrinal issues and concluded that, apart from a tendency to simplify the metaphysical hierarchies of the Athenians, the Alexandrians were very much "orthodox" Neoplatonists.[26] Nevertheless, the whole issue remains unclear and deserves further study, possibly leading to a more nuanced appreciation of the admittedly broad sketch of philosophical diversity painted by Praechter.

Praechter's principal observation that there was a difference between Athens and Alexandria in the approach to the exegesis of texts, suggests that one could create a test case by comparing Proclus's commentary on Plato's *Cratylus* with Ammonius's commentary on Aristotle's *On Interpretation*. Unfortunately, the juxtaposition of these two primary treatises on semiotics and their treatments by an Athenian and an Alexandrian is less promising than it appears since Ammonius himself acknowledges that his work is heavily influenced by Proclus's lectures, which he heard when he studied under him. Proclus, of course, would have been eager to harmonize the Aristotelian, conventionalist view of language with his own, Platonic view that names originated in the intellect of a divine lawgiver and are, as part of a chain of being from the highest to the lowest, directly significant of the higher reality they name. To be sure, some harmonizing along these lines goes on in Ammonius's commentary, but as Ludwig Fladerer has pointed out, Ammonius retains the Aristotelian view that words are conventional entities which symbolically signify whatever they were intended to signify, but that *this* cannot be assumed to be identical with something's nature or essence.[27] The upshot of this view for the project of exegesis is that a philosophical text by, say, Plato or Aristotle cannot be taken to give access to the *truth*, but rather to the *intention of the author*. It remains an open question, further to be investigated by the scholar, whether the author's intended view indeed corresponds to the "truth" in the sense that it accounts for the phenomena in a satisfactory way.

In short, the history of philosophy should be dealt with not in the way Iamblichus or Proclus have dealt with it, as a repository of truths that all fit together in a harmonious way, but critically, in the manner of Aristotle. Ammonius's pupil Philoponus thus takes Proclus to task (in his polemical commentary on Proclus's *On the Eternity of the World*), saying that no reasonable person pays attention to the feebleness of utterances and not to the intention of what has been said, because utterances can give no unimpaired account either of our thoughts or of external states of affairs.[28] There is no doubt in Philoponus's mind that Aristotle disagrees with Plato on important doctrinal issues.[29] Indeed, as Philoponus will demonstrate in a later work, Aristotle is even in disagreement with himself.

Philoponus's pagan rival Simplicius disapproved of this kind of critical reading. No doubt with an eye to how things had gotten out of hand in Alexandria, he writes in the introductory sections of his *Categories* commentary (*CAG* 8, p. 7, 23–32):

> A worthy commentator of Aristotle's writings must not be entirely wanting in the greatness of intellect that was Aristotle's. Moreover, he must be familiar with all of the philosopher's writings and know Aristotle's way (of philosophizing). He must also have unerring judgment, so that he does not show what has been well said to be unreasonable on account of a frivolous misunderstanding; nor, if something needs careful attention, must he show that he is eager to quarrel in each and every way, as if he had inscribed himself into the school of the philosopher. But I also think that in the case of the things said by Aristotle against Plato, (the ideal commentator) must not simply look at the words and accuse the philosophers of disagreement, but he must pay attention to the meaning (*nous*) and search out their agreement (*symphonia*) in most things.[30]

That hermeneutical questions and presuppositions continued to be part of the self-consciousness of a late antique philosopher is evidenced by an instructive passage we read in Elias. In his preface to Aristotle's

*Categories*, he summarizes the qualities of an ideal commentator; a text like this could only have been written by an Alexandrian, not by an Athenian exegete (*CAG* 18.1, pp. 122f. as quoted by Nigel Wilson 1983, 47):

> The commentator should be both commentator and scholar at the same time. It is the task of the commentator to unravel obscurities in the text; it is the task of the scholar to judge what is true and what is false, or what is sterile and what is productive. He must not assimilate himself to the authors he expounds, like actors on the stage who put on different masks because they are imitating different characters. When expounding Aristotle he must not become an Aristotelian and say there has never been so great a philosopher, when expounding Plato he must not become a Platonist and say that there has never been a philosopher to match Plato. He must not force the text at all costs and say that the ancient author whom he is expounding is correct in every respect; instead he must repeat to himself at all times "the author is a dear friend, but so also is truth, and when both stand before me truth is the better friend." He must not sympathize with a philosophical school, as happened to Iamblichus, who out of sympathy for Plato is condescending in his attitude to Aristotle and will not contradict Plato in regard to the theory of ideas. He must not be hostile to a philosophical school like Alexander (of Aphrodisias). The latter, being hostile to the immortality of the intellectual part of the soul, attempts to twist in every way the remarks of Aristotle in his third book on the immortality of the soul which prove that it is immortal. The commentator must know the whole of Aristotle in order that, having first proved that Aristotle is consistent with himself, he may expound Aristotle's works by means of Aristotle's works. He must know the whole of Plato, in order to prove that Plato is consistent with himself and make the works of Aristotle an introduction to those of Plato.[31]

Hermeneutical differences inevitably lead to doctrinal ones, and these eventually broke into the open, most clearly in Simplicius's furious rebuttal of John Philoponus's philosophical effort to undermine the belief in the eternity of the world. In a series of curious treatises, which are partly commentary, partly ad hominem polemics, Philoponus repudiated first a Proclean pamphlet that surveyed the stock arguments of the pagans for eternity and then took on those canonized chapters in Aristotle's oeuvre, notably from the *On the Heavens* and the *Physics*, which had supposedly settled the matter. The polemic against Proclus survives,[32] but the much more important and influential treatise against Aristotle (*On the Eternity of the World against Aristotle*) is known only on the basis of fragments, mainly from Simplicius.[33] Reading the passages Simplicius cites, as well as his own responses, it becomes clear that Philoponus was "reading" his philosophical texts through a different hermeneutical lens.[34] For one thing, being a Christian, he has been liberated from the contention that a man can save or even deify his soul through philosophy. Moreover, the supposed authority of the great thinkers, which was so much at the forefront of traditional Neoplatonists, no longer constrained him. Finally, in the wake of this erosion of authority, there seems no longer any obligation to show, as Simplicius did, that the doctrines of the ancient thinkers were all in harmony with one another.

The Alexandrian grammarian forcefully rejected a number of other central Aristotelian doctrines: out went the concept of ether, which Aristotle thought causes the celestial spheres to rotate in perfect circles; out went the idea of prime matter, interpreted, as it commonly was, as an immaterial and formless substrate. Philoponus thought instead that there could be no ontological level below unqualified three-dimensional extension. But most famously, Philoponus gave new direction to the theoretical explanation of dynamic processes, such as the movement of projectiles and the movement of the celestial bodies. In the course of reflections that span from the early commentaries *On the Soul* and the *Physics* to the late commentary on *Genesis* (entitled *On the Making of the World*), he famously formulated the theory of the impetus.[35] According to this theory, which later profoundly influenced medieval physical and economic theory, a projectile moves in virtue of a force that has been imparted to it and which exhausts itself in the course of the motion. In the case of the heavens, the idea was that the creator sent the celestial bodies spinning at the time of their creation.

Philoponus has to be admired for being a leading force in the history of philosophy, at times far ahead of his time. In his attack on Athenian Neoplatonism, however, he was curiously in tune with the imperial political agenda of his day.

## Philosophy and Politics

An account of the history of philosophy in the Age of Justinian must address the more general political and cultural setting of Greek learning during the fifth and sixth centuries and take the intense political pressure under which the philosophers operated into account. Pagan cult and temple worship had come under attack by Christian Roman emperors since the emperor Constantius in the mid-fourth century. For philosophy and individual philosophers in particular, serious trouble arose first at the beginning of the fifth century. By all accounts, the prestige philosophers tended to enjoy among local elites became a stumbling block for an increasingly ambitious clergy. In Alexandria, the renowned female philosopher Hypatia was caught in the midst of a power struggle between the imperial prefect of Egypt, Orestes, and Cyril, the newly appointed bishop of Alexandria. Hypatia was a powerful public intellectual at the time and on excellent terms with Orestes; in March 415, when she was about sixty years old, a mob of Christians, with or without the patriarch's approval, abducted her, dragged her to a local church, and, using pottery shards to slash her flesh, murdered her in cold blood, a crime that sent shockwaves through the community of scholars and philosophers.[36]

Near the end of the same century, in 488–489, the philosophers in Alexandria became unwittingly associated with a revolt against the emperor Zeno (474–491). In 482 or 483, the rebelling generals Illus and Leontius had sent the grammarian, poet, and soothsayer Pamprepius to Alexandria, apparently "to canvass pagan support for the rebellion."[37] In crushing the revolt, Zeno also cracked down on the circle of Alexandrian philosophers and rhetoricians. Among them were Isidore and Damascius, who fled to Athens fearing for their lives, and Ammonius Hermeiou, who somehow survived the persecutions unscathed. Some forty years later, Justinian attempted to deal pagan philosophy the final blow. We turn now to the events around the year 529 and that famous and unhappy episode known as the closing of the school of Athens.

In the fifth century, Athens seems to have been a relatively safe place for pagans to live, and the Platonic school, reestablished under Plutarch of Athens at the beginning of the century, helped to turn the city into a stronghold of intellectual paganism. Pagan philosophers, their inner circle of intimate students, and the larger group of "auditors" must have been integral to the city's cultural life. Proclus and his successor Marinus first came into conflict with the Christian authorities in Athens and had to stay away from Athens for extended periods.[38]

Under Damascius, who took over as the school's leader around 515, the circle of Neoplatonists apparently enjoyed a surge of interest, with students flocking to Athens from all over the empire. But with Justinian's accession, the situation for pagans, and pagan professionals in particular, became precarious. In the years 529 and perhaps again in 531, increasingly harsh legislation was passed to bar pagans from public office and teaching. Within two years, the Athenian philosophers decided to leave the empire and follow an invitation issued by the young and aspiring Persian king Khusro. Thus, a group of seven resident Athenian philosophers, Damascius of Syria, Simplicius of Cilicia, Eulamius (or Eulalius, according to the Suda) of Phrygia, Priscian of Lydia, Hermes and Diogenes of Phoenicia, and Isidore of Gaza, moved to the Sassanid capital Ctesiphon, some fifty miles southeast of Baghdad, on the west bank of the Tigris. After a brief and disillusioning sojourn they left again, intending to return to the Roman Empire. At that point, their activities are lost to history and open to much speculation.

In the present context, it is neither necessary nor possible to lay out all the relevant and possibly relevant pieces of evidence we possess relating to this episode, weighing their respective value and credibility.[39] Rather, in what follows, I should like to move the imperial legislation relating to this event into the foreground, stressing its unprecedented brutality in order to render more vivid the human experience of the imperial subjects. I am doubtful about a cluster of Christianocentric impressions, often found in the modern accounts, to the effect that the routing of the pagan intelligentsia had its raison d'être in a quite impersonal and entirely reasonable trend to remove the last pockets of pagan resistance to the homogenization of Christian imperial culture.

It is important to note, first of all, that the kind of legal sanctions that disrupted philosophical life in Athens were initially part of a broader legislative initiative that targeted all kinds of Christian heretics, as well as Manichaeans, Samaritans, Jews, and pagans (*CJ* 1.5). The relevant laws of the Code reveal that the major threat to religious and cultural cohesion was in fact not perceived to be posed by pagan teachers of philosophy. It is indeed hard to believe that a small group of private intellectuals and their circle of students, tucked away in an insignificant Greek town, should cause serious concern in the capital.[40] Still, in the broad context of an attempt to confine all kinds of unorthodox and heretic doctrines in order to procure for the empire the "grace of God" (*CJ* 1.5.16.2; 1.11.10.1), something had to be done about the Greek polytheists, and the most obvious thing to do was to bar them from positions of influence. This is precisely what we see in a law published in April 529. The relevant section of this law (1.5.18.4–5) is explicitly directed against heretics, Manichaeans, Samaritans, and pagans, and *all* of these are forbidden to teach and thereby earn a public salary, to serve as advocate or in the military, or to hold public office. Anyone who is not of orthodox creed and holds any such position of influence is to be denounced, and the law then goes on to specify heavy fines for those who fail or refuse to make these denunciations (1.5.18.10–11).

It seems that this law ties in well with the famous remark in John Malalas's *Chronicle* (18.47) which has always been taken as the main piece of evidence for the closing of the Athenian school. Malalas says that "during the consulship of Decius [529], the emperor issued a decree and sent it to Athens ordering that nobody should teach philosophy nor interpret the laws." It is unnecessary to drive a wedge between this reported decree and the law just discussed on the grounds that the law bars pagans from any kind of teaching but the Athenian decree apparently forbids anyone, pagan or Christian, to teach philosophy. For one thing, it is quite reasonable to suppose that by "teaching" the law does not in the first instance mean the teaching of grammar and arithmetic, but the teaching of pagan (or other uncouth) beliefs – the kind of teaching that has an effect on the pupil's own system of beliefs.[41] It is also reasonable to suppose that what Malalas had in mind when he invoked the concept of "philosophy in Athens" was pagan philosophy taught by pagans. The general reason Malalas gives for the decree is a crackdown on blasphemy, and it is not at all obvious that philosophy taught by a Christian should have that result.

However this may be, the important point is that neither the general law 1.5.18 nor the decree specifically sent to Athens could have amounted to a "closing" of the Neoplatonic academy. The *Code* closely juxtaposes teaching and holding public office,[42] barring nonorthodox citizens from teaching and receiving an annual salary in this or some other official capacity. In the Roman Empire, teachers of grammar, rhetoric, and philosophy were typically recipients of public salaries, either imperial or municipal,[43] but this was not the case in Athens, where the Neoplatonists enjoyed considerable income, either from their own wealth or from large private endowments.[44] Moreover, their teaching activity was almost certainly carried out not publicly but in the privacy of the house of the school's leader (*diadochus*).

We do not know the effect this law had on the public teaching of philosophy in Alexandria – presumably, it was none (we must return to this question) – and it seems likewise hard to believe that *CJ* 1.5.18 and the particular missive sent to Athens in 529 (if we can believe Malalas) had any dramatic effect on the operations of the Athenian philosophers, other than restricting the public projection of the school's public activities. It is therefore unsurprising that other evidence suggests that the philosophers stayed put for another two years or so. The Sassanian King Khusro Anoshirvan (531–579), whose fabled inclination to philosophy enticed our philosophers to his court, did not accede to the throne before mid-September of the year 531.[45] During the winter months, it was precarious to cross the Aegean Sea, and the sailing may not have occurred until the following spring of 532. The conclusion must be that the Athenian school was not obliterated in the year 529. At most, this year marks the beginning of the end. The end itself must have been so traumatic that it reminded the philosophers of the fate of Hypatia or the more recent persecutions in Alexandria some forty years earlier. It has often been held, on the evidence of Agathias, that our group of philosophers left for Persia by choice. As Agathias puts it, the philosophers mentioned "had come to the conclusion, since the official religion of the Roman empire was not to their liking, that the Persian state was much superior."[46] To be sure, the propaganda issuing from the Persian court must have posed a considerable temptation,[47] but the magnitude of this temptation can be understood only in light of Justinian's increasingly aggressive and brutal legislation.

Unfortunately, the relevant laws we now turn to, *CJ* 1.11.9 and 10, addressing pagan sacrifice and temples, are undated.[48] Edward Watts argues in a forthcoming article that *CJ* 1.5.18, which he plausibly dates to 529, was followed somewhat later by *CJ* 1.11.9 and 10 between 529 and the year 534, when Justinian published the second edition of the Code. The short paragraph 1.11.9 validates the previous limitations and penalties imposed on pagans (1.11.9.3), adding merely that pagans, and pagan institutions, cannot receive bequests, and that any such bequests are to be confiscated (*CJ* 1.11.1–2). This part of the antipagan legislation could well have been part of the first edition of the *Code* in 529. The next paragraph, 1.11.10, seems to have been added at a slightly later time.[49] Turning to this particular law, one is struck immediately by the detail of the provisions and the magnitude of the penalties imposed on pagans. Pagans are instructed to convert without delay, together with their wives and entire household, or face confiscation of their property (10.1); teachers of pagan doctrine are to be struck off the public payroll, and those who do not also convert face expropriation and exile (10.2–3). Secret pagan sacrifice and idolatry carries the death penalty (10.4). Clearly, a machinery is put into place to wipe out paganism on a broad scale, with a clear conception of the precise targets, giving local authorities sweeping authority to commit the gravest injustices against wealthy and cultivated pagan citizens. In spirit, and we may presume application, this law goes beyond anything that had been signed by previous emperors.

If we suppose that *CJ* 1.11.10 was drafted and published some time in 531, the time when the philosophers left for Persia, it seems compelling to infer that the Athenian philosophers had little choice. No matter what one thinks of the effectiveness of imperial law on the ground, any pagan intellectual reading these imperial injunctions had every reason to believe that the law could be applied in all its terrible force. What we do not know for certain is whether the Athenian clergy and imperial authorities played a sinister role in this affair;[50] archeological evidence suggests that the complex of late antique houses on the north slope of the Areopagus, which were clearly inhabited by pagans and have been plausibly linked with Damascius and his circle, suddenly, at the beginning of the sixth century, passed into the hands of a new Christian owner,[51] perhaps the bishop of Athens.[52] It seems certain, at any rate, that Damascius and his friends did not leave, as Agathias said, because "the Roman empire was not to their liking"; rather, having lost their endowment and property, they were given the choice between exile and execution.[53]

Looking at the events in this way also throws into sharp relief the clause of the peace treaty of September 532 between Justinian and Khusro. If we can believe Agathias, "a clause was inserted in the treaty . . . to the effect that the philosophers should be allowed to return to their homes and to live out their lives in peace without being compelled to alter their traditional religious belief or to accept any view which did not coincide with them. Khusro insisted on the inclusion of this point and made the ratification and continued observance of the truce conditional on its implementation" (2.31.4, Frendo). This, we may surmise, was not only a thoughtful and magnanimous piece of diplomacy on behalf of Khusro[54] but also a matter of life and death for the philosophers, should they ever set foot on Roman territory. Not implausibly, the lobbying for the inclusion of some such clause came from the philosophers themselves.[55]

## The Cultural Significance of Philosophy in the Age of Justinian

Paradoxically, despite Justinian's obliteration of Athenian Neoplatonism, the institutional teaching of pagan philosophy continued to flourish elsewhere in the empire. It is clear that some of the philosophers in Alexandria, notably Olympiodorus, but probably also the authors who wrote the commentaries transmitted under the names of David and Elias, were pagans, teaching Plato and Aristotle well into the second half of the century.

One way to explain the historical paradox would be to say that in actual practice, a fine line was drawn between, as it were, "applied" paganism (with an emphasis on cult and pagan ritual) and merely "theoretical" paganism (with an emphasis on keeping the pagan intellectual heritage alive). The Athenians were vulnerable because they practiced both, whereas the Alexandrians practiced only the latter. But this is not a line the Code draws. Another theory proposed some time ago by Henri Saffrey is that Alexandria was spared the same fate as Athens by the good offices of John Philoponus, who around that time wrote his repudiation of Proclus's *On the Eternity of the World*. But then, why did Philoponus not take further charge of the philosophical affairs of the school?

On balance, it seems that one decisive reason for the survival of the Alexandrian school may have been a monetary one. One of the major purposes of Justinian's antipagan legislation was to forge a legal basis for lucrative expropriations. The Athenian intellectuals had a lot to offer in that regard, but there was nothing to confiscate in Alexandria. Even if this is true, however, it would be a mistake to think of the survival of school philosophy in Alexandria and elsewhere as accidental. The important question that calls out to be answered is why it is that the Age of Justinian appears to us, in comparison with the preceding century, almost as a renaissance period of philosophy, in spite of the imperial efforts to contain it. The evidence suggests that philosophy could still rely on broad cultural support from pagans, closet pagans, and no doubt some of the Christian elite as well. For why should educated Christians of the sixth century be less interested in philosophy and science and speculation than, say, Origen or Augustine? Is it really so surprising that the Athenian school survived so long, and even more surprising that philosophy remained an integral part of higher education? What, in other words, was the social function and significance of philosophy in the Christian Roman Empire?

It would be entirely wrong to think that from the beginning Christians and pagans lived in parallel worlds that offered few points of contact. The early church fathers were steeped in philosophy, even if one might hesitate to count them as philosophers.[56] Christian apologists studied the pagan sages in part because they had to know their religious enemies, but this was no longer a pressing issue at the time of Justinian, when the most threatening real or perceived enemies were fellow Christians of "the other" sect. Schism and factional riots offered a much more serious and palpable reason for concern than the academic pursuits of the few remaining metropolitan pagans.

Somewhat more promising is the observation that a liberal education that included a fair bit of serious philosophy was in many respects a ticket to higher imperial or curial office. John the Lydian, for example, studied philosophy at Constantinople under Agapius, a pupil of Proclus,[57] and even the philosophically-challenged Agathias seems to know his share of Aristotle and Plato.

The most likely answer, however, lies in the fact that to some extent the study of philosophy was a matter of necessity for the Christian elite, for the unavoidable doctrinal differences of the day could be articulated and understood only in a language that was heavily indebted to philosophy. The Bible gave no guidance as to the question of whether Father, Son, and Spirit are of the "same substance," or, more pertinent to the time we are discussing, how precisely the natures of humanity and godhead were combined within one single historical person, Jesus Christ. Anyone who was given to speculation about theological issues such as these had to have a solid grasp of Aristotle's logic as well as the central concepts of Neoplatonic ontology, such as hypostasis, nature, substance, Soul, and Intellect. We can glean, for example, from John Philoponus's letters, addressed to the emperor to convince him of the reasonability of Miaphysitism, how much of an abstract and speculative "tool kit" any two interlocutors who approached such matters had to have at their disposal. It seems that Christianity itself generated a certain pressure and demand for philosophical training, and we may infer that pagan philosophy survived and thrived in part because it rendered vital services to the different Christian communities it was embedded in.

But even this is no entirely satisfactory explanation of the broader significance of philosophy in the Christian society and culture of late antiquity. For the question still remains how it came to be in the first place that the Christians of the first centuries of our era cast their religion in philosophical garb and proceeded to problematize their creed by formulating increasingly speculative refinements to it, thus generating a host of doctrinal problems that could be understood and adjudicated only by an appeal to philosophical argument. In broad strokes, the answer presumably has to be that Christianity brought an entirely new idea into the ancient world, an idea that, scandalous to the world as it was, needed to be understood. The philosophers had always integrated reason and religion in some way, commonly arguing from premises of reason to conclusions of faith – about the One, the celestial hierarchies, the immortality of the soul. Christianity's conclusions of faith, in contrast, were revealed. And the content of *that* faith, with its promise of universal salvation on account of the death of a god who became man, died on the cross, and rose again from the dead, defied reason. What was lacking, initially, was a rational framework on which these doctrines of faith could be construed, discussed, and defended, but no institution offered such a framework other than the logical and metaphysical works of pagan philosophy. And it seems that it was for this reason that the status of classical philosophy in the Christian empire was necessarily an ambivalent one: at the same time an ally and an enemy, a means but no end, a temptation impossible to resist but equally impossible to embrace.

## Notes

1 This monumental work in twenty-five volumes is known under its Latin name as *Commentaria in Aristotelem Graeca*, henceforth abbreviated *CAG*.

2 See Damascius, *History of Philosophy* (a.k.a. *Life of Isidore*), frag. 118B (Athanassiadi). See also the discussion in Leendert G. Westerink, *Anonymous Prolegomena to Platonic Philosophy* (Amsterdam, 1962), x–xiii.

3 The dialogue is often inaccurately referred to as the "Ammonius."

4 On this episode, see the section "Philosophy and Politics."

5 See Alan Cameron, "The Last Days of the Academy at Athens," *Proceedings of the Cambridge Philological Society* 195 (1969): 22.

6 Polymnia Athanassiadi, *Damascius: The Philosophical History* (Athens, 1999).

7 On Simplicius, see esp. Ilsetraut Hadot, *La vie et l'œuvre de Simplicius d'après des sources grecques et arabes. In ead. Simplicius, sa vie, son œuvre, sa survie* (Berlin, 1987), 3–39.

8 Agathias, *Historiarum libri quinque*, ed. Rudolf Keydell (Berlin, 1967), 2.30.3. Isidore of Gaza is not to be confused with Isidore of Alexandria, Damascius's mentor.

9 Two works survive under his name, an epitome of Theophratus's *On Perception* and a response to puzzles (concerning the nature of the human soul and natural phenomena such as sleep, dreams, the seasons, tides, and the poison of snakes) posed by Khusro I, the Persian host of the philosophers (partially extant in Latin). Some scholars think that Priscian is the author of the commentary on Aristotle's *On the Soul*, which the manuscript tradition attributes to Simplicius.

10 Photius, *Bibliotheca*, 8 vols., ed. René Henry. Paris, 1959–1965. Cod. 181; see now Athanassiadi, *Damascius*, Testimonium III.

11 See Elias *In Cat.*, pr. 134, 4. Eutocius wrote commentaries, still extant, on Archimedes and Apollonios of Perge, the latter being dedicated to Anthemius of Tralles, one of the architects of Hagia Sophia.

12 A fairly comprehensive list of works can be found in Clemens Scholten, *Antike Naturphilosophie und christliche Kosmologie in der Schrift "De opificio mundi" des Johannes Philoponos* (Berlin, 1996).

13 See Harold Tarrant, "Olympiodorus and the Surrender of Paganism," *Byzantinische Forschungen* 24 (1997): 185, who also sees Olympiodorus, together with John the Lydian, as the first classicists, "champions of some ancient heritage that needed to be kept alive" (183).

14 Westerink, *Anonymous Prolegomena to Platonic Philosophy*, xv.

15 See Christian Wildberg, "Three Neoplatonic Introductions to Philosophy: Ammonius, David, and Elias," *Hermathena* 149 (1991): 33–51.

16 See Avedis K. Sanjian, ed., *David Anhagt, the "Invincible" Philosopher* (Atlanta, 1986).

17 On Sergius, see Henri Hugonnard-Roche, "Aux origines de l'exégèse orientale de la *Logique* d'Aristote: Sergius de Resh'aina, médecin et philosophe," *Journal asiatique* 277 (1989): 1–17.

18 On Paul the Persian, see Dimitri Gutas, "Paul the Persian on the Classification of the Parts of Aristotle's Philosophy: A Milestone between Alexandria and Baghdad," *Der Islam* 60 (1983): 231–267.

19 These are an "Introduction to Logic" addressed to King Khusro (531–578) and a commentary on Aristotle's *On Interpretation*, both extant in Syriac.

20 On Uranius, see Agathias, *Historiarum libri quinque*, 2.29–32; and Joel T. Walker, "The Limits of Late Antiquity: Philosophy between Rome and Iran," *Ancient World* 33 (2002): 45–69.

21 On John of Scythopolis, see John C. Lamoreaux and Paul Rorem, *John of Scythopolis and the Dionysian Corpus: Annotating the Areopagite* (Oxford, 1998).

22 See Garth Fowden, "The Pagan Holy Man in Late Antique Society," *JHS* 102 (1982): 33–59.

23 Karl Praechter, "Richtungen und Schulen im Neuplatonismus," *Genethliakon für Carl Robert* (Berlin, 1910,) 105–155, reprinted in Praechter, *Kleine Schriften*, ed. Heinrich Dörrie, Collectanea 7 (Hildesheim, 1973), 165–216.

24 See Karl Praechter, "Christlich-neuplatonische Beziehungen," *BZ* 21 (1912): 1–27, and the discussion in Koenraad Verrycken, "The Metaphysics of Ammonius Son of Hermeias," in *Aristotle Transformed*, ed. Richard R. K. Sorabji (London, 1990), 199–204.

25 See, for example, Ilsetraut Hadot, *Le problème du néoplatonisme Alexandrin: Hiéroclès et Simplicius* (Paris, 1978); and Hadot, "The Life and Work of Simplicius in Greek and Arabic Sources," in *Aristotle Transformed: The Ancient Commentators and Their Influence*, ed. Richard R. K. Sorabji (London, 1990), 275–303. Verrycken, "The Metaphysics of Ammonius Son of Hermeias," also briefly discusses the problem.

26 In particular, Verrycken, "The Metaphysics of Ammonius Son of Hermeias," 215–226, argues convincingly that Ammonius did not depart from neoplatonic tradition by interpreting Aristotle's prime mover as both final and efficient cause.

27 See Ludwig Fladerer, *Johannes Philoponos* De opificio mundi. *Spätantikes Sprachdenken und christliche Exegese* (Stuttgart, 1999), 19–164.

28 Philoponus, *Against Proclus*, 116.22–117.12.

29 See, for example, his remarks in *Against Proclus*, 318, 5–12.

30 Simplicius, *CAG*, 8, p. 7, 23–32.

31 Elias, *CAG*, 1.8.1, pp. 122, 25–123, 11, trans. Nigel Wilson, Scholars of Byzantium, 7.

32 This is the "On the Eternity of the World against Proclus" (ed. Rabe), which cites the Proclean arguments verbatim at the beginning of each book. Proclus's treatise has been reedited by Helen S. Lang and A. D. Marco, *On the Eternity of the World / De aeternitate mundi. Proclus.* Greek text with introduction, translation, and commentary (Berkeley, Calif., 2001). Argument 1 is translated from the Arabic by Jon McGinnis.

33 The treatise is extant only in fragments preserved by Simplicius, who quotes Philoponus in order to "comment" on him in the same way he "commented" on Aristotle. Simplicius's polemic is one of the high points of ancient philosophical invective; see Philippe Hoffmann, "Simplicius' Polemics," in *Philoponus and the Rejection of Aristotelian Science*, ed. Richard R. K. Sorabji (London, 1987), 57–83. On the reconstruction of the treatise from those fragments, see Christian Wildberg, "Prolegomena to the study of Philoponus' contra Aristotelem," in Sorabji, *Philoponus and the Rejection of Aristotelian Science*, 197–209; Wildberg, *Philoponus, Against Aristotle on the Eternity of the World* (London, 1987); and Wildberg, *John Philoponus' Criticism of Aristotle's Theory of Aether* (Berlin, 1988). There is good evidence that the *Against Aristotle* was a "hybrid" text in the sense that it appended creationist evidence from the Bible to a very technical discussion of natural philosophy.

34 See Christian Wildberg, "Impetus Theory and the Hermeneutic of Science in Simplicius and Philoponus," *Hyperboreus* 5 (1999): 107–124.

35 See Wildberg, "Impetus Theory and the Hermeneutic of Science," and Ludwig Fladerer, "Johannes Philoponus, Gregor von Nyssa und die Genese der Impetustheorie," *Hommages à Carl Deroux. Tome V – Christianism et Moyen Âge, Néo-latin et survivance de la latinité* (Brussels, 2003).

36 A judicious account of Hypatia's life is offered by Maria Dzielska, *Hypatia of Alexandria* (Cambridge, Mass., 1995).

37 Robert Kaster, *Guardians of Language* (Berkeley, Calif., 1988), 331. On Pamprepius, see 329–332.

38 See Fowden, "The Pagan Holy Man in Late Antique Society," 53.

39 The primary evidence for the closing of the Academy in Athens is found in: *CJ* 5.18.4; 11.9–10; John Malalas, *Chronographia*, 18.47; and Agathias, *Histories*, 2.30ff. The most important and the most recent contributions to the debate are Polymnia Athanassiadi, "Persecution and Response in Late Paganism: The Evidence of Damascius," *JHS* 113 (1993): 1–29; Polymnia Athanassiadi, *Damascius: The Philosophical History. Text with Translation and Notes* (Athens, 1999), appendix 1, 342–347; Henry J. Blumenthal, "529 and Its Sequel: What Happened to the Academy" *Byzantion* 48 (1978): 369–385; Alan Cameron, "The Last Days of the Academy at Athens," *Proceedings of the Cambridge Philological Society* 195 (1969): 7–29; Averil Cameron, *The Mediterranean World in Late Antiquity* (London, 1993), 132–136; John M. Camp, "The Philosophical Schools of Roman Athens," in *The Greek Renaissance in the Roman Empire*, ed. Susan Walker and Averil Cameron, Bulletin of the Institute for Classical Studies supp. 55 (1989): 50–55; Pierre A. Chuvin, *Chronicle of the Last Pagans*, Trans. B. A. Archer (Cambridge, Mass., 1990), 135–141; Paul Foulkes, "Where Was Simplicius?" *JHS* 112 (1992): 143; Alison Frantz, "From Paganism to Christianity in the Temples of Athens," *Proceedings of the American Philosophical Society* 119 (1975): 29–38; Alison Frantz, *The Athenian Agora*, vol. 24, *Late Antiquity, AD 267–700* (Princeton, N.J., 1988), 86–92; Ilsetraut Hadot, "La Vie et l'œuvre de Simplicius d'après des sources grecques et arabes," in *Simplicius,*

*sa vie, son œuvre, sa survie* (Berlin, 1987), 3–39; Ilsetraut Hadot, "The Life and Work of Simplicius in Greek and Arabic Sources," in *Aristotle Transformed: The Ancient Commentators and Their Influence*, ed. Richard R.K. Sorabji (ed.) (London, 1990), 275–303; Gunnar af Hällström, "The Closing of the Neoplatonic School in A.D. 529: An Additional Aspect," *Papers and Monographs of the Finnish Institute at Athens* 1 (1994): 141–165; Judith Herrin, *The Formation of Christendom* (Princeton, N.J., 1987), 77–79; Johannes Irmscher, "Paganismus im Justinianischen Reich," *Klio* 63 (1981): 683–688; A. Kariveri, "The 'House of Proclus' on the Southern Slope of the Acropolis: A Contribution," *Papers and Monographs of the Finnish Institute at Athens* 1 (1994): 115–139; Concetta Luna, review of *Thiel* (1999), *Mmenosyne* 54 (2001): 482–504; Simone v. Riet, "À propos de la biographie de Simplicius," *Revue Philosophique de Louvain* 89 (1991): 506–514; Paul Tannery, "Sur la pèriode finale de la philosophie grecque," *Revue philosophique* 42 (1896): 266–287; Michel Tardieu, "Sâbiens coranique et 'Sâbien' de Harrân," *Journal asiatique* 274 (1986): 1–44; Michel Tardieu, "Les Calendriers en usage à Harrân d'après les sources arabes et le commentaire de Simplicius à la Physique d'Aristote," in Hadot, *Simplicius, sa vie, son oeuvre, sa survie*, 40–57; Michel Tardieu, *Les paysages reliques: Routes et haltes syriennes d'Isidore à Simplicius*. Bibliothèque de l'École des Hautes Études. Sciences religieuse 94 (Louvain, 1990); Rainer Thiel, *Simplikios und das Ende der neuplatonischen Schule in Athen* (Stuttgart 1999); Edward Watts, "Justinian, Malalas, and the End of Athenian Philosophical Teaching in 529," *JRS* 94 (2004): 1–15.

40 It is not clear how many active members the Athenian school had at the time. Invariably, we hear that there were seven (Damascius, Simplicius, Eulamius, Priscian, Hermes, Diogenes, and Isidore), but our sole witness for this is Agathias, who says only that these seven emigrated to Persia, not that they all came from Athens; he simply refers to them broadly as the leading philosophers of his time (2.30.3).

41 The rationale of the law is "that people affected with this kind of fault do not . . . in the form of teachers of whatever discipline attract the souls of simpler people to their own errors" (1.5.18.4).

42 See the clause at 1.5.18.4: "But we allow only those to teach and receive public remuneration who are of orthodox faith."

43 See Kaster, *Guardians of Language*, 114–116, and Polymnia Athanassiadi, "Persecution and Response in Late Paganism: The Evidence of Damascius," *JHS* 113 (1993): n. 15.

44 See, for example, Cameron, "The Last Days of the Academy at Athens," 21.

45 Cameron, "The Last Days of the Academy at Athens," 13, gives the date of accession as September 13, 531.

46 Agathias, *Histories*, 2.30.3, trans. Frendo.

47 For a judicious evaluation of Khusro's cultural policy, see Joel T. Walker, "The Limits of Late Antiquity: Philosophy between Rome and Iran," *Ancient World* 33 (2002): 45–69, and Dimitri Gutas, *Greek Thought, Arabic Culture* (New York, 1998), 25–27.

48 See E. Watts, "Justinian, Malalas, and the End of Athenian Philosophical Teaching in 529," *JRS* 94 (2004): 1–15. On the law's content, see also James A. S. Evans, *The Age of Justinian: The Circumstances of Imperial Power* (London, 1996), 67ff.

49 This is suggested by a number of features. First, a lengthy preamble details why further legislation is being added: quite a number of people have been found out to be pagans, whose presence turns the grace of God into wrath. Then

1.11.10.2 repeats and reiterates the prohibition in 1.5.18.4 against pagan teaching but adds, as forms of punishment, confiscation and exile (10.3). Finally, in contrast to 1.5, the criminal status of pagans is now elevated to that of the Manichaeans, at 1.11.10.4.

50 Justinian imposed penalties on those who failed to denounce heretic and pagan "offenders" (1.5.18.11–13). Bishops were encouraged to keep an eye on local magistrates, and so on. Of course, everybody would only have been "following orders."

51 See Alison Frantz, *The Athenian Agora, XXIV. Late Antiquity, AD 267–700* (Princeton, N.J., 1988), 86–92; John M. Camp, "The Philosophical Schools of Roman Athens," in *The Greek Renaissance in the Roman Empire*, ed. S. Walker and Averil Cameron, *Bulletin of the Institute for Classical Studies* 55 (1989): 50–55.

52 See Athanassiadi, "Persecution and Response in Late Paganism: The Evidence of Damascius," and Athanassiadi, *Damascius*, appendix 1, 345.

53 Agathias himself unwittingly suggests that more was at stake than personal preference when he mentions in passing that the philosophers "were forbidden by law to take part in public life with impunity" (2.30.4; Frendo).

54 Though it may well be, as Athanassiadi puts it, "the only profession of ideological toleration ever signed by Justinian" ("Persecution and Response in Late Paganism," 25).

55 Whether or not the actual phrasing of the clause stems from Damascius, as Athanassiadi believes ("undoubtedly phrased by Damascius" ["Persecution and Response in Late Paganism," 25]), is of little consequence.

56 See, for example, Christopher Stead, *Philosophy in Christian Antiquity* (Cambridge, 1994).

57 See John the Lydian, *On Offices*, 3.26; Kaster, *Guardians of Language* (Berkeley, Calif., 1988), 306–309.

Part 3

# LITERATURE AND THE ARTS

# 14: Art and Architecture in the Age of Justinian

*Joseph D. Alchermes*

The reign of Justinian witnessed extraordinary levels of artistic activity, with the emperor himself an energetic patron of the arts. The court and clerical elites followed his lead, as did others throughout the empire and even beyond its borders in regions where the heritage of imperial Rome was still strong, especially in the former Roman provinces of western Europe. By Justinian's time, Constantinople had become a major center for the arts, rivaling and even surpassing much older cities like Alexandria, Antioch, and Rome. In this chapter we will see how Justinian helped to shape artistic and architectural production in the capital and how this art is reflected in other regions of the empire and of the larger Mediterranean world.

Depictions of the emperor himself illustrate certain essential themes and concepts that characterized Justinianic art and are related to many developments observed in other chapters. Justinian appears as a triumphant conqueror, in accordance with conventions even older than the empire. He is often shown with features derived from the classical past, as ancient iconographic traditions continue to signal the age-old message of authority. Through such images, Justinian makes universal claims to sovereignty and control, aspects of imperial rule particularly emphasized during his reign. Perhaps most importantly, he is pictured as supported by Christ and supporting Christ. In the art of Justinian's age, many strands of old Roman ideology and new religious expression are woven together in a way that is at once imperial and Christian to an extent never before realized. This Christian-imperial artistic matrix, characteristic of the Justinianic age, is fully in keeping with developments in law, political theory, philosophy, and military affairs.

In the pages that follow we will examine these traditional and Christian aspects of Justinianic art and architecture. We will also analyze the evidence for the ways in which imperial patronage and other factors encouraged the diffusion of themes and patterns of representation throughout and beyond the empire. We will evaluate the relationship of Justinianic art to the earlier Roman visual repertoire, point out striking innovations, and identify several features of sixth-century art that adumbrate the developments of the Middle Ages.

## The Image of Justinian: Imperial Tradition and Christianity

The artists of Justinian's day made full use of the traditional repertoire of Roman imperial iconography. Visual emblems of authority, victory, and world rule developed under Augustus and his successors still resonated powerfully. At the same time, Christian images that legitimated imperial rule were closely integrated with Roman tradition. The interweaving of Christian and imperial themes was certainly not a new phenomenon. The faith had helped shape imperial imagery since the days of Constantine in the early fourth century. Nevertheless, we see a growing synthesis of the imperial and the Christian in the remarkable artistic production of the Justinianic epoch.

Imperial tradition fully informs the magnificent golden medallion of Justinian struck around 535 and weighing half a Roman pound, almost six ounces (Plates i and ii).[1] The burly bust of the round-faced emperor fills one side of the disk. Wearing a breastplate and military cloak and crowned with a gem-studded diadem topped by a plumed dress helmet, Justinian is glorious, his exceptional status highlighted by the nimbus (halo) around his head. The inscription acclaims him as "Our lord Justinian, perpetual Augustus." On the reverse of this lavish presentation piece, the armed ruler again appears, this time astride a horse. A winged Victory bearing a palm frond and a trophy of captured weapons ushers along the exultant emperor. Here the inscription lauds Justinian as the "salvation and glory of the Romans." Both the cuirassed, spear-bearing image and the equestrian format are formulas for representing the Roman ruler that by Justinian's day had been in use for well over half a millennium.

Monumental mural decoration directly depicted another venerable and closely related theme, imperial mastery of "barbarian" enemies. For example, the mosaic (now lost) once on the vaulted ceiling of the

Chalke, the vestibule of the imperial palace, pictured Justinian and the empress Theodora at the center of an elaborate composition celebrating the "victories over both the king of the Vandals and the king of the Goths, submissive prisoners of war who approach the imperial couple."[2]

Procopius mentions a colossal equestrian portrait of Justinian that formerly stood near the Chalke in Constantinople's central plaza, the Augoustaion.[3] This lost statue is reflected in a fifteenth-century drawing in Budapest (Plate iv). The historian carefully observed the details of the emperor's dress: breastplate, low boots without greaves (leg protectors), and a remarkable piece of headgear with a crest of swaying plumes. Justinian carries no weapons, holding instead in his left hand the *globus cruciger*, a sphere representing his universal domain surmounted by a cross, a symbol of Christian authority. Procopius emphasizes the potency of this Christianized imperial symbol, "by which alone Justinian has secured both his dominion and his mastery in war." He also interprets the gesture of the emperor's other hand: "Extending his right hand toward the regions of the rising sun and spreading out his fingers, he orders the barbarians in that place to remain at home and to not move forward."

Another more dynamic figure on the well-known Barberini Ivory (Plate iii) in all likelihood also depicts Justinian as victorious and protected by Christ.[4] In the central panel of this originally five-part composite, the equestrian emperor, crowned and armed, looks toward the viewer as his mount rears energetically. Behind the central group stands a submissive bearded figure, clearly non-Roman, as his dress indicates. A Victory hovers above the jubilant Justinian, while beneath his horse a full-bodied woman representing fertility and earthly plenty cradles fruits in her lap as she touches the emperor's boot in a gesture of supportive subservience.

This centerpiece, emphasizing the emperor's vigor, victory, and the abundance they produce, is surrounded by panels that round out its meaning. On the left (and originally, it seems, on the right), a cuirassed soldier offers a statuette of crown-bearing Victory to the triumphant rider. The lowest section illustrates the extent of the emperor's domination: non-Roman peoples carrying tribute hasten toward a trophy-bearing Victory. The strip at the top pictures directly the concept that Procopius saw expressed in the *globus cruciger* of the Augoustaion statue: imperial victory and power are ordained by God. Flying angels derived from classical Victories raise a roundel with a bust of Christ blessing and holding a cross-scepter.[5] The heavenly bodies incised on the disk denote the cosmic authority of Christ and of his earthly representative, the emperor. In this context should be mentioned a nearly contemporary Constantinopolitan image (now lost) that made the same point on a much larger scale: the mosaic of Christ in the apse over the imperial throne in the Chrysotriklinos (Golden Hall), a late sixth-century chamber in the imperial palace.[6] The colossal equestrian portrait and, even more vividly, the Barberini Ivory illustrate the melding of traditional triumphal imagery with Christian elements, demonstrating that the source of imperial victory and authority is the ruler's relationship to the Christian God. The large bronze and small, costly presentation pieces such as the medallion endow the emperor with an air of martial valor, when in fact he was not a battlefield commander. In typical late imperial fashion, however, valor and triumph belong to the perennially victorious emperor, given him by Christ, whom he serves.

## The Image of Justinian in a Christian Context: Ravenna

A powerful fusion of imperial tradition and Christian themes marks the most impressive and best-known portrait of the emperor preserved in Ravenna, the capital of the western empire during the fifth and sixth centuries. Here, in the Church of San Vitale (dedicated 547), the glittering mosaics of the sanctuary include two nearly nine-foot-high panels representing the empress with her retinue (Plate III) and the emperor surrounded by churchmen and members of the royal entourage (Plate IV). The imperial couple appears to participate in religious processions, the Christian equivalent of scenes so familiar in earlier Roman art that depicted the emperor offering sacrifice.[7] Crowned, clad in imperial purple, and carrying a large golden paten or liturgical bowl, Justinian stands at the center of the panel, flanked by courtiers, armed guards, and clerics. An inscription identifies a figure dressed in clerical costume as Archbishop Maximian. In his central position and through his benefaction, though, the emperor here is the protagonist. The pendant mosaic places Theodora and her retinue in a different setting: a courtyard with a scalloped niche and a striped curtain hung above the heads of the empress and her attendants. Two courtiers precede Theodora, drawing the drape at the door and yielding deferentially to the empress and her handmaidens. These women wear luxurious garments so brilliantly colored that Theodora's rich purple mantle (typically worn by men only) seems sober by comparison. The truly dazzling elements of her costume are the tall, jeweled crown with pendant strands of pearls and the heavy necklace covering her shoulders and upper chest; these frame and stand in sharp contrast with her solemn, severe face. Like Justinian, Theodora carries an offering, a gem-encrusted chalice or ritual cup. The importance of the gift and its imperial bearer are underscored by the golden embroidery on the hem of Theodora's cloak: in a pose similar to that of the empress, the three royal Magi extend their arms to the right as they bring gifts to Christ, the infant king. The imperial offerings complement the complex program of the mosaics in the sanctuary, which revolves around the twin theme of offering and sacrifice, ideas related to the ritual performed on the eucharistic altar at its center.

No document records imperial gifts to San Vitale; in any case, no donations were made in person by Justinian and Theodora, who never set foot in Italy. Their conspicuous presence in the church must be interpreted against the backdrop of the political and military events of the decades preceding the dedication of San Vitale in 547. Since the late fifth century, Italy was ruled by non-Romans, first Odoacer and then the Ostrogothic king Theodoric. In 535, Justinian's armies invaded Italy, recovering the capital of Ravenna in 540. Later in the 540s, the mosaics picturing the imperial processions were installed in San Vitale as a token of the allegiance of Ravenna's Romans to their leader in the east.[8] The images of the emperor and of his consort demonstrated imperial solidarity with the Roman population of the city and of the peninsula.[9]

In the traditional view, the processional panels were created after Maximian took up his position in Ravenna (546) but before the death of Theodora (548), at a time when tensions flared between the imperial administration and the Roman Church during the Three Chapters Controversy.[10] Pope Vigilius had been arrested in 545 and later was brought against his will to Constantinople, where he remained until shortly before his death in 555. In 546, Justinian arranged Maximian's elevation to bishop, expecting that the new holder of the important see of Ravenna would prove more cooperative than the pope. The mosaic created soon after Maximian's accession pictures him and his deacons standing next to Justinian in a display of collaboration between the administration in Constantinople and the ecclesiastical authorities in Ravenna.[11]

The imperial bodyguard, with colorful cloaks and shields distinguishing this corps clearly from the other participants in the procession, is prominently represented for rather different reasons. The characteristic costume and weapons indicate their status; certain features differentiate them also in ethnic terms from the courtiers and clerics accompanying Justinian. Viewers would recognize in carefully represented details, such as the long, flowing hair and perhaps also the heavy golden torques (necklaces) worn by the soldiers, that they are of non-Roman, Germanic stock.[12] The army, including the imperial guard in Constantinople, had for centuries recruited Germanic troops, a practice maintained in Justinian's day. The representation of such a group of non-Roman servitors of the eastern emperor must have had particular resonance for the Roman residents of Ravenna. Between 542 and 546, the Ostrogothic king Totila brought Rome and much of Italy (excluding Ravenna) under his control. In contrast to the hostile Goths commanded by Totila, the soldiers pictured in the mosaic were "barbarians" domesticated in the service of the emperor. Not Roman by birth, Justinian's guards instead are naturalized through their loyalty to the Roman sovereign; like the bishop and his clergy, these troops are presented as faithful collaborators and participants in empire.

The works discussed thus far show how through their images the emperor and also the empress presented themselves to their subjects. We now turn to consider briefly the artistic terms of the audience response.

## The Response to the Imperial Image among the Late Roman Public

Throughout the many centuries of the Roman Empire, portraits served both as likenesses of the emperor as well as embodiments of his rule. The official effigy displayed in legal tribunals validated the proceedings conducted by the emperor's judicial representative; for example, the multiple pairs of imperial busts so prominent in the trial scenes of the sixth-century Rossano Gospels (Plate xiv) confirm the authority of Pilate's decision.[13]

Imperial portraits, both male and female, also set trends and inspired imitation among the elite, a pattern that can be observed well into the late empire. The marble bust of a noblewoman (Plate xv), probably from Constantinople, is the most remarkable of the surviving sixth-century representations. Shared elements of fashion and form have encouraged comparison to the portrait of Theodora and other sixth-century works.[14] Though damaged, this rare example of Justinianic life-size portraiture suggests what has been lost with the disappearance of so much that was created in the capital. The skill of the sculptor is manifest in the superbly worked surfaces: the smooth, polished skin of the neck and face, the voluminous folds of the weighty mantle, the lighter cloth of the tunic covering the upper chest and right shoulder, and the seemingly sheer fabric of the snoodlike hair-covering. The sitter's features are masterfully delineated: the delicate, pursed lips, the slightly puffy cheeks, and the focused yet soulful eyes. The artist has effectively characterized the noblewoman as a person of sensitivity and sophisticated intelligence, qualities underlined by the scroll in her right hand, which in Roman portraiture had long been a badge of the learned person.[15] This marble bust demonstrates the persistent taste of the sixth-century elite for portraits that maintained centuries-old visual formulas as well as the remarkable ability of Constantinopolitan sculptors to serve their patrons' wishes for classically inspired art.

## Luxury Objects and Cosmopolitan Taste in the Age of Justinian

By the sixth century, Constantinople had come into its own as an artistic center where precious objects of every sort were produced, including gems, jewelry, plate, and carved ivory. Another luxury good specifically associated with the Justinianic age was silk. The emperor donated to Hagia Sophia, the cathedral of Constantinople, silken sanctuary furnishings decorated with figures done in rich colors, gold, and silver: Christ flanked by Saints Peter and Paul, the imperial couple shown once with Christ, once with Mary. These lavish offerings highlighted imperial piety and publicized imperial largesse: the altar cloth pictured the hospitals and churches founded by Justinian and Theodora. Justinian's achievements were also depicted on another elaborate textile, the embroidered robe in which he was clothed after his death in 565. Corippus's panegyric on Justin II, Justinian's successor, refers to its decoration, imagery like the mosaic in the Chalke that depicted imperial triumph and the submission of conquered enemies.[16]

According to Procopius, Justinian himself introduced silkworm breeding in the empire, when with his encouragement monks from India smuggled silk moth eggs from the East to Constantinople. Possibly as early as the seventh century, the Byzantine silk industry was centered in the capital.[17] Sixth-century carvers who created such splendid works as the Barberini Ivory (Plate iii), the throne of Archbishop Maximian of Ravenna, or the superb panel with an archangel (Plate xvi) did not enjoy such easy access to the raw material of their craft, which in the late empire was imported from faraway India and above all Africa.[18] Ivory provisioning required extensive international networks that centered on patrons and workshops in Constantinople as well as in other economic and cultural hubs.

The winged archangel (usually identified as Michael) seems to rest his heels on the top of a flight of steps deep in the space framed by the intricately carved arch; his arms and wings, however, clearly overlap the columns at the front of the arch. The master carver working on this large plaque (the largest late Roman or Byzantine ivory panel to survive) was not concerned to create a fully convincing spatial setting for the figure; the richly ornamented backdrop frames the angel and serves as a foil for the stiff quills of the wings contrasting in texture with his fluffy curls and the flowing folds of his garments, which cling to and reveal the rounded body volumes. The carefully modeled body and fluid drapery preserve the visual heritage of the classical world, while the dense arrangement of the decorative elements of the intricate architecture recalls the ornament of contemporary buildings like the Church of Sts. Sergius and Bacchus. The Michael panel may well have once been part of a diptych (two plaques joined with hinges on their long sides) linked with a leaf picturing the emperor; such an ivory diptych would represent a luxurious parallel to the coins of Justin I and Justinian, where the archangel and the emperor were similarly paired. Christianized imperial imagery appears in the sumptuary arts available to relatively few as well as in objects, such as coins, that circulated widely.

Elaborately written and illustrated manuscripts were also created in growing numbers in this period. One of the most extravagant, even in its present truncated form, is the so-called Rossano Gospels, usually dated to the sixth century and attributed by some to Constantinople. A Syrian, perhaps Antiochene provenance is more likely; in Justinian's day, Constantinople was one of a number of artistic centers around the Mediterranean.[19] Of the four gospels, only Matthew and part of Mark survive, written in gold and silver on purple-dyed parchment. The gospel text is introduced by more than a dozen miniatures, painted with a vivid dash that continues venerable traditions in Roman art. The leaf pictured here, with the episode of Christ before Pontius Pilate (Plate xiv), is one of the most elaborate. The scene fills the whole page, with the action unfolding in two tiers that together represent a single, unified setting: the tribunal of the Roman governor, presented in terms familiar from experience to the sixth-century viewer. Below (to be understood as in the foreground) stands Christ, flanked by two court officials wearing the long mantles (similar to those of the courtiers in the imperial panels at Ravenna) that indicate their rank. To the right are two men, a shackled, belligerent prisoner and his jailer. An inscription identifies the former as Barabbas, the thief who received amnesty while Christ was condemned to death. This is the outcome for which the audience, pictured above, clamors. Two groups of spectators gesticulate vigorously toward the Roman governor as they attempt to affect his decision, the authority of which is confirmed by the paired imperial busts visible on the table drape and on the panels mounted on poles next to the guards. In this miniature, the lively drama of the upper part contrasts neatly with the majestic composure of the accused Christ below. Lavishly written, richly illustrated books like the Rossano Gospels were rare and prestigious trophies, tangible signs of affluence and taste that only the wealthiest could afford.

Well-off sixth-century patrons also commissioned works of religious content and function crafted of precious metals. A liturgical vessel like the silver-gilt paten, or eucharistic dish (Plate x), dating perhaps to 577, was part of a sizeable set of ritual furnishings belonging to a church in the north Syrian village of Kaper Koraon.[20] The paten, more than a foot in diameter and weighing over two and a half Roman pounds, has a handsome inscription on the rim that names the donor and those for whom the gift was offered. The central circle contains a scene of the Communion of the Apostles. In the gospels, Christ first administered the eucharist to his followers in the context of a meal, the Last Supper. Here the event is instead pictured so that it conforms to current liturgical custom, much as the trial scene discussed above drew on contemporary judicial practice. Christ, shown twice, stands behind a draped altar laden with eucharistic vessels. The group of apostles on the right takes from Christ's hands the consecrated bread, while those on the left drink the consecrated wine from a large chalice.[21] All the components – the processional movement of the communicants, the altar and the equipment on and near it, the columned screen supporting lamps – were familiar elements of the sixth-century eucharistic rite and its physical setting.

## Elite Taste and the Classical Past

Other costly sixth-century silver often features themes drawn from Greco-Roman tradition. A large (sixteen-inch diameter) plate (Plate xvii) probably made in Constantinople pictures Hercules, the classical hero par excellence, as he performs one of his most famous labors, defeating the Nemean lion.[22] The smith has carefully picked out the hero's powerful muscles flexed to fend off the lunging beast. The texture of the lion's thick mane is distinguished from that of the furry legs and of the lighter hide pulled taut over the ribs and haunches. Hercules' determined composure, so characteristic of classical heroes, contrasts with the ferocious snarl of the lion, whose fierceness is emphasized by his oversized, sharp-clawed paws. The hero's scattered weapons and a few landscape elements complete the picture dominated by the dueling pair.

Classically inspired silver like the Hercules plate differs in style and mood from the paten discussed above, where the cramped figures of Christ and the apostles have little corporeal solidity and seem barely modeled. The communicants' clothing all but totally obscures the forms of their bodies. The paten's creator strove to convey the intensity of feeling, the fervor filling Christ's followers as they reverently approach him to partake of the bread and wine miraculously made body and blood. The paten contrasts with more classical works like the Hercules plate, the ivory carving of Michael (Plate xvi), and the David Plate (Plate xxiv), which demonstrate that as late as the sixth and seventh centuries, artisans trained in the Greco-Roman tradition could cater to the taste of wealthy patrons for luxury art featuring classical as well as Christian imagery that maintained the artistic hallmarks of the pre-Christian past.

## Christian Images in the Age of Justinian: Icons

Many sixth-century makers of silver plate and other luxurious furnishings maintained the style and imagery typical of works created earlier in the Empire, even when the figures and scenes represented are clearly Christian. Images in other media, such as panel painting, also show links with earlier Roman art. The celebrated image of the blessing Christ (Plate VI) is one of the oldest extant Christian painted panels. This devotional image, or icon, was created in Constantinople under Justinian or soon thereafter.[23] The icon is preserved in the isolated monastery, now dedicated to St. Catherine, founded by the emperor in the southern Sinai. The panel escaped destruction during the eighth- and ninth-century imperial ban on religious images (Iconoclasm), because by that time, the peninsula was under Muslim control and outside imperial jurisdiction. The life-size half-figure is given a pose and a mien familiar from countless later paintings and representations in other media: set in front of a diminutive niche, the haloed Christ holds a gem-studded gospel book in his left hand as he raises his right arm in a gesture of blessing, his face subtly animated in an expression of grave benevolence. Though two-dimensional, the image has an imposing three-dimensional force generated by the placement of the long bust at the front of the pictorial space and by the careful shading that creates an impression of volume. The sense of presence, enhanced by Christ's size and by his penetrating gaze, provides a powerful encouragement to the Christian devotee to communicate with God through this riveting image.

Literary testimony associates with the Age of Justinian a famous early image of Christ, the Camouliana icon, named for the village in Asia Minor where it was found. According to the legend of its origin, the divine likeness, not painted by human hand, appeared miraculously in a fountain. Soon after, an equally spontaneous duplicate was generated. Much later, the Camouliana image was brought to Constantinople, where it performed further miracles. Its remarkable power impelled emperors to use the icon as a supernatural weapon, bringing it on military campaigns. George of Pisidia credits the deployment of the Camouliana Christ with success in the Persian campaign of 622 and with the deliverance of Constantinople from the Avar siege of 626.[24] The holy image, charged with the divine potency of the figure that it represents, served both in the defense of the Empire and for the devotion of the faithful.

The method of painting employed for the Sinai Christ icon and in many other sixth- and seventh-century devotional images is known as encaustic, in which the pigments are suspended in melted wax. Encaustic painting had been practiced for centuries in the Greco-Roman world. Painters in Roman Egypt, for example, often used the technique for the masklike portraits attached to mummy cases or directly to the wrappings themselves. These mummy portraits and other Roman funerary images have often been seen as pre-Christian precedents for early Christian icons.[25] The Christian icons have much more in common with another category of ancient painting: wooden panels depicting polytheist gods that survive in about thirty examples, most from Roman Egypt.[26] The similarities span a wide range, from imagery, composition, and function to format and methods of manufacture. Both the non-Christian and Christian panels focus attention on the large figures displaying themselves to the viewer in static, frontal poses. At times the presence of diminutive donor figures or inscriptions naming the patron express directly the votive function of the images. The frame of the Christ icon unfortunately does not survive, but other Christian panels preserve features in their frames, identical to those seen in the non-Christian examples, that made it possible to cover the image, both for protection and out of reverence.

## Monumental Christian Art in the Age of Justinian

In its present location at the monastery on Mt. Sinai, the icon of the blessing Christ complements a contemporary image linked to Justinianic Constantinople: the extraordinary apse mosaic of the Transfiguration (Plate VII), the scriptural episode in which Christ briefly shed his human appearance and made visible his divine glory to three apostles, Peter, John, and James (Mt 17.1–13). This stunning composition is the centerpiece of the sanctuary decoration in the main monastic church founded by the emperor himself and constructed between 548 and 565.[27] Against the shimmering gold ground of the apse appears the central figure of Christ set in a brilliant blue mandorla, the oval signifying divine presence and power. Its concentric, subtly gradated blue bands concentrate attention on the transfigured Christ, clad in white garments richly trimmed with gold and blessing with his right hand as he gazes toward the viewer in the nave. His starkly geometric face projects an aura of intensity heightened by the silver bands of divine light radiating from him in all directions. This focal image – Christ and the mandorla – floats against the golden sky, while below, a shallow strip of yellow-gold and green ground provides the surface on which the human participants in this dramatic episode are placed. Inscriptions identify the figures standing to the left and right: Moses and Elijah, turned and gesturing toward Christ. Beneath the mandorla, the awe-struck apostles have fallen to the ground. At the top of the wall above the apse, a pair of mosaic panels depict the two most famous events specifically linked with Mt. Sinai: in one, Moses reverently removes his sandals before God present in the Burning Bush, while in the other he receives from God's hand the tablets of the Law.

The associations of the place clearly inspired the decision to picture these instances of Old Testament theophany, the manifestation of God. In Christian belief, the divine vision experienced by Moses is juxtaposed with and completed in the Transfiguration, the dazzling display of divinity that fills the apse. Here in the sanctuary of Justinian's monastery church, images of historical theophanies formed the backdrop for the liturgical performance that made God present and visible in the eucharist.

## Architectural Patronage and Justinian

Authors active during Justinian's reign, Procopius foremost among them, placed far greater emphasis on the emperor's architectural undertakings than on other areas of artistic patronage. From the very beginning of the empire, massive construction campaigns were both an imperial prerogative and an imperial expectation. Justinian's accomplishments as a patron of architecture stand the test of comparison with the undertakings of even his most energetic predecessors.

The first book of Procopius's *Buildings*, the lengthy survey of Justinianic constructions written about 550, describes the wide range of imperial projects in the capital and its suburbs.[28] Much was occasioned by the devastation of the Nika revolt (532). Justinian sponsored the construction or rebuilding of palaces, the Senate and other government buildings, public squares, markets, colonnaded streets, public baths, cisterns, harbors, lodgings for travelers, hospitals and other charitable institutions, and over thirty churches and religious shrines. Procopius's catalog of Constantinopolitan building gives a good sense of the variety and vibrancy of life in the capital, which for much of Justinian's reign must have seemed to its residents an ongoing construction site.

Justinian's contemporaries note a similar range of building sponsored by the emperor in other parts of his realm. The example of two other cities illustrates the broad span of urbanistic and architectural development. In Antioch, the emperor responded energetically to the catastrophic destruction brought about by earthquakes in the 520s and the Persian sack of 540. Procopius outlines the extensive program of urban renewal: the course of the Orontes River was altered, a shorter circuit of city walls laid out, and the water supply improved. New colonnaded streets, paved and provided with sewers, rose over foundations fashioned from the debris. Procopius also sketchily mentions the public buildings, such as theaters and baths, and the great churches that were part of this redevelopment campaign.[29]

Justinian also set his urban planners to work at the village in the Balkans that was his birthplace, founding a new city named for himself, Justiniana Prima. Procopius again enumerates the principal landmarks: an aqueduct, churches, civic buildings, colonnaded streets, market squares, baths, fountains, and shops.[30] Justinian's city has been identified with the ruins of Caričin Grad near Niš in modern Serbia. Here archaeologists have brought to light a small city with a remarkably varied complement of sixth-century structures (Fig. 5) that validates the reliability of Procopius's list: a walled citadel with the cathedral,

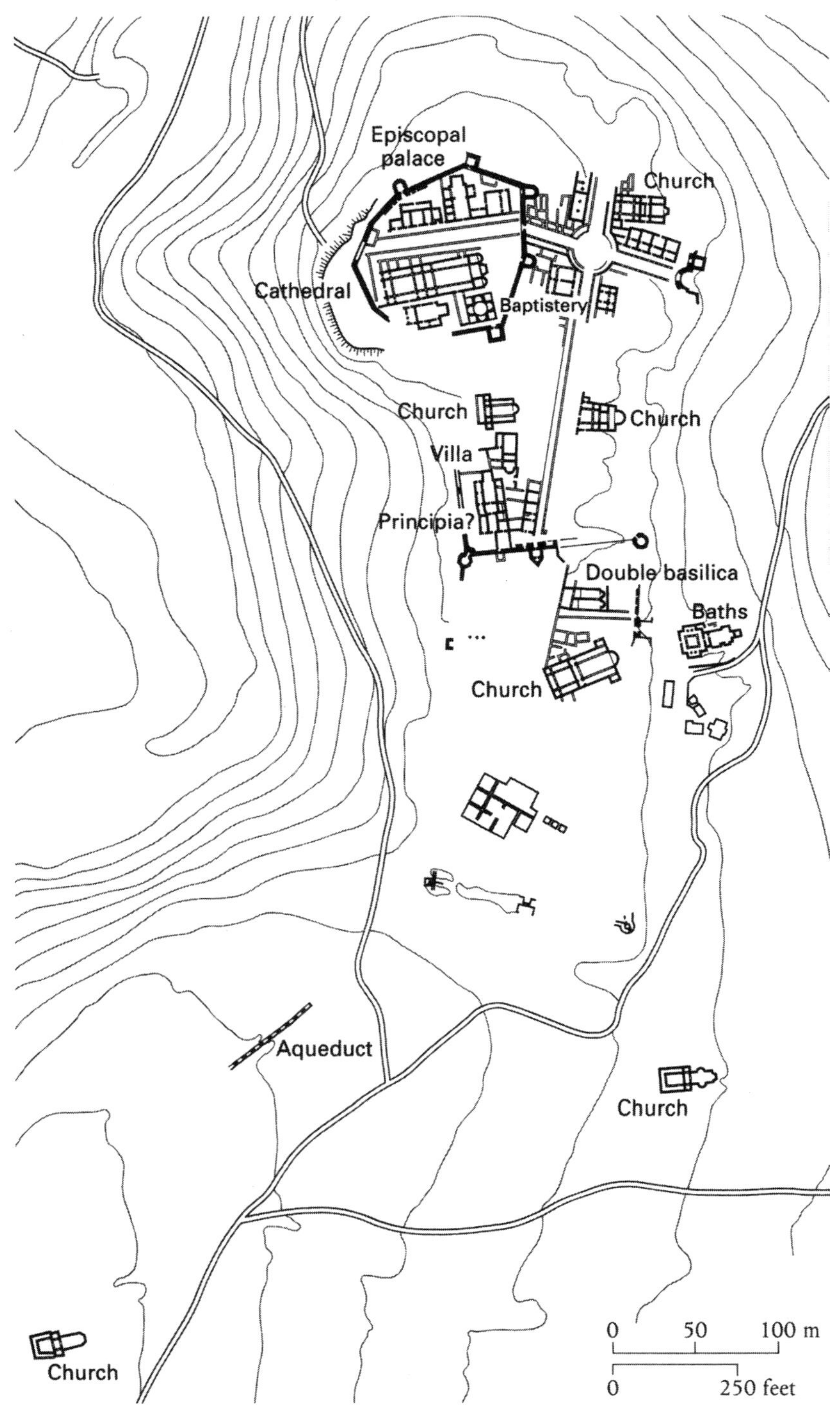


FIGURE 5. Justiniana Prima, sixth century, topographical map

baptistery and archbishop's palace; a main plaza, circular in plan, on which the four main porticoed avenues of the city converge; an aqueduct and other constructions related to the water supply; baths; commercial and residential buildings; and a number of sizeable churches, almost all simple variants on the basic basilica form.

Justiniana Prima represents a remarkable case of a late city foundation where planners reproduced urban features and amenities – colonnaded streets, public plazas, baths, and other buildings – that had long characterized the cityscapes of the eastern Mediterranean.[31] Inserted in this small-scale but traditional urban matrix is an array of religious buildings, dominating the citadel and highly visible in the lower town as well. Justiniana Prima was at once classical and Christian.

Military architecture was another major concern of the emperor. Procopius notes and the archaeological record confirms that fortifications were laid out anew for fresh foundations like Justiniana Prima or were rebuilt at many older sites from the Middle East to Tunisia. Throughout the empire, Justinian also commissioned works of urban infrastructure such as aqueducts and cisterns. More rarely, he is given credit for civic buildings and commercial facilities.[32]

Along with constructions related to defense and to water provisioning, the third main category of architectural patronage that Procopius ascribes to Justinian is the building of churches. The material and literary evidence attests the ecclesiastical construction sponsored by him in all parts of the empire: the churches of Justinian, celebrated as witnesses to his piety and closeness to God, were complemented throughout the Christian world by large numbers of religious buildings commissioned by the emperor's contemporaries.[33] Procopius suggests that the imperial architectural prerogative regarding religious buildings aspired to monopoly. Two priests who served at churches of the Archangel Michael near Constantinople had to secure imperial approval before undertaking restorations, because under Justinian "it was not possible either to build or restore a church except with imperial support, not only in Constantinople but everywhere in the empire."[34] Procopius notes that Justinian had the decrepit structures demolished and replaced with splendid new shrines to Michael.

In building churches, the emperor devoted special attention to locations distinguished by longstanding Christian traditions or of particular prominence in the sixth century: Jerusalem, Bethlehem, Mt. Sinai, Antioch, Ephesus, and above all the capital. In the remote Sinai, the emperor sponsored the construction of the monastery (Plate VIII) with a standard basilica, aisled and timber-roofed. An inscription on one of

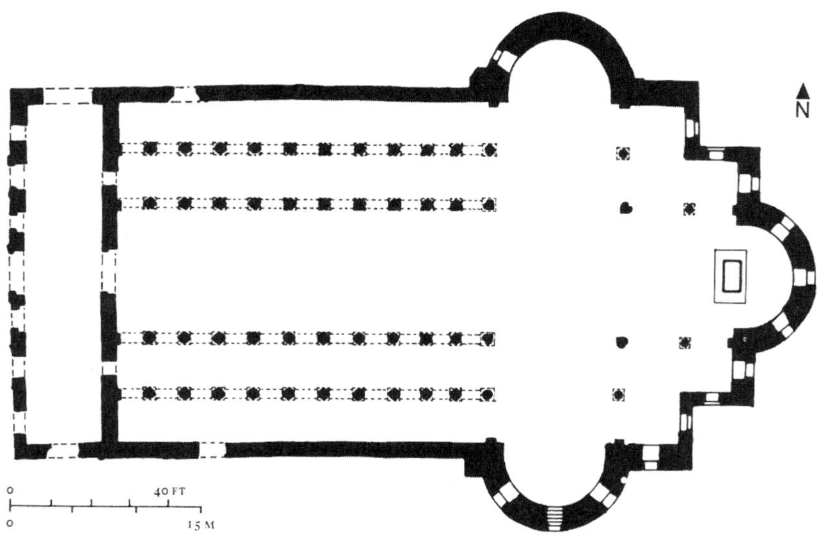


FIGURE 6. Bethlehem, Church of the Nativity, sixth-century reconstruction, plan

the wooden rafters names the builder, Stephen of Aila (near modern Eilat on the Gulf of Aqaba).[35] He was therefore from the region, unlike the mosaicist, who along with the mosaic materials and marble decoration must have been brought to Sinai, presumably from Constantinople.

Buildings in the religious centers of Jerusalem and Bethlehem were conceived on a grander scale and according to a more complex design. Two sixth-century authors refer to the sumptuous Church of the Theotokos (Mother of God), commonly called the Nea (New Church), in Jerusalem.[36] Unfortunately, neither has much to say about the shape of the church complex, of which only scant, but impressive, remains have been identified.[37] In a long excursus on the Nea, Procopius credits it to Justinian alone and focuses on the magnitude of the project, the splendor of the materials, and the obstacles posed by the uneven topography. Procopius's contemporary Cyril of Scythopolis provides additional information about the Nea: begun more than a decade before Justinian came to power, the church was completed under him by Theodore, an architect sent out from Constantinople.

The reconstruction of the Church of the Nativity in Bethlehem, founded originally under the Emperor Constantine, seems instead to date to the end of Justinian's reign or perhaps as late as 600. The most remarkable feature of the new church (Fig. 6) is its spacious, trefoil-plan sanctuary, which replaced the Constantinian octagon built over the grotto where tradition located the birth of Christ. The distinctive

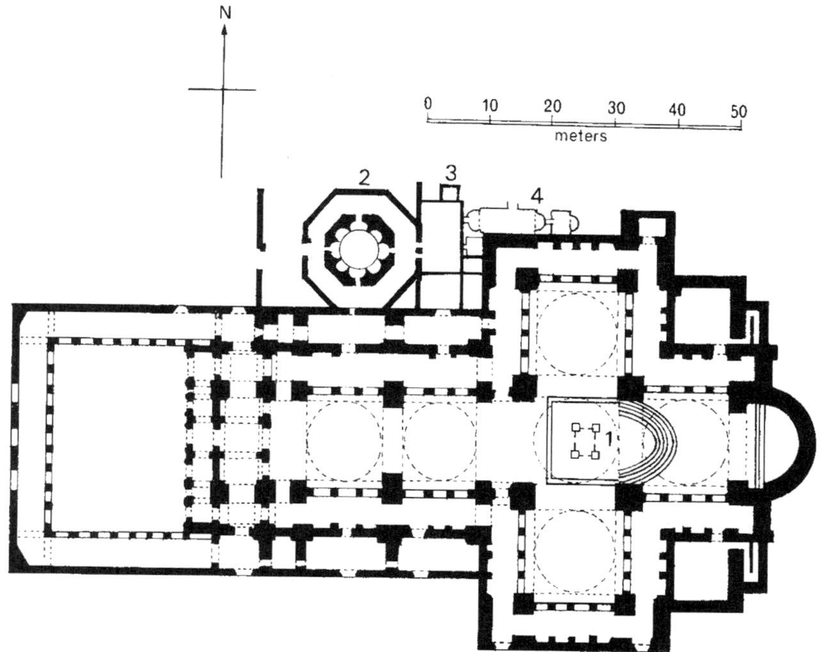


FIGURE 7. St. John, Ephesus, plan, c. 540

design may show links with the architecture of the capital; for example, a few years after the death of Justinian, his successor, Justin II (565–578), apparently commissioned a similar transept and sanctuary at the Church of the Theotokos (Mother of God) in the Blachernae region of Constantinople.[38]

Clear connections in design also bind Justinianic commissions in Constantinople and Ephesus. About 540, Justinian and Theodora sponsored the reconstruction on a much-enlarged scale of the fifth-century church of St. John on the outskirts of Ephesus.[39] A cross-shaped plan (Fig. 7) was laid down, with four domed units on the main east-west axis and two similar volumes north and south of the domed crossing (Figs. 8 and 9). Procopius himself noted that this simple but imposing scheme closely resembled the design of Justinian's Apostoleion (Church of the Apostles) in Constantinople. The Apostoleion had four domed units arranged around a domed core, distinguished from the other four in that its base was pierced with windows. The Apostoleion was demolished in 1462 to permit construction of the mosque of the Turkish sultan Mehmet II, but a general idea of the appearance of the church can be gleaned from various kinds of evidence: sixth-century and later texts

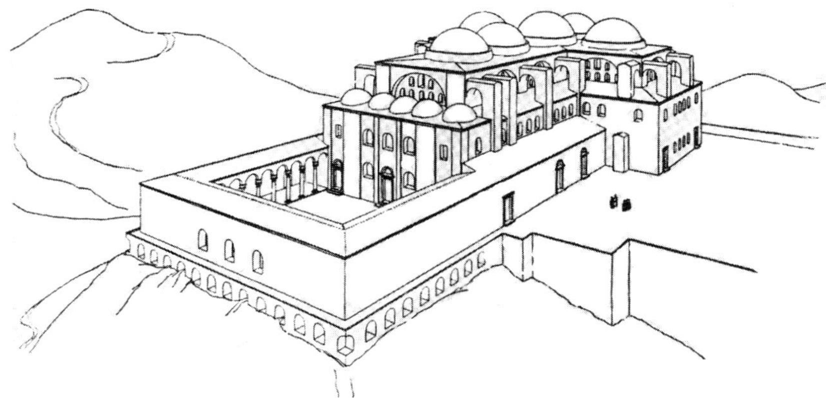

FIGURE 8. St. John, Ephesus, reconstruction of exterior, c. 540

FIGURE 9. St. John, Ephesus, reconstruction of interior, c. 540

that mention the church, Byzantine paintings that picture it, and later designs patterned on it. The prestige of the Constantinopolitan cruciform basilica was enhanced by nearby domed mausolea that served as the preferred place of royal burial from the fourth through the eleventh century. The best-known "replica" of the Apostoleion, the eleventh-century basilica of San Marco in Venice, attests how compelling a sense of imperial power the Constantinopolitan church conveyed, even in the medieval west a half-millennium after its completion under Justinian.[40]

## Sts. Sergius and Bacchus and Hagia Sophia

The two churches that best illustrate the brilliant inventiveness of the emperor's designers were commissioned in the capital by Justinian and survive today. The earlier of the two honored Sergius and Bacchus, soldiers executed around 300 for their Christian beliefs. The later, much larger Church of Divine Wisdom, Hagia Sophia, was the cathedral of Constantinople and supreme creation of late Roman (and Byzantine) architecture.

Procopius identifies Sts. Sergius and Bacchus (Plate xviii) as a work of Justinian, laid out alongside an earlier church dedicated by the emperor to another saintly pair, Peter and Paul, Rome's most famous martyrs. These churches, Procopius adds, stood in the Palace of Hormisdas, the residence of Justinian and Theodora before Justinian's elevation to the imperial rank in 527.[41] The monogrammed capitals and the impressive dedicatory inscription carved in the rich, ground-level entablature (Plate xix) name the royal patrons: the church was probably begun in 527 (the year of Justinian's accession) or soon after and was certainly completed by 536.[42] The perimeter walls, nearly square in plan, form a simple, two-story spatial shell that surrounds a three-story domed octagonal core of remarkably sophisticated design.[43] Eight wedge-shaped piers mark the angles of the octagon: on the east side, a broad arch opens onto an apsed rectangle that served as the bema (sanctuary), while seven narrower arches linked the remaining piers. These eight arches support a sixteen-sided pumpkin dome, in which concave segments (corresponding with the octagon corners below) alternate with flat vault strips pierced by eight arched windows. The complex, lively shape of the lobed dome is matched by the sophisticated design and decoration of the lower levels. The arches of the octagon frame two-story niches of alternating rectangular and semicircular plan. The curving and flat walls of the niches open in two tiers corresponding to the ground-level ambulatory and upper-story gallery, vaulted corridors that envelop the octagon on all sides except the east, where they are interrupted by the bema. At gallery level, each niche opens in a triple arcade, while below paired columns carry the rich entablature, with its elaborate sculpture and the imposing inscription of the imperial founders. The expertly carved lettering and the dynamic forms – at once feathery and flamelike – of the capitals and other architectural sculpture (Plate xix) present a counterpart to the brilliant molding of space, manipulation of light, and interpenetrating volumes of the central core and the enveloping ambulatory and gallery. Whether or not Justinian's church in the palace of Hormisdas is to be considered a "palace chapel," with its ever-changing effects of light and space and refined sculpture, Sts. Sergius and Bacchus represents an architecture developed to appeal to the discriminating taste of the sixth-century elite.[44]

As the construction of Sts. Sergius and Bacchus neared completion, the emergency conditions that followed the Nika revolt in early 532 compelled the emperor to direct his attention to a far greater architectural enterprise. Fires set by the rioters at the city center damaged civic buildings and the imperial palace and devastated the cathedral of Hagia Sophia. After the rebellion was quelled, Justinian's efforts to demonstrate control and assert authority took many forms, including an impressive display of construction spearheaded by the new cathedral, intended as far more than a mere replacement for the earlier church, which had been a large but simple aisled basilica. Notwithstanding the vast size of the new church (coupled with its innovative design) and the many resultant structural and logistical problems, work on Hagia Sophia proceeded with extraordinary rapidity. The church was ready for dedication by the emperor and patriarch on December 27, 537, less than six years after the destruction of the old cathedral.[45]

The smaller, probably earlier Sts. Sergius and Bacchus has several features in common with the huge, new church: the trilevel domed core, the two-story niches whose walls open in column screens, the aisles and galleries enveloping the vaulted centerpiece with an interruption only at the bema, and the spiky, deeply undercut patterns of the architectural sculpture. But the elements shared with Sts. Sergius and Bacchus appear in Hagia Sophia on a vastly enlarged scale. The main dome of the cathedral, one hundred feet in diameter, is divided by forty ribs framing forty curved webs perforated at the base by forty arched windows. Beneath the dome to the north and south (Plate ix, left and right), massive arches encircle heavily fenestrated tympana that rest on two tiers of arcades, seven in the gallery and five at ground level. Originally these tympana were even lighter and seemingly more insubstantial than the present arrangement.[46] Flanking the great dome on the main axis, similar arches frame not windowed tympana but rather the huge voids covered by the eastern and western half domes. Four enormous curved triangular segments called pendentives span the angles at the intersection of the four main arches, mediating between the circular base of the main dome and the square plan of the space beneath it. In the walls below the half domes, vaulted conches (oversized niches) expand further the eastern bema and the entrance area to the west. In this way a longitudinal hall was created, providing a basilical accent complemented by the aisles and galleries that run parallel to the vaulted nave on the north and south flanks. The nave of Hagia Sophia, about 260 feet long with its main dome soaring to a height of more than 180 feet, was the largest open vaulted interior in the ancient and medieval world.

In spite of the many remodelings and major repairs (beginning already in the mid-sixth century) the church has undergone, the interior of Hagia Sophia still offers an unmatched spectacle, from its polychrome stone pavement to the crowns of the nave vaults. A remarkable wealth of costly, colorful materials was deployed in the construction and decoration of the cathedral: richly carved architectural sculpture; a wide range of colored stone columns and variegated marble paneling, all originally from quarries on three continents; gold-ground, floral, and geometric mosaics on the vaults and arches.[47] Of the Justinianic elements that have vanished, the greatest losses are the glittering gold and silver furnishings of the bema and nave, above all the altar, the open, columned screen surrounding it, and the ambo (pulpit) below the central dome.

The dramatic, radically innovative design of the new cathedral was the creation of Anthemius of Tralles and Isidore of Miletus, acclaimed teachers and authors on technical subjects who were firmly grounded in classical scientific theory, especially geometry and mechanics.[48] Unlike the typical late Roman builder, Anthemius and Isidore approached the design of Hagia Sophia from a theoretical perspective, their remarkable vision not blinkered by the constraints of empirical building practice. They certainly demonstrated their ability to think outside the box of the traditional, timber-roofed basilica form: the windowed dome and half-domes, along with the pendentives, are of dimensions unprecedented in the ancient world.[49] Similar inventiveness appears in the nave walls and conches, where Anthemius and Isidore devised unusual arrangements for the arched openings. The normal pattern in classical and late Roman wall design, observed for example in Sts. Sergius and

Bacchus, features tiers of supports and openings in vertical correspondence. In Hagia Sophia, the five broad arcades that join the aisles to the nave are not aligned with the seven narrower arches in the galleries above. A contemporary of Justinian named Paul was struck by the similar lack of vertical alignment in the eastern and western lateral conches. Paul noted the unaccustomed, audacious placement of the seven arched openings in the gallery over the triple arcade of the ground level, so that the bases of the gallery columns stood, seemingly unsupported, over the arched voids below.[50]

The sculptural decoration, particularly of the capitals and of the impost blocks above them, also presents significant divergences from earlier forms. In the capitals and impost blocks of Hagia Sophia, the time-honored distinction between support (capital) and load (impost block) disappears (Plate xx). The surface of both capital and impost are overwhelmed by floral and other decoration comparable in the deep undercutting to the sculpture of Sts. Sergius and Bacchus.[51]

From the very start, the colorful covering of walls and vaults, the abundant but diffused light, the soaring dome, half-domes, and vaults have overwhelmed visitors to Justinian's church, a monument not equaled at any time in the Byzantine millennium. Contemporaries such as Procopius and especially the later medieval authors credit the emperor not only as the patron but also as a moving spirit in matters of design. While the most daring and innovative structural elements of Hagia Sophia must have been devised by Anthemius and Isidore, the emperor himself would have prescribed the colossal scale, perhaps expressing a preference as well for such features as the central dome merged with the enveloping basilica plan.[52] Whatever precise role the emperor played in its creation, Justinian's new cathedral was a most conspicuous demonstration of imperial piety and a most dramatic, majestic stage on which the emperor and his Constantinopolitan subjects could worship.

When Hagia Sophia was dedicated in 537, its immense cupola surpassed even the dome of Hagios Polyeuktos, built around 525 by Anicia Juliana and at the time probably the greatest vaulted church in the capital (today it is in ruins). The patron of Hagios Polyeuktos, a wealthy aristocrat descended from emperors on both sides of her family, spared no expense on construction and opulent decoration. The most revealing element of the decoration is the impressive dedicatory inscription, preserved today only in fragments but fortunately copied by a visitor before the collapse of the church.[53] The dedicatory poem, with its repeated references to the imperial lineage of the pious patron, casts a challenge to the authority of Justin and Justinian, lowborn provincials compared to the Constantinopolitan *grande dame*.

The dedication also boasts that by building this sumptuous church Anicia Juliana surpassed Solomon and his temple in Jerusalem. According to Harrison, the excavator of the site, this relationship was expressed as well in the carved ornamentation: the preponderance of palm trees, pomegranates, and lilies in the architectural decoration was determined by associations with the Jewish temple. The Solomonic reference may have been communicated even more subtly in the very layout of the building, where the designer used as the basis of measurement the royal cubit, the same unit employed in the Jerusalem temple.[54]

It is tempting to consider Justinian's new cathedral a response to the challenge launched by Anicia Juliana with her impressive basilica. In its colossal scale and grandiose dome, Hagia Sophia completely eclipsed the princess's church, dedicated just a decade earlier. Justinian's often-quoted first comment on entering the new cathedral was "Solomon, I have surpassed you!" If this report of the emperor's reaction (furnished by an admittedly suspect source) is reliable, the suggestion that Justinian aimed to diminish the achievement of a rival patron gains further support.[55]

As many have noted, for various reasons Hagia Sophia was never the object of replication or even close imitation either in Byzantium or in the medieval west.[56] Far-flung echoes, however, of smaller-scale domed designs current in Justinian's day can be identified. Ravenna preserves striking instances of this architectural borrowing. One, the church of San Vitale, was cited earlier as the setting for the renowned mosaics of Justinian and Theodora. San Vitale has much in common with the contemporary church of Sts. Sergius and Bacchus.[57] In each case, a three-story vaulted octagonal core is encircled at the lower two levels by a continuous ambulatory and gallery, interrupted only on the east side by the bema. In both churches, two-story niches extend outward from the domed core, their walls pierced with triple openings at each level.

In many ways, however, they differ in design and construction. The enveloping shell of Sts. Sergius and Bacchus is square in plan, while the outer walls of its Ravennate counterpart form an octagon consistent with the shape of the domed center. In San Vitale, all the niches are semicircular and their openings are arched at ground and gallery level. In Sts. Sergius and Bacchus, the niches are of alternating rectangular and semicircular plan, with trabeated openings below and arcades above. The proportions of the Italian church are much steeper than those of its Constantinopolitan counterpart, even taking into account the later raised pavement of the latter. Some components of San Vitale, such as the marble columns, capitals, and paneling, were imported to Ravenna from the area of Constantinople, while others are characteristically western. For example, the dome is constructed not in the brickwork typical of Constantinople, but of hollow clay tubes inserted into one another. The builder of San Vitale clearly drew inspiration and acquired certain materials from the eastern capital but adapted the imported elements to local traditions and taste. San Vitale in Ravenna is a variant, slightly simplified, of the highly sophisticated scheme seen in Sts. Sergius and Bacchus; with its elegant design, brilliant decoration, and compelling imperial images, the Italian church in turn inspired imitation centuries later by Charlemagne in his palace church at Aachen.

## Non-Roman Responses to Imperial Art and Architecture

Constantinopolitan designs like that of Sts. Sergius and Bacchus shaped the essential features of San Vitale, which was completed in the 540s when Ravenna was in imperial hands. Imperial art also had a profound influence on artistic patterns preferred by non-Roman leaders, the "barbarian" rulers who emerged as Roman power collapsed in the west. Often these westerners based their public image on that of the eastern emperors. A gold solidus struck about 540 for the Merovingian king Theudebert (Plate xxi) provides an excellent illustration of this phenomenon of iconographic appropriation: the bust of the Frankish lord is clearly modeled on imperial images like those created for Justinian and his immediate predecessors.[58] The inscription apes imperial coin legends as it hails the Merovingian chief: "Our lord, Theudebert, victor." The presumptuous desire of western leaders for aggrandizement through self-representation based on imperial models did not go unnoticed in contemporary Constantinople. Procopius commented disdainfully on the inappropriateness, even the uselessness, of gold coins struck for upstart Frankish kings; such coins, which substituted the authoritative image of the emperor with that of the western leader, could not be used in transactions even when both parties were non-Roman. The Roman ruler's portrait was necessary to guarantee the quality of the metal.[59]

The lapidary conciseness of imperial coin imagery was replicated by western rulers like Theudebert. At times, non-Roman kings commissioned even more ambitious imitations of imperial patterns of display. The most striking example of late Roman and early Byzantine royal imagery appropriated in this way is a gilded bronze plaque (Plate xxii) that once decorated an elaborate helmet made around 600 at the court of the Lombard king Agilulf.[60] The longhaired, bearded ruler, shown enthroned at the center of the plaque, raises his right arm in the old Roman gesture of speech while he touches his left hand to the sword on his lap. A pair of armed guards flanks the throne, with this inscription above their heads: "To our lord, Agilulf, the king." Personifications of victory race toward the central group, each bearing a drinking horn (or less likely, a cornucopia) and a staff mounted with a plaque inscribed with the word "victory." The winged Victories and the placards on staffs demonstrate a link with the traditional Roman imagery of triumph, while the drinking horns strike a decidedly contemporary Lombard note.[61] To the left and right, paired figures following the Victories proceed ceremonially toward the center from towerlike structures, old Roman shorthand symbols for cities. The outer member of each pair carries as tribute a crown topped with a globe and a cross, the same tokens of Christian rule frequently seen in fifth- and sixth-century imperial art, for example, in the Augoustaion statue of Justinian. In general terms, the acclamatory formulas of the Agilulf plaque can be compared with the symbols of victory and displays of tribute on similarly small-scale imperial objects such as the Barberini Ivory. The coin of Theudebert and the Lombard helmet plaque borrow imagery current at the court in Constantinople but present it in visual terms typical of the sixth- and seventh-century West, with little of the classical refinement and sophistication that were hallmarks of works produced in the Byzantine capital.

Other more ephemeral forms of imperial display also had an effect on western practices: at about the time the helmet plaque was created, Agilulf also mimicked imperial ceremonial and had his son elevated to royal rank in the old Roman circus in Milan before an audience that included a delegation of representatives from Francia.[62] Westerners adapted the visual and ceremonial language of Byzantine rulers to make claims about their status with regard to Byzantium. As Procopius implied, Frankish (and for that matter other non-Roman) leaders hoped to confer upon themselves the authority of the eastern Roman Empire by assuming imperial prerogatives such as issuing coins with imperial visual formulas and legends. They also employed the ceremonial and protocol of the Byzantine court to communicate with one another: the

Lombard elevation ritual was staged in order to impress a crowd that included Frankish legates.

The Frankish coins and the Lombard ceremony represent the numismatic and performative equivalents of the literary production of Cassiodorus, a Roman official in the sixth-century Gothic administration of Italy. As quaestor under King Theoderic, Cassiodorus composed texts strikingly similar in style to the rhetoric of late imperial legislation; many were addressed to the kings of the Visigoths, Burgundians, Franks, and other non-Roman leaders.[63] In the letter to the Byzantine emperor Anastasius that opens Cassiodorus's compilation of royal correspondence composed in Theoderic's name, the king acknowledged the source of the special status of his Italian realm: "Our rule is an imitation of yours, an image of your good way of life, a likeness of the imperial authority that is yours alone. To the degree that we follow you, so much do we take the lead over other peoples."[64]

Theoderic's adherence to Roman imperial ideals is strikingly reflected in his unfinished but still ponderous mausoleum (Plate xxiii) constructed on the outskirts of Ravenna. This grand tomb shows unmistakable connections with monumental architecture created for imperial patrons. The two-story decagon is incomplete in the second level, where an arcaded gallery was probably planned to rest on the massive arches of the ground floor. The most impressive (and distinctly un-Roman) feature of the tomb, however, is the circular monolith that crowns the upper chamber. The exterior and interior surfaces of this huge stone slab, an engineering marvel with an estimated weight of more than 300 tons, are curved to imitate the profile of a masonry dome.[65]

The designer of Theoderic's memorial found essential inspiration for the central-plan domed layout in Roman imperial funerary tradition. Emperors had long chosen domed, central designs for their tombs, many of which Theoderic himself must have known firsthand. Two familiar examples in Rome are the vaulted rotunda of Helena, the mother of Constantine the Great, and the domed mausoleum next to St. Peter's that sheltered the graves of the emperor Honorius and others of his dynasty. Theoderic, who was educated in Constantinople, also surely knew the circular, domed mausoleum built by Constantine the Great adjoining the Constantinopolitan Apostoleion.[66] The Ostrogothic king of Italy, the historic heart of the empire, chose a form for his tomb that linked him to the commemoration of rulers such as Constantine, the founder of the Christian Empire, and the Honorian family, Theoderic's predecessors in Italian rule. Like his Frankish contemporaries and his later Lombard counterparts, Theoderic looked to the Roman Empire, adapting imperial architecture as well as imagery and ceremonial to legitimate his rule and to ennoble his memory.

## EPILOGUE

Patterns of patronage maintained for decades by Justinian continued under his successors, Justin II and the emperors of the later sixth and early seventh centuries.[67] Justin in fact affirmed and even expanded certain aspects of the classical and imperial tradition. For example, in the first year of his reign he revived (and himself filled) the ancient office of consul, with all the spectacle and patronage (artistic as well as political) that this entailed. In the best imperial tradition, he was an energetic patron of architecture and had many statues of himself (and of the empress Sophia) erected throughout the capital.[68]

At the same time, images of the imperial couple were shaped by the ongoing fusion of imperial and Christian concerns, seen for example in the silver cross sent by Justin to the pope in Rome. Here, busts of Justin and Sophia are juxtaposed with images of Christ, recalling the pairing of Justinian and Theodora with Christ or Mary in lost works such as the textile furnishings of Hagia Sophia and in surviving objects like the ivory diptych made in 540 to celebrate the consulship of another nephew of Justinian named Justin. Justin II built the Chrysotriklinos, with its mosaic of Christ decorating the vault above the imperial throne. As Cameron has noted, such images parallel Corippus's panegyric of Justin II, where the theme of the emperor's imitation of Christ is emphasized.[69]

The reigns of Justin and his successors witnessed the burgeoning use of religious images in private devotion and for public purposes. In 574, Justin had the miraculous Camouliana image of Christ conveyed to Constantinople. A decade later, the general Philippikos brought the icon to battle on the eastern frontier, while in the 620s it was credited both for the success of the emperor Heraclius against the Persians and for the lifting of the Avar siege of Constantinople.[70] George of Pisidia's poem on Heraclius's Persian expedition dramatically envisions the emperor's address to the army, as he takes the icon of Christ in his hands and says: "This one, not I, is the universal emperor, lord and general of our armies." George conversely accords Heraclius the status of divinely ordained and protected leader when he acclaims him a "new Moses" and a "new Daniel."[71]

We can conclude with a work of Christian luxury art created during the reign of Heraclius in which classical visual elements predominate: a magnificent solid-silver plate (Plate xxiv) decorated with scenes from the life of David. This plate, the largest in a set of nine, depicts the climactic event of David's youthful career: the confrontation with the Philistine champion, Goliath, as told in 1 Samuel 41–51. At the top is Goliath's contemptuous challenge and David's bold response, while the duel itself fills the central register. The unarmed youth reacts to Goliath's attack by falling back and raising his draped arm, the fluttering cloth affording little protection against the imminent blow. As David whirls the sling, his face shows no sign of strain or concern; his expression instead is as composed and restrained as those of classical Greek athletes depicted more than a millennium earlier. In the lowest register, the Israelite hero energetically seals the victory, taking Goliath's sword to lop off the giant's head. The seventh-century silversmith masterfully presents these three episodes. The well-proportioned bodies of David, Goliath, and the other figures move their limbs convincingly in a landscape indicated by the classical personification and city symbols in the top register and by the plants that sprout from the rocky ground. The textures and surfaces of clothing and weapons are brilliantly differentiated and painstakingly rendered.[72] The plate is animated by the coherent movement and lifelike detail characteristic of Greco-Roman art. In this classically inspired work, a fitting coda to the Age of Justinian, David is imagined as a conquering classical hero, a Christian Hercules, even as George of Pisidia hails Heraclius as a "new Moses."

## Notes

1 Before its disappearance in 1831, the original medallion was duplicated in the electrotype pictured in Plates i, ii: see Cécile Morrisson in *Byzance: L'Art byzantin dans les collections publiques françaises*, ed. Jannic Durand (Paris, 1992), 57–59.

2 Procopius, *Buildings*, 1.10.11. All translations are my own.

3 Procopius, *Buildings*, 1.2.1–12. On the Augoustaion and the Justinian statue, see Wolfgang Müller-Wiener, *Bildlexikon zur Topographie Istanbuls* (Tübingen, 1977), 248–249; and Mango, "The Columns of Justinian and His Successors," in Mango, *Studies on Constantinople* (Aldershot, Eng., 1993), 10:1–20.

4 The stylistic and iconographic parallels proposed by Danielle Gaborit-Chopin (in Durand, *Byzance*, 63–66) suggest a date near the middle of the century, making likely the identification of the rider as Justinian.

5 Images of angels derived from Victories first appeared in imperial art on coins struck for Justin I and his successor Justinian. See Philip Grierson, *Byzantine Coins* (London, 1982), 35, 52, and plate 2, figs. 18, 20–21.

6 The mosaic is the subject of two poems in the *Greek Anthology* 1.106–107. The verses refer to a ninth-century image, but present it as the restoration of much older work.

7 See Irina Andreescu-Treadgold and Warren Treadgold, "Procopius and the Imperial Panels of San Vitale," *Art Bulletin* 99 (1997): 708–723, for a recent review of the sizeable bibliography on these mosaics and an unconvincing attempt to identify certain participants in both processions.

8 Thomas F. Mathews, *Byzantium: From Antiquity to the Renaissance* (New York, 1998), 105.

9 Friedrich Wilhelm Deichmann, *Ravenna. Hauptstadt des spätantikes Abendlandes*, 3 vols. in 5 parts (Wiesbaden, 1958–1976), 1:241–243; 2:48–49, 180–187.

10 See Gray, Chap. 9 in this volume.

11 Andreescu-Treadgold and Treadgold ("Procopius," 721–722) claim that in the Justinian mosaic, the legend "MAXIMIANUS" and the head of the cleric beneath the inscription are alterations of the original scheme which pictured Bishop Victor, Maximian's predecessor in the see of Ravenna. This theory has obvious implications for the precise dating of the processional panels.

12 Valerie A. Maxfield, *The Military Decorations of the Roman Army* (London, 1981), 86–89. In late antiquity, torques were worn by many groups other than the Germanic contingents of the imperial guard. They appear, for example, in images of warrior saints such as Sergius and Bacchus. Alexander P. Kazhdan, ed., *The Oxford Dictionary of Byzantium* (New York, 1991), 3:2098, s.v. "torque."

13 See Hans Belting's synthesis of earlier scholarship on the function and status of imperial images in *Likeness and Presence: A History of the Image before the Era of Art*, trans. Edmund Jephcott (Chicago, 1994), 102–107.

14 James D. Breckenridge summarized the evidence supporting a Justinianic date and noted other proposals in *Age of Spirituality*, ed. Kurt Weitzmann (New York, 1979), 292–295. Harrison tentatively identified the noblewoman as Anicia Juliana, the highborn patron of the church of Hagios Polyeuktos in Constantinople: R. Martin Harrison, *A Temple for Byzantium: The Discovery of Anicia Juliana's Palace-Church in Istanbul* (Austin, Tex., 1989), 36.

15 On scrolls and other emblems of learning in the Greco-Roman world, see most recently Paul Zanker, *The Mask of Socrates: The Image of the Intellectual in Antiquity*, trans. Alan Shapiro (Berkeley, Calif., 1995), esp. 194–197, 210–217, 229–233, 253–256, 267–306.

16 On the sanctuary furnishings of Hagia Sophia, see Paulus Silentiarius, *Descriptio S. Sophiae*, 755–805, in *Johannes von Gaza, Paulus Silentiarius, und Prokopios von Gaza*, ed. Paul Friedländer (Leipzig, 1912), 248–250. The passage is translated by Cyril Mango, *The Art of the Byzantine Empire, 312–1453: Sources and Documents* (Englewood Cliffs, N.J., 1972), 88–89. On the robe of Justinian, see Corippus, *In laudem Iustini Augusti minoris, libri IV*, 272–293.

17 Procopius, *Wars*, 8.17.1–8. Regarding early Byzantine silks, see Anna Muthesius, "From Seed to Samite: Aspects of Byzantine Silk Production," in *Studies in Byzantine and Islamic Silk Weaving* (London, 1995), 120–121. On the silk industry in Constantinople see Anna Muthesius, "Contantinople and Its Hinterland: Issues of Raw Silk Supply," in *Studies in Byzantine and Islamic Silk Weaving*, 315–335 and Nicholas Oikonomides, "Silk Trade and Production in Byzantium from the Sixth to the Ninth Century: The Seals of the Kommerkiarioi," *DOP* 40 (1986): 49–51, for the location of the industry in seventh-century Constantinople.

18 On the throne of Maximian, see Wolgang Fritz Volbach, *Elfenbeinarbeiten der Spätantike und des frühen Mittelalters*, 3rd ed. (Mainz, 1976), 93–94. For the Michael

plaque, see David Buckton, ed., *Byzantium: Treasures of Byzantine Art and Culture* (London, 1994), 73–74. On the supply of ivory used by Byzantine carvers, see Anthony Cutler, *Hand of the Master: Craftsmanship, Ivory, and Society in Byzantium, Ninth–Eleventh Centuries* (Princeton, N.J., 1994), 57–58.

19 Guglielmo Cavallo, *Codex Purpureus Rossanensis* (Rome, 1992), 11–13, discusses the evidence for the date and place of origin.

20 Marlia Mundell Mango, *Silver from Early Byzantium: The Kaper Koraon and Related Treasures* (Baltimore, 1986), 165–170; see also the broader discussion (14–15) regarding the centers of early Byzantine silver production.

21 Two miniatures in the contemporary Rossano Gospels present the Communion of the Apostles in a similar processional scheme: Cavallo, *Codex Purpureus*, plates 6 and 7.

22 On the Hercules plate, see Durand, *Byzance*, 10–11.

23 Kurt Weitzmann, *The Monastery of St. Catherine on Mount Sinai: The Icons*, vol. 1, *From the Sixth to the Tenth Century* (Princeton, N.J., 1976), no. B1, 10–15.

24 Giorgio di Pisidia, *Carmi*, ed. Luigi Tartaglia, 2.1.139–153 and 4.370–373 (Turin, 1998), 80–83, 180–181. Most recently on the Camouliana icon, see Mathews, *Byzantium*, 43–47, and Thomas F. Mathews, *The Clash of Gods: A Reinterpretation of Early Christian Art*, rev. and expanded ed. (Princeton, N.J., 1999), 188–189.

25 For example by Belting, *Likeness*, 78–101, and Robin Cormack, *Painting the Soul: Icons, Death Masks, and Shrouds* (London, 1997), 65–72.

26 The evidence is gathered and analyzed by Mathews: *Byzantium*, 43–47; *Clash*, 177–190; Thomas F. Mathews, "The Emperor and the Icon," *Acta ad archaeologiam et artium historiam pertinentia* 15 (2001): 168–177.

27 George H. Forsyth and Kurt Weitzmann, *The Monastery of St. Catherine on Mt. Sinai* (Ann Arbor, Mich., 1973).

28 On *Buildings*, see Averil Cameron, *Procopius and the Sixth Century* (Berkeley, Calif., 1985), chap. 6, "Procopius and the *Buildings*," especially the cautionary remarks regarding the archaeological value of much of Procopius's panegyric. See also the essays on *Buildings* by various authors gathered in *Antiquité Tardive* 8 (2000).

29 Procopius's observations on Antioch are in *Buildings* 2.10.2–25. See the recent comments of Clive Foss, "Late Antique Antioch," in *Antioch: The Lost City*, ed. Christine Kondoleon (Princeton, N.J., 2000), 23–27.

30 Procopius, *Buildings*, 4.1.19–27. For a concise synthesis of the discoveries made at Caričin Grad, see Djordje Mano-Zissi, "Justiniana Prima (Caričin Grad)," in *Reallexikon zur byzantinischen Kunst* (Stuttgart, 1972–1978), 3:687–717.

31 The circular main plaza in Justiniana Prima has parallels in other cities of the Roman East, most notably in Constantinople, where the forum of that city's namesake, Constantine, had the same plan.

32 Cameron, *Procopius*, 94, 102–103.

33 For general remarks on Justinianic church building, see Cameron, *Procopius*, 86–87.

34 On these churches honoring Michael, see Procopius, *Buildings*, 1.8.1–20.

35 Forsyth and Weitzmann, *St. Catherine*, 19.

36 Procopius, *Buildings*, 5.6.1–26; Cyril of Scythopolis, *Vita Sabae*, 72–73, in Eduard Schwartz (ed.), *Kyrillos von Skythopolis* (Leipzig, 1939), 175–177.

37 Yoram Tsafrir argues that the archaeological record amply confirms Procopius's comments regarding the scale and lavish materials of the Nea in "Procopius and the Nea Church in Jerusalem," *Antiquité Tardive* 8 (2000), 149–164.

38 For the Church of the Nativity, see Richard Krautheimer and Slobodan Ćurčić, *Early Christian and Byzantine Architecture*, 4th ed. (Harmondsworth, 1986), 266–267, 491–492, n. 15. On the lost Constantinopolitan church of the Theotokos, see *Greek Anthology* 1.2–3 and Krautheimer and Ćurčić, *Early Christian and Byzantine Architecture*, 266–267, 492, n. 17.

39 Clive Foss, *Ephesus after Antiquity* (Cambridge, 1979), 88 (and n. 88 for the date).

40 Procopius mentions the Ephesian church in *Buildings* 5.1.6; see also Krautheimer and Ćurčić, *Early Christian and Byzantine Architecture*, 242–245, 489, n. 15.

41 Procopius, *Buildings*, 1.4.1-13. Jonathan Bardill reviews the literary and epigraphic evidence cited in the protracted debate about the nature of Sts. Sergius and Bacchus (palace chapel or monastery church) in "The Church of Sts. Sergius and Bacchus in Constantinople and the Monophysite Refugees," *DOP* 54 (2000): 1–11.

42 Bardill, "Sts. Sergius and Bacchus," 2–4, on the documentary and physical evidence for the date.

43 For important observations regarding the building periods of the central octagon and outer shell, see Helge Svenshon and Rainer H. W. Stichel, "Die Kirche der heiligen Sergios und Bakchos," *Istanbuler Mitteilungen* 50 (2000): 389–409.

44 Krautheimer and Ćurčić, *Early Christian and Byzantine Architecture*, 222–225; and Rowland J. Mainstone, *Hagia Sophia: Architecture, Structure, and Liturgy of Justinian's Great Church* (London, 1988), 154–155. McClanan emphasizes the role of the empress in the project: Anne McClanan, *Representations of Early Byzantine Empresses: Image and Empire* (New York, 2002), 99–102.

45 Mainstone, *Hagia Sophia*, 9, 145–148.

46 Reconstruction of the original fenestration: Mainstone, *Hagia Sophia*, 97–101.

47 No physical or documentary evidence points to the presence of large-scale figural decoration in the sixth-century church. The mosaics in the apse and elsewhere are of medieval date.

48 Mainstone (*Hagia Sophia*, 157) mentions the relevant ancient authors and supplies references to modern studies of their background and training.

49 Certain features in the 530s design may have been so bold that they were structurally unsound and collapsed after suffering damage in the earthquake of 557 (Mainstone, *Hagia Sophia*, 85–91, 213–217). See also Rabun Taylor, "A Literary and Structural Analysis of the First Dome of Justinian's Hagia Sophia, Constantinople," *Journal of the Society of Architectural Historians* 55 (1996): 66–78.

50 Paulus Silentiarius, in Friedländer, *Descriptio*, 392–394. Mainstone (*Hagia Sophia*, 191) provides a translation of the passage from Paul. He also notes (191–194) that a more traditionally aligned elevation was perhaps originally planned and its design altered, the changes dictated by a desire to economize or to speed construction.

51 See most recently Hans Buchwald, "Saint Sophia, Turning Point in the Development of Byzantine Architecture?" in *Die Hagia Sophia in Istanbul*, ed. Volker Hoffman (Bern, 1997), 30–37, with references to earlier studies.

52 For Justinian's role in the planning and construction of the cathedral, see Mainstone (*Hagia Sophia*, 151–154), and even more emphatically, Buchwald ("Saint Sophia," 37–46), with the claim (41) that "St. Sophia, perhaps more than any other known

important building, reflects '*architectural design upon Imperial command.*' " The italics and upper-case "imperial" are his.

53 Design and decoration of the church and sketch of the princess's character: Harrison, *Temple*, 77–135. Buchwald ("Saint Sophia," 43) questions Harrison's reconstruction of the nave as domed.

54 Harrison (*Temple*, 137–144) discusses the sculptural and other evidence for the parallel between Solomon and the Constantinopolitan noblewoman.

55 On Justinian's first reaction to Hagia Sophia, see *Narratio de Aedificatione Templi S. Sophiae*, 27, in *Scriptores Originum Constantinopolitanarum*, ed. Theodor Preger (Leipzig, 1901), 105. On the rivalry between Anicia Juliana and Justinian, see Harrison, *Temple*, 36–41; Mainstone, *Hagia Sophia*, 147–148; and McClanan, *Early Byzantine Empresses*, 94–98.

56 See, most recently, Buchwald, *Hagia Sophia*, 41.

57 Relations between the two churches: Deichmann, *Ravenna*, 2:2, 83–85, and Krautheimer and Ćurčić, *Early Christian and Byzantine Architecture*, 232–237.

58 Philip Grierson and Mark Blackburn, *Medieval European Coinage*, vol. 1, *The Early Middle Ages* (Cambridge, 1986), 116–117. Michael McCormick highlights the relationship with the coin images of the emperor Anastasius (491–518) in *Eternal Victory: Triumphal Rulership in Late Antiquity, Byzantium, and the Early Medieval West* (Cambridge, 1986), 338–339.

59 Procopius, *Wars*, 7.33.5–6. Validating effect of the imperial coin image: most recently Oikonomides, "Silk Trade," 33–53, esp. 36–37 and nn. 20–23.

60 Gian Carlo Menis, ed., *I Longobardi* (Milan, 1990), 96.

61 Drinking horns are often found in early medieval Lombard graves and are prominent in legendary accounts of Lombard celebrations; for references to the latter, see McCormick, *Eternal Victory*, 291 and n. 144.

62 Paul the Deacon, *Historia Langobardorum*, 4.30, ed. Ludwig Bethmann and Georg Waitz (Hannover, 1878), 127.9–11; cited in Chris Wickham, *Early Medieval Italy: Central Power and Local Society 400–1000* (Ann Arbor, Mich., 1981), 34, and McCormick, *Eternal Victory*, 288.

63 On the literary character of Cassiodorus's work as quaestor, see Cassiodorus, *Variae*, translated and with commentary by Sam J. B. Barnish (Liverpool, 1992), xviii–xxx, esp. xviii–xxiii.

64 Cassiodorus, *Variae*, 1.1.3, ed. Theodor Mommsen, *Cassiodori Senatoris Variae* (Berlin, 1894), *MGH AA* 12, 10.

65 On Theodoric's mausoleum, see Mark J. Johnson, "Toward a History of Theodoric's Building Program," *DOP* 42 (1988): 92–96; and Slobodan Ćurčić, "Design and Structural Innovation in Byzantine Architecture before Hagia Sophia," in *Hagia Sophia from the Age of Justinian to the Present*, ed. Robert Mark and Ahmet Ş. Çakmak (Cambridge, 1992), 33–35.

66 On Constantine's tomb, see Cyril Mango, "Constantine's Mausoleum and the Translation of Relics," *BZ* 83 (1990): 51–62, and "Addendum," *BZ* 83 (1990): 454, with reference to the earlier bibliography.

67 Averil Cameron, "The Artistic Patronage of Justin II," *Byzantion* 50 (1980): 62–84.

68 Cameron, "Artistic Patronage," 72–80 (on Justin's construction and monumental decoration), 68–72 (on statuary).

69 On the cross of Justin II, see Christa Belting-Ihm, "Das Justinus-Kreuz in der Schatzkammer der Peterskirche zu Rom," *Jahrbuch der römisch-germanischen*

*Zentralmuseums Mainz* 12 (1965): 142–166; on the diptych of Justin, Belting, *Likeness*, 109–113; on Corippus's encomium, Cameron, "Artistic Patronage," 76.

70 Cameron ("Artistic Patronage," 83) noted that the Camouliana icon was brought to Constantinople under Justin II in 574. For its subsequent use in military operations, see Anna Kartsonis, "The Responding Icon," 64, in *Heaven on Earth: Art and the Church in Byzantium*, ed. Linda Safran (University Park, Penn., 1998).

71 Giorgio di Pisidia, *Carmi*, 2.1.132–136 (new Moses); 2.2.99–100 (imperial address); 2.3.415–425 (new Moses); 5.1.16 (new Daniel).

72 See Ruth E. Leader, "The David Plates Revisited: Transforming the Secular in Early Byzantium," *Art Bulletin* 102 (2000): 407–414, where this and the other David plates are seen as reflections of broad cultural and intellectual patterns current in early medieval Byzantium.

# 15: Literary Culture under Justinian

Claudia Rapp

Justinian's reign is distinguished by its lasting accomplishments in law and architecture. It is also unusually rich in written sources, a treasure trove of documentation that provides insight and detailed knowledge about the sixth century that is rarely matched for other periods in the ancient world or Byzantium. There is no consensus, however, in the evaluation by posterity of the literary activities under Justinian and the emperor's role in fostering them. Scholars of an earlier generation, such as J. B. Bury and Glanville Downey, tend to credit "the favorable atmosphere of the capital" for producing "the glories of Justinian's age" in literature.[1] But critical voices were already heard in Byzantium. The twelfth-century chronicler John Zonaras remarks that "by making the teachers redundant," Justinian was responsible for a new level of "boorishness" (*agroikia*).[2] This refers to Justinian's order in 529 to stop the teaching of philosophy and law in Athens – a measure that effectively shut down the Academy, a bastion of learning in the classical tradition that had been founded by Plato in the fourth century BCE where church fathers like Basil of Caesarea and Gregory of Nazianzus had completed their education.[3] This order was part of Justinian's effort to suppress any teaching by those "who are infected with the sacrilegious foolishness of the Hellenes [i.e. pagans]"[4] in order to enforce Christian uniformity and imperial control on the institutions of higher learning in the empire.[5] Toward the end of his reign, Justinian even ordered the violent persecution of pagan intellectuals in Constantinople.[6] The French scholar Paul Lemerle therefore concludes that "a decline in secular higher education and culture began under Justinian."[7] He bases his judgment on the neglect of authors from classical antiquity, which were neither copied nor commented upon during Justinian's reign. Lemerle's exclusive focus on the preservation of the heritage of classical literature renders him unable to acknowledge that the authors of the sixth century in fact produced a wide variety of literary works, ranging from histories of their own time to poetry in the classical style, and that many authors of the time were beginning to turn their attention to literature inspired by Christian belief and practice.

What role did Justinian play in the literary production of his day? Should he be credited for the ample activities of authors during his reign? This chapter explains the concrete circumstances of literary production and discusses the most important individual authors and the circumstances of their work in order to attempt an answer to these questions.

## Audience

It is important to be cognizant of the practice of literary production and consumption in late antiquity. People could not simply curl up in a corner and get blissfully lost in reading a cheap paperback that they picked up at the corner store. Since the third century AD, manuscripts were written increasingly on parchment and in codex form, gradually replacing the use of papyrus as writing material and the scroll as the book form that were common in classical antiquity. Books were available only in a few copies, as writing material was scarce and expensive. They were luxury objects, their possession a marker of social status. A beautiful example from Justinian's reign is Dioscurides' *De materia medica*, a manual of medicinal herbs. It was commissioned by the aristocratic lady Anicia Juliana, whose lineage could boast connections to several generations of Roman emperors. The beginning of the manuscript shows a portrait of the author, and, on a separate page, of the donor herself. The intended use of such a lavishly executed book of such utilitarian content remains unclear, although it must be noted that a certain degree of medical knowledge was considered a sign of great intellectual refinement in Byzantium. Books were available for purchase on the open market but often also circulated among friends who shared the same interests and tastes. Late antique literati often wrote letters to their acquaintances to ask for the loan of books, so that they could have them copied for their own use.

The professional production of books in the sixth century underwent a noticeable change. According to Gulielmo Cavallo, the great Italian scholar of paleography, the scriptoria of religious establishments and monasteries that had initially only provided for their own use, now began to produce for the market. In Constantinople, the monks in the monastery of the Akoimetoi (Sleepless Monks), for example, copied manuscripts in Greek, Latin, and Syriac. The production of Latin manuscripts in Italy had a long tradition in Rome and also flourished in the new capital of Ravenna. In the production of Greek manuscripts in Constantinople, the imperial chancery, and especially the branch responsible for copying legal documents, exerted its influence on script and writing style. It seems that the same copyists were at work on both legal documents and works of literature.[8] According to Cavallo's calculations, the number of manuscripts, whether written on parchment or on papyrus (or at least, those manuscripts that now survive and can be securely dated), produced during the reign of Justinian was significantly higher than in a comparable period during previous decades.[9] But we are still talking about a relatively small number of surviving books produced under Justinian: about twenty papyri from Egypt that contain Classical Greek authors, and a total of about twenty parchment manuscripts in Greek, Latin, and Syriac.

The professional book dealers in Constantinople had their stalls at a short distance from the Church of Hagia Sophia. Agathias tells us how Uranius, who had come from Syria and made his living as a physician, would position himself there and engage passersby in heated debates about the nature of the Deity, so that he could show off his encyclopedic knowledge. Uranius obviously had no trouble in finding equally educated and opinionated partners for his verbal sparring, which, Agathias notes with disdain, tended to take place toward the evening "in all probability after some drunken orgy."[10] It is interesting to speculate that the men who enjoyed such conversation with the learned and inebriated Uranius were in large part lawyers, who, as we will see below, constituted a significant portion of the literary elite of the capital. For these bookstalls were located in the vicinity of the Royal Stoa, where many lawyers, including Agathias himself, were employed in keeping legal records.[11]

Books were luxury objects, but they were also for sharing. The sharing of books was facilitated by the fact that the boundaries between orality and literacy were not as clearly drawn as they are now. When an author was engaged in the composition of a new work, he would at some point arrange to read a draft to his circle of educated friends, to invite their comments and to bask in their admiration, as the case may be.[12] Only after producing the finished version did he release his text, by giving gift copies to his friends and by allowing the book dealers to make copies on demand. At this point, the dissemination of the work passed out of the control of the author and into the vagaries of the open market. Once someone acquired ownership of a book, he was not the only one to enjoy it. One common way of reading any piece of writing in antiquity and beyond was to read it aloud so that anyone who was present in the room was exposed to the text and reading became a communal activity. We must also bear in mind that a large number of the works that we now think of as literature had their origin as speeches, delivered orally before an audience. This is the way in which the liturgical poetry of Romanos the Melode or the panegyrical speeches of Corippus were first publicized.

We know about an occasion for public recital in Rome in the spring of 544, while the city was under siege by Totila, where the entertainment of hearing an author read from his recently composed work brought together large parts of the population of the city. Arator, a learned subdeacon, had composed a metric paraphrase of the Acts of the Apostles in the style of Virgil. According to the note that precedes the manuscript version of this text, Arator presented his work to Pope Vigilius (the same pope whom Justinian would soon thereafter summon to Constantinople) in the presbyterium of St. Peter. The pope asked to have a part of it read out there and then, in the presence of many bishops, priests, deacons, and most of the other clergy. On the pope's orders, the codex was to be deposited in the archive of the church. But the clergymen in the audience were so enthused that they begged for a public reading, and thus a huge crowd of clergy, monks, noble laymen and "all kinds of people" gathered in the Church of San Pietro in Vincoli a few days later. Arator himself performed the reading, which continued over four (nonconsecutive) days, at a rate of half a book (or volume) per session. The reason for this slow progression was that his admiring audience often asked him to stop and read out a particularly beautiful or interesting passage for a second time.[13] The presence of "all kinds of people" on that occasion alerts us to the fact that the appreciation of literature did not necessarily depend on literacy and recondite learning.

## Being an Author

The question of literacy in the ancient and medieval world has attracted much attention in recent scholarship. A very rough estimate places the level of literacy in the later Roman Empire at around 10 percent. But literacy in this period is not an either/or skill, but rather a fluid concept. William Harris in his book on *Ancient Literacy* follows common wisdom in distinguishing between three kinds: the ability to sign one's name on a document; the craftsmen's literacy (what we might also call functional literacy) that was sufficient for people to go about their jobs; and the application of the Latin word *litteratus* in the strictest sense as "cultivated," referring to someone who could not merely write down words for business or legal transactions, but who was able to compose works of stylistic refinement and elegance of expression.[14] Clearly, the truly erudite literati were only a fraction of the population of the empire. But such educated men constituted the social, economic, and political elite, and their shared erudition and culture played an important role in creating a common bond and asserting their status.[15] On the other hand, people who were known to have no education were able to gain the imperial throne, as did Justinian's uncle and predecessor Justin I.

Very few people in the empire had the wherewithal to attain that lofty level of erudition to be called a literatus – a man of letters in the truest sense. It has been estimated for the tenth century that only three hundred students were receiving a higher education in Constantinople in any given year.[16] Education was not easy to come by, nor was it cheap. After entering elementary school at age seven or eight and learning the basic skills of reading and writing from a *grammaticus*, there would follow, at about the age of thirteen, further years of instruction. At this stage, emphasis was placed on honing one's stylistic expressions and modeling them after the great writers of classical antiquity, so that one could write with eloquence, grace, and ease, and at the same time dazzle one's audience with references and reminiscences to Greek epic and tragedy, phrases from ancient philosophy, or stories from mythology. Obviously, this kind of writing could be fully appreciated only by those who had enjoyed the same kind of education. They would be able to understand the inside jokes, appreciate the erudition in the use of arcane vocabulary, marvel at the artistry that went into the construction of a carefully chosen turn of phrase, and admire the fortuitous selection of an example from classical literature. In short, this kind of education "actually functioned as a caste-marker," as Peter Heather has termed it.[17] Additional specialized study at one of the institutions of higher learning could follow: Berytus and Alexandria were famous for their law schools (although Justinian closed the latter in an effort to concentrate legal studies at Berytus and Constantinople), and Athens was a center for the study of philosophy until Justinian's closure of the Academy in 529. Constantinople itself had a university, founded in 425 under Theodosius II, perhaps with the encouragement of his wife Eudoxia, the daughter of a pagan professor of philosophy in Athens.

After completing one's education, further enhancement of status could be derived by moving from the provinces into the orbit of the imperial court. Educated men from the provinces came to the capital in large numbers to seek their fortune in a job in the imperial administration. They hoped to attract wealthy benefactors, perhaps even the attention of the emperor himself. The chances to succeed were good. It has been estimated that by the early fifth century, there were at least 3,000 desirable jobs, perhaps even twice as many, each in the eastern and the western empire, whether in the imperial or the provincial administration. Many of the highest jobs had a very quick turnover time, often as little as one year, thus creating new openings all the time.[18] This may not have contributed to the efficiency of the administration, but it did allow a greater number of men to enjoy the privilege of being associated, however tenuously, with the imperial court, and to enjoy the increase in status that came with an elevated position.

The desire for recognition, honor, and fame is the personal motivation that drove the erudite men of the sixth century to put pen to paper. As members of the educated elite, they already came from reasonably prosperous backgrounds, and some found opportunities to further increase their prestige and wealth, either through holding office in the imperial administration or through their writing. They flocked to Constantinople, the location of the imperial palace, seat of the patriarch, and a city of golden opportunities. Constantinople covered a large territory, with the western delineation of the urban area of triangular peninsula marked by a massive wall of six kilometers' length, which Theodosius II had built about a century earlier. The number of its inhabitants in the sixth century has been estimated at half a million or slightly more.[19] Spectacular entertainments were put on in the theater: plays, pantomimes, and more titillating performances by female dancers. Theodora herself was said to have been such a woman of the stage before she donned the stiff imperial regalia in which she is depicted later in life. For sports fans, there were the horse races in the hippodrome. These competitions were often accompanied by the raucous activities of the supporters of the two horse-racing teams, the Blues and the Greens. Sometimes, they united to heckle the emperor, seated high up in his loge, with their complaints, voiced in a rhythmical chant, as they did in the devastating Nika riot of 532. The hippodrome itself was a multipurpose structure: in the space under the ascending rows of seats, for about fifty-five meters from the turning post to the imperial loge, it housed the imperial archives. This was the bureaucratic center of the empire. Here, dedicated government officials, secretaries, and scribes went about their daily business of recording and filing documents.

The vast majority of authors in the sixth century came from provincial families of some wealth. Many of them are labeled as *scholasticus*, "lawyer," or "barrister" – a reference to their many years of study, which might also have included the formal study of law. Others held titles such as *notarius* or *cancellarius* that indicate a high position in the administration or in the military.[20] And finally, there are some authors, like Agapetus or Romanos, whose employment was in the church. We know this because, compared to other periods of Byzantine history, the sixth century seems to have been particularly prolific in bringing forth authors of every kind. Our information on their background and careers varies. At the very least, authors are referred to by name, place of origin, and title or profession. This is true, for example, for the poets whose short verses Agathias collected and edited in his *Cycle*. A number of authors took the trouble to formally introduce themselves in their work and thus provide us with valuable biographical detail. This is the case with Procopius at the beginning of his *Wars*; Agathias at the beginning of his *Histories*, John the Lydian in his work *On Offices*, and Menander Protector at the beginning of his historical treatise. In addition, it is sometimes possible to extract further detail about an author's life or any strong views that he harbored from personal remarks scattered in his work. Most of these authors hovered just below the glass ceiling that separated the merely well-to-do from the truly wealthy, status-conscious aristocratic families. Above that, there was only the level of the imperial household. To attract the patronage of these aristocrats was highly desirable, for that could lead to a promotion to a better job, a nice financial reward, perhaps even an introduction at the court.

## PATTERNS OF PATRONAGE

The composition of literary works thus became a vehicle for upward social mobility. This is not without consequence for the content and often also for genres of literature that were being produced. Effusive praise of the (prospective) benefactor and sometimes also his family was the norm. In works that otherwise aim to record or inform, such as Procopius's *Wars*, Agathias's *Histories*, or John the Lydian's *On Offices*, this *captatio benevolentiae* (seeking a favor) is confined to the preface. Other works are devoted entirely to expressing admiration, adulation, and gratitude, combined with a gentle tug on the addressee's purse strings. These are the kinds of works that would first be delivered orally, before an audience on a special occasion, and only later put into circulation in written form.

The two panegyrics by Corippus exemplify this. It is perhaps no coincidence that each of them survives in only one single manuscript.[21] Corippus was a native of Latin-speaking North Africa and probably began his career as a small-town teacher.[22] His first work, the *Iohannis*, praises John Troglyta, Justinian's *magister militum* (master of soldiers) in Africa, for his valiant deeds on the battlefield in the war against the Berbers. It was publicized soon after the end of warfare, in 548, in a recital before an audience in Carthage that most likely included the victorious general himself. Naturally, Corippus bent the truth here and there in order to make his hero look better, as a comparison of his account with that of Procopius shows. He begins his preface "I have presumed, noble princes, to tell about the laurels a conqueror won, and write a poem of celebration in a time of peace." And he ends it with a plea for patronage: "If, amid many triumphs, Carthage may rejoice through my efforts, then let the acclaim, in all justice, be mine and, I pray, your affection as well."[23] His strategy must have been successful, for the next time we hear of him, about twenty years later, he is in the capital delivering a panegyric on Justin II, Justinian's nephew and successor, in the presence of members of the court (he includes mini-panegyrics on several of them). At that point, Corippus hints that he was holding some kind of imperial post, under the supervision of the quaestor Anastasius. He begins his panegyric by praising the emperor but soon moves on to set out his own agenda: "Pious one, stretch out your right hand to a weary old man. . . . You for whom it is right to conquer unvanquished peoples and to lay low barbarian kingdoms, conquer, I beseech you, the fierce anger of my fate. . . . Bereft of my possessions and after suffering many wounds," Corippus explains, he is now seeking to be comforted by the emperor's favor.[24] He then turns, in a second preface, to Anastasius the quaestor, who had apparently encouraged him to write this panegyric.[25] Here we see the patronage of aristocrats at work. Men like Anastasius act as the hinge between the aspirations of the author and the favors that only the emperor can dispense. Anastasius not only gave Corippus employment but also encouraged him to show off his rhetorical skill before the emperor. Corippus recognizes this when he says of his benefactor: "You are the fertile tree, drinking from the imperial spring. Our lord and common benefactor [i.e., the emperor] is the great spring of the court, the spring that enriches all, which stretched your branches over the wide earth and let the people rest in your shade. Grant to me that I may drink from this spring. You supply me with food, the sweet spring [i.e., the emperor, supplies me] with water."[26]

Justinian in his younger years had acted in the same role as a benefactor for literary talent. Some time prior to his accession in 527, while he held a position of power at the right hand of his uncle and predecessor Justin I, he granted the post of *cancellarius* (private secretary with senatorial rank) to Marcellinus Comes. Like Justinian, Marcellinus Comes hailed from the region of Illyricum and spoke Latin. His appointment as *cancellarius* was probably a reward for the composition of his *Chronicle*, which was completed in 518. When Marcellinus updated his work in 534, he showed his gratitude to Justinian by highlighting Justinian's subsequent achievements, from his accession as emperor to his building projects and his victory over the Vandals, which provided a convenient endpoint to his narrative.[27]

The same pattern of patronage based on a shared regional background also operated in the life of John the Lydian. A native of Philadelphia in Lydia, he came to Constantinople at the age of twenty-one, after the completion of his studies, in the hopes of finding employment as a legal secretary. As luck would have it, his fellow countryman Zoticus was just at that time being promoted to the high office of *logothete* of the praetorium and offered John a lucrative position on his staff. "As was natural, then, since I was thankful," John notes in his autobiographical passage near the end of his treatise *On Offices*, "(how, indeed, could I not have been?), I composed a brief panegyric in his honor. Because he had been pleased with it, he issued orders for me to receive from the bank a gold coin for each line."[28]

Further promotions to other positions followed, until John was deemed worthy to marry the daughter of his benefactor. He was soon able to give more time to his studies and eventually attracted the attention of Justinian. At the invitation of the emperor, John delivered an encomium at the court, in the presence of celebrities from Rome. He was also commissioned to write a history of the war with Persia. Both works are now lost. The later years of his public career were spent as a teacher, drawing an imperial salary. By his own account, his learning was his proudest achievement, even more so than the honor he was shown and the wealth he was able to accumulate. On the occasion of his retirement, he became himself the subject of effusive praise in a written decree of Justinian, which he eagerly cites.[29] John, like Corippus, depended for his rising fortune on a succession of factors: his own erudition, aristocratic patronage, a well-paid job in the administration, and finally access to the emperor. Men like these formed the rather numerous group of "civil savants," as Michael Maas has called them, who provide us with the ample literary evidence that the sixth century brought forth.[30]

John the Lydian's history of the Persian war is the only work that we know Justinian commissioned, and it is a work that does not survive. It is a striking fact that Justinian took only minimal interest in supporting the aspiring authors of his day, as he had done as emperor-to-be when he rewarded Marcellinus Comes. Our most important literary sources from Justinian's reign were composed by authors who were employed as civil servants in the imperial administration and depended on aristocratic patronage in their hope for a breakthrough.

Procopius of Caesarea exemplifies the educated man who remains in the distant orbit of the emperor but never gains direct access to him.[31] Procopius is our most extensive source of information for the reign of Justinian. In addition to the *Wars* describing Justinian's military campaigns in Persia, North Africa, and Italy, he also wrote *On Buildings* and the *Anecdota* (or *Secret History*). He came from the landowning provincial aristocracy of Caesarea in Palestine. His education, like that of most of his contemporaries, must have included a background in legal studies. But instead of seeking a sedentary post in the capital, Procopius became the legal adviser and secretary of Belisarius, one of Justinian's most successful generals. He accompanied Belisarius on his campaigns and became virtually a member of his household. Not surprisingly, Procopius's *Wars* concentrate on the figure of Belisarius and his military accomplishments. He proclaimed himself competent for the task of recording these events for posterity because he had been an eyewitness. Procopius borrows this idea of documenting war for the benefit of future generations from his model Thucydides, the great historian of the Peloponnesian War between Athens and Sparta in the fifth century BC. Although his mindset was very much that of a Christian, his desire to emulate the much-admired style of classical Athens led him to write about Christian matters assuming the stance of a distant observer. Not long after the completion of book 8 of his *Wars*, Procopius composed his work *Buildings*. Here the focus shifts from Belisarius to Justinian. The emperor is praised effusively for his territorial gains, his religious policy, his legal codification - in sum, for having "wedded the whole State to a life of prosperity."[32] Justinian's construction of churches, fortifications, bridges, and aqueducts is treated as being of the same magnitude, a token of the emperor's paternal and benevolent care and a sign of his lavish generosity toward all the inhabitants of his empire. The work reads like a panegyric, but it is not clear whether Procopius wrote it either in the hope of receiving a reward, or motivated by the necessity to clear his name from any association with Belisarius, who had been suspected of treason not long before, or indeed out of gratitude for a favor already received. The latter may be hinted at in Procopius's remark that "history shews that subjects who have received benefits have proved themselves grateful toward their benefactors, and that they have repaid them with thank-offerings in generous measure."[33] This passage is our only indication for any direct interaction that Procopius may have had with the emperor.

Procopius's third work, the *Secret History*, seems to undermine all his efforts to curry favor with those in power. In the manner of a tabloid newspaper, Procopius promises to "tell it all," the less than pleasant events and the *true* reasons why everything happened the way it did. At the same time, he announces his intention to recount "the contemptible conduct" of his erstwhile patron Belisarius, as well as of Justinian and Theodora. And he does. He spares us no detail, from Theodora's past as a danseuse in the circus (particularly famous was the number in which she appeared thinly veiled, with some live geese picking grains from unmentionable parts of her body) to the personal cruelty of Belisarius's wife Antonina, who paraded her lover in front of her husband's eyes, and Justinian's strange habit – true to his characterization as evil incarnate – of walking around in the palace with his head under his arm. Although Procopius admits to his fear of discovery by his contemporaries and the certain punishment by the emperor that would follow, he acknowledges his need to give a complete record of Justinian's reign.[34] If there was any contemporary audience for this work, we are not told about it. It is possible that Procopius merely wrote the *Secret History* as his own private joke, to let off steam and to reassure himself of his intellectual integrity after writing the *Wars*. Here, then, is "art for art's sake," literature without a patron and without a financial incentive, although it remains puzzling that the literary urge in its unencumbered form should find its outlet in such an outrageous and unusual piece of writing.

Procopius's account of the political history of Justinian's reign is continued by Agathias.[35] He was a native of Myrina in Asia Minor and came from a reasonably prosperous family (his father was probably a lawyer) that moved to Constantinople when he was still a child. No expenses were spared for his education: Agathias studied rhetoric in Alexandria and then trained as a lawyer in Constantinople. His dreams of a comfortable life that would allow him time for reading and study never seem to have materialized. He complains about having to work hard for a living, and uses this as an excuse for his unpolished style:

> Though I should be at leisure to improve my style by reading through the works of the great writers of antiquity, to survey with critical discernment the entire historical scene and to give my full and unfettered attention to these matters, I am instead kept at my desk in the Basileios Stoa [the same place where the loquacious Uranius was holding forth] from early morning to late evening busying myself with the incessant perusal of innumerable legal documents. And though I resent being overworked I am distressed if I am not, since it is impossible for me to eke out a livelihood without considerable toil and hardship.[36]

But for all his complaints about financial distress, he still had sufficient resources to restore and beautify a public convenience outside the city of Smyrna – a public benefaction that was celebrated in a poem and gained him the honorable title of "father of the city." "I am a place formerly hideous, divided by brick walls, and here the bellies of strangers, natives, and countrymen thunderously relieved themselves. But Agathias, the father of the city, transformed me and made me distinguished instead of most ignoble."[37]

Agathias was about thirty-three years old when Justinian died in 565. His literary production, apart from a few poems, falls during the reigns of Justinian's successors Justin II (565–578) and Tiberius Constantine (578–582), with his *Cycle* of poems published in 567 and his *Histories* in the early 580s. Neither emperor granted Agathias the recognition that he felt was his due. He was not as successful as John the Lydian had been in gaining the ear of the emperor Justinian, nor did he have the indirect access to the court that Procopius may have enjoyed through his employer Belisarius. He seems to be talking about himself when he notes with bitterness that

> It has already been amply demonstrated by some of the most brilliant minds of antiquity that initiative is blunted and all incentive to action destroyed when noble spirits are deprived of their rightful share of acclaim and that in consequence those qualities that have been disparaged, whether they are associated with military success, literary achievement

> or with some other matter of vital concern, cease, much to the detriment of society, to be properly cultivated. I think, moreover, that it requires no great perspicacity to see that the truth of this assertion is continually borne out by our own everyday experience.[38]

Agathias is also highly critical of the efforts of his contemporaries to attract patronage through flattery in whatever they are writing. But this is a sensitive issue for him, and his words ring like sour grapes.

> These authors who claim to be writing history and profess to be historians on the title page of their works, are shown upon closer inspection to be charlatans. For they eulogize living men during their lifetimes, be they emperors or persons otherwise distinguished, not just by their presentation of the facts . . . , but they make it plain to all and sundry that their sole concern is the bestowal of excessive and unjustifiable praise. . . . By so doing they think that they are putting their immediate interests on a sound footing and they imagine that by cultivating whoever happens to be in power they are securing their own advantage, a mistaken calculation since those who are the object of their eulogies are not pleased with this sort of tribute and consider that open adulation is not capable of ensuring their reputation.[39]

But these gripes are only part of the picture. Agathias himself acknowledges that he was encouraged to write his *Histories* by Eutychianus the Younger, who was a member of the imperial secretariat, and thus could well have acted as his patron.[40] His account gives us lovely vignettes of everyday life, such as the story of Anthemius of Tralles, one of the engineers responsible for the lofty dome of Hagia Sophia, who created an artificial earthquake through the use of a steam machine in order to frighten an annoying neighbor.[41] He is also very conscientious in seeking out his materials: his history of the Persian royal family is based directly on Persian sources in the royal archives at Ctesiphon, which Agathias obtained through the good services of Sergius "the Interpreter."[42]

Agathias was well connected among the literati of his day. This is evident from his *Kyklos* or *Cycle* of poems, which has been preserved as part of a larger collection of poems in the so-called *Greek Anthology*. In his own words, this was "as complete a collection as possible of those recent and contemporary epigrams which were as yet unknown and indiscriminately murmured on the lips of some."[43] This work, too, seems to owe its existence to a prominent man, Theodorus the Decurion, a high officer in the military administration, to whom it is dedicated. He may be identical with the governor of Egypt in 577 of the same name. Moreover, the beginning of Agathias's *Kyklos* includes a short encomium on the emperor – the same arrangement of double praise of an aristocratic patron and of the emperor as that adopted by Corippus in his *Praise of Justin II*. Agathias's collection contains epigrams by twenty-three authors. We must assume that he was personally acquainted with most, if not all of them. These poets included officials at the highest level, a prefect, an ex-consul, a proconsul, and a consul. But the largest single group (a total of seven) are lawyers, *scholastici*, like Agathias himself. The painstaking prosopographical work of Averil and Alan Cameron has shown the network of ties that existed among these full-time bureaucrats and small-time poets.[44] The law professor Julian, for example, wrote a poem on the city prefect Gabriel, who in turn was a friend of John the Lydian and the dedicatee of the latter's work *On Months*. Rufinus, another author of epigrams, had been a fellow law student of Agathias and then joined the ceremonial guard of the *domestici*. Paul the Silentiary is also represented with a couple of epigrams that testify to his friendly relations with Agathias.[45] And then there is Damocharis, identified as a "friend and pupil of Agathias," who composed a charming poem on Agathias's mischievous cat that had eaten his favorite pet partridge.[46] Damocharis's early death is, in turn, lamented in a poem by Paul the Silentiary.

As a *silentiarius*, Paul held a position at the imperial court and was perhaps Agathias's best hope for gaining access to the emperor. He was the author of the famous description (*ekphrasis*) of Hagia Sophia, which must have circulated widely already during his lifetime, for Agathias in his *Histories* refers his audience to Paul's treatise: "If anyone who lives far from the capital wishes to get as clear and comprehensive a picture of the church as he would if he were there to view it in person, then he could hardly do better than to read the poem in hexameters of Paul the son of Cyrus and the grandson of Florus."[47] Other short epigrams in Agathias's *Cycle* are taken down directly from monuments, such as the inscription on a bridge built by Justinian over the river Sangarius, the inscription that adorned the beautiful Church of Saint Polyeuctus, built by the noblewoman Anicia Juliana, or indeed the inscriptions found on the statue of Porphyrius, a popular charioteer in the hippodrome races.

Agathias's works thus allow us a glimpse of a world where education defined a man's position in society. Not only did it provide him with the skills to make a living, it also guaranteed his membership in a circle of like-minded intellectuals. There were several such clusters of literati in Justinian's Constantinople, most notably among its Latin-speaking residents from North Africa, Italy, and Illyricum.[48] Authors from North Africa included, in addition to Corippus, Priscian, a professor of Latin and author of a Latin grammar, Victor of Tununna, who completed his *Chronicle* of the world while in exile in Constantinople,[49] and Junillus, the successor of Tribonian as Justinian's *quaestor sacri palatii* (quaestor of the sacred palace) from 542 to 549, during which time he composed his *Handbook of the Basic Principles of Divine Law* (*Instituta regularia divinae legis*).[50] Another literary circle was constituted by the many Italians, refugees from the Gothic wars or diplomats, who were present in Constantinople during Justinian's reign. Among them was Cassidorus Senator, the former secretary to the Ostrogothic king Theoderic and future founder of the scholarly monastery of Vivarium in southern Italy, who composed his longest work, the *Expositio psalmorum* (*Explanation of the Psalms*) during his sojourn in the capital,[51] and Jordanes, who wrote his *Roman History* (*Romana*, now lost) and his *Gothic History* (*Getica*) in Constantinople around the year 551. For the composition of the latter, he managed to secure from Cassiodorus's administrator a three-day loan of the latter's *Gothic History*, a text that does not survive.[52] Authors who shared Justinian's Illyrian background were also prominent in Constantinople. This common regional bond was probably the reason why Marcellinus Comes received a post in the administration from the young Justinian as a reward for his *Chronicle*. Another Illyrian who enjoyed Justinian's favor is Peter the Patrician who held the high post of master of offices for a remarkable twenty-six years. A lawyer and a career diplomat, he was sent by Justinian on missions to Italy and Persia. He also tried his hand as an author, composing a history of the first three centuries of the Roman Empire, recording imperial ceremonies, and writing down the protocols of his diplomatic encounters, sometimes exaggerating his own part. Menander Rhetor, who uses chunks of Peter's work in his own, chides him for this: "Peter, for the sake of his own reputation, has placed somewhat too much emphasis upon himself, in order that he appear to posterity as a very effective and convincing speaker who was able to bring around the unyielding and arrogant spirits of the barbarians."[53] Only traces of Peter's work survive in quotations by later authors, and we do not know whether Justinian took any interest in the literary endeavors of his trusted official.[54]

Justinian's successors took a much more active role than he had in promoting and rewarding contemporary authors. His successor Justin II rewarded Corippus's poem, as has been noted above. And the emperor Maurice (582–602) even created new opportunities for aspiring authors.[55] This is what saved Menander Protector from continuing his life as a lazy young lout and instead prompted him to write the continuation of Agathias's *Histories* from 557–558 to the year 582. In brief autobiographical remarks in his preface, Menander explains that although his father had received no education, he and his brother were sent to study law. "But," he continues,

> I did not take up the profession for which I was trained. For I had no desire to plead cases or to haunt the Royal Stoa and impress the petitioners with my eloquence [a possible jibe against Agathias's pitiful remarks about the difficulties of earning a living?]. I therefore neglected my career for the disgraceful life of an idle layabout. My interests were the gang fights of the "colours" [the Blues and the Greens], the chariot races and the pantomimes, and I even entered the wrestling ring. I sailed with such folly that I not only lost my shirt but also my good sense and all my decency.[56]

But when the emperor Maurice who "loved the Muses, being especially enthusiastic for poetry and history," "offered financial inducements to stimulate slothful intellects" Menander seized the opportunity and began to write his *History*.[57] He seems to gloat over his success, which came so much easier to him than to his predecessors Agathias and Procopius.

The scope of imperial support for literary activity after Justinian's death extends even outside Constantinople, to distant Antioch. Evagrius of Antioch, a prominent lawyer attached to Patriarch Gregory of Antioch, and with connections to the family of the Emperor Maurice, completed his *Ecclesiastical History* there in 593–594. The outbreak of the plague hit his household in several waves:

> I was affected by what are called buboes [swollen lymph nodes caused by the bubonic plague] while I was still attending the elementary teacher, but in the various

> subsequent visitations of these great misfortunes I lost many of my offspring and my wife and other relatives, and numerous servants and estate dwellers. Thus as I write this, while in the 58th year of my life, not more than two years previously while for the fourth time now the misfortune struck Antioch, when the fourth cycle from its outset had elapsed, I lost a daughter and the son she had produced, quite apart from the earlier losses.[58]

Evagrius's work covers the period from the Council of Ephesus in 431 to the reign of the emperor Maurice and is an important source for the religious aspects of Justinian's reign. Evagrius makes frequent use of Procopius's *Wars*, but remarks that its continuation by Agathias, written about a decade earlier, is as yet unavailable to him – a striking affirmation for the potentially slow dissemination of texts from Constantinople.[59] But Evagrius's example also shows that new literary works from the provinces could reach the capital rather quickly. His compilation of administrative documents was rewarded by the emperor Tiberius Constantine (578–582) with the rank of quaestor, and his panegyric on the birth of the emperor Maurice's first son Theodosius in 584 garnered him the elevation to the rank of prefect.[60] Both these works are now lost.

## LITERATURE WITHOUT PATRONAGE

Literary production independent of aristocratic and imperial patronage did exist, but it was located at some distance from the center of power: among authors who were men of the church and among authors who lived in the provinces.

There is the enigmatic Agapetus, for example. All we know about him is that he was a deacon attached to the numerous clergy of Hagia Sophia and that he addressed his work to the emperor Justinian. Agapetus wrote what can justifiably be called the first "Mirror of Princes," seventy-two short maxims of advice on how to be a good ruler. His admonition can be stern: "Let no man feel conceit about nobility of birth. All men alike have clay for their first ancestor [a reference to the creation account in Genesis] – both those who boast themselves in purple and fine linen, and those who are afflicted by poverty and sickness; both those who are crowned with a diadem and those who are attendants in the palace."[61] This treatise enjoyed enormous success: it was one of the first Greek works to be translated into Old Church

Slavonic, and in the sixteenth century no less than twenty printed versions of it were circulated.[62]

Another clergy member in Constantinople, Romanos, was equally innovative and pathbreaking in his writing. He originally came from Emesa in Syria and then served as a deacon in a church in Berytus (Beirut). In this culturally fertile borderland, he was exposed to the tradition of chanting sermons in verse that had been popular in Syriac Christianity for centuries. Legend has it that after he arrived in Constantinople during the reign of Anastasius I, he stood on the pulpit ready to deliver a sermon when the Virgin Mary appeared and gave him a scroll to swallow and with it the gift of poetry, which he immediately used to good effect. He has been known since then as Romanos the Melodist, or the Melode. His poetry uses new construction principles, repeating the complicated accentuated rhythms of the whole stanza, interspersed with shorter refrains and often embellished by an acrostic. The *kontakion* form that he championed remained the dominant form of hymnography until it was eventually superseded by the *Kanon* in the ninth century. The most famous hymn still recited today in the Orthodox Church is attributed to him: the *Akathistos Hymn* on the Virgin Mary.

> Hail, woman in whom all opposites are reconciled.
> Hail, woman who joins virginity and childbirth.
> Hail, woman through whom sin was erased.
> Hail, woman through whom Paradise was reopened.
> Hail, key to the kingdom of Christ.
> Hail, hope of eternal happiness.
> Hail, unwedded Bride![63]

Also from the Syriac-speaking regions of the Byzantine Empire comes John Malalas. We know little about him except that he must have practiced as a lawyer in Antioch – the name Malalas is equivalent to *scholastikos* in Greek – and that at some point in his life he moved to Constantinople, because the focus of his narrative changes. He wrote the first world chronicle that survives in Greek and did so in a rather refreshingly unadorned style.[64] His work was so popular that it was translated into Old Church Slavonic and Georgian. Its Greek version, however, survives in only one incomplete manuscript from the eleventh century. Malalas's *Chronicle* begins with the creation of Adam and then moves quickly through the account of Genesis, the mythical history of ancient Greece, and then on to the foundation of Rome up to his own lifetime, when his account becomes more detailed, ending with the year 565. It contains a curious mixture of political history and local lore, reports on earthquakes and floods, and other newsworthy items such as the story about a dog who performed tricks of memory or the travels of a giant woman through the empire that included a visit to Antioch.[65]

Egypt brought forth another idiosyncratic and innovative author during Justinian's reign, Cosmas Indicopleustes ("the one who travels to India"). Unlike the work of Agapetus, Romanos, and Malalas, Cosmas's work met with little or no interest among contemporaries or later audiences. His *Christian Topography* is indeed a tough act to follow: Cosmas sets out to describe this world and the world above. He advocates a literal interpretation of the Bible in order to show that the universe is constructed on the model of the tabernacle of Moses. At the same time, he manages to insert his own personal reminiscences of his extensive travels, probably as a trader, to Ethiopia and the Red Sea, perhaps even India and Ceylon. His work skillfully integrates the text with illustrations, a combination that later copyists sought carefully to preserve.

This overview of literary activity in the sixth century leaves us with some sobering conclusions regarding the appreciation of literature in Byzantium and Justinian's role in its creation. While modern scholars depend heavily on the formal histories by Procopius and Agathias for their accounts of Justinian's reign, these were not the works that enjoyed the greatest popularity among contemporaries and later generations. That merit fell to Agathias's *Cycle* of poems, Agapetus's *Mirror of Princes*, Malalas's *Chronicle*, and Romanos's liturgical poetry, texts that provided – respectively – light literary enjoyment, moral instruction, infotainment, and spiritual edification. Except for Agathias, none of these authors profited from patronage of any kind. If patronage was forthcoming – as was the case for most of the authors discussed above – the benefactors were aristocrats in the outer orbit of the imperial court. Justinian acted as such a patron prior to his accession in rewarding the *Chronicle* of his fellow Illyrian Marcellinus Comes. After he became emperor, he commissioned John the Lydian to write the history of the Persian wars. These two works, of which the latter does not survive, are the sum total of the concrete evidence for Justinian's support for literature.[66] Unlike Maurice, who was known for his eagerness at reading and study, Justinian did not create any incentives for the production of literature. That this did not result in an overall reduction to a new level of boorishness, as Zonaras had claimed, and that literature nonetheless flourished, is perhaps one of the more remarkable paradoxes of Justinian's reign.

## Notes

This chapter focuses on literature that was written in Constantinople and the Greek-speaking provinces of the East to educate, entertain, and edify the literary elite of the sixth century. It does not attempt a complete record of the production of written works in that period, which would also have to include, among others, handbooks of law and medicine, rhetorical treatises and *ekphraseis*, and the ample production and dissemination of writing by the Christian Church, including hagiography. Nor does it do justice to the important works by Syriac authors, or by Latin authors in Italy and North Africa, which would require a study of their own.

1 J. B. Bury, *History of the Later Roman Empire from the Death of Theodosius I to the Death of Justinian*, 2 vols. (New York, 1958), 2:418; Glanville Downey, *Constantinople in the Age of Justinian* (Norman, Okla., 1960), 154.

2 Zonaras, *Epitome historiarum*, 14.6, ed. Ludwig Dindorf, vol. 3 (Leipzig, 1870), 274, ll. 3–5.

3 Malalas, *Chronographia*, 18.47, Dindorf, 451.

4 *CJ*, I.11.10.2, trans. from Paul Lemerle, *Byzantine Humanism: The First Phase*, trans. Helen Lindsay and Ann Moffatt (Canberra, 1986; first published in French, 1971), 74.

5 For the persecution of "Hellenes" (Christian authors of late antiquity used this word to refer to pagans) in 529, see Malalas, 18.42, Dindorf, 449.

6 Malalas, *Chronographia*, 18.136, Dindorf, 491.

7 Lemerle, *Byzantine Humanism*, 77.

8 Guglielmo Cavallo, "La circolazione libraria nell'età di Giustiniano," in *L'imperatore Giustiniano. Storia e mito*, ed. G. G. Archi (Milan, 1978).

9 Cavallo, "Circolazione," 213–215, 232.

10 Agathias, *Histories*, 2.29.1–5.

11 Agathias, *Histories*, 3.1.4.

12 Roger Starr, "The Circulation of Literary Texts in the Roman World," *Classical Quarterly* 37.1 (1987): 213–223.

13 Arator, *De actibus apostolorum*, ed. Arthur Patch McKinlay, CSEL 72 (Vienna, 1951), xxviii, from the manuscript Vat. Pal. lat. 1716, of the tenth century. See also Cavallo, "Circolazione," 201–202.

14 William V. Harris, *Ancient Literacy* (Cambridge, Mass., 1989).

15 Peter Heather, "Literacy and Power in the Migration Period," *Literacy and Power in the Ancient World*, ed. Alan K. Bowman and Greg Woolf (Cambridge, 1994), 177–197.

16 Lemerle, *Byzantine Humanism*, 298.

17 Heather, "Literacy and Power," 183.

18 Peter Heather, "New Men for New Constantines? Creating an Imperial Elite in the Eastern Mediterranean," *New Constantines: The Rhythm of Imperial Renewal in Byzantium, Fourth–Thirteenth Centuries*, ed. Paul Magdalino (Aldershot, 1994), 18–20.

19 Brian Croke, *Count Marcellinus and His Chronicle* (Oxford, 2001), 80.

20 On the social background of sixth-century historians, see L. Michael Whitby, "Greek Historical Writing after Procopius: Variety and Vitality," in *The Byzantine and Early Islamic Near East, I: Problems in the Literary Source Material*, ed. Averil Cameron and Lawrence I. Conrad (Princeton, N.J., 1992), 28–30.

21 Flavius Cresconius Corippus, *The Iohannis, or, De Bellis Libycis*, intro. and trans. George W. Shea (Lewiston, N.Y., 1998).

22 On Corippus's life, see Flavius Cresconius Corippus, *In laudem Iustini minoris libri IV*, ed., trans., and comm. Averil Cameron (London, 1976), 1–2.

23 Corippus, *Ioannis*, preface 1.

24 Corippus, *In laudem*, preface.

25 Corippus, *In laudem*, panegyric.

26 Corippus, *In laudem*, panegyric, 18–24.

27 On the author, see Brian Croke, *Count Marcellinus and His Chronicle* (Oxford, 2001), esp. 17–35.

28 John Lydus, *On Offices*, 3.27.

29 John Lydus, *On Offices*, 3.26–30.

30 Michael Maas, *John Lydus and the Roman Past: Antiquarianism and Politics in the Age of Justinian* (London, 1992), 29.

31 Detailed discussion of the author and his works in Averil Cameron, *Procopius and the Sixth Century* (Berkeley, Calif., 1985).

32 Procopius, *Buildings*, 1.1.10.

33 Procopius, *Buildings*, 1.1.4.

34 Geoffrey Greatrex, "Procopius the Outsider?" in *Strangers to Themselves: The Byzantine Outsider*, ed. Dion S. Smythe (Burlington, Vt., 2000), argues that the *Secret History* contains material that Procopius had intended for inclusion in his *Wars*, a work that was left unfinished at the time of this death.

35 For the life and works of Agathias, see Averil Cameron, *Agathias* (Oxford, 1970).

36 Agathias, *Histories*, 3.1.4.

37 *Anthologia Palatina*, 9.662.

38 Agathias, *Histories*, 5.20.7.

39 Agathias, *Histories*, preface, 18–19.

40 Agathias, *Histories*, preface, 11–12.

41 Agathias, *Histories*, 5.6.

42 Agathias, *Histories*, 4.30.2–3.

43 Agathias, *Histories*, preface, 8. See also Averil Cameron, "Agathias on the Sassanians," *DOP* 23.4 (1969–1970), 1–150.

44 Alan and Averil Cameron, "The *Cycle* of Agathias," *JHS* 86 (1966): 6–25. See also R. C. McCail, "The *Cycle* of Agathias: New Identifications Scrutinized," *JHS* 89 (1969): 87–96.

45 *Anthologia Palatina*, 5.292–293.

46 *Anthologia Palatina*, 7.588.

47 Agathias, *Histories*, 5.9.7.

48 Brian Croke, *Count Marcellinus and His Chronicle* (Oxford, 2001), 86–93.

49 Brian Croke, "Basiliscus the Boy-Emperor," *Greek, Roman, and Byzantine Studies* 24 (1983): 81–91, reprinted in Croke, *Christian Chronicles and Byzantine History, Fifth–Sixth Centuries* (Aldershot, 1992).

50 Michael Maas, *Exegesis and Empire in the Early Byzantine Mediterranean: Junillus Africanus and the* Instituta Regularia Divinae Legis (Tübingen, 2003), 1–18.

51 James O'Donnell, *Cassiodorus* (Berkeley, Calif., 1979), 131–176.

52 Brian Croke, "Cassiodorus and the Getica of Jordanes," *Classical Philology* 82 (1987): 117–134, reprinted in *Christian Chronicles and Byzantine History*.

53 Menander Protector, frag. 6.2.

54 "Peter Patrikios," *Oxford Dictionary of Byzantium*, vol. 3 (New York, 1991), 1641.

55 On this author and his work, see *The History of Menander the Guardsman*, intro., ed., trans., and annot. R. C. Blockley (Liverpool, 1985).

56 Menander Protector, frag. 1.

57 Menander Protector, frag. 1.

58 Evagrius Scholasticus, *Ecclesiastical History*, 4.29. On the author and his working technique, see also the introduction to the translation by Michael Whitby.

59 Evagrius Scholasticus, *Historia ecclesiastica*, 4.24.

60 Evagrius Scholasticus, *Historia ecclesiastica*, 6.24.

61 Agapetus, *Expositio capitum admonitorium*, PG 86.1, 1163–1186, cap. 4, col. 1165B.

62 Ihor Ševčenko, "Agapetus East and West: The Fate of a Byzantine 'Mirror of Princes,'" *Revue des Études Sud-Est Européennes* 16 (1978): 3–44, reprinted in his *Ideology, Letters, and Culture in the Byzantine World* (London, 1982).

63 *Akathistos Hymn*, 15.

64 The Greek world chronicle by Eusebius of Caesarea (d. c. 339) survives only in the Latin translation by Jerome, and that by Sextus Julius Africanus (d. c. 240) only in fragments.

65 Malalas, *Chronographia*, 18.51.

66 I exclude Procopius's *Buildings*, because that case is based on plausibility rather than hard evidence.

PART 4

# PEOPLES AND COMMUNITIES

# 16: Jews in the Age of Justinian

*Nicholas de Lange*

"Withdrawing behind the rampart of talmudic law and religion, the Jewish people of the sixth century continued to pursue its historic career quietly, almost inarticulately."[1] This judgment of the foremost twentieth-century historian of the Jews writing in English, Salo Wittmayer Baron, encapsulates a commonly held view of the Jews in the Age of Justinian, yet it is a view that can be challenged in every particular. In what follows we shall endeavour to explore the foundations on which such a judgment rests, and hope to show that, insofar as one can speak of a "Jewish people" with a "historic career," the latter was pursued anything but quietly or inarticulately. The sixth century was a time of dramatic change and strident conflict, a time of acute anxiety for Jews as for other minorities of the empire, but also a time of challenge and opportunity, a time that decisively shaped the character of Judaism in momentous ways.

The main obstacle facing anyone attempting to write the history of the Jews in the Age of Justinian is a shortage of securely datable written texts, especially texts written by Jews. Apart from a few characteristically laconic inscriptions, all the dated writings that we have were written by non-Jews, and almost all of these are inherently antagonistic to the Jews as a group. We are bound at every turn to recognise uncertainties and ambiguities in the evidence, to reconstruct the background to an obscure event, or to estimate the distance between ideology and reality. Accordingly we shall begin with an account of the available materials and an assessment of their reliability. But before doing so it is necessary to say a few words about the conventional periodisation of Jewish history during the Roman Empire, since this has an important bearing on how we assess developments in the sixth century.

A series of key moments punctuates the history of the Jews under Roman rule as conventionally described. The sack of the Jerusalem temple in 70 CE and the subsequent failure of the Bar Kochba revolt in 135 represent the loss of national autonomy, and these dates are also thought to indicate the early consolidation of rabbinic Judaism and the "parting of the ways" between Judaism and Christianity. Early rabbinic Judaism (the "Tannaitic age") ends in the early third century with the compilation of the Mishnah, the first authoritative compilation of the law and lore of the rabbis. The compilation of the next major rabbinic text, the Palestinian Talmud or Yerushalmi, an extensive discussion of the materials gathered in the Mishnah, is generally placed in the early fifth century, around the time of the end of the hereditary patriarchs, seen as a crucial moment in Jewish political history because they had been recognised by the Romans as the leaders and representatives of the Jewish community as a legal entity. Marked by acts of aggression and even violence against Jews by Christians, this moment follows not long after the ending of the last serious challenge to Christianity as the religion of the empire on the death of Julian in 363. The next phase goes from the Persian conquest of Jerusalem in 614 to the Arab conquest of Egypt and the Middle East in the 630s and includes the edict decreeing the conversion of all Jews to Christianity, issued by Heraclius in or around 632.[2] It is around this time that the next and greatest monument of rabbinic Judaism, the Babylonian Talmud or Bavli (a more extensive work than the Yerushalmi, not dissimilar in conception), is dated. From the Arab conquests the important Jewish communities of Palestine and Syria were cut off from the empire and politically joined to the centres in what the Jews called Babylon (modern Iraq), and a new page is turned.

This picture of Jewish history, which is the one presented in most of the standard history books, is open to question in all sorts of ways. For our present purpose, the key element is the long-term process by which the Jews lose their autonomy and gradually become subject to the domination of the Christian Church and the Christian empire, and the parallel process by which rabbinic Judaism, as embodied in its most perfect expression, the Babylonian Talmud, becomes established as the monolithic Jewish orthodoxy. Undoubtedly there is a certain truth in this picture: the Jews *did* become subject to the power of the Christians, which was often exercised to segregate, marginalise, and even physically attack them; the rabbis *did* come to exercise enormous power within the Jewish communities both inside and outside the empire, and the Babylonian Talmud *did* come to be recognised not only as the main source of Jewish law but also as a repository of authoritative teaching on virtually every subject. However, these twin developments were by no means unchallenged, nor was their impact on Jewish life immediate and complete. Various contrary forces within both Judaism and Christianity make the reality much more complex.

Again, we note that the conventional picture leaves a long gap of some two centuries between the compilation of the Yerushalmi and the Bavli when nothing much appears to happen. The Age of Justinian falls into this gap. In fact this was an enormously rich and productive period for the Jews of the empire, at least if we can extrapolate from the sparse literary and archaeological remains. In studying these, we have to bear in mind constantly the very fragmentary nature of the evidence. It is clear that an enormous amount has been lost: we have virtually no manuscripts and very few physical monuments, and there are references in the sources to writings that have not survived. As for texts that have been preserved by continuous tradition (either in rabbinic Judaism or in the Christian churches), it is reasonable to be suspicious both about the selection of what was to survive and about the reliability of the written text itself.

## Sources

We have hardly any securely dated Jewish sources from the time of Justinian, and very few that are approximately datable to this period. And yet a considerable body of Jewish writings exists that could have been – indeed is likely to have been – composed at this time. It is simply that the problems of dating are well nigh insuperable. We cannot ignore these writings, then, but we have to be responsible in the use we make of them. All the writings survive in Aramaic, Hebrew, or a mixture of the two. Although we know that Jews in the empire used other languages, particularly Greek (which for many Jews was a sacred language[3]), we know virtually nothing about Jewish writings in Greek, Latin, or other languages.

While Aramaic was a widely used language that is also the vehicle of an important Christian literature, Hebrew was a specially Jewish language. This ancient language of the Jerusalem sanctuary was revived in late antiquity and made into the language of the synagogue (where previously Greek and Aramaic had dominated) as well as the main language of written communication. Texts associated with the synagogue, and with the adjacent house of study, are foremost in the Jewish writings from late antiquity. They include texts of prayers, which were being gradually formalised at this time.[4]

Two types of writing that were to become very important make their appearance among Jews during the fifth and sixth centuries. Both have close parallels in Christian writing, and indeed both may well have originated under Christian influence. One is *midrash* (plural *midrashim*), a selective and often discursive commentary on the biblical readings of the synagogue, seemingly based on actual homilies and lectures; the other is *piyyut* (plural *piyyutim*), hymnody or liturgical poetry.

The origin and early development of the midrashic genre are obscure in the extreme. Insofar as there is a scholarly consensus, it would appear that compilations of traditional material arranged around the regular synagogue readings appointed to be read in synagogues on Sabbaths and festivals began to be made in Palestine in the fifth century; there was no standard, authoritative text, but the various compilations differed in terms of both their content and their arrangement. In all these respects the *midrashim* closely parallel the Christian biblical *catenae* or *seirai*, and it is hard to resist the thought that there must be a connection between the two, although which influenced the other or whether the influences were mutual is impossible to determine.[5]

None of the midrashic compilations can be dated precisely; indeed, according to some scholars they did not attain a fixed form until they had begun to be printed in the sixteenth century. But the scholarly consensus now situates the main phase of compilation in Palestine between the early fifth and early seventh centuries. There is a strong likelihood that works such as Genesis Rabba, Lamentations Rabba, Leviticus Rabba, and Pesikta de Rav Kahana were either compiled in the sixth century or were circulating then as relatively recent writings, and similar compilations on other biblical books were at various stages of compilation.[6]

The term "*piyyut*," thought to derive from the Greek *poietes*, "poet," denotes a poetic composition designed to replace or accompany the prayers of the Hebrew liturgy. The origin of this genre has also been hotly debated, and it used to be suggested that it began in response to the prohibition of rabbinic teaching (referred to in Greek as *deuterosis*) in the synagogue by Justinian (*Novel* 146); there seem, however, to be earlier examples of *piyyutim*, and the consensus today would place the origin in Palestine in the late fourth or early fifth century.[7] By the sixth century it had become well established, and the poets of this time, such as Yannai, Simeon ben Megas, Yehudah, and Qillir, produced works of great subtlety and complexity.[8] The *piyyutim* constitute a valuable, under-exploited resource for studying Jewish beliefs, practices, and attitudes.

*Targum* (plural *targumim*) is the name given to the various Aramaic translations of biblical books, originating either in the synagogue or in the house of study. There are many of them, and they have proved virtually impossible to date. While some *targumim* give a straight Aramaic translation of the Hebrew text, others paraphrase and add new material, and some are so discursive that they hardly deserve the name of translations at all. For example, the so-called Second Targum on Esther contains a great deal of commentary and legend, some of it barely connected to the biblical book of Esther. The first editor of this text dated it to the time of Justinian and described it as a Jewish reaction to the emperor's restrictive policy towards the Jews. Other opinions about the date range, however, from the fourth century to the eleventh, the most commonly accepted view now situating the work in the late seventh or early eighth century.[9]

Of the Greek liturgy of the synagogue at this time, little or nothing survives; we do have, though, some fragments of Greek bibles, in the translation of Aquila, which will be discussed below in the section on Jewish life.

Outside the life of the synagogue, the most characteristic type of Jewish writing in late antiquity consists of legal texts, and pride of place among these are the two Talmuds, the Palestinian and the Babylonian, representing the two main centres of rabbinic scholarship. The Babylonian Talmud, or Bavli, was compiled over a long period of time, culminating in a final redactional phase either just before or just after the Arab conquest of Iraq in the seventh century. However, this activity lies outside the confines of the Roman Empire, and although the Bavli contains a good deal of Palestinian material, this is mainly ascribed to the second, third, and fourth centuries and is therefore not directly relevant to the study of Byzantine Jewry in the sixth century, although it is invaluable for the study of Sasanian Jewry.[10] As for the Palestinian Talmud, or Yerushalmi, its compilation is generally stated to have been completed in the late fourth or early fifth century, as no rabbinic authorities or historical events after this time are mentioned. The arguments in favour of such an early dating are, however, not compelling and have probably been excessively influenced by what is now known to be an erroneous belief that Jewish life in Palestine more or less came to an end after the triumph of Christianity, and particularly after the end of the Jewish patriarchate under Theodosius II.[11] A recent study has suggested that the Yerushalmi may have been completed as late as the early sixth century and draws persuasive comparisons between it and Justinian's *Digest*.[12] While such a view does not necessarily make the Yerushalmi, which is one of the most extensive Jewish texts we have from late antiquity, into a quarry for information about Jewish life and thought at this time, it does modify the general view that by now there was an absence of scholarly legal activity among Jews. Other evidence undermines such a view, including some actual texts dated to this period.[13]

Little is known about Jewish apologetical or polemical writings at this time. A Jewish history of Jesus known as *Toldoth Yeshu* was composed in or around the sixth century, originally in Aramaic.[14] An Arabic apologetic work, *The Account of the Disputation of the Priest*, purporting to be a letter by a converted bishop refuting Christian arguments against Judaism (and displaying a good knowledge of Christianity), was dated to 514 by its original editor, but this dating has lately been shown to be unfounded. It is not impossible, however, that the lost Syriac original was composed during the sixth century.[15]

To summarise so far: there is a wealth of Jewish literature that has a good chance of having existed in the sixth century, if not in its present form then in something like it, but it is hard to be certain in any particular case.

What has transformed our estimate of the religious and cultural as well as the material level of Jewish life in the time of Justinian is the archaeological exploration of Jewish sites, particularly in Galilee. Whereas the Roman laws, beginning with Theodosius II, prohibit the building of new synagogues and even the repair of old ones unless they are in imminent danger of collapse,[16] there are concrete examples of synagogues being built, repaired, and embellished, and the archaeological record suggests that the period in general was one of quiet prosperity for the Jews. We do indeed find cases of synagogues being converted into churches, such as the synagogue of Gerasa (Jerash) in Transjordan, which became a church in 530–531.[17] Yet at the same time throughout the fifth and well into the sixth century we find synagogues being built, enlarged, or repaired. A good example is the excavated and now partly restored synagogue of Sardis in Lydia, which has attracted a good deal of attention because of the prominent city-centre site it occupies and the evidence it provides of Jews and Christians coexisting closely; but no less interesting is the fact that alterations and repairs were made to the synagogue at least until the middle of the sixth century (Plate xxv).[18] The majority of buildings are undated, but a few have inscriptions containing a date, among them a mosaic pavement in Gaza dated 508–509 and the synagogue of Beth Alpha in Galilee, one of the earliest excavated synagogues to attract attention because of its mosaics, dated in the reign of Justin I. (We shall return to these mosaics.) The architecture of the synagogues, their carvings and mosaics, and their inscriptions demonstrate clearly that, whatever their legal status, the Jews were fully integrated in the surrounding culture. The inscriptions are in Greek and Aramaic and contain formulae identical with those in Christian and pagan inscriptions.

Of the texts written by non-Jews, the vast majority issue from the pen of Christians. Some information can also be gleaned, however, from non-Christian writers, in particular the leading Neoplatonist thinkers Damascius and Simplicius.[19] We can detect the involvement of Jews and Samaritans in the philosophical schools, including no less a figure than the Samaritan Marinus of Neapolis, who was the head of the school of Athens after the death of Proclus in 485.

Many Christian writings mention Jews, either as individuals or as a group. In the past these, rather than the Jewish sources just mentioned, were exploited by historians writing about Jews at this time. The results, however, were less than satisfactory, for a number of reasons. In the first place, their outlook is hostile, biased, and ill-informed.[20] Much of what they say can best be classified under the heading of mythology, and they cannot be trusted to give us a reliable picture of Jewish life or thought. As for events that they mention, these tend to be haphazard, and we lack the means to know whether they are isolated or typical occurrences. Most of them are located in out-of-the-way places, and we hear next to nothing about major centres such as Galilee or Constantinople. An exception to all this in some ways are the legal texts, since they are official documents and are intended to apply to the whole empire, or at least the whole of a specified region.[21] It is too tempting, though, to read them as indicating what really happened, rather than what the legislator wanted to happen. As we have already seen, it would be erroneous to deduce from the repeated prohibition on building or repairing synagogue buildings that such buildings were not built or repaired.

For these reasons it would be preferable if historians paid greater attention to internal Jewish sources than to external Christian ones. Since these sources exist, and since they can supply a good deal of information not available from Jewish sources (particularly about the policy of the state and the church towards the Jews) we have to mention them here. But they must always be read with a certain amount of suspicion.

Among the Christian historical writers pride of place must go to Procopius of Caesarea, who mentions matters of Jewish interest in all three of his works.[22] In book 1 of the *Wars*, for example, he mentions the Jews who lived on the island of Iotabe in the Red Sea (1.19.4) and an invasion of the land of the Jewish and pagan Homerites (also known as Himyarites; their territory, Himyar, was in southern Arabia) by the Christian king of Ethiopia (1.20.1), while in book 5 he describes the Jews of Naples helping to defend the city from Belisarius (5.8.41–42 and 5.10.24–26). In *Buildings* he records the forced conversion of the Jews of Borion in Africa to Christianity and of their ancient synagogue to a church (6.2.21–23). In the *Secret History* he writes about the persecution of the Samaritans (11.14–33; 18.34) and complains that Justinian interfered in the Jewish laws, forbidding the Jews to celebrate Passover if it fell earlier than the Christian Easter (28.16–18).[23]

John Malalas refers in his *Chronography* to the war between the Axumites of Ethiopia and the Homerites; he also describes the Samaritan revolts of 529 and 556. In keeping with his well-known interest in the city of Antioch, where in the fourth century John Chrysostom had inflamed Christian sentiments against the local Jews in his sermons, he records two violent attacks on the Jews in the city by the Green faction, as well as an earthquake in 528 that caused the synagogues of Laodicea to collapse, although the churches were spared.[24]

Other contemporary Christian historical sources that make some reference to the Jews include Cyril of Scythopolis, a Palestinian hagiographer with an interest in local events; John of Ephesus; Zacharias of Mytilene, together with his anonymous continuator; and his friend Severus of Antioch.[25]

Legal texts, although they are state documents, have to be classified under the heading of Christian sources, and they constitute a particularly rich source of information not only about the official status of the Jews but also about many aspects of Jewish life.[26]

A good deal of information, about Christian attitudes to Jews but also incidentally about Jewish life and thought, can be gained from polemical writings, as well as from other types of ecclesiastical literature. The sixth century, compared to earlier and later periods, is relatively poor in Christian polemical texts aimed particularly against Judaism.[27] In some cases it is hard for us to assign a date to a text; the absence of any reference to the forced baptism of the Jews under Heraclius or to iconoclasm tends to be considered a sign of a date before the seventh century, but it is probably unwise to be dogmatic on this point. The polemics of this period, compared to those of an earlier date, have been characterised as being much more picturesquely written, with a mass of "novelistic" detail; they deal with mass movements and they make much use of miracles. It has also been noted that they tend to repeat the same arguments endlessly, and that they are often closely linked to a specific issue.[28] The *Disputation of Gregentius and Herbanus*, like some other works of this time, is given an exotic setting in the wars of the Axumites and the Himyarites. All the Jews of Himyar gather to watch their spokesman debate with the bishop. After several days of debate the heavens open, Jesus Christ reveals himself in glory, and the Jews are all baptised.[29] Other disputations that have been ascribed to this time are those bearing the names of Anastasius of Sinai,[30] Timothy and Aquila,[31] and Athanasius and Zacchaeus,[32] as well as the *Disputation on Religion* set in the Sassanian court.[33] A dialogue of a Jewish priest or leader or teacher named Theodosius with his Christian friend Philip appears in a number of different sources, in some of which (notably in the tenth-century lexicon known as the *Suda*, under the rubric "Jesus our Christ and God") it is specifically set in the reign of Justinian.[34] Such overtly polemical texts are, however, not the only Christian writings in which we find anti-Jewish materials: the hymns of Romanos, for example, himself said to have been of Jewish origin, include attacks on the Jews. As hymns reached a wider public than the published disputations (many of which are of frankly academic character), they are particularly valuable in informing us about Christian attitudes to Jews.[35]

Finally, we have various formulae of abjuration or renunciation intended to be pronounced by Jews on accepting baptism and becoming Christians. Some of these have been thought to belong to our period, and they provide an interesting summary of Jewish beliefs and practices. While they cannot be taken at face value (some of the information they contain, for example about Jewish sects, visibly comes from antecedent Christian tradition), they do give us an idea of what Christians thought Jews believed and did, and it is not unlikely that converted Jews had a hand in their composition.[36]

Taking all these various Christian sources together, we see that while they contain a good deal of incidental information about the Jews and Judaism, they leave enormous gaps, and their tone is highly tendentious. Even official and public texts use insulting language that appears astonishingly offensive to us today. This very fact is instructive when we come to consider the legal status of the Jews and the place they held in Roman society, and it is possible to trace a progressive degradation in the terms in which the laws, for example, refer to Jews from the earliest Christian legislation under Constantine to the very aggressive texts issued by Justinian.[37] The Christian sources inform us about certain Christian attitudes, but they cannot be used to reconstruct Jewish life and thought in Justinian's empire.

## The Jews in the Empire

We have no basis whatever for gauging the numbers of Jews in the sixth century, or indeed in the preceding or following centuries.[38] Consequently we are unable to tell whether, as is sometimes asserted, the population was in decline as a result of Christian discrimination and pressure.

In considering the Jews in the Age of Justinian it is difficult to avoid mentioning a related group, the Samaritans, a community with a religion sharing some features with Judaism, centred on Samaria but with a considerable diaspora both in Palestine and further afield.[39] Both Jewish and Christian sources distinguish between Jews and Samaritans, but neither indicates the relations between the two groups. Modern authors do not have a clear policy about whether to treat the Samaritans as a Jewish sect, a completely separate group, or something between the two. If we take our lead from the rabbinic and Roman legal texts, we could justify treating them as a separate group, and there are crucial differences in their respective histories in the sixth century: for example, the Samaritans rose in armed rebellion in 529 and again in 556 (as they had done earlier, in 484) and clearly had their own political agenda.[40] But that is not the end of the story. While the rabbinic sources distinguish the Samaritans from the Jews, they do not exactly classify them as non-Jews, either; the Roman laws sometimes link Jews and Samaritans,[41] and according to Malalas, Jews joined the Samaritan revolt of 556. Moreover, both culturally and geographically the two groups were very close, and it is not at all easy to distinguish between Jewish and Samaritan archaeological remains such as synagogue buildings or tombstones.[42]

The main concentrations of the Jewish population seem to have been in the east, particularly in northern Palestine (Palaestina II) and Syria, but southern Italy also had important communities. Jewish settlements were scattered throughout the empire, from Spain and Africa through Egypt and Arabia to southern and western Asia Minor, to Constantinople, Thessalonica, and Athens, and both southern and, to a lesser extent, northern Italy. Sicily, Sardinia, Crete, Cyprus, and the Aegean islands also had a Jewish presence.[43] The list of places where synagogues were confiscated or destroyed gives an indication of the widespread nature of Jewish settlement: they include Cagliari, Palermo, Terracina, Rome, Ravenna, various towns of Africa in the west, and Constantinople, together with several places in Asia as well as Daphne, near Antioch, in the east.[44] An oblique remark referring to the mid–sixth century suggests that the Jews of Alexandria, a community with a glorious history of centuries, had no synagogue.[45] Jews lived in Jerusalem, but the main centre of religious learning in Palestine was Tiberias, on the western shore of the Sea of Galilee (Map 9).

On the fringes of the empire, both within and without, Jews are sometimes mentioned in the sources as an element in political and military events. For instance, they resisted the reconquest of Italy by Belisarius;[46] they had mounting influence among the Berber tribes of North Africa, some of which were converted to Judaism;[47] and in the east they were accused of siding with the Persian attackers,[48] a reminder of the considerable presence of Jews within the Sasanian Empire during this period of flourishing, when the Babylonian Talmud was being compiled.[49]

The Jewish element among the Himyarites, a group of tribes in southern Arabia, came to prominence when a Jewish ruler, Yusuf Asar, also known as Dhu Nuwas, came to power here around 518. The empire as a matter of policy encouraged the Christian religion both in this region and across the straits in the Horn of Africa.[50] The Jews, who played an important part in the trade of the region, had tended to favour the Persians. These factors no doubt help to explain the episode mentioned by Procopius, when Justinian (probably in the 530s, some years after the death of Dhu Nuwas) brought under Roman control the autonomous Jewish community on the island of Iotabe in the Red Sea.[51] The fighting between Ethiopians and Himyarites is a complex and obscure story. Our exclusively Christian sources blame the invasion of the Himyarite lands by Christian Ethiopians, leading to the overthrow of Dhu Nuwas, on his persecution of Himyarite Christians, culminating in a massacre of Christians in Najran. Whatever the facts, the story serves as a reminder, first that, however powerless the Jews were becoming within the empire, elsewhere they could still exercise power, and second that it is likely that what we know about Jewish populations is only the tip of the iceberg: a good deal was happening that has left no trace whatever.

The story of the Jews of the Arabian peninsula raises a question that may well be asked about Jews elsewhere: Where had they come from? Often they claimed great antiquity in particular locations (the Jews of Borion in Cyrenaica claimed that their temple, converted into a church by Justinian, had been built by King Solomon[52]). Such claims are generally impossible to test, but we do know that some settlements outside the Land of Israel had a history going back centuries, to the conquests of Alexander and before, and in very many places the Jews could claim to have preceded the coming of Christianity. That is not to

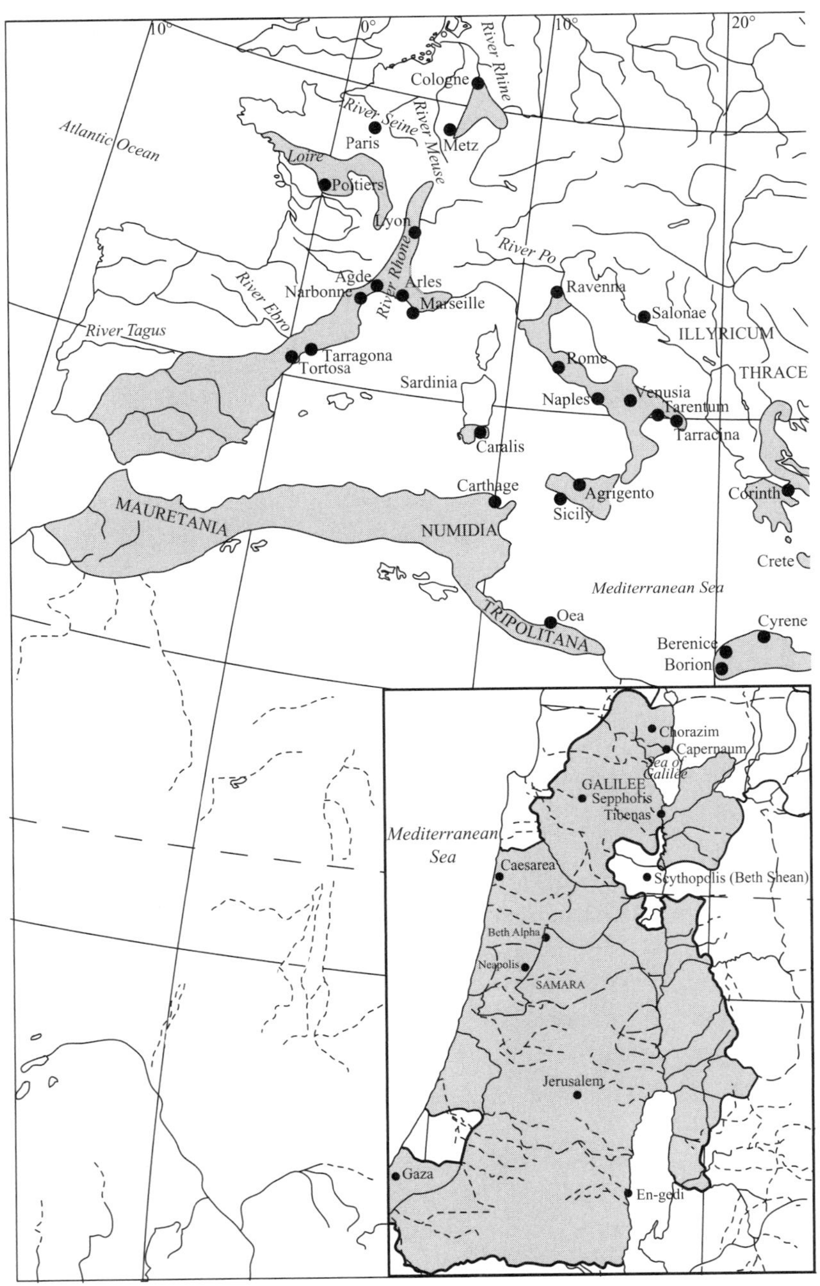


MAP 9. Jews in the Age of Justinian

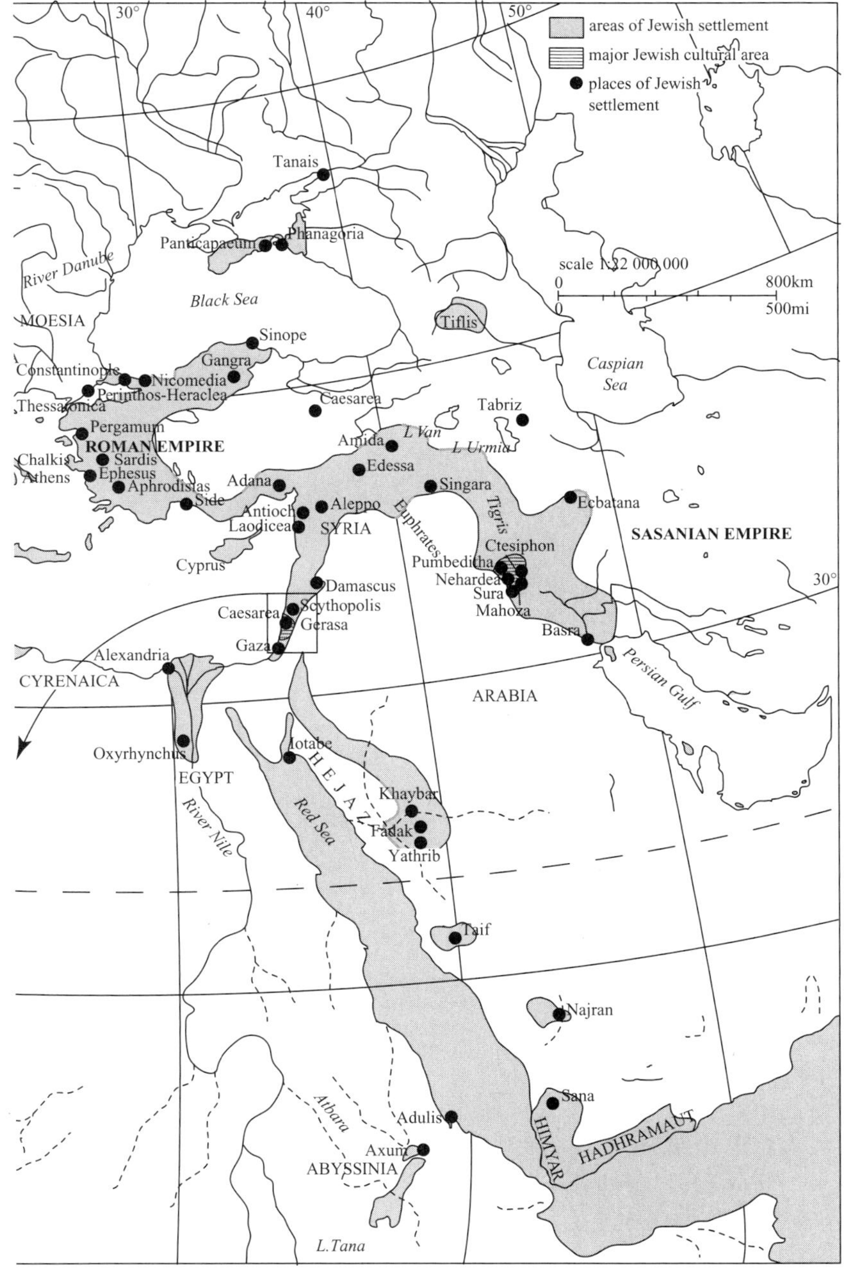
30°
40°
50°
areas of Jewish settlement
major Jewish cultural area
places of Jewish settlement
Tanais
Panticapaeum
Phanagoria
River Danube
scale 1:22 000 000
0
800km
0
500mi
Black Sea
MOESIA
Tiflis
Sinope
Gangra
Constantinople
Nicomedia
Perinthos-Heraclea
Thessalonica
Caesarea
Caspian Sea
Tabriz
Pergamum
ROMAN EMPIRE
Amida
L Van
L Urmia
Chalkis
Sardis
Athens
Ephesus
Edessa
Aphrodisias
Adana
Singara
Side
Antioch
Aleppo
Ecbatana
Laodicea
SYRIA
Euphrates
Tigris
SASANIAN EMPIRE
Ctesiphon
Cyprus
Pumbeditha
Nehardea
Damascus
Sura
30°
Mahoza
Caesarea
Scythopolis
Gerasa
Basra
Gaza
Alexandria
CYRENAICA
Persian Gulf
ARABIA
Iotabe
Oxyrhynchus
EGYPT
HEJAZ
Red Sea
River Nile
Khaybar
Fadak
Yathrib
Taif
Najran
Sana
Athbara
Adulis
HIMYAR
HADHRAMAUT
Axum
ABYSSINIA
L.Tana

say, however, that the population remained fixed, and there is evidence of Jews moving from place to place.

How distinctive were the Jews? We do not hear of any outward sign that would distinguish Jews from non-Jews.[53] Neither clothing nor language marked them out, and they mingled freely with non-Jews, even if in some cities they had their own quarters. They are not associated with any particular occupations, although the range of careers open to them was progressively limited by discriminatory legislation that barred them from the army and civil service. (Belisarius must have been surprised when the opposing Persian commander asked him to postpone a battle because the "Jews and Nazarenes" would not willingly fight during the days of unleavened bread.)[54]

## COMMUNAL LEADERSHIP

We have few indications of how the Jewish communities were organised. Until the 420s the Jewish patriarch was recognised by the state as the head of the Jews of the empire. From that time on, there was no single figure to whom all Jews could look as leader, unless they chose to look to the exilarch in Persia, who exercised a role similar to that of the Roman patriarch. An obscure allusion in a medieval Jewish chronicle asserts that in the year 520 "Mar Zutra the son of the exilarch Mar Zutra arrived in the Land of Israel and was appointed *Resh Pirka*."[55] This obscure title is attested elsewhere only in Justinian's *Novel* 146, which refers to "those whom they call *archiferecites*, or perhaps presbyters or teachers." The title is clearly not one recognised by the state, nor does it seem to be that of a single head of the community. It is probably an honorific, reserved for the leading rabbinic authorities of the academy of Tiberias in Galilee, the principal rabbinic centre in Palestine until the Arab conquest, when it was transferred to Jerusalem. An indication of the far-flung influence of the rabbis of Tiberias is that they periodically visited the Himyarites and aided their ruler Dhu Nuwas in a proselyting campaign among the local Christians and pagans.[56]

The second title mentioned in the *Novel*, that of the presbyters or elders, is well attested on inscriptions from all over the empire. We have a few occurrences of the feminine form, *presbytera*. It is not easy to pinpoint the precise function of the presbyters: was their role purely administrative, or did it have some religious or academic character? The title sometimes seems equivalent to other titles, such as *archon, archisynagogos*, or *phrontistes*, which are normally considered to be primarily at least administrative or honorific. It is possible, however, that both presbyters and archons may have owed their position to their academic or religious authority, and not simply to social eminence. The *Novel* may support this view. In fourth-century legislation, presbyters and the patriarch, like Christian clergy, enjoy similar immunity from liturgies.[57] Special seating was provided for them in synagogues.[58]

The third category mentioned in the *Novel*, that of the teachers or masters, is presumably the same as the rabbis or sages, who figure on every page of the Talmud and Midrash. The basis for their status was their learning: they were the custodians of the "Oral Torah" and served as academic lawyers, teachers and, as need arose, judges.

The leadership of the synagogue (Jewish community) was thus exercised jointly by the learned and the wealthy, categories that were not mutually exclusive. Wealthy grandees are recorded on inscriptions as founders and restorers of synagogue buildings.

## Jewish Life

The synagogue buildings, in which Jews gathered for religious services and for other purposes, were sometimes prominent buildings but outwardly, at least, their architecture did not single them out from other monumental edifices.[59] Indeed, the Talmud envisages a case where a man mistakenly bows to a pagan temple, thinking it is a synagogue (Bavli, Shabbat 72b). While older manuals link architectural plan to chronology, associating sixth-century synagogues with an apsidal plan (a basilica with an apse at one end), it is now clear that no such direct link exists. Synagogues were constructed at the same time, even within a short distance of each other, in different styles, and synagogues of different periods existed side by side. One feature that almost all synagogues shared, and that distinguished them from Christian churches and other buildings, was their symbolic orientation towards Jerusalem. Internally, a prominent focus of attention is a structure to house the Torah scrolls: it may take the form of an apse, a niche, an aedicula (a miniature building), or sometimes a bema (raised platform), on which a wooden ark probably stood.

The synagogue building was the focus of all public Jewish activities, not only worship, and generally consists of an architectural complex containing, besides a main hall, a number of other elements such as an atrium or open court, often equipped with a fountain or water basin, a library and study rooms, a dining hall, storerooms, and living quarters for functionaries of the synagogue and perhaps sometimes for visitors.

Synagogues were often richly decorated with stone carvings, mosaic floors, or frescoes. Very few traces remain of wall decoration,[60] but the abundant remains of mosaic pavements attest to rich decoration in many synagogues. As with the architecture, the artistic decoration is neither uniform nor distinctive. In some cases the same artists decorated synagogues and nearby churches, using the same style and motifs. Unlike synagogues constructed from the seventh century on, sixth-century synagogues were still being adorned with human figures, particularly with Bible scenes, a tradition going back centuries. A good example is the Binding of Isaac (Genesis 22), as shown for example in the sixth-century synagogue of Beth Alpha in Galilee. God is represented by a hand coming down from heaven. Other biblical figures include Noah and his sons, Daniel, and David (represented as Orpheus, taming wild animals by playing the lyre, in a synagogue at Gaza dated 508–509) (Plate xxvi). We also find at Beth Alpha, as elsewhere, in the centre of the nave, a zodiac, with the sun chariot in the centre and the four seasons round about: the meaning and purpose of this mosaic motif has long puzzled scholars (Plate X). No less puzzling is an image, again found at Beth Alpha as elsewhere, showing a shrine in the centre flanked by various symbolic objects, such as palm branches, rams' horns, incense shovels, and the most pervasive and typical Jewish symbol of all, the menorah, or seven-branched lampstand (Plate xxvii). Some have seen in such images as the sun chariot and the Orphic David a certain level of religious syncretism; it is hard, however, to judge whether it is a question of syncretism or simply of an appropriation of well-known motifs.

Although it is hard to be certain, it does seem that in some synagogues human figures are avoided, pointing to an inner Jewish tension about the legitimacy of artistic representations of the human form. There are also instances where human figures have been defaced or removed, although it is not possible to date the damage or determine if it was inflicted by Jews, Christians, or Muslims. From the seventh century, aniconic synagogue art is the rule; whether this was due to the rise of Islam or to internal Jewish developments is impossible to say. The Age of Justinian represents the last flowering of representational art within the synagogue.

Originally the synagogue was primarily a meeting place or communal centre, and there is no reason to think that this changed fundamentally, even if we tend to think of the synagogue as a house of prayer. There certainly were meetings for communal worship, and at their heart was a public reading from the most sacred scripture of the Jews, the Pentateuch or Torah. Very little is known about these practices. Rabbinic writings suggest that in Palestine, at least, the Torah was read in Hebrew on Sabbaths, the whole Torah being read over three or three-and-a-half years. The readings were translated by specially designated translators so that the public could understand; they were followed by an extract from the prophetic writings and explained and developed in homilies. Quotations from such homilies, and perhaps entire homilies, are preserved in the midrashic compilations. There is no reason to doubt the accuracy of this image of synagogue Torah-reading derived from rabbinic sources, but how widespread or uniform it was is unknown. In some synagogues the reading was carried out in Greek, not Hebrew, or the Hebrew reading was translated into Greek rather than Aramaic. Greek was widely used in the diaspora, even in the west, although in some places Latin was used. To judge by the prevalence of Greek inscriptions in synagogues in Palestine, Greek may have served here too as a liturgical language and for the reading of the holy books. Various Greek translations were used, the most popular apparently being that attributed to Aquila, a remarkable rendering into a special form of Greek that was effectively a kind of calqued Hebrew (the vocabulary was Greek, but the grammar Hebrew). This translation served as the basis for further translations into Latin and Romance dialects in the west (Plate xxviii).[61]

The use of Hebrew or Greek for the reading could be hotly contested, as we can see from Justinian's *Novel* 146, dated February 8, 553. The emperor speaks of open conflict between those Jews who wanted the reading to be conducted only in Hebrew and others who wanted a Greek reading as well or instead. It is not made clear whether the turmoil was limited to Constantinople, but in his response, supporting the claim that the sacred books should be read in a language that people can understand, Justinian has the whole Jewish world in mind, apparently:

> We decree, therefore, that it shall be permitted to those Hebrews who want it to read the Holy Books in their synagogues and, in general, in any place where there are Hebrews, in the Greek language before those assembled and comprehending, or possibly in our ancestral language (we speak of the Italian language), or simply in all the other languages, changing language and reading according to the different

> places; and that through this reading the matters read shall become clear to all those assembled and comprehending, and that they shall live and act according to them.[62]

The public readings thus played an important educational role and strengthened communal solidarity. The prayers and hymns contributed to both these ends, as well as catering to the congregation's spiritual needs. As in the case of the readings, we cannot be certain about the use of various languages for prayer and hymnody; it seems likely that Hebrew gradually replaced Greek. Surviving prayers and hymns from this time are almost all in Hebrew, although this is due to the prevalence of Hebrew in the rabbinic tradition – the only continuous Jewish tradition going back to late antiquity. Concerning prayer, we have evidence of long-lasting conflict over the formulation of the liturgy: Should prayers be spontaneous or fixed? Some have attributed the emergence of the *piyyut* (Hebrew hymnody) in our period as a device to sidestep this issue and the gradual ossification of the synagogue prayers. An older explanation, that *piyyut* developed as a result of Christian persecution, has been replaced by a variety of different accounts, some of which emphasize the analogous developments in Christian hymnody at the same time.[63] A *hazzan* (cantor-poet) sang the hymns with the assistance of a professional choir.

## Jewish Attitudes to Church and Empire

Close study of the surviving *piyyutim* reveals much about the attitudes of the *hazzanim*, and presumably also of the congregations they served, to the political conditions of their day, including the increasingly repressive measures aimed at the Jews, and to the hostility of the Christian Church. The cantor-poets of our period, preeminent among whom are Yannai and Eleazar Qillir, call on a tradition of homiletical exposition of the biblical story of Jacob and Esau, the twin brothers who are at odds with each other, in depicting the relations of the Jewish people with the Byzantine Empire.

According to this tradition, Jacob, whose other name is Israel, stands for the people of Israel, while Esau, also known as Edom, represents the empire of Rome.[64] The pain of Roman oppression is thus mitigated by a theological understanding: it is foretold in the holy book and is thus part of a divine dispensation. Edom, the "evil empire," "shall live by the sword" (Genesis 27:39) and indeed is appointed by God as the scourge of the world, including Israel. "There is no successful war in which the descendants of Esau do not have a hand," as one preacher puts it. In the present situation, Israel cannot but yield the power to his brother, but at a future time, in this age or the next, he will take his place. Was it not written"the older brother shall serve the younger" (Genesis 25:23) and prophesied to Jacob "be lord over your brothers, and may your mother's sons bow down to you" (Genesis 27:29)? Many prophetic verses foretell the devastation of Edom. While the second-century rabbis after the war with the Romans under Hadrian speak in apocalyptic fashion of the coming overthrow of Rome, from the third century on a more irenic tone appears, stressing the brotherhood of Jacob and Esau and the idea of a division: military might and political power have been allotted to Esau, while Jacob must make use of his voice in praise and petition to God: "The voice is the voice of Jacob, but the hands are the hands of Esau" (Genesis 27:22). Such a message of acceptance of the status quo makes itself heard in the midrashic compilations of the fifth century, although even at that time an early synagogue poet, Yose ben Yose, can sing: "May the liberators [of Zion] do battle and remove the [royal] mantle from Edom / And place upon the Lord the majesty of power."[65]

With the cantor-poets of the sixth century a more impatient note creeps in, reflecting perhaps the worsening of conditions for the Jews under Justinian. Yannai calls for the destruction of Esau: "Would that the ruler of Dumah [Edom] be humbled and brought low and lick dirt like a worm." "Let there be great slaughter in the land of Edom, a glowing fire in Edom's fields." "Our inheritance is given to strangers; our lands are sold to our enemies," Yannai laments, referring to the burden of taxation that compelled farmers to sell their lands, and perhaps to the advancing Christianisation of Palestine. He rails against Christian beliefs and practices in some of his hymns and warns his flock not to consort with Christians or with the circus factions.

Qillir also rages against the empire and the church writing, "Bring upon Esau's sons, the insolent villains, loss of children and widowhood"; "The powers that subjugate [Your people] worship idols of stone." He compares the imperial dynasty to a lizard growing fat with the aid of heretics, and, like Yannai, he identifies Rome with the fourth beast in the apocalyptic vision of Daniel 7.

The prayers of the synagogue, while they look forward to the restoration of the Davidic kingdom, are more restrained in their invective against the empire, with one notable exception. An old prayer against the Romans and their Jewish stooges, probably formulated at the time of the war under Hadrian, was revised for use against the Christian empire:

> For the apostates let there be no hope; speedily uproot, smash and humble the arrogant empire in our days, may the Christians and heretics perish in an instant, and may all the enemies and persecutors of your people be speedily cut off; break the yoke of the gentiles off our necks: Blessed are you, Lord, Destroyer of the wicked and Humiliator of the arrogant.[66]

Through this prayer we glimpse of the depth of feeling of the Jews in the face of the worsening oppression.

## Conclusions

For the Jews of the Roman Empire, the Age of Justinian was a transitional period. The consolidation of the Christian Church, with its deeply ingrained hostility to Judaism, as an institution of the Roman state gradually eroded the protected status of the Jewish communities and exposed them to discriminatory treatment, ranging from loss of privileges to expropriations and forcible conversion to the state religion.The process was very gradual, as we can see from the legal codes. The Theodosian Code in the fifth century contains more than fifty laws dealing with the Jews. Some protect Jewish rights, others restrict them; the laws are often marked by insulting language, which is an indication of the process of marginalisation. Several laws refer to attacks on synagogues, many of which were destroyed or converted into churches. Justinian, in his own code, retains fewer than half of the earlier laws. Some were perhaps obsolete or superfluous, but among the abandoned laws were some that related to Jewish privileges, and in particular the formal statement of the legality of Judaism, issued by Theodosius the Great (*CTh*, 16.8.9), was omitted by Justinian. The Code severely limits the rights of Jews in the civic, economic, and religious spheres, and the emperor regulated synagogue life. Still, confiscation of synagogues or forcible conversion of Jews remained exceptional in the time of Justinian. With hindsight we can see these incidents as harbingers of much worse to come, and notably the edict of baptism issued by Heraclius I around 632: all the Jews and Samaritans in the empire were to become Christians. Justinian did not go that far, but his conception of a united Christian state did not leave much room for Jews, "heretics," or pagans, and the Jews were the particular object of Christian theological odium from which dissident Christians and pagans were exempt.

The condition of the Jews in the Age of Justinian may seem confusing and contradictory; seen in the longer view, it appears more coherent. The Jews were still relatively numerous, and in some places they were still prosperous and may have felt they could count on the protection of the laws. They still built, repaired, and embellished synagogues. They had a flourishing cultural life, as is often the case in transitional periods. But we can now see how precarious their position was, and irreversible changes were taking place. It was becoming harder for Jews to own slaves, which limited their economic activity, and they were excluded from careers in the army or the administration. The temptation and indeed the pressure on Jews to change their religion increased. While friendship between a Jew and a Christian was still possible, as we can see from the story of Theodosius and Philip, social tensions and animosities were growing, and theological enmity was fostered on both sides.

A significant indicator of the growing rift between Jews and Christians was language. Most of the Jews in the empire spoke Greek, and the upper classes had traditionally enjoyed the benefits of a classical education. The life of the synagogue, including Bible readings, prayers, hymns, and sermons, was generally conducted in Greek, particularly outside Syria and Palestine, where the Aramaic language was still strong. The exclusion of Jews from the various schools where they could acquire a knowledge of Greek grammar and a training for a range of careers (some of which were, in any case, no longer open to them) had a profound effect on Jewish culture, as well as on relations between Jews and non-Jews. In Palestine and perhaps elsewhere they set up their own schools, attached to synagogues, where they studied the Hebrew scriptures and their traditional rabbinic interpretation; at more advanced schools they could acquire a training in rabbinic law. The main languages of these schools were Hebrew and Aramaic. These languages came to play an increasing part in the synagogue, as we can see from Justinian's *Novel* 146. But the emperor's support for Greek and Latin in the synagogue was undermined by other developments for which he was perhaps ultimately responsible: how could these languages survive in the synagogue without an educated clergy at home in Greek and Latin culture? Over the following centuries Hebrew made increasing inroads in the synagogue, and this had an effect not only on the religious culture of the Jews but on their relations with their Christian neighbors. Greek continued to be the spoken language of Byzantine Jews, but it was no longer a language of high culture for them. The mark of an educated Jew was mastery of Hebrew, as it was eventually (before 1000) for Jews worldwide. And the higher education was a preparation to become a rabbi, that is, a teacher and judge within the religious and legal system represented by the Talmuds.

Thus the story of the Jews in the Age of Justinian is an episode in a much longer history, an episode that indicates profound changes both for the Roman Empire and for the Jewish communities in it.

## Notes

1 Salo W. Baron, *A Social and Religious History of the Jews*, 2nd ed. (New York, 1957), 3:3.

2 Gilbert Dagron and Vincent Déroche, "Juifs et Chrétiens dans l'Orient du VIIe siècle," *Travaux et Mémoires* 11 (1991): 17–273, esp. 28–32.

3 Vittore Colorni, "L'uso del greco nella liturgia del giudaismo ellenistico e la novella 146 di Giustiniano," *Annali de storia del diritto* 8 (1964): 19–80.

4 See Nicholas de Lange, "The Revival of the Hebrew Language in the Third Century," *Jewish Studies Quarterly* 3 (1996): 342–358; "Hebraism and Hellenism: The Case of Byzantine Jewry," *Poetics Today* 19 (1998): 129–145; "Etudier et prier à Byzance," *Revue des études juives* 158 (1999): 51–59. On synagogue literature, see Steven Fine, ed., *Sacred Realm: The Emergence of the Synagogue in the Ancient World* (New York, 1996); and Lee I. Levine, *The Ancient Synagogue: The First Thousand Years* (New Haven, Conn., 1999).

5 Nicholas de Lange, "Midrash et Byzance: Sur une traduction française du Midrach Rabba (Notes Critiques)," *Revue d'histoire des religions* 206 (1989): 171–181. On the catenae, see Robert Devreesse, "Chaînes exégétiques grecques," in *Dictionnaire de la Bible*, suppl. 1 (Paris, 1928), 1048–1233.

6 Günter Stemberger, *Introduction to the Talmud and Midrash*, trans. Markus Bockmuehl, 2nd ed. (Edinburgh, 1996).

7 Leon J. Weinberger, *Jewish Hymnography: A Literary History* (London, 1998): 20–21.

8 Weinberger, *Jewish Hymnography*, 28–72; Wout J. van Bekkum, "The Byzantine Identity of the Poet Yehudah," *Bulletin of Judaeo-Greek Studies* 7 (Winter 1990): 13–17.

9 Mordechai Rabello, *Giustiniano, ebrei e samaritani all luce delle fonti storico-letterarie, ecclesiastiche e giuridiche* (Milan, 1987–1988), 455–470.

10 The Bavli remains an important source for the study of Sasanian Jewry at the time of its compilation. See Jacob Neusner, *A History of the Jews in Babylonia*, vol. 5, *Later Sasanian Times* (Leiden, 1970).

11 Mentioned in *C.Th.*, 16.8.29 (dated 429), and so probably to be dated in the 420s.

12 Catherine Hezser, "The Codification of Legal Knowledge in Late Antiquity: The Talmud Yerushalmi and Roman Law Codes," in *The Talmud Yerushalmi and Graeco-Roman Culture*, ed. Peter Schäfer, vol. 1 (Tübingen, 1998), 581–641.

13 For example, collections of legal rulings of the rabbis of Palestine. See Rabello, *Giustiniano*, 483–491.

14 Samuel Krauss, *The Jewish-Christian Controversy from the Earliest Times to 1789*, ed. William Horbury, vol. 1 (Tübingen, 1996), 12ff.

15 Daniel J. Lasker and Sarah Stroumsa, *The Polemic of Nestor the Priest*, 2 vols. (Jerusalem, 1996). On the dating and history of the work, see 1:13–26.

16 For the law that new synagogues were not to be built, see *C.Th.*, 16.8.25 and 27 (423 CE) and *Novel* 3 (438), cf. *CJ*, 1.9.18, and *Nov.*, 131.14 (545); Theodosius protects synagogues in *C.Th.*, 16.8.21 (412), 16.8.25, 26, and 27 (423). Justinian's edict relating to Africa (*Nov.*, 37.8 [535]) goes much further: synagogues are to be converted into churches. Procopius (*Buildings*, 6.2.21–23) shows that this was no empty threat: the ancient synagogue of Borion was turned into a church and the Jews were forcibly converted to Christianity.

17 The synagogue occupied a prominent location at the highest point of the city. See Annabel J. Wharton, *Refiguring the Post Classical City: Dura Europos, Jerash, Jerusalem, and Ravenna* (Cambridge, 1995), 69.

18 John S. Crawford, "Jews, Christians, and Polytheists in Late-Antique Sardis," in *Jews, Christians, and Polytheists in the Ancient Synagogue*, ed. Steven Fine (London, 1999), 190–200.

19 Rabello, *Giustiniano*, 444–446; Menachem Stern, *Greek and Latin Authors on Jews and Judaism*, vol. 2 (Jerusalem, 1980), 671–688. For Damascius, see Polymnia Athanassiadi, ed., *Damascius, The Philosophical History* (Athens, 1999).

20 Lawrence Lahey, "The Christian-Jewish Dialogues through the Sixth Century (excluding Justin)," in *Jewish Believers in Jesus*, vol. 1, *The First Five Centuries*, ed. Oskar Skarsaune and Reidar Hvalvik (Peabody, Mass., forthcoming).

21 J. W. Parkes, *The Conflict of the Church and the Synagogue* (London, 1934), 245–256.

22 See Rabello, *Giustiniano*, 157–281.

23 Perhaps a persecutory measure, and certainly an intrusion, as Procopius states, it should be set in the context of Christian divisions about the calendar. Some Christians insisted on fixing the date of Easter according to that of the Jewish Passover. In certain years Passover could fall a month earlier than the Orthodox Easter, before the spring equinox, and it is this practice that the emperor seems to have been concerned to stamp out. Rabello, *Giustiniano*, 279–281; Sacha Stern, *Calendar and Community: A History of the Jewish Calendar, Second Century BCE – Tenth Century CE* (Oxford, 2001), 85–87.

24 Rabello, *Giustiniano*, 313–434; on Antioch, see Parkes, *Conflict*, 243–245.

25 Rabello, *Giustiniano*, 439–449.

26 Texts in Rabello, *Giustiniano*, 667–892; English translation in Amnon Linder, *The Jews in Roman Imperial Legislation* (Detroit, Mich., 1987). More recent bibliography includes Johannes Irmscher, "The Jews under the Reign of Justinian," *Eos* 78 (1990): 155–161; and Eberhard Klingenberg, "Justinians Novellen zur Judengesetzgebung," in *Festschrift für Hermann Lange zum 70. Geburtstag am 24. Januar 1992*, ed. D. Medicus et al. (Stuttgart, 1992), 139–161. For bibliography on Novel 146, see n. 62.

27 Vincent Déroche, "La Polémique anti-judaïque au VIe et au VIIe siècle. Un mémento inédit, les Képhalaia," *Travaux et mémoires* 11 (1991): 275–311; see Nicholas de Lange, "Jews and Christians in the Byzantine Empire: Problems and Prospects," in *Christianity and Judaism*, ed. D. Wood (Oxford, 1992), 15–32.

28 Déroche, "La Polémique," 290. On the use of miracles, see Parkes, *Conflict*, 283.

29 Parkes, *Conflict*, 283–285; Krauss, *The Jewish-Christian Controversy*, 48–49. On the date, see Déroche, "La polémique," 276–277, and Lahey, "The Christian-Jewish Dialogues."

30 Dated to the sixth century by Parkes, *Conflict*, 280–282.

31 R. G. Robertson, *The Dialogue of Timothy and Aquila* (Cambridge, Mass., 1986), 372–383; see Déroche, "La polémique," 276, which connects polemic against Aquila to Novel 146.

32 On the date, see Déroche, "La polémique," 276.

33 On the date, see Déroche, "La polémique," 277–278.

34 Parkes, *Conflict*, 290; P. W. van der Horst, "Jesus and the Jews According to the Suda," *Zeitschrift für die neutestamentliche Wissenschaft* 84 (1993): 268–277. Among other polemical works of this period are parts of the *Questions to Antiochus the Duke* (Krauss, *Controversy*, 63; Déroche, "La polémique," 279) and José Declerck, ed., *Anonymus dialogus cum Iudaeis seculi ut videtur sexti* (CCSG 30), Turnhout, 1994. A slightly later author, John Moschos (c. 550–619), refers in his *Spiritual Meadow* (172) to his own debates with Jews in Alexandria, at the instigation of a layman who possessed a large library of books for the purpose. See de Lange, "Jews and Christians," 26; Lahey, "The Christian-Jewish Dialogues."

35 Krauss, *Controversy*, 62.

36 Rabello, *Giustiniano*, 619–656; English translation of two different Greek texts in Parkes, *Conflict*, 397–400.

37 Parkes, *Conflict*, 225–269.

38 Brian McGing, "Population and Proselytism: How Many Jews Were There in the Ancient World?" in *Jews in the Hellenistic and Roman Cities*, ed. John R. Bartlett (London, 2002), 88–106.

39 Alan D. Crown, "The Samaritans in the Byzantine Orbit," *Bulletin of the John Rylands Library* 69 (1986): 96–138, and "The Samaritan Diaspora," in *The Samaritans*, ed. A. D. Crown (Tübingen, 1989), 195–217, and, more generally, Alan D. Crown, Reinhard Pummer, and Abraham Tal, eds., *A Companion to Samaritan Studies* (Tübingen, 1993).

40 On these events, see Rabello, *Giustiniano*, 409–422, 428–432, and 148–150 respectively.

41 See Andrew Sharf, *Byzantine Jewry from Justinian to the Fourth Crusade* (London, 1971), 28; and for the laws themselves Rabello, *Giustiniano*, 720–729 and 806–809.

42 Reinhard Pummer, "Samaritan Synagogues and Jewish Synagogues: Similarities and Differences," in *Jews, Christians, and Polytheists in the Ancient Synagogue*, ed. S. Fine (London, 1999), 118–160; and the important caveat of Pieter W. van der Horst, *Japheth in the Tents of Shem: Studies on Jewish Hellenism in Antiquity* (Louvain, 2002), 257–258.

43 See the map in Nicholas de Lange, *Atlas of the Jewish World* (New York, 1984), 30–31. On the Samaritan diaspora, see Crown, "The Samaritan Diaspora"; and Pieter W. van der Horst, "The Samaritan Diaspora in Antiquity," in his *Essays on the Jewish World of Early Christianity* (Fribourg, 1990), 138–146.

44 See the map in de Lange, *Atlas of the Jewish World*, 34. Such actions were generally illegal but were carried out nonetheless, often by violence. John of Ephesus (c. 507–586) boasts of turning seven synagogues in Asia into churches (*Lives of the Eastern Saints*, PO 18, 681).

45 Sharf, *Byzantine Jewry*, 27; Rabello, *Giustiniano*, 90.

46 Rabello, *Giustiniano*, 56.

47 Sharf, *Byzantine Jewry*, 35; Rabello, *Giustiniano*, 78; Haim Z. Hirschberg, *A History of the Jews in North Africa*, 2nd rev. ed., vol. 1 (Leiden, 1974), 39–57.

48 Sharf, *Byzantine Jewry*, 27; Rabello, *Giustiniano*, 104–105.

49 Neusner, *A History of the Jews in Babylonia*, vol. 5 (Leiden, 1970).

50 Sharf, *Byzantine Jewry*, 31–32; Michael Avi-Yonah, *Geschichte der Juden im Zeitalter der Talmud* (Berlin, 1962), 252–254; Rabello, *Giustiniano*, 90; Gordon D. Newby, *A History of the Jews of Arabia from Ancient Times to Their Eclipse under Islam* (Columbia, S.C., 1988), 34–48.

51 Sharf, *Byzantine Jewry*, 33; Avi-Yonah, *Geschichte*, 254; Rabello, *Giustiniano*, 171–178.

52 Procopius, *Buildings*, 6.2.22.

53 Parkes, *Conflict*, 274–275. Elisabeth Revel-Neher has suggested that Jewish men wore *tefillin*, leather-cased amulets on their foreheads and upper arms, in public: "L'iconographie judéo-chrétienne en milieu byzantin: Une source de connaissance pour l'histoire du monde juif à l'époque pre-chrétienne et talmudique," *Mélanges André Neher* (Paris, 1975), 307–316.

54 The story is reported by Zacharias of Mytilene (Hamilton and Brooks, *Chronicle*, 9.6). See Parkes, *Conflict*, 260, on Jews in the Persian army.

55 Rabello, *Giustiniano*, 479–482; Moshe Gil, *A History of Palestine, 634–1099*, trans. E. Broido (Cambridge, 1992), 495.

56 Sharf, *Byzantine Jewry*, 32; Avi-Yonah, *Geschichte*, 253; Newby, *History of the Jews of Arabia*, 46.

57 *C.Th.*, 16.8.4, 16.8.13, cf. 12.1.165.

58 Lee I. Levine, *The Ancient Synagogue: The First Thousand Years* (New Haven, Conn., 1999), 407–408.

59 Levine, *The Ancient Synagogue*, 302.

60 Levine, *The Ancient Synagogue*, 339–340. The only extensive remains of wall paintings are from the third-century synagogue at Dura-Europos on the Euphrates, currently displayed at the National Archaeological Museum in Damascus; see Carl H. Kraeling, *The Excavations at Dura-Europos*, vol. 8, part 1, *The Synagogue* (New Haven, Conn., 1967). Some synagogues had decorated marble revetments.

61 See D.-S. Blondheim, *Les Parlers judéo-romans et la Vetus Latina* (Paris, 1925).

62 Translation from Amnon Linder, ed., *The Jews in Roman Imperial Legislation* (Detroit, 1987), 408. See also Rabello, *Giustiniano*, 814–828; Giuseppe Veltri, "Die Novelle 146 *ΠΕΡΙ ΕΒΡΑΙΩΝ*. Das Verbot des Targumvortrags in Justinians Politik," in *Die Septuaginta zwischen Judentum und Christentum*, ed. M. Hengel and A. M. Schwemer (Tübingen, 1994), 116–130; Albert I. Baumgarten, "Justinian and the Jews," in *Rabbi Joseph H. Lookstein Memorial Volume*, ed. Leo Landman (New York, 1980), 37–44; Rose-Marie Seyberlich, "Die Judenpolitik Kaiser Justinians I," in *Byzantinische Beiträge*, ed. J. Irmscher (Berlin, 1964), 73–80. We cannot judge how effective this ruling was; eventually all communities went over to reading the Torah in Hebrew, although an Aramaic or Greek translation may have followed. Certain other readings, such as that of the Book of Jonah on the Day of Atonement, continued to be in Greek until recent times in some synagogues.

63 For various explanations, see Eric Werner, *The Sacred Bridge: The Interdependence of Liturgy and Music in Synagogue and Church during the First Millennium*, vol. 1 (London, 1959), 234–237; and Levine, *The Ancient Synagogue*, 552–553.

64 See Nicholas R. M. de Lange, "Jewish Attitudes to the Roman Empire," in *Imperialism in the Ancient World*, ed. P. D. A. Garnsey and C. R. Whittaker (Cambridge,

1978), 255–281; Mireille Hadas-Lebel, "Jacob et Esaü ou Israel et Rome dans le Talmud et le Midrash," *Revue de l'Histoire des Religions* 201 (1984): 369–392.

65 This and the following quotations are translated by Weinberger, *Jewish Hymnography*, 34–39.

66 Translated in de Lange, "Jews and Christians in the Byzantine Empire," 15–32 (here 27–28). Some versions of the prayer begin "For the Christians let there be no hope."

PLATE i. Medallion of Justinian, obverse with bust of the emperor, c. 535, Bibliothèque Nationale, Cabinet des Médailles, Paris. Photo: Bibliothèque Nationale de France, Paris

PLATE ii. Medallion of Justinian, reverse with equestrian image of the emperor, c. 535, Bibliothèque Nationale, Cabinet des Médailles, Paris. Photo: Bibliothèque Nationale de France, Paris

PLATE iii. Justinian Triumphant (the "Barberini Ivory"), c. 532, Musée du Louvre, Paris. Photo: Chuzeville – Louvre, Paris, France. © Réunion des Musées Nationaux/Art Resource, N.Y.

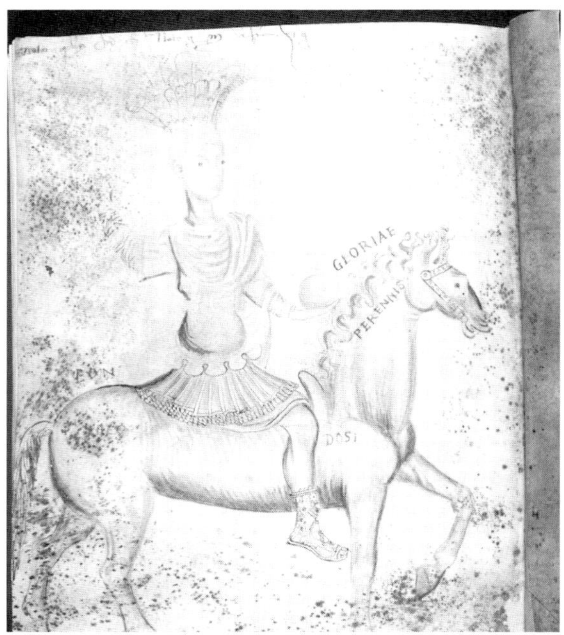


PLATE iv. Fifteenth-century drawing of the colossal statue of Justinian once in the Augoustaion, Cod. Ital. 2, University Library, Budapest

PLATE V. Qalbloze (Syria), between Antioch and Qalʿat Semʿan. Pilgrim church, built in the fifth century and expanded in the sixth century. See Georges Tchalenko, *Villages antiques de la Syrie du Nord. Le Massif du Bélus à l'époque romaine*, I (Paris, 1953), 343–344. Photo: L. Van Rompay

PLATE VI. Tall Biʿa, near Raqqaʿ (Syria), the ancient city of Callinicum, sixth-century monastery. Symeonis mosaic. Photo: Deutsche Orient-Gesellschaft, Grabung Tall Biʿa, photo Anwar ʿAbd al-Ghafour

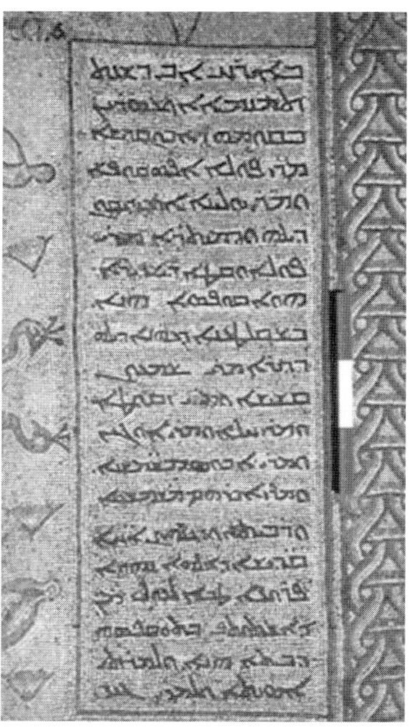

PLATE vii. Tall Bi'a, near Raqqa' (Syria). The ancient city of Callinicum, sixth-century monastery, Syriac inscription mentioning bishop Paul, dated 509. Photo: Deutsche Orient-Gesellschaft, Grabung Tall Bi'a, photo Anwar 'Abd al-Ghafour

PLATE viii. Ms. Florence. Biblioteca Medicea Laurenziana Plut., I, 56, Rabbula Gospels (586 AD) F.13.b: Christ's Ascension into heaven, with, in the lower register, Mary and the apostles. Courtesy Biblioteca Medicea Laurenziana

PLATE ix. Ms. Florence. Biblioteca Laurenziana, Plut., I, 56, Rabbula Gospels (586 AD) F. 9b: Canon Tables for the Gospels of Matthew and John, with representations of the evangelists Matthew (right) and John (left), holding a codex or a scroll containing their Gospel. Courtesy Biblioteca Laurenziana

PLATE x. Silver paten with the Communion of the Apostles, 577(?), Dumbarton Oaks, Washington, D.C. Photo: Dumbarton Oaks, Byzantine Photograph and Fieldwork Archives, Washington, D.C.

PLATE xi. Tin-lead pilgrim's ampulla cast around the year 600 with scenes from Golgotha on one side and the Marys approaching the tomb of Christ on the other. Diameter 4.6 cm. Dumbarton Oaks, Byzantine Collection, Washington, D.C. Photo: Dumbarton Oaks

PLATE xii. Reverse side of Plate xi. Photo: Dumbarton Oaks

PLATE xiii. Reliquary box with sliding lid, formerly in the Sancta Sanctorum, filled with *eulogiae* from the Holy Land: stones, dirt, wood, and cloth. The lid depicts five scenes from the life of Christ (see detail, Plate V). Photo: Museo Sacro, Vatican

PLATE xiv. Christ before Pilate, folio 8v, Rossano Gospels, sixth century, Rossano, Biblioteca Arcivescovile. Photo: Scala/Art Resource, N.Y.

PLATE XV. Bust of a lady of rank, sixth century, Metropolitan Museum of Art. Photo: The Metropolitan Museum of Art, the Cloisters Collection, 1966 (66.25)

PLATE XVI. Archangel (Michael?) on a leaf of an ivory diptych, second quarter of the sixth century, British Museum. Photo: © Copyright the British Museum

PLATE XVII. Hercules and the Nemean lion, silver plate, sixth century, Bibliothèque Nationale, Cabinet des Médailles, Paris. Photo: Bibliothèque Nationale de France, Paris

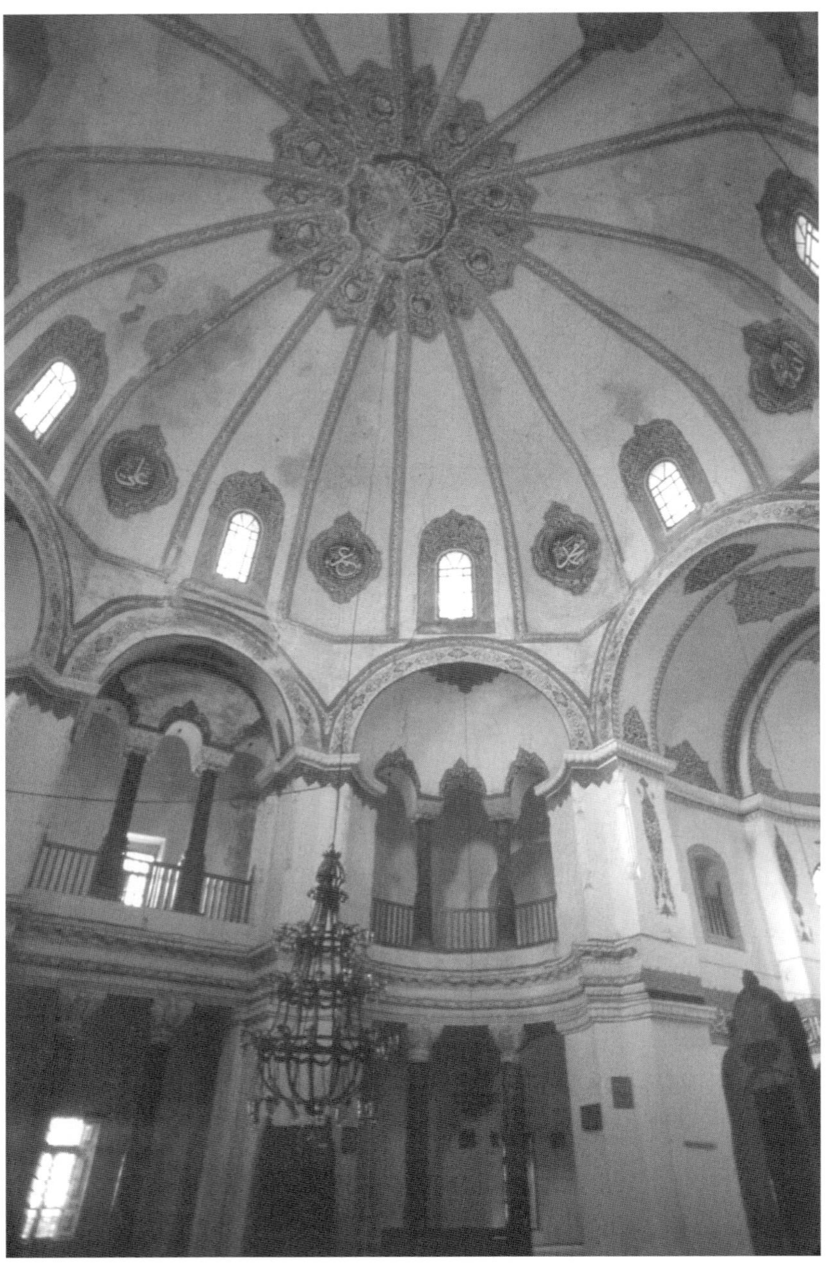

PLATE XVIII. Sts. Sergius and Bacchus, Istanbul, interior and dome, c. 530. Photo: Vanni/Art Resource, N.Y.

PLATE XIX. Sts. Sergius and Bacchus, Istanbul, ground-level capitals and entablature, c. 530. Photo: Thomas F. Mathews

PLATE XX. Hagia Sophia, Istanbul, capital and impost, 532–537. Photo: Vanni/Art Resouce, N.Y.

PLATE XXI. Gold solidus of King Theudebert, c. 540, Bibliothèque Nationale, Cabinet des Médailles, Paris. Photo: Bibliothèque Nationale de France, Paris

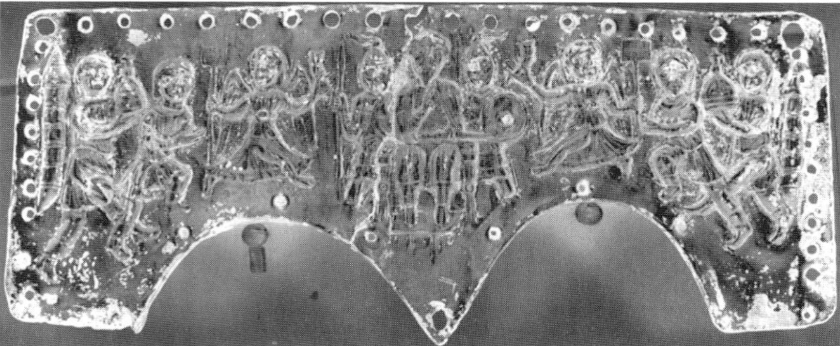

PLATE XXII. Gilded bronze helmet plaque representing King Agilulf, c. 600, Museo del Bargello, Florence. Photo: Museo del Bargello, Florence

PLATE xxiii. Mausoleum of King Theodoric, Ravenna, c. 525. Photo: Joseph D. Alchermes

PLATE xxiv. David and Goliath, silver dish, 629–630, Metropolitan Museum of Art. Photo: The Metropolitan Museum of Art, Gift of J. Pierpont Morgan, 1917 (17.190.396)

PLATE XXV. The Synagogue of Sardis, the largest ancient synagogue known. Fourth or fifth century. Photo: İnci Türkoğlu

PLATE XXVI. Synagogue mosaic from Gaza, showing King David as Orpheus taming the wild beasts with his music. Sixth century. Beersheva Museum, Israel. Photo: Collection N. de Lange

PLATE XXVII. Gold ex voto from a synagogue showing seven-branched lampstand, ram's horn and ?*lulab*. Legend: In fulfilment of a vow of Jacob, archegos, ?pearl-setter. Third through sixth centuries. Photo: Jewish Museum, London

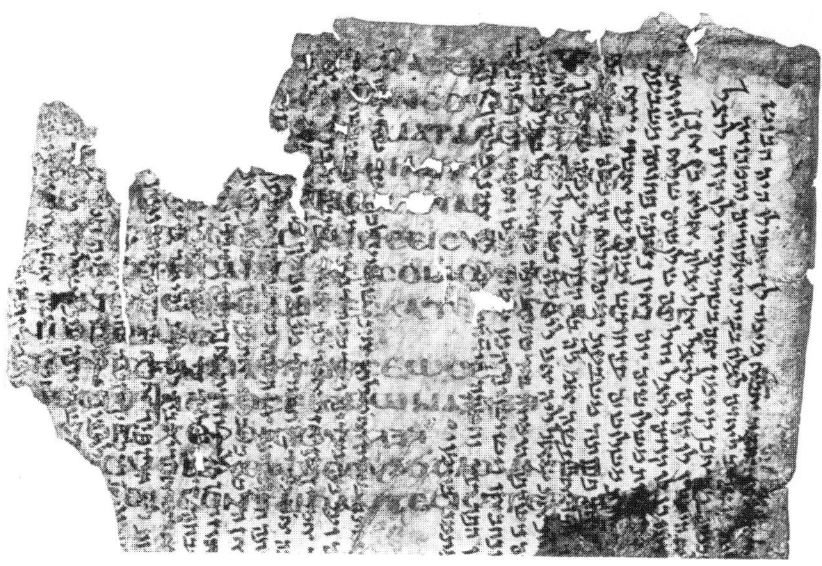

PLATE XXVIII. Fragment of a Jewish Greek Bible (Aquila's version). Palimpsest found in the Cairo Genizah. This finely written Greek biblical text, probably intended for use in a synagogue, was reused later for writing a Hebrew text. Shown here: Psalm 91:4–10. Probably sixth century. University Library, Cambridge, T-S 20.50. By kind permission of the Syndics of Cambridge University Library

PLATE xxix. Sergiopolis (Resafa), modern Syria, north and east walls looking north. Sixth century. Photo: Geoffrey Greatrex

PLATE xxx. Zenobia, modern Syria, looking west. In the centre, a church. Above lies the citadel, and at the right-hand side the headquarters of the local commander. Photo: Geoffrey Greatrex

# 17: The Age of Justinian

## Gender and Society

*Leslie Brubaker*

### Sex and Gender in the Age of Justinian

Sex and gender are not the same. Sex is biologically determined: except in extremely unusual circumstances, humans are born male or female. Gender is historically determined and relies on social practices that change across time and geographical location: codes of behavior that are culturally specific teach women and men to act in ways "appropriate" to their sex. That is why it is sometimes said that a woman is "acting like a man" or that a man is "acting like a woman": they are behaving in ways that are believed, at the time, to be more suitable to the opposite sex. Masculinity and femininity are not, however, universal qualities shared by all cultures but are understood in different ways by different groups, and this understanding changes over time.[1] Procopius – a sixth-century historian closely associated with Justinian and his general Belisarius – provides a good example of how gender roles were understood in the Age of Justinian when, in his *History of the Wars*, he describes the "manly valor" of Amazon women on the battlefield. In Procopius's mind, men rather than women were the appropriate warriors: women who fought well must, by definition, exhibit male traits and be described in masculine terms. This gender "transgression" troubled Procopius sufficiently that he took pains to explain it away, arguing that "there never was a race of women endowed with the qualities of men and . . . human nature did not depart from its established norm." Instead, according to Procopius, the Amazon women took up arms only out of "sheer necessity," after all of their husbands had been killed in Asia (*Wars*, 8.3.7–11). Sixth-century social practice determined that fighting was an appropriate attribute of masculinity, not of femininity; it followed that women would engage in warfare only under extremely unusual circumstances such as the absence of men to defend them.

Along with fighting, another masculine characteristic expressed by Procopius was the ability to rule well. He described Amalasuintha, Theoderic's daughter, who was regent for her young son after 526, as "displaying to a great extent the masculine temper." From Procopius, this was high praise: Amalasuintha displayed no "womanly weakness" but played what he saw as a male role in the proper "male" way (*Wars*, 5.2.3. 21). While Procopius was normally hostile to women exercising political power, if they had to do it (and regency for children was the only acceptable context for this), the "male" way was the only way to do it well.

## Eunuchs

Alongside males and females, what is sometimes called a "third gender" also existed in the Byzantine world. Eunuchs, castrated males who could normally be recognised by their lack of facial hair, played a significant role in Byzantium. They were active in the church; in administrative and court culture as, for example, guardians of the imperial bedchamber; and in the military: for example, Justinian's great general, Narses (c. 490–574), was a eunuch.[2] Byzantine responses to eunuchs were usually cast in comparative terms, with their behavior evaluated by comparison with what were considered to be appropriate masculine or feminine characteristics. For this reason, gender stereotypes are often brought into sharp relief when applied to eunuchs. The stereotypes themselves were, however, generated not by Byzantine attitudes to eunuchs but by beliefs about masculinity and femininity, for which reason we will concentrate on men and women in the remainder of this chapter.

## Why Is Gender Analysis Important for Historians?

How a culture defines appropriate masculine and feminine roles is important for historians to understand because it helps us to see how that culture represented itself to itself. The relationship between those who hold power and those who do not is, normally, defined by those in power; the beliefs of the powerful group justify and reinforce these social hierarchies. The presentation and manipulation of gender roles thus sheds considerable light on how the Byzantines structured their world and their hierarchies of power.

In Roman and Byzantine society, the "powerful" were elite men, like Procopius, and the social constructs that they believed in reinforced their own worth. As the two selections from Procopius have shown, the language of power is filled with gendered rhetoric, and failure to understand the references can lead to misinterpretations of the past.[3] A third example from Procopius provides a case in point. In 532, during urban riots in Constantinople, Justinian and his courtiers debated whether to flee or to face out the mob. Procopius was not with the emperor at the time, so the imprecision of his remark that "many opinions were expressed" is unsurprising: he was not an eyewitness to the event but was at best reporting on it secondhand. Immediately following this vague comment, Procopius nonetheless has the empress Theodora deliver a long speech in which she argues that "for one who has been an emperor it is unendurable to be a fugitive" before delivering her coup de grâce: "I approve a certain ancient saying that royalty is a good burial shroud" (*Wars*, 1.24.32–41). Procopius's sudden shift to the verbatim reportage of a speech he cannot have heard is not the only unusual feature of this passage. In the context of the *History of the Wars*, the whole episode is exceptional. Across the eight volumes of the *Wars*, Theodora appears a mere eight times, and on seven of these occasions she is simply mentioned in passing.[4] The "burial shroud" episode is the only time that Procopius pays any real attention to her, and it is the only time she speaks in the entire work. Either Procopius was sufficiently impressed by reports of Theodora's courage that he elaborated on it here – a prospect that, as we shall see, is unlikely – or he is using the story to make another point.

The writers Procopius emulated had no qualms about authorial invention. His historical model was Thucydides, the fifth-century BC author of the *History of the Peloponnesian War*, and his rhetorical model was Menander Rhetor, who wrote in the third century AD. Both discussed and accepted made-up narrative. In Thucydides, "the speeches are given in the language in which, as it seemed to me, the several speakers would express, on the subjects under consideration, the sentiments most befitting the occasion" (*Peloponnesian War* 1.22.1–2). Though he described public speeches rather than speeches recorded in historical accounts, Menander went even further: "If it is possible to invent, and to do this convincingly, do not hesitate" (*Treatise* 2.371.11–14 [83]).

Attentive reading suggests that this is precisely what Procopius did, and he framed his account with opening and closing sentences that reveal exactly how the "burial shroud" narrative plays into the main story line. Procopius has Theodora begin by acknowledging "the belief that a woman ought not to be daring among those who are holding back from fear," and he concludes: "When the empress had spoken thus, all were filled with boldness" (*Wars*, 1.24.33, 38). From this it becomes apparent that Theodora's speech is a "rhetorical set-piece," with wavering men shamed into acting manly by a woman "acting out of character."[5] By depicting men as fearful (the way the Byzantines believed women behaved) and a woman as daring (the way the Byzantines believed a man behaved), Procopius inverted Byzantine gender stereotypes to indicate the gravity of the occasion: the situation was so bad that the natural order was reversed, with men quaking like women and a woman speaking like a man.

Despite its many peculiarities, the "burial shroud" episode was accepted as historically accurate until the late twentieth century, when Procopius's skilful use of gender was first noticed by Elizabeth Fisher and his careful rhetorical constructions were analyzed by Averil Cameron.[6] In this case, the two go hand in hand. Without careful assessment of the gendered language, we would both misinterpret the past and fail to appreciate Procopius's skill at reconstructing the sense of the terror he imagined that the emperor and his courtiers felt during the riots of 532.

## The Roman Background

In the Age of Justinian, the Byzantine social group about which we know the most is the urban elite of Constantinople. Its members called themselves Romans, and they were still, throughout the first half of the sixth century, largely bound by Roman social conventions. Procopius, like most of the other writers of the period, is representative of this class in many ways, one of which is that his understanding of gender roles followed Roman practice. To him, as to earlier elite Romans, the core social grouping was the family, headed by the father. Legal and social conventions located everything and everyone in relation to him: women, children, and slaves were categorised according to their relationship to the head of the household. Roman sources esteemed men who exhibited self-control, moderation, and pursuit of the common good; the ideal Roman woman was beautiful, gentle, and modest, a good mother, faithful to her husband, and dedicated to her home and family. The four great imperial male virtues defined by Menander in the third century – courage, justice, temperance, and wisdom – simply elaborated the virtues of elite Roman males in general. Menander largely ignored imperial women, except as adjuncts to male activity. In this he is typical of Roman authors, whose descriptions of women's actions usually had little to do with any actual activity engaged in by any particular woman, but were instead used as ways to characterize the dominant male in her life (father, husband, or son).[7]

## The Impact of Christianity

Apart from those who dedicated themselves to perpetual virginity, Christianity imposed only relatively minor modifications on the social construct of gender for most elite Byzantines. Insistence on chastity outside marriage now applied to men as well as to women, at least in theory; the sexual act in general was more strictly regulated; the rationale for divorce was tightened; and Christian piety and philanthropy replaced Roman *pietas* (devotion to the gods).[8] Christian imperial virtues were defined around 400 by John Chrysostom, patriarch of Constantinople, as philanthropy, wisdom, and piety. Sounding very much like earlier Romans, Chrysostom wrote: "The true ruler is he who masters his passions of anger, envy, and lust, and subordinates everything to the laws of God; who, keeping his mind free, will not let pleasure dominate his soul."[9] Feminine virtues also continued Roman precepts, particularly the ideal of the wife as gentle, modest, and dedicated to family and home. The good empress augmented the properties of the ideal wife with elite largesse: she was pious, philanthropic, humble, and chaste.[10] Procopius described the ideal imperial bride as "in the highest degree both well-born and blessed with a nurture sheltered from the public eye, a woman who had not been unpracticed in modesty, and had dwelt with chastity, who was not only surpassingly beautiful but also still a maiden" (*Secret History* 10.2–3).

## Procopius, Justinian, and Theodora

Procopius provides considerable information about the construction of gender in mid-sixth-century Constantinople, particularly when he considers Justinian and Theodora. As we have already seen, Procopius considered war to be a masculine rather than a feminine arena, and thus his *History of the Wars* virtually ignored the empress.

His second major work, *Buildings*, celebrated Justinian's building campaigns, with particular emphasis on the imperial patronage of churches. Like Eusebius in his *Life of Constantine*, written two hundred years earlier, Procopius used the emperor's construction program to establish his piety and to locate him firmly in the tradition of the idealized builder-rulers of the Old Testament and of Roman imperial builders such as Augustus. This was a male imperial role and, in *Buildings*, Procopius's Justinian plays it to perfection.[11] In fact, however, Theodora was closely associated with many of the commissions that Procopius linked solely with Justinian: her monogram joins his in a number of buildings, notably Hagia Sophia and the Church of Sts. Sergius and Bacchus, both rebuilt after the Nika riots in 532. Nonetheless, as in *Wars*, the empress appears only occasionally: Procopius tells us that she was portrayed with Justinian on the Chalke Gate that led into the imperial palace; that her statue stood in the courtyard of the Arkadianai baths on the eastern shore of Constantinople; and that she and Justinian built a hospice close to the sea at Stadion (*Buildings* 1.10.17; 1.11.8; 1.11.27). The most significant reference concerns the Convent of Repentance, founded by "the emperor Justinian and the empress Theodora, who always shared a common piety in all that they did," as a refuge for women who had been forced into prostitution by poverty. With this commission, according to Procopius, the imperial couple banished "the very name of brothel-keepers, and they set free from a licentiousness fit only for slaves the women who were struggling with extreme poverty, providing them with independent maintenance, and setting virtue free" (*Buildings* 1.9.1–10). Apart from the convent, Procopius mentions Theodora only in the context of secular civic monuments, which were far less important to him, leaving the lone religious commission associated with the empress in *Buildings* – and her single participatory role in the imperial building campaign – a monastery for women. We know, from other sources and from the preserved monograms, that this is inaccurate. But it is clear what Procopius has done: he has imposed the hierarchy of Byzantine gender on his distribution of imperial patronage.

Theodora is, then, largely absent from the public imperial arenas celebrated in *Wars* and *Buildings*. Her main role is reserved for Procopius's *Secret History*, the most important of his writings for our understanding of gender in the mid-sixth century. Unlike the laudatory *Buildings*, and the relatively neutral *Wars*, the *Secret History* is an invective in which Procopius attacks Justinian using every trick in the book. We do not know why Procopius wrote the *Secret History*, which is so offensive that it can never have been publicly circulated. It is useless as a source of information about "what really happened," but the *Secret History* is a goldmine of information about mid-sixth-century Byzantine social systems and it is particularly informative about appropriate gender roles.[12]

## The Secret History

Procopius structured the *Secret History* as an inversion of the imperial panegyric (*enkomion*, or encomium); he developed Justinian into a demonic and barbaric character, lacking all masculine and imperial virtues. As a secondary theme, Procopius turned Theodora into an extraordinary example of everything a mid-sixth-century Byzantine woman should not be. One of his main rhetorical strategies is to portray Justinian as "unmanly" and Theodora as "unwomanly": to Procopius, such inversions overturned the social order and represented the grossest possible insult, thereby indicating to us just how important gendered roles were in sixth-century Byzantium.

Procopius subverted a model that had been developed in the third century by Menander, who codified the formula of imperial praise followed by most later Greek authors. According to Menander, one should first emphasize the prestige of the emperor's family, stressing any "miraculous happenings" associated with his birth and childhood, which the speaker may invent "because the audience has no choice but to accept the *enkomion* without examination" (*Treatise* 2.368–371, quotations 371.8–9, 12–14 [77–83]). Procopius followed Menander's advice to fabricate details but, instead of praising Justinian's family, tells us that they were illiterate, boorish, and descended from slaves and barbarians; rather than report any good omens surrounding his birth, Procopius reports that Justinian's mother claimed that he was the son of a demon (*Secret History* 6.11–28; 12.18–19).

Menander follows the glories of the imperial youth with a catalogue of the emperor's accomplishments, followed by actions in times of war and of peace, and divided into the four imperial virtues we have already mentioned (courage, justice, temperance, and wisdom) (*Treatise* 2.372–376, quotation 372.3–4 [83–93]). Procopius's Justinian displays none of these masculine attributes. On the contrary, an entire section (chapter 11) of the *Secret History* details Justinian's senseless wars and persecutions, and elsewhere Procopius notes that "during his reign the whole earth was constantly drenched with human blood" (18.30). He consistently paints the emperor as driven by greed rather than justice: "without any hesitation he shattered the laws when money was in sight" (27.33). Far from being temperate and wise, Procopius's Justinian is "like a cloud of dust in instability" (22.30–31), who "never paused for a thorough investigation before reaching a decision" (8.28–29), and "never was able to adhere to settled conditions, but he was naturally inclined to make confusion and turmoil everywhere" (18.12).

Menander then praised imperial successes and made comparisons with earlier rulers to demonstrate how the current emperor surpassed his predecessors (*Treatise* 2, 377.1–10 [93]). Procopius condemns Justinian for ruining the empire and compares him with the Roman emperor Domitian (AD 81–96; *Secret History* 8.13–21), who was detested by the Byzantines for his loathsome behavior and treated by them as an Antichrist figure.[13]

At the end of the oration, Menander writes that "you will speak of the prosperity and good fortune of the cities: the markets are full of goods . . . the earth is tilled in peace . . . piety toward God is increased" (*Treatise* 2.377.11–30, quotation 377.9–14 [93–95]). No hint of this appears in the *Secret History*, where Procopius claims that "practically the whole population found itself suddenly reduced to beggary" (25.25); that Roman peace was shattered (11.5); and that while Justinian "ruled over the Romans, neither good faith nor belief in God remained secure, no law remained fixed, no transaction safe, no contract valid" (13.24). In short, Procopius's portrait of Justinian neatly reverses all of the imperial male virtues established by Menander to present him as the anti-emperor, the exact opposite of the virtuous Roman ruler.

Procopius also enlists Theodora in this enterprise. In part, he does this by following the same pattern he used for Justinian: the empress is portrayed as the betrayal of all Roman feminine virtues. But her more important role is to expose Justinian's weaknesses.

As we have seen, Procopius described the ideal imperial bride as "well-born and . . . sheltered from the public eye," modest, chaste, beautiful, and a virgin. The Theodora of the *Secret History* is none of these things. She was the daughter of a bear-keeper (9.2), in the public eye from an early age (9.6–8), immodest, shameless (9.14), short and sallow (10.11), and a former prostitute. In the latter context, before her marriage, Procopius describes her appropriation of various male sexual roles: according to the *Secret History*, she had anal intercourse (9.10), pursued men (9.15), and was a "slave to pleasure" (9.16).

Female status was largely dependent on marriage and the production of legitimate heirs to carry on a husband's family line. So, to condemn Theodora, Procopius accused her of an "unwomanly" disregard of the sanctity and honor of marriage and motherhood. This becomes a major theme of the *Secret History*. Chastity before marriage was vital for women, so Procopius has Theodora force Belisarius's only daughter into losing her virginity in order to guarantee her grandson's marriage to the girl (5.21). Fathers arranged advantageous marriages for their children carefully in order to maximize social status, so Procopius portrays Theodora as usurping paternal authority by regulating all people's marriages (17.28–37). Because they were necessary to continue the family line, legitimate children – and especially boys – were a woman's main claim to social standing, and motherhood was a prime female virtue. It comes as little surprise that Procopius claims that, far from being an exemplary mother, Theodora had many abortions (10.3, 9.19) and later murdered her surviving son (17.16–23). In Procopius's story, Theodora's example polluted all women and destroyed the ideal of the Roman family (17.24–26).

Procopius plays on the Byzantine view of woman as vehicles of emotion (as opposed to rational men) in his picture of Theodora's inability to control her passions.[14] She betrays the rules of female decorum by laughing loudly on inappropriate occasions (9.14), treating everything as a joke (15.24), mocking patricians (15.25–35) and law courts (15.23), and by being "unusually clever and full of gibes" (9.13–14).

Because Roman and Byzantine gender constructs assigned public roles to men and private, domestic roles to women, most of Procopius's tales about Theodora avoid the public arena. As we have seen, she is for this reason largely absent from *Wars* and *Buildings*. But in the *Secret History*, Procopius evidently felt that he could leave no stone unturned, and he introduced, at least briefly, Theodora's relationship with church and state. Inevitably, given the nature of the work, she perverted both. Procopius casts doubt on Theodora's piety by describing her desecration and violation of sacred places (3.25; 16.22; 17.10–11) and pictures her as a "slave-instructor" of the government (15.16–17).

In Theodora, Procopius created the perfect anti-woman. Rather than a modest and self-effacing Roman matron, Procopius's empress inverts all qualities that late Roman culture valued in a woman. But, throughout the *Secret History*, Procopius also used Theodora to highlight Justinian's failures, especially his bad judgment and his weak character.[15] To Procopius, Justinian's lack of judgment is exemplified by his selection of Theodora as his wife: "And I think that I need make mention of nothing else whatever in regard to the character of this man. For this marriage would be amply sufficient to show full well all the maladies of his soul, since it serves as both an interpreter and a witness and recorder of his character" (10.3–5). As to his weak character, Procopius tells us that the emperor was "both an evil-doer and easily led into evil," and "an easy prey, to those who wished to deceive him" (8.22).[16] This, in Procopius's narrative, allowed Theodora to manipulate him: "She could win over her husband quite against his will to the action she desired" (13.19). Following old Roman formulae that equated the virtue of male self-control with the ability to be in command of one's family,[17] Procopius emasculated Justinian by portraying him as unable to control his own wife.

Procopius's understanding of appropriate gender roles is clear. Men dominated the public sphere of politics, warfare, and civic works. Good men were well-born, Roman, physically courageous and morally strong, just, wise, pious, moderate, and self-controlled. Women were seen largely within a private sphere; when status decreed that they could act outside of it, they commissioned minor works or buildings for other women. Good women were well-born, modest, chaste, beautiful, sheltered, pious, dutiful wives, and caring mothers. These patterns of behavior follow Roman precedent. They remained sufficiently important to Procopius that he relied on their inversion alone to condemn Theodora; he brought rhetorical strategies based on both gender and imperial roles into play to vilify Justinian.

## Gender and the Law

The legal systems in place during the sixth century are quite informative about perceptions of gender roles. Like the literature written by Procopius, however, laws cannot be understood as "facts." Laws tell us about the ideal world imagined and constructed by legislators and lawyers, but the extent to which the lawyers' world related to the real one and how much legal detail most people actually knew are both open to question. What is considered to be socially acceptable behavior is rarely successfully determined by legislation; normally, it is negotiated by consensus, managed and channeled by the dominant social group. Legislation codifies and authorizes the practice of this group and mediates between past and present conceptions of appropriate actions. In a slightly different way from the gender constructs used by Procopius, the gender roles embedded in Byzantine legal codes provide a perspective on Byzantine hierarchies of power.

The main legal sources for the sixth century are the various law codes compiled for Justinian. The ranking status throughout is free men, with freed men (slaves who have been given their freedom) as a separate category. The normative legal gender is male, and most laws deal exclusively with men's affairs. Women are presented as dependent on men: a daughter is under the authority of her father, and a wife takes on her husband's rank irrespective of her own family's status. The appearance of women in the law codes is virtually always restricted to legislation dealing with marriage, the family, or the protection of female virtue. Women are consistently omitted from references to public life in the law codes, and their legal rights are relatively limited. Only widows have greater legal authority (over their children, for example): like Procopius's Amazons, they are allowed to transgress conventional "female" roles because they are in the extreme position of having no male protector.[18]

These basic legal precepts enshrine ideas about the appropriate roles of men and women that are very similar to Procopius's, but their application differs somewhat from his. A comparison between Procopius's stance and legal attitudes towards adultery provides a case in point. Procopius discussed adultery in the *Secret History* when, as part of his attack on Theodora, he accused her of destroying the sanctity of Roman marriage. Procopius claimed that, following the empress's example, "practically all the women had become corrupt in character" and with Theodora's help treated their husbands "outrageously" and became adulteresses (*Secret History* 17.24–26). Procopius treats adultery as a social scandal, a moral corruption perpetuated by wives on husbands.

Legislation about adultery also focused on wifely action, but it was not couched in moralistic terms. Instead, laws about adultery were designed primarily to ensure legitimate heirs to the (man's) family property. Unmarried women, with no husband for whom to produce heirs, were therefore not involved: in legal terms, sex between a married man and an unmarried woman was simply fornication. Adultery occurred only when there was a possibility that illegitimate heirs might be produced; in other words, when a married woman had sex with a man (married or unmarried) who was not her husband. Given the social importance of the family structure, this was a serious offence, and both the man and the woman involved might be penalized. Only a man, however, could obtain a divorce by accusing his wife of adultery; the claim was justified because she had thrown the legitimacy of his heirs into question. If, however, a husband was unfaithful to his wife with an unmarried woman, she had no legal recourse unless he was also a culpable criminal.[19]

The gender issues at stake here have less to do with appropriate or inappropriate sexual behavior than they do with property law. Underpinning the adultery legislation is the legal position that, their wives' dowries aside, men controlled the family, the family's property, and its dispensation. Procopius treated adultery as social corruption; the law treated it as an abuse of inheritance rights. Both, however, reinforced male status as head of the family and household. Despite their different approaches, the gendered rules of etiquette and the gendered rules of inheritance coincided.

## Gender and Public Life

Procopius's rhetoric and the law codes tell us how gender roles were constructed in the mid-sixth century, but they do not tell us how men and women actually lived their lives. Other evidence suggests that, while the understanding of appropriate masculine and feminine behavior expressed by Procopius and legislation was widely accepted, the rules were not always followed. If we accepted the ideal social systems described in our sources, we would expect to find few women visible outside a domestic environment, yet it is clear that this was not the case. Women went to church and participated in religious processions; they appeared in public and engaged in family business; and some worked outside the home, either reputably (for example, as scribes) or not (for example, as innkeepers or prostitutes).[20] Elite women could be commemorated by statues, erected in crowded thoroughfares, and they sometimes commissioned objects and buildings that were very much in the public sphere. One aristocratic woman, Patricia, even became city governor of Antaiopolis in Egypt in 553, although she seems to have had a male co-governor who acted in public for her. It may be added that Theodora, too, had an accepted public role, which we can tell from sources that are more reliable than Procopius's narrative. She was a building patron, as we have seen, but she was also sought out as the special patron of one well-documented Egyptian village, Aphrodito, probably in 540–541, which indicates that quite remote inhabitants of the empire recognized and valued her political protagonism.[21]

## Gender and Patronage

In the late Roman and early Byzantine period, patronage – the sponsorship and support of a person, object, or monument – was normally the prerogative of men, and the term itself is gendered: the word patronage derives from the Latin *pater* (father) and its derivative *patronus* (protector, defender). But although the concepts of protection and support were closely linked with male roles, throughout the sixth century elite women also sponsored people and, especially, things.

In the Age of Justinian, two figures stand out as patrons of monuments: Justinian himself, as commemorated in Procopius's *Buildings*, and the *patrikia* Anicia Juliana. Anicia Juliana (c. 462–c. 528) was the western emperor Olybrius's daughter and, as her name indicated to all, a member of the wealthy and ancient Roman Anicius family. Her lineage ran back through Theodosius I to Constantine the Great, and during the first quarter of the sixth century she was probably both the most aristocratic and the wealthiest inhabitant of Constantinople. She commissioned at least three buildings in the capital and its immediate suburbs: a church dedicated to St. Polyeuktos near the Anicii family estates, probably constructed between 524 and 527, the massive substructures of which survive to this day; the church of St. Euphemia in the Olybrios district, the precise date of which is unknown; and, around the year 512, a church in the Honoratae district.[22]

The dedication inscriptions of the first two of these buildings are recorded in a Byzantine collection of epigrams now known as the *Greek Anthology*. Epigrams 12 to 17 were found at St. Euphemia and tell us that Anicia Juliana's grandmother, Licinia Eudoxia, founded the church, probably in the 440s or early 450s, Juliana's mother Placidia embellished the building at some point between 461 and 472, and Anicia Juliana in turn completed it before her death in 527–528. Shortly before her death, Anicia Juliana rebuilt St. Polyeuktos, another church that had been established by one of her female ancestors, this time her great-grandmother Aelia Eudocia, wife of Theodosius II. Once again, Juliana commemorated the female family line in an inscription that is recorded in the *Greek Anthology* and is still partially preserved. It begins:

> Eudocia the empress, eager to honor God, first built here a temple of Polyeuktos the servant of God. But she did not make it as great and beautiful as it is . . . because her prophetic soul told her that she would leave a family well knowing how better to adorn it. Whence Juliana, the glory of her blessed parents, inheriting their royal blood in the fourth generation, did not disappoint the hopes of the empress, the mother of a noble race, but raised this from a small temple to its present size and beauty (*Greek Anthology* 1.10).

The long inscription, and another that was also once inscribed on the building, consistently invokes Juliana's family. Her parents (for example,

"Who hath not heard of Juliana, how in her pious care she glorified even her parents by fair-fashioned works"), her son and grandchildren ("preserve her gladly with her son and his daughters, and may the immeasurable glory of the most beneficient family survive as long as the sun drives his burning chariot"), and her ancestors Constantine and Theodosius are all glorified.

Comparison with Justinian's (preserved) inscription at his Church of Sts. Sergius and Bacchus is instructive. The emperor's inscription reads:

> Other sovereigns have honored dead men whose labor was unprofitable, but our sceptered Justinian, fostering piety, honors with a splendid abode the servant of Christ, begetter of all things, Sergius. . . . May he [St. Sergius] in all things guard the rule of the sleepless sovereign [Justinian] and increase the power of the God-crowned Theodora whose mind is adorned with piety, whose constant toil lies in unsparing efforts to nourish the destitute.[23]

Beyond the obviously gendered contrast between how piety is constructed for Justinian (who builds) and Theodora (who nurtures), the difference between Anicia Juliana's and Justinian's dedication inscriptions is striking. Juliana honors her family; Justinian asks for divine protection.

This difference is not unique: nearly all female commissions of the fifth and sixth centuries invoke family, while very few male commissions do so. What we see here is women – and in this case a very important, high-status *patrikia* – so encased in the web of gender-appropriate behavior that their acts, even when they replicate male activities, are defined not in terms of power negotiation but in terms of promoting family values.

Anicia Juliana could, however, have traced her lineage back to Theodosius and, ultimately, to Constantine through either the male or the female sides of her heritage: if she had been interested simply in promoting family status, she would not have focused on her female line of descent. The stress on Juliana's female lineage associated her with an empress renowned for her piety – Aelia Eudocia – but, beyond that, it also linked her with a long chain of female commissions that evoked Constantine the Great's mother Helena (c. 250–c. 330). By the early fifth century, Helena was legendary for her piety and her buildings. She was believed to have discovered the True Cross in Jerusalem in

326 and was held responsible for a sequence of important churches and chapels. Helena's reputation was such that, across the fifth and sixth centuries, imperial women were honored as the "new Helena" and some – notably Aelia Eudoxia (wife of the emperor Arcadius), Aelia Galla Placidia (c. 388–450, daughter of Theodosius I), and Aelia Eudocia (Juliana's great-grandmother) – emulated Helena's example through their building campaigns.[24] None of these buildings survive, but where inscriptions were recorded it is clear that the "Helena commissions" celebrated family as well as the saintly empress. They form a particularly gender-specific group of monuments that is significant for its joining of the conventional Byzantine linkage of women and family to a different kind of gendered association: the female role model.

## Gender and the Church

Initially, in terms of gender roles, the main impact of Christianity was the attempted regulation of sexual behavior. One immediate effect was new legislation concerning divorce. Divorce had not been an issue of great concern under Roman law, which held that mutual consent was sufficient justification to end a marriage. In 331, however, Constantine I, apparently under the influence of Christianity, imposed tight legislation that restricted the reasons for divorce: for example, a woman could divorce her husband only if she could demonstrate that he was a murderer, a poisoner, or that he desecrated graves. Under Justinian, mutual consent was abandoned as a justification for divorce entirely.[25] These changes affected secular law codes; canon law – the legislation drafted by church councils to regulate Christian life – was more intrusive.

Following the Bible, the church believed that marriage was indissoluble under all circumstances except specific types of adultery. Whether divorced or left single by the death of a spouse, Christians ought not remarry, though one remarriage was tolerated. Civil and canon law did not, in this instance, agree, because the church claimed to expect Christians to live by higher standards than was legally necessary.[26]

The church also followed Old Testament strictures that forbade men and women from participating in religious activities when they were "polluted": women could neither attend church nor take communion when they were menstruating or had just given birth; men could not take communion, though they could attend church, after involuntary nocturnal seminal emission; and, to be permitted to take communion, couples must abstain from sexual relations the night and morning before.[27]

Gender differences, too, were observed within the church hierarchy. Men were excluded from certain areas of the church – usually sections of the side aisles on the ground floor and parts of the upper galleries – but after suitable training could join the ranks of the clergy. Women over the age of forty might be ordained as deaconesses, but no other official roles were available to them within the church hierarchy. Even in monasteries for women, the ranking clergy were, following canon law, male.[28]

Religious literature such as lives of the saints (hagiography) perpetuated this division, and generally reinforced social conventions. Most Byzantine saints so honored were male, and good females – often nameless – appear in their roles as family members, and usually as mothers. When women were considered holy, they – like Procopius's good female ruler, Amalasuintha – were believed to have transcended "womanly weakness" and to have become "honorary males." As with other literature of the period, like the *Secret History* discussed earlier, this portrayal of women was grounded in expectations about male behavior.[29]

## Changing Gender Strategies in the Sixth Century: The Transformation of the Social World

Theodora died in 548, Justinian in 565. They were succeeded by Justinian's nephew, Justin II, who died in 578, and his wife Sophia, perhaps Theodora's niece, who outlived her husband by over twenty years. It is during their reign that we begin to find evidence for significant shifts in the presentation of gender that continued over the next century.

The lengthy poem written by Corippus on Justin's accession, *In Praise of Justin II*, is an unusual text in many ways. In terms of its presentation of gender roles, it breaks from Procopius's model in one significant way: Sophia, always playing the idealized role of the perfect wife, is an active participant in the narrative. When, for example, Corippus described Justin's prayer to Christ and God, to receive their blessing on his accession, he followed it immediately with a transcription of Sophia's prayer to the Virgin (*Praise* 2.1–83).

Sophia's role in Corippus's poem is matched by other representations. Shortly after their coronations, Justin II reinstated the old idea of including a portrait of the empress on coins. This had last occurred in 491 on the marriage nomismata (the highest-value Byzantine gold coins) struck to commemorate the wedding of Ariadne and Anastasius, which showed the emperor on its front and an image of the emperor and empress crowned by Christ on the back. As a commemorative issue, the marriage nomisma was unusual: normally, between 383 and 491 the so-called empress coins portrayed the empress alone, in profile on the front, while the reverse presented a range of formulaic inscriptions, personifications and, from the time of Aelia Eudoxia (400–404) onwards, a cross in a wreath – a clear indication of the lasting identification of imperial women with Helena and the True Cross.

Justin's coinage looks quite different from these earlier coins, and it initiated a sequence that was continued from 565 until 641, across the reigns of five imperial couples. Now, the empress never appears alone on coins; instead, either the imperial couple is shown as a pair or the emperor appears on the front and the empress on the back. Across the entire span of seventy-six years, with the single exception of two issues dated to 572–573, the emperor is named but the empress remains anonymous.

The new coinage might be interpreted as representing the shared nature of imperial authority under Justin II and Sophia. Against this, however, is the problem that the empress is anonymous and appeared only on low-denomination coins, never on the gold nomismata. Rather than signaling Sophia's importance, subsequent practice suggests that the joint portrait indicates that the empress was losing significance in her own right. For while the Justin II/Sophia issues were numerous and continued to be minted throughout Justin's lifetime, subsequent emperors issued coins portraying their wives only at the start of their rule. The joint imperial portrait seems to have been considered appropriate as an inauguration image, as an expression of imperial unity, necessary only at the beginning of a reign; the empress was no longer an essential component of, or even a participant in, the empire's day-to-day ideological program.[30]

That the gendered balance of power was shifting is also evident in the realms of patronage and the church. Anicia Juliana's commissions were the last to promote female relatives. After the mid-sixth century, commissions celebrating secular women ceased, and a competing female role model – the Virgin Mary, also commemorated in church dedications across the fifth century – replaced them entirely. Unlike Helena or Juliana's maternal ancestors, by uniting the conflicting roles of virgin and mother, Mary set an example no Byzantine woman could hope to follow. Also unlike secular women, the presentation of the Virgin Mary was, at least officially, controlled by the church. And, in terms of gender, theirs was not a tolerant regime. The next church council to enact new canon law, the Council in Trullo held in 692, lauded the family but rigorously enforced gender boundaries: cross-dressing, for example, was condemned. Most significantly, women were no longer allowed to speak in church and so were effectively barred from participating in the responses to the spoken liturgy.[31]

## Conclusion

As expressed in the sources, gender roles became increasingly Christianized after the reign of Justinian. While there were, as we have seen, considerable restrictions on women's and men's roles in the gender representations of Justinian's reign, there was actually more space for especially female action than during the next two centuries. More and more, the Christian imagery in our sources tends to exclude women, whatever they actually did – and in this connection it is worth noting that the restricted, but certainly existent, role of women in public life continued to be recognized in law. But they are decreasingly evident in other sources. Procopius demonized Theodora as a means of attacking her husband, and his narrative is useless as a description, but – through his reliance on gender constructs to further his particular rhetorical strategy – he admitted "woman" as a character type on the Byzantine stage. We will not find her again in this role for two hundred years.

## Notes

I thank Mary Harlow and Chris Wickham for comments on an earlier draft of this chapter.

1 For a good overview, see Dominic Montserrat, "Reading Gender in the Roman World," in *Experiencing Rome*, ed. Janet Huskinson (London, 2000), 153–181.

2 On eunuchs, see Kathryn Ringrose, *The Perfect Servant: Eunuchs and the Social Construction of Gender in Byzantium* (Chicago, 2003); Matthew Kuefler, *The Manly Eunuch: Masculinity, Gender Ambiguity, and Christian Ideology in Late Antiquity* (Chicago, 2001); Shaun Tougher, "Social Transformation, Gender Transformation? The Court Eunuch, 300–900," in *Gender in the Early Medieval World*, ed. Leslie Brubaker and Julia Smith (Cambridge, 2005).

3 See the classic study by Joan Scott, "Gender, a Useful Category of Historical Analysis," conveniently reprinted in her *Gender and the Politics of History*, rev. ed. (New York, 1999), 28–50.

4 This is her first appearance. The subsequent seven are in *Wars*, 1.25.4–5; 1.25.22; 1.25.30; 2.30.49; 4.9.13; 7.30.3; 7.31.13. In contrast, both Justinian and Belisarius

appear over twenty times each in book 1 alone, and Belisarius's wife Antonina appears nineteen times across the eight volumes.

5 Quotations from Averil Cameron, *Procopius and the Sixth Century* (Berkeley, Calif., 1985), 69.

6 Elizabeth Fisher, "Theodora and Antonia," *Arethusa* 11 (1978): 253–280; and Cameron, *Procopius.*

7 The literature on this topic is extensive. See, for example, Suzanne Dixon, *The Roman Mother* (London, 1988); Susan Treggiari, *Roman Marriage: Iusti Coniuges from the Time of Cicero to the Time of Ulpian* (Oxford, 1991); Martha Vinson, "Domitia Longina, Julia Titi, and the Literary Tradition," *Historia* 38 (1989): 431–450; Kate Cooper, "Insinuations of Womanly Influence: An Aspect of the Christianisation of the Roman Aristocracy," *JRS* 82 (1992): 150–164; Amy Richlin, "Julia's Jokes, Galla Placidia, and the Roman Use of Women as Political Icons," in Barbara Garlick, et al., *Stereotypes of Women in Power: Historical Perspectives and Revisionist Views* (New York, 1992), 65–91; Gillian Clark, *Women in Late Antiquity, Pagan and Christian Lifestyles* (Oxford, 1993); Susan Fischler, "Social Stereotypes and Historical Analysis: The Case of the Imperial Women at Rome," in *Women in Ancient Societies, an Illusion of the Night*, ed. Léonie Archer, Susan Fischler and Maria Wyke (Houndmills, 1994), 115–133; and Mary Harlow and Ray Laurence, *Growing Up and Growing Old in Ancient Rome* (London, 2001), all with extensive bibliographies. For Menander's list of imperial virtues, see his *Treatise* 2.373.7–8 [85].

8 See, for example, Averil Cameron, "Virginity as Metaphor: Women and the Rhetoric of Early Christianity," in *History as Text: The Writing of Ancient History*, ed. Averil Cameron (London, 1989), 184–205; Elizabeth Clark, "Patrons Not Priests: Gender and Power in Late Antique Christianity," *Gender and History* 2 (1990): 253–273; Elizabeth Clark, "Ideology, History, and the Construction of 'Woman' in Late Ancient Christianity," *JEChrSt* 2.2 (1994): 155–184; Elizabeth Clark, "Holy Women, Holy Words: Early Christian Women, Social History, and the 'Linguistic Turn,'" *JEChrSt* 6.3 (1998): 413–430; Elizabeth Clark, "The Lady Vanishes: Dilemmas of a Feminist Historian after the 'Linguistic Turn,'" *ChHist* 67 (1998), 1–31; and Martha Vinson, "The Christianization of Sexual Slander: Some Preliminary Observations," in *Novum Millennium: Studies on Byzantine History and Culture Dedicated to Paul Speck*, ed. Claudia Sode and Sarolta Takács (Aldershot, 2001), 415–424.

9 See Francis Dvornik, *Early Christian and Byzantine Political Philosophy, Origins and Background*, vol. 2, Dumbarton Oaks Studies 9 (Washington, D.C., 1966), 695. For further discussion of male virtue in the wake of Christianity, see Cooper, "Insinuations"; Liz James, *Empresses and Power in Early Byzantium* (London, 2001), 12–13; Mary Harlow, "In the Name of the Father: Procreation, Paternity, and Patriarchy," and Gillian Clark, "The Old Adam: the Fathers and the Unmaking of Masculinity," both in *Thinking Men: Masculinity and Its Self-Representation in the Classical Tradition*, ed. Lyn Foxhall and John Salmon (London, 1998), 155–169 and 170–182. All contain additional bibliography.

10 James, *Empresses and Power*, 12–16.

11 Cameron, *Procopius*, 84–112; Averil Cameron and Stewart Hall, eds., *Eusebius, Life of Constantine* (Oxford, 1999); Glanville Downey, "Justinian as a Builder," *Art Bulletin* 32 (1950): 262–266.

12 See Leslie Brubaker, "Sex, Lies, and Textuality: The *Secret History* of Prokopios and the Rhetoric of Gender in Sixth-Century Byzantium," in *Gender in the Early Medieval World*, ed. Leslie Brubaker and Julia Smith (Cambridge, 2005).

13 Cameron, *Procopius*, 57.

14 See Clark, *Women in Late Antiquity*, 120–126. For examples, see *Secret History*, 25.2; 25.5–9; 26.22.

15 So too Cameron, *Procopius*, 71.

16 For more examples, see, for example, *Secret History*, 8.26; 8.10; 19.11–12.

17 See Vinson, "Domitia Longina"; Cooper, "Insinuations"; Fischler, "Social Stereotypes"; and Clark, "The Lady Vanishes."

18 See Caroline Humfress, "Law and Legal Practice in the Age of Justinian," Chap. 7 of this volume, and Clark, *Women in Late Antiquity*, 6–62; Antii Arjava, *Women and the Law in Late Antiquity* (Oxford, 1996); Joëlle Beaucamp, "La Situation juridique de la femme à Byzance," *Cahiers de Civilisation Médiévale* 20 (1977): 145–176; Joëlle Beaucamp, *Le Statut de la femme à Byzance (4e–7e siècle)*, 2 vols., Travaux et mémoires du Centre de recherché d'histoire et civilisation de Byzance monographies, 5–6 (Paris, 1990–1992); and Marie Theres Fögen, "Legislation in Byzantium: A Political and Bureaucratic Technique," in *Law and Society in Byzantium, Ninth–Twelfth Centuries*, ed. Angeliki Laiou and Dieter Simon (Washington, D.C., 1994), 53–70.

19 See the references in n. 18, and Bernard Stolte, "Desires Denied: Marriage, Adultery, and Divorce in Early Byzantine Law," in *Desire and Denial in Byzantium*, ed. Liz James (Aldershot, 1999), 77–86.

20 See Angeliki Laiou, "The Role of Women in Byzantine Society," *JÖB* 31.1 (1981): 233–260; Alice-Mary Talbot, "Women," in *The Byzantines*, ed. Guglielmo Cavallo (Chicago, 1997), 117–143; and Kim Haines-Eitzen, "'Girls Trained in Beautiful Handwriting': Female Scribes in Roman Antiquity and Early Christianity," *JEChrSt* 6.4 (1998): 629–646.

21 For Patricia, see *The Prosopography of the Later Roman Empire*, vol. 3, *A.D. 527–641*, ed. John Martindale (Cambridge, 1992), 970; for Theodora, see Harold Bell, "An Egyptian Village in the Age of Justinian," *JHS* 64 (1944): 31. I thank Chris Wickham for this reference.

22 See Cyril Mango and Ihor Ševčenko, "Remains of the Church of St. Polyeuktos at Constantinople," *DOP* 15 (1961): 243–247; Martin Harrison, *A Temple for Byzantium: The Discovery and Excavation of Anicia Juliana's Palace-Church in Istanbul* (London, 1989); Leslie Brubaker, "Memories of Helena: Patterns of Imperial Female Matronage in the Fourth and Fifth Centuries," in *Women, Men, and Eunuchs: Gender in Byzantium*, ed. Liz James (London, 1997), 52–75; and Leslie Brubaker, "The Vienna Dioskorides and Anicia Juliana," in *Byzantine Garden Culture*, ed. Antony Littlewood, Henry Maguire, and Joachim Wolschke-Bulmahn (Washington, D.C., 2002), 189–214.

23 English translation from Cyril Mango, "The Church of Saints Sergius and Bacchus at Constantinople and the Alleged Tradition of Octagonal Palatine Churches," *JÖB* 21 (1972): 190.

24 Brubaker, "Memories of Helena."

25 Fögen, "Legislation in Byzantium," 56–58; Stolte, "Desires Denied."

26 John Meyendorff, "Christian Marriage in Byzantium: The Canonical and Liturgical Tradition," *DOP* 44 (1990): 99–107; Clark, *Women in Late Antiquity*, 17–21.

27 Robert Taft, "Women at Church in Byzantium: Where, When – and Why?" *DOP* 52 (1998): 27–87.

28 Susan Ashbrook Harvey, "Women in Early Syrian Christianity," in *Images of Women in Antiquity*, ed. Averil Cameron and Amélie Kuhrt (Detroit, 1983), 288–298; Catia Galatariotou, "Holy Women and Witches: Aspects of Byzantine Conceptions of Gender," *Byzantine and Modern Greek Studies* 9 (1984–1985): 55–94; Alice-Mary Talbot, "A Comparison of the Monastic Experience of Byzantine Men and Women," *GOTR* 30 (1985): 1–20; Judith Herrin, "Public and Private Forms of Religious Commitment among Byzantine Women," in *Women in Ancient Societies, an Illusion of the Night*, ed. Léonie Archer, Susan Fischler, and Maria Wyke (Houndmills, 1994), 181–203; Taft, "Women at Church in Byzantium"; Joëlle Beaucamp, "Exclues et aliénées: Les Femmes dans la tradition canonique byzantine," in *Strangers to Themselves: The Byzantine Outsider*, ed. Dion Smythe (Aldershot, 2000), 87–103.

29 Susan Ashbrook Harvey, "Women in Early Byzantine Hagiography: Reversing the Story," in *"That Gentle Strength": Historical Perspectives on Women and Christianity*, ed. Lynda Coon, Katherine Haldane, and Elisabeth Summers (Charlottesville, Va., 1990), 16–59; Gillian Cloke, *This Female Man of God: Women and Spiritual Power in the Patristic Age, AD 350–450* (London, 1995); Aideen Hartney, "Manly Women and Womanly Men: The *Subintroductae* and John Chrysostom," in *Desire and Denial in Byzantium*, ed. Liz James (Aldershot, 1999), 41–48.

30 For Sophia, see Averil Cameron, "The Empress Sophia," *Byzantion* 45 (1975): 5–21; for the coinage, see Leslie Brubaker and Helen Tobler, "The Gender of Money: Byzantine Empresses on Coins (324–802)," *Gender and History* 12.3 (2000): 572–594.

31 Judith Herrin, "'Femina Byzantina': The Council of Trullo on Women," *DOP* 46 (1992): 97–105.

# 18: Justinian and the Barbarian Kingdoms

*Walter Pohl*

## The Empire and Its Barbarians

In the early summer of 552, the Ostrogothic king Totila faced a large Byzantine army arrayed near Busta Gallorum, in central Italy, for the battle that would decide the fate of his kingdom. He was desperately waiting for reinforcements to arrive. To win time, he rode into the empty space between the two armies, clad in gold-plated armor, with purple adornments hanging from cheek plates, helmet, and spear, and began to perform a war dance. Procopius reports, "He wheeled his horse around in a circle and then turned him again to the other side and so made him run round and round. And as he rode he hurled his javelin into the air and caught it again as it quivered above him, then passed it rapidly from hand to hand, shifting it with consummate skill, and he gloried in his practice in such matters, falling back on his shoulders, spreading his legs and leaning from side to side." Although the reinforcements arrived, the Goths lost the battle, and Totila died in flight the following night.[1]

Courage, splendor, skill at martial arts, and archaic barbarian customs: Procopius's famous report reflects a familiar image of the barbarian kings who ruled the West in the time of Justinian.[2] The glory and the fall of these barbarian kings is part of our grand narrative of Justinian's achievements. His reconquests removed barbarian rulers from some of the former heartlands of the western empire and reestablished direct imperial rule. But by concentrating on the wars against the Vandals, the Ostrogoths, and in some measure also against the Visigoths, Justinian made the empire vulnerable to the attacks by new and more ferocious barbarians: Slavs, Avars, Lombards, Berbers, and others. This was already the view of contemporary historians, most of all, Procopius.[3] In several volumes of his *Wars*, he criticized Justinian's conquests. Later, his sweeping and devastating denunciation of Justinian's rule in the *Secret History* culminated in pointed questions: where had all the money gone that the Emperor had squeezed from his subjects? Was it hidden somewhere in the palace? Or, as many maintained, had it all gone to the barbarians?[4]

At the end of Justinian's rule, his barbarian policy, in spite of its spectacular successes, was generally considered a failure; northern barbarians had once again begun to threaten the Thracian hinterland of the capital. This chapter will take a look at the dynamics of this development, and it will also suggest some modifications to the traditional grand narrative of events. Both Procopius and many modern historians have pictured the barbarians as the enemies, as the others, in their accounts of Justinian's reign. There are, however, many ways in which the emperor and his barbarian adversaries were inextricably linked in their conflicting bids for power.[5] This was not simply a "clash of cultures" between a Christian civilization and its uncivilized, pagan or heretical enemies.

The theater of ambitions of both Byzantines and barbarians was Rome. The Roman *res publica* (polity) was a unique basis on which to build power – not the imperial title; none of Justinian's adversaries ever openly challenged his unique position as Roman emperor. This explains, for instance, Procopius's remark that even among the Moors – the Berbers of north Africa – whom he regards as the most hardy barbarians, "it was a law that no one should be a ruler over them, even if he was hostile to the Romans, until the emperor of the Romans should give him the tokens of the office."[6] In that sense, few of the enemies of Rome in the sixth century were actually enemies of the Roman order; they only objected to the direct rule of Justinian's generals and his tax collectors, and sometimes also of his bishops.

When Gelimer, the last king of the Vandals, retreated after his defeat to a remote stronghold in the Atlas mountains and was besieged there by Byzantine troops, he first turned down an offer of honorable surrender. Instead, he asked his Roman interlocutor for three gifts: a lyre, one loaf of bread, and a sponge. The sponge was intended for his swollen eye, "and being a skilful harpist he had composed an ode relating to his present misfortune, which he was eager to chant to the accompaniment of the lyre while he wept out his soul."[7] This anecdote reveals that in the century during which they controlled the rich provinces of Roman north Africa, the Vandal elite had become "the most luxurious nation we know," as Procopius states with some gusto. They enjoyed daily

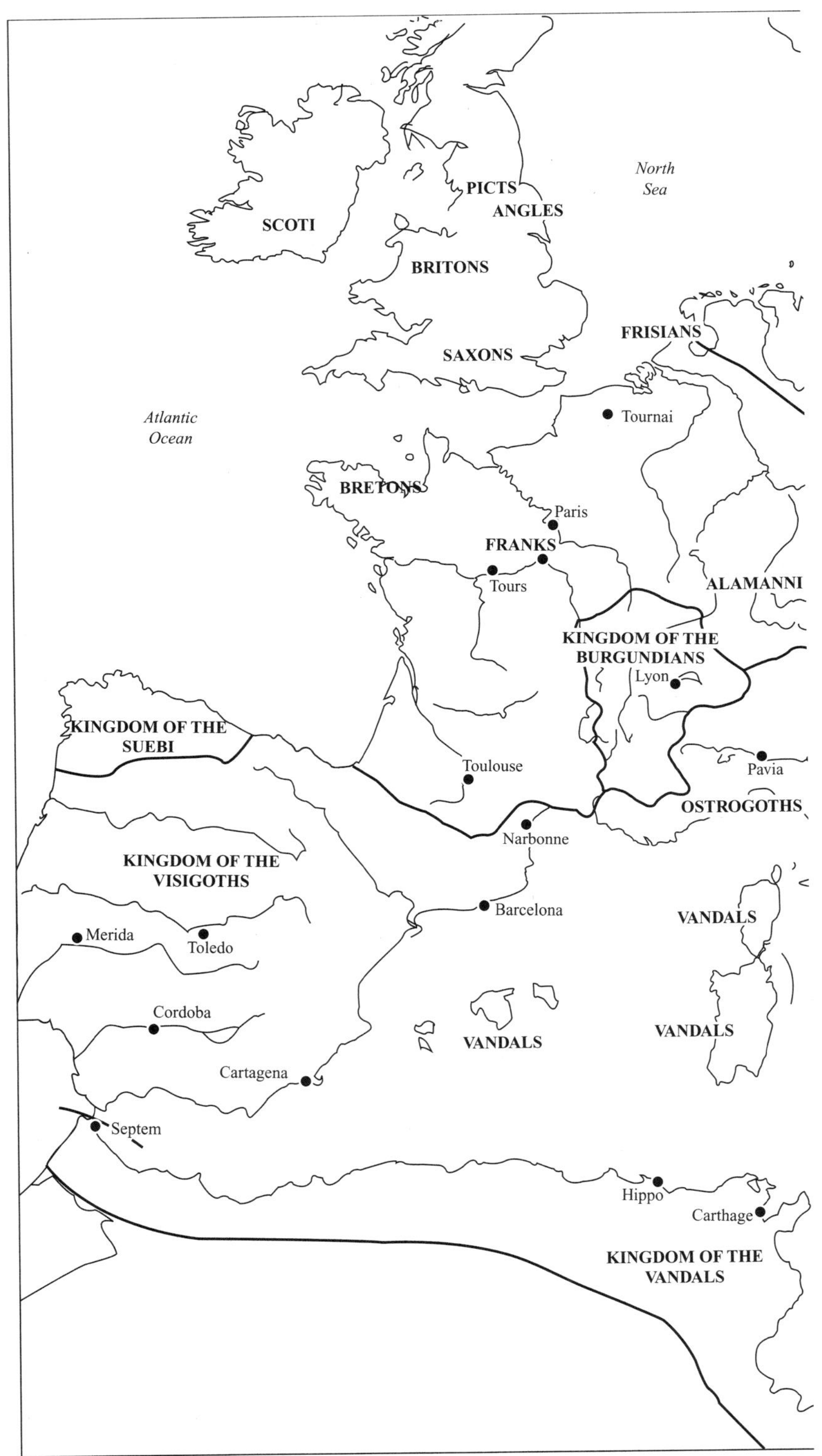


MAP 10. Barbarian kingdoms, c. 527

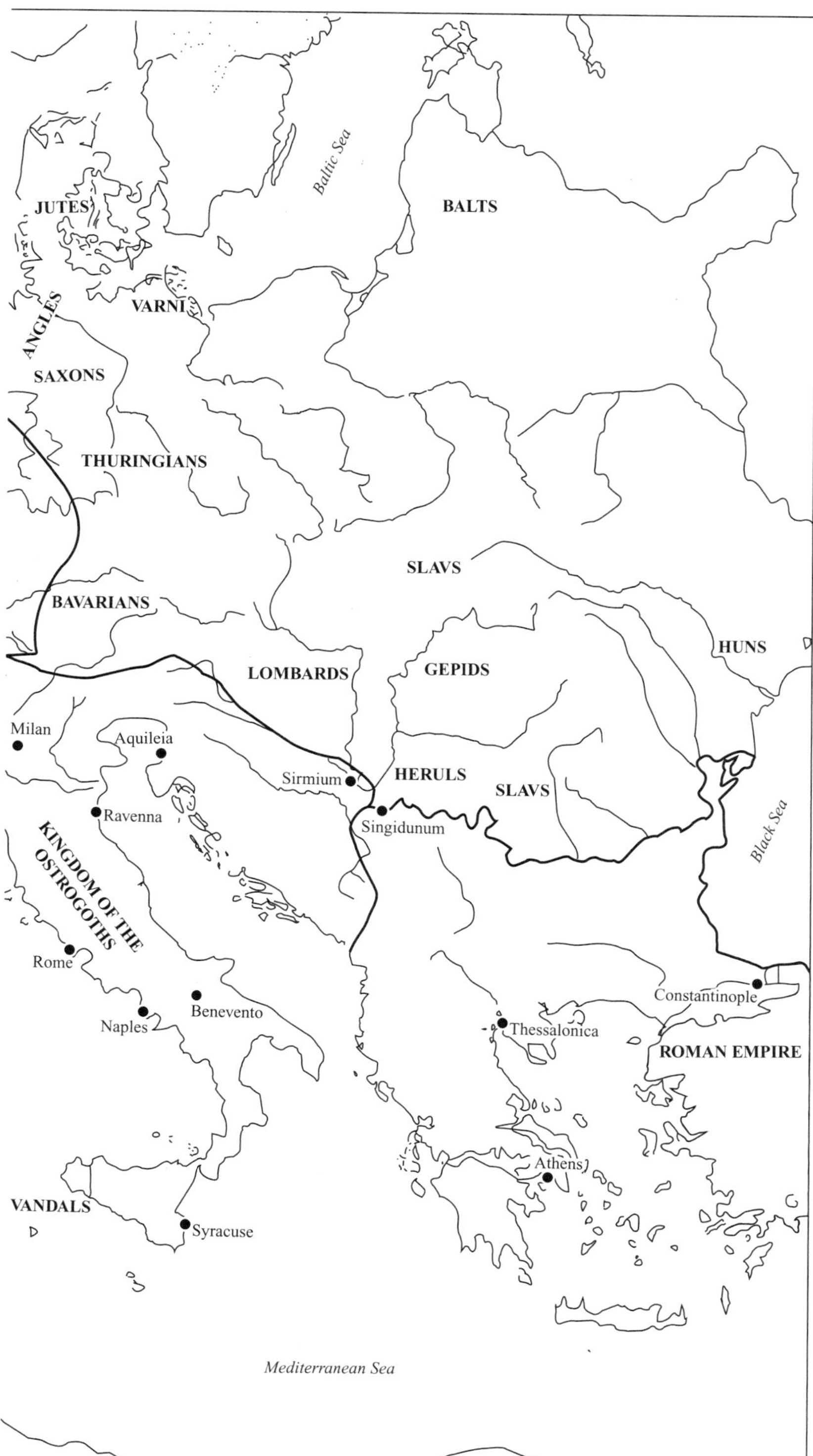
Baltic Sea
JUTES
BALTS
ANGLES
VARNI
SAXONS
THURINGIANS
SLAVS
BAVARIANS
HUNS
LOMBARDS
GEPIDS
Milan
Aquileia
Sirmium
HERULS
SLAVS
Singidunum
Ravenna
KINGDOM OF THE OSTROGOTHS
Black Sea
Rome
Benevento
Constantinople
Naples
Thessalonica
ROMAN EMPIRE
Athens
VANDALS
Syracuse
Mediterranean Sea

baths and excellent meals, the theater and the hippodrome, dancers and mimes, silk garments and lush gardens.[8] Not all barbarians were able to live their lives in such late Roman luxury, but most of them strove to, and many had at least modest success. The majority of barbarians on Roman soil must have understood that in order to accumulate such wealth, they had to leave some of the Roman economic and administrative structure in place (Map 10).

Nineteenth-century historians often viewed the Roman lifestyle of the late Vandals as decadence. Like Procopius, they employed this idea of decadence in moralizing ways to explain the fall of the Vandal kingdom, implying that baths, gardens, and theaters put the nation's liberty at risk. Late-twentieth-century historians have preferred the paradigm of acculturation, of romanization of barbarians. Again, perhaps, this model relies too much on the assumption of two distinct cultures, "Roman" and "Germanic." Sixth-century Roman culture is not difficult to conceptualize. In many respects the cultural profile of Justinian's empire shows a surprising homogeneity of forms of expression, for instance in church architecture, funeral inscriptions, administrative hierarchies, or the writing of polite letters – although in other respects, the distance between the refined "Roman" court culture of Constantinople and the civilization of "Roman" villages in the Alps, along the Danube, or in northern Gaul was immense.

But what exactly was "Germanic" culture in former Roman provinces? Certainly not Gelimer's lyre, and perhaps not even Totila's gold-plated armor. Among the population of however remote Germanic origin, many spoke Germanic dialects, but others Latin or even Greek. "Germanic" names were still widely, if not exclusively given, but there is no trace of any corresponding sense of Germanic identity, or of any specifically Germanic cultural sphere. Not surprisingly, the only longer text preserved in a Germanic language from late antiquity is Wulfila's Gothic translation of the Bible in a manuscript from Ostrogothic Italy, the luxurious sixth-century *Codex Argenteus*. By contrast, the Gothic origin myth was written down in Latin by the Roman senator Cassiodorus. Barbarians might be Germanic or classical pagans, Arians or even Catholics, and most likely they did not care to distinguish neatly among all of those creeds. Some buried their dead with grave goods, others the Roman way, and their costume and attire often was a mix of Roman and barbarian taste that had come to distinguish the ambitious specialized warriors on whose courage and abilities power was built, regardless of their origin. In sixth-century material culture, therefore, one can hardly distinguish between "Germanic" and "non-Germanic." Just as a barbarian king would do, the Byzantine commander Narses, before the battle at Busta Gallorum, incited his soldiers by "holding in the air bracelets and necklaces and golden bridles on poles and displaying other incentives to bravery in the coming struggle."[9]

As far as the origin of its soldiers was concerned, the Roman army of the sixth century was perhaps the most barbarian of all.[10] This is what Procopius has King Totila say in his speech to his army before the battle at the Busta Gallorum: "The vast number of the enemy [i.e., the Roman army] is worthy only to be despised, seeing that they present a collection of men from the greatest possible number of nations," for instance Huns, Heruls, and Lombards.[11] Discipline was always an issue in the wars fought under Justinian. When the general Belisarius on the way to the Vandal war had two Huns executed for murder committed in a drunken brawl, some of his barbarian units maintained that it was "not to be subject to the laws of the Romans that they had entered the alliance."[12] And when the Lombard contingents returned to their homeland in Pannonia after the victory at Busta Gallorum, "they kept setting fire to whatever buildings they chanced upon and violating by force the women who had taken refuge in the sanctuaries."[13] Especially those barbarians fighting under their own leaders, or even their own kings (such as the Heruls who fought on the Byzantine side in the Gothic War), did not regard themselves so much as subjects of the emperor as his allies. Barbarians fought barbarians in Justinian's wars, and often all of them received Roman money for most of the time.

Sixth-century authors were quite aware of the problems this entailed and sometimes lamented the times when Roman citizens had fended for themselves and had been regarded as unsurpassed in their courage. On the other hand, the army had been predominantly barbarian for well over three centuries, and the Christian empire, in spite of all setbacks, had remained the hegemonic power in the Mediterranean world. There was no shortage of men willing and able to fight for the empire, as long as money was available for their pay.[14] The long-term structural problems of having to maintain a force of hundreds of thousands of soldiers mostly of barbarian origin were not unknown to contemporary observers. Civil society tended to consider soldiers a nuisance at best, regardless of whom they fought for. Procopius's emphatic description of the disciplined behavior of the Byzantine troops when they entered Carthage in 533 makes it very clear that normally "Roman soldiers were not accustomed to enter a subject city without confusion," insolence, or threat.[15] When they stormed Naples in 535, "a great slaughter took place," and the Byzantine soldiers behaved as soldiers normally did, killing men, raping women, and selling the survivors into slavery.[16] This corresponded to old prejudices against barbarians, but the only distinction was not between Romans and barbarians any more: on the one hand, there were relatively disciplined troops (including Goths, Vandals, and other "integrated" barbarians) who behaved badly. On the other hand, there were those who were more savage, for instance Huns, Heruls, or Lombards (whether in imperial service or not), who behaved worse, killing men and raping women, even in churches. The imperial authorities who had sent these troops could hardly inspire a sense that these were "their" troops in the Roman population. Additionally, the financial load of maintaining such a huge army burdened the Roman taxpayers, and overtaxation and shortage in funds for the costs of war constantly threatened this balance from both sides. After the victory against the Vandals in 534, just as after the initial triumph against the Goths in 540, the arrival of Roman tax officials soon eroded loyalties with the empire among the Roman population. The administrator Alexander, called "the Scissors," became an emblem in Italy of the hated Byzantine bureaucracy. The empire's means to finance imperial politics were limited. Ironically, it was Justinian's political success that, in the long run, made things much worse, because it overstretched the empire's resources.

## Barbarian "Kingdoms of the Empire"

When, in the fifth century, barbarian kingdoms had formed on Roman territory, their kings had mostly been barbarian generals in Roman service, or at least holders of high imperial titles.[17] They were, to a varying degree, members of a Romano-barbarian military aristocracy, and in many respects, Gothic or Burgundian kings resembled the "last Roman" Aetius and other commanders of Roman origin. There was, however, a difference. Roman generals may have had their private armies. For example, during Justinian's reign, Belisarius commanded a strong force of his own. But the loyalty of these troops to their commander was personal, and after his death they were disbanded or entered the service of another powerful man. Roman armies sometimes also had a strong sense of loyalty to a successful commander and might even raise him as an emperor, but such constellations had no lasting impact, either. After the victories of Belisarius against Vandals and Goths, there was gossip that he might usurp the kingdom or even revive the western empire, but he wisely abstained from such ambitions.[18] When Belisarius left Africa, two other officers in Roman service, Stotzas and Gontharis, made bids for kingship, but both failed quickly.[19] No kingdom without a people had any lasting success. The only exception was Odoacer, who took power in Italy in 476 and sent the last western emperor into exile. His power was based on an army composed of smaller ethnic groups from the middle Danube, in whom he inspired some sense of belonging, not least by keeping his own identity ambiguous. But when Theoderic, king of the Ostrogoths, attacked in 493, Odoacer's kingdom collapsed after fierce resistance.

All other kingdoms established on Roman soil were ethnically defined. Often, their kings also carried an ethnic title, such as *rex Vandalorum* (king of the Vandals), although that was not always the case (Theoderic simply styled himself as *rex*, because an ethnic definition might have estranged his non-Gothic Italian subjects, Romans or barbarians).[20] Ethnic solidarities seem to have prevented dissolution of barbarian armies in times of crisis, and Gothic history offers numerous examples of this cohesion. Traditional research has taken the ethnic character of barbarian kingdoms for granted – it regarded Goths or Vandals as rather homogeneous and self-assured peoples who had come from the forests of Germania to establish their kingdoms on Roman soil. Only recently, historians and archaeologists have begun to understand the complex process in which both barbarian kingdoms and identities were formed on Roman territory.[21]

All barbarian kingdoms of the fifth and sixth centuries carried names that had already been known for centuries. Most of them (Goths, Vandals, Burgundians, Lombards, Suebi) were from the first century AD or earlier, and some, such as the Franks and the Alamanni, appeared in the third century AD. However, migrations, social transformation seen especially in the rise of specialized warriors, and the arrival in Roman provinces dramatically changed the composition of these groups and led to a crisis of identity. The impact of the Huns between about 375 and the death of Attila in 453 further destabilized many ethnic communities. It was only after at least a generation of experience in a late Roman environment and a long process of integration that any barbarian group succeeded in establishing a relatively stable kingdom on Roman territory. Only barbarian groups that had sooner or later been accepted as federates (allies of the empire) and had continued to negotiate in spite of recurrent armed conflict could eventually reach the necessary degree of stability. The Visigoths, for example, had crossed the lower Danube in 375–376 and were settled in southwestern Gaul in 418, where their kingdom could finally find a solid basis. The Vandals crossed the Rhine in 406–407, together with the Alans and Suebi; after a troubled period on the Iberian penisula, Geiseric's kingdom gained firm ground with the conquest of Carthage in 439. The Burgundians had been precariously settled west of the Rhine soon after the Vandals had crossed it, but only when Aetius moved them to the region around Geneva and Lyon could the kingdom of the Gibichung dynasty become more firmly entrenched. The Frankish kings had been regional commanders in northwestern Gaul for at least a generation before Clovis, with brutality, cunning, and the support of Roman bishops, established a unified Frankish kingdom in Gaul under the rule of the Merovingian family around 500. At around the same time, in 493, Theoderic founded the kingdom of the Ostrogoths in Italy after defeating Odoacer, forty years after his Goths had entered the province of Pannonia and twenty years after he had led them into the Balkan provinces and the hinterland of Constantinople.

All of these kingdoms relied on extensive cooperation between barbarian military elites and the Roman population, represented by civilian officials and, increasingly, by Catholic bishops.[22] Ostrogothic rule in Italy, most notably, was based on a lasting alliance with the senate of Rome, and some of its most conspicuous members, such as Cassiodorus and Liberius, were responsible for the smooth functioning of the civil administration. Although himself a heretic and "Arian," in the polemic terminology of the day, Theoderic's advice was sought when the papacy was troubled by the Laurentian schism in the beginning of the sixth century. In Gaul, bishops such as Caesarius of Arles, Avitus of Vienne, and Remigius of Reims supported, advised, and also admonished Visigothic, Burgundian, and Frankish kings. The Vandals had been relatively less integrated when they came to Africa and received additional negative publicity from orthodox authors when the successors of Geiseric, in the late fifth century, launched a pro-Arian policy with repressive measures against the Catholic hierarchy. Victor of Vita dwelt on the barbarian and ruthless character of Vandal rule, but his main worries in fact were that a consensus between the Vandal elite and important parts of the Roman population could thus be reached at the expense of the Catholic clergy.[23] And in any case, Huneric's anti-Catholic measures were only based on imperial law originally directed against the Arians.

In all kingdoms, barbarians were a small minority, and among them, only a part had come into the country as members of the conquering ethnic group. To belong to the ruling gens entailed privilege, for instance the *libertas Gothorum*, or "Gothic freedom," as it was called in the Ostrogothic kingdom.[24] Therefore, access to the dominant identity was both sought for and restricted. In the long run, successful kingdoms would see the expansion of their leading identities to include increasing parts of the subject population. Social mobility in both directions would allow descendants of Romans or of other barbarian peoples to rise into the dominant social and ethnic group, but at the same time some of the offspring of the conquerors became poor or lost their status of free citizens. Both processes threatened to unsettle the balance of the rule of an armed minority. Living in Roman provinces that were still relatively wealthy spurred the ambitions of many, and often sharp internal conflict fatally weakened the barbarian kingdoms. These were the opportunities that Justinian exploited in the case of the Ostrogoths and the Vandals. At the same time, the transformation of the ethnic communities on Roman soil progressed fast. Their identity was regarded as derived from noble and ancient origins – a point explicitly propagated by Theoderic's Roman aide, Cassiodorus – but the old names described a new reality, responding to the need of giving a common focus to a new military elite of rather varied descendance.[25]

Given the rather precarious character of the rule of an armed minority over the population of Roman provinces, it is surprising to see how little resistance from the majority of the population most barbarian regimes actually encountered. One reason must have been that loyalties to the late Roman imperial system had already weakened. To many provinces, barbarian rule in fact brought political consolidation, putting an end to incessant factional struggle. The two first barbarian rulers of Italy, Odoacer and Theoderic, taken together reigned for more than half a century without major opposition (except for the war they fought against each other). Such a long period of peace had been unimaginable under the late western emperors, when civil war had hardly ever stopped, even during the reigns of the most successful rulers, Constantine and Theodosius "the Great."

A second reason for the widespread loyalty to barbarian rulers was that the settlement of barbarian soldiers did not impinge too heavily on the civil population. The debate about the modalities of barbarian accommodation so far seems to indicate that there was not a single model of how barbarians received their share of wealth.[26] Regardless of whether they received tax shares (as often seems to have been the case initially) or land (which was inevitable as a long-term solution), or tax income from specific landowners that gradually came to be regarded as land rent, barbarian warriors more or less enjoyed the social positions Roman soldiers had always occupied, though they received a rather lower percentage of the redistributed wealth.

Most of the peoples in whose name new kingdoms had been established were, in the sense of nineteenth-century scholarship, "Germanic." That means they originally spoke a Germanic language and had once lived in or near "Germania," the territories beyond the Rhine and Danube not ruled by Rome. This definition continues to inspire misleading ideas about their common cultural identity. But exactly at the point when "Germanic" peoples began to enter the Empire on a massive scale at the end of the fourth century, the term "Germani" lost its meaning. By the time of Justinian, the Franks were identified with the "Germani" – or rather, that was regarded as their ancient name. The inclusive term, never as popular in the Greek east as in the Latin west, disappeared from contemporary use. Goths, Gepids, often the Vandals, and also the non-Germanic Alans were called "Gothic peoples" and, if at all, subsumed under the category of Scythians, not Germans. And indeed, as already observed above, what modern scholars have regarded as "Germanic" in the post-Roman kingdoms was in reality far from any common culture and identity.[27] The barbarian element in the post-Roman regna (kingdoms) was far from being purely Germanic. The Vandal kings in Africa, for instance, prided themselves of the title *rex Vandalorum et Alanorum* (king of the Vandals and Alans), and the Lombard invasion in Italy in 568 comprised Sarmatians, Bulgarians and Roman provincials along with "Germanic" Lombards and "Gothic" Gepids.

In short, these were Christian kingdoms based on late-Roman infrastructure and a high degree of Latin literacy. The wealth of historiographic and hagiographic texts, of law codes and letters, of poetry and inscriptions, of philosophical and theological writings transmitted to us from most of them is hardly inferior to the body of evidence preserved from the period of the late Roman Empire before it. The economy had been through a period of decline in the fifth century, which becomes visible in the drop in long-distance trade and the crisis of the cities in many parts of the West.[28] Yet in the first decades of the sixth century, recovery seemed possible. Although there were sixth-century authors who began to regard the end of empire in the west as a fatal development,[29] on the whole, little seemed to indicate that the ancient world had come to an end.

To call the post-Roman states around the western Mediterranean in the time of Justinian "barbarian kingdoms" may thus be a little misleading. Of course, their ruling elites were, in the eyes of a Roman, barbarians, and thus corresponded to an old stereotype through which classical civilization had stylized its perceptions of the world beyond its frontiers. Barbarians living in the heartlands of the Mediterranean world had, however, always been a well-known phenomenon. They would always remain barbarians even though they might successfully adapt to Greek or Roman ways. That barbarians had actually seized power in some of the core areas of the Roman world was certainly regarded as a threat, or as divine punishment. But in the sixth century, one might still be confident that most of them would become as thoroughly romanized as the Vandals described by Procopius, or that they would, as Pope Pelagius II uttered after the Lombard invasion, soon "pass like smoke."[30] In that sense, Justinian simply intended to remove what the Romans of his day considered an anomaly: barbarian rule over the heartlands of the Roman state. At the same time, these barbarian rulers had long become familiar members of a Christian elite who knew as well as the emperor and his officials how to govern Roman provinces.

## POST-ROMAN KINGDOMS IN THE AGE OF JUSTINIAN

In 500, the barbarian kingdoms in the west seemed to be thriving: the Ostrogoths in Italy under Theoderic, the Franks in northern Gaul under Clovis, the Burgundians in the Loire valley under Gundobad, the Visigoths in southern Gaul and Spain under Alaric II, and the Vandals in Africa under Thrasamund (Map 11). Conflict was, however, imminent. When Justinian succeded to the throne in 527, the Visigoths had been pushed out of most of Gaul by the Franks (508), and the Burgundians would, within a few years, also succumb to Frankish power (531–534). The sons of Clovis, among whom the Frankish kingdom had been partitioned, continued the expansionist policy of their father. The demonstrative pro-Catholic stance of the Merovingians won them the active support of Gallic bishops, and the sympathy of the Byzantines; Agathias wrote that of all the barbarian peoples, the Franks were most like the Romans in almost every way: "Their system of government, administration and laws are modelled more or less on the Roman pattern, apart from which they uphold similar standards with regard to contracts, marriage and religious observance. They are in fact all Christians and adhere to the strictest orthodoxy. They also have magistrates in their cities and priests and celebrate the feasts in the same way as we do, and, for a barbarian people, strike me as extremely well-bred and civilized

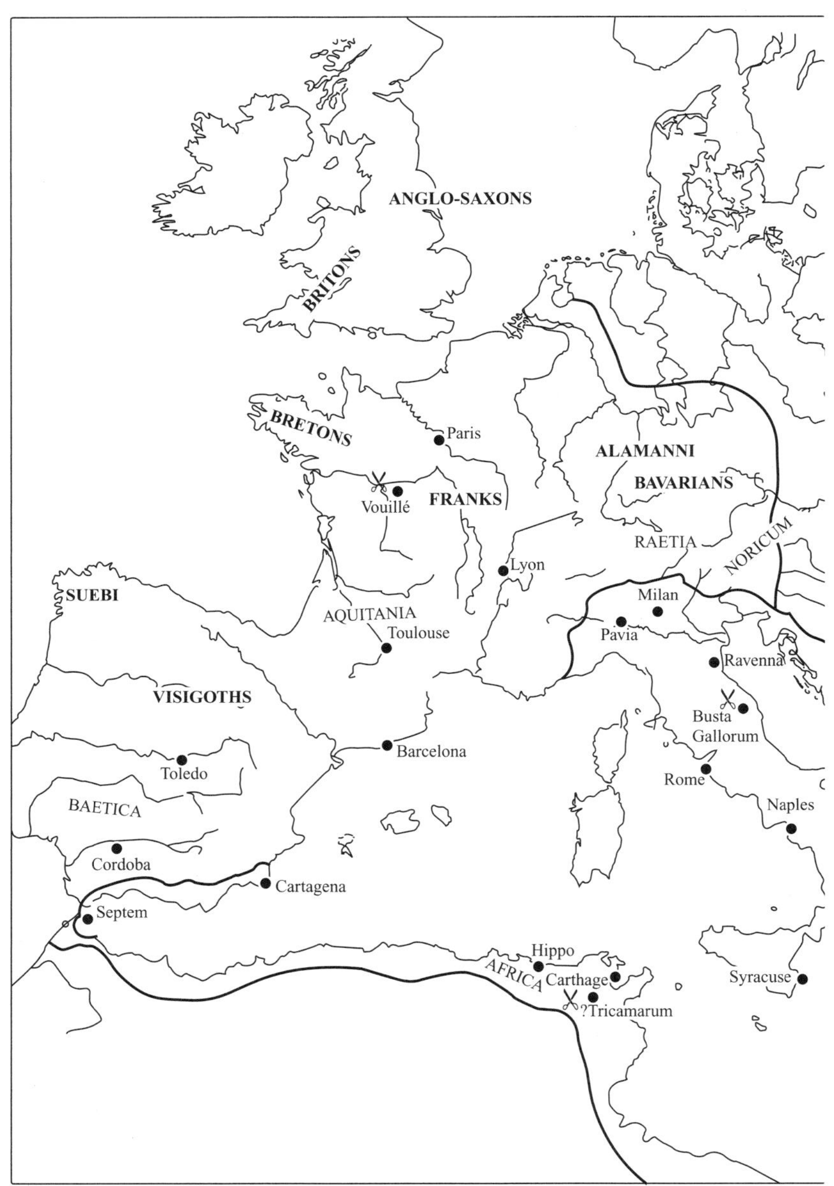


MAP 11. Kingdoms after the conquest

and practically the same as ourselves except for their uncouth style of dress and peculiar language."[31]

In the fifth century, the Franks had been minor players in the periphery of the empire in northeastern Gaul; now they established a

regional hegemony and put all their neighbors under constant pressure, extending their sphere of influence as far as Pannonia, the North Sea, and the Mediterranean.[32] Rather than seeing the Merovingian kings as barbarians from Germania who had overrun Roman Gaul, we can see them as having achieved what Rome had not been able to do in half a millennium: they were in fact the first rulers of Gaul to control wide regions east of the Rhine, a periphery of proud peoples who, being cut off from the richer provinces of the empire, lacked the resources to compete with the Franks. Clovis had already subdued the Alamanni in the southwestern Germania. In the 530s, the Thuringian kingdom under Herminafrid, a faithful ally of the Ostrogoths, was crushed. The Saxons to the north had to accept Frankish overlordship, and the newly formed people of the Bavarians came to be ruled by dukes imposed by Frankish kings.[33] King Theudebert I (534–547) proudly claimed that he would march on Constantinople, uniting all barbarian peoples under his banner. But in reality, Byzantines and Franks had little reason for conflict and shared a number of common political interests, notably against the barbarian rulers of Italy.

In Italy, Theoderic's death in 526 opened a cycle of crisis.[34] Already in the last years of his rule, the long-established consensus with the Gothic regime among senators and bishops had begun to erode.[35] Senatorial factions in Rome, worried about the prospect of a succession crisis after the death of the king who had no son, began to turn to Constantinople for support. Theoderic reacted harshly against what he perceived as treason, but the death penalties against Symmachus and the highborn philosopher Boethius only made things worse. Theoderic's daughter Amalasuintha, who ruled during her son Athalaric's minority, had to face opposition from a reactionary faction of noble Goths who claimed that integration had been pushed too far, and that traditional Gothic values should be maintained. When young Athalaric died, Amalasuintha attempted to stabilize her regime by sharing the rule with her unpopular, and thoroughly romanized, cousin Theodahad. But in an unexpected move, he sided with the opposition to remove her from power, late in 534.

Similar conflicts of succession shook the Vandal kingdom in the early 530s.[36] Geiseric, who had reigned in Africa for almost half a century (d. 477), had established a particular system of succession in his family, called tanistry by modern scholars after old Irish parallels.[37] According to this system, the oldest surviving member of all branches of Geiseric's family was destined to rule, normally at the expense of the son of a deceased king. For a few decades, this system prevented open conflict over the succession. But in 530, Gelimer, although the probable successor of the reigning king Hilderic, overthrew the ruler who enjoyed excellent contacts with Justinian and the support of the Catholic bishops. In spite of protests from Constantinople, Gelimer systematically extinguished Hilderic's branch of the family, the descendants of the Theodosian princess Eudocia. Justinian waited for peace with Persia, but in 533, against the warnings of influential circles in Constantinople, sent a fleet of 500 ships and 30,000 sailors carrying an army of 10,000 infantry and 5,000 cavalry under the command of Belisarius to attack the Vandal kingdom. Previous Byzantine attempts to recapture Carthage in the fifth century had failed miserably, but this time, fortune was with them. Although numerically inferior, Justinian's army soon overcame Vandal resistance in 533–534 and reestablished direct Roman rule in one of the richest provinces of the empire.

Late in 534 the Ostrogothic king Theodahad staged his coup against Amalasuintha. He knew this could serve as a pretext for Justinian's intervention and tried to negotiate, but without any clear strategy. In 535, the emperor unleashed his successful armies against the Goths in Italy. Even at an early stage in the war, the resistance of many major Italian cities against the invaders showed that Gothic rule was well rooted in the peninsula. The "Roman" invaders from the east were often regarded as "Greeks," whereas many Italians remained loyal to the Goths as defenders of the "Roman" population in Italy. Naples closed its gates to the army of Belisarius and was taken only after a bloody siege. Rome changed hands several times. Soon the civilian population suffered heavy casualties. Cities and their water supplies were destroyed, and the population of stormed cities massacred or sold off as slaves. The defeated military garrisons, however, were usually treated honorably and sometimes even received into the victorious army. In 539, a Frankish army intervened and devastated parts of northern Italy. When the Gothic king Witigis, successor to the unfortunate Theodahad, surrendered in Ravenna in 540, most parts of the peninsula had suffered heavy damage from the war.

Worse was yet to come. The reintroduction of direct Byzantine rule and the arrival of the tax officials provoked such opposition that within a year or two Italy flared up in rebellion, and the new Gothic king Totila successfully recaptured most of the peninsula. In his detailed account of the vicissitudes of the Gothic war, Procopius portrays the gradual collapse of the ancient landscape in the old heartland of the empire. Destruction of the infrastructure, the decimation of the population, hunger, and the plague affected region after region, and only a few parts were better off (among them Ravenna, which remained in Byzantine hands). The impact on the city of Rome was also massive: the destruction of most aqueducts, the end of the senate, and a sharp drop in population made the effects of the war on the ancient capital much more sustained than the sack by the Visigoths in 410 or by the Vandals in 455. Paradoxically, Justinian's attempt to bring back Roman rule to Rome and Italy did more damage than any of the barbarian invasions the peninsula had endured so far and weakened the basis for Roman restoration considerably. Even after his decisive victory against Totila in 552, Justinian's successful general Narses, who remained in Italy, had to face remaining Gothic resistance, a Frankish-Alamannic invasion, a Herul uprising and other threats. When the Lombards invaded Italy in 568, they encountered hardly any organized resistance. The peninsula had been impoverished and fragmented, and Byzantium could hope to control only its coastal areas and the imperial cities of Ravenna and Rome.[38]

The Frankish defeat of the Visigothic kingdom at the battle of Vouillé in 508 led to a crisis of the Visigothic monarchy.[39] Against Visigothic resistance, Theoderic, king of the Ostrogoths, took the Visigothic throne as well. Soon after his death, the Ostrogothic governor Theudis, who had married a rich Roman heiress and could thus afford a considerable private army, grabbed power and ruled until 548. When Vandals and Ostrogoths came under attack from the Byzantines, he ignored their pleas for help. The Visigoths now ruled over most of the Iberian peninsula. Only the northwest, a region too remote for other powers to dispute, remained under the control of the Suebian kingdom. The Visigothic strip of Gallic coastline around Narbonne was in easy reach of Frankish armies and repeatedly contested. In spite of the extension of the realm, the military capacities of the Visigothic kingdom were limited. Thus, when Theudis attempted to exploit the difficulties that the Byzantines faced in the Gothic war in the mid-540s for an attack on Septem/Ceuta, to control both sides of the Strait of Gibraltar, he was defeated.

When Theudis was murdered in 548, a series of bitter inner conflicts ensued. Under King Agila (549–554), a civic uprising in Cordoba and the rebellion of Athanagild, supported by the Roman aristocracy in Baetica, shook the south of the kingdom. It is not unlikely that they were quite deliberately providing a case for Byzantine intervention; Athanagild appealed for help to Justinian, who promptly sent an army under Liberius in 552. At the time, Liberius was in his late eighties; he had already supervised the accommodation of the Ostrogoths in Italy in 493 and had served Theoderic and Amalasuintha until she was murdered, so he must have enjoyed some reputation among the Goths. Procopius, however, had a low opinion of his military talents. His appointment indicates that Justinian's expedition was hardly intended to subdue the third barbarian kingdom around the western Mediterranean completely, but rather to establish some presence there, to hold Visigothic offensive plans in check, and to interfere, if possible, in their internal conflicts. The Byzantine force occupied the city of Carthago Spartaria, modern Cartagena, and other towns along the southeastern coast of the peninsula, but they soon encountered resistance from their former ally Athanagild, who prevailed in the struggle for kingship. The extent of Byzantine territories should not be overestimated, but they provided a basis from which to exert some influence in the rich and conflict-ridden province of Baetica; the last Byzantine strongholds were recaptured by the Visigoths only around 624.[40]

Justinian's attacks demonstrated the vulnerability of the barbarian kingdoms around the Mediterranean. These kingdoms had provided some stability after the turmoil during much of the fifth century and had more or less left Roman infrastructures, and the Roman elites, in place, giving them some degree of autonomy in civic life. Still, the barbarian kings had to preserve a double consensus, within their own, predominantly barbarian armies, and among Roman *possessores* (wealthy landholders) and aristocrats. Of course, successful barbarians had become wealthy landowners, too, and adopted a late Roman lifestyle, like the noble Vandals Procopius describes. But that created new tensions between those barbarians who had and those who had not (or rather, not so fully) embraced Roman ways. In the long run, barbarian rulers faced the same problems of eroding loyalty that the western Emperors before them had not been able to overcome. Even so, inner dissent would never have been sufficient to change the system. The question was who would defend it when it came under attack from outside.

Just as barbarian invasions had done away with Roman rule in the fifth century, Roman invasions now toppled the barbarian kings who had replaced it, exploiting similar fault lines within the system. The initial success, both in Africa and in Italy, was remarkable. But in many respects, the renewed Byzantine regime was more unstable than the barbarian kingdoms it had swept away; before long, much of Italy would fall to the Lombards, and Byzantine Africa would eventually be overwhelmed by the Islamic expansion. Problems started immediately after the reconquest. It is no coincidence that the decisive victory at Tricamarum and the collapse of the Vandal kingdom are described almost exactly in the middle of Procopius's history of the Vandal war; the rest is an account of the problems of reestablishing Roman rule – something historians overlook. Berber attacks, rivalries and conflicts among the new elite, and rebellions of Byzantine troops undermined

Justinian's success in north Africa. Victory against the Ostrogoths came after five years, with the capitulation of Witigis in 540, but then, sparked by massive resistance to Byzantine restoration, the war dragged on for another thirteen years. It was the fiercest resistance put up by any of the barbarian kingdoms in the Mediterranean, showing that half a century of Ostrogothic rule had permeated late Roman society more deeply than in the other kingdoms. The Visigothic kingdom collapsed after a single battle had been lost against the Islamic conquerors in 711, and the Lombards were subdued by Charlemagne in 774 after a prolonged siege of their capital at Pavia.

## BARBARIANS OF THE NORTH

In Justinian's day, communication between Byzantium and the kingdoms of the Vandals, Goths, and Franks was still intense, and there was a sense that they were all part of a Roman and Christian world with its focus in Constantinople. But there were numerous barbarian peoples beyond that sphere of late Roman civilization who still regarded the empire as the center of their ambitions, whether as allies or as enemies (which most of them were in turn, or even simultaneously) (Map 12). Power among the external barbarians depended to a considerable extent on a steady flow of gold and precious objects from Byzantium. Warlords could maintain their positions only by satisfying their warriors' ambitions, by giving them both opportunities for deeds of valor and for plunder and extensive gifts in times of peace. The Roman subsidies and presents fed into this circulation of prestige goods, whether these were directly of Roman origin or reworked by barbarian craftsmen. Successful leadership among the barbarians beyond the frontiers, where the late Roman economy could not be directly exploited, thus depended on a well-calculated balance between attacks on Roman provinces and treaties and negotiations with the emperor. Whether local warlords, kings of medium-sized barbarian peoples, or rulers of huge steppe empires, barbarian leaders depended on the riches of the late Roman world. On the other hand, the Byzantine Empire depended on the barbarians' moderation in both raids and negotiations, and on the diligence of diplomacy in maintaining the balance between the warlords and the empire, and thus holding them in check.[41]

The sixth century was a period of unusually far-reaching political contacts and perspectives. For instance, the horizon of Byzantine diplomacy routinely included the steppe empires to the north of Sasanian

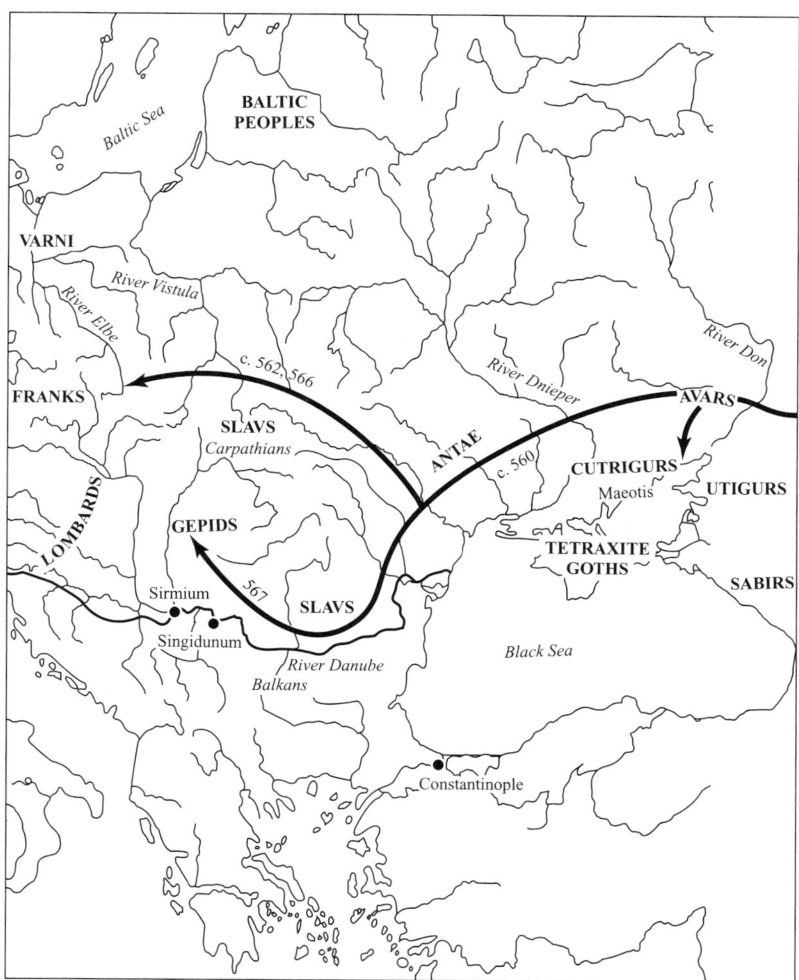


MAP 12. Northern barbarians, c. 560

Persia. The successors of Justinian even established regular relations with the newly founded khaganate of the Turks, with its center near the T'ien-shan mountains. But even barbarian rulers on Roman territory had contacts far beyond the old frontiers of the empire. Theoderic the Ostrogoth had a diplomatic exchange with the south coast of the Baltic Sea, and the Heruls of Singidunum sent envoys to the Isle of Thule, probably southern Scandinavia, to invite a prince from their supposed ancient homeland to become their king.[42] Close relations between north and south, east and west are also attested in the archaeological evidence; for instance, gold bracteates (coinlike medallions) from Scandinavia and the "Germanic" animal style of decoration were distributed over almost all of Europe.[43]

Some regions that had for a long time been part of the Roman world had, however, become less accessible and more remote. The British Isles are an obvious example.[44] Since Roman troops withdrew in the beginning of the fifth century, Britain had come to be associated with barbarism, heresy, and dark legends. Procopius recounts a grisly story how sailors living along the south coast of the English Channel had to ship the souls of the dead across to Britain at night.[45] However, late Roman life did not come to an end entirely when the empire withdrew its troops. Regional Romano-British kingdoms withstood Pictish and Irish attacks and engaged Saxons and Angles as federates.[46] Soon these immigrants from the continent, including Frisians and Jutes, established their own kingdoms in the east of England, while the British kings continued to rule over much of the western parts of the island. Latin inscriptions, even with proper consular dating, can still be found in the sixth century, even in remote parts of Wales. And Gildas's work *The Destruction of Britain*, written between the late fifth and the mid–sixth centuries, for all its lament about the ruin of Britain demonstrates a surprising continuity of Latin education and Christian literacy in the British kingdoms.[47] A Frankish embassy that arrived in Constantinople under Justinian brought a few Angles from Britain to bolster their claim of overlordship over the island. This was surely exaggerated, but relations between the Franks and the kingdoms of Angles and Saxons must have been rather close.[48] From a Byzantine perspective, though, both Britain and the recently Christianized Ireland were only a very remote concern.

Another part of the empire where the Roman infrastructure had more or less collapsed in the fifth century was the middle Danube region; but here, the interest of Byzantine diplomacy was much more immediate. This was a region where, since the late fourth century, barbarian groups had built up their strength, waiting for an opportunity to march into Italy or the Balkan provinces.[49] As long as the Ostrogothic kingdom controlled the southern parts of Pannonia and held the ancient imperial residence of Sirmium, situated on the Save river west of Singindunum (Belgrade), Justinian was not particularly concerned with the region, except for the small and unstable federate kingdom of the Heruls near Singindunum. But soon after the Gothic war began, the Gepids, whose kingdom stretched along the Tisza river and into the ancient province of Dacia, occupied Sirmium.[50] The strategic position along the road that connected the Balkans with Italy became especially important when Justinian changed his strategy in the Gothic war in the late 540s and planned to send an army to Italy overland instead of reinforcements by sea.

Justinian sought new allies to hold the Gepids in check and concluded a treaty with the Lombards under King Audoin. They had settled along the Danube west of Vienna in the 490s and gradually extended their kingdom into Pannonia. Justinian now granted them the province of Pannonia and parts of Noricum, a diplomatic gesture that did not give them anything they had not had before but amounted to encouraging them in the imminent conflict with their Gepid neighbors. Procopius gives a detailed account of the events and even includes well-written speeches by the Lombard and Gepid ambassadors who appear in turn to ask Justinian for support.[51] This literary stylization of a conflict between two kingdoms in the middle Danube region dramatizes a situation in which the emperor can play off two barbarian kingdoms of roughly equal power against each other, and in which both point to their federate (allied) status and their loyalty to the Byzantines to achieve some armed help. That Justinian could offer military support in a war between barbarians was quite unusual and due to the buildup of an army in Illyricum that was destined to march into Italy as soon as possible. Justinian, predictably, decided to support the Lombards, but the Byzantine troops in the area remained more or less aloof. In the years 549–552, three wars between Lombards and Gepids ended with Audoin's victory. He soon reestablished friendly relations with Gepid neighbors. War broke out again after Justinian's death, ending in the destruction of the Gepid kingdom in 567. This gave the Lombard king Alboin the military resources necessary to invade Italy in the following year.

North of the lower Danube, but also in the northern and southern foothills of the Carpathian mountains, a new people had established itself in the course of the sixth century: the Slavs. They were first noticed during Justinian's reign, when they began to attack the Balkan provinces, alone or in alliances with Huns or Gepids. They formed no "barbarian kingdoms" at all but rather lived in small rural communities or regional confederacies. Occasionally larger groups would join their forces for a raid on imperial territory. The origin, expansion, and identity of the early Slavs is one of the major historiographic problems of the period.[52] The old model of large-scale Slavic migrations from an "original homeland" (of hotly debated location) was built largely on speculation and on the fact that Jordanes also called the Slavs "Venethi." That is not proof of any ethnic continuity between the Venethi mentioned by early imperial authors and the Slavs, but simply the traditional name used for their eastern neighbours by speakers of Germanic languages – and Jordanes knew his Gothic.

In many respects, the Slavic expansion that gained momentum under Justinian, and that led to the Slavicization of great parts of eastern Europe within less than a century after his death, constituted an alternative to the barbarian kingdoms founded on Roman territory by highly specialized and hierarchy-minded warriors who exploited late Roman infrastructure and aimed at winning prestige, high status, and wealth. Social differentiation among the early Slavs took a long time to develop. Hierarchies were precarious and political power was always contested, so that most known leaders of early Slavic groups were in fact of foreign origin, such as the impostor who claimed to be the Roman general Chilbudios or the Gepid pretender Hildigis.[53] The rural Slavic communities must have offered an attractive alternative of peasant life in personal freedom to many disappointed lower-class barbarians and Romans.[54] Byzantine and western perceptions of a broad Slavic identity probably played a part in the spread of these identities,[55] as it had done with the "Germani" in the days of Julius Caesar and Augustus. Unlike the Germans of the early imperial age, however, names of specific ethnic groups were late to appear among the Slavs (with the exception of the Antae east of the Carpathians, who were seen as related to the Slavs). The reign of Justinian witnessed the first wave of Slavic raids into the Balkan provinces, which contributed to the growing sense of insecurity in the European hinterland of Constantinople in his later years.

In the steppes north of the Black Sea, Hunnic peoples – the name designates their common steppe culture, rather than any common origin – continued to live in a delicate balance of power between Cutrigurs, Utigurs, Bulgars, and others. For a while, the Cutrigurs were the most aggressive, advancing as far as the Long Wall of Constantinople on a major raid led by Zabergan in 559. Justinian had to ask the retired general Belisarius to lead an improvised force against the barbarians.[56] He also instigated the Utigurs to plunder the homeland of the Cutrigurs.[57] The situation is characteristic of the later years of Justinian. Diplomacy and money were employed to keep a delicate balance along the northern frontier. Subsidies of a few tens of thousands of solidi were routinely paid, implicitly as a price to keep the peace. Additional gifts and payments motivated barbarians to attack other enemies of the empire.

In the last years of Justinian's reign the balance of smaller powers along the northern frontiers of the empire was shattered by the arrival of a new steppe people, the Avars.[58] They were a heterogeneous group of fugitives from the expanding Turkish power in central Asia. The Avars' westward momentum brought them to the European plains as victorious builders of a new steppe empire. In 558, they arrived north of the Caucasus and at once sent an embassy to Justinian with a request for an alliance and subsidies, and with the promise to destroy his enemies. Justinian, as Menander remarks, accepted their offer, considering that "whether the Avars prevailed or were defeated, both eventualities would be to the Romans' advantage."[59] This seemingly sober judgment turned out to be a serious mistake. In the following years, the Avars subdued all the other northern barbarians group by group: Sabirs, Utigurs, Cutrigurs, Bulgars, Antae, Slavs, and others. In the early 560s, they reached the lower Danube and increased the pressure on Byzantium, at first without attempting a direct attack; instead, they launched an expedition against the Franks and defeated their King Sigibert near the Elbe river.[60] Within a few years, the Avars had established a hegemony among the northern barbarians, and a monopoly to negotiate with the Byzantines, crushing the balance so studiously maintained by Byzantine diplomacy. Soon after Justinian's death, the victory of the Lombards over the Gepids and their subsequent migration to Italy gave the Avars under their khagan Baian undisputed control over the Carpathian basin, where they established the center of their empire. The successors of Justinian had to face devastating attacks of the Avars, culminating in the siege of Constantinople of 626. Avar raids also opened the gates for Slavic settlements in the Balkan provinces, and eventually for the decay and fall of the Roman order in much of the Balkan peninsula.

## Conclusion

Unlike most late antique emperors, Justinian inspired some confidence that the glory of Rome had finally returned. But the high hopes soon gave way to disappointment, even among those who had supported him. The cost of imperial politics enraged taxpayers, and as it turned out that even spectacular military success could not buy lasting peace and stability, and that not even the capital could feel quite safe from the attack of northern barbarians, harsh judgments of Justinian's policy prevailed. As the bitter polemic of Procopius's *Secret History* makes clear, most of the criticism was directed against individuals (Justinian, Theodora, corrupt officials and incompetent officers) and their intrigues. The imperial pretensions that Justinian's triumphs had blown up beyond measure now prevented a sober assessment of the actual balance of power. If Justinian had brought Gelimer and Witigis to their knees, why did he fail to rid Rome of marauding bands of Huns or Slavs? Even a benevolent critic such as Menander, who looked back to the time of Justinian as a generally more successful period than his own, believed that in old age, Justinian's body was too weak to cope with the barbarians, and "his bold and warlike spirit had become feeble."[61] He had no doubt that otherwise Justinian would have "crushed and utterly destroyed" the Avars.

When Justin II succeded to the throne in the autumn of 565, he was determined to make the barbarians feel imperial power once again. In its description of the harsh reception of an Avar embassy, the panegyric poem that Corippus wrote on occasion of his accession shows the contempt with which barbarians were now to be treated.[62] Justin's display of arrogance and his moratorium on subsidies were to have disastrous consequences. An empire that believes its own propaganda is bound to underestimate its enemies and to create more enemies by treating those who hesitate with contempt. Justinian had been subtler in his handling of barbarians and on the whole more realistic in both war and diplomacy.

What contemporaries did not realize was that Justinian's success had set a dynamic in motion that was bound to undermine it in the end. The emperor had successfully sent his armies against barbarians governing rich provinces where the Byzantine troops could hope for glory and plunder. That had created claims and pretensions among the army and its officers that could hardly be met once the spectacular reconquests were over. Defending the empire against northern barbarians was certainly less rewarding for ambitious soldiers. This is a logic that expansionist politics often follow.

In sixth-century Byzantium, however, a second spiral created growing problems as well. In the early sixth century, the intensity of conflicts was somewhat lower in many parts of the Roman world, the influx of ambitious soldiers into the Empire had diminished, and barbarian societies both inside and outside the empire had become more stable. Justinian's offensives had created new demand for barbarian soldiers and therefore new ambitions that made themselves felt far beyond the frontiers of empire. Once again, barbarians could make a fortune by providing military service. Barbarian communities came under new pressures, and the influence of aggressive warriors who knew how to negotiate with the empire as well as how to exploit its weaknesses grew. As in preceding centuries, Byzantium could not hope to harness all these ambitions to its needs. Conflicts, even between barbarians, became sharper. The Lombard king Wacho (d. 540) was a cautious politician who avoided getting involved in the Gothic war. His successor Audoin risked three wars against the Gepids around 550 but advocated reconciliation after his victory. His son Alboin fought the next Gepid war, 565–567, until the enemy was destroyed, and marched on to Italy. Justinian had defeated barbarians comfortably settled in the heartlands of the Roman world, but he helped create new forces of hungry barbarians who increasingly threatened the empire. His successors would see his empire crumble, but again paradoxically: because of the long-term failure of his barbarian policy, Justinian would soon be remembered mainly for his triumphs against the barbarian kingdoms and not for their long-term consequences.

## Notes

1 Procopius, *Wars*, 8.31. For the context, see H. Wolfram, *History of the Goths* (Berkeley, 1988); Stein, *Bas-Empire*, 2:597–604; P. Heather, *The Goths* (Oxford, 1996), 270ff.; and W. Pohl, *Die Völkerwanderung. Eroberung und Integration* (Stuttgart, 2002).

2 See the fundamental study by J. M. Wallace-Hadrill, *Early Germanic Kingship in England and on the Continent* (Oxford, 1971), and the survey of the sources by M. Reydellet, *La Royauté dans la littérature Latine de Sidoine Apollinaire à Isidore de Séville* (Rome, 1981).

3 Averil Cameron, *Procopius and the Sixth Century* (Berkeley, Calif., 1985).

4 Procopius, *Anecdota*, 30.34.

5 Pohl, *Völkerwanderung;* see also H. Wolfram, *The Roman Empire and Its Germanic Peoples* (Berkeley, 1997).

6 Procopius, *Wars*, 3.25.

7 Procopius, *Wars*, 4.6.

8 Procopius, *Wars*, 4.6.

9 Procopius, *Wars*, 8.31.

10 Cf. P. Southern and K. R. Dixon, *The Late Roman Army* (New Haven, Conn., 1996), 46–52; M. Whitby, "The Army, c. 420–602," *CAH* 14:288–314, esp. 306ff.

11 Procopius, *Wars*, 8.30.

12 Procopius, *Wars*, 3.12.

13 Procopius, *Wars*, 8.33.

14 J. Haldon, *Warfare, State, and Society in the Byzantine World, 565–1024* (London, 1999).

15 Procopius, *Wars*, 3.21.

16 Procopius, *Wars*, 5.10.29; see W. Pohl, "Perceptions of Barbarian Violence," in *Violence in Late Antiquity*, ed. H. Drake, forthcoming.

17 See W. Pohl, ed., *Kingdoms of the Empire: The Integration of Barbarians in Late Antiquity* (Leiden, 1997).

18 Procopius, *Wars*, 4.8: "For some officers slandered him to the Emperor, charging him, without any grounds whatever, with seeking to set up a kingdom [*tyrannis*] for himself"; 6.30.1 (*tyrannis*), 6.30.6 (*Gotthon basileia*).

19 Procopius, *Wars*, 4.15–24 (Stotzas), 4.25–28 (Guntharis).

20 H. Wolfram, *Intitulatio I. Lateinische Königs- und Fürstentitel bis zum Ende des 8. Jahrhunderts* (*Mitteilungen des Instituts Für Österreichische Geschichtsforschung*, Ergänzungsband 21, Köln-Wien, 1967); for a skeptical opinion, see A. Gillett, "Was Ethnicity Politicized in the Earliest Medieval Kingdom?" in *On Barbarian Identity: Critical Approaches to Ethnogenesis Theory*, ed. A. Gillett (Turnhout, 2002), 85–122.

21 W. Pohl, "Telling the Difference: Signs of Ethnic Identity," in *Strategies of Distinction: The Construction of Ethnic Communities, 300–800*, ed. W. Pohl and H. Reimitz, Transformation of the Roman World 2 (Leiden, 1998), 17–69; and W. Pohl, "Ethnicity, Theory, and Tradition: A Response," in *On Barbarian Identity – Critical Approaches to Ethnogenesis Theory*, ed. A. Gillett (Turnhout, 2002), 221–240. See also, using various approaches, H. Wolfram, "Origo et Religio: Ethnic Traditions and Literature in Early Medieval Texts," in *Early Medieval Europe* 3 (1994): 19–38; P. Amory, *People and Identity in Ostrogothic Italy, 489–544* (Cambridge, 1997); and P. J. Geary, *The Myth of Nations: The Medieval Origins of Europe* (Princeton, N. J., 2001).

22 Chalcedonian Christians in Western Europe are conventionally called Catholic.

23 Translation and commentary: Victor of Vita, *History of the Vandal Persecution*, trans. J. Moorhead (Liverpool, 1992).

24 Wolfram, *Goths*.

25 Wolfram, "Origo et Religio"; Pohl, "Ethnicity, Theory, and Tradition."

26 W. Goffart, *Barbarians and Romans A.D., 418–584: The Techniques of Accommodation* (Princeton, N. J., 1980); J. Durliat, *Les finances publiques de Dioclétien aux Carolingiens (284–889)* (Sigmaringen, 1990); W. Liebeschuetz, "Cities, Taxes, and the Accommodation of the Barbarians: The Theories of Durliat and Goffart," and W. Pohl, "The Empire and the Lombards: Treaties and Negotiations in the Sixth Century," both in *Kingdoms of the Empire: The Integration of Barbarians in Late Antiquity*, ed. W. Pohl (Leiden, 1997), 135–152 and 75–134; and H. Wolfram, "Die dauerhafte Ansiedlung der Goten auf römischem Boden. Eine endlose Geschichte," *Mitteilungen des Instituts Für Österreich Geschichtsforschung* 12 (2004) 11–35.

27 W. Pohl, *Die Germanen* (Munich, 2000); and Pohl, *Völkerwanderung*.

28 J. H. W. G. Liebeschuetz, *The Decline and Fall of the Ancient City* (Oxford, 2001); G. P. Brogiolo and B. Ward-Perkins, eds., *The Idea and the Ideal of the Town between Late Antiquity and the Early Middle Ages*, Transformation of the Roman World 4 (Leiden, 1999); C. Wickham, *Land and Power: Studies in Italian and European Social History, 400–1200* (London, 1994), esp. 77–118; R. Hodges and W. Bowden, eds., *The Sixth Century: Production, Distribution, and Demand* (Leiden, 1998).

29 W. Goffart, *Rome's Fall and After* (London, 1989), esp. 81–110.

30 MGH *Ep*, 3.449; Pohl, "The Empire and the Lombards," 101.

31 Agathias, *Histories*, 1.2.

32 I. N. Wood, *The Merovingian Kingdoms, 450–751* (London, 1994); P. J. Geary, *Before France and Germany: The Creation and Transformation of the Merovingian World* (New York, 1988); J. Drinkwater and H. Elton, eds., *Fifth-Century Gaul: A Crisis of*

*Identity?* (Cambridge, 1992); R. Mathisen, *Roman Aristocrats in Barbarian Gaul: Strategies for Survival in an Age of Transition* (Austin, Tex., 1993).

33 I. N. Wood, "The Frontiers of Western Europe: Developments East of the Rhine in the Sixth Century," in Hodges and Bowden, *The Sixth Century*, 231–253.

34 Wolfram, *Goths*; Heather, *Goths*.

35 J. Moorhead, *Theoderic in Italy* (Oxford, 1992).

36 For the history of the Vandal kingdom, see C. Courtois, *Les Vandales et l'Afrique* (Paris, 1955); the essay collection by F. M. Clover, *The Late Roman West and the Vandals* (Aldershot, 1993); *L'Afrique Vandale et Byzantine. Première partie, Antiquité Tardive* 10 (2002); A. Merrills, ed., *Vandals, Romans, and Berbers: New Perspectives on Late Antique Africa* (forthcoming).

37 I. N. Wood, "Royal Succession and Legitimation in the Roman West, 419–536," in *Staat im frühen Mittelalter*, ed. S. Airlie, W. Pohl, and H. Reimitz (Vienna, forthcoming).

38 C. Wickham, *Early Medieval Italy: Central Power and Local Society, 400–1000* (London, 1981); C. La Rocca, ed., *Italy in the Early Middle Ages: Short Oxford History of Medieval Italy* 1 (Oxford, 2002).

39 R. Collins, *Early Medieval Spain: Unity in Diversity, 400–1000* (Basingstoke, Eng., 1995).

40 G. Ripoll, "On the Supposed Frontier between the *Regnum Visigothorum* and Byzantine *Hispania*," in *The Transformation of Frontiers: From Late Antiquity to the Carolingians*, ed. W. Pohl, I. N. Wood, and H. Reimitz (Leiden, 2000).

41 W. Pohl, *Die Awaren. Ein Steppenvolk in Mitteleuropa, 567–822 n. Chr.* (Munich, 2002; English trans. forthcoming). See also J. Shepard and S. Franklin, eds., *Byzantine Diplomacy* (London, 1992).

42 Procopius, *Wars*, 6.15.

43 H. Roth, *Die Kunst der Völkerwanderungszeit*, Propyläen Kunstgeschichte, Ergänzungsband 4 (Frankfurt am Main, 1979).

44 I. N. Wood, "The End of Roman Britain," in *Gildas: New Approaches*, ed. M. Lapidge and D. Dumville (Woodbridge, 1984), 1–26; S. Bassett, ed., *The Origins of Anglo-Saxon Kingdoms* (London, 1989); B. Yorke, *Kings and Kingdoms of Early Anglo-Saxon England* (London, 1990); K. Dark, *Civitas to Kingdom: British Political Continuity, 300–800* (London, 1994); M. E. Jones, *The End of Roman Britain* (Ithaca, N.Y., 1996); E. James, *Britain in the First Millennium* (London, 2000).

45 Procopius, *Wars*, 8.20.

46 E. Chrysos, "Die Römerherrschaft in Britannien und ihr Ende," *Bonner Jahrbücher* 191 (1991): 247–276.

47 M. Lapidge and D. Dumville, eds., *Gildas: New Approaches* (Woodbridge, 1984).

48 Procopius, *Wars*, 8.20.10; cf. I. N. Wood, *The Merovingian North Sea* (Alingsås, 1983).

49 H. Wolfram, *Grenzen und Räume. Geschichte Österreichs vor seiner Entstehung* (Vienna, 1995), 17–70.

50 W. Pohl, "Die Gepiden und die Gentes an der mittleren Donau nach dem Zerfall des Attilareiches," in *Die Völker an der mittleren und unteren Donau im 5. und 6. Jahrhundert*, ed. H. Wolfram and F. Daim (Vienna, 1980), 240–305.

51 Procopius, *Wars*, 7.33–35, 8.18, 8.25, 8.27; Pohl, "The Empire and the Lombards"; Stein, *Bas-Empire*, 2:531.

52 The best overview is P. M. Barford, *The Early Slavs: Culture and Society in Early Medieval Eastern Europe* (Ithaca, N.Y., 2001). See also F. Curta, *The Making of the Slavs: History and Archaeology of the Lower Danube Region, c. 500–700* (Cambridge, 2001); Pohl, *Awaren*, 94–127.

53 Procopius, *Wars*, 7.14 and 7.35.

54 Pohl, *Awaren*, 125–127.

55 See Curta, *The Making of the Slavs.*

56 Agathias, *Histories*, 5.14–15.

57 Agathias, *Histories*, 5.25; Menander, frag. 2.

58 Pohl, *Awaren*. For a short synthesis in English, see W. Pohl, "A Non-Roman Empire in Central Europe: The Avars," in *Regna et Gentes: The Relationship between Late Antique and Early Medieval Peoples and Kingdoms in the Transformation of the Roman World*, ed. H. W. Goetz, J. Jarnut, and W. Pohl (Leiden, 2003), 571–595.

59 Menander Protector, *History*, frag. 5.2, trans. Blockley 51.

60 Gregory of Tours, *Histories*, 4.29.

61 Menander Protector, *History*, frag. 5.2.

62 Corippus, *In laudem Iustini Augusti Minoris*, 3.231 ff.

# 19: Byzantium and the East in the Sixth Century

*Geoffrey Greatrex*

In 551 a Persian ambassador, Yazdgushnasp, travelled to Constantinople. The journey from the Roman frontier at Dara took three months; en route he was entertained and provided for by local officials and envoys of the emperor. Once in the imperial capital, he and his retinue were lodged at imperial expense. Within a few days, he was summoned to the palace to meet Justinian and his counsellors. Once the Persian had prostrated himself several times before the emperor and greeted him in the name of the Persian king, Justinian replied to him, "How fares our brother in God? We rejoice in his good health." Gifts were then exchanged, and the audience concluded. Detailed negotiations began in earnest a few days later.[1]

Here we see one aspect of Romano-Persian relations as they had evolved over three centuries. Diplomatic language permitted the two rulers to address one another as equals, even as brothers. Persian diplomats could claim that the two empires were the "two lamps of the world"; and "as with (two) eyes, each one should be adorned by the brightness of the other."[2] Later in the sixth century, the emperor Maurice even intervened during a civil war in Persia to restore Khusro II to the throne. His decision flew in the face of the advice of several of his counsellors, however: the polite phrases of diplomats must not be allowed to obscure the abiding mistrust of Persia felt by most Romans.[3] More typical of the Roman view is the following judgement from the historian Agathias, writing in the 580s, here commenting on the decision of the emperor Arcadius in the early fifth century to appoint the Persian king Yazdgerd I as the guardian of his young son Theodosius II: "How could it be a good thing to hand over one's dearest possessions to a stranger, a barbarian, the ruler of one's bitterest enemy, one whose good faith and sense of justice were untried, and, what is more, one who belonged to an alien and heathen faith?" (*Histories*, 4.26.6, trans. Averil Cameron).

Centuries of warfare could scarcely be effaced by elaborate protocol. In the words of Nina Garsoïan, "Behind the bland courtesy of diplomatic clichés ran a deep vein of enmity, and, what was perhaps still more damaging, mutual contempt."[4] For the Sasanian Persians, whose rulers claimed descent from an obscure figure named Sasan, were but the latest eastern power to challenge the Romans, having overthrown their Parthian overlords in the 220s. Greek-speaking Romans of the eastern empire looked to an even remoter past, tracing hostilities back to the wars between Greece and the Achaemenid Persians in the fifth century BC. The Persians were thus for many Romans a source equally of fascination, fear, and revulsion. Historians such as Procopius and Agathias go out of their way to recount amazing tales concerning Persian kings but note with horror certain of their practices, such as their failure to bury their dead and the incestuous marriage practices of the nobility.[5]

Of the importance and power of the Persians there could be no doubt. Their empire, stretching roughly from the Indus in the east to the Roman frontiers in the west, and from the steppes of Central Asia in the north to the southern shores of the Persian Gulf in the south, was equal in size to the eastern Roman Empire. They had proved to be a far more redoubtable foe than the Parthians had ever been. The power of their kings was largely uncontested throughout their domains, while their military technology (for instance, in the case of siege warfare) was notably superior to their predecessors'. Roman dealings with other peoples in the east, such as the Huns to the north of the Caucasus, the Iberians, Lazi, and Armenians in the Caucasus, the Arabs of the Syrian steppes or of southern Arabia, were mediated above all by a calculation of how they might affect relations with Persia. Alliances were forged or broken, depending on their reliability and usefulness in gaining an advantage in negotiations or warfare with Persia: thus Justin I welcomed the Iberian king Gourgenes, hitherto a Persian ally, to his court in the mid-520s, promising to defend his country against Persian reprisals, but his nephew quickly abandoned it when it suited him, and the Eternal Peace agreed in 532 merely permitted refugee Iberians to remain in the Roman Empire if they wanted.[6]

We shall begin with an overview of Romano-Persian relations up to the early sixth century, in order to appreciate the background to Justinian's policies in the East. We shall then briefly examine the position of the Persian kingdom in the sixth century, before moving on to offer a concise narrative of eastern events during Justinian's reign. We shall next turn to the margins of empire, from the Caucasus to southern Arabia, in order to grasp the complexity of foreign relations in the sixth century and to appreciate the delicate balance that existed between the two powers. This will allow an assessment of how the emperor attempted to come to grips with the East and of how successful his strategies were. As we shall see, the two powers were capable of peaceful co-existence, as had happened in the fifth century, and yet various factors drove them apart in the sixth; in particular, the weakness of the Persian crown, combined with the emptiness of the Persian treasury, tempted Persian kings to invade Roman territory on several occasions. This naturally led to outright warfare, which tended to become more protracted as the century progressed, as well as eroding the trust which had developed between the two powers. Justin I and Justinian, as will emerge, sought to reverse this process: they were almost always prepared to negotiate with the Persians, and on two occasions Justinian concluded a peace treaty with them, even at some cost to the Roman treasury.

## Rome and Persia in Late Antiquity

Both Justin I and Justinian inherited an empire at war with Persia. Although for most of their reigns the two powers remained at war, Justinian was able at the end of his reign to come to terms with Persia and to bequeath to his successor a peaceful and stable eastern frontier. The treaty negotiated by Justinian and his *magister officiorum* Peter was due to last half a century, but after only ten years it was deliberately broken by Justin II, Justinian's nephew and successor, and a new phase of hostilities, destined to drag on for nearly twenty years, was begun. Clearly, Roman policy in the East was far from consistent: much depended on the emperor concerned, and sudden changes were possible. As we shall see, however, both Justinian and Justin II could find many precedents for their policies in earlier Roman dealings with the Persians.

In the late 330s, an anonymous writer prefaced an itinerary of Alexander the Great's conquests in the East dedicated to the young Emperor Constantius with the injunction, "You have a hereditary duty towards the Persians, inasmuch as they have trembled for so long at Roman arms."[7] Constantius, however, declined to embark on the ambitious campaign envisaged for him by his adviser and planned by his father Constantine.[8] Instead, he vigorously defended the eastern provinces and, despite some setbacks, succeeded in preserving the Roman frontier intact. It was thus left to his successor Julian to take the offensive. Despite Persian attempts to negotiate a peace, the new emperor assembled a large army and advanced down the river Euphrates, following the traditional Roman invasion route trodden earlier by the emperors Trajan, Septimius Severus, and Carus. Like them, he reached the city of Ctesiphon, but unlike his predecessors, he was unable to capture it. In the ensuing retreat to Roman territory, the emperor himself and a large proportion of his army were killed.[9]

Julian's disastrous defeat had several important consequences. The most obvious one was the cession to the Persians of a substantial tract of territory between the Tigris and Euphrates, including the city of Nisibis. For this surrender both Julian and his successor, Jovian, who agreed to the hand over, were widely criticised.[10] But a further consequence, less frequently noticed, was the shattering of Roman illusions of conquest in the East. Indeed, Julian was the last emperor ever to undertake an unprovoked attack on the Persians (with the exception of Justin II, whose ambitions were rather more limited). For the rest of the fourth century, eastern emperors preferred to adopt a more passive eastern policy, meeting Persian aggression when it occurred – usually in Armenia – and trying to resolve differences by diplomacy. Gradually a more peaceful relationship evolved, and diplomatic protocols were established, by which each side notified the other of a change of ruler, and at least two types of embassy (major and minor) were distinguished. By the early fifth century the emperor Arcadius felt sufficiently confident in the good faith of the Persian king Yazdgerd I to nominate him as the guardian of his young son Theodosius II in order to protect him from rival claimants to the throne.[11] An important element in the improvement of relations between the powers was the declaration of independence by the Persian church at a synod in 424, which removed the possibility of western bishops interfering in its affairs: hitherto, Persian Christians had suffered because of suspicions concerning their loyalty, whereas now they were able to govern themselves and to develop their own doctrines, which over time distanced them further from their western coreligionists.[12] For the rest of the fifth century, relations between the two sides remained peaceful, punctuated by two brief wars in 421–422 and 440. The war that broke out in 502 lasted somewhat longer but proved equally inconclusive and was effectively brought to an end by a truce in 506. It was not until twenty years later that hostilities recommenced; however, because no peace had intervened since 506, the war of 502–532 is generally treated as one conflict, despite the long interval.[13]

Such, in brief, is the history of Romano-Persian relations before the reign of Justinian. The future emperor, already a figure of some importance at the imperial court at the time of his uncle's accession, will undoubtedly have been aware of these events from the outset of his reign. He could read for himself accounts of the wars and diplomatic contacts in both secular and church historians; while these were apt to be tendentious and to exaggerate the extent of Roman successes (notably in the case of Theodosius II's war of 421–422), he will also have had access to more sober campaign reports submitted by the commanders themselves, as well as diplomatic records.[14] Specialists in diplomacy with the East will have been particularly valuable to him: the family of Euphrasius undertook numerous missions to the Arabian peninsula, while that of Rufinus was on excellent terms with the Persian royal family and the Persian court generally.[15] Other sources of information were close at hand, for Constantinople was a magnet to ambitious men from all over the empire (such as Justinian's uncle himself had once been). Among Justin's household were men such as Peter, a native of Arzanene captured while still a boy, later promoted to active commands in the northeast; and at some point during Justin's reign, Justinian recruited a talented Armenian, Sittas, as one of his bodyguards, later to become one of his foremost generals.[16]

What conclusions might be drawn by Justinian from such sources? Whether or not he cherished ambitions in the West from the start, the benefits of a peaceful eastern frontier were obvious: the recent war during Anastasius's reign had highlighted the vulnerability of Roman cities and armies, as well as requiring the mobilisation and despatch of substantial forces to the region. The Persian king Kavadh made it clear before, during, and after his attack that his only objective was financial: if Anastasius had been willing to give him a subsidy in the first place, the whole war could have been avoided. As Justinian will have been aware, Roman emperors in the past had provided funds to the Persians, although "this payment was not made as tribute, as many supposed it to be."[17] In 440, a serious war had even been averted by the provision of gifts to the Persian king Yazdgerd II. There were, of course, dangers in such a compliant policy. Persian demands grew more frequent, and in the end the Persians were satisfied only with annual fixed payments. Arguably, this in itself was not necessarily disadvantageous for the Romans, since it provided an ongoing incentive to the Persians to keep the peace, and, at five hundred pounds of gold per year, was not exorbitantly expensive; in fact, this was the solution Justinian finally adopted in 562, although he preferred to make several years' payments together.[18] The real danger in such a policy was the appearance it gave – that the Romans were, in effect, tributaries of the Persians. This could be and was exploited by the Persians, but its impact closer to home was more damaging: the people (and many of the nobility) of Constantinople and the eastern provinces preferred a tougher approach to the traditional enemy. There was general resentment at the lavish hospitality accorded to the Persian ambassador Yazdgushnasp in the 550s, particularly at a time when hostilities were still active in the Caucasus. Roman commanders, unhappy with the softer line being pursued by the emperor, might even sabotage or undermine negotiations on the frontier on occasion.[19]

As we shall see, Justinian appears to have maintained a consistent policy towards Persia right from the outset of his reign; in today's terms, one might call it "constructive engagement." Persian embassies were treated with courtesy and proposals for peace well received. Hostile incursions were met by force (when possible), but invasions of Persian domains were undertaken seldom and only in response to Persian attacks. Justinian was prepared to pay for peace, whether a general peace or a truce confined to part of the frontier, but took steps so as not to be perceived as weak or too ready to make concessions. He therefore sought to separate his payments from the actual terms of agreements, for instance in the treaty of 562, no doubt to give them the appearance of being voluntary.[20] Maximum publicity was given to any success against the Persians, such as the victory of Belisarius at Dara in 530. Monuments were erected, works of history commissioned, and epigrams composed, in order to emphasise the emperor's success and his victory over the traditional enemy[21] (See Fig. 1). Such propaganda must not be taken at face value; rather, it assuaged public opinion and served to emphasise the emperor's personal involvement in the victory, even though he rarely left the capital.

## Persia in the Sixth Century

The sixth century in many ways marked the apogee of Sasanian rule. Not only was Persia itself prosperous and powerful, but the ruling dynasty, at least under Kavadh (488–496, 499–531) and Khusro I (531–579), was also firmly established in its ascendancy. In the late fifth century, however, Persian prospects had seemed very bleak. During the reign of Peroz (459–484), a new and dangerous enemy, the Hephthalite Huns, appeared on the vulnerable northeastern frontier of the Persian Empire. Two campaigns by the king against the Hephthalites proved spectacularly unsuccessful; in the second, Peroz himself and many of his sons perished. At the same time, the kingdom was struck by a long drought.[22] Thus, as a result of military disasters and declining revenues, Peroz's successor Balash (484–488) found the Persian treasury empty. When he failed to resolve this problem, the army and the Zoroastrian clergy removed him in favour of Peroz's son Kavadh. Although he too was subsequently ousted from the throne in 496, he was able to recover it three years later with the military support of the Hephthalites. Until his death in 531 his rule went unchallenged, and he was able to ensure the succession of his preferred son, Khusro I.[23]

Internal instability had also threatened the Persian Empire during Kavadh's reign. At some point during his rule, a popular movement, usually known as that of the Mazdakites, after its founder, Mazdak, but also called the sect of the Zaradushtakan, rose to prominence. Much debate still surrounds all aspects of this uprising – when exactly it broke out (before or after Kavadh's expulsion), what precisely its followers believed, and to what extent it was supported by Kavadh. We may here briefly note that its followers, drawn from the common people, seem to have favoured the communal holding of various goods, as of women too, thereby challenging conventional inheritance patterns. The movement thus undermined and set itself against the entrenched landholding aristocracy, as also against the Zoroastrian church – two of the pillars of Persian society. Whether out of genuine sympathy or political calculation, Kavadh lent his support to the Mazdakites; in this way he was able to strengthen his own grip on power and avoid being ousted again by the nobles and clergy, as Balash was in 488 and he himself had been in 496. But by the end of his reign, the Mazdakites themselves had become a threat. Therefore Khusro, having attained the throne, conducted a purge of the sect, eliminating its followers, together with his older brother Kaoses, whom the Mazdakites had hoped to make king in his place.[24]

The rise of the Mazdakites was undoubtedly linked to the difficulties besetting the Persian kingdom at the time, but it should not obscure the fact that during the sixth century the heartlands of the Persian Empire – Lower Mesopotamia and Khuzistan – continued to prosper: under the Sasanians the region was more densely populated and cultivated than at any point hitherto (Map 13). Cities expanded, major irrigation works were undertaken (under Khusro I), and new populations transplanted there from Roman territory (and elsewhere).[25]

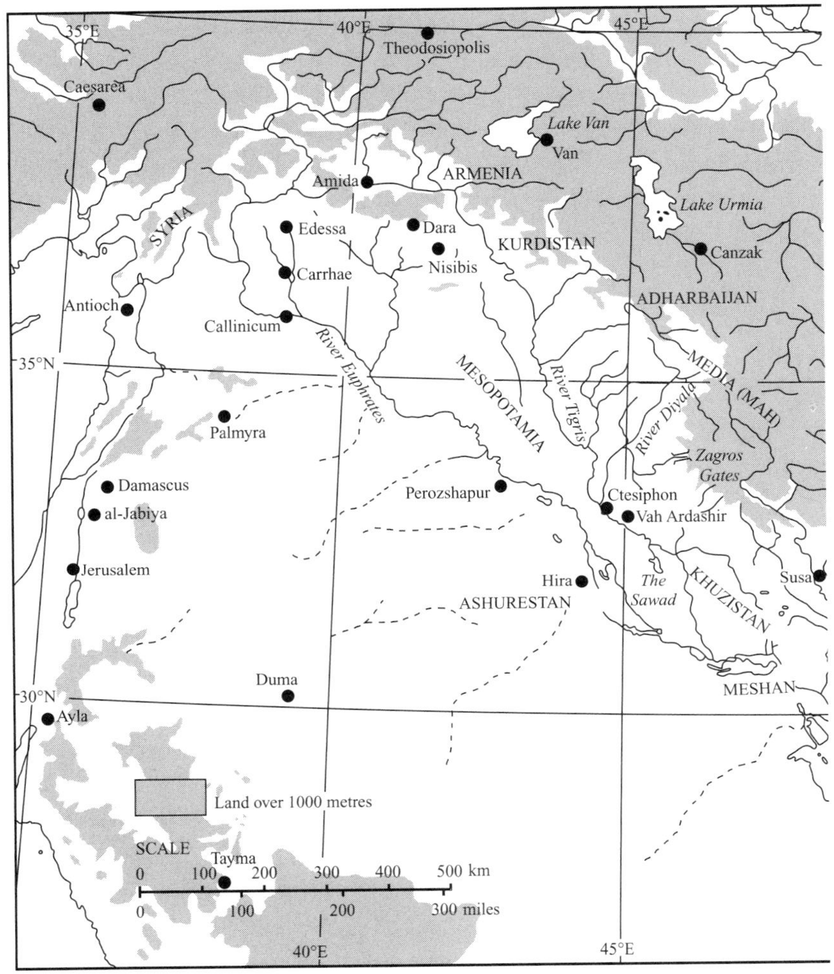


MAP 13. Sasanid Iran

Trade, particularly with the East, also represented a significant source of wealth. Already in the fourth century AD, one Roman writer had noted how the Persians benefited from their commerce with all their neighbours.[26] By the sixth century, Persians were actively involved in trade in the Indian Ocean; at the same time, archaeological evidence suggests that Lower Mesopotamia was the major beneficiary of this development, while other ports in the Persian Gulf, such as Oman and Bahrain, declined.[27] We shall return in due course to this point.

Increased revenues from this trade, combined with the depopulation of certain areas as a result of the upheavals of the Mazdakite

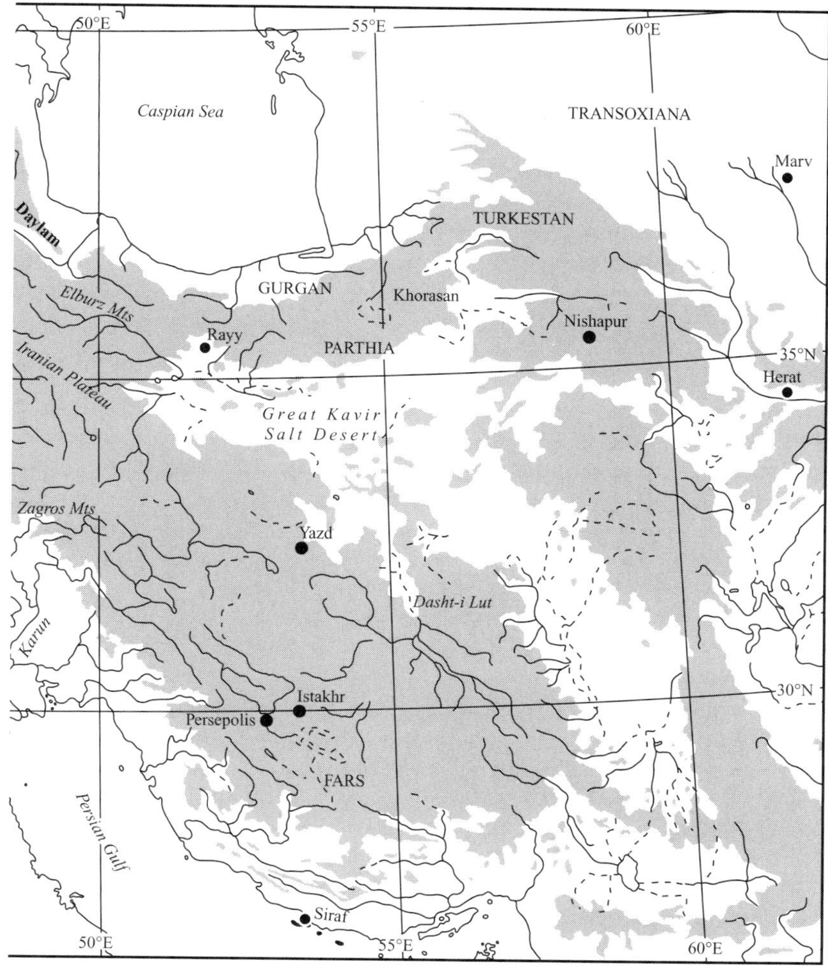


movement, provided an opportunity for the Sasanian kings to strengthen their position at the expense of the nobility and clergy. It is clear that Kavadh initiated and Khusro completed an important series of reforms to the structure of the state, but the precise details of when and how they did so remain uncertain: our sources are late and their interpretation disputed. However, the following features may be noted. A land survey of Lower Mesopotamia was begun under Kavadh and completed under Khusro. A new taxation system was then introduced, according to which state incomes were fixed in advance, rather than fluctuating from year to year. Khusro eliminated the differences between taxes on royal land and those on land belonging to magnates and emphasised the egalitarian nature of his new system, no doubt to conciliate those who had supported the Mazdakites.[28] The army too was subject to reform. Hitherto the Persian king had depended to a great extent on troops raised by the leading families of Persia to constitute his army. The most important of these were the heavy cavalry units, drawn from the upper echelons of Sasanian society, under the overall command of a supreme commander, the *Eran-spahbed*, himself a member of one of the seven noble houses of Persia. Under Khusro, this supreme command was divided up into four regional commands, each with considerable autonomy, while other aspects of the system were centralised. Henceforth soldiers were paid by the state, as well as, in the case of frontier troops, being endowed with property; subsidies were also established for the recruitment of cavalry, whereby the state furnished men with the mounts, weapons, and pay necessary for service. In principle, we should expect these reforms to have produced a more numerous and effective army. Yet the evidence suggests that even late in Khusro's reign, problems remained: considerable numbers of frontier peoples were being recruited for Persian service, in return for which they were granted lands to settle, a concession that implies a shortage of available manpower.[29]

In general, the reigns of Kavadh and Khusro saw an increase in the extent of royal power; the landed nobility remained important, but now an aristocracy of service – those who had been rewarded or promoted by the king – came to the fore. But even as this process took root, the dispersal of lands to soldiers and foreign settlers, removing lands from royal control, undermined the power of the king, while tensions also arose in the tax-raising process. The reign of Khusro I was in many respects a golden age for Persia, as tradition enshrined it, but his reforms failed to eliminate fundamental weaknesses in the state.[30]

## THE HISTORY OF THE EASTERN FRONTIER UNDER JUSTIN I AND JUSTINIAN

### *The War under Justin I and Justinian (518–532)*

The accession of Justin I occasioned no perceptible change in relations between Rome and Persia. Sporadic Arab raids continued to be the chief menace to the frontier provinces; in one of these, two senior Roman commanders were captured and were recovered only by negotiation several years later. Although the defection of the new king of Lazica, Tzath, to the Roman side in 521 was condemned by the Persian king

Kavadh, no fighting broke out between the two sides in the Caucasus at this point. A few years later, the elderly Kavadh took a remarkable (but not unprecedented) diplomatic initiative, proposing that Justin adopt his son Khusro, in order to secure his accession to the Persian throne. According to Procopius (*Wars*, 1.11.10), both Justin and Justinian were delighted by this approach and were quite ready to accept the Persian proposal. Their resolve was shaken, however, by the imperial quaestor Proculus, who argued that the Persians were seeking to wrest control of the Roman Empire by a subterfuge: Khusro would be entitled, as Justin's son, to inherit control of it. Nevertheless, Justin despatched high-ranking officials to the frontier to arrange an adoption "by arms," the normal procedure for foreign rulers. It is clear that the negotiations were proceeding smoothly – Khusro was even waiting nearby to take part in the adoption ceremony – when they were deliberately sabotaged by hard-liners on both sides, unwilling to make concessions. This episode, described in detail only by Procopius, deserves emphasis. Justin and Justinian were eager for peace from the start, and had their delegates been more disciplined, war might never have broken out again a few years later. The hostility towards such dealings with Persia on the part of senior officials, in this case Proculus and the chief commander in the East, Hypatius, is also significant and was a factor Justinian would always have to contend with.[31]

Following the death of his uncle, Justinian took active steps to strengthen the defences of the East, creating a new commander-in-chief for Armenia and the northeast, reorganising the Armenian provinces, and restoring the fortifications of Palmyra and other cities close to the frontier. Despite rising tensions and some confrontations along the eastern frontier, negotiations continued; Kavadh repeated the demands for money he had been making since the 490s, while Justinian rebuffed him. In order to break the stalemate, Kavadh in 530 ordered a full-scale invasion of Roman Mesopotamia, only for his army to be decisively defeated outside the walls of the recently built Roman fortress of Dara; a simultaneous attack on Roman Armenia was equally unsuccessful. Undeterred, Kavadh sent another force of Arabs and Persians up the Euphrates early in 531. Taking the Romans by surprise, it penetrated as far as Gabbulon, causing panic in Antioch, but was then forced back by the *magister militum per Orientem* (master of soldiers in the East), Belisarius. While the general would have preferred to allow the invaders to depart unchallenged, his soldiers were eager to avenge themselves for the destruction caused by this raid and earlier incursions. Belisarius found himself obliged to give battle, and in April 531 the

Persians emerged the victors near Callinicum. Negotiations continued nevertheless, but the death of Kavadh in late 531 changed the situation. Justinian seized the opportunity offered, refusing to allow his ambassadors to proceed and to acknowledge Khusro as king, no doubt hoping to foment internal strife in Persia. When Khusro swiftly secured his position, however, Justinian soon resumed talks and agreed to a truce. In the following year, a peace was agreed.[32]

## *The Eternal Peace (532–540)*

Never before had the two powers agreed to a peace of indefinite duration. On both sides there was, it seems, considerable optimism about the future of their relations. Khusro returned forts in Lazica and Armenia to the Romans, while Justinian's chief concession was a one-time payment to the Persians of 11,000 pounds of gold. John Malalas reports, "The two rulers agreed and stated explicitly in the treaty that they were brothers according to the ancient custom, and that if one of them required money or men in a military alliance, they should provide it without dispute" (Malalas, *Chronographia*, 18.76, trans. Jeffreys and Scott, revised).

On the face of it, the two powers had returned to the golden days of the fifth century, when the Romans had indeed provided financial help, albeit intermittently. Scraps of evidence from the 530s appear to confirm a spirit of cooperation between the two powers. Certainly Justinian took the opportunity it gave him to redeploy many of the forces that had defended the East to undertake his campaigns to reconquer first North Africa, then Italy. But already by 539 Khusro was seeking a pretext to break the peace. Behind the renewal of war, clearly the responsibility of the Persians, we may detect two main factors: first, the ongoing needs of the depleted Persian treasury; and second, the deterioration of the defences of the Roman East, providing the Persians with a perfect opportunity to seize large amounts of property and manpower at little cost. As we shall see, Khusro was interested neither in fighting pitched battles nor in annexing Roman territory: his main goal in violating the peace was riches.[33]

## *Justinian's Second Persian War (540–562)*

In 540 Khusro broke the Eternal Peace and led his army up the Euphrates, avoiding the newly strengthened fortresses of Mesopotamia and aiming instead for the more weakly defended Syria. Pausing briefly to extort money from cities en route in return for passing them by, he sacked Beroea and continued westwards, while the Romans vainly sought to deflect him by further payments. In June 540 the most important city of the Roman East, Antioch, fell into Persian hands and was systematically plundered; many of its citizens were deported to Persia, where a new city, modelled on their own, was built for them. After a brief visit to the port of Seleucia, Khusro withdrew eastwards, demanding more gold as he proceeded.[34]

The campaign of 540 was without doubt a huge success for Khusro, but it was not to be repeated. By the following year Belisarius had returned to the East from Italy and undertaken a counterattack into Persian Mesopotamia (Assyria), thereby forcing the king, then seeking to press his advantage in the Caucasus, to return to deal with the situation. Further Persian invasions of Mesopotamia in 542 and 543 made little headway, and in 545 a truce was agreed, bringing hostilities in the area to an end. In the north, particularly in Lazica, campaigning dragged on for another ten years, probably because the scope for gains was larger here than in the heavily fortified south, without achieving any decisive result. A truce was finally concluded here too in 557, paving the way for negotiations for a definitive peace.[35] Five years later, the two sides agreed to a comprehensive peace treaty, the terms of which are preserved in detail by the Roman historian Menander Protector. The treaty differed in two significant ways from the Eternal Peace. On the one hand, it more modestly proposed a duration for the peace of fifty years, and on the other, it laid down that the Romans were to pay a fixed sum (approximately five hundred pounds of gold) per year (initially in instalments covering several years) to the Persians. Justinian had evidently concluded that without such an annual payment, there was little incentive for the Persians to abide by any peace. It was a logical conclusion, but to many Romans, and not least his successor Justin II, his solution appeared dangerous and indicative of weakness.[36]

Justin consequently embarked on an attack on Persia in 572, relying partly on an alliance with the Turks, the new power challenging Persia to the northeast, and partly on the Armenians, aggrieved at Persian attempts to enforce Zoroastrianism in Persarmenia. The Persians quickly gained the upper hand in the war, capturing the important border fortress of Dara. Under the emperors Tiberius (574–582) and Maurice (582–602), the situation stabilised and negotiations were pursued, but it was not until the Persian king Hormizd IV (578–91) was overthrown and Maurice gave military support to his son Khusro II (591–628) that the Romans were able to bring the war to a conclusion.

Because of Maurice's aid, they obtained very favourable terms, extending the frontiers of the empire deep into what had been Persarmenia. But Maurice's intervention provided Khusro with an excellent pretext for Khusro II to follow his example in the wake of Maurice's overthrow and the accession of Phocas in 602. Persian armies proceeded to overrun almost the entire eastern empire, seizing Syria, Egypt, Armenia, and Palestine; one Persian force even reached Constantinople in 626. Only with the greatest difficulty was the emperor Heraclius (610–641) able to turn the tide against the invaders and to undermine Khusro's position by laying waste the heartlands of the Persian Empire. The two sides then came to terms, but it was too late: both powers had exhausted themselves through decades of warfare. Consequently they were unable to defeat the Arab armies that came forth to wrest their territories from them in the 630s. As Peter the Patrician had predicted, by squandering their resources, the two sides were "conquered by those who ought not to defeat them."[37]

## JUSTINIAN AND THE FRONTIER PEOPLES BETWEEN ROME AND PERSIA

A glance at some maps illustrating the extent of the Roman and Persian empires might give the impression of a neat frontier line dividing the two powers, stretching from the Caucasus mountains in the north to the Syrian desert in the south (Maps 14 and 15). The reality, however, was far more complex, as one might expect if one considers the nature of the terrain in question: neither the mountainous districts of Armenia and the Caucasian kingdoms nor the Syrian steppes have ever been easy for an external power to control. As we shall see, both the Romans and the Persians struggled to impose their authority on these frontier zones; sometimes they employed negotiation, at other times they resorted to coercion. In some cases it is difficult even to determine the precise status of a region or people – whether it was actually in the Roman Empire or outside it. For example, to the north of Roman Mesopotamia lay a region that, until the late fifth century, was governed by five Armenian satraps, even though it was considered to be part of the empire. Beyond it to the north lay Armenia Interior, a Roman province from the late fourth century onwards, which was integrated only gradually into the structure of the empire.[38] As will become clear, during the sixth century a concerted attempt was made to consolidate the Roman grip on the frontier territories.

One final point must be made before discussing the particular regions in detail, and that concerns the role of Christianity. While the importance of Christianity to the empire and Justinian's keen interest in matters of faith and doctrine are dealt with in several chapters in this volume, its relevance in this case lies in the fact that he was the first emperor to perceive the political benefits of missionary activity beyond the frontiers. By this means the empire was able to bring foreign peoples into its orbit without the need to deploy any troops and thus to increase its influence and power at little cost. In the long term, as Byzantine military power waned, this commonwealth, bound together by the ties of religion, would prove an ever more useful instrument of empire.[39]

We may broadly distinguish two types of missionary activity. On the one hand, there were missions sent out by imperial initiative; both the Tzani and the Abasgi in the Caucasus were converted by this method. When, in both cases, the peoples proved recalcitrant, troops were deployed and the people subjugated by force. Here we see two obvious instances of Christianity being used overtly as a tool of empire by which Roman influence could be entrenched in the Caucasus.[40] On the other hand, Justinian was always willing to exploit opportunities that presented themselves, such as the cases of the kings Tzath and Gourgenes. It was likewise through a visit to Constantinople by a foreign king, in this case a certain Grod, that Roman control of the Crimea was established in 528, not without some difficulty.[41] Now in all the cases discussed so far, the kingdoms or peoples involved were brought directly into the Roman political orbit, sometimes by force. But opportunities also arose further afield, a notable one being that of the Nobatae (Nubians), to the south of Egypt, who were converted to Christianity during the reign of Justinian through the efforts of the monk Julian. There is no reason to suppose that Justinian wished to annex Nubia to the empire, but here too there were political dividends to be had: in the fifth century, for instance, the king of the Nobatae, Silko, had waged a successful war against the Blemmyes, a tribe that frequently molested Roman Egypt.[42] Still further afield, the common bond of Christianity allowed the Romans to expand their role in the Red Sea through their support of their Christian ally, the Ethiopians.[43] This leads to an important point. Neither the Nobatae, who were converted by anti-Chalcedonians, nor the Ethiopians were orthodox Christians. Despite the fact that both Justin and Justinian often took a hard line in dealing with the opponents of Chalcedon inside the empire, in the conduct of foreign policy doctrinal differences receded into the background. The

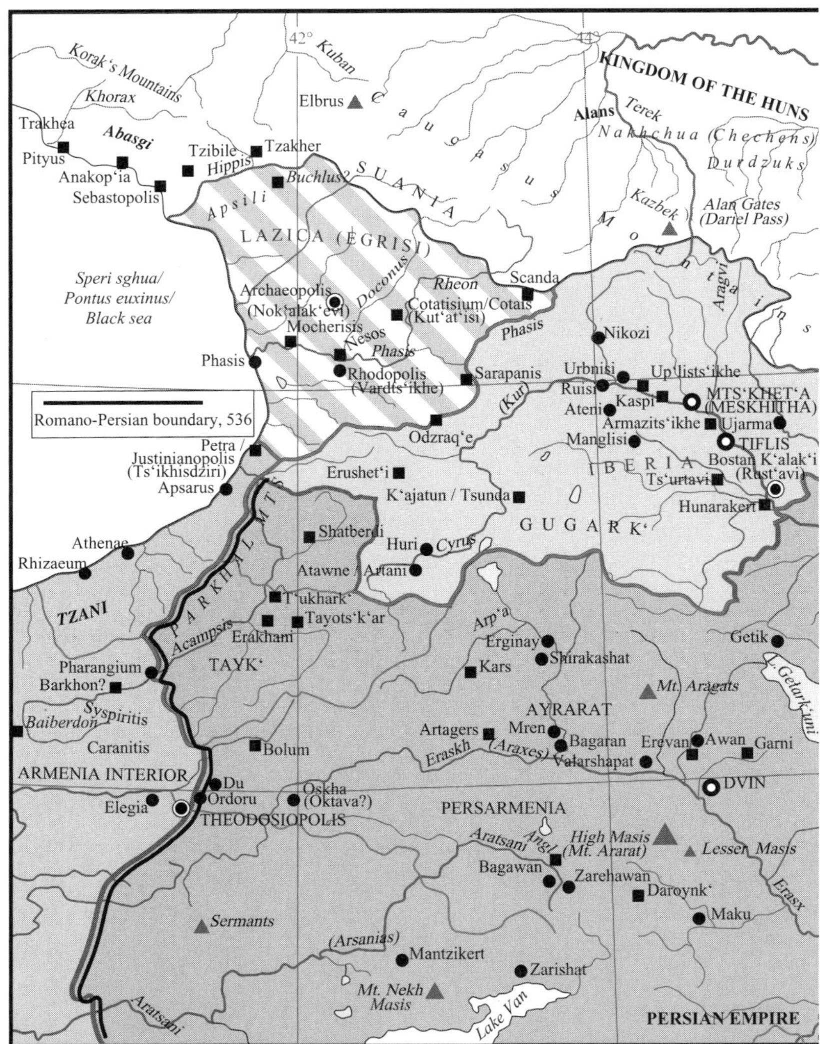


MAP 14. The Roman-Persian borderlands in the Caucasus

charred Bible sent by the Ethiopian king to Justin as proof of the persecutions being carried out in Himyar symbolised the need for Christians to unite against their enemies.[44] Nevertheless, Christians outside the Roman Empire were not necessarily all loyal allies of the emperor. The Christians of Persia, for instance, had their own separate church, whose doctrines differed from both those of the Chalcedonians and their so-called Monophysite opponents; although they were intermittently

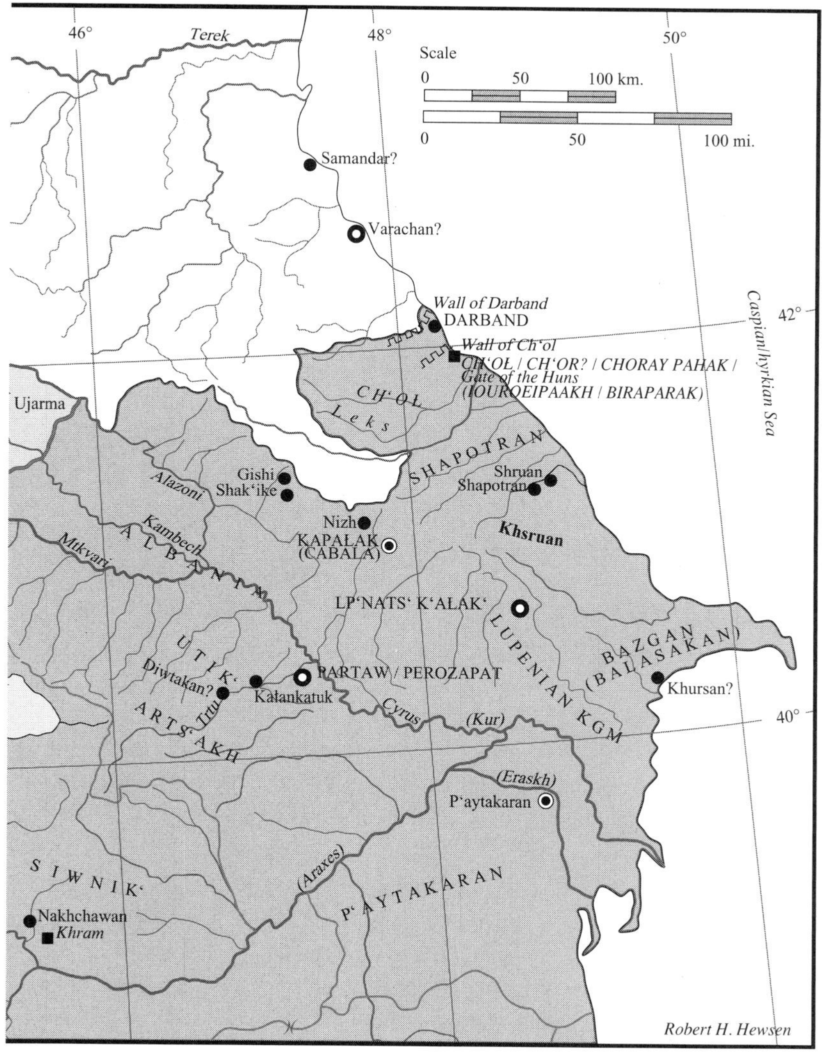


persecuted in the sixth century, it is difficult to detect any pro-Roman sympathies among them. Indeed, in times of persecution by supporters of Chalcedon within the empire, opponents of the council might flee for refuge across the border to escape oppression, as John of Tella did in the 530s.[45]

Probably the most important frontier region between Rome and Persia lay in the Caucasus and the Armenian highlands. Not only was it densely populated, offering a ready source of skilled soldiers, and rich in

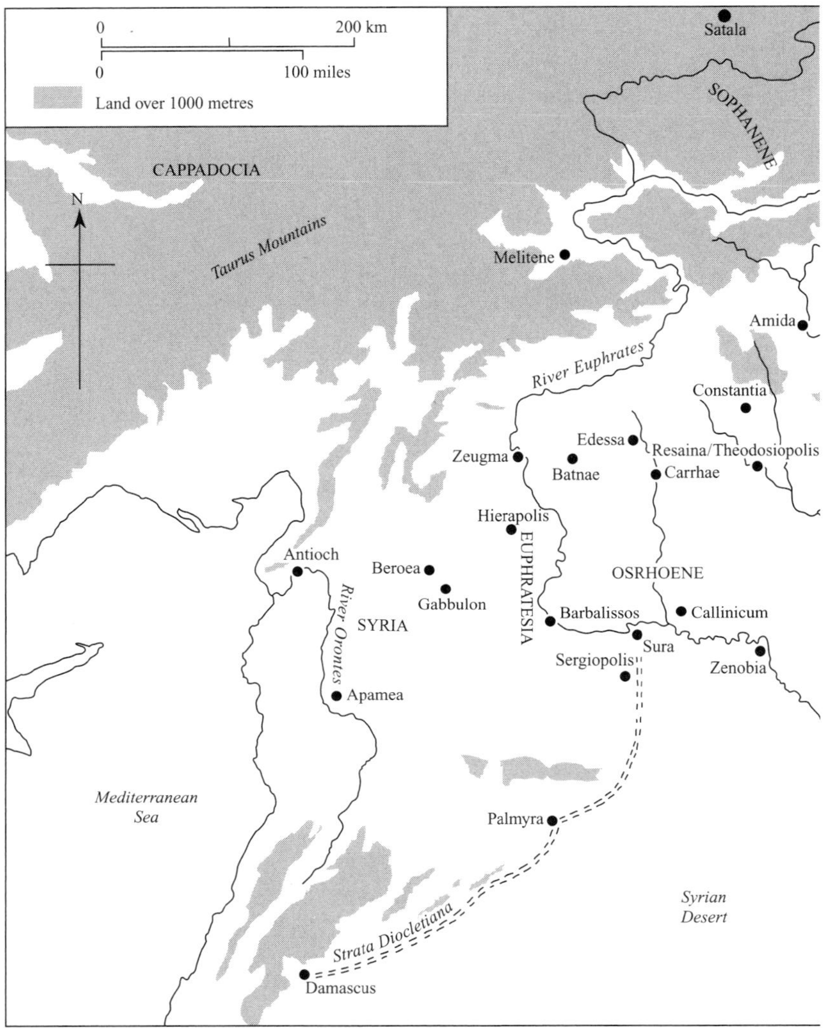


MAP 15. Northern Mesopotamia and adjacent regions

certain resources (such as gold), but the Caucasus range itself provided a barrier against the incursions of the foreign peoples of the north.[46] Control of the region thus conferred many benefits, and throughout the fifth and sixth centuries the two powers struggled to gain the upper hand. For the most part, the Persians were more successful, consistently dominating the eastern Caucasus and at times extending their power as far as the Black Sea. But it consequently fell to them to guard the passes across the mountains and to protect the region (and their

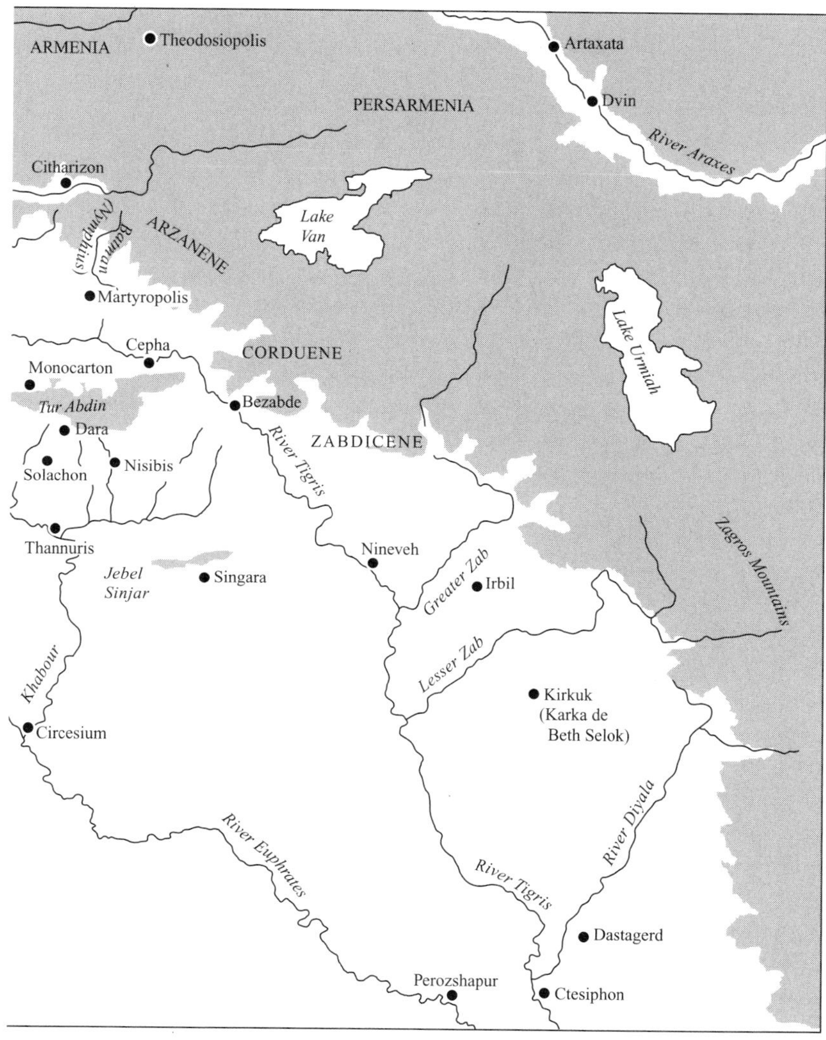


own lands in northern Iran) from invasions, an onerous and expensive task. Frequently they turned to the Romans for financial or military assistance; rarely did they receive any, since the Roman emperors were well aware that the Persians were more vulnerable to such incursions than they were.[47] The main obstacle to Roman and Persian ambitions, however, lay not in invasions from the north, but in the nature of the terrain itself and its inhabitants. Neither power was ever able to subjugate the region (or indeed any part of it) entirely, despite strenuous efforts. The physical geography of this mountainous region militated against them: wintry conditions confine military campaigning to less than half of the year through much of the area, and the rugged terrain tends to benefit small forces rather than large armies.[48] The whole area formed a patchwork of fiercely independent peoples, some of whom shared a common culture and language – such as the Armenians – but who were rarely united under a single ruler. Neat labels such as "Armenia" and "Iberia" must consequently be treated with caution: Armenians and Iberians could frequently be found on both sides of the struggle between the major powers. In the year 530, for instance, a Persian army, incorporating Armenian and other non-Persian contingents, invaded Roman Armenia, where it was defeated by the Roman commanders Sittas (himself an Armenian) and Dorotheus outside the city of Satala. Shortly afterwards, as a consequence of the Roman victory, two Armenian leaders, the brothers Narses and Aratius, deserted the Persians and received a warm welcome from the Romans; their example was soon followed by their younger brother, who simultaneously handed over to the Romans an important border fortress. Meanwhile other Armenians, such as a certain Symeon, preferred to take the opportunity of the war to assert their independence. Symeon therefore ceased to supply the Persians with gold from the mine he controlled, handed over his territory to the Romans, and kept the gold for himself. The Persian king Kavadh was eager to avenge this loss, but "the Persians were not able against the will of the Romans to force the inhabitants of the place to terms because they were baffled by the difficult country."[49]

Right from the start, Justinian and his uncle had to work out how best to perserve and extend Roman influence in this region. Success would allow them to hold more securely the frontier lands already in their possession, such as the Armenian provinces and the barely pacified territories of the Tzani, and to stem the westward advance of Sasanian power, which by 518 extended to the western Caucasus. They would also be better able to maintain contacts with tribes beyond the Caucasus, such as the Sabir Huns, who might become useful allies against the Persians. An opportunity soon presented itself:

> During his reign Tzath, the king of the Lazi, grew angry and departed from Persian territory. (This was) while the Persians were ruled by Kavadh, a friend of Tzath, king of the Lazi, who had once been subject to the rule of Kavadh. Thus whenever a king of the Lazi happened to die, his successor, though from the race of the Lazi, was appointed and

> crowned by the king of the Persians. The king of the Lazi had rejected the belief of the Hellenes and so as not to be appointed by Kavadh, the Persian king, and not to perform sacrifices and all the other Persian customs, as soon as his father Damnazes died, he immediately went up to the Emperor Justin in Byzantium, put himself at his disposal and asked to be proclaimed king of the Lazi and to become a Christian. He was received by the emperor, baptized, and, having become a Christian, married a Roman wife named Valeriana, the granddaughter of Oninus the patrician and former *curopalates*, and he took her back with him to his own country (Malalas, *Chronographia*, 17.9, trans. Jeffreys and Scott, revised).

This episode, recounted in detail by several Byzantine chroniclers, is significant. The indirect nature of Persian rule is clear: Tzath was clearly destined to succeed his father Damnazes to the throne, although he was expected to await ratification by the Persians. Furthermore, the role of Christianity is paramount. To become a Christian is to align oneself with the Roman Empire, and the emperor himself welcomes the shift in allegiance, cementing it by a marriage to a Roman noblewoman. Despite protests from Kavadh, Justin stood by his actions and Tzath retained his throne. Others were not slow to follow the Lazic king's example: discontent with Zoroastrian practices encouraged the Iberian king Gourgenes, for instance, to defect to the Romans a few years later. In fact, as Procopius notes, the Iberians were already Christians, as were the Armenians. This was the trump card of the Romans in their dealings with the region, even if differences over points of doctrine occasionally soured relations. For while Armenia and Iberia were in many respects heavily influenced culturally and politically by Iran, as Nina Garsoïan has shown, their religion linked them inextricably to the Romans. No matter how tolerant some Persian kings might be of these peoples, there was always the danger of them making common cause with their fellow Christians across the border.[50]

Much of the Caucasus, then, was fertile ground for Roman diplomacy. Other parts, influenced by their neighbours, would also prove receptive. In the late 530s, for instance, the Abasgi were converted to Christianity by one of their own number, despatched by Justinian for this very purpose.[51] Even within the empire in this region, some isolated peoples remained to be converted: high up in the mountains southwest of Lazica, the fractious Tzani had defied attempts to subjugate them for centuries. Justinian, however, succeeded where others had failed by a combination of evangelisation and vigorous military campaigns. As Procopius rather optimistically declared, "they [the Tzani] immediately changed their belief to piety, all of them becoming Christians, and they altered their manner of life to a milder way, giving up all brigandage and always marching with the Romans whenever they went against their enemies."[52] The 520s and 530s were indeed an encouraging period for Roman ambitions in the Caucasus, yet already by 540 the tide was turning against them. The problem came with the encroachment of Roman troops, commanders, and regulations in the region. For Justinian aimed not only at extending Roman influence through diplomacy but also at fully integrating all the remotest parts of his domains into the empire. Thus in 536 he issued a decree "that the Armenians should follow Roman laws in all ways." The whole provincial structure was changed, fortifications were built or improved, and Roman troops took up positions throughout the region; in Lazica, a new city was even established at Petra.[53] All this proved too much for the Armenians and Lazi to bear. First the Armenians appealed to the Persians for help, followed in quick succession by the Lazi, dismayed at the corrupt administration of their territory by the Roman general John Tzibus. A Persian invasion in 541 met with much local support, and Khusro was able to seize and garrison the city of Petra.[54]

The subsequent vicissitudes of the region follow a similar pattern. Already by 542 certain Armenians had begun to transfer their loyalties back to the Romans, while Persian plans to consolidate their hold on Lazica soon persuaded the Lazic king Gubazes to throw in his lot with the emperor again. For the next twenty years the region would be the scene of sporadic campaigning by the two major powers, constantly seeking to attract the aid of local peoples. As neither proved capable of gaining a decisive advantage, the war gradually lost momentum until at last the general peace was concluded in 562.[55]

Justinian's penchant for regularisation and consolidation is also in evidence in his dealings with Rome's Arab allies (Map 16, Ch. 20). From the very start of Roman expansion into the Near East, the new power had relied on local allies. While most of these were gradually absorbed into the empire, certain regions, notably marginal steppe lands in the hands of nomadic or seminomadic tribes, were never taken over.[56] In the fourth and fifth centuries, some of these tribes were converted to Christianity and came to ally themselves with the Romans; meanwhile, across the Syrian desert to the east, one tribe in particular, the Lakhmids, emerged as the privileged ally of the Persians. At the start of the sixth century, tribal movements close to the frontier led to the supplanting of the Salîhids as Rome's principal ally by the Ghassanids, a tribe ruled by the Jafnid dynasty.[57] During the conflicts between Rome and Persia in the late 520s and early 530s, as well as during the 540s, the Jafnid king Harith campaigned alongside the Romans on several occasions. Initially, however, Harith seemed a poor match for the Lakhmid ruler Mundhir, who raided the provinces of the Roman East with impunity throughout the 520s.[58] It was largely in response to these raids that Justinian, once established as sole emperor, sought ways to improve the defences of the vulnerable eastern provinces. Part of his solution lay in the improvement of frontier fortifications, such as at Palmyra, Zenobia (Plate xxx), Martyropolis, and Dara, but he was also aware of weaknesses in the command structure. The establishment of a separate supreme commander for the northeastern frontier, the *magister militum per Armeniam et Pontum Polemoniacum et gentes* (master of soldiers for Armenia, Pontus Polemoniacus, and surrounding peoples), cut down on the responsibilities of the chief commander of the East, the *magister militum per Orientem* (master of soldiers for the East); there were changes too at the level of the local commanders (*duces*).[59] Until this time, Rome's Arab allies had been poorly organised: each province had not only its own commander (a *dux*, usually) but also an allied Arab commander, known as a phylarch (or tribal chief). Thus, in response to one of Mundhir's raids in 528, Malalas reports, "On learning this, the emperor Justinian wrote to the *duces* of Phoenice, Arabia and Mesopotamia and to the phylarchs of the provinces to go after him and pursue him and his army" (*Chronographia* 18.16).

By the time the force was assembled, Mundhir was long gone. The emperor's solution, implemented in the following year, was to elevate Harith to a supreme phylarchate (chiefdom). Henceforth he would coordinate the allied Arab forces of the eastern provinces. It was a bold stroke; Procopius calls it unprecedented.[60] Initially, there were problems. The Roman defeat at Callinicum in April 531 was attributed by many to treachery on the part of Arab allies; modern scholars plausibly suggest that some phylarchs, jealous of Harith's promotion, may have abandoned him at the battle, thus giving rise to the accusations. But Harith's position was never called into question. In the late 540s he pursued a bitter war with Mundhir after his adversary had captured and killed his son; by c. 550 he had gained the upper hand, and even Procopius then admits "that it was known from this that Harith was not squandering Roman chances [in favour of] the Persians." A few years later, Mundhir died in battle; Harith himself visited Constantinople in

563 and ended his days as a patrician, one of the highest dignities of the empire.[61]

Justinian's support for Harith and the Jafnids was well judged. His confidence in the dynasty may have been based in part on their obvious devotion to Christianity. For in this case, as frequently when dealing with peoples outside the empire, the emperor not only tolerated, but even actively supported, anti-Chalcedonian Christians. Indeed, through the intervention of Theodora, Harith was able to secure the appointment of two anti-Chalcedonian bishops for the eastern provinces in the early 540s; we know also of monasteries supported by the dynasty.[62] The promotion of Harith allowed Justinian to scale back Roman defences south of the Euphrates, where already in the fifth century Roman forts along the road from Sura to Damascus, known as the Strata Diocletiana, had started to be abandoned. Even further south, in the three provinces of Palestine, the Ghassanids proved valuable allies: either Harith or his brother Abu Karib, for instance, helped to crush a Samaritan uprising in 529. The mobile cavalry forces of the Ghassanids were better adapted to desert warfare, while the cost of the annual subsidies paid to them will have been considerably less than supporting all the soldiers previously stationed here.[63]

In this case, therefore, Justinian refrained from seeking to incorporate a foreign people into the empire or from imposing orthodoxy on them. Nonetheless, the provinces of the East were subject to extensive reorganisation during the 530s and 540s in an attempt to achieve greater efficiency. As in Armenia, the emperor undertook to make sure that Roman law was observed throughout the region: he was particularly keen, for instance, to ensure that close-kin marriages in Mesopotamia, which continued to take place in the sixth century, should be stamped out.[64] But when it came to the arid steppe lands of the Strata Diocletiana, the emperor preferred a more cautious approach. The Jafnid rulers were accorded wide-ranging powers and collaborated successfully with the Roman administration for the most part. The city of Sergiopolis, dedicated to the martyr Sergius, who was particularly venerated by the tribesmen, grew in this period into a major pilgrimage centre, where Harith and his successors could meet with other phylarchs in November each year (Plate xxix).[65] The full wisdom of Justinian's support for the Jafnids was revealed only after his death: both Justin II and Maurice, like many Romans suspicious of the Arabs, attempted to dispense with the aid of the Ghassanids, in both cases with disastrous consequences.[66]

## Southern Arabia and the Question of Trade

There was one further area, southern Arabia, in which the two powers vied for supremacy, relying in this case almost exclusively upon local allies. The outcome of the struggle here was unlikely ever to have any significant impact on the main frontier area in Mesopotamia, but its importance should not be underrated.

The issue that sparked Justinian's interest in the region was trade. From as early as the first century AD, large quantities of Roman gold and silver had flowed out of the empire to the East as the market for imported goods such as spices, perfumes, and silk expanded.[67] This last item grew to be of particular importance in late antiquity. As an indicator of social standing, it inspired strong demand and could fetch high prices. Trade in silk was tightly regulated: only certain designated officials, the *kommerkiarioi*, were permitted to buy it, and even they could not exceed a specified amount in the price they paid for it. Silk could be purchased only in designated foreign cities, moreover: ever since the reign of Diocletian, the Romans had insisted on limiting trade with Persia to a handful of border cities, a restriction maintained in Justinian's treaty of 562.[68] The reason for all this regulation is not hard to perceive, for although silk was not actually produced in Persia, but rather in China and, from the early fifth century, in Sogdia, Persian merchants had established a complete monopoly in the provision of silk to the Roman Empire. This was clearly a very lucrative situation for Persian traders, and by extension the Persian state.[69] Around 530, however, an opportunity presented itself to cut out the middleman and cease benefiting the Persian treasury.

Since the start of the sixth century, Roman interest in the Red Sea had been growing (Map 16, Ch. 20). In 498 a Roman *dux*, Romanus, had recaptured the island of Iotabe, at the mouth of the Gulf of Aqaba, and, as the chronicler Theophanes states, "gave it back to the Roman traders to inhabit under its own laws, to import goods from the Indies and to bring the assessed tax to the emperor."[70] Roman traders became active in the Red Sea, dealing with both Ethiopians (also known as Axumites) and Himyarites (in modern-day Yemen) alike. One of our chief sources for Roman contacts with this region is the work of an Alexandrian merchant, Cosmas, known as Indicopleustes (the sailor to India). Despite his title, however, and the fact that he provides information on trade routes as far as Sri Lanka and even beyond, it is likely that he relied on others for his descriptions of these regions. Indeed, few Roman traders ventured further East than Himyar, and their knowledge of the Indian Ocean was very limited.[71] In the 510s a Jewish Himyarite ruler, Dhu Nuwas, sought to stem the rise of Roman and Ethiopian influence in the region. He executed some Roman merchants, organised the persecution of Christians in his kingdom, and even attempted to form an alliance with the Lakhmids.[72] However, his efforts served only to persuade the Romans and Ethiopians to make common cause against him, culminating in a successful invasion of Himyar in 525 by the Ethiopian king Ella Asbeha and the imposition of an Ethiopian ruler; the Romans contributed a substantial fleet to the operation.[73] It was this favourable situation, perhaps coupled with the renewal of major hostilities to the north, that prompted the emperor to seek a new way to bypass the Persian silk monopoly: "He purposed that the Ethiopians, by purchasing silk from India and selling it among the Romans, might themselves gain much money, while causing the Romans to profit in only one way, namely, that they no longer be compelled to pay over their money to their enemy" (Procopius, *Wars*, 1.20.9, trans. Dewing).

The emperor's logic was sound, but he underestimated the strength of the Persian grip. As Procopius relates (*Wars*, 1.20.12), Sasanian traders completely dominated the Indian Ocean and were able to buy up all the silk arriving in Sri Lanka from further east; consequently, the Ethiopian traders were never able to buy directly from the exporters.[74] With the conclusion of the Eternal Peace in 532 and the overthrow of the Ethiopian ruler of Himyar around the same time, the initiative came to nothing. Southern Arabia continued to interest the major powers, however. A striking indication of its importance comes in an inscription from Marib of 542. During a war between the new ruler of Himyar, a Christian named Abraha, and his rivals, the dam at Marib, vital for the irrigation of a large area, collapsed. The warring parties united to rebuild it, and in the inscription recording the work it is reported that embassies arrived not only from the Lakhmid chief Mundhir and the Jafnid rulers Harith and Abu Karib, but also from both the Persian and the Roman rulers. What exactly their mission was is unclear, but the gathering was clearly an important one. Eventually, in 570, following an appeal from the Himyarites, the Persians intervened directly and annexed the kingdom to their empire.[75]

The issue of the silk trade did not disappear with the failure of Justinian's Ethiopian venture. Although silkworms were introduced to the Roman Empire in the early 550s by eastern monks, Roman dependence on imported silk remained strong. In the late 560s a new opportunity to bypass the Persians presented itself: a Sogdian ambassador arrived in Constantinople, holding out the prospect not only of unmediated supplies of silk but also of an alliance with the Turks, a new power in central Asia that proposed to destroy the Persian Empire in conjunction with the Romans. The prospect proved irresistible to Justin II, and thus he was persuaded to embark on a new war with Persia in 572.[76]

## Conclusion

Justinian emerges above all as a pragmatist in his dealings with Persia and the frontier peoples of the East. Unlike Julian or Justin II, he cherished no ambitions of destroying his powerful neighbour. Instead he preferred to rely on diplomacy, skilfully combined with missionary campaigns, to strengthen Roman influence beyond the imperial frontier; at the same time he sought to consolidate the defences of the eastern provinces by upgrading defensive installations and by relying more heavily on Arab phylarchs. Where possible, he tried to reduce Roman dependence on trade with Persia. The two peace treaties concluded by the emperor testify to the consistency of his policy. Both represent an attempt to end hostilities with the traditional foe for good: the emperor was well aware that Roman resources could be deployed far more effectively elsewhere, as was proved by the remarkable conquests of Belisarius in the West in the 530s. The damage inflicted on the eastern provinces by the resumption of war in 540 has sometimes led to accusations that Justinian neglected the interests of the East in his absorption with the reconquest of the western empire. The accusation is unwarranted. Throughout his reign, the emperor was prepared to invest both men and funds in the defence of the east: in 542 a Roman force of 30,000 was operating in Armenia, while in the 550s a similarly large army campaigned in the Caucasus. The devastation caused by the invasion of 540 was quickly repaired and the defences of Syria greatly strengthened; work continued in the region right up until Justinian's death and beyond.[77]

It may be, however, that the emperor's pragmatism was excessive. The annual payment of some five hundred pounds of gold to the Persians proved to be a source of resentment and embarrassment to many Romans, as has been noted. According to one source, John of Epiphania, the primary reason for the outbreak of war in 572 was that "the Emperor Justin no longer deigned to make an annual payment to the Medes of the 500 lbs. of gold, on which condition the treaty had previously been agreed, or to make the Roman state tributary to the Persians in perpetuity."[78]

Throughout the war that followed, the Romans repeatedly insisted that they wanted to conclude a peace "on equal terms," that is, without any money changing hands. They had a point: no emperor before Justinian had conceded to the Persians a regularised annual payment, which therefore affronted the Romans all the more. Nevertheless, even the peace finally concluded on such terms in 591 was to last only eleven years.[79]

## Notes

1 See G. Greatrex and S. N. C. Lieu, *The Roman Eastern Frontier and the Persian Wars: Part II, 363–628 A.D., A Narrative Sourcebook* (hereafter *REF*) (London, 2002), 123–128, for a detailed account of the reception of a Persian embassy in Constantinople.

2 Peter the Patrician, frag. 13, trans. in M. H. Dodgeon and S. N. C. Lieu, *The Roman Eastern Frontier and the Persian Wars, A.D. 226–363: A Documentary History* (hereafter *REF*) (London, 1994), 131–132. See Theophylact Simocatta, *History*, 4.11.2, with G. Greatrex, *Rome and Persia at War, 502–532* (hereafter *RPW*) (Leeds, 1998), 17; and N. G. Garsoïan, "Byzantium and the Sasanians," *Cambridge History of Iran* (Cambridge, 1983), 3:574–579.

3 M. Whitby, *The Emperor Maurice and His Historian* (Oxford, 1988), 298–299.

4 Garsoïan, "Byzantium and the Sasanians," 591.

5 See, for example, Procopius, *Wars* 1.3–5; and Agathias, *Histories*, 4.24–29. On disgust at Persian practices, see Agathias, *Histories*, 2.24.1, 2.30.5–31.1; and Procopius, *Wars*, 1.12.4. See Garsoïan, "Byzantium and the Sasanians," 575–577.

6 Greatrex, *RPW*, 140–145, 215.

7 Anonymous, *Itinerarium Alexandri*, 5, translated in Dodgeon and Lieu, *REF*, 177.

8 John the Lydian, *On Offices*, 3.34, with G. Fowden, *Empire to Commonwealth* (Princeton, N.J., 1993), 93–97.

9 Dodgeon and Lieu, *REF*, chap. 9, and J. F. Matthews, *The Roman Empire of Ammianus* (London, 1989), 130–161.

10 Greatrex and Lieu, *REF*, 1–13.

11 R. C. Blockley, *East Roman Foreign Policy* (hereafter *ERFP*) (Leeds, 1992), 42–52, 152–163; J. Bardill and G. Greatrex, "Antiochus the *Praepositus*: A Persian Eunuch at the Court of Theodosius II," *DOP* 50 (1996): 171–197; Greatrex and Lieu, *REF*, 16–34.

12 See n. 45 on the Persian church generally. On the synods held in the early fifth century, starting in 410, see S. Brock, "The Church of the East in the Sasanian Empire up to the Sixth Century and Its Absence from the Councils in the Roman Empire," in *Syriac Dialogue* (Vienna, 1994), 69–76; and see J. Wiesehöfer, *Ancient Persia from 550 B.C. to 650 A.D.* (London, 1996), 201–205, on the changing situation of the Persian Christians from the third century onwards.

13 See Greatrex, *RPW*, 13, 73–165; and Greatrex and Lieu, *REF*, 31–81.

14 On the nature of these sources, see A.D. Lee, *Information and Frontiers* (Cambridge, 1993), 35–48; and J. D. Howard-Johnston, "The Official History of Heraclius' Persian Campaigns," in E. Dąbrowa, ed., *The Roman and Byzantine Army in the East* (hereafter *RBAE*) (Cracow, 1994), 57–87.

15 On Euphrasius, see *PLRE* 2, Euphrasius 3. Euphrasius's grandson Nonnosus wrote a work on his travels in Arabia. On Rufinus, see *PLRE* 2, Rufinus 13. See Lee, *Information and Frontiers*, 47.

16 On Peter, see *PLRE* 2, Petrus 27. On Sittas, see *PLRE* 3, Sittas 1. Malalas, *Chronographia*, 18.10 shows Justinian accepting input from Sittas in his reorganisation of Armenia.

17 Quotation from Joshua the Stylite, chap. 8, trans. F. R. Trombley and J. W. Watt, *The Chronicle of Pseudo-Joshua the Stylite* (Liverpool, 2000), 9; see Greatrex, *RPW*, 14–18.

18 By way of comparison, in 443 Theodosius II had been compelled to pay the Huns 2,100 pounds of gold per year (see Blockley, *ERFP*, 64).

19 Procopius, *Wars*, 8.11.1–7, 15.1–20. In 556 a riot broke out in the hippodrome in the presence of a Persian ambassador (Malalas, *Chronographia*, 18.121). See Agathias, *Histories*, 5.24.1, on popular discontent with subsidies to foreign peoples.

20 Menander Protector, *History*, frag. 6.1.162–174. This also accounts for his preference for giving a lump sum in 532 rather than continued payments.

21 For monuments, see a column at Hierapolis, ascribing the ending of the war to "Justinian alone, by divine counsel," trans. in Greatrex and Lieu, *REF*, 97. See also fig. 1. On works of history, see John the Lydian, *On Offices*, 3.28. On the epigrams, see Greatrex, *RPW*, 185.

22 R. N. Frye, "The Political History of Iran under the Sasanians," *Cambridge History of Iran*, 147–148; and Greatrex, *RPW*, 45–8.

23 Frye, "The Political History," 148–151; M. Morony, "Sasanids," *Encyclopedia of Islam*, 2nd ed. (1995): 76–77; and Greatrex, *RPW*, 48–52.

24 P. Crone, "Kavad's Heresy and Mazdak's Revolt," *Iran* 29 (1991): 21–42, M. Whitby, "The Persian King at War," 248–250, in Dąbrowa, *RBAE*, Z. Rubin, "The Reforms of Khusro Anūshirwān," in Cameron, *States, Resources, Armies*, 229–231, Wiesehöfer, *Ancient Persia*, 208–210.

25 J. D. Howard-Johnston, "The Two Great Powers in Late Antiquity: A Comparison," in Cameron, *States, Resources, Armies*, 198–203 (upbeat); see St. J. Simpson, "Mesopotamia in the Sasanian Period: Settlement Patterns, Arts and Crafts," in J. Curtis, ed., *Mesopotamia and Iran in the Parthian and Sasanian Periods* (London, 2000), 57–66. M. Morony, "Land Use and Settlement Patterns in Late Sasanian and Early Islamic Iraq," in Cameron and King, *Land Use*, 221–230, is more cautious.

26 *Expositio totius mundi et gentium*, chap. 19. See Dodgeon and Lieu, *REF*, 221; and Wiesehöfer, *Ancient Persia*, 194.

27 Howard-Johnston, "The Two Great Powers," 204–205; see A. Wink, *Al-Hind: The Making of the Indo-Islamic World*, vol. 1 (Leiden, 1996), 48–50; and D. Whitehouse, "Sasanian Maritime Activity," in J. Reade, ed., *The Indian Ocean in Antiquity* (London, 1996), 339–344. See T. Daryaee, "The Persian Gulf Trade in Late Antiquity," *Journal of World History* 14 (2003): 1–16, on the increase in trade in the Persian Gulf in the sixth and seventh centuries.

28 See Morony, "Sasanids," 77–78; Wiesehöfer, *Ancient Persia*, 190–191; and Rubin, "The Reforms," 243–254.

29 See Rubin, "The Reforms," esp. 283–294, for the fullest treatment of these reforms; Wiesehöfer, *Ancient Persia*, 198–199; and S. Shahbazi, "Army. 5. The Sasanian Period," *EIr* 2 (1987): 496–498; and Howard-Johnston, "The Two Great Powers," 214–219. See also now R. Gyselen, *The Four Generals of the Sasanian Empire: Some Sigillographic Evidence* (Rome, 2001).

30 Wiesehöfer, *Ancient Persia*, 172–174, Rubin, "The Reforms," 292–295. The greatest defeat of the Persian army at the hands of the Romans (near Melitene in 576; see Greatrex and Lieu, *REF*, 153–158) in the sixth century took place *after* the reforms had been carried through.

31 See Procopius, *Wars*, 1.11, with Greatrex, *RPW*, 130–138.

32 Greatrex, *RPW*, 168–212; and Greatrex and Lieu, *REF*, 82–97.

33 See Greatrex and Lieu, *REF*, 97–102 on the 530s and the causes of war.

34 Procopius, *Wars*, 2.5–13, with Greatrex and Lieu, *REF*, 102–108.

35 D. Braund, *Georgia in Antiquity* (Oxford, 1994), 296–311; and Greatrex and Lieu, *REF*, 111–122.

36 See Menander Protector, *History*, frag. 6.1 for the terms of the peace, to be found also in Greatrex and Lieu, *REF*, 131–134.

37 Quotation from Menander Protector, *History*, frag. 6.1.95–96, trans. Blockley. See Greatrex and Lieu, *REF*, 135–228 for events from 572 to 630. J. D. Howard-Johnston, "Heraclius' Persian Campaigns and the Revival of the East Roman Empire, 622–630," *War in History* 6 (1999): 1–44, offers an excellent analysis of the Romano-Persian war that broke out in 603. See W. Kaegi, *Heraclius, Emperor of Byzantium* (Cambridge, 2003), chaps. 2–5.

38 N. Adontz, *Armenia in the Period of Justinian*, trans. N. G. Garsoïan (Lisbon, 1970), 25–53, with N. G. Garsoïan, "Armenia Megale kai eparkhia Mesopotamias," in *Eupsychia. Mélanges offerts à Hélène Ahrweiler* (Paris, 1998), 251–262.

39 I. Engelhardt, *Mission und Politik in Byzanz* (Munich, 1974), 5; Fowden, *Empire to Commonwealth*, chap. 5, esp. 100–104; and see Moorhead, *Justinian*, 143.

40 See Procopius, *Wars*, 1.15.25, and *Buildings*, 3.6.7–12 on the Tzani. Strictly speaking, their lands were already part of the empire. See Procopius, *Wars*, 8.3.18–21, 8.9.10–30 on the Abasgi (though compare 2.29.15, where he claims that the Abasgi had long been Christians).

41 Malalas, *Chronographia*, 18.14, with Evans, *Justinian*, 91–92, and Moorhead, *Justinian*, 141–143.

42 See T. Eide et al., *Fontes Historiae Nubiorum*, vol. 3 (Oslo, 1998), 1147–1153, for Silko's victories; and Siegfried Richter, *Studien zur Christianisierung Nubiens* (Wiesbaden, 2002), 42–114, for discussion of the Nobatae.

43 See the section "Southern Arabia and the Question of Trade."

44 Cf. A. Vasiliev, *Justin I* (Cambridge, Mass., 1950), 250–252, Engelhardt, *Mission und Politik*, 36, 75. Even within the empire, Justinian sometimes gave his backing to opponents of Chalcedon, for example, to John of Ephesus, who converted thousands of pagans in Asia Minor in the 540s; see Evans, *Justinian*, 249.

45 On John, see Greatrex and Lieu, *REF*, 101. On the Persian church, see Wiesehöfer, *Ancient Persia*, 204–205, and S. Brock, "Christians in the Sasanian Empire: A Case of Divided Loyalty," in *Religion and National Identity: Studies in Church History*, vol. 18, ed. S. Mews (Oxford, 1982), 1–19. There is no trace of disloyalty to the empire among anti-Chalcedonians during the wars with Persia, however, cf. Whitby, *Emperor Maurice*, 213–215.

46 See Adontz, *Armenia*, 224–225, on the Armenian army in late antiquity (although his figure of 120,000 men is improbably high); and Procopius on the wealth of Dvin, *Wars*, 2.25.1–3, with M. Chaumont, "Armenia and Iran II," *EIr* 2 (1987): 433; and R. H. Hewsen, *Armenia: A Historical Atlas* (Chicago, 2001), 17–19; see D. Braund, "Procopius on the Economy of Lazica," *Classical Quarterly* 41 (1991): 221–225, on Lazica.

47 Braund, *Georgia*, 273–276, Greatrex, *RPW*, 122–130.

48 See J. D. Howard-Johnston and N. Ryan, *The Scholar and the Gypsy* (London, 1992), 78–85, with Whitby, *Emperor Maurice*, 201–202, and Hewsen, *Armenia*, 14–19.

49 Details in Procopius, *Wars* 1.15, and Greatrex, *RPW*, 185–190. See also Hewsen, *Armenia*, 87–88.

50 On Christianity in Lazica, see Braund, *Georgia*, 277–281. On Christianity in Iberia and Armenia, see Fowden, *Empire to Commonwealth*, 104–109; Braund, *Georgia*, 283–286; and Hewsen, *Armenia*, 72. On Iranian influences in Armenia, see N. G. Garsoïan and J.-P. Mahé, *Des Parthes au Califat* (Paris, 1997), chap. 1.

51 Procopius, *Wars*, 8.3.13–21.

52 Procopius, *Buildings*, 3.6.7, and *Wars*, 1.15.25. See Braund, *Georgia*, 289; and Greatrex, *RPW*, 129–130.

53 *Novel* 31, trans. in Adontz, *Armenia*, 143–144, and chap. 7 on the reforms generally, with Hewsen, *Armenia*, 84–86. See also Braund, *Georgia*, 292–295, on Roman encroachments in Lazica.

54 Procopius, *Wars*, 2.3 on Armenian complaints, 2.15 on Lazic. See also Braund, *Georgia*, 295–296. Even the Tzani eventually revolted in 558; see Greatrex and Lieu, *REF*, 122.

55 For details, see Greatrex and Lieu, *REF*, 116–122. After 542, fighting was confined essentially to Lazica and the surrounding area.

56 On types of nomad, see F. M. Donner, "The Role of Nomads in the Near East in Late Antiquity," in *Tradition and Innovation in Late Antiquity*, ed. F. M. Clover and R. S. Humphreys (Madison, Wis., 1989), 73–85; see also Hoyland, *Arabia*, 89–91, 96–102.

57 I. Shahîd. *Byzantium and the Arabs in the Fifth Century* (hereafter *BAFIC*), (Washington, D.C., 1989), 120–131; I. Shahîd. *Byzantium and the Arabs in the Sixth Century* (hereafter *BASIC*), (Washington, D.C., vol. I, 1995) chap. 1; M. Sartre, *Trois études sur l'Arabie romaine* (Brussels, 1982), 155–162, Hoyland, *Arabia*, 239–240. On the Arab allies of both powers generally, see Hoyland, *Arabia*, 78–83, and Donner, Chap. 20 in this volume.

58 Shahîd, *BASIC*, III A and C; and Greatrex and Lieu, *REF*, 92–93, 108–109.

59 On the fortification work, see M. Whitby, "Procopius and the Development of Defences in Upper Mesopotamia," in *The Defence of the Roman and Byzantine East*, ed. P. Freeman and D. Kennedy (Oxford, 1986), 717–735. On the administrative changes, see Greatrex, *RPW*, 153–155.

60 *Wars*, 1.16.47. See Sartre, *Trois études*, 170–172; and Shahîd, *BASIC*, 95–109.

61 See Procopius, *Wars*, 2.28.13 for the quotation and Harith's victory; see Greatrex and Lieu, *REF*, 129, for the final defeat of Mundhir in 554. On the progress of Harith's career, see Shahîd, *BASIC*, 236–288.

62 See Shahîd, *BASIC*, 735–793; and E. Key Fowden, *The Barbarian Plain* (Princeton, N. J., 1999), 143–144.

63 On the crushing of the revolt, see Shahîd, *BASIC*, 82–95; and Greatrex, *RPW*, 161. See W. Liebeschuetz, "The Defences of Syria in the Sixth century," in C. B. Rüger, ed., *Studien zu den Militärgrenzen Roms II* (Cologne, 1977), 487–499, on the withdrawal of Roman forces from Syria; and see P. J. Casey, "Justinian, the *Limitanei*, and Arab-Byzantine Relations in the Sixth Century," *JRA* 9 (1996): 214–222.

64 Justinian, *Novel* 154 of 535–536.

65 Whitby, *Emperor Maurice*, 210–211; and Key Fowden, *Barbarian Plain*, 131–173.

66 Shahîd, *BASIC*, 346–364, 540–549; and Greatrex and Lieu, *REF*, 136, 166.

67 See J. I. Miller, *The Spice Trade of the Roman Empire* (Oxford, 1969), chap. 13; G. K. Young, *Rome's Eastern Trade* (London, 2001), 24–26, 201–207.

68 See N. Oikonomides, "Silk Trade and Production in Byzantium from the Sixth to the Ninth Century: The Seals of Kommerkiarioi," *DOP* 40 (1986): 33–35; more detail appears in J.-P. Callu, "I commerci oltre i confini dell'Impero," in *Storia di Roma*, vol. 3.1, *L'età tardoantica* (Turin, 1993), 487–491; see also Moorhead, *Justinian*, 164–167. From 408, the three cities where trade could be conducted were Artaxata, Nisibis, and Callinicum, *CJ* 4.63.4 (trans. in Greatrex and Lieu, *REF*, 33–34); see also Menander Protector, *History*, frag. 6.1 (the treaty of 562).

69 Callu, "I commerci," 491, 501–510. On the growth of Sasanian commerce in the fifth and sixth centuries, see D. Whitehouse and A. Williamson, "Sasanian Maritime Trade," *Iran* 11 (1973): 29–49, updated as Whitehouse, "Sasanian Maritime Activity," in *Meccan Trade and the Rise of Islam*, ed. P. Crone (Oxford, 1987), 40–42; and see Wiesehöfer, *Ancient Persia*, 195–196; and n. 27 here.

70 Theophanes, A.M. 5990, trans. Mango and Scott. The revenues to the state were considerable: one *dux* of Palestine was funded in part by the dues collected at the port of Clysma, cf. M. Sartre, *Inscriptions grecque et latines de la Syrie XIII* (Paris, 1982), 107–119 (no. 9046); and Z. Rubin, "Byzantium and Southern Arabia" in D. H. French and C. S. Lightfoot, eds., *The Eastern Frontier of the Roman Empire* (Oxford, 1989), 400.

71 E. Frézouls, "Cosmas Indicopleustes et l'Arabie," in *L'Arabie Préislamique et son environnement historique et culturel*, ed. T. Fahd (Leiden, 1989), 458–460, downplays Roman involvement even in the Red Sea, but see J.-F. Salles, "Fines Indiae – Ardh el-Hind," in Dąbrowa, *RBAE*, 173, n. 36; and Callu, "I commerci," 516–523. Rubin, "Byzantium and Southern Arabia," 400, argues that direct trading links with the Far East were made possible by the Red Sea route.

72 See Greatrex, *RPW*, 227–229; Hoyland, *Arabia*, 51–53; and Rubin, "Byzantium and Southern Arabia."

73 Vasiliev, *Justin I*, 295–297; and Greatrex, *RPW*, 230–231.

74 See Malalas, *Chronographia*, 18.56. For competition between Romans and Persians in Sri Lanka, see Cosmas Indicopleustes, *Topographie chrétienne*, ed. and trans. W. Wolska-Conus, vol. 3 (Paris, 1973), 11.17–18, with n. 69 above.

75 For a translation of the inscription, see S. Smith, "Events in Arabia in the Sixth Century A.D.," *BSOAS* 16 (1954): 437–441. See also Hoyland, *Arabia*, 55–7, 87–88; and Shahîd, *BASIC*, 364–372.

76 See Menander Protector, *History*, frag. 10 with Whitby, *Emperor Maurice*, 218; and Greatrex and Lieu, *REF*, 129, 136–137.

77 On the figures, see Procopius, *Wars*, 2.24.13; and Agathias, *Histories*, 3.8.2 (though both should be treated with caution). On investment in fortifications (not always at

the emperor's own initiative), see Whitby, *Emperor Maurice*, 211–212; and Greatrex and Lieu, *REF*, 242–244.

78 Chap. 2, *FHG* 4.274, trans. in Greatrex and Lieu, *REF*, 141–142.

79 See Menander Protector, *History*, frag. 20.2, for the Roman insistence, trans. in Greatrex and Lieu, *REF*, 159. There is some debate still about whether the Romans had agreed to regular payments in the fifth century, but none has yet been demonstrated; see Greatrex, *RPW*, 15–17.

# 20: The Background to Islam

*Fred M. Donner*

Muhammad, the prophet of Islam (d. 632 CE), who was born around the time of Justinian's death in 565,[1] is associated with changes that heralded the arrival of a new world unimaginable when Justinian was on the throne, and which we associate with the rise of Islam itself during the seventh century. Some of these changes, of course, must be attributed to distinctive features of Muhammad's teachings, which, in turn, were shaped in part by his own unique character and life experiences (and, believing Muslims would insist, by the revelations God vouchsafed to him). Yet in a number of ways, it makes sense to try to see the rise of Islam in the context of social and intellectual developments in the late antique world.[2] For no matter how original or unheralded Muhammad's ideas and message may have been, his own outlook and understanding were inevitably shaped in part by the historical situation in which he lived. Likewise, the reception of Muhammad's message by those around him would have been shaped by the concepts they had been exposed to in their lives. In both cases, this historical context derived from the institutions and ideas that prevailed in the immediately preceding generation – the Age of Justinian.

## Problems of Perception

Attaining a clear historical view of the beginnings of Islam in historical perspective, however, has never been easy. Indeed, it is fair to say that despite the many "historical" works written about Islam's beginnings, we still do not have a very good idea of what the movement begun by Muhammad was all about, and how it fit into the historical context of the late antique Near Eastern world.

There are many reasons for this.[3] A major impediment to achieving a truly historical view of Islam's origins arises from the nature of our sources of information about it. Contemporary documentation in the strict sense is almost totally lacking for the crucial earliest chapters of Islam's origins in the early seventh century; instead, we have a large body of literary sources that describe what happened. These were compiled by members of the Muslim community during the several centuries after the life of the prophet and provide us with sometimes voluminous detail. But, being retrospective rather than contemporary, these literary sources pose for the would-be historian challenging problems because of the likelihood that they contain, alongside possibly accurate memories of what happened, idealizations and distortions of all kinds. One notes, for example, that this literary tradition expresses a "salvation-historical" presentation of events (that is, a narration that depicts events as evidence of God's unfolding plan for the establishment of His favored community). This includes the portrayal of the early Islamic community's expansion as a series of military conquests of quasi-miraculous character; the presentation of Islam's rise as a sudden and decisive break with the past, and a concomitant tendency to minimize continuities between Muhammad's preaching and community and the ideas and practices current in other traditions, particularly in contemporary Christianity and Judaism; and, as part of this, a probable tendency to overemphasize the pagan environment in which the prophet acted. Modern historians have for the most part been forced to rely on these traditional Islamic narratives to construct their picture of "what actually happened," because there is little else to work with. But this picture has not always been historically plausible, and it has proven difficult for historians to identify and free themselves completely from the sources' salvation-historical perspective.[4] Many of their presentations of early Islam thus are, as one of the most acute critics of the traditional sources has aptly put it, little more than "Muslim chronicles in modern languages and graced with modern titles."[5]

Another difficulty derives from the fact that Western writings about Islam began not with scholarship, but with long centuries of anti-Islamic polemic.[6] Even though Western writers began during the Enlightenment to attempt to understand Islam and its beginnings in a more detached and scholarly manner, the heritage of polemical attitudes toward Islam was not easy to shake off. One example might be seen in the tendency, once widespread among Western scholars, to view passages in the Qur'an in a purely reductionist manner – that is, as being little more than distorted "borrowings" from the Old and New

Testaments – without paying adequate attention to broader issues such as the purpose and overall character of the Qur'anic passages. This kind of polemical or quasi-polemical attitude survives vestigially even today, although it tends now to be found more in Western popular opinions about Islam than in scholarship.

Other obstacles to a proper historical understanding of Islam's beginnings are rooted in salient attitudes found in recent and contemporary Western culture – in particular, deeply ingrained nationalist and secularizing ideologies. The profound influence of now-discredited theories of "race" on virtually all aspects of Western culture between the eighteenth and twentieth centuries produced, as one of its manifestations, a tendency to view all of history in nationalist terms (a tendency still widely current in many areas, both within the West and outside it).[7] This nationalist optic distorted many studies of early Islam, notably by leading historians to attribute events to the actions of presumed national groups that did not yet exist as collectivities, at least not in the political and communal sense in which these groups are currently conceived (such as "Arabs"). In the process, the importance of other historical causes, such as religious motivations, was often obscured or completely overlooked.[8]

At the same time, there has been a curious tendency in much Western scholarship on the rise of Islam to minimize, or even to discount altogether, the religious character of these events. Some scholars were devout adherents of another religion (usually Christianity or Judaism) and so, consciously or unconsciously, felt impelled to undercut Muhammad's claim to prophecy. Other scholars were so thoroughly securalist in outlook that they felt uncomfortable with any form of religious explanation. Whatever the reason, one sees a widespread tendency in Western scholarship to explain Islam's appearance primarily as a result of "real," that is, social and economic factors, and a reluctance to entertain the possibility that religious belief may have motivated many people to act (sometimes even against their own economic or social interests) and so contributed fundamentally to driving the complex movement we call the rise of Islam.

Any effort to see Islam's appearance in its proper historical context must, then, overcome these numerous challenges: the dearth of true documentation, the salvation-historical and other idealizing features of the Islamic sources on which we must rely, the lingering heritage of anti-Islamic polemic, and the straitjacket of rigidly nationalist or secularist perceptions.

The remainder of this chapter will review briefly a number of historical phenomena in which the cultures and history of the late antique Near East seem to provide a meaningful context for ideas and events that we associate with the beginnings of Islam. It is hoped that by highlighting such factors, we can begin to contextualize the rise of Islam in ways that are, from the point of view of the historian, more plausible than many earlier descriptions of it, without detracting from Islam's claims to originality or diminishing the importance of its impact.

## The Role of the Great Powers

A fundamental feature of the background against which Islam first appeared was the presence of the two great powers of the late antique Near East, the Byzantine (the later Roman) Empire and the Sasanian Persian Empire, and the complex relationship between them, which wavered unsteadily between grudging mutual recognition and open conflict.[9] This ancient rivalry dated back to Rome's earliest expansion into the eastern Mediterranean, when it came into conflict with the Sasanians' predecessors, the Parthian Arsacids (ruled 248 BCE–224 CE) for control of important border regions coveted by both, particularly northern Mesopotamia and Armenia, and for control of trade routes and trade revenues (Map 16). These issues continued to divide the Byzantines and the Sasanians, to which were added also a religious and cultural dimension to the conflict, pitting Byzantine Christianity and Hellenistic culture against the Zoroastrian (Magian) religion and Iranian culture of the Sasanians. Between the beginning of the Byzantine era in the 330s and the rise of Islam in the early seventh century, the Byzantines and Sasanians were formally at war with one another no fewer than seven times (mainly in the fourth and sixth centuries), on some occasions for periods of a decade or more. Justinian spent lots of energy reconquering the West but like his predecessors and successors was engaged also in war with the Persians, particularly in the period 540–562, when the Sasanians invaded Syria and tried to bring Colchis (Lazica, at the eastern end of the Black Sea) under their control.

Arabia was seldom the central concern of either the Byzantines or the Sasanians, but the protracted military struggle between the two powers had a definite impact on Arabia in the decades preceding Muhammad's birth and preaching there.[10] Both empires, hoping to outflank the other, tried in various ways to extend their own influence over key regions of the peninsula and to thwart the influence of their rival. On the northern fringes of Arabia, the two empires established special ties with powerful Arabic-speaking families, whose leaders

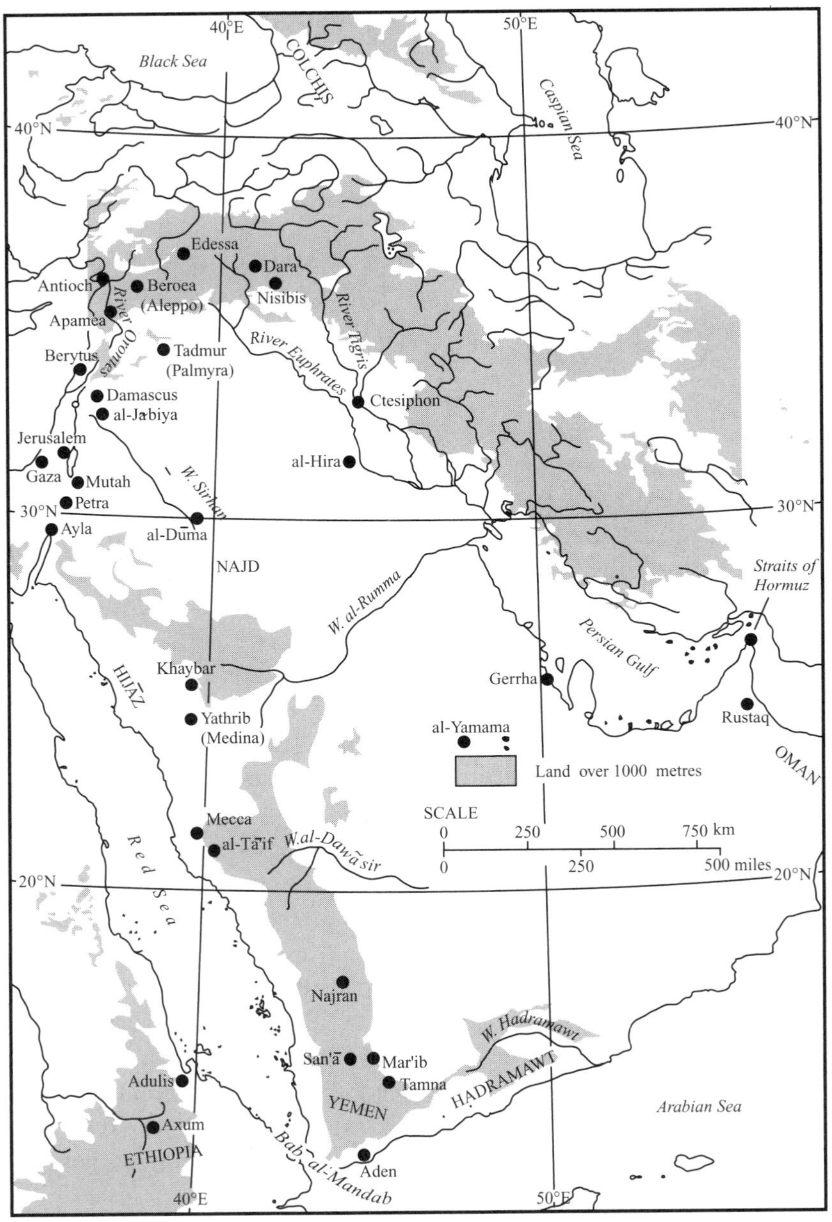


MAP 16. The Arabian Peninsula and adjacent areas in late antiquity

they recognized as "kings" and supplied with monetary subsidies and weapons. The Jafnid family of the tribe of Ghassan, based at al-Jabiya in the Jawlan (Golan) plateau overlooking the Sea of Galilee, were as early as 502 recognized by the Byzantines as *foederati* of the empire; one of the Jafnid rulers, al-Mundhir ibn al-Harith, was even given a crown by the Byzantines in 580. The Jafnids (presumably leading the rest of the Ghassanids) were charged by the Byzantines with preventing other Arabic-speaking groups in their vicinity, particularly pastoral nomadic ones, from raiding settled districts on the Byzantines' eastern frontier in Syria and so disrupting the Byzantines' tax base. The Jafnids were also, on occasion, required to contribute contingents to the Byzantine army when it went on campaign against the Sasanians. In Justinian's time, the Jafnids, under their chief al-Harith ibn Jabala, played an important role at the disastrous battle of Callinicum (531) and in the Assyrian campaign of 541. The Jafnids also warded off and fought against the Sasanian's clients, the Nasrids (see below); once (570) they even burned the Nasrid capital at al-Hira in Iraq. The Byzantines also apparently had a more tenuous agreement with the powerful Arabian group of Kinda, although we know much less about it.[11]

The Sasanians' client relationship with the Nasrid family resembled that of the Byzantines with the Jafnids. The Nasrids, who were part of the tribe of Lakhm, were based in the town of al-Hira on the western steppe fringe of central Iraq.[12] They also had important alliances with (or protectorates over) local chiefs in the eastern Arabian coastal region and in Oman and even maintained standing garrisons or outposts in some of these areas, such as the town of Rustaq in northern Oman.[13] Even distant South Arabia[14] was not beyond the reach of Byzantine and Sasanian interference. The Byzantines were distressed by the activities of the Yemeni ruler Dhu Nuwas (Yusuf Ash'ar), who was Jewish and who persecuted the local Christians. Dhu Nuwas had even written to the Nasrid king al-Mundhir in al-Hira, encouraging him to exterminate his Christian subjects.[15] The Byzantines responded by encouraging the kings of Axum (Ethiopia) to invade Yemen in 525 and to overthrow Dhu Nuwas. Although an Ethiopian general, Abraha, made himself independent ruler of Yemen some years later, Yemen during Justinian's reign was still firmly in the Byzantine sphere of influence. After nearly half a century of Axumite rule over Yemen, however, the locals rose in rebellion around 572, led by Sayf ibn Dhi Yazan, and called upon the Sasanians to support him (if the Sasanians had not had a hand in organizing this uprising in the first place). The Great King Khusro II sent a Sasanian expeditionary force which made

Yemen a province of the Sasanian empire under a governor, backed by a Sasanian garrison. It remained so until the time of Muhammad in the 620s CE.

All of these activities had repercussions deep in the Arabian peninsula. Most Arabian communities and pastoral groups, particularly those in the north of the peninsula, were aware of the Byzantine-Sasanian rivalry and must have been constrained to accommodate to it somehow, whether by allying themselves openly with one power or the other or by carefully trying to preserve their neutrality. The Nasrid kings of al-Hira seem to have had some influence in the affairs of Yathrib (later Medina) in the sixth century, and may have been, for a time, able to appoint a governor there.[16] They may also have had supporters in Mecca and striven to establish a kind of protectorate over it.[17] Similarly, there is some evidence to suggest that, on the eve of Muhammad's career, the Byzantines (probably through their Jafnid allies) may have come close to establishing an alliance with one of the leaders of Quraysh, the main family of Mecca, although in the end the town seems to have remained neutral.[18]

The effect of this rivalry on the intellectual life of Arabia – in particular, on the conceptual outlook of Muhammad and his first followers, who shaped the rise of Islam – is harder to determine. It might be suggested that the Sasanians' virtual encirclement of Arabia following their conquest of Yemen in the 570s and their occupation of Syria and Egypt in the first decade of the seventh century impelled the inhabitants of Arabia to seek a broader, integrating movement in order to resist the increasing pressure of Sasanian political control and Zoroastrian religion. This, some have speculated, might have been either a "nativist" (consciously Arab) identity movement, or rallying around a hitherto neglected Abrahamic monotheism, with close affinities to Christianity and Judaism, that was resurrected (or discovered for the first time).[19] But, as noted above, such ruminations are speculation. The Qur'an, which is notoriously and maddeningly vague in its allusions to historical events, never refers to the Persians or to their religion, Zoroastrianism (Magianism), but speaks frequently of Jews (presumably because Jews lived in Yathrib/Medina) and, less frequently, of Christians (called Nasara). Its only direct reference to the Byzantine-Sasanian rivalry seems to be the celebrated opening verses from Surat al-Rum (30): "The Romans are defeated in the nearest land, but after their defeat they shall be victorious in a few years. The determination [of these events], beforehand and afterward, is God's. And on that day the Believers shall rejoice" (verses 2–4). This passage seems to imply a sympathy for the Byzantine side, assuming that the "defeat" mentioned in verses 2 and 3 refers to a Byzantine defeat by the Sasanians (presumably related to the war of 603–630), but the passage is so ambiguous that it is difficult to be sure.[20] Moreover, if the mention of the "possessors of the elephant" in Surat al-Fil (105) does indeed refer to the attack on Mecca by an army from the Yemeni regime of Abraha's successors, as most commentators assume, this would suggest some hostility to the Byzantines' Ethiopian allies, at least when they tried to attack Mecca.[21]

The great powers, Byzantine and Sasanian, both espoused a concept of universal rule with a strong component of cultural mission that harked back at least to Alexander and the states of his successors in the Near East, including Parthian Iran. This concept of universal rule was adopted by the Romans and, in Christianized form, by the Byzantines; the Sasanians, too, viewed themselves as sovereigns with a claim to universal authority.[22] An expression of this idea on the Byzantine side is found in Justinian's edict of 554 to the people of Constantinople (*Novel* 132): "We believe that the first and greatest blessing for all mankind is the confession of the Christian faith, true and beyond reproach, to the end that it may be universally established and that all the most holy priests of the whole globe may be joined together in unity."[23] Justinian was so determined to establish the Chalcedonian formula for the faith as the only one that he enacted harsh legislation against Nestorians and other Christian "heretics" and even attempted to make Jews, Samaritans, and other non-Christians espouse the formula. Above all, he attempted to eradicate paganism, ordering pagans to embrace Christianity or be stripped of their possessions, closing the pagan academy in Athens and forbidding pagans to teach.[24] The idea of a distinctive religious message underpinning a God-guided kingdom that would – or should – embrace all mankind, and that was particularly hostile to paganism, was thus another part of the intellectual environment in which Muhammad and his Believers worked and acted, another part of the heritage of Justinian and his age.

Commerce formed one of the arenas in which the Byzantines and Sasanians competed in the decades preceding the rise of Islam. The two empires struggled to control – and hence, to tax – the movement of luxury goods (in particular of silk, and of pepper and other spices and aromatics) that flowed from their areas of production in East and South Asia to centers of consumption in the Mediterranean basin.[25] Commercial concerns were almost certainly among the reasons for major offensives launched by the empires or their proxies on several occasions, including the Axumite occupation of Yemen in 525 CE, the Persian occupation of Yemen in the 570s CE, and possibly the Persian invasion of Byzantium's whole eastern half (Syria, Egypt, and much of Anatolia) in the final Byzantine-Persian war beginning in 602.

The role of the Asian-Mediterranean commerce in Arabia and the importance of it (or of changes in it) to the rise of Islam have been hotly debated in recent Western scholarship. The Muslim sources themselves describe Muhammad as having been a merchant involved in trading ventures organized in his native town of Mecca, but it was the Jesuit scholar Henri Lammens who, in the years around 1900, first described Mecca as a wealthy "merchant republic" dealing in precious luxury goods, and identified this commerce as a key factor in the rise of Islam. He implied that the trading interests of the Meccan tribe of Quraysh, to which Muhammad belonged and from which much of the leadership of his movement was drawn after his death, underlay Islam's rapid early expansion.[26] Lammens's notion that Mecca was a nexus of luxury trade established itself as the consensus view among Western scholars through much of the twentieth century and was further refined in numerous detailed studies by such scholars as William Montgomery Watt and Róbert Simon.[27] Despite an occasional critical voice,[28] this theory held sway until 1987, when Patricia Crone published a book that seriously challenged – some would say demolished – it.[29] But her analysis still left open the possibility that the Meccans (and Muhammad) may have engaged in commerce on a much more modest scale, and in more mundane goods like hides, raisins, and grain. It has been argued that the mining of gold may have been a significant feature of the west-Arabian economy on the eve of Islam,[30] and that Sasanian involvement in Arabian trade, mining, and industrial activity may have stimulated an economic expansion in Arabia on the eve of Islam.[31] In sum, while the older theory of Lammens that posited a highly-developed commercial economy in Mecca based on luxury trade should probably now be rejected, it still remains possible that a more modest level of commerce, and other economic activity, could have contributed (both in economic terms and in terms of organizational and management skills) to the orientation and success of Muhammad's religious movement.

Trade has received much attention in discussions of the rise of Islam – and it remains a subject of some dispute. Less clear still are the general economic developments (including demographic changes) in the Near East in the century or so leading up to the appearance of Islam. The evidence, both textual and archaeological, is spotty, and patterns vary from area to area, as do interpretations of it.[32] Parts of southern Syria (modern Jordan) and the Negev, for example, seem to have experienced an increase in church-building from the latter sixth century until the eighth, suggesting prosperity in the local communities.[33] But in general the sixth century, particularly the latter half of the sixth century, seems to have been one of marked decline in major urban centers of the Levant. Antioch and other major cities of northern Syria were devastated by Sasanian invasions in 540, 573, and 611–613, including in some instances having sizable parts of their population deported to Iran. The north Syrian countryside, too, seems to have undergone major changes, with farmers and magnates being replaced by pastoral nomads in some districts.[34] The "Justinianic plague" pandemic that first hit the Near East in 540 and recurred every decade or so until the mid-eighth century affected densely-settled urban centers more severely than small towns, villages, or the region's nomadic populations. The demographic decline caused by the plague (the exact degree of which can only be guessed at) weakened demand for commercial goods and undermined the ability of cities to recover from other shocks, such as war destruction and the numerous very destructive earthquakes that shook the Near East in the sixth century.[35] The plague does not, however, seem to have spread to Arabia itself, raising the possibility that, by weakening the areas neighboring Arabia while leaving it relatively untouched, plague may have contributed significantly to the shift in power that coincides with the rise of Islam.

Late antique society – whether in the Byzantine or Sasanian domains – was highly stratified and class-conscious, and this fact may also be seen as part of the historical and social background against which Islam arose. The Sasanian empire and its official faith of Zoroastrianism were structured around a virtual caste system, according to which people were born into and lived their whole lives as members of one of four discrete social classes – Zoroastrian clergy (including judges), "warriors" (free, landed gentry), scribes, and "cultivators" (including merchants and craftsmen), in descending order. (Moreover, slaves and aliens were effectively noncitizens, not considered to be part of the society.) Zoroastrian priestly rituals were centered on fire temples, but the maintenance of separate fire temples for each class reinforced this ideology of social differentiation and helped ensure that "inappropriate" contact between people from different classes did not occur.[36] Byzantine society was not so rigidly divided in theory, but in practical terms social differentiations were sharp and, for the most part, enduring. The army did provide an avenue of social mobility (even to the top of the social pyramid, as numerous emperors rose through the army), but only for the relatively small number of people who were part of it. Generally, a small and highly privileged elite (*potentiores*), most of whom disposed of great wealth derived from vast landed estates, or sometimes from commerce, dominated the overwhelming majority of the population in the Byzantine empire – the *humiliores* – who were poor.[37]

The extreme stratification that prevailed in most late antique societies sometimes engendered popular reaction, as in the case of the Mazdakite movement in the Sasanian/Zoroastrian context, which from the fifth century CE called for a more egalitarian structuring of society.[38] In the Byzantine/Christian context, the emphasis on piety helped override social stratification, because pious behavior was something that was readily recognized and could help a person overcome lowly ascribed status. The activities of the "holy men" who, according to Peter Brown, were such a prominent feature of the late antique Christian world, may also have worked to blunt class differences, because such people could hail from all strata of society and could serve as intermediaries between different classes and groups.[39]

Arabia on the eve of Islam represented, however, something of an exception to this picture of extreme social stratification. In northern and central Arabia at least, the relatively meager level of resources and organization of society into kinship groups ("tribes") helped undermine the tendency toward social stratification that marked other parts of the Near East. The fact that the Qur'an projects a fundamentally egalitarian view of society may be taken, perhaps, as a reflection of its Arabian milieu; alternatively, we may wish to see the Qur'an's and early Islam's persistent emphasis on egalitarianism and the equality of all humans before their Creator as a reaction against the class-riven visions of society emanating from the Fertile Crescent area.

Another feature of the late antique world, and of the two great empires, that may be significant as part of the background of Islam is the contemporary emphasis on laws or legal codes.[40] All states pay some attention to establishing laws, but there seems to have been a special emphasis on the codification of laws in the late antique world. In the Byzantine domains, this took the form of successive efforts to systematize the complex mass of Roman law, undertaken particularly by the emperors Theodosius II (r. 408–450) and Justinian, after both of whom law codes were named. Justinian's *Corpus iuris civilis*, a massive compilation consisting of three separate works (*Codex Iustinianus; Institutes; Digest*), was drawn up over a five-year period early in his reign and is the most ambitious of these efforts to codify Roman law.[41] Farther west, various barbarian kingdoms of Europe issued codes or collections of royal decrees.[42] The Sasanians, too, engaged in a thoroughgoing compilation of their legal system, particularly under the Great King Khusro II Parviz (r. 591–628). He sponsored the compilation of the *Matakdan i hazar datastan*, or *Book of a Thousand Judicial Decisions*, the culmination of earlier efforts to collect and comment on judicial decisions, Zoroastrian religious law, books on duties of officials, royal decrees, relevant court records, and other documents bearing on the law in order to create a practical guide for judges.[43]

This emphasis on codification of basic texts also extended into the religious realm, constituting almost a bureaucratization of religious belief.[44] The preparation of authoritative Latin, Syriac, and other versions of both the Old and New Testaments was undertaken during the second through fifth centuries. It was during the Sasanian period that the books of the Avesta, or Zoroastrian scripture, were definitively compiled in written form (even though their contents dated to much earlier times), and the compilation of the Zand or commentary on the Avesta was also effected at this time. The same centuries saw the compilation, by Jewish sages, of the Palestinian and Babylonian Talmuds, which are in essence extensive commentaries on the rabbinic text known as the Mishnah.

The result of these activities was that discrete religious confessions came to be defined as much as anything by the fact that they had their own codified holy books. This idea may be the ultimate source of the Qur'an's use of the term *ahl al-kitab*, or "people of the book," to refer to earlier recipients of the monotheist message (particularly Christians and Jews).[45] From the perspective of an imperial government that identified itself with a particular faith, moreover, as both the Byzantine and Sasanian governments did, this sharp definition of religious confessions was a valuable tool for the formulation of imperial policy and the maintenance of social control. Communities following a particular confession could be administered by their own hierarchs, and the codification of religious texts helped give them legal force. The legal orientation of the late antique world may have contributed also to the Qur'an's sense of the importance of legal guidance (*huda*) – a term the Qur'an applies above all to itself – for ensuring the salvation of the Believer.

## The Religious Background

Although many works have emphasized the specifically Arabian religious background to Islam, recent work reveals that we must view

Islam's origins not only in its Arabian context, but rather against the much wider backdrop of the rich and varied religious and cultural traditions of the late antique Near East. We must consider Islam's relationship to religious traditions best known to us from lands adjacent to Arabia – Syria, Mesopotamia, Egypt, Iran, Ethiopia – with which Arabia stood, as we have seen, in intimate contact, to see how they may have contributed to its formation and reception.[46]

The Islamic sources (and, following their lead, much Western scholarship on early Islam) traditionally emphasized the existence in Mecca and elsewhere in Arabia of pagans (idolators, polytheists) who revered idols representing astral deities such as the sun, the moon, and Venus.[47] These pagans were generally identified with the Qur'an's *mushrikun*, those who "associate [something with God]" and thereby deny His uniqueness, and seem to have formed at least part of the immediate background against which Muhammad's preaching and the Qur'an must be viewed. The Qur'an's insistence that God will judge us on the Last Day according to our actions in this life, and on that basis either reward or punish us in the afterlife, implies a general orientation in favor of the concept of free will. This may be read as a reaction against the pervasive fatalism of Arabian paganism, which rejected the idea of an afterlife and viewed worldly existence as determined by blind fate (*dahr*; see Qur'an 45:24).[48] Viewing the Qur'an's teachings and the career of Muhammad against the backdrop of paganism, of course, highlights both the originality of Muhammad's message in the Arabian environment and the uniqueness of his role as a reformer bringing monotheism to these polytheistic communities, and it is hardly surprising that it would be emphasized by later Muslim tradition, and hence adopted by Western scholarship as well.

On the other hand, there is evidence for an indigenous Arabian notion of henotheism – the belief that, while many gods existed, one was supreme among them. Its Arabian form focused on Allah as a "high God" who existed above the lesser gods of the "pagan" pantheons. There is also some evidence for an indigenous Arabian monotheism called *hanifiyya*. The latter may have been linked to recognition of the people of Arabia as descendants of Abraham, and of Mecca's Ka'ba as a shrine to this "religion of Abraham," even in pre-Islamic times.[49]

Moreover, the fact that the Qur'an is replete with references to figures (especially prophets) and events that were part of the Old and New Testament lore reveals that the Qur'an's original audience must also have been familiar with monotheism in its Christian and Jewish variants.[50] This is not to say that Muhammad's early followers were originally Jews or Christians, but it does imply that Judaism and Christianity were present in Muhammad's vicinity. The Qur'anic evidence is bolstered by the traditional biography of Muhammad, produced by the Muslim community during the two centuries after his death; this relates in some detail Muhammad's interactions with what are described as large Jewish communities of western Arabia, particularly with those of Yathrib (Medina), which became his base of operations for the last decade of his life, and other communities farther north, such as Khaybar and Tayma'.[51] G. Hawting has recently argued that the Qur'an's references to *mushrikun* are hyperbolic: that is, they refer not to actual pagans, but rather to monotheists considered inadequately rigorous in their monotheism.[52] G. Lüling has gone farther and suggested that Arabia was largely Christianized in Muhammad's day, and that the Ka'ba may have been a Christian church.[53] C. Luxenberg has proposed that some problematic words and phrases in the Qur'an are actually not in the Arabic language at all, but are rather a transliterated form of Syriac[54] – the literary vehicle of the Syrian and Mesopotamian Monophysite and Nestorian churches between the fourth and eighth centuries CE – suggesting a powerful resonance between the Qur'an and the late antique Christian tradition. These hypotheses remain tentative and still require further investigation, but the evidence as a whole forces us to recognize that Arabia alone (and its presumed paganism) can no longer be viewed as the full setting in which the Qur'an and Muhammad's mission must be viewed. Rather, Islam's origins must be situated in the context of religious trends current in the broader Near Eastern world of the sixth and early seventh centuries CE – a time when this region was intensely engaged in interreligious polemic among various, mostly monotheistic, religious groups, including Jews, several varieties of Christians, and perhaps Zurvanite Zoroastrians.[55]

An important feature of the late antique religious environment in the Near East was the widespread currency of apocalypticism, a complex of eschatological ideas centering on the imminent anticipation of the end of the world. Usually this was expected to be marked by cataclysmic events – natural and sociopolitical – that would usher in the final resurrection of the dead, the Last Judgment, and the dispatch for eternity of all people to heaven or hell. The titanic struggle between the Byzantine and the Sasanian Empires seems to have coincided with a spate of apocalyptic thought and writing in the Near East.[56] By the sixth and seventh centuries, these ideas had been current in the Near East for more than five hundred years. The continuing attraction of apocalypticism in the Byzantine Empire and elsewhere in the Near East throughout the late antique period and into early Islamic times is revealed by the translation and reissue of earlier apocalyptic texts (such as the Tiburtine Sibyl, a fourth-century text translated into Greek in Baalbek during the sixth century)[57] and by the production of entirely new ones during the seventh century and later, such as the late seventh-century works of Pseudo-Methodius, Pseudo-Athanasius, and even the *History* of Sebeos.[58]

Apocalyptic ideas seem to have penetrated Arabia, too, by Muhammad's day and thus may be taken as another dimension of the intellectual background against which Islam arose. Whether Muhammad himself and his earliest followers were charged with apocalyptic enthusiasm remains a subject of debate. The evidence on this point is ambiguous; the text of the Qur'an seems at times to be concerned with establishing a just social order, and in other ways implies belief in a future on earth, but it also speaks with great frequency of the Last Day using powerful eschatological imagery, exhorts its hearers to be constantly mindful of its approach, and offers other hints that the end was considered imminent.[59] Whatever the situation with Muhammad and the earliest Believers may have been on this score, it is hardly surprising, in view of the prevalance of apocalyptic ideas throughout the Near East, that apocalyptic writings began to appear in the Islamic community soon after the time of the prophet. Apocalyptic "predictions" were often presented as utterances of the prophet Muhammad in the *hadith* literature that crystallized in the eighth and following centuries CE.[60] Likewise, a number of rebellions or uprisings in the early Islamic community embraced apocalyptic imagery to give force and appeal to their claims.[61]

Another feature of the late antique religious environment was a widespread concern for individual piety, sometimes to the point of ascetic self-denial. It may in some cases have been associated with apocalyptic concerns, because the conviction that the Judgment was near could incline people to be more punctilious about their religious duties in an effort to ensure their salvation.

This pious attitude was especially marked in Egypt and Syria, but it also was found in most other parts of the Near East.[62] It involved a keen awareness of the need to prepare for death and the life after death, and a turning away from the more public, socially connected cults of classical antiquity. Peter Brown has typified this "new mood" as one that encouraged the drawing of sharp boundaries around the worshipers: "The invisible chasm between the 'saved' and the 'damned' stood like a deep moat round the little groups, pagan and Christian alike, that came to chisel out a position for themselves at the expense of the time-honoured consensus of traditional public worship."[63]

We have little direct evidence to show how deeply this orientation toward piety had penetrated the societies of the Arabian peninsula on the eve of the rise of Islam. But it seems plausible to assume that late antique piety formed the direct background for the understanding of piety in the earliest Muslim community, if for no other reason than because the Qur'an itself has parallels to many late antique practices in this regard. Certainly the Qur'an shows an acute awareness of the distinction between "saved" and "damned," Believer (*mu'min*) and unbeliever (*kafir*).

Another feature of the Near Eastern religious background to Muhammad's mission that we should not overlook is the very concept of prophecy itself. Although the Jewish rabbis had decided that the age of true prophecy had ended in the first century CE – in the sense that there were after that time no more authentic prophets, defined as individuals who received God's revelations – a tradition of belief in active prophecy nevertheless continued in some late antique religious communities, including some branches of Christianity, although prophecy may have become in some cases entirely unmoored from the Judeo-Christian tradition.

The notion of prophecy was probably not always clearly defined in late antiquity and may have been understood in various ways by different groups. For some, prophecy seems to have meant what we might simply call the occasional onset of "inspiration," a special felicity in interpreting scripture or in deciding what to do in a given situation, presumably under divine influence, or the skillful interpretation of dreams and omens, or inspired prognostication.[64] But others understood prophecy in a much more active way, including being the recipient of divine revelations taking written form. Mani, who preached in Iraq in the later third century (he was executed by the Sasanian chief minister Kartir, a determined Zoroastrian, in 276), presented himself as a prophet who had received divine revelations and compiled them in a book. Like Muhammad, Mani saw himself as one in a long series of prophets, including many known to Judaism and Christianity, and called himself the "seal" of the prophetic series.[65]

An active attitude toward prophecy was also espoused by the Christian sect called the Montanists, named after their founder Montanus, who along with his associates Priscilla and Maximilla in the late second century believed they had received revelations from God. Montanists established communities in central Anatolia, Alexandria, and elsewhere, clinging stubbornly to the idea that individual members of the community could, like their founders, be the recipients of prophetic revelations. Despite the church's increasingly strong disapproval of such ideas and its efforts to suppress them, Montanists continue to be mentioned through Justinian's time and until the eve of Islam's appearance.[66]

In Arabia, it is noteworthy that according to the Islamic sources themselves, Muhammad and his followers had to confront a number of rival prophets (called, naturally, "false prophets" by Muslim tradition) who, like him, claimed to be receiving divine revelations. The best-known of these, Maslama (Musaylima) of the Hanifa tribe, was based in the rich oasis of al-Yamama in eastern Arabia (modern Riyadh), and he and his followers put up stiff resistance to the spread of the early Islamic state during the so-called *ridda* wars (wars of apostasy) immediately following Muhammad's death in 632.[67] Several other such "false prophets" (and even one prophetess, Sajah) are reported to have been active in northeastern Arabia, in the Najd, in Yemen, and in Oman.[68] These reports, despite their sketchy character, reveal that Muhammad's claim to prophecy was not *sui generis*. Rather, they make it clear that the late antique tradition of active prophecy was very much alive in Arabia during the sixth and seventh centuries CE, and it is against this background that Muhammad's prophetic claims, and their reception, must be understood.

## Conclusion

The various facets of life in the late antique Near East that we have touched on – political, economic, social, legal, and religious – all formed parts of the background against which Islam first emerged and gradually assumed its distinctive lineaments. It is important to remember, however, that they constitute a background, not a blueprint; they were not, in themselves, "seeds" for a religious movement whose advent no one could have predicted before it happened, even less an inventory of causes or components of the movement itself. The religious movement that began with the prophet Muhammad and soon came to be identified as Islam was, like all such movements, historically unique – shaped by forces that defy historical analysis in part because they are rooted in the individual psyche of key actors and in part because they are vulnerable to the inscrutable interplay of intention and chance. In this sense, no historical event can be fully explained by its context, and each remains unique. We can, however, contextualize Islam's origins to a certain extent by seeing it against beliefs, practices, and institutions that came to resonate with its teachings and actions as a movement, or that – once it had appeared on the historical stage – can be seen to have helped prepare the way for its acceptance.

## Notes

In this article no diacritical marks are used when romanizing words from oriental languages, except for the *'ayn* (') and *hamza* (').

1 The traditional date for Muhammad's birth is often given as 570 CE; the conflicting traditions are examined in Lawrence I. Conrad, "Abraha and Muhammad: Some Observations apropos of Chronology and Literary Topoi in the Early Arabic Historical Tradition," *BSOAS* 50 (1987): 225–240, which favors a date around 552 CE.

2 One of the first attempts to see early Islam in this way – rather than adopting the early Islamic sources' own vision, which sees the rise of Islam as marking a sudden break with the past – was Peter Brown, *The World of Late Antiquity, AD 150–750* (London, 1971). See also Walter E. Kaegi, *Byzantium and the Early Islamic Conquests* (Cambridge, 1992), esp. chap. 2, "The Byzantine Empire in an Era of Accelerating Change," 26–46, on institutional continuity; also his "Variable Rates of Seventh-Century Change," in *Tradition and Innovation in Late Antiquity*, ed. Frank M. Clover and R. Stephen Humphreys (Madison, Wis., 1989), 191–208. A useful compilation and analysis of the non-Muslim primary sources from many languages that describe the rise of Islam is Robert Hoyland, *Seeing Islam as Others Saw It*, Studies in Late Antiquity and Early Islam 13 (Princeton, N.J., 1997).

3 A slightly more developed version of the points covered here appears in my *Seeing the Rise of Islam in Historical Perspective: The First Wadie Jwaideh Memorial Lecture, delivered November 4, 2002* (Bloomington, Ind., Department of Near Eastern Languages and Cultures, 2003).

4 On the complexities of the narrative accounts, see Fred M. Donner, *Narratives of Islamic Origins: The Beginnings of Islamic Historical Writing* (Princeton, N.J., 1998). An important recent study reexamining the "pagan background" is Gerald R. Hawting, *The Idea of Idolatry and the Emergence of Islam: From Polemic to History* (Cambridge, 1999).

5 Patricia Crone, *Slaves on Horses: The Evolution of the Islamic Polity* (Cambridge, 1980), 13.

6 The classic treatment of early Western writings on Islam is Norman Daniel, *Islam and the West: The Making of an Image* (Edinburgh, 1960; rev. ed., Oxford, 1993).

7 For an introduction, see Ashley Montagu, *Man's Most Dangerous Myth: The Fallacy of Race* (New York, 1974); and George L. Mosse, *Toward the Final Solution: A History of European Racism* (Madison, Wis., 1985).

8 See Fred M. Donner, "Modern Nationalism and Medieval Islamic History," *Al-'Usur al-Wusta* 13 (2001): 21–22.

9 See Geoffrey Greatrex, "Byzantium and the East in the Sixth Century," Chap. 19 in this volume. On the Byzantine empire, see J. A. S. Evans, *The Age of Justinian: The Circumstances of Imperial Power* (London, 1996), and Mark Whittow, *The Making of Byzantium, 600–1025* (Berkeley, Calif., 1996). On the Sasanians, see Ze'ev Rubin, "The Sasanid Monarchy," *CAH* 14:638–661 (chap. 22a); Michael Morony, "Sasanids," *Encyclopedia of Islam* (2).

10 See Lawrence I. Conrad, "The Arabs," *CAH* 14 (chap. 22c); and Robert Hoyland, *Arabia and the Arabs: From the Bronze Age to the Coming of Islam* (London, 2001).

11 On the Byzantines' relations with Ghassan and Kinda, see the exhaustive work of Irfan Shahîd, *Byzantium and the Arabs in the Sixth Century* (Washington, D.C., 1995–2002). See also his summary treatment, "Ghassan," *Encyclopedia of Islam* (2). The Sasanian Great King Kavadh is also reported to have had contact with Kinda; see Clifford E. Bosworth, "Iran and the Arabs before Islam," *Cambridge History of Iran* (Cambridge, 1983), 3:593–613 (chap. 16).

12 On Sasanian influence in Arabia, see Bosworth, "Iran and the Arabs." The classic study of the Lakhmids is Gustav Rothstein, *Die Dynastie der Lahmiden in al-Hira* (Berlin, 1899). See also Irfan Shahîd, "Lakhmids," *Encyclopedia of Islam* (2); M. J. Kister, "Al-Hira: Some Notes on Its Relations with Arabia," *Arabica* 15 (1968): 143–169.

13 See Monique Kevran, "Suhar," and G. Rex Smith, "Rustak," in *Encyclopedia of Islam* (2).

14 Yemen is roughly 3,500 kilometres as the crow flies from the Byzantine capital at Constantinople (modern Istanbul) – about as far as Constantinople is from Scotland – and over 2,000 km from the Sasanian capital at Ctesiphon (near modern Baghdad).

15 M. R. Al-Assouad, "Dhu Nuwas," *Encyclopedia of Islam* (2).

16 Kister, "Al-Hira," esp. 144–149; Bosworth, "Iran and the Arabs," 600–601.

17 Suliman Bashear, *Muqaddima fi l-ta'rikh al-akhar* (Jerusalem, 1984), 130–131. Bosworth, "Iran and the Arabs," 600, notes references to *zindiqs* in Mecca, perhaps remnants of the Sasanian monarch Kavadh's adoption of Mazdakism and the Kindite interregnum in al-Hira.

18 On the episode of 'Uthman ibn al-Huwayrith, see William Montgomery Watt, *Muhammad at Mecca* (Oxford, 1953), 15–16.

19 Patricia Crone, *Meccan Trade and the Rise of Islam* (Princeton, N.J., 1987), 246–250, makes the former suggestion (Arab nativism) explicitly and seems to hint at the latter. The nativist idea is also touched on in Uri Rubin, "*Hanifiyya* and Ka'ba: An Inquiry into the Arabian Pre-Islamic Background of *Din Ibrahim*," *Jerusalem Studies in Arabic and Islam* 13 (1990): 85–112. See also Hoyland, *Arabia and the Arabs*, 229–247 (chap. 9), "Arabhood and Arabisation," which seems to adopt this notion.

20 The Sasanian Great King Khusro II began his invasion of Byzantine territory in Anatolia in 603; northern Syria was invaded in 611, and Antioch Apamaea taken; Damascus was conquered in 613, Jerusalem in 614, and Egypt fell in 619. Heraclius's campaigns of reconquest began in Anatolia in 622, focused from 627 on Mesopotamia and Iraq, and resulted in the fall of Khusro II in 628. Heraclius returned to Constantinople and made a triumphant visit to Jerusalem in 630 to return fragments of the True Cross. See Geoffrey Greatrex and Samuel N. C. Lieu, eds., *The Roman Frontier and the Persian Wars, Part II, A.D. 363–630: A Narrative Sourcebook*

(London, 2002), chap. 13, "The Persian Takeover of the Near East" (182–197) and chap. 14, "The Roman Recovery under Heraclius (622–630)," (198–228).

21 On this attack – probably to be identified with the campaign on Haliban in 547 CE – see Bosworth, "Iran and the Arabs," 606, which cites the relevant scholarship discussing the problems raised by this identification.

22 On this theme, see John H. Marks, *Visions of One World: Legacy of Alexander* (Guilford, Conn., 1985); and Garth Fowden, *Empire to Commonwealth: Consequences of Monotheism in Late Antiquity* (Princeton, N.J., 1993). Also see Charles Pazdernik, "Justinianic Ideology and the Power of the Past," Chap. 8 in this volume.

23 Quoted in P. N. Ure, *Justinian and His Age* (Harmondsworth, Eng., 1951), 122.

24 A summary of Justinian's religious policies is provided in Pauline Allen, "The Definition and Enforcement of Orthodoxy," *CAH* 14:811–835 (chap. 27), esp. 820–828.

25 See Touraj Daryaee, "The Persian Gulf Trade in Late Antiquity," *Journal of World History* 14 (2003): 1–16.

26 See especially Henri Lammens, "La République marchande de la Mecque vers l'an 600 de notre ère," *Bullétin de l'Institut Egyptien*, 5th ser., no. 4 (1910): 23–54, and *La Mecque à la veille de l'hégire* (Beirut, 1924).

27 Watt, *Muhammad at Mecca;* Róbert Simon, *Meccan Trade and Islam: Problems of Origin and Structure* (Budapest, 1989; the Hungarian original of this work first appeared in 1975). Like many other works, my own *Early Islamic Conquests* (Princeton, N.J., 1981) accepted this theory without full critical scrutiny; it was assumed "proven."

28 See especially G.-H. Bousquet's review of Watt's *Muhammad at Mecca*, "Une explication Marxiste de l'Islam par un ecclésiastique épiscopalien," *Hésperis* 41 (1954), 231–247, which calls into question the notion of Mecca as a center of "capitalist" commerce on which Watt builds his work, explicitly mentioning (at least in passing) the work of Lammens himself (238).

29 Crone, *Meccan Trade and the Rise of Islam.* In his review of this work, the historian Hugh Kennedy terms it a "thorough demolition job" against the traditional Meccan trade hypothesis: *Middle East Studies Association Bulletin* 22 (1988): 54–55.

30 Gene Heck, "Gold Mining in Arabia and the Rise of the Islamic State," *Journal of the Economic and Social History of the Orient* 42 (1999): 364–395; Heck, "'Arabia without Spices': An Alternate Hypothesis," *Journal of the American Oriental Society* 123 (2003), forthcoming.

31 Michael Morony, "The Late Sasanian Economic Impact on the Arabian Peninsula," *Name-ye Iran-e Bastan* 1.2 (2001–2002): 25–37.

32 Two important studies that appeared in the same year and draw on much common evidence provide a striking contrast. J. A. S. Evans, *The Age of Justinian: The Circumstances of Imperial Power* (London, 1996), 225–240, sketches the deterioration of towns and institutions in Syria during the sixth century under the impact of repeated earthquakes, invasions, and plague and outlines the difficulty the emperor had in rebuilding ruined towns; in Evans' view, "by 600, the amenities of urban life which still existed a century earlier had disappeared in most of [the cities of the classical world]" (225). Mark Whittow, *The Making of Byzantium, 600–1025* (Berkeley, Calif., 1996), 53–68, argues, on the contrary, that the "decline" of Syria during the sixth century has been overstated by modern scholars and alleges that western Asia Minor, Cilicia, Syria, Palestine, and Egypt provide evidence of "the

empire's continuing prosperity in 600" (59). Although not an expert in these matters, I find the evidence provided by Evans, Trombley (see n. 34), and others more convincing than that adduced by Whittow, although Whittow is undoubtedly correct to stress that we must not equate change with decline.

33 See Clive Foss, "The Near Eastern Countryside in Late Antiquity: A Review Article," in *The Roman and Byzantine Near East: Some Recent Archaeological Research*, ed. J. H. Humphrey, *Journal of Roman Archaeology*, suppl. 1 (1995), 213–234, which summarizes some of the archaeological evidence.

34 Frank R. Trombley, "War and Society in Rural Syria ca. 502–613 A.D.: Observations on the Epigraphy," *BMGS* 21 (1997): 154–209.

35 Foss, "The Near Eastern Countryside"; Hugh Kennedy, "The Last Century of Byzantine Syria: A Reinterpretation," *Byzantinische Forschung* 10 (1985): 141–183. On the plague and its impact, see Lawrence I. Conrad, *The Plague in the Early Medieval Near East* (PhD diss., Princeton University, 1981); and Evans, *The Age of Justinian*, 160–165. Whittow, *Making of Byzantium*, 66–68, attempts to minimize the impact of the plague, in keeping with his general interpretation.

36 See A. Perikhanian, "Iranian Society and Law," *Cambridge History of Iran* 3:627–680, esp. 631–646. Also Jamsheed Choksy, "Sassanians," in *Late Antiquity: A Guide to the Postclassical World*, ed. G. W. Bowersock, Peter Brown, and Oleg Grabar (Cambridge, Mass., 1999), 682–685; Richard N. Frye, "Parthian and Sasanian History of Iran," in *Mesopotamia and Iran in the Parthian and Sasanian Periods: Rejection and Revival c. 238 B.C.–A.D. 642*, ed. John Curtis (London, 2000), 17–22.

37 A concise overview of Byzantine social structure in the later sixth century is found in John F. Haldon, *Byzantium in the Seventh Century: The Transformation of a Culture* (Cambridge, 1990), 26–31; see also Whittow, *Making of Byzantium*, 53–68. Mercantile wealth is discussed in Linda Jones Hall, "The Case of Late Antique Berytus: Urban Wealth and Rural Sustenance – A Different Economic Dynamic," in *Urban Centers and Rural Contexts in Late Antiquity*, ed. Thomas S. Burns and John W. Eadie (East Lansing, Mich., 2001), 63–76.

38 Patricia Crone, "Kavad's Heresy and Mazdak's Revolt," *Iran* 29 (1991): 21–42; Ehsan Yarshater, "Mazdakism," *Cambridge History of Iran*, 3:991–1024.

39 On the "holy man," see Peter Brown, "The Rise and Function of the Holy Man in Late Antiquity," *JRS* 61 (1971): 80–101; and Peter Brown, "Town, Village, and Holy Man: The Case of Syria," in *Assimilation et résistance à la culture gréco-romaine dans le monde ancien* (Madrid, 1976), 213–220, both reprinted in Peter Brown, *Society and the Holy in Late Antiquity* (Berkeley, Calif., 1982). Also see Peter Brown, "Holy Men," *CAH* 14: 781–810 (chap. 26); Han J. W. Drijvers, "The Saint as Symbol: Conceptions of the Person in Late Antiquity and Early Christianity," in *Concepts of Person*, ed. Hans G. Kippenberg, Y. B. Kuiper, and A. F. Sanders (Berlin, 1990), 137–157.

40 See Caroline Humfress, "Law and Legal Practice in the Age of Justinian," Chap. 7 in this volume.

41 A fascinating glimpse of the procedures followed in compilation of Justinian's *Digest* is A. M. Honoré, *Justinian's Digest: Work in Progress* (Oxford, 1971). The same author has provided a useful overview of the codification of Byzantine law in his article "Law Codes" in Bowersock, Brown, and Grabar, *Late Antiquity*, 539–540. More generally, see Detlef Liebs, "Roman Law," *CAH* 14: 238–259 (chap. 9).

42 For an overview, see T. M. Charles-Edwards, "Law in the Western Kingdoms between the Fifth and the Seventh Century," *CAH* 14: 260–287 (chap. 10).

43 See Perikhanian, "Iranian Society and Law," 628–631.

44 See Humfress, Chap. 7, and Nicholas de Lange, "Jews in the Age of Justinian," Chap. 16 in this volume.

45 On this concept in the Qur'an, see Georges Vajda, "Ahl al-kitab," *Encyclopedia of Islam* (2). Zoroastrians are not mentioned in the Qur'an, but later Muslims debated the status of Zoroastrians and the mainstream view included them among the *ahl al-kitab*.

46 A pioneering experiment to do this was Patricia Crone and Michael Cook, *Hagarism: The Making of the Islamic World* (Cambridge, 1977). The shortcomings of some aspects of *Hagarism's* historical reconstruction should not diminish our appreciation of the value of the attempt or obscure the impact the book had.

47 The classic studies are Julius Wellhausen's *Reste arabischen Heidentums* (Berlin, 1887) and Toufic Fahd, *Le Panthéon de l'Arabie centrale à la veille de l'hégire* (Paris, 1968). See also Uri Rubin, "The Ka'ba: Aspects of Its Ritual Functions and Position in Pre-Islamic and Early Islamic Times," *Jerusalem Studies in Arabic and Islam* 13 (1986): 97–131; and Michael Lecker, "Idol Worship in Pre-Islamic Medina (Yathrib)," *Le Muséon* 106 (1993): 331–346.

48 See Helmer Ringgren, *Studies in Arabian Fatalism* (Uppsala-Wiesbaden, 1955).

49 See Hamilton A. R. Gibb, "Pre-Islamic Monotheism in Arabia," *Harvard Theological Review* 55 (1962): 269–280; William Montgomery Watt, "Belief in a 'High God' in Pre-Islamic Mecca," *Journal of Semitic Studies* 16 (1971): 35–40; and Rubin, "Hanifiyya and Ka'ba."

50 A classic overview of the Old Testament material found in the Qur'an is Heinrich Speyer, *Die biblischen Erzählung im Qoran* (Grafenhainchen, 1931). The New Testament parallels in the Qur'an, which are greatly outweighed by those with the Old Testament, are discussed in Richard Bell's *The Origin of Islam in Its Christian Environment* (London, 1926).

51 An overview of what can be learned about these Jewish communities, not a little of it derived from the *Sira* and similar works, is found in Gordon Darnell Newby, *A History of the Jews of Arabia* (Columbia, S.C., 1988). An English translation of the *Sira* is Alfred Guillaume, *The Life of Muhammad* (Oxford, 1955). The *Sira* makes far less mention of Christians and does not portray Christian communities as being present in western Arabia. The penetration of Christianity in other parts of Arabia is surveyed in J. Spencer Trimingham, *Christianity among the Arabs in Pre-Islamic Times* (London, 1979).

52 Hawting, *The Idea of Idolatry and the Emergence of Islam*; see my review in *Journal of the American Oriental Society* 121 (2001): 336–338.

53 Günter Lüling, *Die Wiederentdeckung des Propheten Muhammad* (Erlangen, 1981).

54 Christoph Luxenberg, *Die syro-aramäische Lesart des Koran. Ein Beitrag zur Entschlüsselung der Koransprache* (Berlin, 2000).

55 On the latter, see R. C. Zaehner, *Zurvan, A Zoroastrian Dilemma* (Oxford, 1955).

56 On this as background to Islam, see my "The Sources of Islamic Conceptions of War," in *Just War and Jihad: Historical and Theoretical Perspectives on War and Peace in Western and Islamic Traditions*, ed. John Kelsay and James Turner Johnson (Westport, Conn., 1991), 30–69, esp. 43–48; Gerrit J. Reinink, "Heraclius, the

New Alexander: Apocalyptic Prophecies during the Reign of Heraclius," in *The Reign of Heraclius (610–641): Crisis and Confrontation*, ed. Bernard H. Stolte and Gerrit J. Reinink (Leuven, 2002), 81–94; Wout Jac. van Bekkum, "Jewish Messianic Expectations in the Age of Heraclius," in Stolte and Reinink, *Reign of Heraclius*, 95–112.

57 See Paul J. Alexander, *The Oracle of Baalbek: The Tiburtine Sibyl in Greek Dress* (Washington, D.C., 1967).

58 See Paul J. Alexander, *The Byzantine Apocalyptic Tradition* (Berkeley, Calif., 1985); Francisco Javier Martinez, *Eastern Christian Apocalyptic in the Early Muslim Period: Pseudo-Methodius and Pseudo-Athanasius* (PhD diss., Catholic University of America, 1985); John Haldon, "The Works of Anastasius of Sinai: A Key Source for the History of Seventh-Century East Mediterranean Society and Belief," in *The Byzantine and Early Islamic Near East*, vol. 1, *Problems in the Literary Source Material*, ed. Averil Cameron and Lawrence I. Conrad, Studies in Late Antiquity and Early Islam 1 (Princeton, N.J., 1992), 107–147; Gerrit J. Reinink, "Ps.-Methodius: A Concept of History in Response to the Rise of Islam," in Cameron and Conrad, *The Byzantine and Early Islamic Near East*, 149–187; Han J. W. Drijvers, "The Gospel of the Twelve Apostles: A Syrian Apocalypse from the Early Islamic Period," in Cameron and Conrad, *The Byzantine and Early Islamic Near East*, 189–213; Walter E. Kaegi, "Byzantine Sardinia and Africa Face the Muslims: A Rereading of Some Seventh-Century Evidence," *Bizantistica* 3 (2001): 1–24, helps clarify the outlook of Ps.-Methodius. Walter Kaegi informs me that the role of apocalyptic expectations in the construction of Sebeos's *History* is noted in Timothy W. Greenwood, *A History of Armenia in the Seventh and Eighth Centuries* (PhD diss., Oxford University, 2000), which I have not seen.

59 For example, Qur'an 16 (al-Nahl): 77: "God's are the hidden things of the heavens and the earth; the matter of the Hour is like the fleeting glance, or even nearer." For a general overview, see Uri Rubin, "Al-Sa'a (2)," *Encyclopedia of Islam* (2).

60 For an overview, see Arendt J. Wensinck, *A Handbook of Muhammadan Tradition* (Leiden, 1927), s.v. "Hour," which indexes many purported sayings of Muhammad dealing with the coming of the end. See also Wilferd Madelung, "Apocalyptic Prophecies in Hims in the Umayyad Age," *Journal of Semitic Studies* 31 (1986): 141–185; and David Cook, *Studies in Muslim Apocalyptic* (Princeton, N.J., 2003).

61 For example, the Abbasid revolution, or the anti-Abbasid rebellion of Abu l-'Umaytir in Syria, on which see Paul M. Cobb, *White Banners: Contention in Abbasid Syria, 750–880* (Albany, N.Y., 2001), 55–65.

62 Two classic treatments of late antique piety are Arthur Vööbus, *A History of Asceticism in the Syrian Orient*, 2 vols. (Louvain, 1958–1960); and Derwas Chitty, *The Desert a City* (Oxford, 1966). See also Peter Brown, "Asceticism," *CAH* 13, chap. 20, and the references in n. 39 herein on the "holy man."

63 Brown, *The World of Late Antiquity*, 57.

64 On the survival of various concepts of prophecy into the late antique period, see Rebecca Gray, *Prophetic Figures in Late Second Century Jewish Palestine: The Evidence from Josephus* (New York, 1993). My thanks to Charles Jones for guiding me to this important study.

65 On Manichaeism, see Samuel N. C. Lieu, *Manichaeism in the Later Roman Empire and Medieval China* (Tübingen, 1992). L. J. R. Ort, *Mani: A Religio-Historical Description of His Personality* (Leiden, 1967), 117–127, discusses Mani's forerunners.

Garth Fowden, "Religious Communities," in Bowersock, Brown, and Grabar, *Late Antiquity*, 95, emphasizes parallels between Mani and Muhammad.

66 Ronald E. Heine, *The Montanist Oracles and Testimonia* (Macon, Ga., 1989) provides Montanist texts; Stephen Gero, "Montanus and Montanism According to a Medieval Syriac Source," *Journal of Theological Studies* n.ser. 28 (1977): 520–524, discusses persecution of Montanists under Justinian.

67 On al-Yamama, see Abdullah al-Askar, *Al-Yamama in the Early Islamic Era* (Riyadh, 2002); Musaylima and religious questions are dealt with on 77–117. Also M. J. Kister, "The Struggle against Musaylima and the Conquest of Yamama," *Jerusalem Studies in Arabic and Islam* 27 (2002): 1–56.

68 The best discussion of the movements subsumed by Muslim historians under the rubric *al-ridda*, which includes the political activities of the various "false prophets," remains Elias S. Shoufani, *Al-Riddah and the Muslim Conquest of Arabia* (Toronto, 1972). The religious activities of these figures is obscure, but their claim to have been prophets is not in doubt. One can read descriptions of their activities in al-Tabari, *The History of al-Tabari*, vol. 10, *The Conquest of Arabia* (Albany, N.Y., 1993); it is hostile to them, of course, but for the best known of them, Maslama, it provides at least a caricature of his religious preachings.

# Bibliography

## Primary Sources


Acacian Schism. *Publizistische Sammlungen zum Acacianischen Schisma.* Ed. Eduard Schwartz. Munich, 1934.

Acts of Church Councils. *ACO* 4. 1, ed. J. Straub. Berlin, 1971.

———. *ACO* 4. 2, ed. Eduard Schwartz, Berlin: 1914.

Agapetus. *Ekthesis. Expositio capitum admonitorium.* Ed. J. P. Migne. PG 86.1, 1163–1186. Paris, 1867. Partial trans. in Ernest Baker, *Social and Political Thought in Byzantium.* Oxford, 1957.

Agathias. *Agathiae Myrinaei Historiarum libri quinque.* Ed. Rudolf Keydell, *Histories.* trans. Joseph D. Frendo. Berlin, 1975.

Ammianus Marcellinus. *Rerum Gestarum libri qui supersunt,* ed. Wolfgang Seyfarth, Liselotte Jacob-Karau, and Ilse Ulmann. Leipzig, 1978. Trans. John C. Rolfe, *Ammianus Marcellinus.* Cambridge, Mass., 1935–1939.

Anonymous. *Itinerarium Alexandri,* ed. R. Tabacco. Florence, 2000.

———. *On Political Science.* (See *Peri politikês epistêmês*)

———. *On Strategy.* In *Three Byzantine Military Treatises,* ed. and trans. George T. Dennis. Washington, D.C., 1985. 1–136.

*Anthologia Graeca* (*The Greek Anthology*). Trans. William Paton. 5 vols. London, 1916–1918.

*Anthologia Palatina.* In *Anthologie grecque, première partie: Anthologie palatine,* ed. and French trans. Pierre Waltz. 6 vols. Paris, 1960.

Arator. *De actibus apostolorum.* Ed. Arthur Patch McKinlay. CSEL 72. Vienna, 1951.

Augustus. *Res gestae.* In *Res gestae divi Augusti,* trans. P. A. Brunt and J. M. Moore, Oxford, 1967.

Anonymous of Piacenza. In John Wilkinson, trans., *Jerusalem Pilgrims before the Crusades,* Warminster, 2002, pp. 129–151.

Cassiodorus. *Cassiodori Senatoris Variae.* Ed. Theodor Mommsen (Berlin, 1865–1894), *MGH AA* 12, 10.

———. *Variae.* Trans. S. J. B. Barnish. Liverpool, 1992.

*Codex Theodosianus.* In *Theodosiani libri XVI cum Constitutionibus Sirmondianis: Et Leges novellae ad Theodosianum pertinentes,* ed. T. Mommsen and P. M. Meyer. Berlin, 1905. English trans. C. Pharr et al., *The Theodosian Code and Novels, and the Sirmondian Constitutions.* Princeton, N. J., 1952.

*Collectio Avellana* (*imperatorum pontificum aliorum inde ac a. XVII usque ad a. DLIII datae*). Ed. O. Guenther. CSEL 35.1–2. Prague, 1895.

Constantine VII Porphyrogenitus. *De cerimoniis aulae Byzantinae*. In *Constantini Porphyrogeniti imperatoris de cerimoniis aulae Byzantinae libri duo*, ed. J. J. Reiske. Bonn, 1829.

Corippus, Flavius Cresconius. *Iohannis*. Ed. James Diggle and Francis R. D. Goodyear. Cambridge, 1970.

———. *The* Iohannis *or* De bellis libycis *of Flavius Cresconius Corippus*. Trans. George W. Shea. Lewiston, Me., 1998.

———. *In laudem Iustini minoris libri IV*. Ed., trans., and comm. Averil Cameron. London, 1976.

Cosmas Indicopleustes. *Chronicon Paschale. 284–628 AD*. Ed. M. Whitby and M. Whitby. Liverpool, 1989.

———. *Topographie chrétienne*. Ed. Wanda Wolska-Conus. 3 vols. Paris, 1968–1973.

———. *The Christian Topography of Cosmos, an Egyptian Monk*. Trans. William McCrindle. London, 1897.

Cyril of Edessa. *Six Explanations of the Liturgical Feasts by Cyrus of Edessa. An East Syrian Theologian of the Mid-Sixth Century*. Ed. William F. Macomber. CSCO 355–356/Syr. 155–156. Louvain, 1974.

Cyril of Scythopolis. *Life of Sabas (Vita Sabae)*. In *Kyrillos von Skythopolis*, ed. Eduard Schwartz. *Texte und Untersuchungen* 49.2 (Leipzig, 1939): 85–200.

———. *Cyril of Scythopolis: The Lives of the Monks of Palestine*. Ed. R. M. Price and John Binns. Cistercian Studies 114. Kalamazoo, Mich. 1991.

Description of Hagia Sophia. *Narratio de Aedificatione Templi S. Sophiae*. In *Scriptores originum Constantinopolitanarum*, ed. Theodor Preger, Leipzig, 1901.

Dionysius, Pseudo-. *Corpus Dionysiacum*. Ed. Beate Suchla et al. 2 vols. Berlin, 1990–1991.

———. *The Complete Works*. Trans. Colm Luibheid with forward and notes by Paul Rorem. New York, 1987.

Egeria. *Travels*. In *Égérie, Journal de voyage*, ed. and trans. Pierre Maraval. SC 296. Paris, 1982.

———. *Egeria's Travels to the Holy Land*. Ed. John Wilkinson. 3rd ed. Warminster, Eng., 1999.

Ennodius. *Magni Felicis Ennodi opera*. Ed. Friedrich Vogel. *MGH AA* 7. Berlin, 1885.

Eusebius. *Life of Constantine*. Ed. and trans. Averil Cameron and Stewart Hall. Oxford, 1999.

Evagrius Scholasticus. *Ecclesiastical History*. Ed. J. Bidez and L. Parmentier. London, 1898. Repr. Amsterdam, 1964. Trans. M. Whitby as *The Ecclesiastical History of Evagrius Scholasticus*. Liverpool, 2000.

*Expositio totius mundi et gentium*. Ed. and trans. J. Rougé. Paris, 1966.

Facundus. *Pro defensione Trium Capitulorum*. Ed. Jean-Marie Clément and Roland Vander Plaetse. CCSL 90A. Turnhou, Belgium, 1974.

Ferrandus. *Epistolae et opuscula*. Ed. Jean-Paul Migne. Patrologia Latina 96. Paris, 1865.

*Fragmenta Historicorum Graecorum*, vol. 4. Ed. Carolus Müller. Paris, 1851.

Gaius. *Institutiones*. Ed. E. Seckel and B. Kübler. 7th ed. Leipzig, 1935. English trans. W. M. Gordon and O. F. Robinson as *The Institutes of Gaius*. Ithaca, N.Y., 1988.

George Cedrenus. *Historiarum Compendium*. Ed J.-P. Migne. Paris 1889–1894. *PG* 121: 23–1166.

George of Pisidia/Giorgio di Pisidia. *Carmi*. Ed. Luigi Tartaglia. Turin, 1998.

Gildas. *De excidio Britonum*. Ed. M. Winterbottom. London, 1978.

*Greek Anthology (Anthologia Graeca).* Ed. and trans. William Paton. 5 vols. 67–68, 84–86. Cambridge, Mass., 1916–1918.

Innocentius. *Letter to the Thomas, Priest of Thessalonica, about the Conversations with the Severians, ACO* 4.2.169–184.

*Ius Graeco-romanum.* Ed. J. and P. Zepos. 8 vols. Athens 1931 and Aalen, 1962.

Jerome. *Selected Letters.* Cambridge, Mass, 1933.

John Chrysostom. *On the Priesthood.* NPNF 1.9.33–83.

John of Beit-Aphtona [?]. See in S. Brock, "The Conversations with the Syrian Orthodox under Justinian (532)." *OCP* 47 (1981):92–113.

John of Ephesus. *John of Ephesus. Lives of the Eastern Saints,* I–III. Ed. Ernest W. Brooks. PO 17.1, 18.4, 19.2. Paris, 1923–1925. Reprint, Turnhout, Belgium, 1974.

———. *Ecclesiastical History,* vol. 2. Partially preserved in *The Chronicle of Zuqnin, Parts III and IV,* ed. and trans. A. Harrak. Toronto, 1999. 49–137.

———. *Ecclesiastical History: Part 3.* Ed. E. W. Brooks. CSCO 105–106/Syr 54–55. Louvain, 1952; first published 1935–1936.

John the Lydian. *Ioannis Laurentii Lydi, De magistratibus populi Romani libri tres.* Ed. Richard Wünsch. Leipzig, 1903.

———. *On Powers, or, The Magistracies of the Roman State.* Ed., trans., and comm. Anastasius C. Bandy. Philadelphia, 1983.

———. *John Lydos, On the Magistracies of the Roman Empire.* Trans. Thomas F. Carney. *Bureaucracy in Traditional Society: Romano-Byzantine Bureaucracies Viewed from Within,* 3. Lawrence, Kan., 1971.

———. *De mensibus.* In *Ioannis Lydi liber de mensibus.* Ed. R. Wünsch. Leipzig, 1898. Reprint, Stuttgart, 1967.

John Malalas. *Chronographia.* In *Ioannis Malalae Chronographia,* ed. Johannes Thurn. Berlin, 2000.

John Philoponus. *De aeternitate mundi contra Proclum (On the Eternity of the World).* Ed. Hugo Rabe. Leipzig, 1899.

John of Nikiou. *The Chronicle of John, Bishop of Nikiou.* Trans. R. H. Charles. London, 1916.

Jordanes. *The Gothic History of Jordanes.* Trans. Charles C. Mierow. Cambridge, 1915.

Julian. *Dictatum de Consiliariis.* In *Iuliani Epitome Latina Novellarum Iustiniani,* ed. Gustav Hänel. Leipzig, 1873. 198–201.

Junillus Africanus. *Instituta Regularia Divinae Legis,* in *Exegesis and Empire in the Early Byzantine Mediterranean: Junillus Africanus and the Instituta Regularia Divinae Legis,* by Michael Maas. Tübingen, 2003. Includes the 1880 edition by Heinrich Kihn and an English translation.

*Jus Graeco-romanum.* Ed. I. and P. Zepos. 8 vols. Athens, 1931. Reprint, Aalen, 1962.

Justinian. *Drei dogmatische Schriften Justinians.* Ed. E. Schwartz. Munich, 1939. Reprint, Milan, 1973. Trans. K. P. Wesche as *On the Person of Christ.* Crestwood, N.Y., 1991.

———. *Institutiones, Digesta.* Ed. P. Krüger and T. Mommsen. 16th ed. Vol. 1 of *Corpus iuris civilis.* Berlin, 1928. English trans. of *Institutiones* P. Birks and G. MacLeod as *Justinian's Institutes.* Ithaca, N.Y., 1987. English trans. of *Digesta* Alan Watson et al. as *The Digest of Justinian.* Rev. ed. Philadelphia, 1998.

———. *Codex Iustinianus.* Ed. P. Krüger. 11th ed. Vol. 2 of *Corpus iuris civilis.* Berlin, 1929.

———. *Novellae.* Ed. R. Schöll and G. Kroll. 6th ed. Vol. 3 of *Corpus iuris civilis.* Berlin, 1928.

Leontius of Jerusalem. *Against the Monophysites*. PG 86.2. Paris, 1865. 1769A–1901A.

*Liber Pontificalis*. Ed. Louis Duchesne. 2nd ed. Paris, 1955–1957. Trans. Raymond Davis as *The Book of the Pontiffs: The Ancient Biographies of the First Ninety Bishops of Rome to AD 715*. 2nd ed. Liverpool, 2000.

Liberatus. *Breuiarium causae Nestorianorum et Eutychianorum*. Ed. Jean-Paul Migne. PL 68. Paris, 1866.

*Life of St. Nicholas of Sion*. Ed. and trans. Ihor Ševčenko and Nancy Patterson Ševčenko. Brookline, Mass., 1984.

*Life of Symeon the Younger. La vie ancienne de S. Syméon Stylite le jeune (521–592)*. Ed. Paul van den Ven. 2 vols. Brussels: Société des Bollandistes, 1962–1970.

Livy (T. Livius). *Ab urbe condita*. In *Titi Livi Ab urbe condita*, ed. R. M. Ogilvy. Vol. 1, books 1–5. 2nd ed. Oxford, 1974. English trans. Aubrey De Sélincourt as *The Early History of Rome*. Rev. ed. London, 2002.

Marcellinus Comes. *Chronicle*. Ed. Theodor Mommsen. Berlin, 1894.

———. *The Chronicle of Marcellinus: A Translation and Commentary (with a Reproduction of Mommsen's Edition of the Text)*. Ed. Brian Croke. Sydney, 1995.

Martyrs of Najrân. *The Martyrs of Najrân. New Documents*. Ed. Irfan Shahîd. Brussels, 1971.

Maurice. *Das Strategikon des Maurikios*. Ed. George T. Dennis. Vienna, 1981. Trans. George T. Dennis as *Maurice's Strategikon: handbook of Byzantine military strategy*. Philadelphia, 1984.

Menander Protector. *The History of Menander the Guardsman*. Trans. Roger C. Blockley. Liverpool, 1985.

Menander Rhetor. *The Art of Rhetoric*. Ed. and trans. Donald Russell and Nigel Wilson. Oxford, 1981.

Miracles of Cosmas and Damian. *Miracles of Cosmas and Damian*. Trans. Ludwig Deubner as *Kosmas und Damian: Texte und Einleitung*. Leipzig, Teubner, 1907. French trans. A.-J. Festugière as *Sainte Thècle, Saints Côme et Damien, Saints Cyr et Jean (Extraits), et Saint Georges*. Paris, 1971. 83–213.

Miracles of Saint Demetrius. *Miracles of Saint Demetrius*. Ed. Paul Lemerle as *Le plus anciens recueils des Miracles de Saint Démétrius*. 2 vols. Paris, 1979–1981.

Monophysites. *Vitae virorum apud Monophysitas celeberrimorum. Pars prima*. Ed. Ernest W. Brooks CSCO 7–8/Syr. 7–8. 1907. Reprint, Louvain, 1955.

*Papyri*

*P. Mich.* 13: *The Aphrodite Papyri in the University of Michigan Papyrus Collection*. Ed. and trans. Pieter J. Sijpesteijn. Terra, 1977.

*P. Oxy.*: *The Oxyrhynchus Papyri*. Ed. and trans. Bernard P. Grenfell and Arthur S. Hunt. London, 1898–1999.

*P. Ital.*: *Die nichtliterarischen lateinischen Papyri Italiens aus der Zeit 445–700*. Ed. J.O. Tjader. Lund, 1955.

Paul the Deacon. *Historia Langobardorum*. Edited by Ludwig Bethmann and Georg Waitz. Hannover, 1878.

Paulus Silentiarius. *Descriptio S. Sophiae*. In Paul Friedländer (ed.), *Johannes von Gaza, Paulus Silentiarius, und Prokopios von Gaza*. Leipzig, 1912. 755–805.

*Peri politikês epistêmês. Menae patricii cum Thoma referendario de scientia politica dialogus quae exstant in codice Vaticano palimpsesto*. Ed. Carlo Maria Mazzucchi. Milan, 1982.

Pelagius the Deacon/Pelagius diaconus. *In defensione Trium Capitulorum*. Ed. Robert Devreese. Rome, 1957.

Pelagius the Pope/Pelagius I Papa. *Epistulae quae supersunt*. Ed. Pius M. Gassò and Columba M. Batlle. Montserrat, 1956.

Photius. *Bibliotheca*. 8 Vols. Ed. René Henry. Paris, 1959–1965.

Piacenza Pilgrim. *Travels*. In *Itineraria et Alia Geographica*. CCSL 175. Turnhout, Belgium, 1965. 127–153. English trans. John Wilkinson, in *Jerusalem Pilgrims Before the Crusades*. Warminster, Eng., 2002.

Procopius. *Procopii Caesariensis opera omnia*. 4 vols. Ed. Jacob Haury and Gerhard Wirth. Leipzig 1962–1964. Vols. 1–2, *Bella* (Wars), 1–4, 5–8. Vol. 3. *Historia arcana* (*Anecdota, Secret History*). Vol. 4. *De aedificiis* (*Buildings*).

———. *Buildings, History of the Wars, and Secret History*. Trans. H. B. Dewing and G. Downey. Cambridge, Mass, 1914–1940.

———. *Secret History*. Trans. Richard Atwater. Ann Arbor, 1961.

Ps.-Joshua the Stylite. *Chronicle*. Trans. Frank R. Trombley and John W. Watt. Liverpool, 2000.

Romanos the Melodist. *Hymns. Sancti Romani Melodi Cantica: Cantica Genuina*. Ed. Paul Maas and C. A. Trypanis. Oxford, 1963.

———. *St. Romanos the Melodist,* Kontakia: On the Life of Christ. Trans. Ephrem Lash. San Francisco, 1995.

———. *Sacred Song from the Byzantine Pulpit: Romanos the Melodist*. Trans. R. J. Schork. Gainesville, Fl., 1995.

———. *Kontakia of Romanos, Byzantine Melodist*. Trans. Marjorie Carpenter. 2 vols. Columbia, MO, 1970.

Seneca, L. Annaeus. *De clementia*. In *L. Annaei Senecae De clementia libri duo*, ed. Ermanno Malaspina. Alexandria, 2001. English trans. J. M. Cooper and J. F. Procopé in *Seneca: Moral and Political Essays*. Cambridge, 1995.

Severus of Antioch. *The Sixth Book of the Select Letters of Severus Patriarch of Antioch in the Syriac Version of Athanasius of Nisibis*, I, 1–2. *Text*, II, 1–2. *Translation*. Ed. Ernest W. Brooks. London, 1902–1904.

———. *Sévère d'Antioche. La polémique antijulianiste*. Ed. Robert Hespel. CSCO 244/Syr. 104. Louvain, 1964.

Stephen of Heracleopolis Magna. *A Panegyric on Apollo Archimandrite of the Monastery of Isaac by Stephen Bishop of Heracleopolis Magna*. Ed. K. H. Kuhn. CSCO 395/Copt. 40. Louvain, 1978.

Suetonius Tranquillus, C. *Divus Augustus, Tiberius*. In *C. Suetoni Tranquilli Opera*, ed. M. Ihm. Stuttgart, 1961. English trans. R. Graves. *The Twelve Caesars*. London, 1976.

Themistius. *Orations*. In *Orationes quae supersunt*, ed. H. Schenkl, G. Downey, and A. F. Norman. 3 Vols. Leipzig, 1965–1974. English trans. Peter Heather and David Moncur in *Politics, Philosophy, and Empire in the Fourth Century: Select Orations of Themistius*. Liverpool, 2001.

Theophanes Confessor. *Chronographia*. Ed. Carl de Boor. Leipzig, 1883. Trans. Cyril Mango and Roger Scott as *The Chronicle of Theophanes Confessor.* In *Byzantine and Near Eastern History, AD 284–813*. Oxford, 1997.

Theophylact Simocatta. *History*. Ed. Carl de Boor and Peter Wirth. Stuttgart, 1972.

———. *The History of Theophylact Simocatta*. Trans. Michael and Mary Whitby. Oxford, 1985.

Thomas of Marga. *The Book of Governors. The Historia Monastica of Thomas Bishop of Marga A.D. 840*, I–II. Ed. E. A. Wallis Budge, London, 1893. Reprint, Piscataway, N.J., 2003.

Thucydides. *Historiae* (History). Ed. H. S. Jones, corr. J. E. Powell. 2 vols. Oxford, 1942.

———. *History of the Peloponnesian War*. Rev. ed. and trans. Charles Smith. Loeb Classical Library 108. London, 1928.

Victor of Tununna/Vittore da Tununna. *Chronica: Chiesa e impero nell'età di Giustiniano*. Ed. and trans. Antonio Placanica. Florence, 1997.

Victor of Vita. *History of the Vandal Persecution*. Trans. J. Moorhead. Liverpool, 1992.

Zacharias Scholasticus. *Ecclesiastical History*. CSCO 38–39. Trans. F. J. Hamilton and E. W. Brooks as *The Syriac Chronicle Known as That of Zachariah of Mitylene*. London, 1899.

———. *Life of Severus*. Ed. and trans. Marc-Antoine Kugener. PO 2. Paris, 1907. 46–92.

Zonaras. *Epitome historiarum*. Ed. Ludwig Dindorf. Leipzig, 1870.

## Collections of Translations

Maas, Michael. *Readings in Late Antiquity*. London, 2000.

Mango, Cyril. *The Art of the Byzantine Empire, 312–1453: Sources and Documents*. Englewood Cliffs, N.J., 1972.

Norris, R. A., Jr., ed. and trans. *The Christological Controversy*. Philadelphia, 1980.

Rusch, W. G., ed. and trans. *The Trinitarian Controversy*. Philadelphia, 1980.

*The Seven Ecumenical Councils*. Nicene and Post-Nicene Fathers, ser. 2, vol. 14. New York, 1900.

Stevenson, J., ed., and rev. W. H. C. Frend. *Creeds, Councils, and Controversies*. London, 1989.

———. eds. *A New Eusebius*. London, 1987.

## Secondary Sources

Aalders, G. J. D. "NOMOS EMΨYXOS." In *Politeia und Res Publica*, ed. Peter Steinmetz, 315–329. Wiesbaden, 1969.

Abadie-Reynal, Catherine. "Céramique et commerce dans le bassin égéen du IVe au VIIe siècle." In *Hommes et richesses dans l'Empire byzantin*. Vol. 1. *IVe–VIIe Siecle*, ed. C. Abadie-Reynal et al., 143–159. Paris, 1989.

Adontz, Nicholas. *Armenia in the Period of Justinian*. Trans. Nina G. Garsoïan. Lisbon, 1970.

Al-Askar, Abdullah. *Al-Yamama in the Early Islamic Era*. Riyadh, 2002.

Al-Assouad, M. R. "Dhu Nuwas." In *Encyclopaedia of Islam*, 2nd ed., vol. 2, ed. Bernard Lewis, et al., 243–245. Leiden, 1965.

Alchermes, Joseph D. "*Spolia* in Roman Cities of the Late Empire: Legislative Rationales and Architectural Reuse." *DOP* 48 (1994): 167–178.

Alexander, Paul J. *The Byzantine Apocalyptic Tradition*. Berkeley, Calif., 1985.

———. *The Oracle of Baalbek: The Tiburtine Sibyl in Greek Dress*. Washington, D.C., 1967.

Alföldi, Andreas. *Die monarchische Repräsentation im romischen Kaiserreiche*. Darmstadt, 1970.

Allen, Pauline. "The 'Justinianic' Plague." *Byzantion* 49 (1979): 5–20.

———. "Neo-Chalcedonism and the Patriarchs of the Sixth Century." *Byzantion* 50 (1980): 5–17.

———. "The Definition and Enforcement of Orthodoxy." *CAH*, vol. 14, 3rd ed, ed. Averil Cameron, 811–835. Cambridge, 2000.

Alston, Richard. "Managing the Frontiers: Supplying the Frontier Troops in the Sixth and Seventh Centuries." In *The Roman Army and the Economy*, ed. Paul Erdkamp, 398–419. Amsterdam, 2002.

———. "Urban Population in Late Roman Egypt and the End of the Ancient World." In *Debating Roman Demography*, ed. Walter Scheidel, 161–204. Leiden, 2001.

al-Tabari, Muhammad ibn Jarir. *The History of al-Tabari*. Vol. 10: *The Conquest of Arabia*. Trans. Fred M. Donner. Albany, N.Y. 1993.

Amory, Patrick. *People and Identity in Ostrogothic Italy, 489–554*. Cambridge, 1997.

Anastos, Milton V. "Justinian's Despotic Control over the Church as Illustrated by His Edicts on the Theopaschite Formula and his Letter to Pope John II in 533." In *Mélanges Georges Ostrogorsky*, ed. Franjo Barisic, 2:1–11. Reprinted in *Studies in Byzantine Intellectual History*, ed. Milton V. Anastos. London, 1979.

Andreescu-Treadgold, Irina, and Warren Treadgold. "Procopius and the Imperial Panels of S. Vitale." *Art Bulletin* 99 (1997): 708–723.

Antonopoulos, Panagiotes. *Petros Patrikios: Byzantine Diplomat, Official and Author*. Athens, 1990.

Arjava, Antii. *Women and the Law in Late Antiquity*. Oxford, 1996.

Armstrong, Arthur H., ed. *The Cambridge History of Later Greek and Early Medieval Philosophy*. Cambridge, 1967.

Arthur, Paul. *Naples: From Roman Town to City-State*. London, 2002.

Athanassiadi, Polymnia. "Persecution and Response in Late Paganism: The Evidence of Damascius." *JHS* 113 (1993): 1–29.

———. *Damascius: The Philosophical History*. Text with Translation and Notes. Athens, 1999.

Avigad, Nahman. *Discovering Jerusalem*. Nashville, Tenn., 1980.

———. "A Building Inscription of the Emperor Justinian and the Nea in Jerusalem (Preliminary Note)." *Israel Exploration Journal* 27 (1977): 145–151.

Avi-Yonah, Michael. "The Economics of Byzantine Palestine." *Israel Exploration Journal* 8 (1958): 39–51.

———. *Geschichte der Juden im Zeitalter der Talmud*. Berlin, 1962.

———. *The Jews under Roman and Byzantine Rule: A Political History from the Bar Cochba War to the Arab Conquest*. New York, 1976.

Bagnall, Roger. *Egypt in Late Antiquity*. Princeton, N.J., 1993.

Bagnall, Roger S., Alan Cameron, S. R. Schwartz, and K. A. Worp. *Consuls of the Later Roman Empire*. Atlanta, 1987.

Baillie, M. G. L. *Exodus to Arthur: Catastrophic Encounters with Comets*. 2nd ed. London, 2000.

Baldovin, John F. *The Urban Character of Christian Worship: The Origins, Development, and Meaning of Stational Liturgy*. Rome, 1987.

Balty, Jean Ch. "Apamée au VIe siècle: Témoinages archéologiques de la richesse d'une ville." In *Hommes et richesses dans l'Empire byzantine*, ed. C. Abadie-Reynal et al., 1:79–92. Paris, 1989.

Banaji, Jairus. "Rural Communities in the Late Empire: Economic and Monetary Aspects." PhD diss., University of Oxford, 1992.

Bardill, Jonathan. "The Golden Gate in Constantinople: A Triumphal Arch of Theodosius I." *AJA* 103 (1999): 671–696.

———. "The Great Palace of the Byzantine Emperors and the Walker Trust Excavations." *JRA* 12 (1999): 216–230.

———. "The Church of Sts. Sergius and Bacchus in Constantinople and the Monophysite Refugees." *DOP* 54 (2000): 1–11.

Bardill, Jonathan, and Geoffrey Greatrex. "Antiochus the *Praepositus*, a Persian Eunuch at the Court of Theodosius II." *DOP* 50 (1996): 171–197.

Barford, Paul M. *The Early Slavs: Culture and Society in Early Medieval Eastern Europe*. Ithaca, N.Y., 2001.

Barker, Ernest. *Social and Political Thought in Byzantium*. Oxford, 1957.

Barnish, Samuel J. B. "Pigs, Plebeians, and *Potentes*: Rome's Economic Hinterland, c. 350–600 AD." *Proceedings of the British School at Rome* 55 (1987): 157–185.

Baron, Salo Wittmayer. *A Social and Religious History of the Jews*. 2nd ed. Vol. 3. New York, 1957.

Bashear, Suliman. *Muqaddima fi l-ta'rikh al-akhar*. Jerusalem, 1984.

Bassett, Steven, ed. *The Origins of Anglo-Saxon Kingdoms*. London, 1989.

Baum, Wilhelm, and Dietmar W. Winkler. *The Church of the East: A Concise History*. London, 2003.

Bauer, F. A. "Urban Space and Ritual: Constantinople in Late Antiquity." *Acta ad archaeologiam et artium historiam pertinentia* 15 (2001), 27–61.

Baynes, Norman H. "Eusebius and the Christian Empire." *Annuaire de l'Institut de Philologie et d'Histoire Orientale* 2 (1934): 13–18. Reprinted in Baynes, *Byzantine Studies and Other Essays*, 168–172. London, 1960.

Beaucamp, Joëlle. "La situation juridique de la femme à Byzance." *Cahiers de civilisation médiévale* 20 (1977): 145–176.

———. *Le Statut de la femme à Byzance (4e–7e siècle)*. 2 vols. Travaux et mémoires du Centre de recherché d'histoire et civilisation de Byzance monographies 5–6. Paris, 1990–1992.

———. "Exclues et aliénées: les femmes dans la tradition canonique byzantine." In *Strangers to Themselves: the Byzantine Outsider*, ed. Dion Smythe, 87–103. Aldershot, Eng., 2000.

Beck, Hans-Georg. "Konstantinopel. Zur Sozialgeschichte einer frühmittelalterlichen Hauptstadt." *BZ* 58 (1965): 11–45. Reprinted in H.-G. Beck, *Ideen und Realitäten in Byzanz*. London, 1972.

———. "Grossstadt-Probleme: Konstantinopel vom 4–6 Jahrhundert." In *Studien zur Frühgeschichte Konstantinopels*, ed. Beck, 3–19. Munich, 1973.

Bell, Catherine. "Performance." In *Critical Terms for Religious Studies*, ed. Mark C. Taylor, 205–224. Chicago, 1998.

Bell, Harold. "An Egyptian Village in the Age of Justinian." *JHS* 64 (1944): 21–36.

Bell, Richard. *The Origin of Islam in Its Christian Environment*. London, 1926.

Belting, Hans. *Likeness and Presence: A History of the Image before the Era of Art*. Trans. Edmund Jephcott. Chicago, 1994.

Belting-Ihm, Christa. "Das Justinus-Kreuz in der Schatzkammer der Peterskirche zu Rom." *Jahrbuch der römisch-germanischen Zentralmuseums Mainz* 12 (1965): 142–166.

Benedict, Carol. *Bubonic Plague in Nineteenth-Century China*. Stanford, Calif., 1996.

Berger, A. *Untersuchungen zu den Patria Konstantinopoleos*. Bonn, 1988.

———. "Regionen und Straßen im frühen Konstantinopel." *IstMitt* 47 (1997): 349–414.

———. "Streets and Public Spaces in Constantinople." *DOP* 54 (2000): 161–172.

———. "Imperial and Ecclesiastical Processions in Constantinople." In *Byzantine Constantinople: Monuments, Topography and Everyday Life*, ed. N. Necipoglu, 73–87. Leiden, 2001.

Bergman, Robert P. *Vatican Treasures: Early Christian, Renaissance, and Baroque Art from the Papal Collections*. Cleveland, Ohio, 1998.

Bickermann, Elias. "Justinian." *Encyclopaedia Judaica* 9 (1932): col. 617–620.

Biraben, Jean-Noël, and Jacques Le Goff. "The Plague in the Early Middle Ages." In *Biology of Man in History: Selections from the "Annales: Économies, Sociétés, Civilisations,"* ed. Robert Forster and Orest Ranum, 48–80. Baltimore, 1975. Trans. of "La Peste dans le haut moyen age." *Annales* ESC 24 (Nov.–Dec. 1969): 1484–1510.

Bleicken, Jochen. *Staatliche Ordnung und Freiheit in der römischen Republik*. Frankfurter althistorische Studien, Heft 6. Kallmünz, 1972.

Blockley, Robert C. *East Roman Foreign Policy*. Leeds, 1992.

Blondheim, D.-S. *Les Parlers judéo-romans et la Vetus Latina*. Paris, 1925.

Blumenthal, Henry J. "529 and Its Sequel: What Happened to the Academy?" *Byzantion* 48 (1978): 369–385.

———. *Alexandria as a Center of Greek Philosophy in Later Classical Antiquity*. Illinois Classical Studies 18 (1993): 307–325.

———. "Were Aristotle's Intentions of Writing the *De anima* Forgotten in Late Antiquity?" *Documenti e studi sulla tradizione filosofica medievale* 8 (1997): 143–157.

Boak, Arthur E. R. *The Master of the Offices in the Later Roman and Byzantine Empire*. New York, 1919. Reprinted in Boak and J. E. Dunlop, *Two Studies in Late Roman and Byzantine Administration*. New York, 1924.

Bodson, Liliane. "Le Vocabulaire des maladies pestilentielles et épizootiques." *Centre Jean-Palerne Mémoires* 10 (1991): 215–241.

Bono, P., J. Crow, and R. Bayliss. "The Water Supply of Constantinople: Archaeology and Hydrogeology of an Early Medieval City." *Environmental Geology* 40 (2001): 1325–1333.

Bosworth, Clifford Edmund. "Iran and the Arabs before Islam." In *Cambridge History of Iran*, ed. William Fisher, 3:593–613. Cambridge, 1968–1991.

Bourdieu, Pierre. *The Logic of Practice*. Trans. Richard Nice. Cambridge, 1990.

Bousquet, G. H. "Une explication Marxiste de l'Islam par un ecclésiastique épiscopalien." *Hésperis* 41 (1954): 231–247.

Bowersock, Glen. *Hellenism in Late Antiquity*. Ann Arbor, Mich., 1990.

Bowersock, Glen W., Peter Brown, and Oleg Grabar, eds. *Late Antiquity: A Guide to the Postclassical World*. Cambridge, Mass., 1999.

Brandes, Wolfram, and John Haldon. "Towns, Tax, and Transformation: State, Cities and Their Hinterlands in the East Roman World, c. 500–800." In *Towns and Their Territories between Late Antiquity and the Early Middle Age*, ed. Gian Pietro Brogiolo, Nancy Gauthier, and Neil Christie, 141–172. Leiden, 2000.

Brands, Gunnar, and Hans-Georg Severin, eds. *Die Spätantike Stadt und Ihre Christianisierung*. Frühes Christentum-Byzanz, Series B: Studien und Perspektiven 11. Wiesbaden, 2003.

Braund, David. "Procopius on the Economy of Lazica." *Classical Quarterly* 41 (1991): 221–225.

———. *Georgia in Antiquity: A History of Colchis and Transcaucasian Iberia, 550 BC–AD 562.* Oxford, 1994.

Brightman, Frank E. *Liturgies Eastern and Western.* Vol. 1. Oxford, 1896. Reprint, Oxford 1965.

Brock, Sebastian. "The Conversations with the Syrian Orthodox under Justinian (532)." *OCP* 47 (1981): 87–121.

———. "Christians in the Sasanian Empire: A Case of Divided Loyalty." In *Religion and National Identity*, ed. Stuart Mews. *Studies in Church History* 18 (1982): 1–19.

———. "The Church of the East in the Sasanian Empire up to the Sixth Century and Its Absence from the Councils in the Roman Empire." In *Syriac Dialogue: First Non-official Consultation on Dialogue within the Syriac Tradition.* Vienna, 1994.

Brock, Sebastian, and David G. K. Taylor. *The Hidden Pearl: The Syrian Orthodox Church and Its Ancient Aramaic Heritage.* Vol. 2. Rome, 2001.

Brogiolo, Gian Pietro, and Bryan Ward-Perkins, eds. *The Idea and Ideal of the Town between Late Antiquity and the Early Middle Ages.* Leiden, 1999.

Brogiolo, Gian Pietro, Nancy Gauthier, and Neil Christie. *Towns and Their Territories between Late Antiquity and the Early Middle Ages.* Leiden, 2000.

Brooks, Ernest W. *The Sixth Book of the Select Letters of Severus Patriarch of Antioch in the Syriac Version of Athanasius of Nisibis*, vol. 1.1–2. *Text*, vol. 2.1–2. *Translation.* London, 1902–1904.

———. *Vitae virorum apud Monophysitas celeberrimorum. Pars prima.* CSCO 7–8/Syr. 7–8. 1907. Reprint, Louvain, Belgium, 1955.

———. *John of Ephesus: Lives of the Eastern Saints.* Vols. 1–3. PO 17.1; 18.4; 19.2. Paris 1923–1925. Reprint, Turnhout, 1974.

———. "The Patriarch Paul of Antioch and the Alexandrine Schism of 575." *BZ* 30 (1929–1930): 468–476.

Browe, Peter. "Die Judengesetzgebung Justinians." *Analecta Gregoriana* 8 (1935): 109–146.

Brown, Peter. "Asceticism." *CAH*, vol. 13, 3rd ed., ed. Iorwerth Edwards, 601–603. Cambridge, 1970.

———. "The Rise and Function of the Holy Man in Late Antiquity." *JRS* 61 (1971): 80–101.

———. *The World of Late Antiquity, AD 150–750.* London, 1971.

———. "Town, Village, and Holy Man: The Case of Syria." In *Assimilation et résistance à la culture gréco-romaine dans le monde ancien: Travaux du VIe Congrès Internationale d'Études Classiques (Madrid, Septembre 1974)*, ed. D. M. Pippidi, 213–220. Bucharest, 1976.

———. *The Making of Late Antiquity.* Cambridge, Mass., 1978.

———. *Society and the Holy in Late Antiquity.* Berkeley, Calif., 1982.

———. *The Body in Society: Men, Women, and Sexual Renunciation in Early Christianity.* New York, 1988.

———. *Power and Persuasion in Late Antiquity: Towards a Christian Empire.* Madison, Wis., 1992.

———. "Holy Men." *CAH*, vol. 14, 3rd ed, ed. Averil Cameron, 781–810. Cambridge, 2000.

———. *Poverty and Leadership in the Later Roman Empire.* Hanover, N.H., 2002.

Brown, Thomas S. *Gentlemen and Officers: Imperial Administration and Aristocratic Power in Byzantine Italy, A.D. 554–800*. London, 1984.

Browning, Robert. "The Continuity of Hellenism in the Byzantine World: Appearance and Reality." In *Greece Old and New*, ed. Tom Winnifrith and Penelope Murray, 111–128. New York, 1983.

———. *Justinian and Theodora*. 2nd ed. London, 1987.

Brubaker, Leslie. "Memories of Helena: Patterns of Imperial Female Matronage in the Fourth and Fifth Centuries." In *Women, Men and Eunuchs: Gender in Byzantium*, ed. Liz James, 52–75. London, 1997.

———. "Icons before Iconoclasm?" In *Morfologie sociali e culturali in Europa fra tarda antichità e alto Medioevo*, 2:1215–54. Spoleto, 1998.

———. "The Vienna Dioskorides and Anicia Juliana." In *Byzantine Garden Culture*, ed. Antony Littlewood, Henry Maguire and Joachim Wolschke-Bulmahn, 189–214. Washington, D.C., 2002.

———. "Sex, Lies, and Textuality: The *Secret History* of Procopius and the Rhetoric of Gender in Sixth-Century Byzantium." In *Gender in the Early Medieval World*, ed. Leslie Brubaker and Julia Smith. Cambridge, 2005.

Brubaker, Leslie, and John F. Haldon. *Byzantium in the Iconoclast Era (ca. 680–850): A History*. Cambridge, 2003.

Brubaker, Leslie, and Helen Tobler. "The Gender of Money: Byzantine Empresses on coins (324–802)." *Gender and History* 12 (2000): 572–594. Reprinted in *Gendering the Middle Ages*, ed. Pauline Stafford and Anneke Mulder-Bakker, 42–64. Oxford, 2001.

Brunt, Peter A. "Lex de imperio Vespasiani." *JRS* 67 (1977): 95–116.

———. "*Libertas* in the Republic." In Brunt, *The Fall of the Roman Republic and Related Essays*, 281–350. Oxford, 1988.

Buchwald, Hans. "Saint Sophia, Turning Point in the Development of Byzantine Architecture?" In *Die Hagia Sophia in Istanbul*, ed. Volker Hoffman, 30–37. Bern, 1997.

Buckland, W. W. *A Text-Book of Roman Law from Augustus to Justinian*. 3rd ed. rev. Peter Stein. Cambridge, 1963.

Buckton, David, ed. *Byzantium: Treasures of Byzantine Art and Culture*. London, 1994.

Budge, Ernest A. Wallis, ed. *The Book of Governors: The Historia Monastica of Thomas Bishop of Marga, A.D. 840*. Vols. 1–2. London, 1893. Reprint, Piscataway, N.J., 2003.

Bundy, David D. "Jacob Baradaeus: The State of Research, a Review of Sources, and a New Approach." *Le Muséon* 91 (1978): 45–86.

Bury, John B. "The Nika Riot." *JHS* 17 (1897): 92–119.

———. *History of the Later Roman Empire from Arcadius Irene (395 A.D to 800 A.D)*. 2 vols. London, 1889.

———."The Ceremonial Book of Constantine Porphyrogennetos." *English Historical Review* 22 (1907): 209–227.

———. *History of the Later Roman Empire from the Death of Theodosius I to the Death of Justinian*. 2 vols. New York, 1923. Reprint 1958.

Callu, Jean-Pierre. "I commerci oltre i confini dell' Impero." In *Storia di Roma*, vol. 3.1, *L'età tardoantica*, 487–524. Turin, 1993.

*The Cambridge Ancient History*. 3rd ed. Vol. 13: *The Late Empire, A.D. 337–425*, ed. Averil Cameron and Peter Garnsey. Cambridge, 1998. Vol. 14: *Late Antiquity. Empire and Successors, A.D. 425–600*, ed. Averil Cameron, Bryan Ward-Perkins, and Michael Whitby. Cambridge, 2000.

*Cambridge History of Iran*. Vol. 3, ed. Ehsan Yar-Shater. Cambridge, 1983.

Cameron, Alan. "The Last Days of the Academy at Athens." *Proceedings of the Cambridge Philological Society* 195 (1969): 7–29.

———. *Circus Factions: Blues and Greens at Rome and Byzantium*. Oxford, 1976.

Cameron, Alan, and Averil Cameron. "The Cycle of Agathias." *JHS* 86 (1966): 6–25.

Cameron, Alan, and Diane Schauer. "The Last Consul: Basilius and His Diptych." *JRS* 72 (1982): 126–145.

Cameron, Averil. "Agathias on the Sassanians." *DOP* 23–24 (1969–1970): 1–150.

———. *Agathias*. Oxford, 1970.

———. "The Empress Sophia." *Byzantion* 45 (1975): 5–21.

———. "The Artistic Patronage of Justin II." *Byzantion* 50 (1980): 62–84.

———. *Procopius and the Sixth Century*. London, 1985.

———. "The Construction of Court Ritual: The Byzantine *Book of Ceremonies*." In *Rituals of Royalty Power and Ceremonial in Traditional Societies*, ed., D. Cannadine and S. Price, 106–136. Cambridge, 1987.

———. "Virginity as Metaphor: Women and the Rhetoric of Early Christianity." In *History as Text: The Writing of Ancient History*, ed. Averil Cameron, 184–205. London, 1989.

———. "Gelimer's Laughter: The Case of Byzantine Africa." In *Tradition and Innovation in Late Antiquity*, ed. Frank M. Clover and R. Stephen Humphreys, 171–190. Madison, Wis., 1989.

———. *Christianity and the Rhetoric of Empire*. Berkeley, Calif., 1991.

———. *The Mediterranean World in Late Antiquity*. London, 1993.

———. "Byzantium and the Past in the Seventh Century: The Search for Redefinition." In *The Seventh Century: Change and Continuity*, ed. Jacques Fontaine and J. N. Hilgarth, 250–276. London, 1992.

———. "The Language of Images: The Rise of Icons and Christian Representation." In *The Church and the Arts*, ed. Diana Wood, 1–42. Oxford, 1992.

———. "Byzantines and Jews: Some Recent Work on Early Byzantium." *Byzantine and Modern Greek Studies* 20 (1996): 249–274.

———. "The "Long" Late Antiquity." In *Classics in Progress: Essays on Ancient Greece and Rome*, ed. T. P. Wiseman, 165–191. Oxford, 2002.

Cameron, Averil, and Judith Herrin, eds. *Constantinople in the Early Eighth Century: The Parastaseis Syntomoi Chronikai*. Leiden, 1984.

Cameron, Averil, and Lawrence I. Conrad, eds. *The Byzantine and Early Islamic Near East, vol. 1, Problems in the Literary Source Material*. Princeton, N.J. 1992.

Camp, John M. "The Philosophical Schools of Roman Athens." In *The Greek Renaissance in the Roman Empire*, ed. S. Walker and Averil Cameron. *Bulletin of the Institute for Classical Studies* 55 (1989): 50–55.

Carmichael, Ann G. "Bubonic Plague." In *The Cambridge World History of Human Disease*, ed. Kenneth F. Kiple, 628–631. Cambridge, 1993.

Casey, P. John. "Justinian, the *Limitanei*, and Arab-Byzantine Relations in the Sixth Century." *Journal of Roman Archeology* 9 (1996): 214–222.

Castrén, Paavo. "Paganism and Christianity in Athens and Vicinity during the Fourth to Sixth Centuries A.D." In *The Idea and Ideal of the Town between Late Antiquity and the Early Middle Ages*, ed. Gian Pietro Brogiolo and Bryan Ward-Perkins, 211–223. Leiden, 1999.

Cavallo, Guglielmo. "La circolazione libraria nell'età di Giustiniano." In *L'imperatore Giustiniano. Storia e mito*, ed. Gian Gualberto Archi, 201–236. Milan, 1978.

———. *Codex Purpureus Rossanensis*. Rome, 1992.

Ceccheli, Carlo, Giuseppe Furlani, and Mario Salmi. *The Rabbula Gospels: Facsimile Edition of the Miniatures of the Syriac Manuscript Plut. I,56 in the Medicaean-Laurentian Library*. Olten, 1959.

Chadwick, Henry. "Philosophical Tradition and the Self." In *Late Antiquity: A Guide to the Postclassical World*, ed. Glen W. Bowersock, Peter Brown, and Oleg Grabar, 60–81. Cambridge, Mass., 1999.

———. *The Church in Ancient Society: From Galilee to Gregory the Great*. Oxford, 2001.

Charanis, Peter. *Church and State in the Later Roman Empire: The Religious Policy of Anastasius the First, 491–518*. Madison, Wis., 1939.

Charles-Edwards, Thomas. "Law in the Western Kingdoms between the Fifth and the Seventh Century." *CAH* 14:260–287.

Chaumont, Marie-Louise. "Armenia and Iran II." *Encyclopaedia of Islam*, 2nd ed., 418–438. Leiden, 1987.

Chesnut, Roberta C. *Three Monophysite Christologies*. Oxford, 1976.

Chitty, Derwas. *The Desert a City*. Oxford, 1966.

Choksy, Jamsheed K. "Sassanians." In *Late Antiquity: A Guide to the Postclassical World*, ed. G. W. Bowersock, Peter Brown, and Oleg Grabar, 682–685. Cambridge, Mass., 1999.

Christ, Wilhelm v. *Geschichte der griechischen Literatur*. Handbuch der Altertumswissenschaft 7. 2. Teil: *Die nachklassische Periode der griechischen Literatur, 2. Hälfte, Von 100 bis 530 nach Christus*, revised by W. Schmid und O. Stählin. Munich, 1924.

Christie, Neil, and Loseby, Simon T., eds. *Towns in Transition: Urban Evolution in Late Antiquity and the Early Middle Ages*. Aldershot, Eng., 1996.

Chrysos, Evangelos. "Die Römerherrschaft in Britannien und ihr Ende." *Bonner Jahrbucher* 191 (1991): 247–76.

———. *Die Bischofslisten des V. ökumenischen Konzils (553)*. Bonn, 1966.

Chuvin, Pierre. *A Chronicle of the Last Pagans*. Trans. B. A. Archer. Cambridge, Mass., 1990.

Clark, Elizabeth. "Patrons Not Priests: Gender and Power in Late Antique Christianity." *Gender and History* 2 (1990): 253–273.

———. "Ideology, History, and the Construction of 'Woman' in Late Ancient Christianity." *Journal of Early Christian Studies* 2 (1994): 155–184.

———. "Holy Women, Holy Words: Early Christian Women, Social History, and the 'Linguistic turn.'" *Journal of Early Christian Studies* 6 (1998): 413–430.

———. "The Lady Vanishes: Dilemmas of a Feminist Historian after the 'linguistic turn.'" *Church History* 67 (1998): 1–31.

Clark, Gillian. *Women in Late Antiquity, Pagan and Christian Lifestyles*. Oxford, 1993.

———. *This Female Man of God: Women and Spiritual Power in the Patristic Age, AD 350–450*. London, 1995.

———. "The Old Adam: The Fathers and the Unmaking of Masculinity." In *Thinking Men: Masculinity and Its Self-Representation in the Classical Tradition*, ed. Lyn Foxhall and John Salmon, 170–182. London, 1998.

Claude, Dietrich. *Die byzantinische Stadt im 6. Jahrhundert*. Munich, 1969.

Clauss, Manfred. *Der Magister Officiorum in der Spätantike*. Munich, 1980.

Clover, Frank M. "Carthage and the Vandals." In *Excavations at Carthage 1978, Conducted by the University of Michigan*, vol. 7, ed. J. H. Humphrey, 1–22. Ann Arbor, Mich., 1982.

———. "*Felix Karthago*." In *Tradition and Innovation in Late Antiquity*, ed. Frank M. Clover and R. Stephen Humphreys, 129–169. Madison, Wis., 1989.

———. *The Late Roman West and the Vandals*. Aldershot, Eng., 1993.

Coates-Stephens, Robert. "Housing in Early Medieval Rome." *Papers of the British School at Rome* 64 (1996): 239–259.

———. "The Walls and Aqueducts of Rome in the Early Middle Ages, AD 500–1000." *JRS* 88 (1998): 166–178.

Cobb, Paul M. *White Banners: Contention in Abbasid Syria, 750–880*. Albany, N.Y. 2001.

Cody, Aelred. "Dayr al-Baramus, History." In *The Coptic Encyclopedia*, ed. Aziz S. Atiya vol. III, 789–791. New York, 1991.

———. "Dayr al-Suryan, History." In *The Coptic Encyclopedia*, ed. Aziz S. Atiya vol. III, 876–879. New York, 1991.

Cohn, Samuel K., Jr. *The Black Death Transformed: Disease and Culture in Early Renaissance Europe*. London, 2002.

Coleman-Norton, Paul Robinson. *Roman State and Christian Church: A Collection of Legal Documents to AD 535*. 3 vols. London, 1966.

Collins, Roger. *Early Medieval Spain. Unity in Diversity, 400–1000*. Basingstoke, Eng., 1995.

Colorni, Vittore. "L'uso del greco nella liturgia del giudaismo ellenistico e la novella 146 di Giustiniano." *Annali de storia del diritto* 18 (1964): 19–80.

Congourdeau, Marie-Hélène. "La Société byzantine face aux grandes pandémies." In *Maladie et société à Byzance*, ed. Evelyne Patlagean, 21–41. Spoleto, 1993.

Conrad, Lawrence I. "Abraha and Muhammad: Some Observations apropos of Chronology and Literary Topoi in the Early Arabic Historical Tradition." *Bulletin of the School of Oriental and African Studies* 50 (1987): 225–240.

———. "The Plague in the Early Medieval Near East." PhD diss., Princeton University, 1981.

———. "*Ṭāʿūn* and *Wabāʾ*: Conceptions of Plague and Pestilence in Early Islam." *Journal of the Economic and Social History of the Orient* 25 (1982): 268–307.

———. "Epidemic Disease in Central Syria in the Late Sixth Century: Some New Insights from the Verse of assān ibn Thābit." *Byzantine and Modern Greek Studies* 18 (1994): 12–58.

———. "Die Pest und ihr soziales Unfeld in Nahen Osten des frühren Mittelalters." *Der Islam* 73 (1996): 81–112.

———. "The Arabs." *CAH* 14:678–700.

Conte, Gian Biagio. *Latin Literature: A History*. Trans. Joseph B. Solodow, revised by Don Fowler and Glenn W. Most. Baltimore, 1987.

Cook, David. *Studies in Muslim Apocalyptic*. Princeton, N.J. 2003.

Cooper, Kate. "Insinuations of Womanly Influence: An Aspect of the Christianisation of the Roman Aristocracy." *JRS* 82 (1992): 150–164.

Cormack, Robin. *Painting the Soul: Icons, Death Masks, and Shrouds*. London, 1997.

Courtois, Courtois. *Les Vandales et l'Afrique*. Paris, 1955.

Cowe, S. Peter. "Philoxenus of Mabbug and the Synod of Manazkert." *Aram* 5 (1993) 115–129.

Cranz, F. Edward. "Kingdom and Polity in Eusebius of Caesarea." *Harvard Theological Review* 45 (1952): 47–66.

Crawford, John S. "Jews, Christians, and Polytheists in Late-Antique Sardis." In *Jews, Christians, and Polytheists in the Ancient Synagogue*, ed. Steven Fine, 190–200. London, 1999.

Crawford, John Stephens, et al. *The Byzantine Shops at Sardis*. Cambridge, Mass., 1990.

Croke, Brian. "Justinian's Bulgar Victory Celebration." *Byzantinoslavica* 41 (1980): 188–195. Reprinted in B. Croke, *Christian Chronicles and Byzantine History, 5th–6th Centuries*. London, 1992.

———. "Byzantine Earthquakes and Their Liturgical Commemoration." *Byzantion* 51 (1981): 112–147. Reprinted in B. Croke, *Christian Chronicles and Byzantine History*.

———. "Basiliscus the Boy-Emperor." *Greek, Roman, and Byzantine Studies* 24 (1983): 81–91. Reprinted in Croke, *Christian Chronicles and Byzantine History*.

———. "A.D. 476: The Manufacture of a Turning Point." *Chiron* 13 (1983): 81–119.

———. "Cassiodorus and the Getica of Jordanes." *Classical Philology* 82 (1987): 117–134. Reprinted in B. Croke, *Christian Chronicles and Byzantine History*.

———. "Malalas, the Man and His Work." In *Studies in John Malalas*, ed. E. M. Jeffreys with B. Croke and R. Scott, 1–25. Sydney, 1990.

———. *The Chronicle of Marcellinus: Translation and Commentary*. Sydney, 1995.

———. *Count Marcellinus and His Chronicle*. Oxford, 2001.

Croke, Brian, and James Crow. "Procopius and Dara." *JRS* 73 (1983): 143–159.

Croke, Brian, and Roger Scott. "Byzantine Chronicle Writing." In Elizabeth Jeffreys, *Studies in John Malalas*, 25–54.

Crone, Patricia. *Slaves on Horses: The Evolution of the Islamic Polity*. Cambridge, 1980.

———. *Meccan Trade and the Rise of Islam*. Oxford, 1987.

———. "Kavad's Heresy and Mazdak's Revolt." *Iran* 29 (1991): 21–42.

Crone, Patricia, and Michael Cook. *Hagarism: The Making of the Islamic World*. Cambridge, 1977.

Crow, James. "The Long Walls of Thrace." In *Constantinople and its Hinterland*, ed. C. Mango and G. Dagron, 109–124. London, 1995.

Crow, James, and Ricci, A. "Investigating the Hinterland of Constantinople: Interim Report on the Anastasian Long Wall." *JRA* 10 (1997): 235–262.

Crown, Alan D. "The Samaritans in the Byzantine Orbit." *Bulletin of the John Rylands Library* 69 (1986): 96–138.

———. "The Samaritan Diaspora." In *The Samaritans*, ed. Crown, 195–217. Tübingen, 1989.

Cunningham, Andrew. "Transforming Plague: The Laboratory and the Identity of Infectious Disease." In *The Laboratory Revolution in Medicine*, ed. Cunningham and Penry Williams, 209–244. Cambridge, 1992.

———. "Identifying Disease in the Past: Cutting the Gordian Knot." *Asclepio* 54 (2002): 13–34.

Ćurčić, Slobodan. "Design and Structural Innovation in Byzantine Architecture before Hagia Sophia." In *Hagia Sophia from the Age of Justinian to the Present*, ed. Robert Mark and Ahmet Çakmak, 33–35. Cambridge, 1992.

Curta, Florin. *The Making of the Slavs: History and Archaeology of the Lower Danube Region, c. 500–700*. Cambridge, 2001.

Curtis, John, ed. *Mesopotamia and Iran in the Parthian and Sasanian Periods: Rejection and Revival, c. 238 B.C.–A.D. 642*. London, 2000.

Cutler, Anthony. "The Making of the Justinian Diptychs." *Byzantion* 54 (1984): 75–115.

———. *Hand of the Master: Craftsmanship, Ivory, and Society in Byzantium, Ninth–Eleventh Centuries*. Princeton, N.J., 1994.

Dąbrowa, Edward. *The Roman and Byzantine Army in the East*. Cracow, 1994.

Dagron, Gilbert. "Aux origines de la civilisation byzantine: Langue de culture et langue d'état." *RH* 489 (1969): 29–76.

———. *Naissance d'une capitale*. Paris, 1974.

———. "Le Christianisme dans la ville byzantine." *DOP* 31 (1977): 1–25.

———. *Constantinople imaginaire*. Paris, 1984.

———. "'Ainsi rien n'échappera à la réglementation,' État, Église, corporations, confréries: À propos des inhumations à Constantinople (IVe–Xe siècles)." In *Hommes et richesses dans l'Empire byzantin*, vol. 2, ed. V. Kravari, J. Lefort, and C. Morrisson, 157–61. Paris, 1991.

———. *Emperor and Priest: The Imperial Office in Byzantium*. Trans. Jean Birrell. Cambridge, 2003.

Dagron, Gilbert, and Vincent Déroche. "Juifs et Chrétiens dans l'Orient du VII$^{e}$ siècle." *Travaux et Mémoires* 11 (1991): 17–273.

Daniel, Norman. *Islam and the West: The Making of an Image*. Edinburgh, 1960. Rev. ed., Oxford, 1993.

Daniélou, Jean. *The Bible and the Liturgy*. Notre Dame, Ind., 1956. Original French edition, Paris, 1951.

Dark, Ken. *Civitas to Kingdom: British Political Continuity, 300–800*. London, 1994.

Dark, Ken and Özgumüs, F. "The Last Roman Imperial Palace? Rescue Archaeology in Istanbul." *Minerva* 12 (2001): 52–55.

Daryaee, Touraj. "The Persian Gulf Trade in Late Antiquity." *Journal of World History* 14 (2003): 1–16.

Davies, Oliver. *Roman Mines in Europe*. Oxford, 1935.

Davies, Wendy. "Local Participation and Legal Ritual in Early Medieval Texts." In *The Moral World of the Law*, ed. Peter Coss, 48–61. Cambridge, 2000.

Davis, Stephen J. *The Cult of Saint Thecla: A Tradition of Women's Piety in Late Antiquity*. New York, 2001.

de Lange, Nicholas. "Jewish Attitudes to the Roman Empire." In *Imperialism in the Ancient World*, ed. P. D. A. Garnsey and C. R. Whittaker, 235–281. Cambridge, 1978.

———. "Midrash et Byzance: Sur une tradition française du Midrach Rabba (Notes Critiques)." *Revue d'histoire des religions* (206) 1989: 171–181.

———. "Jews and Christians in the Byzantine Empire: Problems and Prospects." In *Christianity and Judaism*, ed. Diana Wood, 15–32. Oxford, 1992.

———. "The Hebrew Language in the European Diaspora." In *Studies on the Jewish Diaspora in the Hellenistic and Roman Periods*, ed. Benjamin Isaac and A'haron Oppenheimer, Te'uda 12, 111–137. Tel Aviv, 1996.

———. "The Revival of the Hebrew Language in the Third Century." *Jewish Studies Quarterly* 3 (1996): 342–358.

———. "Hebraism and Hellenism: The Case of Byzantine Jewry." *Poetics Today* 19 (1998): 129–145.

———. "Etudier et prier à Byzance." *Revue des études Juives* 158 (1999): 51–59.

Declerck, José, ed. *Anonymus dialogus cum Iudaeis seculi ut videtur sexti*. Turnhout, Belgium, 1994.

Deichmann, Friedrich Wilhelm. *Ravenna. Hauptstadt des spätantikes Abendlandes.* 3 vols. in 5 parts. Wiesbaden, 1958–1976.

Delmaire, Roland. "Le déclin des largesses sacrées." In *Hommes et richesses dans l'Empire byzantine*, ed. Catherine Abadie-Reynal et al., vol. 1, 265–278. Paris, 1989–1991.

———. *Largesses sacrées et* res privatae: *L'*aerarium *imperial et son administration du IVe au VIe siècle.* Rome, 1989.

———. *Les institutions du Bas-Empire romain de Constantin à Justinien*, vol. 1, *Les institutions civiles palatines.* Paris, 1995.

Delogu, Paolo. "Reading Pirenne Again." In *The Sixth Century: Production, Distribution, and Demand*, ed. Richard Hodges and William Bowden, 15–40. Leiden, 1998.

Demicheli, Anna Maria. "La politica religiosa di Giustiniano in Egitto. Riflessi sulla chiesa egiziana della legislazione ecclesiastica giustinianea." *Aegyptus. Rivista italiana di egittologia e papirologia* 58 (1983): 217–257.

Devignat, Rene. "Variétés de l'espèce *Pasteurella pestis*: Nouvelle hypothèse." *Bulletin of the World Health Organisation* 4 (1951): 247–263.

Diefenbach, S. "Zwischen Liturgie und *civilitas*. Konstantinopel im 5. Jahrhundert und die Etablierung eines städtischen Kaisertums." In R. Warland (ed.), *Bildlichkeit und Bildorte von Liturgie. Schauplätze in Spätantike, Byzanz und Mittelalter*, 21–47. Wiesbaden, 2002.

Devresse, Robert. "Chaînes exégétiques grecques." In *Dictionnaire de la Bible*, suppl. 1 (Paris, 1928), 1048–1233. Cited in ch 16, n. 5 (p 939).

Dihle, Albrecht. *Greek and Latin Literature of the Roman Empire from Augustus to Justinian.* Trans. Manfred Malzahn. London, 1994.

Di Segni, Leah. "The Involvement of Local, Municipal, and Provincial Authorities in Urban Building in Late Antique Palestine and Arabia." In *The Roman and Byzantine Near East: Some Recent Archaeological Research*, JRA Supplementary Series 14, ed. John Humphrey, 312–332. Ann Arbor, Mich., 1995.

———. "Metropolis and Provincia in Byzantine Palestine." In *Caesarea Maritima: A Retrospective after Two Millenia*, ed. Avner Raban and Kenneth G. Holum, 575–589. Leiden, 1996.

———. "Epigraphic Evidence for Building in Palaestina and Arabia (4th–7th c.)." In *The Roman and Byzantine Near East: Some Recent Archaeological Research*, vol. 2, JRA Supplementary Series 31, ed. John Humphrey, 149–178. Portsmouth, R.I., 1999.

Dixon, Suzanne. *The Roman Mother.* London, 1988.

Dodgeon, Michael, and Samuel N. C. Lieu. *The Roman Eastern Frontier and the Persian Wars A.D. 226–363.* London, 1991.

Donceel-Voûte, Pauline. *Les pavements des églises byzantines de Syrie et du Liban. Décor, archéologie et liturgie.* 2 vols. Louvain-la-Neuve, 1988.

Donner, Fred M. *The Early Islamic Conquests.* Princeton, N.J., 1981.

———. "The Role of Nomads in the Near East in Late Antiquity." In *Tradition and Innovation in Late Antiquity*, ed. Fred M. Clover and R. Stephen Humphreys, 73–85. Madison, Wis., 1989.

———. "The Sources of Islamic Conceptions of War." In *Just War and Jihad: Historical and Theoretical Perspectives on War and Peace in Western and Islamic Traditions*, ed. John Kelsay and James Turner Johnson. Westport, Conn., 1991.

———. *Narratives of Islamic Origins: The Beginnings of Islamic Historical Writing.* Princeton, N.J., 1998.

———. "Modern Nationalism and Medieval Islamic History." *Al-'Usur al-Wusta* 13 (2001): 21–22.

——— Review of *The Idea of Idolatry*, by Gerald R. Hawting. *Journal of the American Oriental Society* 121 (2001): 336–338.

———. *Seeing the Origins of Islam in Historical Perspective: The First Wadie Jwaideh Memorial Lecture, delivered November 4, 2002.* Bloomington, Ind., 2003.

Donner, Herbert. *The Mosaic Map of Madaba.* Kampen, 1992.

Downey, Glanville. "Justinian as Achilles." *Transactions and Proceedings of the American Philological Association* 71 (1940): 68–78.

———. "Justinian as a Builder." *Art Bulletin* 32 (1950): 262–266.

———. *Constantinople in the Age of Justinian.* Norman, Okla., 1960.

———. *A History of Antioch in Syria from Seleucus to the Arab Conquest.* Princeton, N.J., 1961.

———. *Gaza in the Early Sixth Century.* Norman, Okla., 1963.

Draguet, René. *Julien d'Halicarnasse et sa controverse avec Sévère d'Antioche sur l'incorruptibilité du corps du Christ.* Universitas Catholica Lovaniensis. Dissertationes ad gradum magistri in Facultate Theologica consequendum conscriptae II, 12. Louvain, 1924.

Drijvers, Han J. W. "The Saint as Symbol: Conceptions of the Person in Late Antiquity and Early Christianity." In *Concepts of Person*, ed. Hans G. Kippenberg, Y. B. Kuiper, and A. F. Sanders, 137–157. Berlin, 1990.

———. "The Gospel of the Twelve Apostles: A Syrian Apocalypse from the Early Islamic Period." In *The Byzantine and Early Islamic Near East*, vol. 1, *Problems in the Literary Source Material*, edited by Averil Cameron and Lawrence I. Conrad, 189–213. Princeton, N.J., 1992.

Drinkwater, John, and Hugh Elton, eds. *Fifth-Century Gaul: A Crisis of Identity?* Cambridge, 1992.

Driver, Thomas F. *Liberating Rites: Understanding the Transformative Power of Ritual.* Boulder, 1998.

Dubrov, Gregory W. "A Dialogue with Death: Ritual Lament and the *Threnos Theotokou* of Romanos Melodos." *Greek, Roman, and Byzantine Studies* 35 (1994): 385–405.

Dunbabin, Katherine M. D. "*Baiarum Grata Voluptas*: Pleasures and Dangers of the Baths." *Proceedings of the British School at Rome* 57 (1989): 6–46.

Dunn, Archibald. "The Transition from *polis* to *kastron* in the Balkans (III–VII cc.): General and Regional Perspectives." *Byzantine and Modern Greek Studies* 18 (1994): 60–80.

Durand, Jannic, ed. *Byzance: L'Art byzantin dans les collections publiques françaises.* Paris, 1992.

Durliat, Jean."La Peste du VIe siècle: Pour un nouvel examen des sources byzantines." In *Hommes et richesses dans l'Empire byzantin IVe–VIIe siècles*, ed. Catherine Abadie-Reynal et al., 107–119. Paris, 1989.

———. *De la ville antique à la ville byzantine. Le problème des subsistances.* Rome, 1990.

———. *Les Finances publiques de Dioclétien aux Carolingiens (284–889).* Sigmaringen, 1990.

———. "La Approvisionnement de Constantinople." In *Constantinople and Its Hinterland*, ed. Cyril Mango and Gilbert Dagron, 19–34. London, 1995.

Duval, Noel. "L'Architecture religieuse de Tcharitchin Grad." In *Villes et peuplement dans l'Illyricum protobyzantin*. Collection de l'École française de Rome 77, 397–482. Paris, 1984.

Dvornik, Francis. *Early Christian and Byzantine Political Philosophy*. 2 vols. Washington, D.C., 1966.

Edmondson, J. C. "Mining in the Later Roman Empire and Beyond." *JRS* 79 (1989): 84–102.

Elton, Hugh. *Warfare in Roman Europe, AD 350–425*. Oxford, 1996.

Engelhardt, Isrun. *Mission und Politik in Byzanz: Ein Beitrag zur Strukturanalyse byzantinischer Mission zur Zeit Justins und Justinians*. Munich, 1974.

Ensslin, Wilhelm. "Gottkaiser und Kaiser von Gottes Gnaden." *Sitzungsberichte der Bayerischen Akademie der Wissenshaften zu München, phil.-hist. Abt.* 6 (1943): 1–133.

Esbroeck, Michel van. "The Aphthartodocetic Edict of Justinian and Its Armenian Background." *Studia Patristica* 33 (1997): 578–585.

Evans, James A. S. *The Age of Justinian: The Circumstances of Imperial Power*. London, 1996.

———. *The Empress Theodora*. Austin, Tex., 2002.

Fahd, Toufic. *Le Panthéon de l'Arabie centrale à la veille de l'hégire*. Paris, 1968.

Feissel, Denis. "Magnus, Mégas et les curateurs des 'maisons divines' de Justin II à Héraclius." *Travaux et mémoires* 9 (1985): 465–476.

Fiey, Jean Maurice. *Jalons pour une histoire de l'Église en Iraq*. CSCO 310/Subs. 36. Louvain, 1970.

Fine, Steven, ed. *Sacred Realm: The Emergence of the Synagogue in the Ancient World*. New York, 1996.

Fischler, Susan. "Social Stereotypes and Historical Analysis: The Case of the Imperial Women at Rome." In *Women in Ancient Societies, an Illusion of the Night*, ed. Léonie Archer, Susan Fischler, and Maria Wyke, 115–33. Houndmills, 1994.

Fisher, Elizabeth. "Theodora and Antonia." *Arethusa* 11 (1978): 253–280.

Fladerer, Ludwig Johannes. *Philoponos De opificio mundi. Spätantikes Sprachdenken und christliche Exegese*. Stuttgart, 1999.

———. *Philoponus, Gregor von Nyssa und die Genese der Impetustheorie. Hommages à Carl Deroux. Tome V – Christianism et Moyen Âge, Néo-latin et survivance de la latinité*. Brussels, 2003.

Fögen, Marie Theres. "Legislation in Byzantium: A Political and Bureaucratic Technique." In *Law and Society in Byzantium, Ninth–Twelfth Centuries*, ed. Angeliki Laiou and Dieter Simon, 53–70. Washington, D.C., 1994.

Forsyth, George H., and Kurt Weitzmann. *The Monastery of St. Catherine on Mt. Sinai*. Ann Arbor, Mich., 1973.

Foss, Clive. *Ephesus after Antiquity: A Late Antique, Byzantine, and Turkish City*. Cambridge, 1979.

———. "The Near Eastern Countryside in Late Antiquity." In *The Roman and Byzantine Near East: Some Recent Archaeological Research*, JRA Supplementary Series 14, ed. J. Humphrey, 218–223. Ann Arbor, Mich., 1995.

———. "Syria in Transition, A.D. 550–750: An Archaeological Approach." *DOP* 51 (1997): 189–269.

———. "Late Antique Antioch." In *Antioch: The Lost City*, ed. Christine Kondoleon, 23–27. Princeton, N.J., 2000.

Foss, Clive, and Winfield, D. *Byzantine Fortifications*. Pretoria, 1986.

Foulkes, Paul. "Where Was Simplicius?" *JHS* 112 (1992): 143.

Fowden, Elizabeth Key. *The Barbarian Plain: Saint Sergius between Rome and Iran*. Berkeley, Calif., 1999.

Fowden, Garth. "The Pagan Holy Man in Late Antique Society." *JHS* 102 (1982): 33–59.

———. *Empire to Commonwealth: Consequences of Monotheism in Late Antiquity*. Princeton, N.J., 1993.

———. "Religious Communities." In *Late Antiquity: A Guide to the Postclassical World*, ed. G. W. Bowersock, Peter Brown, and Oleg Grabar, 82–106. Cambridge, Mass., 1999.

Frank, Georgia. "'Taste and See': The Eucharist and the Eyes of Faith in the Fourth Century." *Church History* 70 (2001): 619–643.

———. *The Memory of the Eyes: Pilgrims to Living Saints in Christian Late Antiquity*. Berkeley, Calif., 2000.

Frankfurter, David. *Religion in Roman Egypt: Assimilation and Resistance*. Princeton, N.J., 1998.

Frantz, Alison. "From Paganism to Christianity in the Temples of Athens." *DOP* 19 (1965): 185–205.

———. "Pagan Philosophers in Christian Athens." *Proceedings of the American Philosophical Society* 119 (1975): 29–38.

———. *Late Antiquity, AD 267–700*. The Athenian Agora 24. Princeton, N.J., 1988, 86–92.

Frend, William H. C. *The Rise of the Monophysite Movement: Chapters in the History of the Church in the Fifth and Sixth Centuries*. Cambridge, 1972. Reprinted with corrections, Cambridge, 1979.

———. "Old and New Rome in the Age of Justinian." In *Relations between East and West in the Middle Ages*, ed. Derek Baker, 11–28. Edinburgh, 1973.

Frézouls, Edmond. "Cosmas Indicopleustes et l'Arabie." In *L'Arabie Préislamique et son environnement historique et culturel*, ed. Toufic Fahd, 441–460. Leiden, 1989.

Frösén, Jaakko, Antti Arjava, and Marjo Lehtinen, eds. *The Petra Papyri*, vol. 1. Amman, 2002.

Frye, Richard N. "The Political History of Iran under the Sasanians." In *Cambridge History of Iran*, vol. 3, ed. Ehsan Yarshater, 116–177. Cambridge, 1983.

———. "Parthian and Sasanian History of Iran." In *Mesopotamia and Iran in the Parthian and Sasanian Periods: Rejection and Revival c. 238 B.C.–A.D. 642*, ed. John Curtis. London, 2000.

Gabra, Gawdat. *Coptic Monasteries: Egypt's Monastic Art and Architecture*. Cairo, 2002.

Gager, John G. *Curse Tablets and Binding Spells from the Ancient World*. New York, 1992.

Gagos, Traianos, and Peter van Minnen. *Settling a Dispute: Towards a Legal Anthropology of Late Antique Egypt*. Ann Arbor, Mich., 1994.

Galatariotou, Catia. "Holy Women and Witches: Aspects of Byzantine Conceptions of Gender." *Byzantine and Modern Greek Studies* 9 (1984–1985): 55–94.

Garland, Linda. *Byzantine Empresses*. London, 1999.

Garsoïan, Nina G. "Byzantium and the Sasanians." In *Cambridge History of Iran*, vol. 3, ed. Ehsan Yarshater, 574–592. Cambridge, 1983.

———. "Armenia Megale kai eparkhia Mesopotamias." In *Eupsychia. Mélanges offerts à Hélène Ahrweiler*, ed. Hélène Ahrweiler and Michel Balard, 239–264. Paris, 1998.

Garsoïan, Nina G. and Jean-Pierre Mahé. *Des Parthes au Califat*. Paris, 1997.

———. *L'Église arménienne et le grand schisme d'Orient*. CSCO 574/Subs. 100. Louvain, 1999.

Gawlikowski, Michal. "The Syrian Desert under the Romans." In *The Early Roman Empire in the East*, ed. Susan E. Alcock, 37–54. Oxford, 1997.

Geary, Patrick J. *Before France and Germany: The Creation and Transformation of the Merovingian World*. New York, 1988.

———. *The Myth of Nations: The Medieval Origins of Europe*. Princeton, N.J., 2001.

Gero, Stephen. "Montanus and Montanism according to a Medieval Syriac Source." *Journal of Theological Studies*, n.s., 28 (1977): 520–524.

Gerostergios, Asterios. *Justinian the Great, the Emperor and Saint*. Belmont, MA, 1982.

Gibb, Hamilton A. R. "Pre-Islamic Monotheism in Arabia." *Harvard Theological Review* 55 (1962): 269–280.

Gibbon, Edward. *Decline and Fall of the Roman Empire*. London, 1776–1788.

Gillett, Andrew. "Was Ethnicity Politicized in the Earliest Medieval Kingdom?" In *On Barbarian Identity – Critical Approaches to Ethnogenesis Theory*, ed. Andrew Gillett, 85–122. Turnhout, Belgium, 2002.

Goehring, James E. *Ascetics, Society, and the Desert: Studies in Egyptian Monasticism*. Harrisburg, Pa., 1999.

Goffart, Walter A. "Zosimus, the First Historian of Rome's Fall." *American Historical Review* 76 (1971): 412–441.

———. *Barbarians and Romans, A.D. 418–584: The Techniques of Accommodation*. Princeton, N.J., 1980.

———. *Rome's Fall and After*. London, 1989.

Goldberg, P. J. P. "Introduction." In *The Black Death in England*, ed. Mark Ormrod and Phillip Lindley, 1–15. Stamford, Eng., 1996.

Gonosova, Anna. "Exotic Taste: The Lure of Sasanian Persia." In *Antioch, the Lost Ancient City*, ed. Christine Kondoleon, 130–145. Princeton, N.J., 2000.

Goodenough, E. R. "The Political Theory of Hellenistic Kingship." *Yale Classical Studies* 1 (1928): 55–102.

Grabar, André. *Les Ampoules de Terre Sainte (Monza, Bobbio)*. Paris, 1958.

Gray, Patrick T. R. *The Defense of Chalcedon in the East*. Studies in the History of Christian Thought 20. Leiden, 1979.

———. "'The Select Fathers': Canonizing the Patristic Past." *Studia Patristica* 23 (1989): 21–36.

———. "Covering the Nakedness of Noah: Reconstruction and Denial in the Age of Justinian." In *Conformity and Non-Conformity in Byzantium*, ed. Lynda Garland, 193–206. Byzantinische Forschungen 24. Amsterdam 1997.

———. "Through the Tunnel with Leontius of Jerusalem: The Sixth-Century Transformation of Theology." In *The Sixth Century: End or Beginning?*, ed. Pauline Allen and Elizabeth Jeffreys, 187–196. Brisbane, 1996.

Gray, Patrick T. R., and M. W. Herren. "Columbanus and the Three Chapters Controversy." *Journal of Theological Studies*, n.s., 45 (1994): 160–170.

Gray, Rebecca. *Prophetic Figures in Late Second Century Jewish Palestine: The Evidence from Josephus*. New York, 1993.

Greatrex, Geoffrey. "The Nika Riot: A Reassessment." *JHS* 117 (1997): 60–86.

———. *Rome and Persia at War, 502–532*. Leeds, 1998.

———. "Procopius the Outsider?" In *Strangers to Themselves: The Byzantine Outsider*, ed. Dion S. Smythe, 215–218. Burlington, Vt., 2000.

Greatrex, Geoffrey, and Samuel N. C. Lieu, eds. *The Roman Eastern Frontier and the Persian Wars, Part II: A.D. 363–630: A Narrative Sourcebook*. London, 2002.

Greene, Kevin. *The Archaeology of the Roman Economy*. Berkeley, Calif., 1986.

Greenwood, Timothy William. "A History of Armenia in the Seventh and Eighth Centuries." PhD diss., University of Oxford, 2000.

Grierson, Philip. *Byzantine Coins*. London, 1982.

Grierson, Philip, and Mark Blackburn. *Medieval European Coinage*. Vol. 1, *The Early Middle Ages*. Cambridge, 1986.

Grillmeier, Alois, and Theresia Hainthaler. *Christ in Christian Tradition. 2/2. The Church of Constantinople in the Sixth Century*. Trans. John Cawte and Pauline Allen. Louisville, Ky., 1995.

———. *Christ in Christian Tradition. 2/4. The Church of Alexandria with Nubia and Ethiopia after 451*. Trans. O. C. Dean Jr. Louisville, Ky., 1996.

Grosdidier de Matons, José. "Liturgie et Hymnographie: Kontakion et Canon." *DOP* 34–35 (1980–1981): 31–43.

Grosse, Robert. *Römische Militärgeschichte von Gallienus bis zum Beginn der byzantinischen Themenverfassung*. Berlin, 1920.

Grümel, Venance. *Les Regestes des actes du patriarcat de Constantinople*, vol. 1, *Les Actes des patriarches*. Fasc. 1: *Les regestes de 381 à 715*. Istanbul, 1932. Reprint, Paris, 1972.

Guidi, Ignazio. *Chronica Minora* I. CSCO 1/Syr. 1. 1903. Reprint, Louvain, 1955.

Guidoboni, Emanuela, ed. *I terremoti prima del Mille in Italia e nell'area mediterranea*. Bologna, 1989.

Guilland, R. *Études de topographie de Constantinople byzantine*, 2 vols. Berlin, 1969.

Guillaume, Alfred. *The Life of Muhammad. A Translation of Ibn Ishaq's "Sirat Rasul Allah."* Oxford, 1955.

Guillaumont, Antoine. "Justinien et l'Église de Perse." *DOP* 23–24 (1969–1970): 39–66.

———. "Un colloque entre orthodoxes et théologiens nestoriens de Perse sous Justinien." *Académie des Inscriptions et Belles Lettres. Comptes rendus* (1970): 201–207.

Gunn, Joel. D., ed. *The Years without Summer: Tracing AD 536 and Its Aftermath*. British Archaeological Reports Intermediate Series 872. Oxford, 2000.

Gutas, Dimitri. *Greek Thought, Arabic Culture*. New York, 1998.

Haas, Christopher. *Alexandria in Late Antiquity: Topography and Social Conflict*. Baltimore, 1997.

Haas, Frans A. J. de. *John Philoponus' New Definition of Prime Matter: Aspects of Its Background in Neoplatonism and the Ancient Commentary Tradition*. Leiden, 1997.

Hadas-Lebel, Mireille. "Jacob et Esaü en Israel et Rome dans le Talmud et le Midrash." *Revue de l'histoire des religions* 201 (1984): 369–392.

Hadot, Ilsetraut. *Le problème du néoplatonisme Alexandrin: Hiéroclès et Simplicius*. Paris, 1978.

———. "La vie et l'œuvre de Simplicius d'après des sources grecques et arabes." In Hadot, *Simplicius, sa vie, son œuvre, sa survie*, 3–39. Berlin and New York, 1987.

———. "The Life and Work of Simplicius in Greek and Arabic sources." In *Aristotle Transformed: The Ancient Commentators and their Influence*, ed. Richard R. K. Sorabji, 275–303. London, 1990.

Hagedorn, D., and K. A. Worp. "Von ΚΥΡΙΟΣ zu ΔΕΣΠΟΤΗΣ: Eine Bemerkung zur Kaisertitulatur im 3./4. Jhdt." *Zeitschrift für Papyrologie und Epigraphik* 39 (1980): 165–177.

Hahn, Cynthia. "Loca Sancta Souvenirs: Sealing the Pilgrim's Experience." In *The Blessings of Pilgrimage*, ed. Robert Ousterhout, 85–96. Urbana, Ill., 1990.

Haines-Eitzen, Kim. "'Girls Trained in Beautiful Handwriting': Female Scribes in Roman Antiquity and Early Christianity." *Journal of Early Christian Studies* 6 (1998): 629–646.

Hainthaler, T. "Johannes Philoponus, Philosoph und Theologe in Alexandria." In *Jesus der Christus im Glauben der Kirche*. Band 2/4: *Die Kirche von Alexandrien mit Nubien und Äthiopien nach 451*, ed. Alois Grillmeier, 109–149. Freiburg, 1990.

Haldon, John F. *Recruitment and Conscription in the Byzantine Army, c. 550–950*. Vienna, 1979.

———. *Byzantine Praetorians: An Administrative, Institutional and Social Survey of the Opsikion and Tagmata, c. 580–900*. Bonn, 1984.

———. *Constantine Porphyrogenitus, Three Treatises on Military Expeditions*. Corpus Fontium Historiae Byzantinae, Series Vindobonensis 28. Vienna, 1990.

———. "The Works of Anastasius of Sinai: A Key Source for the History of Seventh-Century East Mediterranean Society and Belief." In *The Byzantine and Early Islamic Near East*, vol. 1, *Problems in the Literary Source Material*, Studies in Late Antiquity and Early Islam 1.1, ed. Averil Cameron and Lawrence I. Conrad, 107–147. Princeton, N.J. 1992.

———. *Byzantium in the Seventh Century: The Transformation of a Culture*. Cambridge, 1990. 2nd rev. ed., Cambridge 1997.

———. *Warfare, State, and Society in the Byzantine World, 565–1024*. London, 1999.

———. *The Byzantine Wars*. Stroud, 2000.

Hall, Linda Jones. "The Case of Late Antique Berytus: Urban Wealth and Rural Sustenance – A Different Economic Dynamic." In *Urban Centers and Rural Contexts in Late Antiquity*, ed. Thomas S. Burns and John W. Eadie, 63–76. East Lansing, Mich., 2001.

Halleux, André de. *Philoxène de Mabbog. Sa vie, ses écrits, sa théologie*. Universitas Catholica Lovaniensis. Dissertationes ad gradum magistri in Facultate Theologica vel in Facultate Iuris Canonici consequendum conscriptae III, 8. Louvain, 1963.

Hällström, Gunnar. "The Closing of the Neoplatonic School in A.D. 529: An Additional Aspect." *Papers and Monographs of the Finnish Institute at Athens* 1 (1994): 141–165.

Halsall, Guy. "Towns, Societies, and Ideas: The Not So Strange Case of Late Roman and Early Merovingian Metz." In *Towns in Transition*, ed. Neil Christie and Simon T. Loseby, 235–261. Aldershot, Eng. 1996.

Hannestad, Knud. "Les Forces militaires d'après la Guerre Gothique de Procope." *Classica et Mediaevalia* 21 (1960): 136–183.

Hardy, Edward R. "The Egyptian Policy of Justinian." *DOP* 22 (1968): 21–41.

Harl, Kenneth W. "Sacrifice and Pagan Belief in Fifth- and Sixth-Century Byzantium." *Past and Present* 128 (1990): 7–27.

Harlow, Mary. "In the Name of the Father: Procreation, Paternity, and Patriarchy." In *Thinking Men: Masculinity and Its Self-Representation in the Classical Tradition*, ed. Lyn Foxhall and John Salmon, 155–169. London, 1998.

Harlow, Mary, and Ray Laurence. *Growing Up and Growing Old in Ancient Rome*. London, 2001.

Harries, Jill. *Law and Empire in Late Antiquity*. Cambridge, 1999.

Harris, William V. *Ancient Literacy*. Cambridge, Mass., 1989.

Harrison, R. Martin. *A Temple for Byzantium: The Discovery of Anicia Juliana's Palace-Church in Istanbul.* Austin, Tex., 1989.

Hartney, Aideen. "Manly Women and Womanly Men: The *Subintroductae* and John Chrysostom." In *Desire and Denial in Byzantium*, ed. Liz James, 41–48. Aldershot, Eng. 1999.

Harvey, Susan Ashbrook. "Women in Early Syrian Christianity." In *Images of Women in Antiquity*, ed. Averil Cameron and Amélie Kuhrt, 288–298. Detroit, 1983.

———. *Asceticism and Society in Crisis: John of Ephesus and The Lives of the Eastern Saints.* Berkeley, Calif., 1990.

———. "Women in Early Byzantine Hagiography: Reversing the Story." In *"That Gentle Strength": Historical perspectives on Women and Christianity*, ed. Lynda Coon, Katherine Haldane, and Elisabeth Summers, 16–59. Charlottesville, Va; 1990.

———. "Theodora the 'Believing Queen': A Study in Syriac Historiographical Tradition." *Hugoye: Journal of Syriac Studies* 4 (2001), available at syrcom.cua.edu/hugoye/Vol14No2/HV4N2Harvey.html.

———. "Spoken Words, Voiced Silence: Biblical Women in Syriac Tradition." *Journal of Early Christian Studies* 9 (2001): 105–131.

Hawting, Gerald R. *The Idea of Idolatry and the Emergence of Islam: From Polemic to History.* Cambridge, 1999.

Hayes, John W. *Late Roman Pottery.* London, 1972.

———. "Problèmes de la céramique des VIIe–IXe siècles à Salamine et à Chypre." In *Salamine de Chypre, histoire et archéologie: État des recherches*, Colloques internationaux du CNRS 578, ed. Marguerite Yon, 375–387. Paris, 1980.

———. "Pottery of the Sixth and Seventh centuries." In *Acta XIII Congressus Internationalis Archaeologiae Christianae*, ed. Emilio Marin and Victor Saxer, 3:541–550. Citta del Vaticano, 1993.

———. *Excavations at Saraçhane in Istanbul.* Vol. 2, *The Pottery.* Princeton, N.J., 1992.

———. *The Goths.* Oxford, 1996.

Heather, Peter. "Literacy and Power in the Migration Period." *Literacy and Power in the Ancient World*, ed. Alan K. Bowman and Greg Woolf. Cambridge, 1994.

———. "New Men for New Constantines? Creating an Imperial Elite in the Eastern Mediterranean." In *New Constantines: The Rhythm of Imperial Renewal in Byzantium, Fourth–Thirteenth Centuries*, ed. Paul Magdalino, 11–33. Aldershot, Eng., 1994.

Heck, Gene. "Gold Mining in Arabia and the Rise of the Islamic State." *Journal of the Economic and Social History of the Orient* 42 (1999): 364–395.

———. "'Arabia without Spices.' An Alternate Hypothesis." *Journal of the American Oriental Society* 123 (2003), forthcoming.

Heine, Ronald E. *The Montanist Oracles and Testimonia.* Macon, Ga., 1989.

Hendy, Michael. *Studies in the Byzantine Monetary Economy, c. 300–1450.* Cambridge, 1985.

Henry, Patrick, III. "A Mirror for Justinian: The *Ekthesis* of Agapetus Diaconus." *Greek, Roman, and Byzantine Studies* 8 (1967): 281–308.

Herrin, Judith. *The Formation of Christendom.* Oxford, 1987.

———. "Byzance: Le Palais et la ville." *Byzantion* 61 (1991), 213–230.

———, "'Femina Byzantina': The Council of Trullo on Women." *DOP* 46 (1992): 97–105.

———. "Public and Private Forms of Religious Commitment among Byzantine Women." In *Women in Ancient Societies, an Illusion of the Night*, ed. Leonie Archer, Susan Fischler, and Maria Wyke, 181–203. Houndmills, Eng., 1994.

Hespel, Robert. *Sévère d'Antioche. La Polémique antijulianiste.* CSCO 244/Syr. 104. Louvain, 1964.

Hewsen, Robert H. *Armenia: A Historical Atlas.* Chicago, 2001.

Hezser, Catherine. "The Codification of Legal Knowledge in Late Antiquity: The Talmud Yerushalmi and Roman Law Codes." In *The Talmud Yerushalmi and Graeco-Roman culture*, ed. Peter Schäfer, 1:581–641. Tübingen, 1998.

Hirschfeld, Yizhar. "Some Aspects of the Late-Antique Village of Shivta." *JRA* 16 (2003): 395–408.

Hirst, L. Fabian. *The Conquest of Plague.* Oxford, 1953.

Hodges, Richard. "Henri Pirenne and the Question of Demand in the Sixth Century." In *The Sixth Century: Production, Distribution and Demand*, ed. Richard Hodges and William Bowden, 3–14. Leiden, 1998.

Hodges, Richard, and William Bowden, eds. *The Sixth Century: Production, Distribution, and Demand.* Leiden, 1998.

Hoffmann, Dietrich. "Der *numerus equitum Persoiustinianorum* auf einer Mosaikinschrift von Sant' Eufemia in Grado." *Aquileia Nostra* 32–33 (1961–1962): 81–98.

Hoffmann, Philippe. "Simplicius' Polemics." In *Philoponus and the Rejection of Aristotelian Science*, ed. Richard R. K. Sorabji, 57–83. London, 1987.

———. "Damascius." *Dictionnaire des philosophes antiques*, ed. Richard Goulet, 2:541–593. Paris, 1989.

Holum, Kenneth. "The End of Classical Urbanism at Caesarea Maritima, Israel." In *Studia pompeiana et classica in Honor of Wilhelmina F. Jashemski*, ed. Robert I. Curtis, 2:89–93. New Rochelle, N.Y., 1989.

———. "The Survival of the Bouleutic Class at Caesarea in Late Antiquity." In *Caesarea Maritima: A Retrospective after Two Millennia*, ed. Avner Raban and Kenneth Holum, 615–627. Leiden, 1996.

———. "The Christianizing of Caesarea Maritima." In *Die spätantike Stadt und ihre Christianisierung*, ed. Gunnar Brands and Hans-Georg Severin, 151–164. Wiesbaden, 2003.

Holum, Kenneth, Avner Raban, and Joseph Patrich, eds. *Caesarea Papers 2. JRA* Supplementary Series 35. Portsmouth, R.I., 1999.

Holum, Kenneth, et al. *King Herod's Dream: Caesarea on the Sea.* New York, 1988.

Honigmann, Ernest. *Évêques et évêchés monophysites d'Asie antérieure au VI^e siècle.* CSCO 127 / Subs. 2. Louvain, 1951.

Honoré, Anthony. "Some Constitutions Composed by Justinian." *JRS* 65 (1975): 107–123.

———. "Law Codes." In *Late Antiquity: A Guide to the Postclassical World*, ed. G. W. Bowersock, Peter Brown, and Oleg Grabar, 539–540. Cambridge, Mass., 1999.

———. *Justinian's Digest: Work in Progress.* Oxford, 1971.

———. *Tribonian.* Ithaca, N.Y., 1978.

———. "Justinian's Codification: Some Reflections." *Bracton Law Journal* 25 (1993): 29–37.

Horden, Peregrine, and Nicholas Purcell. *The Corrupting Sea: A Study of Mediterranean History.* Oxford, 2000.

Horton, Fred. "A Sixth-Century Bath in Caesarea's Suburbs and the Transformation of Bathing Culture in Late Antiquity." In *Caesarea Maritima: A Retrospective after Two Millennia*, ed. Avner Raban and Kenneth G. Holum, 177–189. Leiden, 1996.

Howard-Johnston, James D. "The Official History of Heraclius' Persian Campaigns." In *The Roman and Byzantine Army in the East*, ed. E. Dabrowa, 57–87. Krakow, 1994.

———. "The Great Powers in Late Antiquity: A Comparison." In *States, Resources, Armies*, ed. Averil Cameron, 157–226. Princeton, N.J., 1995.

———. "Heraclius' Persian Campaigns and the Revival of the East Roman Empire, 622–630." *War in History* 6 (1999): 1–44.

Howard-Johnston, James D., and Nigel Ryan. *The Scholar and the Gypsy*. London, 1992.

Hoyland, Robert. *Seeing Islam as Others Saw It*. Studies in Late Antiquity and Early Islam 13. Princeton, N.J., 1997.

———. *Arabia and the Arabs: From the Bronze Age to the Coming of Islam*. London, 2001.

Humphrey, John. *Roman Circuses: Arenas for Chariot Racing*. London, 1986.

Hunger, Herbert. "Kaiser Justinian I (527–565)." *Anzeiger der österreichischen Akademie der Wissenschaften, Wien, phil.-hist. Klasse* 102 (1965): 339–356.

———. *Die hochsprachliche profane Literatur der Byzantiner*. Munich, 1978.

———. "Romanos Melodos, Dichter, Prediger, Rhetor – und sein Publikum." *Jahrbuch für Österreichischen Byzantinistik* 34 (1984): 15–42.

Innemée, Karel C. "Deir al-Baramus: Excavations at the So-Called Site of Moses the Black, 1994–1999." *Bulletin de la Société d'archéologie copte* 39 (2000): 123–135.

Innemée, Karel C., and Lucas Van Rompay. "La Présence des Syriens dans le Wadi al-Natrun (Égypte). À propos des découvertes récentes de peintures et de textes muraux dans l'Église de la Vierge du Couvent des Syriens." *Parole l'Orient* 23 (1998): 167–202.

Irmscher, Johannes. "Paganismus im Justinianischen Reich." *Klio* 63 (1981): 683–688.

———. "La legislazione di Giustiniano sugli Ebrei." *Augustinianum* 28 (1988): 361–365.

———. "The Jews under the Reign of Justinian." *Eos* 78 (1990): 155–161.

Isaac, Benjamin. *The Limits of Empire: The Roman Army in the East*. Oxford, 1990.

James, Edward. *Britain in the First Millennium*. London, 2000.

James, Liz. *Empresses and Power in Early Byzantium*. London, 2001.

Janin, R. *Constantinople byzantine*. Paris, 1964.

———. "Les Processions religieuses à Byzance." *Revue des études byzantines* 24 (1966): 69–88.

———. *Les Églises et les monastères*. Paris, 1969.

Jansma, T. "Encore le Credo de Jacques de Saroug. Nouvelles recherches sur l'argument historique concernant son orthodoxie." *L'Orient syrien* 10 (1965): 75–88, 193–236, 331–370, 475–510.

Jeffreys, Elizabeth, Michael Jeffreys, and Robert Scott. *The Chronicle of John Malalas: A Translation*. Melbourne, 1986.

Johnson, David W. "Anti-Chalcedonian Polemics in Coptic Texts, 451–641." In *The Roots of Egyptian Christianity*, ed. Birger A. Pearson and James E. Goehring, 216–234. Philadelphia, 1986.

Johnson, Mark J. "Toward a History of Theodoric's Building Program." *DOP* 42 (1988): 73–96.

Jones, Arnold H. M. *The Later Roman Empire, 284–602: A Social, Economic, and Administrative Survey*. 3 vols. Oxford, 1964.

———. *The Greek City from Alexander to Justinian*. 2nd ed. Oxford, 1967.

———. "The Economic Life of the Towns of the Roman Empire." *Recueils de la Société Jean Bodin* 7 (1955): 161–192. Reprinted in *The Roman Economy: Studies in Ancient Economic and Social History*, ed. P. A. Brunt, 35–60. Oxford, 1974.

Jones, Michael E. *The End of Roman Britain*. Ithaca, N.Y., 1996.

Kaegi, Walter E. *Byzantium and the Decline of Rome*. Princeton, N.J., 1968.

———. "Variable Rates of Seventh-Century Change." In *Tradition and Innovation in Late Antiquity*, ed. Frank M. Clover and R. Stephen Humphreys, 191–208. Madison, Wis., 1989.

———. *Byzantium and the Early Islamic Conquests*. Cambridge, 1992.

———. "Byzantine Sardinia and Africa Face the Muslims: A Rereading of Some Seventh-Century Evidence." *Bizantistica* 3 (2001): 1–24.

Kaldellis, Anthony. *Procopius of Caesarea: Tyranny, History, and Philosophy at the end of Antiquity*. Philadelphia, 2004.

Kalla, Gábor. "Christentum am oberen Euphrat. Das byzantinische Kloster von Tall Biᶜa." *Antike Welt* 30 (1999): 131–142.

Kaplan, Michel. "Quelques aspects des 'maisons divines' de Justin II à Héraclius." In *Mélanges N. Svoronos*, ed. Vasiles Kremmydas, Chrysa A. Maltezou and Nikalaos M. Panagiotakes, 70–96. Paris, 1986.

———. *Les Hommes et la terre à Byzance du VIe au XIe siècles*. Paris, 1992.

Kariveri, Arja. "The 'House of Proclus' on the Southern Slope of the Acropolis: A Contribution." *Papers and Monographs of the Finnish Institute at Athens* 1 (1994): 115–139.

Kartsonis, Anna."The Responding Icon." In *Heaven on Earth: Art and the Church in Byzantium*, ed. Linda Safran, 59–80. University Park, Pa., 1998.

Kaster, Robert A. *Guardians of Language: The Grammarian and Society in Late Antiquity*. Berkeley, Calif., 1988.

Kazhdan, Alexander P., ed. *The Oxford Dictionary of Byzantium*. New York, 1991.

Keenan, James G. "Egypt." *CAH*, vol. 14, ed. Averil Cameron, Bryan Ward-Perkins, and Michael Whitby, 612–637. Cambridge, 2000.

Kelly, John Norman Davidson. *Early Christian Doctrines*. San Francisco, 1978.

———. *The Oxford Dictionary of Popes*. Oxford Paperback Reference. Oxford, 1988.

Kennedy, Hugh. "From Polis to Madina: Urban Change in Late Antique and Early Islamic Syria." *Past and Present* 106 (1985): 3–27.

———. "The Last Century of Byzantine Syria: A Reinterpretation." *Byzantinische Forschungen* 10 (1985): 141–183.

———. Review of *Meccan Trade*, by Patricia Crone. *Middle East Studies Association Bulletin* 22 (1988): 54–55.

Kevran, Monique. "Suhar." *Encyclopaedia of Islam*. 2d ed., vol. 9., ed. C. E. Bosworth et al. (1997): 774–776.

Key Fowden, Elizabeth. *The Barbarian Plain*. Princeton, N.J., 1999.

Keys, David. *Catastrophe: An Investigation into the Origins of the Modern World*. London, 1999.

Kingsley, Sean and Michael Decker, eds. *Economy and Exchange in the East Mediterranean in Late Antiquity*. Oxford, 2001.

Kister, Michael J. "Al-Hira: Some Notes on Its Relations with Arabia." *Arabica* 15 (1968): 143–169.

———. "The Struggle against Musaylima and the Conquest of Yamama." *Jerusalem Studies in Arabic and Islam* 27 (2002): 1–56.

Kleyn, Hendrik Gerrit. *Het Leven van Johannes van Tella door Elias. Syrische tekst en Nederlandsche vertaling*. Leiden, 1882.

———. *Jacobus Baradaeüs. De Stichter der Syrische Monophysietische Kerk*. Leiden, 1882.

Klingenberg, Eberhard. "Justinians Novellen zur Judengesetzgebung." In *Festschrift für Hermann Lange zum 70. Geburtstag am 24. Januar 1992*, ed. Dieter Medicus et al., 139–161. Stuttgart, 1992.

Klingshirn, William E. *Caesarius of Arles: The Making of a Christian Community in Late Antique Gaul*. Cambridge, 1994.

Koder, Johannes. "Fresh Vegetables for the Capital." In *Constantinople and Its Hinterland*, ed. C. Mango and G. Dagron, 49–56. London, 1965.

———. "Climatic Change in the Fifth and Sixth Centuries?" In *The Sixth Century: End or Beginning?*, ed. Pauline Allen and Elizabeth Jeffreys, 270–285. Brisbane, 1996.

Koenen, Ludwig. "The Carbonized Archive from Petra." *JRA* 9 (1996): 177–188.

Kraeling, Carl H. *The Excavations at Dura-Europos*. Vol. 8, part 1, *The Synagogue*. New Haven, Conn., 1967.

Kraeling, Carl, ed. *Gerasa of the Decapolis*. New Haven, Conn. 1938.

Krauss, Samuel. *Studien zur byzantinisch-jüdische Geschichte*. Vienna, 1914.

———. *The Jewish-Christian Controversy from the Earliest Times to 1789*. Ed. William Horbury. Vol. 1. Tübingen, 1996.

Krautheimer, Richard. *Three Christian Capitals: Topography and Politics*. Berkeley, Calif., 1983.

———. *Rome: Profile of a City, 312–1308*. Princeton, N.J., 1980 repr. 2000.

Krautheimer, Richard, and Slobodan Ćurčić. *Early Christian and Byzantine Architecture*. 4th ed. Harmondsworth, Eng., 1986.

Krebernik, Manfred. "Schriftfunde aus Tall Bi<sup>c</sup>a 1990, I. Funde aus dem byzantinischen Kloster." *Mitteilungen der Deutschen Orient-Gesellschaft zu Berlin* 123 (1991): 41–57.

Krueger, Derek. "Writing as Devotion: Hagiographical Composition and the Cult of the Saints in Theodoret of Cyrrhus and Cyril of Scythopolis." *Church History* 66 (1997): 707–719.

———. "Writing and Redemption in the Hymns of Romanos the Melodist." *Byzantine and Modern Greek Studies* 27 (2003): 2–44.

Krumbacher, Karl. *Geschichte der Byzantinischen Literatur*. Munich, 1891.

Kuefler, Matthew. *The Manly Eunuch: Masculinity, Gender Ambiguity, and Christian Ideology in Late Antiquity*. Chicago, 2001.

Külzer, Andreas. *Disputationes graecae contra Iudaeos: Untersuchungen zur byzantinischen antijüdischen Dialogliteratur und ihrem Judenbild*. Byzantinisches Archiv 18. Stuttgart, 1999.

Kuhn, K. H. *A Panegyric on Apollo Archimandrite of the Monastery of Isaac by Stephen Bishop of Heracleopolis Magna*. CSCO 395/Copt. 40. Louvain, 1978.

La Rocca, Cristina, ed. *Italy in the Early Middle Ages*. Vol. 1 of *Short Oxford History of Medieval Italy*. Oxford, 2002.

Lahey, Lawrence. "Jewish Biblical Interpretation and Genuine Jewish-Christian Debate in the Dialogue of Timothy and Aquila." *Journal of Jewish Studies* 51 (2000): 281–96.

———. "The Christian-Jewish Dialogues through the Sixth Century (Excluding Justin)." In *Jewish Believers in Jesus*. vol. 1, *The First Five Centuries*, ed. Oskar Skarsaune and Reidar Hvalvik. Peabody, Mass., forthcoming.

Laiou, Angeliki. "The Role of Women in Byzantine Society." *Jahrbuch der Österreichischen Byzantinistik* 31 (1981): 233–260.

Lammens, Henri. "La République marchande de la Mecque vers l'an 600 de nôtre ère." *Bulletin de l'Institut Égyptien*, 5th ser., 4 (1910): 23–54.

———. *La Mecque à la veille de l'hégire*. Beirut, 1924.

Lanata, Giuliana. *Legislazione e natura nelle novelle giustinianee*. Naples, 1984.

Lang, Uwe Michael. *John Philoponus and the Controversies over Chalcedon in the Sixth Century: A Study and Translation of the* Arbiter. Louvain, 2001.

Langhammer, Walter. *Die rechtliche und soziale Stellung der Magistratus Municipales und der Decuriones in der Übergangsphase der Städte von sich selbstverwaltenden Gemeinden zu Vollzugsorganen des spätantiken Zwangsstaates (2.–4. Jahrhundert der römischen Kaiserzeit)*. Wiesbaden, 1973.

Laniado, Avshalom. *Recherches sur les notables municipaux dans l'Empire protobyzantin*. Paris, 2002.

Lapidge, Michael, and David Dumville, eds. *Gildas: New Approaches*. Wodbridge, U.K., 1984.

Lavan, Luke. "The Late-Antique City: A Bibliographic Essay." In *Recent Research in Late-Antique Urbanism*, ed. Luke Lavan, 9–26. Portsmouth, R. I., 2001.

———. "The *praetoria* of Civil Governors in Late Antiquity." In *Recent Research in Late-Antique Urbanism*, ed. Luke Lavan, 39–56. Portsmouth, R. I., 2001.

Leader, Ruth E. "The David Plates Revisited: Transforming the Secular in Early Byzantium." *Art Bulletin* 102 (2000): 407–414.

Lecker, Michael. "Idol Worship in Pre-Islamic Medina (Yathrib)." *Le Muséon* 106 (1993): 331–346.

Lee, A. D. *Information and Frontiers. Roman Foreign Relations in Late Antiquity*. Cambridge, 1993.

———. "Warfare and the State in Late Antiquity." In *The Cambridge History of Graeco-Roman Warfare*, ed. Hans van Wees, Philip Sabin, and Michael Whitby. Forthcoming.

Lee, A. D., and Jonathan Shepard. "A Double Life: Placing the *Peri presbeon*." *Byzantinoslavica* 52 (1991): 15–39.

Lee, Tae-Soo. *Die griechische Tradition der aristotelischen Syllogistik in der Spätantike*. Göttingen, 1984.

Lehmann, Clayton Miles, and Holum, Kenneth G. *The Greek and Latin Inscriptions of Caesarea Maritima*. Boston, 2000.

Lemerle, Paul. *Byzantine Humanism: The First Phase*. Trans. Helen Lindsay and Ann Moffatt. Canberra, 1986.

Lendon, J. E. *Empire of Honour: The Art of Government in the Roman World*. Oxford, 1997.

Lepelley, Claude, ed. *La Fin de la cité antique et le début de la cité médévale de la fin du IIIe siècle à l'avèvenement de Charlemagne, Actes du colloque tenu à l'Université de Paris X-Nanterre les 1, 2 et 3 avril 1993*. Bari, 1996.

Levine, Lee I. *The Ancient Synagogue: The First Thousand Years*. New Haven, Conn., 1999.

Lewit, Tamara. "'Vanishing Villas': What Happened to Élite Rural Habitation in the West in the Fifth–Sixth c.?" *JRA* 16 (2003): 260–274.

Leyerle, Blake. "Landscape as Cartography in Early Christian Pilgrimage Narratives." *Journal of the American Academy of Religion* 64 (1996): 119–143.

Liebeschuetz, J. H. W. G. "The Defences of Syria in the Sixth Century." In *Studien zu den Militärgrenzen Roms II*, ed. C. B. Rüger, 487–499. Cologne, 1977.

———. "Cities, Taxes, and the Accommodation of the Barbarians: The Theories of Durliat and Goffart." In *Kingdoms of the Empire: The Integration of Barbarians in Late Antiquity*, The Transformation of the Roman World 1, ed. Walter Pohl, 135–152. Leiden, 1997.

———. *The Decline and Fall of the Roman City*. Oxford, 2001.

Liebs, Detlef. "Roman Law." *CAH*, vol. 14, ed. Averil Cameron, Bryan Ward-Perkins, and Michael Whitby, 238–259. Cambridge, 2000.

Lieu, Samuel N. C. *Manichaeism in the Later Roman Empire and Medieval China*. Tübingen, 1992.

Lifshitz, Baruch. *Donateurs et fondateurs dans les synagogues juives*. Paris, 1967.

Linder, Amnon, ed. *The Jews in Roman Imperial Legislation*. Detroit, 1987.

Lingas, Alexander. "The Liturgical Place of the Kontakion in Constantinople." In *Liturgy, Architecture, and Art in the Byzantine World: Papers of the XVIII International Byzantine Congress (Moscow, 8–15 August 1991) and Other Essays Dedicated to the Memory of Fr. John Meyendorff*, ed. Constantine C. Akentiev, 50–57. St. Petersburg, 1995.

Little, Lester K., ed. *The Justinianic Plague, 541–767 AD* . Proceedings of conference held at the American Academy in Rome, December 2001. Forthcoming.

Llewellyn, Peter. "The Laurentian Schism: Priests and Senators." *Church History* 45 (1976): 417–427.

Lokin, Johannes Henricus Antonius. "The Novels of Leo and Justinian." *Journal of Juristic Papyrology* 28 (1998): 131–140.

Ludwig, E. M. "Neo-Chalcedonism and the Council of 553." DD diss., Graduate Theological Union, Berkeley, Calif., 1983.

Lüling, Günter. *Die Wiederentdeckung des Propheten Muhammad*. Erlangen, 1981.

Luna, Concetta. Review of *Thiel* (1999). *Mnemosyne* 54 (2001): 482–504.

Luxenberg, Christoph. *Die syro-aramäische Lesart des Koran. Ein Beitrag zur Entschlüsselung der Koransprache*. Berlin, 2000.

Lynch, John P. *Aristotle's School*. Berkeley, Calif., 1972.

Maas, Michael. "Roman History and Christian Ideology in Justinianic Reform Legislation." *DOP* 40 (1986): 17–31.

———. *John Lydus and the Roman Past: Antiquarianism and Politics in the Age of Justinian*. New York, 1992.

———. "Junillus Africanus' *Instituta Regularia Divinae Legis* in Its Justinianic Context." In *The Sixth Century: End or Beginning?*, ed. Paulene Allen and Elizabeth Jeffreys, 131–144. Brisbane, 1996.

———. "*Mores et Moenia*: Ethnography and the Decline of Urban Constitutional Autonomy in Late Antiquity." In *Integration und Herrschaft: Ethnische Identitaten und kulturelle Muster im fruhen Mittelalter*, ed. Walter Pohl and Max Diesenberger, 25–35. Vienna, 2002.

———. *Exegesis and Empire in the Early Byzantine Mediterranean: Junillus Africanus and the "Instituta Regularia Divinae Legis."* With a contribution by Edward G. Matthews, Jr. Tübingen, 2003.

———. "'Delivered from Their Ancient Customs': Christianity and the Question of Cultural Change in Early Byzantine Ethnography." In *Conversion in Late Antiquity and the Early Middle Ages: Seeing and Believing*, ed. Kenneth Mills and Anthony Grafton, 152–188. Rochester, N.Y., 2003.

MacCormack, Sabine. *Art and Ceremony in Late Antiquity*. Berkeley, Calif., 1981.

MacCoull, Leslie S. B. "Another Look at the Career of John Philoponus." *Journal of Early Christian Studies* 3, (1995): 269–279.

———. "'When Justinian Was Upsetting the World': A Note on Soldiers and Religious Coercion in Sixth-Century Egypt." In *Peace and War in Byzantium, Essays in Honor of George T. Dennis*, ed. Timothy S. Miller and John Nesbitt, 106–113. Washington, D.C., 1995.

Macdonald, Jeffrey Lee. "The Christological Works of Justinian." PhD diss., Catholic University of America, Washington, 1995.

Macomber, Willliam F. *Six Explanations of the Liturgical Feasts by Cyrus of Edessa: An East Syrian Theologian of the Mid-Sixth Century*. CSCO 355–356/Syr. 155–156. Louvain, 1974.

Macrides, Ruth, and Paul Magdalino. "The architecture of ekphrasis: Construction and Context of Paul the Silentiary's Poem on Hagia Sophia." *Byzantine and Modern Greek Studies* 12 (1988); 47–82.

Maddicott, J. R. "Plague in Seventh-Century England." *Past and Present* 156 (1997): 7–54.

Madelung, Wilferd. "Apocalyptic Prophecies in Hims in the Umayyad Age." *Journal of Semitic Studies* 31 (1986): 141–185.

Magdalino, Paul. "Aristocratic Oikoi in the Tenth and Eleventh Districts of Constantinople." In *Byzantine Constantinople: Monuments, Topography and Everyday Life*, ed. N. Necipoglu, 53–69. Leiden, 2000.

———. "The Maritime Neighbourhoods of Constantinople: Commercial and Residential Functions, Sixth to Twelfth Centuries." *DOP* 54 (2000), 209–226.

———. "Medieval Constantinople: Built Environment and Urban Development." In *The Economic History of Byzantium: From the Seventh through the Fifteenth Century*, ed. A. Laiou, 529–37. Washington, D.C., 2002.

Magoulias, H. J. "The Lives of Byzantine Saints as Sources of Data for the History of Magic in the Sixth and Seventh Centuries A.D.: Sorcery, Relics, and Icons." *Byzantion* 37 (1967): 228–269.

Mahony, Stephanie, and John Hale. "The Villa of Torre de Palma (Alto Alentejo)." *JRA* 9 (1996): 275–294.

Mainstone, Rowland J. *Hagia Sophia: Architecture, Structure, and Liturgy of Justinian's Great Church*. London, 1988.

Mango, Cyril. *The Brazen House: A Study of the Vestibule of the Imperial Palace of Constantinople*. Copenhagen, 1959.

———. "The Church of Saints Sergius and Bacchus at Constantinople and the Alleged Tradition of Octagonal Palatine Churches." *Jahrbuch der Österreischischen Byzantinistik* 21 (1972): 189–193.

———. *The Art of the Byzantine Empire, 312–1453*. Toronto, 1986.

———. "The Development of Constantinople as an Urban Centre." In *The Seventeenth International Byzantine Congress: Main Papers*, 117–136. New Rochelle, N.Y., 1986, Reprinted in Mango, *Studies on Constantinople*. London, 1993.

———. "Constantine's Mausoleum and the Translation of Relics." *BZ* 83 (1990): 51–62. "Addendum." *BZ* 83 (1990): 454.

———. *Le Développement urbain de Constantinople*. Rev. ed. Paris, 1990.

———. "Constantine's Column." In Mango, *Studies on Constantinople*, 3:1–6. London, 1993.

———. "The Columns of Justinian and His Successors." In Mango, *Studies on Constantinople*, 10:1–20. London, 1993.

———. "The Water Supply of Constantinople." In Mango and Dagron, *Constantinople and Its Hinterland*, 9–18. London, 1995.

———. "The Triumphal Way of Constantinople and the Golden Gate." *Dumbarton Oaks Papers* 54 (2000): 173–88.

———. "New Religion, Old Culture." In *The Illustrated History of Byzantium*, ed. Mango, 97–114. Oxford, 2002.

Mango, Cyril, and Ihor Ševčenko. "Remains of the Church of St. Polyeuktos at Constantinople." *DOP* 15 (1961): 243–247.

Mango, Marlia Mundell. "Where Was Beth Zagba?" *Harvard Ukrainian Studies* 7 (1983): 405–430.

———. *Silver from Early Byzantium: The Kaper Koraon and Related Treasures*. Baltimore, 1986.

———. "The Commercial Map of Constantinople." *DOP* 54 (2000): 189–207.

———. "The Porticoed Street at Constantinople." In *Byzantine Constantinople: Monuments, Topography, and Everyday Life*, ed. N. Necipoglu, 29–51, The Medieval Mediterranean: Peoples, Economies, and Cultures, 400–1500 33. Leiden, 2001.

Marks, John H. *Visions of One World: Legacy of Alexander*. Guilford, Conn., 1985.

Markus, Robert A. "Carthage, Prima Iustiniana, Ravenna: An Aspect of Justinian's *Kirchenpolitik*." *Byzantion* 44 (1979): 279–289.

———. "Justinian's Ecclesiastical Politics and the Western Church." In *Sacred and Secular: Studies on Augustine and Latin Christianity*. Aldershot, U.K. 1994. English trans. of "La politica ecclesiastica di Giustiniano e la chiesa d'Occidente," in *Il mondo del diritto nell'epoca giustinianea: caratteri e problematiche*, ed. G. G. Archi, 113–124. Ravenna, 1984.

———. *Gregory the Great and His World*. Cambridge, 1997.

Martindale, John, ed. *The Prosopography of the Later Roman Empire*, vol. III, *AD 527–641*. Cambridge, 1992.

Martinez, Francisco Javier. "Eastern Christian Apocalyptic in the Early Muslim Period: Pseudo-Methodius and Pseudo-Athanasius." PhD diss., Catholic University of America, 1985.

Mathew, Gervase. *Byzantine Aesthetics*. London, 1963.

Mathews, Thomas F. *The Early Churches of Constantinople: Architecture and Liturgy*. University Park, Pa., 1971.

———. *Byzantium: From Antiquity to the Renaissance*. New York, 1998.

———. *The Clash of Gods: A Reinterpretation of Early Christian Art*. Rev. ed. Princeton, N.J., 1999.

———. "The Emperor and the Icon." *Acta ad archaeologiam et artium historiam pertinentia* 15 (2001): 163–177.

Mathisen, Ralph. *Roman Aristocrats in Barbarian Gaul: Strategies for Survival in an Age of Transition*. Austin, Tex., 1993.

Matthews, John. "Ammianus and the Eternity of Rome." In *The Inheritance of Historiography, 350–900*, ed. Christopher Holdsworth and T. P. Wiseman, 17–29. Exeter, 1986.

———. *The Roman Empire of Ammianus*. London, 1989.

———. *Laying Down the Law: A Study of the Theodosian Code*. New Haven, Conn., 2000.

Mattingly, David, and R. Bruce Hitchner. "Roman Africa: An Archaeological Review." *JRS* 85 (1995): 165–213.

Maxfield, Valerie A. *The Military Decorations of the Roman Army*. London, 1981.

Mazal, Otto. *Justinian I. und seine Zeit. Geschichte und Kultur des Byzantinischen Reiches im 6. Jahrhundert*. Cologne, 2001.

McCail, R. C. "The Cycle of Agathias: New Identifications Scrutinized." *JHS* 89 (1969): 87–96.

McClanan, Anne. *Representations of Early Byzantine Empresses: Image and Empire*. New York, 2002.

McCormick, Michael. *Eternal Victory: Triumphal Rulership in Late Antiquity, Byzantium, and the Early Medieval West*. Cambridge, Mass., 1986.

———. "Emperor and Court." *CAH*, vol. 14, ed. Averil Cameron, Bryan Ward-Perkins, and Michael Whitby, 135–163. Cambridge, 2000.

———. *Origins of the European Economy: Communications and Commerce, A.D. 300–900*. Cambridge, 2001.

———. "Rats, Communications, and Plague: Towards an Ecological History." *Journal of Interdisciplinary History* 34 (2003): 1–25.

McDonald, William Lloyd. *The Architecture of the Roman Empire*. Vol. 2, *An Urban Appraisal*. New Haven, 1986.

McKenzie, Judith. "Glimpsing Alexandria from Archaeological Evidence." *Journal of Roman Archeology* 16 (2003): 35–63.

Meier, Mischa. *Das andere Zeitalter Justinians. Kontingenzerfahrung und Kontingenzbewaltigung im 6. Jahrhundert n. Chr.* Goettingen, 2003.

Meinardus, Otto F. A. *Two Thousand Years of Coptic Christianity*. Cairo, 1999.

Menis, Gian Carlo, ed. *I Longobardi*. Milan, 1990.

Merrills, Andrew, ed. *Vandals, Romans and Berbers: New Perspectives on Late Antique Africa*. Burlington, VT, 2004.

Merton, Thomas. "Time and the Liturgy." In *Seasons of Celebration*, ed. Thomas Merton, 45–61. New York, 1977.

Metzger, Ernest, ed. *A Companion to Justinian's Institutes*. Ithaca, N.Y., 1998.

Meyendorff, John. "Christian Marriage in Byzantium: The Canonical and Liturgical Tradition." *DOP* 44 (1990): 99–107.

———. *Christ in Eastern Christian Thought*. Washington, 1969.

———. "Eastern Liturgical Theology." In *Christian Spirituality: Origins to the Twelfth Century*, ed. Bernard McGinn and John Meyendorff, 350–363. New York, 1985.

———. *Imperial Unity and Christian Divisions: The Church 450–680 A.D.* Church History 2. Crestwood, N.Y., 1989.

Meyer, Marvin, et al. *Ancient Christian Magic: Coptic Texts of Ritual Power*. San Francisco, 1994.

Millar, Fergus. *The Emperor in the Roman World*. Ithaca, N.Y., 1977.

———. "Ethnic Identity in the Roman Near East, 325–450: Language, Religion, and Culture." *Mediterranean Archaeology* 11 (1998): 159–176.

Miyakawa, Hisayuki, and Arnulf Kollautz. "Ein Dokument zum Fernhandel zwischen Byzanz und China zur Zeit Theophlyakts." *BZ* 77 (1984): 6–19.

Modéran, Yves. "La Renaissance des cités dans l'Afrique du VIe siècle d'après une inscription récemment publiée." In *La fin de la cité antique*, edited by Claude Lepelley, 85–11. Bari, 1996.

———. "Les Églises et la reconquista byzantine: L'Afrique." In *Histoire du christianisme*, vol. 3, ed. Luce Pietri, 699–704. Paris, 2000.

Momigliano, Arnaldo. "Gli Anicii e la storiografia latina del VI secolo D.C." In *Rendiconti dell'Accademia dei Lincei, classe di scienze morali, storiche e filosofiche*, 8. Serie 9, 11–12 (1956): 279–297, repr. in *Secondo contributo alla storia degli studi classici*. Rome, 1960. 231–253, 249–290. Geneva, 1956.

Montagu, Ashley. *Man's Most Dangerous Myth: The Fallacy of Race*. New York, 1974.

Montserrat, Dominic. "Reading Gender in the Roman World." In *Experiencing Rome*, ed. Janet Huskinson, 153–181. London, 2000.

Moorhead, John. "The Laurentian Schism, East and West in the Roman Church." *Church History* 47 (1978): 125–136.

———. "Italian Loyalties during Justinian's Gothic War." *Byzantion* 53 (1983): 575–596.

———. *Theoderic in Italy*. Oxford, 1992.

———. *Justinian*. London, 1994.

———. *The Roman Empire Divided, 400–700*. London, 2001.

Morford, M. "How Tacitus Defined Liberty." *Aufsteig und Niedergang der römischen Welt* II 33.5 (1991): 3420–3450.

Morony, Michael. "Land Use and Settlement Patterns in Late Sasanian and Early Islamic Iraq." In *Land Use*, ed. Averil Cameron and Geoffrey King, 221–230. Princeton, N.J., 1994.

———. "Sasanids." In *Encyclopaedia of Islam*, 2nd ed., vol. 9, ed. C. E. Bosworth, et al., 70–83. Leiden, 1997.

———. "The Late Sasanian Economic Impact on the Arabian Peninsula." *Name-ye Iran-e Bastan* 1.2 (2001–2002): 25–37.

Morrison, Donald. "Philoponus and Simplicius on Tekmeriodic Proof." In *Method and Order in Renaissance Philosophy of Nature*, ed. Daniel A. Di Liscia, Eckhard Kessler, and Charlotte Methuen, 1–22. Aldershot, Brookfield, Vt., 1997.

Morrisson, Cecile, and Jean-Pierre Sodini. "The Sixth-Century Economy." In *The Economic History of Byzantium from the Seventh through the Fifteenth Century*, ed. Angeliki Laiou, et al., 171–220. Washington, D.C., 2002.

Mosse, George L. *Toward the Final Solution: A History of European Racism*. Madison, Wis., 1985.

Müller, Albert. "Das Heer Justinians (nach Procop und Agathias)." *Philologus* 71 (1912): 101–138.

Müller-Wiener, Wolfgang. *Bildlexikon zur Topographie Istanbuls*. Tübingen, 1977.

Muthesius, Anna. "Constantinople and Its Hinterland: Issues of Raw Silk Supply." In Muthesius, *Studies in Byzantine and Islamic Silk Weaving*, 315–335. London, 1995.

———. "From Seed to Samite: Aspects of Byzantine Silk Production." In *Studies in Byzantine and Islamic Silk Weaving*, 119–134. London, 1995.

Naumann, R. "Neue Beobachtungen am Theodosiosbogen und Forum Tauri in Istanbul." *IstMitt* 26 (1976): 117–141.

Newby, Gordon D. *A History of the Jews of Arabia from Ancient Times to Their Eclipse under Islam*. Columbia, S.C., 1988.

Nicholas, Barry. *An Introduction to Roman Law*. Oxford, 1962.

Nicol, Donald M. "Byzantine Political Thought." In *The Cambridge History of Medieval Political Thought*, ed. James Henderson Burns, 51–79. Cambridge, 1988.

Noble, Thomas F. X. "Theoderic and the Papacy." In *Teoderico il grande e i goti d'Italia: Atti del XIII Congresso internazionale di studi sull'Alto Medioevo Milano 2–6 novembre 1992*, ed. Centro italiano di studi sull'alto medioevo, 395–423. Spoleto, 1993.

O'Donnell, James J. "The Demise of Paganism." *Traditio* 35 (1979): 45–88.

———. *Cassiodorus*. Berkeley, Calif., 1979.

Obolensky, Dimitri. *The Byzantine Commonwealth. Eastern Europe, 500–1453*. New York, 1971.

Oehler, Klaus. "Die Kontinuität in der Philosophie der Griechen bis zum Untergang des bzyantinischen Reiches." In Oehler, *Antike Philosophie und bzyantinisches Mittelalter*, 15–37. Munich, 1969.

Oikonomides, Nicolas. "Silk Trade and Production in Byzantium from the Sixth to the Ninth Century: The Seals of Kommerkarioi." *DOP* 40 (1986): 33–53.

Ort, L. J. R. *Mani: A Religio-Historical Description of his Personality*. Leiden, 1967.

Owens, E. J. *The City in the Greek and Roman World*. New York, 1991.

*The Oxford Dictionary of Byzantium*, 3 vols. New York, 1991.

Panella, Clementina. "Gli scambi nel Mediterraneo Occidentale dal IV al VII secolo dal punto di vista di alcune 'merci.'" In *Hommes et richesses dans l'empire byzantin*, ed. Catherine Abadie-Reynal, et al., 1:129–141. Paris, 1989–1991.

Parkes, James. *The Conflict of the Church and the Synagogue*. London, 1934.

Patlagean, Evelyne. *Pauvreté économique et pauvreté sociale à Byzance, 4e–7e siècles*. Paris, 1977.

Patrich, Joseph. "Warehouses and Granaries in Caesarea Maritima." In *Caesarea Maritima: A Retrospective after Two Millennia*, ed. Avner Raban and Kenneth G. Holum, 146–176. Leiden, 1996.

Pazdernik, Charles F. "'Our Most Pious Consort Given Us by God': Dissident Reactions to the Partnership of Justinian and Theodora, AD 525–548." *Classical Antiquity* 13 (1994): 256–281.

———. "Procopius and Thucydides on the Labors of War: Belisarius and Brasidas in the Field." *Transactions and Proceedings of the American Philological Association* 130 (2000): 149–187.

Peacock, D. P. S., and D. F. Williams. *Amphorae and the Roman Economy*. London, 1986.

Peleg, Yoav. "The Dams of Caesarea's Low-Level Aqueduct." In *The Aqueducts of Israel*, ed. David Amit, Joseph Patrich, and Yizhar Hirschfeld, 141–147. Portsmouth, R.I., 2002.

Percival, John. *The Roman Villa*. London, 1976.

Perikhanian, A. "Iranian Society and Law." *Cambridge History of Iran*, vol. 3, ed. Ehsan Yarshater, 627–680. Cambridge, 1983.

Philippson, Alfred. *Das Mittelmeergebiet: seine geographische und kulturelle Eigenart*. Leipzig, 1904.

Pietri, Charles. "Aristocratie et société cléricale dans l'Italie chrétienne au temps d'Odoacre et de Théodoric." *MélRome* 93 (1981): 417–467.

———. "La géographie de l'Illyricum ecclésiastique et ses relations avec l'église de Rome (Ve–VIe siècles)." In *Villes et peuplement dans l'Illyricum protobyzantin*, 21–62. Rome, 1984.

Pirenne, Henri. "Mahomet et Charlemagne." *La Revue Belge de Philologie et d'Histoire* 1(1922): 77–86.

———. "Un contraste économique: Mérovingiens et Carolingiens." *La Revue Belge de Philologie et d'Histoire* 2(1923): 223–235.

———. *Medieval Cities*. Princeton, 1925.

———. *Economic and Social History of Medieval Europe*. New York, 1937.

———. *Mohammed and Charlemagne*. New York, 1939, French ed., 1937.

Platt, Colin. *King Death: The Black Death and Its Aftermath in Late-Medieval England*. London, 1996.

Pohl, Walter. "Die Gepiden und die Gentes an der mittleren Donau nach dem Zerfall des Attilareiches." In *Die Völker an der mittleren und unteren Donau im 5. und 6. Jahrhundert*, ed. Herwig Wolfram and Falko Daim, 240–305. Vienna, 1980.

———. "The Empire and the Lombards: Treaties and Negotiations in the Sixth Century." In *Kingdoms of the Empire: The Integration of Barbarians in Late Antiquity*, ed. Pohl, 75–134. Leiden, 1997.

———. ed. *Kingdoms of the Empire: The Integration of Barbarians in Late Antiquity*. Vol. 1 of *Transformation of the Roman World*. Leiden, 1997.

———. "Telling the Difference – Signs of Ethnic Identity." In *Strategies of Distinction: The Construction of Ethnic Communities, 300–800*, ed. Walter Pohl and Helmut Reimitz, 17–69. Leiden, 1998.

———. *Die Germanen*. Munich, 2000.

———. "Ethnicity, Theory, and Tradition: A Response." In *On Barbarian Identity – Critical Approaches to Ethnogenesis Theory*, ed. Andrew Gillett, 221–240. Turnhout, Belgium, 2002.

———. *Die Völkerwanderung. Eroberung und Integration*. Stuttgart, 2002.

———. *Die Awaren. Ein Steppenvolk in Mitteleuropa, 567–822 n.Chr.* Munich, 2002.

———. "A Non-Roman Empire in Central Europe: The Avars." In *Regna et Gentes: The Relationship between Late Antique and Early Medieval Peoples and Kingdoms in the Transformation of the Roman World*, ed. Hans-Werner Goetz, Jorg Jarnut, and Walter Pohl, 571–595. Leiden, 2003.

———. "Perceptions of Barbarian Violence." In *Violence in Late Antiquity*, ed. Harold Drake. Forthcoming.

Pollitzer, Robert. *Plague*. Geneva, 1954.

Porath, Yosef. "The Water-Supply to Caesarea: A Re-assessment." In *The Aqueducts of Israel*, ed. David Amit, Joseph Patrich, and Yizhar Hirschfeld, 104–140. Portsmouth, R.I., 2002.

Poulter, Andrew J. "Nicopolis ad Istrum: The Anatomy of a Graeco-Roman City." In *Die römische Stadt im 2. Jahrhundert n. Chr.*, ed. Hans-Joachim Schalles, Henner von Hesberg, and Paul Zanker, 60–86. Bonn, 1992.

———. "The Use and Abuse of Urbanism in the Danube Provinces during the Later Roman Empire." In *The City in Late Antiquity*, ed. John Rich, 99–135. London, 1992.

Poulter, Andrew J., et al. *Nicopolis ad Istrum: A Roman, Late Roman, and Early Byzantine City, Excavations 1985–1992*. London, 1995.

Praechter, Karl. *Richtungen und Schulen im Neuplatonismus. Genethliakon für Carl Robert*, 105–155. Berlin, 1910. Reprinted in Praechter, *Kleine Schriften*, ed. Heinrich Dörrie, 165–216, Collectanea 7. Hildesheim, 1973.

———. "Christlich-neuplatonische Beziehungen." *BZ* 21 (1912): 1–27.

Pringle, Denys. *The Defence of Byzantine Africa from Justinian to the Arab Conquest*. Oxford, 1981.

Pringsheim, Fritz. "Justinian's Prohibition of Commentaries to the *Digest*." *Revue internationale des droits de l'antiquité* 2nd ser., 5 (1950): 383–415.

Pummer, Reinhard. *The Samaritans*. Leiden, 1987.

———. "Samaritan Synagogues and Jewish Synagogues: Similarities and Differences." In *Jews, Christians, and Polytheists in the Ancient Synagogue*, ed. S. Fine, 118–160. London, 1999.

Quasten, Johannes. *Patrology*. Westminster, Eng., 1983–1986.

Raban, Avner, and Kenneth G. Holum, eds. *Caesarea Maritima: A Retrospective after Two Millennia*. New York, 1996.

Raban, Avner, and Shalom Yankelevitz. "Excavation of the Byzantine/Early Islamic Bath in Area TPS, 1995." In *Caesarea Papers, vol. 3*, ed. Kenneth G. Holum and Jennifer Stabler. Forthcoming.

Rabello, Alfredo M. *Giustiniano, Ebrei e Samaritani all luce delle fonti storico-letterarie, ecclesiastiche e giuridiche*. 2 vols. Milan, 1987–1988.

Raoult, Didier, et al. "Molecular Identification by 'Suicide PCR' of Yersinia Pestis as the Agent of Medieval Black Death." *Proceedings of the National Academy of Sciences of the U.S.A.* 97 (2000): 12880–12883.

Rapp, Claudia. "A Medieval Cosmopolis: Constantinople and Its Foreign Inhabitants." In *Alexander's Revenge: Hellenistic Culture through the Centuries*, ed. J. Ma and N. Van Deusen, 153–172. Reykjavik, 2002.

Rappe, Sara. "Scepticism in the Sixth Century? Damascius' Doubts and Solutions Concerning First Principles." *Journal of the History of Philosophy* 36 (1998): 337–363.

Ravegnani, Giovanni. *Soldati di Bisanzio in età Giustinianea*. Rome, 1988.

Reinink, Gerrit J. "Ps.-Methodius: A Concept of History in Response to the Rise of Islam." In *The Byzantine and Early Islamic Near East. Vol. 1, Problems in the Literary Source Material*, ed. Averil Cameron and Lawrence I. Conrad, 149–187. Princeton, N.J., 1992.

———. "Heraclius, the New Alexander: Apocalyptic Prophecies during the Reign of Heraclius." In *The Reign of Heraclius (610–641): Crisis and Confrontation*, ed. Berhard H. Stolte and Gerrit J. Reinink, 81–94. Louvain, Belgium, 2002.

Reydellet, Marc. *La Royauté dans la littérature Latine de Sidoine Apollinaire à Isidore de Séville*. Rome, 1981.

Reynolds, Leighton D., and Nigel G. Wilson. *Scribes and Scholars: A Guide to the Transmission of Greek Literature*. Oxford, 1968.

Reynolds, Paul. *Trade in the Western Mediterranean A.D. 400–700: The Ceramic Evidence*. Oxford, 1995.

Rich, John, ed. *The City in Late Antiquity*. London, 1992.

Rich, John, and Andrew Wallace-Hadrill, eds. *City and Country in the Ancient World*. London, 1991.

Richlin, Amy. "Julia's Jokes, Galla Placidia, and the Roman Use of Women as Political Icons." In *Stereotypes of Women in Power: Historical Perspectives and Revisionist Views*, ed. Barbara Garlick et al., 65–91. New York, 1992.

Richter, Siegfried. *Studien zur Christianisierung Nubiens*. Wiesbaden, 2002.

Riet, Simone van. "A propos de la biographie de Simplicius." *Revue Philosophique de Louvain* 89 (1991): 506–514.

Ringgren, Helmer. *Studies in Arabian Fatalism*. Uppsala Universitets Årsskrift, 1955, no. 2. Uppsala, 1955.

Ringrose, Kathryn. *The Perfect Servant: Eunuchs and the Social Construction of Gender in Byzantium*. Chicago, 2003.

Ripoll Lopez, Gisela. "On the Supposed Frontier between the *Regnum Visigothorum* and Byzantine *Hispania*." In *The Transformation of Frontiers – from Late Antiquity to the*

*Carolingians*, ed. Walter Pohl, Ian N. Wood, and Helmut Reimitz, 95–115. Leiden, 2000.

Robinson, Olivia. *The Sources of Roman Law: Problems and Methods for Ancient Historians* London, 1997.

Robinson, Olivia F., T. D. Fergus, and William M. Gordon. *European Legal History: Sources and Institutions*. 3rd ed. London, 2000.

Roller, Matthew B. *Constructing Autocracy: Aristocrats and Emperors in Julio-Claudian Rome*. Princeton, N.J., 2001.

Rorem, Paul, and John C. Lamoreaux. *John of Scythopolis and the Dionysian Corpus: Annotating the Areopagite*. Oxford, 1998.

Rösch, Gerhard. *ONOMA BASILEIAS. Studien zum offiziellen Gebrauch der Kaisertitel in spätantiker und frühbyzantinischer Zeit*. Vienna, 1978.

Ross, Marvin C. *Catalogue of the Byzantine and Early Mediaeval Antiquities in the Dumbarton Oaks Collection*. Vol. 1, *Metalwork, Ceramics, Glass, Glyptics, Painting*. Washington, D.C., 1962.

Roth, H. *Die Kunst der Völkerwanderungszeit*. Frankfurt am Main, 1979.

Rothstein, Gustav. *Die Dynastie der Lahmiden in al-Hira*. Berlin, 1899.

Roueché, Charlotte. "Acclamations in the Late Roman Empire." *JRS* 74 (1984): 181–199.

———. *Aphrodisias in Late Antiquity*. JRS Monographs 5. London, 1989.

———. *Performers and Partisans at Aphrodisias in the Roman and Late Roman Periods*. JRS Monographs 6. London, 1993.

Rousseau, Philipp. "Inheriting the Fifth Century: Who Bequeathed What?" In *The Sixth Century, End or Beginning?*, ed. Pauline Allen and Elizabeth Jeffreys, 1–19. Brisbane, 1996.

Rubin, Berthold. *Das Zeitalter Iustinians*, vol. I. Berlin, 1960. vol. 2 ed. Carmelo Capizzi, Berlin: 1995.

Rubin, Uri. "The Ka'ba: Aspects of Its Ritual Functions and Position in Pre-Islamic and Early Islamic Times." *Jerusalem Studies in Arabic and Islam* 8 (1986): 97–131.

———. "Al-Sa'a." *Encyclopaedia of Islam*. 2nd ed, vol. 8, ed. C. E. Bosworth, et al. (1995): 654–657.

———. "Hanifiyya and Ka'ba: An Inqiury into the Arabian Pre-Islamic Background of Din Ibrahim." *Jerusalem Studies in Arabic and Islam* 13 (1990): 85–112.

Rubin, Ze'ev. "Byzantium and Southern Arabia." In *The Eastern Frontier of the Roman Empire*, ed. David H. French and Chris S. Lightfoot, 383–420. Oxford, 1989.

———. "The Reforms of Khusro Anshirwn." In *The Byzantine and Early Islamic Near East*. Vol. 3, *States, Resources, Armies*, ed. Averil Cameron, 227–297. Princeton, N.J., 1995.

———. "The Sasanid Monarchy." *CAH*, vol. 14, 3rd ed., Ed. Averil Cameron, Bryan Ward-Perkins, and Michael Whitby, 638–61, Cambridge, 2000.

Saffrey, Henri D. "Le chrétien Jean Philopon et la survivance de l'école d'Alexandrie au VIe siècle." *Revue des etudes grecques* 67 (1954): 396–410.

Sallares, Robert. "Ecology, Evolution, and Epidemiology of Plague." In *Justinianic Plague*, ed. Lester Little. Forthcoming.

Sambursky, Samuel. *The Physical World of Late Antiquity*. London, 1962.

Saradi, Helen. "The *Kallos* of the Byzantine City: The Development of a Rhetorical *Topos* and Historical Reality." *Gesta* 34 (1995): 37–56.

Saradi-Mendelovici, Helen. "The Demise of the Ancient City and the Emergence of the Medieval City in the Eastern Roman Empire." *Échos du Monde Classique/Classical Views*, n.s., 7 (1988): 365–401.

Sarkissian, Karekin. *The Council of Chalcedon and the Armenian Church*. London, 1965.

Sarris, Peter. "Rehabilitating the Great Estate: Aristocratic Property and Economic Growth in the Late Antique Eastern Empire." In *Recent Research on the Late Antique Countryside*, ed. William Bowden, Luke Lavan, and Carlos Machado, 55–71. Leiden, 2003.

———. "The Justinianic Plague: Origins and Effects." *Continuity and Change* 17 (2002): 169–182.

Sartre, Maurice. *Inscriptions grecques et latines de la Syrie XIII*. Paris, 1982.

———. *Trois études sur l'Arabie romaine*. Brussels, 1982.

———. *Bostra des origines à l'Islam*. Paris, 1985.

Schattauer, Thomas H. "The Koinonicon of the Byzantine Liturgy: An Historical Study." *OCP* 49 (1983): 91–129.

Schiller, A. Arthur. *Roman Law: Mechanisms of Development*. New York, 1978.

Schmidt, Andrea B. "Die *Refutatio* des Timotheus Aelurus gegen das Konzil von Chalcedon. Ihre Bedeutung für die Bekenntnisentwicklung der armenischen Kirche Persiens im 6. Jh." *Oriens Christianus* 73 (1989): 149–165.

Scholten, Clemens. *Antike naturphilosophie und christliche Kosmologie in der Schrift "De opificio mundi" des Johannes Philoponos*. Berlin, 1996.

Schreckenberg, Heinz. *Die christlichen Adversus-Judaeos-Text und ihr literarisches und historische Umfeld (1.–11. Jh)*. 3rd ed. Frankfurt am Main, 1995.

Schwartz, Seth. *Imperialism and Jewish Society, 200 BCE to 640 CE*. Princeton, N.J., 2001.

Scott, Joan. "Gender, a Useful Category of Historical Analysis." In Scott, *Gender and the Politics of History*, rev. ed. 28–50. New York, 1999.

Scott, Roger. "The Classical Tradition in Byzantine Historiography." In *Byzantium and the Classical Tradition*, ed. Margaret Mullett and Roger Scott, 61–74. Birmingham, 1981.

Scott, Susan, and Christopher J. Duncan. *Biology of Plagues: Evidence from Historical Populations*. Cambridge, 2001.

Segel, Judah Benzion. *Edessa: The Blessed City*. Oxford, 1970.

Ševčenko, Ihor. "Agapetus East and West: The Fate of a Byzantine 'Mirror of Princes.'" *Revue des Études Sud-Est Européennes* 16 (1978): 3–44. Reprint in *Ideology, Letters, and Culture in the Byzantine World*, by Ihor Ševčenko. London, 1982.

Shahbazi, S. "Army. 5. The Sasanian Period." *Encyclopedia of Iran* (1987): 496–499.

Shahîd, Irfan. "Ghassan." *Encyclopaedia of Islam*. 2nd ed., vol. 2, ed. Bernard Lewis, et. al. Leiden, Belgium. 1020–1021. 1965.

———. "Lakhmids." *Encyclopaedia of Islam*, 2nd ed., vol. 5. ed. C. E. Bosworth, et. al. 632–634. 1986.

———. *Byzantium and the Arabs in the Fifth Century*. Washington, D.C., 1989.

———. *Byzantium and the Arabs in the Sixth Century*, 2 vols. Washington, D.C., 1995–2002.

———. *The Martyrs of Najrân: New Documents*. Subsidia Hagiographica 49. Brussels, 1971.

Sharf, Andrew. *Byzantine Jewry from Justinian to the Fourth Crusade*. London, 1971.

Shaw, Brent. "War and Violence." In *Late Antiquity: A Guide to the Postclassical World*, ed. Glen Bowersock, Peter Brown, and Oleg Grabar, 130–169. Cambridge, Mass., 1999.

Sheldon-Williams, I. P. "The Greek Christian Platonist Tradition from the Cappadocians to Maximus and Eriugena." In *The Cambridge History of Later Greek and Early Medieval Philosophy*, ed. Arthur Hilary Armstrong, 425–533. Cambridge, 1967.

Shepard, Jonathan, and Simon Franklin, eds. *Byzantine Diplomacy*. London, 1992.

Shereshevski, Joseph. *Byzantine Urban Settlements in the Negev Desert*. Beer-Sheva, 1991.

Shoufani, Elias. *Al-Riddah and the Muslim Conquest of Arabia*. Toronto, 1972.

Shrewsbury, John Findlay Drew. *A History of Bubonic Plague in the British Isles*. Cambridge, 1970.

Simon, Róbert. *Meccan Trade and Islam: Problems of Origin and Structure*. Trans. Feodora Sos. Budapest, 1989.

Simpson, St. John. "Mesopotamia in the Sasanian Period: Settlement Patterns, Arts and Crafts." In *Mesopotamia and Iran in the Parthian and Sasanian Periods*, ed. John Curtis, 57–66. London, 2000.

Small, Alistair M., and Robert J. Buck. *The Excavations of San Giovanni di Ruoti*. Vol. 1. *The Villas and their Environment*. Toronto, 1994.

Smith, G. Rex. "Rustak." *Encyclopaedia of Islam*. 2nd ed., vol. 9, ed. C. E. Bosworth, et al., 636. Leiden, Belgium, 1997.

Smith, Sidney. "Events in Arabia in the Sixth Century A.D." *Bulletin of the School of Oriental and African Studies* 16 (1954): 425–468.

Sodini, Jean-Pierre. "La Contribution de l'archéologie à la connaissance du monde byzantin (IVe–VIIe siècles)." *DOP* 47 (1993): 139–184.

———. "Le Commerce des marbres à l'époque protobyzantine." In *Hommes et richesses dans l'Empire byzantin*. Vol. I: *IVe–VIIe siècle*, edited by Catherine Abadie-Reynal, 163–186. Paris, 1989.

Sonderegger, Erwin. *Simplikios, Über die Zeit: ein Kommentar zum Corollarium de tempore*. Göttingen, 1982.

Sorabji, Richard R. K. *Time, Creation and the Continuum*. 193–231. London, 1983.

———. ed. *Philoponus and the Rejection of Aristotelian Science*. London, 1987.

———. *Matter, Space, and Motion*. 227–248. London, 1988.

Sotinel, Claire. "Autorité pontificale et pouvoir impérial sous le règne de Justinien: Le pape Vigile." *MélRom* 104, no. 1 (1992): 439–463.

———. "Silverius," "Vigilius," "Pelagius I." In *Enciclopedia dei Papi*, ed. Instituto di Enciclopedia Italiana, 506–536. Rome, 2000.

Southern, Pat, and Karen Dixon. *The Late Roman Army*. New Haven, Conn., 1996.

Speyer, Heinrich. *Die biblischen Erzählung in Qoran*. Grafenhainchen, 1931.

Spieser, Jean-Michel. "L'Évolution de la ville byzantine de l'époque paléochrétienne à l'iconoclasme." In *Hommes et richesses dans l'Empire byzantin*. Vol. 1, *IVe–VIIe siècle*, ed. Catherine Abadie-Reynal, 97–106. Paris, 1989.

———. "La Céramique byzantine médiévale." In *Hommes et richesses dans l'Empire byzantin*. Vol. 2, *VIIIe–XVe siècle*, ed. Catherine Abadie-Reynal, 249–260. Paris, 1991.

Starr, Joshua. *The Jews in the Byzantine Empire, 641–1204*. Athens, 1939.

Starr, Roger. "The Circulation of Literary Texts in the Roman World." *Classical Quarterly* 37 (1987): 213–223.

Stathakopoulos, Dionysios. "Die Terminologie der Pest in Byzantinsichen Quellen." *Jahrbuch der Österreichischen Byzantinistik* 48 (1998): 1–7.

———. "The Justinianic Plague Revisited." *Byzantine and Modern Greek Studies* 24 (2000): 256–276.

———. *Famine and Pestilence in the Late Roman and Early Byzantine Empire: A Systematic Survey of Subsistence Crises and Epidemics*. Birmingham Byzantine and Ottoman Monographs 9. Aldershot, 2003.

———. "Crime and Punishment: The Plague in the Byzantine Empire, 541–749." In *Justinianic Plague*, ed. Lester Little. Forthcoming.

Stead, Christopher. *Divine Substance*. Oxford, 1977.

———. *Philosophy in Christian Antiquity*. Cambridge, 1994.

Steel, Carlos. *The Changing Self: A Study on the Soul in Later Neoplatonism: Iamblichus, Damascius, Priscianus*. Brussels, 1978.

Stein, Ernest. *Histoire du Bas-Empire*. Vol. 1, *De l'état romain à l'état byzantin (284–476)*. Paris, 1959. Vol. 2, *De la disparition de l'empire d'Occident à la mort de Justinien (476–565)*. Paris, 1949. Both reprinted Amsterdam, 1968.

Stein, Peter. *Roman Law in European History*. Cambridge, 1999.

Steinwenter, Artur. "Nomos Empsychos. Zur Geschichte einer politischen Theorie." *Anzeiger der Akademie der Wissenschaften, Wien, phil.-hist. Klasse* 83 (1946): 250–268.

Stemberger, Günter. *Introduction to the Talmud and Midrash*. Trans. Markus Bockmuehl. 2nd ed. Edinburgh, 1996.

Stolte, Bernard. "Desires Denied: Marriage, Adultery, and Divorce in Early Byzantine Law." In *Desire and Denial in Byzantium*, ed. Liz James, 77–86. Aldershot, Eng., 1999.

Stolte, Berhard H., and Gerrit J. Reinink, eds. *The Reign of Heraclius (610–641): Crisis and Confrontation*. Louvain, 2002.

Stothers, R. B., and M. R. Rampino. "Volcanic Eruptions in the Mediterranean before A.D. 630 from Written and Archaeological Sources." *Journal of Geophysical Research* 88 (1983): 6357–6371.

Striker, Cecil. "Work at Kalenderhane Camii in Istanbul." *DOP* 29 (1975): 306–318.

Stroumsa, Sarah. "Al-Farabi and Maimonides on the Christian Philosophical Tradition: A Re-Evaluation." *Der Islam* 68 (1991): 263–287.

Suerman, Harald. *Die Gründungsgeschichte der Maronitischen Kirche*. Orientalia Biblica et Christiana 10. Wiesbaden, 1998.

Svenshon, Helge, and Rainer H. W. Stichel. "Die Kirche der heiligen Sergios und Bakchos." *IstMitt* 50 (2000): 389–409.

Syme, Ronald. *The Roman Revolution*. Oxford, 1939.

Taft, Robert F. *The Great Entrance: A History of the Transfer of Gifts and other Pre-anaphoral Rites of the Liturgy of St. John Chrysostom*. 2nd ed. Rome, 1978.

———. *A History of the Liturgy of St. John Chrysostom*. Vol. 4, *The Diptychs*. Rome, 1991.

———. *The Liturgy of the Hours in East and West: The Origins of the Divine Office and Its Meaning for Today*. 2nd ed. Collegeville, Minn., 1993.

———. "Women at Church in Byzantium: Where, When – and Why?" *DOP* 52 (1998): 27–87.

———. *The Precommunion Rites*. Rome, 2000.

Talbert, Richard J. A. *Barrington Atlas of the Greek and Roman World*. Princeton, N.J., 2000.

Talbot, Alice-Mary. "Women." In *The Byzantines*, ed. Guglielmo Cavallo, 117–43. Chicago, 1997.

———. "A Comparison of the Monastic Experience of Byzantine Men and Women." *Greek Orthodox Theological Review* 30 (1985): 1–20. Reprinted in Talbot, *Women and Religious Life in Byzantium*. Aldershot, 2001.

Tannery, Paul. "Sur la pèriode finale de la philosophie grecque." *Revue philosophique* 42 (1896): 266–287.

Tardieu, Michel. "Sâbiens coranique et 'Sâbien' de Harrân." *Journal asiatique* 274 (1986): 1–44.

———. "Les Calendriers en usage à Harrân d'après les sources arabes et le commentaire de Simplicius à la Physique d'Aristotle." In *Simplicius, sa vie, son oeuvre, sa survie*, ed. I. Hadot, 40–57. Berlin, 1987.

———. *Les Paysages reliques. Routes et haltes syriennes d'Isidore à Simplicius*. Bibliothèque de l'École des Hautes Études. Sciences religieuses 94. Louvain, 1990.

Tarrant, Harold. "Olympiodorus and the Surrender of Paganism." *Byzantinische Forschungen* 24 (1997): 181–192.

Tate, Georges. *Les Campagnes de la Syrie du nord*. Vol. 1. Bibliothèque archéologique et historique 133. Paris, 1992.

Taylor, Rabun. "A Literary and Structural Analysis of the First Dome of Justinian's Hagia Sophia, Constantinople." *Journal of the Society of Architectural Historians* 55 (1996): 66–78.

Tchalenko, Georges. *Villages antiques de la Syrie du Nord. Le Massif du Bélus à l'époque romaine*, 3 vols. Paris, 1953–1958.

Teall, John L. "The Barbarians in Justinian's Armies." *Speculum* 40 (1965): 294–322.

Teixidor, Javier. *Bardesane d'Edessa. La première philosophie syriaque*. Paris, 1992.

Thiel, Rainer. *Simplikios und das Ende der neuplatonichen Schule in Athen*. Stuttgart, 1999.

Thompson, Edward A. *Romans and Barbarians: The Decline of the Western Empire*. Madison, Wis., 1982.

Thurman, William S. "A Juridical and Theological Concept of Nature in the Sixth Century AD." *Byzantinoslavica* 32 (1971): 77–85.

Tougher, Shaun. "Social Transformation, Gender Transformation? The Court Eunuch, 300–900." In *Gender in the Early Medieval World*, ed. Leslie Brubaker and Julia Smith. Cambridge, 2005.

Treadgold, Warren. *Byzantium and Its Army 284–1081*. Stanford, Calif., 1995.

Treggiari, Susan. *Roman Marriage:* Iusti coniuges *from the time of Cicero to the time of Ulpian*. Oxford, 1991.

Trimingham, J. Spencer. *Christianity among the Arabs in Pre-Islamic Times*. London, 1979.

Trombley, Frank R. "Korykos in Cilicia Trachis: The Economy of a Small Coastal City in Late Antiquity (*Saec.* V–VI) – A Précis." *Ancient History Bulletin* 1 (1987): 16–23.

———. "War and Society in Rural Syria, ca. 502–613 A.D.: Observations on the Epigraphy." *Byzantine and Modern Greek Studies* 21 (1997): 154–209.

Tsafrir, Yoram. "Procopius and the Nea Church in Jerusalem." *Antiquité Tardive* 8 (2000): 149–164.

Tsafrir, Yoram, and Gideon Foerster. "Urbanism at Scythopolis-Bet Shean in the Fourth to Seventh Centuries." *DOP* 51 (1997): 85–146.

Twigg, Graham. *The Black Death: A Biological Reappraisal*. London, 1984.

———. "Bubonic Plague: Doubts and Diagnoses." *Journal of Medical Microbiology* 42 (1995): 383–385.

Ullmann, Walter. *Gelasius I (492–496): Das Papsttum an der Wende der Spätantkike zum Mittelalter*. Stuttgart, 1981.

Ure, Percy N. *Justinian and His Age.* Harmondsworth, Eng., 1951.

Uthemann, Karl-Heinz. "Kaiser Justinian als Kirchenpolitiker und Theologe." *Augustinianum* 39 (1999): 5–83.

Vajda, Georges. "Ahl al-kitab." *Encyclopaedia of Islam.* 2nd ed., vol. 1., ed. H. A. R. Gibb, et. al. (1960): 264–266.

van Bekkum, Wout Jac. "Jewish Messianic Expectations in the Age of Heraclius." In *The Reign of Heraclius (610–641): Crisis and Confrontation*, ed. Bernard H. Stolte and Gerrit J. Reinink, 95–112. Louvain, 2002.

van der Horst, Pieter W. "The Samaritan Diaspora in Antiquity." In *Essays on the Jewish World of Early Christianity*, by Pieter W. van der Horst, 138–146. Freiburg, 1990.

———. "Jesus and the Jews according to the Suda." *Zeitschrift für die neutestamentliche Wissenschaft* 84 (1993): 268–277.

———. "Samaritans at Rome?" In *Japheth in the Tents of Shem: Studies on Jewish Hellenism in Antiquity*, by Pieter W. van der Horst, 251–260. Louvain, 2002.

van der Wal, Nicolaas, and Bernard H. Stolte, eds. *Collectio Tripartita: Justinian on Religious and Ecclesiastical Affairs.* Groningen, 1994.

Van Roey, Albert. "Les débuts de l'Église jacobite." In *Das Konzil von Chalkedon. Geschichte und Gegenwart*, vol. 2, ed. A. Grillmeier and H. Bacht. 339–360. Würzburg, 1953.

———. "La controverse trithéite jusqu'à l'excommunication de Conon et d'Eugène (557–569)." *Orientalia Lovaniensia Periodica* 16 (1985): 141–165.

Vassilaki, Maria. *Mother of God: Representations of the Virgin in Byzantine Art.* Milan, 2000.

Vasiliev, Alexander. *Justin I: An Introduction to the Epoch of Justinian the Great.* Cambridge, Mass., 1950.

Vavřinek, Vladimir. "The Eastern Roman Empire or Early Byzantium? A Society in Transition." In *From Late Antiquity to Early Byzantium*, ed. Vladimir Vavrinek. Prague, 1985.

Veltri, Giuseppe. "Die Novelle 146 περὶ ἑβραιῶν. Das Verbot des Targumvortrags in Justinians Politik." In *Die Septuaginta zwischen Judentum und Christentum*, ed. Martin Hengel and Anna M. Schwemer, 116–130. Tübingen, 1994.

Verbeke, Gerard. "Levels of Human Thinking in Philoponus."In *After Chalcedon: Studies in Theology and Church History*, ed. Carl Laga, Joseph A. Munitz, and Lucas van Rompay, 451–70. Leuven, 1985.

Veyne, Paul. *Le Pain et le Cirque: Sociologie historique d'un pluralisme politique.* Paris, 1976.

Vikan, Gary. *Byzantine Pilgrimage Art.* Washington, 1982.

———. "Pilgrims in Magi's Clothing: The Impact of Mimesis on Early Byzantine Pilgrimage Art." In *The Blessings of Pilgrimage*, ed. Robert Ousterhout, 97–107. Urbana, Ill., 1990.

———. "Early Byzantine Pilgrimage *Devotionalia* as Evidence of the Appearance of Pilgrimage Shrines." *Jahrbuch für Antike und Christentum* 20 (1995–1997): 1:337–388.

Vinogradoff, Paul. *Roman Law in Mediaeval Europe.* 1909. Reprint, Holmes Beach, Fla., 1994.

Vinson, Martha. "Domitia Longina, Julia Titi, and the Literary Tradition." *Historia* 38 (1989): 431–450.

———. "The Christianization of Sexual Slander: Some Preliminary Observations." In *Novum Millennium: Studies on Byzantine History and Culture*, ed. Claudia Sode and Sarolta Takács, 415–424. Aldershot, Eng., 2001.

Volbach, Wolgang Fritz. *Elfenbeinarbeiten der Spätantike und des frühen Mittelalters*. 3rd ed. Mainz, 1976.

Vööbus, Arthur. *A History of Asceticism in the Syrian Orient*. 2 vols. Louvain, 1958–1960.

Wacher, John. *The Towns of Roman Britain*. Berkeley, Calif., 1974.

Walker, Joel T. "The Limits of Late Antiquity: Philosophy between Rome and Iran." *Ancient World* 33 (2002): 45–69.

Wallace-Hadrill, Andrew. "*Civilis princeps*: Between Citizen and King." *JRS* 72 (1982): 32–48.

Wallace-Hadrill, John Michael. *Early Germanic Kingship in England and on the Continent*. Oxford, 1971.

Walmsley, A. K. "Byzantine Palestine and Arabia: Urban Prosperity in Late Antiquity." In *Towns in Transition*, ed. Neil Christie and Simon T. Loseby, 126–158. Aldershot, Eng., 1996.

Ward-Perkins, Bryan. *From Classical Antiquity to the Middle Ages: Urban Public Building in Northern and Central Italy, AD 300–850*. Oxford, 1984.

———. "Land, Labour, and Settlement." *CAH*, vol. 14, ed. Averil Cameron, Bryan Ward-Perkins, and Michael Whitby, 315–345. Cambridge, 2000.

———. "Specialized Production and Exchange." *CAH*, vol. 14, ed. Averil Cameron, Bryan Ward-Perkins, and Michael Whitby, 346–391. Cambridge, 2000.

———. "Reconfiguring Sacred Space from Pagan Shrines to Christian Churches." In *Die spätantike Stadt und Ihre Christianisierung*, ed. Gunnar Brands and Hans-Georg Severin, 285–290. Wiesbaden, 2003.

Watson, Alan. *The Spirit of Roman Law*. Athens, Ga., 1995.

Watt, William Montgomery. *Muhammad at Mecca*. Oxford, 1953.

———. "Belief in a 'High God' in Pre-Islamic Mecca." *Journal of Semitic Studies* 16 (1971): 35–40.

Watts, Edward. "Justinian, Malalas, and the End of Athenian Philosophical Teaching in 529." *JRS* 94 (2004): 1–15.

Weinberger, Leon J. *Jewish Hymnography: A Literary History*. London, 1998.

Weitzmann, Kurt. *The Monastery of St. Catherine on Mount Sinai: The Icons*. Vol. 1, *From the Sixth to the Tenth Century*. Princeton, N.J., 1976.

———. ed. *Age of Spirituality*. New York, 1979.

Wellhausen, Julius. *Reste arabischen Heidentums*. Berlin, 1887.

Wensinck, Arent Jan. *A Handbook of Muhammadan Tradition*. Leiden, 1927.

Werner, Eric. *The Sacred Bridge: The Interdependence of Liturgy and Music in Synagogue and Church during the First Millennium*. Vol. 1. London, 1959.

Wesche, Kenneth P. "The Defense of Chalcedon in the Sixth Century." PhD diss., Fordham University, 1986.

———. "Leontius of Jerusalem: Monophysite or Chalcedonian?" *St. Vladimir's Theological Quarterly* 31 (1987): 65–95.

Wessel, Klaus, and Marcell Restle, eds. *Reallexikon zur byzantinischen Kunst*. Stuttgart, 1972–1978.

Westerink, Leendert G. *Anonymous Prolegomena to Platonic Philosophy*. Amsterdam, 1962.

———. *Ein astrologisches Kolleg aus dem Jahre 564*. *BZ* 64(1971):6–21.

———. *The Greek Commentaries on Plato's Phaedo*. Amsterdam, 1976–1977.

Wharton, Annabel J. *Refiguring the Post Classical City: Dura Europos, Jerash, Jerusalem, and Ravenna*. Cambridge, 1995.

Whitaker, C. R. "Berber." In *Late Antiquity. A Guide to the Postclassical World*, ed. Glen Bowersock, Peter Brown, and Oleg Grabar. Cambridge, Mass., 1999.

Whitby, Michael. "Procopius and the Development of Defences in Upper Mesopotamia." In *The Defence of the Roman and Byzantine East*, ed. Philip Freeman and David L. Kennedy, 717–735. Oxford, 1986.

———. *The Emperor Maurice and His Historian: Theophylact Simocatta on Persian and Balkan Warfare*. Oxford, 1988.

———. "Greek Historical Writing after Procopius: Variety and Vitality." *The Byzantine and Early Islamic Near East*. Vol. 1, *Problems in the Literary Source Material*, ed. Averil Cameron and Lawrence I. Conrad, 25–80. Princeton, N.J., 1992.

———. "Recruitment in Roman Armies from Justinian to Heraclius (ca. 565–615)." In *The Byzantine and Early Islamic Near East*, vol. 3, *States, Resources, and Armies*, ed. Averil Cameron, 61–124. Princeton, N.J., 1995.

———. "*Deus nobiscum*: Christianity, Warfare, and Morale in Late Antiquity." In *Modus Operandi: Essays in Honour of Geoffrey Rickman*, ed. Michel Austin, et al., 191–208. London, 1998.

———. "The Army, c. 420–602." *CAH*, vol. 14, ed. Averil Cameron, Bryan Ward-Perkins, and Michael Whitby, 288–314. Cambridge, 2000.

———. "The Successors of Justinian." *CAH*, vol. 14, ed. Averil Cameron, Bryan Ward-Perkins, and Michael Whitby, 86–111. Cambridge, 2000.

White, Hugh G. Evelyn. *The Monasteries of the Wadi 'n Natrun*. Vol. 2, *The History of the Monasteries of Nitria and of Scetis*. New York, 1932.

Whitehouse, David. "Sasanian Maritime Activity." In *The Indian Ocean in Antiquity*, ed. Julian Reade, 339–349. London, 1996.

Whitehouse, David, and A. Williamson. "Sasanian Maritime Trade." *Iran* 11 (1973): 29–49.

Whittow, Mark. "Ruling the Late Roman and Early Byzantine City: A Continuous History." *Past and Present* 129 (1990): 3–29.

———. *The Making of Byzantium, 600–1025*. Berkeley, Calif., 1996.

Wickham, Chris. *Early Medieval Italy: Central Power and Local Society, 400–1000*. London, 1981.

———. *Land and Power: Studies in Italian and European Social History, 400–1200*. London, 1994.

———. "Overview: Production, Distribution, and Demand." In *The Sixth Century: Production, Distribution, and Demand*, ed. Richard Hodges and William Bowden, 279–292. Leiden, 1998.

Wickham, L. R. "John Philoponus and Gregory of Nyssa's Teaching on the Resurrection: A Brief Note." In *Studien zu Gregor von Nyssa und der christlichen Spätantike*, ed. Hubertus Drobner and Christoph Klock, 205–210. Leiden, 1990.

Wieacker, Franz. *A History of Private Law in Europe, with Particular Reference to Germany*. Trans. Tony Weir. Oxford, 1995.

Wiesehöfer, Josef. *Ancient Persia from 550 B.C. to 650 A.D.* London, 1996.

Wightman, G. J. *The Walls of Jerusalem: From the Canaanites to the Mamluks*. Mediterranean Archaeology Supplements 4. Sydney, 1993.

Wildberg, Christian. "Prolegomena to the Study of Philoponus' contra Aristotelem." In *Philoponus and the Rejection of Aristotelian Science*, ed. Richard R. K. Sorabji, 197–209. London, 1987.

———. *John Philoponus' Criticism of Aristotle's Theory of Aether*. Peripatoi 16. Berlin, 1988.

———. "Three Neoplatonic Introductions to Philosophy: Ammonius, David, and Elias." *Hermathena* 149 (1991): 33–51.

———. "Impetus Theory and the Hermeneutic of Science in Simplicius and Philoponus." *Hyperboreus* 5 (1999): 107–124.

Wilken, Robert. *The Land Called Holy: Palestine in Christian History and Thought*. New Haven, Conn., 1992.

Wilson, Nigel G. *Scholars of Byzantium*. Baltimore, 1983.

Wink, Andre. *Al-Hind: The Making of the Indo-Islamic World*. Vol. 1. *Early medieval India and the expansion of Islam, 7th–11th centuries*. Leiden, 1996.

Wirszubski, Chaim. *Libertas as a Political Idea at Rome during the Late Republic and Early Principate*. Cambridge, 1950.

Wolfram, Herwig. *Intitulatio I. Lateinische Königs- und Fürstentitel bis zum Ende des 8. Jahrhunderts. Mitteilungen des Instituts für Österreichische Geschichtsforschung*, Ergänzungsband 21. Cologne, 1967.

———. *History of the Goths*. Berkeley, Calif., 1988.

———. "Origo et Religio: Ethnic Traditions and Literature in Early Medieval Texts." *Early Medieval Europe* 3 (1994): 19–38.

———. *Grenzen und Räume. Geschichte Österreichs vor seiner Entstehung*. Vienna, 1995.

———. *The Roman Empire and its Germanic Peoples*. Berkeley, Calif., 1997.

———. "Die dauerhafte Ansiedlung der Goten auf römischem Boden. Eine endlose Geschichte." *Mitteilungen des Instituts für Österreichische Geschichtsforschung*. Forthcoming.

Wood, Ian N. "Royal Succession and Legitimation in the Roman West, 419–536." In *Staat im frühen Mittelalter*, ed. Stuart Airlie, Walter Pohl, and Helmut Reimitz. Vienna, forthcoming.

———. *The Merovingian North Sea*. Alingss, 1983.

———. "The End of Roman Britain." In *Gildas: New Approaches*, ed. Michael Lapidge and David Dumville, 1–26. Woodbridge, UK. 1984.

———. *The Merovingian Kingdoms, 450–751*. London, 1994.

———. "The Frontiers of Western Europe: Developments East of the Rhine in the Sixth Century." In *The Sixth Century: Production, Distribution, and Demand*, ed. Richard Hodges and William Bowden, 231–253. Leiden, 1998.

Wood, James, and Sharon DeWitte-Aviña. "Was the Black Death Yersinial Plague?" *Lancet, Infectious Diseases* 3 (2003): 327.

Wright, William. *Catalogue of Syriac Manuscripts in the British Museum, Acquired since the Year 1838*. 3 vols. London, 1870–1872.

Wu, Lien-Teh. *Plague: A Manual for Medical and Public Health Workers*. Shanghai, 1936.

Yar-Shater, Ehsan. "Mazdakism." In *Cambridge History of Iran*, vol. 3, ed. H. A. R. Gibb, et al., 991–1024, Cambridge, 1960.

Yegül, Fikret. *Baths and Bathing in Classical Antiquity*. Cambridge, 1992.

Yorke, Barbara. *Kings and Kingdoms of Early Anglo-Saxon England*. London, 1990.

Young, Gary K. *Rome's Eastern Trade*. London, 2001.

Zaehner, Robert Charles. *Zurvan: A Zoroastrian Dilemma.* Oxford, 1955.

Zanker, Paul. *The Mask of Socrates: The Image of the Intellectual in Antiquity.* Trans. Alan Shapiro. Berkeley, Calif., 1995.

Zayadine, Fawzi, ed. *The Jerash Archaeological Project.* Amman, 1986.

Zuckerman, Constantine. "The Military Compendium of Syrianus Magister." *Jahrbuch der Österreichischen Byzantinistik* 40 (1990): 209–224.

# Index